Emerging Technologies in Intelligent Applications for Image and Video Processing

V. Santhi
VIT University, India

D. P. Acharjya
VIT University, India

M. Ezhilarasan
Pondichery Engineering College, India

A volume in the Advances in Computational
Intelligence and Robotics (ACIR) Book Series

Information Science
REFERENCE
An Imprint of IGI Global

Published in the United States of America by
    Information Science Reference (an imprint of IGI Global)
    701 E. Chocolate Avenue
    Hershey PA, USA 17033
    Tel: 717-533-8845
    Fax: 717-533-8661
    E-mail: cust@igi-global.com
    Web site: http://www.igi-global.com

Library of Congress Cataloging-in-Publication Data

Names: Santhi, V., 1971- editor. | Acharjya, D. P., 1969- editor. |
    Ezhilarasan, M., 1968- editor.
Title: Emerging technologies in intelligent applications for image and video
    processing / V. Santhi, D.P. Acharjya, and M. Ezhilarasan, editors.
Description: Hershey PA : Information Science Reference, [2016] | Includes
    bibliographical references and index.
Identifiers: LCCN 2015037583| ISBN 9781466696853 (hardcover) | ISBN
    9781466696860 (ebook)
Subjects: LCSH: Image processing--Industrial applications. | Diagnostic
    imaging--Industrial applications. | Diagnostic imaging.
Classification: LCC TA1637 .E46 2016 | DDC 006.6--dc23 LC record available at http://lccn.loc.gov/2015037583

This book is published in the IGI Global book series Advances in Computational Intelligence and Robotics (ACIR) (ISSN: 2327-0411; eISSN: 2327-042X)

British Cataloguing in Publication Data
A Cataloguing in Publication record for this book is available from the British Library.

All work contributed to this book is new, previously-unpublished material. The views expressed in this book are those of the authors, but not necessarily of the publisher.

For electronic access to this publication, please contact: eresources@igi-global.com.

Advances in Computational Intelligence and Robotics (ACIR) Book Series

ISSN: 2327-0411
EISSN: 2327-042X

MISSION

While intelligence is traditionally a term applied to humans and human cognition, technology has progressed in such a way to allow for the development of intelligent systems able to simulate many human traits. With this new era of simulated and artificial intelligence, much research is needed in order to continue to advance the field and also to evaluate the ethical and societal concerns of the existence of artificial life and machine learning.

The **Advances in Computational Intelligence and Robotics (ACIR) Book Series** encourages scholarly discourse on all topics pertaining to evolutionary computing, artificial life, computational intelligence, machine learning, and robotics. ACIR presents the latest research being conducted on diverse topics in intelligence technologies with the goal of advancing knowledge and applications in this rapidly evolving field.

COVERAGE

- Evolutionary computing
- Adaptive and Complex Systems
- Neural Networks
- Agent technologies
- Brain Simulation
- Computational Intelligence
- Intelligent control
- Cognitive Informatics
- Artificial Intelligence
- Machine Learning

IGI Global is currently accepting manuscripts for publication within this series. To submit a proposal for a volume in this series, please contact our Acquisition Editors at Acquisitions@igi-global.com or visit: http://www.igi-global.com/publish/.

Titles in this Series

For a list of additional titles in this series, please visit: www.igi-global.com

Handbook of Research on Design, Control, and Modeling of Swarm Robotics
Ying Tan (Peking University, China)
Information Science Reference • copyright 2016 • 854pp • H/C (ISBN: 9781466695726) • US $465.00 (our price)

Handbook of Research on Emerging Perspectives in Intelligent Pattern Recognition, Analysis, and Image Processing
Narendra Kumar Kamila (C.V. Raman College of Engineering, India)
Information Science Reference • copyright 2016 • 477pp • H/C (ISBN: 9781466686540) • US $255.00 (our price)

Handbook of Research on Advanced Hybrid Intelligent Techniques and Applications
Siddhartha Bhattacharyya (RCC Institute of Information Technology, India) Pinaki Banerjee (Goldstone Infratech Limited, India) Dipankar Majumdar (RCC Institute of Information Technology, India) and Paramartha Dutta (Visva-Bharati University, India)
Information Science Reference • copyright 2016 • 653pp • H/C (ISBN: 9781466694743) • US $285.00 (our price)

Research Advances in the Integration of Big Data and Smart Computing
Pradeep Kumar Mallick (Institute for Research and Development, India)
Information Science Reference • copyright 2016 • 374pp • H/C (ISBN: 9781466687370) • US $210.00 (our price)

Innovative Research in Attention Modeling and Computer Vision Applications
Rajarshi Pal (Institute for Development and Research in Banking Technology, India)
Information Science Reference • copyright 2016 • 456pp • H/C (ISBN: 9781466687233) • US $200.00 (our price)

Handbook of Research on Swarm Intelligence in Engineering
Siddhartha Bhattacharyya (RCC Institute of Information Technology, India) and Paramartha Dutta (Visva-Bharati University, India)
Engineering Science Reference • copyright 2015 • 743pp • H/C (ISBN: 9781466682917) • US $335.00 (our price)

Handbook of Research on Advancements in Robotics and Mechatronics
Maki K. Habib (The American University in Cairo, Egypt)
Engineering Science Reference • copyright 2015 • 994pp • H/C (ISBN: 9781466673878) • US $515.00 (our price)

Handbook of Research on Advanced Intelligent Control Engineering and Automation
Ahmad Taher Azar (Benha University, Egypt) and Sundarapandian Vaidyanathan (Vel Tech University, India)
Engineering Science Reference • copyright 2015 • 794pp • H/C (ISBN: 9781466672482) • US $335.00 (our price)

www.igi-global.com

701 E. Chocolate Ave., Hershey, PA 17033
Order online at www.igi-global.com or call 717-533-8845 x100
To place a standing order for titles released in this series, contact: cust@igi-global.com
Mon-Fri 8:00 am - 5:00 pm (est) or fax 24 hours a day 717-533-8661

Dedicated to

My beloved parents Thiru. G. Vaithiyanathan and Smt. V. Rajam
V. Santhi

My beloved mother Smt. Pramodabala Acharjya
D. P. Acharjya

My beloved mother Smt. Rathinambal Murugesan
M. Ezhilarasan

Editorial Advisory Board

Table of Contents

Section 1
Image and Video Enhancement, Restoration, and Segmentations

Li-Wei Kang, National Yunlin University of Science and Technology, Taiwan
Chia-Mu Yu, Yuan Ze University, Taiwan
Chih-Yang Lin, Asia University, Taiwan
Chia-Hung Yeh, National Sun Yat-Sen University, Taiwan

Jacob D'Avy, University of Tennessee, USA
Wei-Wen Hsu, Old Dominion University, USA
Chung-Hao Chen, Old Dominion University, USA
Andreas Koschan, University of Tennessee, USA
Mongi Abidi, University of Tennessee, USA

Punyaban Patel, Chhatrapati Shivaji Institute of Technology, India
Bibekananda Jena, Purushottam Institute of Engineering and Technology, India
Bibhudatta Sahoo, National Institute of Technology Rourkela, India
Pritam Patel, National Institute of Technology Agartala, India
Banshidhar Majhi, National Institute of Technology Rourkela, India

Manami Barthakur, Gauhati University, India
Kandarpa Kumar Sarma, Gauhati University, India

Section 2
Image and Video Compression, Indexing, and Retrieval

Section 3
Image and Video Processing in Public Safety

Section 4
Image and Video Classification, Clustering, and Applications

Detailed Table of Contents

Section 1
Image and Video Enhancement, Restoration, and Segmentations

Chapter 1

Li-Wei Kang, National Yunlin University of Science and Technology, Taiwan
Chia-Mu Yu, Yuan Ze University, Taiwan
Chih-Yang Lin, Asia University, Taiwan
Chia-Hung Yeh, National Sun Yat-Sen University, Taiwan

The chapter provides a survey of recent advances in image/video restoration and enhancement via spare representation. Images/videos usually unavoidably suffer from noises due to sensor imperfection or poor illumination. Numerous contributions have addressed this problem from diverse points of view. Recently, the use of sparse and redundant representations over learned dictionaries has become one specific approach. One goal here is to provide a survey of advances in image/video denoising via sparse representation. Moreover, to consider more general types of noise, this chapter also addresses the problems about removals of structured/unstructured components (e.g., rain streaks or blocking artifacts) from image/video. Moreover, image/video quality may be degraded from low-resolution due to low-cost acquisition. Hence, this chapter also provides a survey of recently advances in super-resolution via sparse representation. Finally, the conclusion can be drawn that sparse representation techniques have been reliable solutions in several problems of image/video restoration and enhancement.

Chapter 2

Jacob D'Avy, University of Tennessee, USA
Wei-Wen Hsu, Old Dominion University, USA
Chung-Hao Chen, Old Dominion University, USA
Andreas Koschan, University of Tennessee, USA
Mongi Abidi, University of Tennessee, USA

Segmenting an image into meaningful regions is an important step in many computer vision applications such as facial recognition, target tracking and medical image analysis. Because image segmentation is an ill-posed problem, parameters are needed to constrain the solution to one that is suitable for a given application. For a user, setting parameter values is often unintuitive. We present a method for automating segmentation parameter selection using an efficient search method to optimize a segmentation objective function. Efficiency is improved by utilizing prior knowledge about the relationship between a segmentation parameter and the objective function terms. An adaptive sampling of the search space is created which focuses on areas that are more likely to contain a minimum. When compared to parameter optimization approaches based on genetic algorithm, Tabu search, and multi-locus hill climbing the proposed method was able to achieve equivalent optimization results with an average of 25% fewer objective function evaluations.

Punyaban Patel, Chhatrapati Shivaji Institute of Technology, India
Bibekananda Jena, Purushottam Institute of Engineering and Technology, India
Bibhudatta Sahoo, National Institute of Technology Rourkela, India
Pritam Patel, National Institute of Technology Agartala, India
Banshidhar Majhi, National Institute of Technology Rourkela, India

Images very often get contaminated by different types of noise like impulse noise, Gaussian noise, spackle noise etc. due to malfunctioning of camera sensors during acquisition or transmission using the channel. The noise in the channel affects processing of images in various ways. Hence, the image has to be restored by applying filtration process before the high level image processing. In general the restoration techniques for images are based up on the mathematical and the statistical models of image degradation. Denoising and deblurring are used to recover the image from degraded observations. The researchers have proposed verity of linear and non-linear filters for removal of noise from images. The filtering technique has been used to remove noisy pixels, without changing the uncorrupted pixel values. This chapter presents the metrics used for measurement of noise, and the various schemes for removing of noise from the images.

Manami Barthakur, Gauhati University, India
Kandarpa Kumar Sarma, Gauhati University, India

Stereoscopic vision in cameras is an interesting field of study. This type of vision is important in incorporation of depth in video images which is needed for the ability to measure distances of the object from the camera properly i.e. conversion of two dimensional video image into three dimensional video. In this chapter, some of the basic theoretical aspects of the methods for estimating depth in 2D video and the current state of research have been discussed. These methods are frequently used in the algorithms for estimating depth in the 2D to 3D video techniques. Some of the recent algorithms for incorporation depth in 2D video are also discussed and from the literature review a simple and generic system for incorporation depth in 2D video is presented.

Section 2
Image and Video Compression, Indexing, and Retrieval

This chapter focus mainly on different wavelet transform algorithms as Burt's Pyramid, Mallat's Pyramidal Algorithm, Feauveau's non dyadic structure and its application in Image compression.This chapter focus on mathematical concepts involved in wavelet transform like convolution, scaling function, wavelet function, Multiresolution analysis, inner product etc, and how these mathematical concepts are liked to image transform application. This chapter gives an idea towards wavelets and wavelet transforms. Image compression based on wavelet transform consists of transform, quantization and encoding. Basic focus is not only on transform step, selection of particular wavelet, wavelets involved in new standard of image compression but also on quantization and encoding, Huffman code, run length code. Difference in between JPEG and JPEG2000, Quantization and sampling, wavelet function and wavelet transform are also given. This chapter is also giving some basic idea of MATLAB to assist readers in understanding MATLAB Programming in terms of image processing.

The Motion Estimation is an indispensable module in the design of video encoder. It employs Block Matching algorithm which involves searching a candidate block in the entire search window of the reference frame taking up to 80% of the total video encoding time. In order to increase the efficiency, several Block Matching Algorithms are employed to minimize the computational time involved in block matching. The chapter throws light on an efficient approach to be applied to the existing Block Matching Search techniques in HEVC which outperforms the various Block Matching algorithms. It involves two steps namely – Prediction and Refinement. The prediction step considers two parameters such as the temporal correlation and the direction to predict the MV of the candidate block. Several combinations of the search points are formulated in the refinement step of the algorithm to minimize the search time. The results depict that the Efficient Motion Estimation schemes provide a faster search minimizing the computational time upon comparison with the existing Motion Estimation algorithms.

Chapter 7

Nidhi Goel, University of Delhi, India
Priti Sehgal, University of Delhi, India

Image retrieval (IR) systems are used for searching of images by means of diverse modes such as text, sample image, or both. They suffer with the problem of semantic gap which is the mismatch between the user requirement and the capabilities of the IR system. The image data is generally stored in the form of statistics of the value of the pixels which has very little to do with the semantic interpretation of the image. Therefore, it is necessary to understand the mapping between the two modalities i.e. content and context. Research indicates that the combination of the two can be a worthwhile approach to improve the quality of image search results. Hence, multimodal retrieval (MMR) is an expected way of searching which attracts substantial research consideration. The main challenges include discriminatory feature extraction and selection, redundancy identification and elimination, information preserving fusion and computational complexity. Based on these challenges, in this chapter, authors focus on comparison of various MMR systems that have been used to improve the retrieval results.

Chapter 8

N. Puviarasan, Annamalai University, India
R. Bhavani, Annamalai University, India

In Content based image retrieval (CBIR) applications, the idea of indexing is mapping the extracted descriptors from images into a high-dimensional space. In this paper, visual features like color, texture and shape are considered. The color features are extracted using color coherence vector (CCV), texture features are obtained from Segmentation based Fractal Texture Analysis (SFTA). The shape features of an image are extracted using the Fourier Descriptors (FD) which is the contour based feature extraction method. All features of an image are then combined. After combining the color, texture and shape features using appropriate weights, the quadtree is used for indexing the images. It is experimentally found that the proposed indexing method using quadtree gives better performance than the other existing indexing methods.

Section 3
Image and Video Processing in Public Safety

Chapter 9

M. Kalaiselvi Geetha, Annamalai University, India
J. Arunnehru, Annamalai University, India
A. Geetha, Annamalai University, India

Automatic identification and early prediction of suspicious human activities are of significant importance in video surveillance research. By recognizing and predicting a criminal activity at an early stage, regrettable incidents can be avoided. Initially, an action recognition framework is developed for identifying the suspicious actions using interest point based 2D and 3D features and transform based approaches. This is subsequently followed by a novel approach for predicting the suspicious actions for crime prevention in real-world scenario. The prediction problem is formulated probabilistically and a novel approach that employs the mixture models for prediction is introduced. The developed system yields promising results for predicting the actions in real-time.

Chapter 10

Iris Identification System: A New Perspective 232

N. Poonguzhali, Pondicherry Engineering College, India
M. Ezhilarasan, Pondicherry Engineering College, India

Recent research on iris is not only on recognition; emerging trends are also in medical diagnostics, personality identification. The iris based recognition system rely on patterns/textures present in the iris, the color of the iris, visible features present in the iris, geometric features of the iris and the SIFT features. An overview of biometric generation is presented. Human iris can be viewed as a multilayered structure in its anterior view. The iris consists of three zones, the pupillary zone, collarette and the ciliary zone. The texture features present in the pupillary zone and collarette are used for identification. As these features are closer to the pupil they are not affected by the occlusion caused by eyelid or eyelashes. The geometric features of the iris can also be used for human identification. The structure of the iris is more related to the geometric shape and hence the extraction of these features is also possible. An overview of the performance metrics to evaluate a biometric system is also presented.

Chapter 11

Object Classification and Tracking in Real Time: An Overview.. 250

Amlan Jyoti Das, Gauhati University, India
Navajit Saikia, Assam Engineering College, India
Kandarpa Kumar Sarma, Gauhati University, India

Algorithms for automatic processing of visual data have been a topic of interest since the last few decades. Object tracking and classification methods are highly demanding in vehicle traffic control systems, surveillance systems for detecting unauthorized movement of vehicle and human, mobile robot applications, animal tracking, etc. There are still many challenging issues while dealing with dynamic background, occlusion, etc. in real time. This chapter presents an overview of various existing techniques for object detection, classification and tracking. As the most important requirements of tracking and classification algorithms are feature extraction and selection, different feature types are also included.

Chapter 12

Gait Based Biometric Authentication System with Reduced Search Space 296

L. R. Sudha, Annamalai University, India
R. Bhavani, Annamalai University, India

Deployment of human gait in developing new tools for security enhancement has received growing attention in modern era. Since the efficiency of any algorithm depends on the size of search space, the aim is to propose a novel approach to reduce the search space. In order to achieve this, the database is split into two based on gender and the search is restricted in the identified gender database. Then highly discriminant gait features are selected by forward sequential feature selection algorithm in the confined space. Experimental results evaluated on the benchmark CASIA B gait dataset with the newly proposed combined classifier kNN-SVM, shows less False Acceptance Rate (FAR) and less False Rejection Rate (FRR).

Chapter 13

Lung Disease Classification by Novel Shape-Based Feature Extraction and New Hybrid Genetic
Approach: Lung Disease Classification by Shape-Based Method 321

    Bhuvaneswari Chandran, Annamalai University, India
    P. Aruna, Annamalai University, India
    D. Loganathan, Pondicherry Engineering College, India

The purpose of the chapter is to present a novel method to classify lung diseases from the computed tomography images which assist physicians in the diagnosis of lung diseases. The method is based on a new approach which combines a proposed M2 feature extraction method and a novel hybrid genetic approach with different types of classifiers. The feature extraction methods performed in this work are moment invariants, proposed multiscale filter method and proposed M2 feature extraction method. The essential features which are the results of the feature extraction technique are selected by the novel hybrid genetic algorithm feature selection algorithms. Classification is performed by the support vector machine, multilayer perceptron neural network and Bayes Net classifiers. The result obtained proves that the proposed technique is an efficient and robust method. The performance of the proposed M2 feature extraction with proposed hybrid GA and SVM classifier combination achieves maximum classification accuracy.

Chapter 14

Fingerprint Iris Palmprint Multimodal Biometric Watermarking System Using Genetic
Algorithm-Based Bacterial Foraging Optimization Algorithm 347

    S. Anu H. Nair, Annamalai University, India
    P. Aruna, Annamalai University, India

With the wide spread utilization of Biometric identification systems, establishing the authenticity of biometric data itself has emerged as an important issue. In this chapter, a novel approach for creating a multimodal biometric system has been suggested. The multimodal biometric system is implemented using the different fusion schemes such as Average Fusion, Minimum Fusion, Maximum Fusion, Principal Component Analysis Fusion, Discrete Wavelet Transform Fusion, Stationary Wavelet Transform Fusion, Intensity Hue Saturation Fusion, Laplacian Gradient Fusion, Pyramid Gradient Fusion and Sparse Representation Fusion. In modality extraction level, the information extracted from different modalities is stored in vectors on the basis of their modality. These are then blended to produce a joint template which is the basis for the watermarking system. The fused image is applied as input along with the cover image to the Genetic Algorithm based Bacterial Foraging Optimization Algorithm watermarking system. The standard images are used as cover images and performance was compared.

Section 4
Image and Video Classification, Clustering, and Applications

Chapter 15

Color Features and Color Spaces Applications to the Automatic Image Annotation 378

    Vafa Maihami, Semnan University, Iran
    Farzin Yaghmaee, Semnan University, Iran

Nowadays images play a crucial role in different fields such as medicine, advertisement, education and entertainment. Describing images content and retrieving them are important fields in image processing.

Automatic image annotation is a process which produces words from a digital image based on the content of this the image by using a computer. In this chapter, after an introduction to neighbor voting algorithm for image annotation, we discuss the applicability of color features and color spaces in automatic image annotation. We discuss the applicability of three color features (color histogram, color moment and color Autocorrelogram) and three color spaces (RGB, HSI and YCbCr) in image annotation. Experimental results, using Corel5k benchmark annotated images dataset, demonstrate that using different color spaces and color features helps to select the best color features and spaces in image annotation area.

Shanmuga Sundari Ilangovan, VIT University, India
Biswanath Mahanty, INHA University, Republic of Korea
Shampa Sen, VIT University, India

Biomedical imaging techniques had significantly improved the health care of patients. Image guided therapy has reduced the high risk of human errors with improved accuracy in disease detection and surgical procedures. The chapter provides an overview of existing imaging methods and current imaging approaches and their potential to unravel the challenges in medical field. First part of the chapter picture outs the basic concepts and mechanism of various imaging techniques that are currently in use. The second part explains about the features of image processing system and future trends in image guided therapy extended with a short discussion on radiation exposure in medical imaging. The authors trust the chapter to be beneficial to the beginners in the area of medical science and to the clinicians.

Priya Kandan, Annamalai University, India
P. Aruna, Annamalai University, India

Age-related macular degeneration is an eye disease, that gradually degrades the macula, a part of the retina, which is responsible for central vision. It occurs in one of the two types, DRY and WET age-related macular degeneration. In this chapter, to diagnose Age-related macular degeneration, the authors have proposed a new EYENET model which was obtained by combining the modified PNN and modified RBFNN and hence it poses the advantages of both the models. The amount of the disease spread in the retina can be identified by extracting the features of the retina. A total of 250 fundus images were used, out of which 150 were used for training and 100 images were used for testing. Experimental results show that PNN has an accuracy of 87%, modified PNN has an accuracy of 90% RBFNN has an accuracy of 80%, modified RBFNN has an accuracy of 85% and the proposed EYENET Model has an accuracy of 94%. This infers that the proposed EYENET model outperforms all other models.

Computed tomography images are widely used in the diagnosis of ischemic stroke because of its faster acquisition and compatibility with most life support devices. This chapter presents a new approach to automated detection of ischemic stroke using k-means clustering technique which separates the lesion region from healthy tissues and classification of ischemic stroke using texture features. The proposed method has five stages, pre-processing, tracing midline of the brain, extraction of texture features and feature selection, classification and segmentation. In the first stage noise is suppressed using a median filtering and skull bone components of the images are removed. In the second stage, midline shift of the brain is calculated. In the third stage, fourteen texture features are extracted and optimal features are selected using genetic algorithm. In the fourth stage, support vector machine, artificial neural network and decision tree classifiers have been used. Finally, the ischemic stroke region is extracted by using k-means clustering technique.

Preface

In recent years data are accumulated at a dramatic pace. The data can be qualitative, quantitative, images or in terms of videos. But, the real challenge lies in converting huge data into knowledge. Therefore, it is essential to develop new computational theories and tools to assist human in extracting knowledge from the high dimensional data. Study of these new theories in image and video processing is quite interesting and challenging. Therefore, there is a growing demand of image and video processing in diverse application areas, such as secured data communication, biomedical imaging, biometrics, remote sensing, texture understanding, pattern recognition, content-based data retrieval, data compression, imaging industry and so on. For the last few decades image and video processing has been considered as an important research area to find solution in many real life applications. The importance of image and video processing is exhibited in almost all existing engineering and scientific fields. Digital image and video processing are carried out through many classical algorithms but it fails to serve the purpose of advanced real life problems. In such circumstances, the use of computational intelligent approaches is essential to address the challenges.

Computational intelligence techniques have firmly established themselves as feasible alternate mathematical tools for more than a decade. They have been extensively employed in many systems and application domains, especially in signal processing, automatic control, industrial and consumer electronics, robotics, finance, manufacturing systems, electric power systems, and power electronics. Image and video processing is also an extremely potent area which has attracted the attention of many researchers who are interested in the development of new computational intelligence based techniques and their suitable applications, in both research and in real world problems. The development of powerful computers is a boon to implement computational intelligence techniques in image and video processing systems. In order to achieve intelligence based processing, high performance computer could exploit parallelism of current and upcoming computer architectures. This edited book presents a large number of interesting applications using various intelligent computing techniques. It will help those researchers who have interest in this field to keep insight into different concepts and their importance for applications in real life. This has been done to make the edited book more flexible and to stimulate further interest in topics.

Image and video processing is active area of current research for its potential application to many real life problems. Therefore, it is challenging for human beings in analyzing, processing and transforming huge image or video data into knowledge. It is very difficult to analyze and extract expert knowledge from a universe due to lack of computing resources available. Therefore, it is an active area of current research in computer science, electronics, electrical and information technology. The objective of this edited book is to provide the researchers the recent advances in the fields of image and video processing which are required to achieve in depth knowledge in the concerned field to solve problems in real.

To achieve these objectives, both theoretical advances and its applications to real life problems will be stressed upon. This has been done to make the edited book more flexible and to stimulate further research interest in topics. It is expected that besides providing up to date knowledge in the field this edited volume will provide a launch pad for future research.

Many of the researchers in different organizations across the globe have been doing research in image and video processing. To keep abreast with this development, it is an effort to bring the recent advances in image and video processing in a cohesive manner. The main objective is to bring most of the major developments in the above mentioned area in a precise manner, so that it can serve as a handbook for many researchers. Also, many of the universities have introduced this topic as a course at the postgraduate level. We trust and hope that this book will help the researchers, who have interest in Computational Intelligence in image and video processing, to keep insight into recent advances and their importance in real life applications.

This book comprises of four sections. First section broadly covers image and video enhancement, restoration, segmentation algorithms with its applications. The second section of the edited book discusses about image and video compression algorithms as it is required to save bandwidth and memory requirements in digital communication and in storage applications. It also discusses about various method of image indexing and retrieval processes. Third section discusses about methods for providing public safety through image and video processing techniques. Section 4 will be stressed upon various applications of image and video processing in various fields. Each section provides the current research trends in the concerned field of study.

In order to perform high level image processing it is required to remove noise from image and video signal. In general image and video data unavoidably suffer from noises due to sensor imperfection or poor illumination. The process of removing noise from images could be called as image enhancement. Similarly reverting the degraded images back to its original quality is called image restoration. Chapter 1 provides insight into recent advances in image and video restoration and enhancement via sparse representation. Moreover, this chapter also addresses the problems about removals of structured and unstructured components such as rain streaks and blocking artifacts from image and video. Chapter 3 deals with various noise models and its removal mechanisms. It also discuss about various metrics to measure quality of images. The degraded images could be restored using mathematical and statistical models of image degradation. It gives fundamental knowledge and insight into various noise removal mechanisms. In addition, image and video quality may be degraded due to low-cost acquisition. Hence, in this chapter various mechanisms to remove noise from images are presented including survey of recent advances in super-resolution via sparse representation and basics of various noises types and removal mechanisms.

Segmenting an image into meaningful regions is an important step in many computer vision applications such as facial recognition, target tracking and medical image analysis. Because image segmentation is an ill-posed problem, parameters are needed to constrain the solution to one that is suitable for a given application. For a user, setting parameter values is often unintuitive. In chapter 2, a method for automatically selecting segmentation parameters using an efficient search method is proposed to optimize a segmentation objective function. The algorithm efficiency is improved by utilizing prior knowledge about the relationship between a segmentation parameter and the objective function terms. An adaptive sampling of the search space is created which focuses on areas that are more likely to contain a minimum. Stereoscopic vision in cameras is an interesting field of study, as it incorporates depth in video images which is required to measure distances of the object from the camera properly. It could be used to convert two dimensional video images into three dimensional video. In chapter 4, some of the basic theoretical aspects of the methods for estimating depth in 2D video and the current state of research have been discussed.

Digital image and video compression techniques plays a major role in reduction of bandwidth requirement in transmission and memory requirement in storage. Data compression could be carried out using any transformation techniques but discrete cosine transformation technique is predominantly used as literature survey. Chapter 5 focuses mainly on different wavelet transform algorithms as Burt's pyramid, Mallat's pyramidal algorithm, Feauveau's non-dyadic structure and its application in image compression. It also presents mathematical concepts involved in wavelet transform like convolution, scaling function, wavelet function, multiresolution analysis, inner product etc. The motion estimation is an indispensable module in the design of video encoder. It employs block matching algorithm which involves searching a candidate block in the entire search window of the reference frame taking up to 80% of the total video encoding time. In order to increase the efficiency, several block matching algorithms are employed to minimize the computational time involved in block matching. Chapter 6 throws light on an efficient approach that can be to be applied to the existing block matching search techniques in HEVC which outperforms the various block matching algorithms.

In image retrieval systems, images are searched by means of text information, sample images, or using both. But this kind image retrieval schemes suffers with the problem of semantic gap which is the mismatch between the user requirement and the capabilities of the image retrieval system. Therefore, it is necessary to understand the mapping between the image content and its context. Chapter 7 discusses about multimodal retrieval system and is an expected way of searching that attracts substantial research consideration. Similarly in content based image retrieval applications, the indexing process is referred as mapping of descriptors into a high-dimensional space. Chapter 8 uses features like color, texture and shape as descriptors for retrieval applications. The color features are extracted using color coherence vector, texture features are obtained using segmentation based fractal texture analysis and shape features are extracted using the Fourier descriptors. The above said three features color, texture and shape are combined using appropriate weights. The concept of quad tree is used for indexing images for retrieval.

Due to advancement in technology in recent world, it is very easy to make unauthorized modification in others digital content. Hence security and safety has become very serious issue and it needs to be addressed. In chapter 9, automatic identification and early prediction of suspicious human activities are presented elaborately for surveillance research. By recognizing and predicting a criminal activity at an early stage, regrettable incidents can be avoided. Recent research on iris recognition could also be used very well for personality identification and it could be used in public safety. Chapter 10 gives insight into iris based recognition system which rely on patterns and textures present in the iris, the color of the iris, visible features present in the iris, geometric features of the iris, and the SIFT features. These geometric features of the iris can be used for human identification and crime reduction.

Similarly, object tracking and classification methods are highly demanding in vehicle traffic control systems, surveillance systems for detecting unauthorized movement of vehicle and human, mobile robot applications, animal tracking, etc. Chapter 11 presents an overview of various existing techniques for object detection, classification and tracking. As the most important requirements of tracking and classification algorithms are feature extraction and selection, different feature types are also included. Chapter 12 proposes a novel approach for deployment of human gait in developing new tools for security enhancement.

Chapter 13 presents classification mechanism for computed tomography images there by it could be possible to assist physicians in the diagnosis of lung diseases. The method is based on a new approach which combines a proposed M2 feature extraction method and a novel hybrid genetic approach with different types of classifiers. Chapter 14 presents biometric identification systems, establishing the authenticity of biometric data itself as an important issue. In this chapter, the multimodal biometric system is implemented using the different fusion schemes such as average fusion, minimum fusion, maximum fusion, principal component analysis fusion, In modality extraction level, the information extracted from different modalities is stored in vectors on the basis of their modality. These are then blended to produce a joint template which is the basis for the watermarking system. The fused image is applied as input along with the cover image to the genetic algorithm based bacterial foraging optimization algorithm watermarking system. The standard images are used as cover images and performances are compared in this chapter.

Image retrieval using its contents is playing a major role in recent days. Automatic image annotation is a process which produces words from a digital image based on the content of the image by using a computer. The automatic annotation process is discussed elaborately in chapter 15. Biomedical imaging techniques have significantly improved the health care of patients. Image guided therapy has reduced the high risk of human errors with improved accuracy in disease detection and surgical procedures. Chapter 16 provides an overview of existing imaging methods, current imaging approaches and their potential to unravel the challenges in medical field. Age-related macular degeneration is an eye disease that gradually degrades the macula, a part of the retina, which is responsible for central vision. In chapter 17, to diagnose age-related macular degeneration, a new EYENET model which combines the modified PNN and modified RBFNN is presented. Computed tomography images are widely used in the diagnosis of ischemic stroke because of its faster acquisition and compatibility with most life support devices. Chapter 18 presents a new approach to automated detection of ischemic stroke using k-means clustering technique which separates the lesion region from healthy tissues and classification of ischemic stroke using texture features.

We continued our effort to keep the book reader-friendly. By a problem solving approach, we mean that researchers learn the material through real life examples that provide the motivation behind the concepts and its relation to the real world problems. At the same time, readers must discover a solution for the non-trivial aspect of the solution. We trust and hope that the book will help the readers to further carryout their research in different directions.

V. Santhi
VIT University, India

D.P. Acharjya
VIT University, India

M. Ezhilarasan
Pondichery Engineering College, India

Acknowledgment

It is with great sense of satisfaction that we present our book entitled *Emerging Technologies in Intelligent Applications for Image and Video Processing* and wish to express our views to all those who helped us both direct and indirect way to complete this work. First of all we would like to thank the authors those who have contributed to this edited book. We acknowledge, with sincere gratitude the kindness of the School of Computer Science and Engineering, VIT University, India to provide an opportunity to carry out this research work. In addition, we are also thankful to VIT University, India for providing facilities to complete this project.

While writing, contributors have referred several books and journals; we take this opportunity to thank all those authors and publishers. We are extremely thankful to the editorial board, reviewers for their support during the process of evaluation. At last but not the least, we thank the production team of IGI Global, USA for encouraging us and extending their full cooperation and help in timely completion of this edited book.

V. Santhi
VIT University, India

D.P. Acharjya
VIT University, India

M. Ezhilarasan
Pondichery Engineering College, India

Section 1
Image and Video Enhancement, Restoration, and Segmentations

Chapter 1
Image and Video Restoration and Enhancement via Sparse Representation

Li-Wei Kang
National Yunlin University of Science and Technology, Taiwan

Chia-Mu Yu
Yuan Ze University, Taiwan

Chih-Yang Lin
Asia University, Taiwan

Chia-Hung Yeh
National Sun Yat-Sen University, Taiwan

ABSTRACT

The chapter provides a survey of recent advances in image/video restoration and enhancement via spare representation. Images/videos usually unavoidably suffer from noises due to sensor imperfection or poor illumination. Numerous contributions have addressed this problem from diverse points of view. Recently, the use of sparse and redundant representations over learned dictionaries has become one specific approach. One goal here is to provide a survey of advances in image/video denoising via sparse representation. Moreover, to consider more general types of noise, this chapter also addresses the problems about removals of structured/unstructured components (e.g., rain streaks or blocking artifacts) from image/video. Moreover, image/video quality may be degraded from low-resolution due to low-cost acquisition. Hence, this chapter also provides a survey of recently advances in super-resolution via sparse representation. Finally, the conclusion can be drawn that sparse representation techniques have been reliable solutions in several problems of image/video restoration and enhancement.

INTRODUCTION

With the rapid development of multimedia and network technologies, displaying and delivering digital multimedia contents (e.g., image/video data) through the Internet and heterogeneous devices has become more and more popular. However, digital images/videos usually unavoidably suffer from noises, which may arise from sensor imperfection, poor illumination, or communication errors (Buades, Coll, & Morel, 2005; Elad, 2010; Ohta, 2007). Image/video noise is usually random variation of brightness

DOI: 10.4018/978-1-4666-9685-3.ch001

or color information in digital images/videos. For example, a typical model of image noise is Gaussian and additive, which is independent at each pixel, and independent of the signal intensity. The principal sources of Gaussian noise in digital images/videos arise during acquisition, e.g., sensor noise, caused by poor illumination, high temperature, or transmission (Nakamura, 2005; Boncelet, 2005).

In addition, to consider more types of image noise, digital images/videos may usually also suffer from bad weather effects, such as, rain streaks (Garg & Nayar, 2007; Bossu, Hautière, & Tarel, 2011; Shehata et al., 2008), snow (Bossu, Hautière, & Tarel, 2011), or haze (or fog) (He, Sun, & Tang, 2011; Yeh, Kang, Lee, & Lin, 2013) (e.g., outdoor surveillance video), compression artifacts (for storage and transmission) (Shen & Kuo, 1998; List, Joch, Lainema, Bjontegaard, & Karczewicz, 2003; Yeh, Ku, Fan Jiang, Chen, & Jhu, 2012), or other undesired components (e.g., induced by image synthesis, manipulation, or editing) (Parra & Sajda, 2003; Haykin & Chen, 2005). On the other hand, besides noises, image/video quality may be also degraded from low-resolution (LR) due to low-cost acquisition system (Park, Park, & Kang, 2003; Farsiu, Robinson, Elad, & Milanfar, 2004; Freeman, Jones, & Pasztor, 2002, Freedman & Fattal, 2011).

To achieve image/video restoration and enhancement, several approaches, such as denoising (Shao, Yan, Li, & Liu, 2014; Buades, Coll, & Morel, 2005), removal of blocking artifacts (deblocking) (Shen & Kuo, 1998; List, Joch, Lainema, Bjontegaard, & Karczewicz, 2003; Yeh, Ku, Fan Jiang, Chen, & Jhu, 2012), removal of rain streaks (deraining) (Garg & Nayar, 2007; Bossu, Hautière, & Tarel, 2011; Shehata et al., 2008), removal of undesired components (Parra & Sajda, 2003; Haykin & Chen, 2005), and enhancement of resolution (Park, Park, & Kang, 2003; Farsiu, Robinson, Elad, & Milanfar, 2004; Freeman, Jones, & Pasztor, 2002, Freedman & Fattal, 2011) for image/video have been proposed. Several of them have been shown to lead to good results.

In recent years, sparse representation techniques (Dong, Shi, Ma, & Li, 2015; Starck, Fadili, Elad, Nowak, & Tsakalides, 2011; Baraniuk, Candès, Elad, & Ma, 2010; Elad, Figueiredo, & Ma, 2010; Elad, 2010; Olshausen & Field, 1996; Bruckstein, Donoho, & Elad, 2009) have been popular in these applications and have been shown to achieve state-of-the-art performances. Sparse representation, also known as sparse coding (Elad, 2010; Olshausen & Field, 1996; Bruckstein, Donoho, & Elad, 2009), is a technique of finding a sparse representation for a signal with a small number of nonzero or significant coefficients corresponding to the atoms in a dictionary (Giryes & Elad, 2014; Rubinstein, Peleg, & Elad, 2013; Elad, 2012; Rubinstein, Bruckstein, & Elad, 2010; Mairal, Bach, Ponce, & Sapiro, 2010; Aharon, Elad, & Bruckstein, 2006). It has been successfully applied to different types of signal decomposition applications (Fadili, Starck, Bobin, & Moudden, 2010; Kang, Yeh, Chen, & Lin, 2014). For examples, image/video denoising or restoration (Elad & Aharon, 2006; Mairal, Elad, & Sapiro, 2008; Mairal, Bach, & Ponce, 2012; Guo, Qu, Du, Wu, & Chen, 2014; Sun, Gao, Lu, Huang, & Li, 2014; Zhang, Zhao, & Gao, 2014; He, Wang, Zhang, Xu, & Lu, 2015; Liu, Zhang, Guo, Xu, & Zhou, 2015), deraining (Kang, Yeh, Chen, & Lin, 2014, Kang, Lin, & Fu, 2012; Kang, Lin, Lin, & Lin, 2012; Huang, Kang, Yang, Lin, & Wang, 2012; Huang, Kang, Wang, & Lin, 2014; Chen, Chen, & Kang, 2014; Chen & Hsu, 2013), deblocking (Jung, Jiao, Qi, & Sun, 2012; Yeh, Kang, Chiou, Lin, & Fan Jiang, 2014), removal of other components (Fadili, Starck, Bobin, & Moudden, 2010; Bobin, Starck, Fadili, Moudden, & Donoho, 2007; Starck, Elad, & Donoho, 2005), image/video super-resolution (Yang, Wright, Huang, & Ma, 2010; Yang, Wang, Lin, Cohen, & Huang, 2012; Dong, Zhang, Shi, & Wu, 2011; Ren, Liu, & Guo, 2013; Yang, Huang, & Yang, 2010; Yang & Wang, 2013; Tsai, Huang, Yang, Kang, & Wang, 2012; Kang, Chuang, Hsu, Lin, & Yeh, 2013; Peleg & Elad, 2014; Romano, Protter, & Elad, 2014; Zhang, Liu, Yang, & Guo, 2015; Kang, Hsu, Zhuang, Lin, & Yeh, 2015), and image/video recognition, classification, or understanding

(Wright, Yang, Ganesh, Sastry, & Ma, 2009; Kang et al., 2011; Guha & Ward, 2012; Yuan, Liu, & Yan, 2012; Hsiao, Kang, Chang, & Lin, 2015).

Moreover, sparse representation-inspired image/video signal restoration and enhancement techniques have been also successfully applied to different fields of applications in multimedia. For example, Chang et al. (2014) proposed a joint destriping and denoising framework by integrating the unidirectional total variation and sparse representation regularizations for remote sensing images. In addition, Guo et al. (2015) presented a global noise reduction approach based on the sparse representation and nonlocal means algorithm to enhance the qualities of both ultrasound images and magnetic resonance images. Moreover, Huang et al. (2015) proposed a cloud removal method for reconstructing the missing information in cloud-contaminated regions of a high-resolution optical satellite image based on sparse representation. On the other hand, Liu et al. (2015) proposed a latent fingerprint enhancement algorithm by combining the total variation model and multi-scale patch-based sparse representation for identifying and convicting criminals in law enforcement agencies. For other related image denoising applications, Tzoumas et al. (2014) presented a spatio-spectral denoising framework for multispectral optoacoustic imaging based on sparse signal representation. Furthermore, Zhao and Yang (2015) proposed a hyperspectral image denoising technique based on sparse representation and low-rank constraint.

On the other hand, for resolution enhancement applications, Chavez-Roman and Ponomaryov (2014) proposed a single image super resolution method based on wavelet domain interpolation with edge extraction via a sparse representation for remote sensing images. In addition, Walha et al. (2015) presented a resolution enhancement method for textual images via multiple coupled dictionaries and adaptive sparse representation selection. Moreover, Zhang et al. (2015) presented an algorithm for producing a high-resolution version for a low-resolution magnetic resonance image using sparse representation, nonlocal similarity and sparse derivative prior.

In this chapter, the main goal is to provide a comprehensive survey on the recent advances in image/video restoration and enhancement techniques via spare representation. The concept and the technical details in sparse representation, including sparse coding and dictionary learning algorithms, will be first introduced (Olshausen & Field, 1996; Bruckstein, Donoho, & Elad, 2009; Mairal, Bach, Ponce, & Sapiro, 2010; Aharon, Elad, & Bruckstein, 2006). Then, reviews of recent advances in signal decomposition via sparse representation (Fadili, Starck, Bobin, & Moudden, 2010; Kang, Yeh, Chen, & Lin, 2014) and their applications in image/video denoising or restoration (Elad & Aharon, 2006; Mairal, Elad, & Sapiro, 2008; Mairal, Bach, & Ponce, 2012; Huang, Kang, Wang, & Lin, 2014), deraining (Kang, Lin, & Fu, 2012; Kang, Lin, Lin, & Lin, 2012; Huang, Kang, Yang, Lin, & Wang, 2012; Huang, Kang, Wang, & Lin, 2014; Chen, Chen, & Kang, 2014; Chen & Hsu, 2013), deblocking (Jung, Jiao, Qi, & Sun, 2012; Yeh, Kang, Chiou, Lin, & Fan Jiang, 2014), and removal of undesired components (Bobin, Starck, Fadili, Moudden, & Donoho, 2007; Starck, Elad, & Donoho, 2005) will be given, where some of them are contributions of the authors (Kang, Yeh, Chen, & Lin, 2014; Kang, Lin, & Fu, 2012; Kang, Lin, Lin, & Lin, 2012; Huang, Kang, Yang, Lin, & Wang, 2012; Huang, Kang, Wang, & Lin, 2014; Chen, Chen, & Kang, 2014; Yeh, Kang, Chiou, Lin, & Fan Jiang, 2014).

Moreover, reviews of the recent advances in image/video super-resolution (SR) via sparse representation (Yang, Wright, Huang, & Ma, 2010; Yang, Wang, Lin, Cohen, & Huang, 2012; Dong, Zhang, Shi, & Wu, 2011; Ren, Liu, & Guo, 2013; Yang, Huang, & Yang, 2010; Yang & Wang, 2013; Tsai, Huang, Yang, Kang, & Wang, 2012; Kang, Chuang, Hsu, Lin, & Yeh, 2013), including the authors' self-learning-based SR method (Tsai, Huang, Yang, Kang, & Wang, 2012) and SR framework for a highly compressed image/video (Kang, Chuang, Hsu, Lin, & Yeh, 2013; Kang, Hsu, Zhuang, Lin, & Yeh, 2015) will be also provided. This chapter will also provide comparative studies among the reviewed sparse representation frameworks as well as their applications. Finally, this chapter will be concluded by discussing some further developments in sparse representation techniques and applications. It should be noted that this chapter focuses on the survey on image/video restoration and enhancement via sparse representation. For other applications of sparse representation or the essential techniques of sparse representation (e.g., dictionary learning or calculation of sparse coefficients), readers are referred to other good tutorial papers or special issue papers (e.g., Baraniuk, Candès, Elad, & Ma, 2010; Elad, Figueiredo, & Ma, 2010; Rubinstein, Bruckstein, & Elad, 2010; Fadili, Starck, Bobin, & Moudden, 2010; Elad, 2012; Shao, Yan, Li, & Liu, 2014; Starck, Fadili, Elad, Nowak, & Tsakalides, 2011).

The rest of this chapter is organized as follows. In the "background" section, the concepts of sparse coding and dictionary learning techniques as well as the MCA (morphological component analysis)-based signal decomposition framework via sparse representation (which forms the basis of image/video denoising via sparse representation) are briefly reviewed. The section of "image/video denoising via sparse representation" reviews recently representative sparse representation frameworks for image/video denoising as well as the authors' contributions. In the section of "image/video super-resolution via sparse representation," recently representative sparse representation frameworks for image/video super-resolution as well as the authors' contributions are reviewed. Finally, the "conclusion and future research direction" section concludes this chapter.

BACKGROUND

Sparse representation of signals has been widely investigated by signal and image processing communities in the past decades (Dong, Shi, Ma, & Li, 2015). Under the framework of sparse representation or sparse coding, many researches have been conducted on the related issues of the design of basis functions (or learning of dictionaries) and their applications. Exemplar studies of the dictionary learning is to train an over-complete dictionary from training data, e.g., the K-SVD (K-singular value decomposition) (Aharon, Elad, & Bruckstein, 2006), multiscale dictionary learning (Mairal, Sapiro, & Elad, 2008), and online dictionary learning (Mairal, Bach, Ponce, & Sapiro, 2010) algorithms.

In this section, the concept of sparse coding (Elad, 2010) and dictionary learning (Mairal, Bach, Ponce, & Sapiro, 2010; Aharon, Elad, & Bruckstein, 2006) techniques as well as the conventional MCA (morphological component analysis)-based signal decomposition framework (which forms the basis of image/video denoising via sparse representation) (Fadili, Starck, Bobin, & Moudden, 2010; Bobin, Starck, Fadili, Moudden, & Donoho, 2007; Starck, Elad, & Donoho, 2005), are briefly introduced. Then, the frameworks of image/video restoration and enhancement based on sparse representation as well as their comparative results or performance evaluations will be addressed in details in the following sections.

Sparse Coding and Dictionary Learning

Sparse coding (Olshausen & Field, 1996) is a technique of finding a sparse representation for a signal with a small number of nonzero or significant coefficients corresponding to the atoms in a dictionary (Mairal, Bach, Ponce, & Sapiro, 2010; Aharon, Elad, & Bruckstein, 2006). The pioneering work in sparse coding proposed by Olshausen and Field (Olshausen & Field, 1996) states that the receptive fields of simple cells in mammalian primary visual cortex can be characterized as being spatially localized, oriented, and bandpass. It was shown by Olshausen & Field (1996) that a coding strategy that maximizes sparsity is sufficient to account for these three properties, and that a learning algorithm attempting to find sparse linear codes for natural scenes will develop a complete family of localized, oriented, and bandpass receptive fields.

By considering the sparse representation for an image consisting of several components, to construct a dictionary D_s to sparsely represent each patch b_s^k extracted from the component I_s of an image I, where $I = \sum_{s=1}^{S} I_s$. A set of available training exemplars y^k, $k = 1, 2, \ldots, P$, may be used to learn a dictionary D_S sparsifying y^k by solving the following optimization problem (Mairal, Bach, Ponce, & Sapiro, 2010; Aharon, Elad, & Bruckstein, 2006):

$$\min_{D_s, \theta^k} \sum_{k=1}^{P} \left(\frac{1}{2} \left\| y^k - D_s \theta^k \right\|_2^2 + \lambda \left\| \theta^k \right\|_1 \right), \tag{1}$$

where θ^k denotes the sparse coefficient vector of y^k with respect to D_s and λ is a regularization parameter. Equation (1) can be efficiently solved by performing a dictionary learning algorithm, such as the online dictionary learning (Mairal, Bach, Ponce, & Sapiro, 2010) or K-SVD (K-singular value decomposition) (Aharon, Elad, & Bruckstein, 2006) algorithms, where the sparse coding step is usually achieved via the OMP (orthogonal matching pursuit) algorithm (Mallat & Zhang, 1993).

MCA-Based Signal Decomposition via Sparse Representation

The key idea of MCA is to utilize the morphological diversity of different features contained in the signal to be decomposed and to associate each morphological component to a dictionary of atoms (Fadili, Starck, Bobin, & Moudden, 2010; Bobin, Starck, Fadili, Moudden, & Donoho, 2007; Starck, Elad, & Donoho, 2005). Suppose an image I of N pixels is a superposition of S components (called morphological components), denoted by $I = \sum_{s=1}^{S} I_s$, where I_s denotes the s-th component, such as the geometric or textural component of the image I. To decompose I into I_s, $s = 1, 2, \ldots, S$, the MCA algorithm iteratively minimizes the following energy function:

$$E\left(\{I_s\}_{s=1}^{S}, \{\theta_s\}_{s=1}^{S} \right) = \frac{1}{2} \left\| I - \sum_{s=1}^{S} I_s \right\|_2^2 + \tau \sum_{s=1}^{S} E_s \left(I_s, \theta_s \right), \tag{2}$$

where θ_s denotes the sparse coefficients corresponding to I_s with respect to the dictionary D_s, τ is a regularization parameter, and E_s is the energy function defined according to the type of D_s (global or local dictionary). The MCA algorithm solve the equation (2) by iteratively performing for each component I_s, the following two steps: (i) update of the sparse coefficients: this step performs sparse coding (Bruckstein, Donoho, & Elad, 2009) to solve θ_s or $\left\{ \theta_s^p \right\}_{p=1}^{P}$, where θ_s^p represents the sparse coefficients of the p-th patch b_s^p extracted from I_s, and P is the total number of extracted patches, to minimize $E_s \left(I_s, \theta_s \right)$ while fixing I_s; and (ii) update of the components: this step updates I_s or $\left\{ b_s^p \right\}_{p=1}^{P}$ while fixing θ_s or $\left\{\theta_s^p\right\}_{p=1}^P$. Finally, the image decomposition is achieved by iteratively performing the MCA algorithm to solve I_s (while fixing D_s) and the dictionary learning algorithm to learn D_s (while fixing I_s) until convergence. More details about MCA can be found in (Fadili, Starck, Bobin, & Moudden, 2010; Fadili, Starck, Elad, & Donoho, 2010; Bobin, Starck, Fadili, Moudden, & Donoho, 2007; Peyré, Fadili, & Starck, 2007; Starck, Elad, & Donoho, 2005).

IMAGE/VIDEO DENOISING VIA SPARSE REPRESENTATION

In this section, recently representative sparse representation frameworks for image/video denoising as well as the authors' contributions (including removals of Gaussian noises, undesired components, rain streaks, and blocking artifacts) are provided.

Image Denoising via Sparse and Redundant Representations over Learned Dictionaries

Image/video noise removal or denoising problem is important and challenging (Buades, Coll, & Morel, 2005). The major goal is to design an algorithm that can remove unstructured or structured noise from an image/video which is acquired in the presence of an additive noise. Numerous contributions for image denoising in the past 50 years addressed this problem from many and diverse points of view. For example, spatial adaptive filters, stochastic analysis, partial differential equations, transform-domain methods, splines, approximation theory methods, and order statistics are some of the directions explored to address this problem (Elad & Aharon, 2006).

Recently, the use of sparse and redundant representations over learned dictionaries has become one specific approach towards image/video denoising, which has proven to be effective and promising (Elad & Aharon, 2006). Based on the assumption that image/video signals admit a sparse decomposition over a redundant dictionary, by using the K-SVD dictionary training algorithm (Aharon, Elad, & Bruckstein, 2006; Elad & Aharon, 2006) obtained a dictionary describing the image content effectively. They proposed two training options, where one is using the corrupted image itself and the other one is training on a set of pre-collected high-quality images. They have shown how such Bayesian treatment leads to a simple and effective denoising algorithm, which achieves state-of-the-art image denoising performance for Gaussian noises. Moreover, similar idea has been successfully extended to solve more general image restoration problems, such as removing nonhomogeneous noise or recovering missing information (e.g., text removal and inpainting (Mairal, Elad, & Sapiro, 2008) and binary artifacts removal from video-game images (Mairal, Bach, & Ponce, 2012)).

Removal of Undesired Image/Video Components Based on MCA-Based Signal Decomposition via Sparse Representation

To consider more general types of image/video noise removal, Starck *et al.* proposed a novel signal decomposition framework, called morphological component analysis (MCA) based on sparse representation of signals (Fadili, Starck, Bobin, & Moudden, 2010; Fadili, Starck, Elad, & Donoho, 2010; Bobin, Starck, Fadili, Moudden, & Donoho, 2007; Peyré, Fadili, & Starck, 2007; Starck, Elad, & Donoho, 2005). By assuming that each signal is the linear mixture of several layers (the so-called morphological components) that are morphologically distinct, MCA achieves signal decomposition relying on two principles, *i.e.*, sparsity and morphological diversity of different components. That is, each morphological component is sparsely represented in a specific transform domain, and the latter is highly inefficient in representing the other content in the mixture. A typical example is to decompose an image into its building components (e.g., geometric and textural parts), which has been recently investigated and extended to the applications of image analysis, synthesis, enhancement, restoration, and content editing.

More specifically, in the case of decomposing an image I into two components I_s, $s = 1, 2$, a key step of MCA described by the equation (2) is to properly select a dictionary built by combining two sub-dictionaries D_s, $s = 1, 2$, D_1 and D_2 can be either global or local dictionaries and should be mutually incoherent, that is, D_1 can provide sparse representation for I_1, but not for I_2, and vice versa. To decompose I into geometric (I_1) and textural (I_2) components, global wavelet or global curvelet is used as D_1, whereas global DCT or local DCT is used as D_2 in (Fadili, Starck, Bobin, & Moudden, 2010; Fadili, Starck, Elad, & Donoho, 2010; Bobin, Starck, Fadili, Moudden, & Donoho, 2007; Starck, Elad, & Donoho, 2005). A comprehensive description of dictionary selections and related parameter settings for different kinds of image decomposition can be found in Table 2 of (Fadili, Starck, Elad, & Donoho, 2010). On the other hand, in (Peyré, Fadili, & Starck, 2007), a global wavelet/curvelet basis is also used as D_1, whereas D_2 is constructed through a local dictionary learning process described by the equation (1). Finally, to decompose an image into two components, both D_1 and D_2 are required to sparsely represent each component individually. More details about traditional MCA methods, such as parameter settings, can be found in (Fadili, Starck, Bobin, & Moudden, 2010; Fadili, Starck, Elad, & Donoho, 2010; Bobin, Starck, Fadili, Moudden, & Donoho, 2007; Peyré, Fadili, & Starck, 2007; Starck, Elad, & Donoho, 2005).

Removal of Rain Streaks from a Single Image/Video Based on MCA-Based Signal Decomposition via Sparse Representation

To further apply MCA to solve more realistic problem, the authors first considered the problem of rain streaks removal from a single image. The major goal is to enhance the quality of an image captured from a digital camera/camera-phone in a rainy day for further applications (e.g., image feature extraction for image retrieval or recognition). However, it should be noted that it is impossible to directly apply the traditional MCA (the equation (2)) to solve the rain streak removal problem. The main reasons include: (i) traditional MCA algorithms usually use a fixed dictionary based on wavelets/curvelets to represent the geometric component of an image. In addition, to represent the textural component of an image, either a fixed or a learned dictionary is used. However, it is not easy to select a proper fixed dictionary to represent rain streaks due to its variety; and (ii) in traditional MCA algorithms, learning a dictionary for representing textural component usually assumes that a set of exemplar patches for the texture to be represented can be either known in advance or extracted from an image to be decomposed itself. Nevertheless, in practice, it is usually not easy to select correct rain patches in a single rain image automatically. Therefore, rather than using a fixed dictionary, assuming prior training exemplar patches available, or resorting to tuning parameters for the used dictionary, the authors proposed self-learning-based MCA framework via sparse representation to achieve rain streak removal from a single image (Kang, Lin, & Fu, 2012).

To decompose an input image into two or more morphological components, the authors proposed to first decompose the high-frequency (HF) part of the image, since the image components to be preserved and those to be removed (e.g., rain streaks or noise patterns) are typically mixed in an image. Unlike prior traditional MCA-based image decomposition works which require the collection of training data for observing the image dictionaries, the authors proposed to advocate the learning of the dictionaries directly from the input image itself, so that the image components associated with undesirable patterns can be automatically identified and extracted, while most original image details can be preserved.

As an example shown in Figure 1 (Kang, Lin, & Fu, 2012), for an input rain image I, a filter (e.g., the bilateral filter (Tomasi & Manduchi, 1998) or guided filter (He, Sun, & Tang, 2013)) is first applied to roughly decompose I into the low-frequency (LF) part (I_{LF}) and HF part (I_{HF}). Then, the authors proposed to learn a dictionary D_{HF} via the online dictionary learning (Mairal, Bach, Ponce, & Sapiro, 2010) based on the training patches extracted from I_{HF} itself to further decompose I_{HF}, where D_{HF} can be further divided into two sub-dictionaries, D_{HF_G} and D_{HF_R} ($D_{HF} = [D_{HF\_G} \mid D_{HF\_R}]$), for representing the non-noise (e.g., non-rain) and noise (e.g., rain) components of I_{HF}, respectively. Here, the method performs unsupervised clustering (e.g., the K-means algorithm) with the HoG (histogram of oriented gradients) feature (Dalal & Triggs, 2005) extracted from each dictionary atom, used to represent the dictionary atom for clustering (partitioning) D_{HF} into D_{HF_G} and D_{HF_R}, where the diversities of them have been well verified. As a result, the rain streaks removal problem for the image I is formulated as an MCA-based signal decomposition problem via sparse representation as:

$$\min_{\theta_{HF}^k \in R^m} \left\| b_{HF}^k - D_{HF}\theta_{HF}^k \right\|_2^2 s.t. \left\| \theta_{HF}^k \right\|_0 \leq L, \tag{3}$$

where $b_{HF}^k \in R^n$ represents the k-th patch extracted from I_{HF}. $\theta_{HF}^k \in R^m$ are the sparse coefficients of b_{HF}^k with respect to $D_{HF} \in R^{n \times m}$, $n \leq m$, and L denotes the sparsity or maximum number of nonzero coefficients of θ_{HF}^k. The equation (3) can be solved via l_1-minimization (a sparse coding technique) (Bruckstein, Donoho, & Elad, 2009), and then each patch b_{HF}^k can be reconstructed and used to recover either the non-rain or rain component of I_{HF}, depending on the corresponding nonzero coefficients in θ_{HF}^k, i.e., the used atoms from D_{HF_G} or D_{HF_R}. Finally, integrating the recovered non-rain component with I_{LF}, the rain-removed version of I can be produced. More details and experimental results of this framework can be found in (Kang, Lin, & Fu, 2012). In summary, the detail steps of the proposed MCA-based single image rain streaks removal framework (Kang, Lin, & Fu, 2012) is summarized in Table 1.

Then, this MCA-based single image rain streaks removal framework (Kang, Lin, & Fu, 2012) can be extended to removal of rain streaks from a video with static scene without significant moving objects (Kang, Lin, Lin, & Lin, 2012). By averaging a number of successive frames in a static scene of a rain video, the rain streaks can be eliminated in this "average frame," which can be used to replace the filtered image (LF part) in the original single-image-based method (Kang, Lin, & Fu, 2012). Therefore, the rain streaks in the following frames of the same scene can be removed accordingly. In addition, to further improve the performance of single image rain removal, the authors relied on the fact that in most rain images, the rain streaks are present in the entire image and with similar gradients. Therefore, the dictionaries learned from different context categories should share common atoms which indicate the rain patterns. This observation inspired the authors to present a context-aware framework for single image

Table 1. Proposed MCA-based single image rain streaks removal algorithm (Kang, Lin, & Fu, 2012)

Input: a rain image I.
Output: the rain-removed version I^{Non_Rain} of I.
1. Apply the bilateral filter to obtain the LF part I_{LF} and HF part I_{HF}, such that $I = I_{LF} + I_{HF}$.
2. Extract a set of image patches $y^k \in R^n$, $k = 1, 2, ..., P$, from I_{HF}. Apply the online dictionary learning for sparse coding algorithm to solve

$$\min_{D_{HF} \in R^{n \times m}, \theta^k \in R^m} \frac{1}{P} \sum_{k=1}^{P} \left(\frac{1}{2} \left\| y^k - D_{HF} \theta^k \right\|_2^2 + \lambda \left\| \theta^k \right\|_1 \right)$$

to obtain the dictionary D_{HF} consisting of the atoms that can sparsely represent y^k, $k = 1, 2, ..., P$.
3. Extract HoG feature descriptor for each atom in D_{HF}. Apply K-means algorithm to classify all of the atoms into two clusters based on their HoG feature descriptors.
4. Identify one of the two clusters as "rain sub-dictionary," D_{HF_R} and the other one as "geometric sub-dictionary," D_{HF_G}.
5. Apply MCA by performing OMP (orthogonal matching pursuit) to solve

$$\min_{\theta_{HF}^k \in R^m} \left\| b_{HF}^k - D_{HF} \theta_{HF}^k \right\|_2^2 \quad s.t. \quad \left\| \theta_{HF}^k \right\|_0 \leq L$$

for each patch $b_{HF}^k \in R^n$, $k = 1, 2, ..., P$, in I_{HF} with respect to $D_{HF} = [D_{HF\_G} | D_{HF\_R}]$.
6. Reconstruct each patch b_{HF}^k to recover either geometric component I_{HF}^G or rain component I_{HF}^R of I_{HF} based on the corresponding sparse coefficients obtained from Step 5.
7. Return the rain-removed version of I via $I^{Non\_Rain} = I_{LF} + I_{HF}^G$.

Figure 1. (a) Block diagram of the proposed rain streak removal method; and (b) illustration of the proposed method based on two learned dictionaries (Kang, Lin, & Fu, 2012)

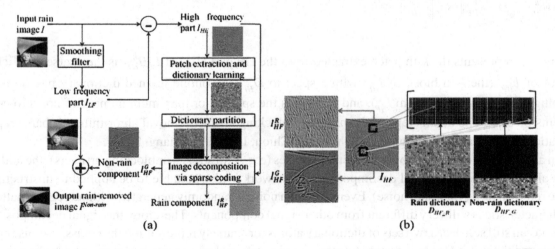

rain removal, which learns context information in an unsupervised setting, while the rain patterns can be automatically identified and removed from dictionaries learned for each context category (Huang, Kang, Yang, Lin, & Wang, 2012; Huang, Kang, Wang, & Lin, 2014). Moreover, to further improve the rain removal performance, the authors also proposed a single-color-image-based rain removal framework by formulating rain removal as an MCA-based image decomposition problem (Chen, Chen, & Kang, 2014).

Similar to (Kang, Lin, & Fu, 2012), an input color rain image is also first decomposed into LF part and HF part by a low-pass filter (the guided image filter (He, Sun, & Tang, 2013) was used here). Different from (Kang, Lin, & Fu, 2012), to separate rain streaks from the HF part, a hybrid feature set, including HoG (Dalal & Triggs, 2005), DoF (depth of field) (Meur, Baccino, & Roumy, 2011), and Eigen color (Tsai, L.-W. et al., 2008), is employed to further decompose the HF part. As a result, better rain removal performance for a single color image can be obtained (Chen, Chen, & Kang, 2014).

Extension to Removal of Blocking Artifacts and Gaussian Noises from a Single Image/Video

To investigate other multimedia applications of the signal decomposition framework, the authors proposed to extend the sparse representation-based framework to blocking artifacts removal (or deblocking) of compressed images/videos (Yeh, Kang, Chiou, Lin, & Fan Jiang, 2014). Inspired by (Kang, Lin, & Fu, 2012), the authors proposed a self-learning-based post-processing framework for image/video deblocking by properly formulating deblocking as an MCA-based signal decomposition problem via sparse representation. Without the need of any prior knowledge (e.g., the positions where blocking artifacts occur, the algorithm used for compression, or the characteristics of image/video to be processed) about the blocking artifacts to be removed, the method automatically learns two dictionaries for decomposing an input decoded image/video frame into its "blocking component" and "non-blocking component" to achieve the removal of blocking artifacts (Yeh, Kang, Chiou, Lin, & Fan Jiang, 2014). More specifically, to remove the blocking artifacts for a compressed image (or video frame) I via the author's framework via sparse representation, the problem can be formulated as:

$$\min_{\theta_{HF}^k} \left\| b_{HF}^k - D_{HF}\theta_{HF}^k \right\|_2^2 \; s.t. \left\| \theta_{HF}^k \right\|_0 \leq L \; , \tag{4}$$

where b_{HF}^k represents the k-th patch extracted from the HF part (I_{HF}) of I. θ_{HF}^k is the sparse coefficient vector of b_{HF}^k (the k-th block of I_{HF}) with respect to D_{HF} (the online learned dictionary based on the training patches extracted from I_{HF}), and L denotes the sparsity or maximum number of nonzero coefficients of θ_{HF}^k. The detail steps of the proposed blocking artifact removal algorithm via sparse representation is summarized in Figure 2 (Yeh, Kang, Chiou, Lin, & Fan Jiang, 2014).

In addition, other than removing structured noises (e.g., rain streaks or blocking artifacts), the authors have also found that the signal decomposition framework is also suitable to be applied to unstructured noise removal (e.g., Gaussian noise). Even Gaussian noise is randomly generated without regular pattern, its characteristic is still very different from other signal components. Therefore, the signal decomposition method can still self-learn two sets of dictionary atoms for sparsely representing the Gaussian-noise component and the noise-free component to achieve noise removal of an input noisy image. Unlike existing denoising methods (e.g., (Buades, Coll, & Morel, 2005; Elad & Aharon, 2006; Mairal, Elad, & Sapiro, 2008)), it is not required to know the standard deviation of such noise to be given in advance, which makes the method more practical for real-world applications. More details and experimental results of this framework can be found in (Huang, Kang, Wang, & Lin, 2014).

Figure 2. Summarization of the proposed self-learning-based image deblocking algorithm via sparse representation (Yeh, Kang, Chiou, Lin, & Fan Jiang, 2014)

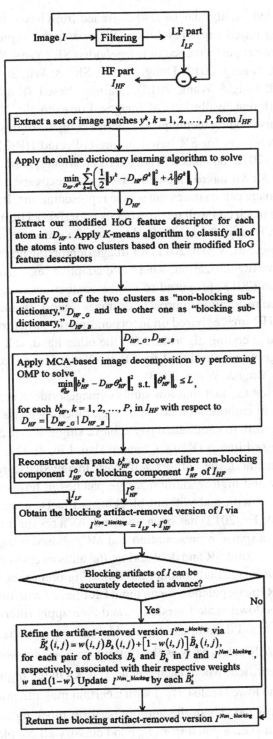

IMAGE/VIDEO SUPER-RESOLUTION VIA SPARSE REPRESENTATION

Other than noises, image/video quality may be also degraded from low-resolution (LR) due to low-cost acquisition system. Learning-based super-resolution (SR) via sparse representation has been recently shown to achieve state-of-the-art performance in image/video SR (Yang, Wright, Huang, & Ma, 2010; Yang, Wang, Lin, Cohen, & Huang, 2012; Dong, Zhang, Shi, & Wu, 2011; Ren, Liu, & Guo, 2013; Yang, Huang, & Yang, 2010; Yang & Wang, 2013). Learning-based SR approaches focus on modeling the relationship between different resolutions of images. For example, Yang, Wright, Huang, & Ma (2010) proposed to apply sparse coding techniques to learn a compact representation for high-resolution/ low-resolution (HR/LR) patch pairs for SR based on pre-collected HR/LR image pairs. Then, Yang, Wang, Lin, Cohen, & Huang (2012) advanced (Yang, Wright, Huang, & Ma, 2010) to propose a coupled dictionary training approach for SR based on patch-wise sparse recovery, where the learned couple dictionaries relate the HR/LR image patch spaces via sparse representations. It is guaranteed that the sparse representation of a LR image patch can well reconstruct its underlying HR image patch, which cannot be guaranteed in (Yang, Wright, Huang, & Ma, 2010). Moreover, a sparse representation based framework was proposed in (Dong, Zhang, Shi, & Wu, 2011) for image deblurring and SR based on adaptive sparse domain selection and adaptive regularization, where two adaptive regularization terms are introduced. In addition, Ren, Liu, & Guo (2013) proposed to utilize context-aware sparsity prior to enhance the performance of sparsity-based restoration approach for image denoising and SR. This method mitigates the artifacts in the produced HR images based on incorporating the structural correlations of dictionary atoms into the employed sparse coding algorithm. On the other hand, self-learning frameworks based on self-similarity of an image were introduced for SR in (Yang, Huang, & Yang, 2010; Tsai, Huang, Yang, Kang, & Wang, 2012; Yang & Wang, 2013).

Furthermore, by considering the fact that low-quality images/videos are usually not only with low-resolution, but also suffer from compression artifacts (e.g., blocking artifacts), the authors proposed a self-learning-based SR framework to simultaneously achieve single-image SR and compression artifact removal for a highly-compressed image (Kang, Chuang, Hsu, Lin, & Yeh, 2013; Kang, Hsu, Zhuang, Lin, & Yeh, 2015). In this method, the authors self-learn image sparse representation for modeling the relationship between low and high-resolution image patches in terms of the learned dictionaries, respectively, for image patches with and without blocking artifacts, where the signal decomposition characteristic in (Kang, Lin, & Fu, 2012) has been involved. As a result, image SR and deblocking can be simultaneously achieved via sparse representation and MCA-based image decomposition.

More specifically, to achieve joint SR and deblocking, the authors convert the problem into the high-frequency domain of the input image and conduct the following preprocessing tasks. To model the relationship between LR and HR image patches, for an input LR image I with blocking artifacts, the authors first down-scale I to obtain its down-scaled version I^d, and then apply filtering to decompose I into the LF part (I_{LF}) and HF part (I_{HF}), and decompose I^d into I_{LF}^d and I_{HF}^d, that is $I = I_{LF} + I_{HF}$, and $I^d = I_{LF}^d + I_{HF}^d$. Then, two sets of HR/LR patch pairs as the training samples for learning the dictionaries used for SR and deblocking are identified, where each patch ($x_i \in X$) in the higher scale (I_{HF}) and its corresponding patch ($y_i \in \Upsilon$) in the lower scale (I_{HF}^d) with a certain magnification factor to form a coupled training patch pair can be extracted. Then, the authors perform blocking artifact detection on the HR part of each coupled patch pair (i.e., a patch from I_{HF}) and classify all coupled patch pairs into two sets of "blocking" and "non-blocking" patch pairs: { X^B, Υ^B } and { X^N, Υ^N }.

Based on the two sets of training samples, the authors propose to learn two sets of dictionaries, respectively, for SR of non-blocking patches and joint SR and deblocking of blocking patches. Then, the SR of each input LR non-blocking patch b_p^N (in I_{HF}) can be formulated as the following sparse representation problem:

$$\widehat{\theta}_p^N = \arg \min_{\theta_p^N} \left\| b_p^N - D_N^{\mathrm{LR}} \theta_p^N \right\|_2^2 + \lambda \left\| \theta_p^N \right\|_1, \tag{5}$$

where D_N^{LR} denotes the learned LR dictionary of non-blocking atoms, θ_p^N is the sparse representation of b_p^N with respect to D_N^{LR}, $\widehat{\theta}_p^N$ is the solution of θ_p^N for minimizing the equation (5), and λ is a parameter controlling the sparsity penalty and representation fidelity. As a result, the SR result B_p^N of b_p^N can be obtained as follows:

$$B_p^N = D_N^{HR} \widehat{\theta}_p^N, \tag{6}$$

where D_N^{HR} is the learned HR dictionary of non-blocking atoms, which leads to the same sparse representation $\widehat{\theta}_p^N$ for an HR patch as that for its corresponding LR patch with respect to D_N^{LR}.

Moreover, the authors formulate the joint SR and deblocking for each input LR blocking patch b_p^B (in I_{HF}) as an MCA-based image decomposition problem via sparse representation:

$$\widehat{\theta}_p^B = \arg \min_{\theta_p^B} \left\| b_p^B - D_B^{\mathrm{LR}} \theta_p^B \right\|_2^2 + \lambda \left\| \theta_p^B \right\|_1, \tag{7}$$

where the definitions of θ_p^B and $\widehat{\theta}_p^B$ are similar to those in the equation (5), and $D_B^{\mathrm{LR}} = \left[D_{B\_N}^{\mathrm{LR}} \mid D_{B\_B}^{\mathrm{LR}} \right]$ is the learned LR dictionary based on the training samples with blocking artifacts, which can be further partitioned into $D_{B\_N}^{\mathrm{LR}}$ and $D_{B\_B}^{\mathrm{LR}}$, consisting of the non-blocking and blocking atoms, respectively. As a result, the joint SR and deblocking result B_p^B of b_p^B can be obtained by:

$$B_p^B = D_{B\_N}^{HR} \widehat{\theta}_{p\_N}^B, \tag{8}$$

where $D_{B\_N}^{HR}$ is obtained from the partition of the learned HR dictionary D_B^{HR} based on the training samples with blocking artifacts, which can be further partitioned into $D_{B\_N}^{HR}$ and $D_{B\_B}^{HR}$, including the non-blocking and blocking atoms, respectively, and $\widehat{\theta}_{p\_N}^B$ is the sparse representation of b_p^B obtained by solving the equation (7) with the coefficients corresponding to the atoms in $D_{B\_B}^{\mathrm{LR}}$, being set to zero. More details and experimental results of this framework can be found in (Kang, Chuang, Hsu, Lin, & Yeh, 2013; Kang, Hsu, Zhuang, Lin, & Yeh, 2015)..

COMPARATIVE STUDIES AND EVALUATION RESULTS

In this section, some experimental results (Kang, Yeh, Chen, & Lin, 2014) of the authors' signal decomposition frameworks for rain streaks removal (Kang, Lin, & Fu, 2012; Kang, Lin, Lin, & Lin, 2012, Huang, Kang, Wang, & Lin, 2014; Chen, Chen, & Kang, 2014), blocking artifacts removal (Yeh, Kang, Chiou, Lin, & Fan Jiang, 2014), Gaussian noises removal (Huang, Kang, Wang, & Lin, 2014), and joint super-resolution and deblocking (Kang, Chuang, Hsu, Lin, & Yeh, 2013; Kang, Hsu, Zhuang, Lin, & Yeh, 2015) for images/videos were presented. The compared results with those of some state-of-the-art approaches (Elad & Aharon, 2006; Yang, Wang, Lin, Cohen, & Huang, 2012; Tomasi & Manduchi, 1998; He, Sun, & Tang, 2013; List, Joch, Lainema, Bjontegaard, & Karczewicz, 2003; Kim & Sim, 2011; Hou & Andrews, 1978) were also provided. More experimental results and discussions can be found in (Kang, Lin, & Fu, 2012; Kang, Lin, Lin, & Lin, 2012, Huang, Kang, Wang, & Lin, 2014; Chen, Chen, & Kang, 2014; Kang, Chuang, Hsu, Lin, & Yeh, 2013; Kang, Hsu, Zhuang, Lin, & Yeh, 2015).

To evaluate the performance of image/video rain removal, several natural/synthetic rain images/videos from the Internet (with ground-truth images/videos for a few of them) were collected, as exemplified in Figure 3 for the test images with ground-truth ones (non-rain versions). Figures 4 and 5 (Kang, Yeh, Chen, & Lin, 2014) show some single image and video rain removal results, respectively. Based on Figure 4, the authors' frameworks (Kang, Lin, & Fu, 2012; Huang, Kang, Wang, & Lin, 2014; Chen, Chen, & Kang, 2014) significantly outperform existing approaches (Elad & Aharon, 2006; Tomasi & Manduchi, 1998; He, Sun, & Tang, 2013) used for comparisons in single image rain removal. The results demonstrate that although these existing denoising filter-based methods (Elad & Aharon, 2006; Tomasi & Manduchi, 1998; He, Sun, & Tang, 2013) can remove most rain streaks, they both simultaneously remove most image details as well. On the other hand, the proposed methods (Kang, Lin, & Fu, 2012; Huang, Kang, Wang, & Lin, 2014; Chen, Chen, & Kang, 2014) successfully removed most rain streaks while preserving most non-rain image details in these test cases. In addition, by advancing the techniques of context-constrained image segmentation, categorization, and sparse coding, the proposed context-aware method (Huang, Kang, Wang, & Lin, 2014) can outperform the MCA-based method (Kang, Lin, & Fu, 2012) which may remove parts of non-rain components as well due to the heuristic dictionary partition. Furthermore, the proposed visual depth guided method (Chen, Chen, & Kang, 2014) can recover/protect non-rain component while removing rain streaks, which can, to the best of the authors' knowledge, achieve the state-of-the-art performance in single image rain removal. Moreover, according to Figure 5, the proposed video rain removal method (Kang, Lin, Lin, & Lin, 2012) also outperforms the proposed single image-based method (lack of temporal information) (Kang, Lin, & Fu, 2012) and the state-of-the-art video-based method (based on very accurate rain detection result and simple interpolation-based method) (Garg & Nayar, 2007) in the static video case.

On the other hand, to objectively (or numerically) evaluate the performance of the proposed rain removal frameworks via sparse representation for the rain images with ground-truth (the corresponding non-rain versions), two numerical metrics are employed. The first one is the classical metric called the peak signal-to-noise ratio (PSNR in dB), defined as:

$$PSNR\left(I, \widehat{I}\right) = 10\log_{10} \frac{255^2}{\frac{1}{MN}\sum_{i=1}^{M}\sum_{j=1}^{N}\left[I\left(i,j\right) - \widehat{I}\left(i,j\right)\right]^2}, \qquad (9)$$

Figure 3. Examples of test images with ground-truth ones (non-rain versions) used for performance measurements and comparisons among the evaluated rain removal approaches, including the authors' frameworks. From the left column to right column: the original non-rain images, the corresponding rain versions, and the corresponding rain-removed versions by the authors' method proposed in (Kang, Lin, & Fu, 2012).

Figure 4. Single image rain removal results (Kang, Yeh, Chen, & Lin, 2014): (a) the original non-rain image; (b) the rain image of (a); the rain-removed versions of (b) via the: (c) bilateral filtering (Tomasi & Manduchi, 1998); (d) guided filtering (He, Sun, & Tang, 2013); (e) K-SVD-based denoising (Elad & Aharon, 2006); (f) proposed MCA-based (Kang, Lin, & Fu, 2012); (g) proposed context-aware-based (Huang, Kang, Wang, & Lin, 2014); and (h) proposed visual depth guided (Chen, Chen, & Kang, 2014) methods.

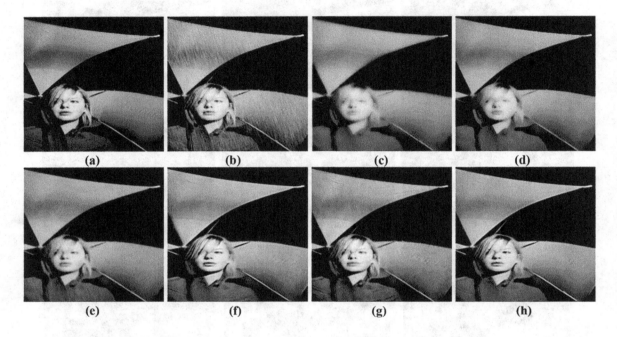

Figure 5. Video rain removal results (Kang, Yeh, Chen, & Lin, 2014): (a) the original rain video frame; and the rain-removed versions of (a) via the: (b) video-based method proposed in (Garg & Nayar, 2007); (c) proposed MCA-based (Kang, Lin, & Fu, 2012); and (d) proposed video-based (Kang, Lin, Lin, & Lin, 2012) methods.

where I and $\widehat{I}$ (with the same image size) denotes, respectively, a reference image (e.g., non-rain image) and the distorted image (e.g., the rain-removed version of a rain version of I), M and N denotes the height and width of an image, respectively. $I(i,j)$ and $\widehat{I}(i,j)$ denotes the pixel value of the (i,j)-th pixel of I and $\widehat{I}$, respectively. Moreover, the well-known visual information fidelity (VIF) metric (Sheikh & Bovik, 2006) is also employed for image quality assessment. VIF was developed by quantifying the information that is present in the reference image and how much of this reference information can be extracted from the distorted image. In the range of [0, 1], VIF has been shown to outperform the PSNR metric to better fit the human visual system. In both of the two metrics, the larger the measurement value is, the better the image quality will be. The PSNR and VIF results of the rain removal for the test images are summarized in Tables 2 and 3, respectively. Based on Tables 2 and 3 and Figure 4, although the bilateral filter and the K-SVD denoising filter can remove most rain streaks, they both simultaneously remove much image detail as well. Both the proposed MCA-based and context-aware-based methods successfully remove most rain streaks while preserving most non-rain image details in these test cases, thereby improving both the subjective and objective visual quality significantly.

In addition, to evaluate the performance of the proposed blocking artifacts removal method (Kang, Yeh, Chen, & Lin, 2014), H.264/AVC-decoded video sequences were used. Figure 6 shows some de-blocking results obtained by the H.264/AVC without filtering, H.264/AVC with in-loop filter (List, Joch, Lainema, Bjontegaard, & Karczewicz, 2003), dual non-local Kuan's (DNLK) filter based on a DCT domain Kuan's filter with non-local parameter estimation (Zhang, Ouyang, & Cham, 2011), signal adaptive weighted sum (SAWS) technique (Kim & Sim, 2011), and the proposed method (Kang, Yeh, Chen, & Lin, 2014), as well as their PSNR performance comparisons. It can be found from Figure 6 that the proposed method (Kang, Yeh, Chen, & Lin, 2014) outperforming the H.264/AVC with in-loop filter (List, Joch, Lainema, Bjontegaard, & Karczewicz, 2003), DNLK, and SAWS (Kim & Sim, 2011) methods can remove blocking artifacts from the original H.264/AVC-decoded versions while preserving acceptable visual quality, mainly benefiting from the proposed self-learning-based image decomposition strategy.

Table 2. The PSNR results for the test images by different evaluated rain removal methods

	Bilateral Filtering (Tomasi & Manduchi, 1998)	K-SVD (Elad & Aharon, 2006)	Proposed MCA-Based (Kang et al., 2012)	Proposed Context-Aware-Based (Huang et al., 2014)
Figure 3(a)	19.21	19.43	19.56	19.87
Figure 3(b)	20.07	20.56	21.66	21.90
Figure 3(c)	24.26	24.65	24.50	24.94

Table 3. The VIF results for the test images by different evaluated rain removal methods

	Bilateral Filtering (Tomasi & Manduchi, 1998)	K-SVD (Elad & Aharon, 2006)	Proposed MCA-Based (Kang et al., 2012)
Figure 3(a)	0.33	0.34	0.52
Figure 3(b)	0.31	0.41	0.57
Figure 3(c)	0.21	0.21	0.38

Figure 6. Deblocking results for the Foreman video sequence (Kang, Yeh, Chen, & Lin, 2014): (a) the rate-PSNR performances; the deblocked frames obtained by the: (b) the H.264/AVC-decoded frame with No filter; (c) the H.264/AVC-decoded frame with loop filer; (d) DNLK; (e) SAWS; and (f) proposed blocking artifacts removal methods.

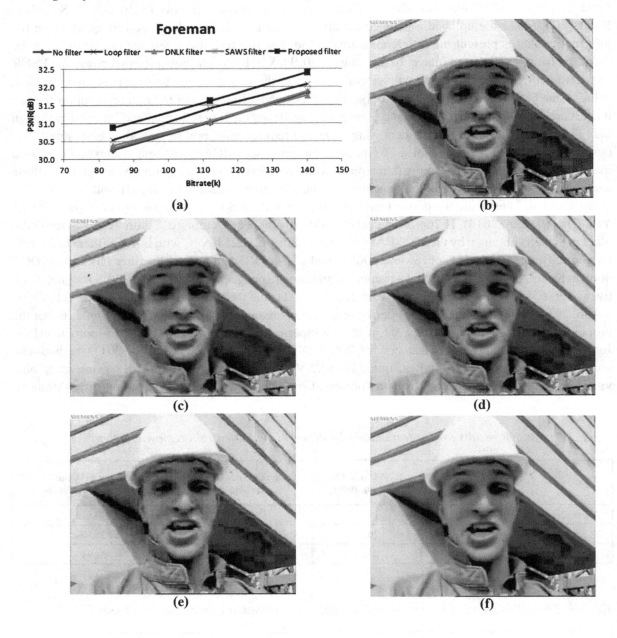

Figure 7. Image denoising results (Kang, Yeh, Chen, & Lin, 2014): (a) the original noise-free image; (b) the Gaussian noisy version of (a); and the noise-removed versions of (b) via the: (c) K-SVD-based denoising (Elad & Aharon, 2006); and (d) proposed denoising (Huang, Kang, Wang, & Lin, 2014) methods.

Moreover, to evaluate the performance of the proposed Gaussian noise removal method (Huang, Kang, Wang, & Lin, 2014), the K-SVD-based denoising method (Elad & Aharon, 2006) was used for comparison, and the results (with the standard deviation value "σ" of the Gaussian noise set to 25) were shown in Figure 7. The exact value of the parameter σ is required for the K-SVD method, while it is not required to be known in advance for the proposed method. It is assumed that this parameter is not exactly known in practical and simply set a larger standard deviation value σ = 35 for the experiment. As a result, the proposed method (Huang, Kang, Wang, & Lin, 2014) quantitatively and qualitatively outperformed the other (Elad & Aharon, 2006) without needing to know the standard deviation of Gaussian noise to be removed. In addition, some objective denoising results, in terms of PSNR, conducted on several standard test images with σ = 25 are also presented in Table 4, where it can be observed that the proposed Gaussian noise removal method outperforms these state-of-the-art approaches.

Furthermore, to evaluate the performance of the proposed joint super-resolution (SR) and deblocking method (Kang, Hsu, Zhuang, Lin, & Yeh, 2015), the method was compared with a baseline SR method (bicubic interpolation (Hou & Andrews, 1978)) and a state-of-the-art learning-based SR method via sparse coding (ScSR) (Yang, Wang, Lin, Cohen, & Huang, 2012). Figure 8 shows the SR results for a highly compressed JPEG image with quality factor (QF) set to 15. It can be observed from Figure 8 that the proposed joint SR and deblocking method (Kang, Hsu, Zhuang, Lin, & Yeh, 2015) outperforms

Table 4. The denoising results in terms of PSNR (in dB) for the standard test images by different evaluated Gaussian noise removal methods

	Bilateral Filtering (Tomasi & Manduchi, 1998)	K-SVD (Elad & Aharon, 2006)	BM3D (Dabov et al., 2007)	Proposed Gaussian Noise Removal Method (Huang et al., 2014)
Pepper	25.03	27.84	29.42	29.27
Lena	24.38	27.02	29.21	29.25
House	26.06	29.79	32.29	31.87
Cameraman	24.92	28.78	28.45	28.88
Boat	24.18	25.65	27.48	27.81

those obtained by the pure SR approaches (Yang, Wang, Lin, Cohen, & Huang, 2012; Hou & Andrews, 1978) used for comparisons, where blocking artifacts are significantly magnified while directly enlarging the image.

On the other hand, since SR is a process to artificially enhance the resolution of an image or based on hallucination, the PSNR metric is sometimes not suitable to evaluate the SR results. Based on the fact that the hallucinated image data may be different from the original version, but may fit the human perception, a subjective user study to evaluate the performances of various SR schemes for 9 test images were employed. In the subjective paired comparisons test (Lee, 2014), 20 subjects are shown with two side-by-side upscaled images obtained by different SR methods (in a random order) at a time, and are asked to choose their preference from the two compared images. For a test image, the method with the highest times preferred by subjects is determined to the best. Therefore, for example, if one method is preferred 80% of the time, it implies all test images (obtained by this method) are preferred on average 80% of the time. The subjects include 15 males and 5 females, whose ages range from 25 to 30. The test device is a full-HD 24-inch LCD display with color temperature 6500K. In the subjective test, the proposed joint SR and deblocking method (Kang, Hsu, Zhuang, Lin, & Yeh, 2015), Cascade type I (SR followed by deblocking based on BM3D denoising (Dabov, Foi, Katkovnik, & Egiazarian, 2007)), Cascade type II (deblocking based on BM3D, followed by SR), and only SR (Yang, Wang, Lin, Cohen, & Huang, 2012) are compared. Each SR method is pairwise compared with the others by totally 3×9×20=540

Figure 8. SR results: (a) the original high-resolution image; and the SR versions of the input low-resolution (LR) image (LR and JPEG-compressed version of (a) with QF = 15) via the: (b) bicubic (Hou & Andrews, 1978); (c) ScSR (Yang, Wang, Lin, Cohen, & Huang, 2012); and (d) proposed (Kang, Chuang, Hsu, Lin, & Yeh, 2013) methods.

Table 5. Winning frequency matrix of subjective paired comparisons among the four evaluated SR methods

	Proposed (Kang et al., 2015)	Cascade I (SR + BM3D)	Cascade II (BM3D + SR)	Only SR (Yang et al., 2012)	Average
Proposed (Kang et al., 2015)	-	70.56%	82.22%	94.44%	82.41%
Cascade I (SR + BM3D)	29.44%	-	50.56%	81.67%	53.89%
Cascade II (BM3D + SR)	17.78%	49.44%	-	79.44%	48.89%
Only SR (Yang et al., 2012)	5.56%	18.33%	20.56%	-	14.81%

times, meaning that 180 comparisons are made between any two methods for the 9 test images. Table 5 demonstrates the winning frequency matrices (Lee, 2014) of the 20 subjects' preferences in subjective paired comparisons on the SR results obtained using the four different methods, where the numbers in each row indicate the times of the method preferred than the compared ones in the column. It indicates that, compared to the other methods, the proposed method achieves better subjective visual quality in about 82% of the paired comparisons.

CONCLUSION AND FUTURE RESEARCH DIRECTIONS

In this chapter, a brief review and comparative studies for the recent advances in image/video restoration and enhancement via spare representation have been presented. The use of sparse and redundant representations over learned dictionaries has recently become one specific approach for image denoising and achieved stare-of-the-art performance. Furthermore, MCA (morphological component analysis)-based signal decomposition framework via sparse representation has been developed to remove more general types of noises. Based on these developments, the authors proposed a novel framework called self-learning-based signal decomposition based on MCA via sparse representation. This framework mainly relying on the uses of sparsity and morphological diversity in signal mixtures has demonstrated state-of-the-art performances in variety of applications, including image/video rain streaks removal (Kang, Yeh, Chen, & Lin, 2014, Kang, Lin, & Fu, 2012; Kang, Lin, Lin, & Lin, 2012; Huang, Kang, Yang, Lin, & Wang, 2012; Huang, Kang, Wang, & Lin, 2014; Chen, Chen, & Kang, 2014), blocking artifacts removal (Yeh, Kang, Chiou, Lin, & Fan Jiang, 2014), Gaussian noise removal (Huang, Kang, Wang, & Lin, 2014), and joint super-resolution and deblocking (Kang, Hsu, Zhuang, Lin, & Yeh, 2015). The major contribution of the authors' framework is three-fold: (i) to the best of the authors' knowledge, the framework is among the first to achieve both structured and unstructured noise removal in a self-learning manner while preserving geometrical details in an image, where no temporal or motion information among successive images is required; (ii) the proposed automatic MCA-based signal decomposition framework is adapted to several denoising applications in multimedia; and (iii) the learning of the proposed framework for decomposing noises from an image is fully automatic and self-contained, where no extra training samples are required in the dictionary learning stage. For future works, more real applications of the signal decomposition framework as well as efficient implementation strategy of the related methods will be further investigated.

REFERENCES

Aharon, M., Elad, M., & Bruckstein, A. M. (2006). The K-SVD: An algorithm for designing of overcomplete dictionaries for sparse representation. *IEEE Transactions on Signal Processing, 54*(11), 4311–4322. doi:10.1109/TSP.2006.881199

Baraniuk, R. G., Candès, E. J., Elad, M., & Ma, Y. (2010). Applications of sparse representation and compressive sensing. *Proceedings of the IEEE, 98*(6), 906–909. doi:10.1109/JPROC.2010.2047424

Bobin, J., Starck, J. L., Fadili, J. M., Moudden, Y., & Donoho, D. L. (2007). Morphological component analysis: An adaptive thresholding strategy. *IEEE Transactions on Image Processing, 16*(11), 2675–2681. doi:10.1109/TIP.2007.907073 PMID:17990744

Boncelet, C. (2005). Image noise models. In A. C. Bovik (Ed.), *Handbook of Image and Video Processing*. Academic Press.

Bossu, J., Hautière, N., & Tarel, J. P. (2011). Rain or snow detection in image sequences through use of a histogram of orientation of streaks. *International Journal of Computer Vision, 93*(3), 348–367. doi:10.1007/s11263-011-0421-7

Bruckstein, A. M., Donoho, D. L., & Elad, M. (2009). From sparse solutions of systems of equations to sparse modeling of signals and images. *SIAM Review, 51*(1), 34–81. doi:10.1137/060657704

Buades, A., Coll, B., & Morel, J. M. (2005). A review of image denoising algorithms, with a new one. *Multiscale Modeling & Simulation, 4*(2), 490–530. doi:10.1137/040616024

Chang, Y., Yan, L., Fang, H., & Liu, H. (2014). Simultaneous destriping and denoising for remote sensing images with unidirectional total variation and sparse representation. *IEEE Geoscience and Remote Sensing Letters, 11*(6), 1051–1055. doi:10.1109/LGRS.2013.2285124

Chavez-Roman, H., & Ponomaryov, V. I. (2014). Super resolution image generation using wavelet domain interpolation with edge extraction via a sparse representation. *IEEE Geoscience and Remote Sensing Letters, 11*(10), 1777–1781. doi:10.1109/LGRS.2014.2308905

Chen, D.-Y., Chen, C.-C., & Kang, L.-W. (2014). Visual depth guided color image rain streaks removal using sparse coding. *IEEE Transactions on Circuits and Systems for Video Technology, 24*(8), 1430–1455. doi:10.1109/TCSVT.2014.2308627

Chen, Y.-L., & Hsu, C.-T. (2013). A generalized low-rank appearance model for spatio-temporally correlated rain streaks. In *Proceedings of IEEE Int. Conf. Comput. Vis.* Sydney, Australia. doi:10.1109/ICCV.2013.247

Dabov, K., Foi, A., Katkovnik, V., & Egiazarian, K. (2007). Image denoising by sparse 3D transform-domain collaborative filtering. *IEEE Transactions on Image Processing, 16*(8), 2080–2095. doi:10.1109/TIP.2007.901238 PMID:17688213

Dalal, N., & Triggs, B. (2005). Histograms of oriented gradients for human detection. In *Proceedings of IEEE Conf. Comput. Vis. Pattern Recognit.* San Diego, CA: IEEE. doi:10.1109/CVPR.2005.177

Dong, W., Shi, G., Ma, Y., & Li, X. (2015). Image restoration via simultaneous sparse coding: Where structured sparsity meets Gaussian scale mixture. *International Journal of Computer Vision*, *114*(2-3), 217–232. doi:10.1007/s11263-015-0808-y

Dong, W., Zhang, L., Shi, G., & Wu, X. (2011). Image deblurring and super-resolution by adaptive sparse domain selection and adaptive regularization. *IEEE Transactions on Image Processing*, *20*(7), 1838–1857. doi:10.1109/TIP.2011.2108306 PMID:21278019

Elad, M. (2010). *Sparse and redundant representations: from theory to applications in signal and image processing*. Springer. doi:10.1007/978-1-4419-7011-4

Elad, M. (2012). Sparse and redundant representation modeling - what next? *IEEE Signal Processing Letters*, *19*(12), 922–928. doi:10.1109/LSP.2012.2224655

Elad, M., & Aharon, M. (2006). Image denoising via sparse and redundant representations over learned dictionaries. *IEEE Transactions on Image Processing*, *15*(12), 3736–3745. doi:10.1109/TIP.2006.881969 PMID:17153947

Elad, M., Figueiredo, M. A. T., & Ma, Y. (2010). On the role of sparse and redundant representations in image processing. *Proceedings of the IEEE*, *98*(6), 972–982. doi:10.1109/JPROC.2009.2037655

Fadili, J. M., Starck, J. L., Bobin, J., & Moudden, Y. (2010). Image decomposition and separation using sparse representations: An overview. *Proceedings of the IEEE*, *98*(6), 983–994. doi:10.1109/JPROC.2009.2024776

Fadili, J. M., Starck, J. L., Elad, M., & Donoho, D. L. (2010). MCALab: Reproducible research in signal and image decomposition and inpainting. *IEEE Computational Science & Engineering*, *12*(1), 44–63. doi:10.1109/MCSE.2010.14

Farsiu, S., Robinson, M., Elad, M., & Milanfar, P. (2004). Fast and robust multiframe super resolution. *IEEE Transactions on Image Processing*, *13*(10), 1327–1344. doi:10.1109/TIP.2004.834669 PMID:15462143

Freedman, G., & Fattal, R. (2011). Image and video upscaling from local self-examples. *ACM Transactions on Graphics*, *30*(2), 1–11. doi:10.1145/1944846.1944852

Freeman, W. T., Jones, T. R., & Pasztor, E. C. (2002). Example-based super-resolution. *IEEE Computer Graphics and Applications*, *22*(2), 56–65. doi:10.1109/38.988747

Garg, K., & Nayar, S. K. (2007). Vision and rain. *International Journal of Computer Vision*, *75*(1), 3–27. doi:10.1007/s11263-006-0028-6

Giryes, R., & Elad, M. (2014). Sparsity-based poisson denoising with dictionary learning. *IEEE Transactions on Image Processing*, *23*(12), 5057–5069. doi:10.1109/TIP.2014.2362057 PMID:25312930

Guha, T., & Ward, R. K. (2012). Learning sparse representations for human action recognition. *IEEE Transactions on Pattern Analysis and Machine Intelligence*, *34*(8), 1576–1588. doi:10.1109/TPAMI.2011.253 PMID:22745001

Guo, D., Qu, X., Du, X., Wu, K., & Chen, X. (2014). Salt and pepper noise removal with noise detection and a patch-based sparse representation. *Advances in Multimedia*, *2014*, 682747:1–682747:14.

Guo, Y., Chai, H., & Wang, Y. (2015). A global approach for medical image denoising via sparse representation. *Int. J. of Bioscience. Biochemistry and Bioinformatics*, *5*(1), 26–35.

Haykin, S., & Chen, Z. (2005). The cocktail party problem. *Neural Computation*, *17*(9), 1875–1902. doi:10.1162/0899766054322964 PMID:15992485

He, K., Sun, J., & Tang, X. (2011). Single image haze removal using dark channel Prior. *IEEE Transactions on Pattern Analysis and Machine Intelligence*, *33*(12), 2341–2353. doi:10.1109/TPAMI.2010.168 PMID:20820075

He, K., Sun, J., & Tang, X. (2013). Guided image filtering. *IEEE Transactions on Pattern Analysis and Machine Intelligence*, *35*(6), 1397–1409. doi:10.1109/TPAMI.2012.213 PMID:23599054

He, N., Wang, J.-B., Zhang, L.-L., Xu, G.-M., & Lu, K. (2015). Non-local sparse regularization model with application to image denoising. *Multimedia Tools and Applications*. doi:10.1007/s11042-015-2471-2

Hou, H. S., & Andrews, H. C. (1978). Cubic splines for image interpolation and digital filtering. *IEEE Transactions on Acoustics, Speech, and Signal Processing*, *26*(6), 508–517. doi:10.1109/TASSP.1978.1163154

Hsiao, J.-K., Kang, L.-W., Chang, C.-L., & Lin, C.-Y. (2015). *Learning-based leaf image recognition frameworks. In Intelligent Systems in Science and Information*. Springer International Publishing Switzerland.

Huang, B., Li, Y., Han, X., Cui, Y., Li, W., & Li, R. (2015). Cloud removal from optical satellite imagery with SAR imagery using sparse representation. *IEEE Geoscience and Remote Sensing Letters*, *12*(5), 1046–1050. doi:10.1109/LGRS.2014.2377476

Huang, D.-A., Kang, L.-W., Wang, Y.-C. F., & Lin, C.-W. (2014). Self-learning based image decomposition with applications to single image denoising. *IEEE Transactions on Multimedia*, *16*(1), 83–93. doi:10.1109/TMM.2013.2284759

Huang, D.-A., Kang, L.-W., Yang, M.-C., Lin, C.-W., & Wang, Y.-C. F. (2012). Context-aware single image rain removal. In *Proceedings of IEEE Int. Conf. Multimedia and Expo*. Melbourne, Australia: IEEE. doi:10.1109/ICME.2012.92

Jung, C., Jiao, L., Qi, H., & Sun, T. (2012). Image deblocking via sparse representation. *Signal Processing Image Communication*, *27*(6), 663–677. doi:10.1016/j.image.2012.03.002

Kang, L.-W., Chuang, B.-C., Hsu, C.-C., Lin, C.-W., & Yeh, C.-H. (2013). Self-learning-based single image super-resolution of a highly compressed image. In *Proceedings of IEEE Int. Workshop Multimedia Signal Process*. (pp. 224–229). Sardinia, Italy: IEEE. doi:10.1109/MMSP.2013.6659292

Kang, L.-W., Hsu, C.-C., Zhuang, B., Lin, C.-W., & Yeh, C.-H. (2015). Learning-based joint super-resolution and deblocking for a highly compressed image. *IEEE Transactions on Multimedia*, *17*(7), 921–934. doi:10.1109/TMM.2015.2434216

Kang, L.-W., Hsu, C.-Y., Chen, H.-W., Lu, C.-S., Lin, C.-Y., & Pei, S.-C. (2011). Feature-based sparse representation for image similarity assessment. *IEEE Transactions on Multimedia*, *13*(5), 1019–1030. doi:10.1109/TMM.2011.2159197

Kang, L.-W., Lin, C.-W., & Fu, Y.-H. (2012). Automatic single-image-based rain streaks removal via image decomposition. *IEEE Transactions on Image Processing, 21*(4), 1742–1755. doi:10.1109/TIP.2011.2179057 PMID:22167628

Kang, L.-W., Lin, C.-W., Lin, C.-T., & Lin, Y.-C. (2012). Self-learning-based rain streak removal for image/video. In *Proceedings of IEEE Int. Sym. Circuits Syst.* Seoul, Korea: IEEE. doi:10.1109/IS-CAS.2012.6271635

Kang, L.-W., Yeh, C.-H., Chen, D.-Y., & Lin, C.-T. (2014). Self-learning-based signal decomposition for multimedia applications: a review and comparative study. In *Proceedings of APSIPA Annual Summit and Conf.* Angkor Wat, Cambodia: APSIPA.

Kim, J., & Sim, C.-B. (2011). Compression artifacts removal by signal adaptive weighted sum technique. *IEEE Transactions on Consumer Electronics, 57*(4), 1944–1952. doi:10.1109/TCE.2011.6131175

Lee, J.-S. (2014). On designing paired comparison experiments for subjective multimedia quality assessment. *IEEE Transactions on Multimedia, 16*(2), 564–571. doi:10.1109/TMM.2013.2292590

List, P., Joch, A., Lainema, J., Bjontegaard, G., & Karczewicz, M. (2003). Adaptive deblocking filter. *IEEE Transactions on Circuits and Systems for Video Technology, 13*(7), 614–619. doi:10.1109/TC-SVT.2003.815175

Liu, M., Chen, X., & Wang, X. (2015). Latent fingerprint enhancement via multi-scale patch based sparse representation. *IEEE Trans. Information Forensics and Security, 10*(1), 6–15. doi:10.1109/TIFS.2014.2360582

Liu, Q., & Zhang, C., Guo, Xu, H., & Zhou, Y. (2015). Adaptive sparse coding on PCA dictionary for image denoising. *The Visual Computer*.

Mairal, J., Bach, F., & Ponce, J. (2012). Task-driven dictionary learning. *IEEE Transactions on Pattern Analysis and Machine Intelligence, 34*(4), 791–804. doi:10.1109/TPAMI.2011.156 PMID:21808090

Mairal, J., Bach, F., Ponce, J., & Sapiro, G. (2010). Online learning for matrix factorization and sparse coding. *Journal of Machine Learning Research, 11*, 19–60.

Mairal, J., Elad, M., & Sapiro, G. (2008). Sparse representation for color image restoration. *IEEE Transactions on Image Processing, 17*(1), 53–69. doi:10.1109/TIP.2007.911828 PMID:18229804

Mairal, J., Sapiro, G., & Elad, M. (2008). Learning multiscale sparse representation for image and video restoration. *SIAM Multiscale Modeling and Simulation, 7*(1), 214–241. doi:10.1137/070697653

Mallat, S., & Zhang, Z. (1993). Matching pursuits with time-frequency dictionaries. *IEEE Transactions on Signal Processing, 41*(12), 3397–3415. doi:10.1109/78.258082

Meur, O. L., Baccino, T., & Roumy, A. (2011). Prediction of the inter-observer visual congruency (IOVC) and application to image ranking. In *Proceedings of ACM Conf. Multimedia.* ACM.

Nakamura, J. (2005). *Image Sensors and Signal Processing for Digital Still Cameras.* CRC Press. doi:10.1201/9781420026856

Ohta, J. (2007). *Smart CMOS Image Sensors and Applications.* CRC Press. doi:10.1201/9781420019155

Olshausen, B. A., & Field, D. J. (1996). Emergence of simple-cell receptive field properties by learning a sparse code for natural images. *Nature*, *381*(13), 607–609. doi:10.1038/381607a0 PMID:8637596

Park, S. C., Park, M. K., & Kang, M. G. (2003). Super-resolution image reconstruction: A technical overview. *IEEE Signal Processing Magazine*, *20*(3), 21–36. doi:10.1109/MSP.2003.1203207

Parra, L., & Sajda, P. (2003). Blind source separation via generalized eigenvalue decomposition. *Journal of Machine Learning Research*, *4*, 1261–1269.

Peleg, T., & Elad, M. (2014). A statistical prediction model based on sparse representations for single image super-resolution. *IEEE Transactions on Image Processing*, *23*(6), 2569–2582. doi:10.1109/TIP.2014.2305844 PMID:24815620

Peyré, G., Fadili, J., & Starck, J. L. (2007). Learning adapted dictionaries for geometry and texture separation. In *Proceedings of SPIE*. SPIE.

Ren, J., Liu, J., & Guo, Z. (2013). Context-aware sparse decomposition for image denoising and super-resolution. *IEEE Transactions on Image Processing*, *22*(4), 1456–1469. doi:10.1109/TIP.2012.2231690 PMID:23221827

Romano, Y., Protter, M., & Elad, M. (2014). Single image interpolation via adaptive nonlocal sparsity-based modeling. *IEEE Transactions on Image Processing*, *23*(7), 3085–3098. doi:10.1109/TIP.2014.2325774 PMID:24860029

Rubinstein, R., Bruckstein, A. M., & Elad, M. (2010). Dictionaries for sparse representation modeling. *Proceedings of the IEEE*, *98*(6), 1045–1057. doi:10.1109/JPROC.2010.2040551

Rubinstein, R., Peleg, T., & Elad, M. (2013). Analysis K-SVD: A dictionary-learning algorithm for the Analysis sparse model. *IEEE Transactions on Signal Processing*, *61*(3), 661–677. doi:10.1109/TSP.2012.2226445

Shao, L., Yan, R., Li, X., & Liu, Y. (2014). From heuristic optimization to dictionary learning: A review and comprehensive comparison of image denoising algorithms. *IEEE Trans. Cybernetics*, *44*(7), 1001–1013. doi:10.1109/TCYB.2013.2278548 PMID:24002014

Shehata, M. S., Cai, J., Badawy, W. M., Burr, T. W., Pervez, M. S., Johannesson, R. J., & Radmanesh, A. (2008). Video-based automatic incident detection for smart roads: The outdoor environmental challenges regarding false alarms. *IEEE Transactions on Intelligent Transportation Systems*, *9*(2), 349–360. doi:10.1109/TITS.2008.915644

Sheikh, H. R., & Bovik, A. C. (2006). Image information and visual quality. *IEEE Transactions on Image Processing*, *15*(2), 430–444. doi:10.1109/TIP.2005.859378 PMID:16479813

Shen, M.-Y., & Kuo, C.-C. J. (1998). Review of postprocessing techniques for compression artifacts removal. *Journal of Visual Communication and Image Representation*, *9*(1), 2–14. doi:10.1006/jvci.1997.0378

Starck, J. L., Elad, M., & Donoho, D. L. (2005). Image decomposition via the combination of sparse representations and a variational approach. *IEEE Transactions on Image Processing*, *14*(10), 1570–1582. doi:10.1109/TIP.2005.852206 PMID:16238062

Starck, J. L., Fadili, J., Elad, M., Nowak, R. D., & Tsakalides, P. (2011). Introduction to the issue on adaptive sparse representation of data and applications in signal and image processing. *J. Sel. Topics Signal Process.*, *5*(5), 893–895. doi:10.1109/JSTSP.2011.2162154

Sun, D., Gao, Q., Lu, Y., Huang, Z., & Li, T. (2014). A novel image denoising algorithm using linear Bayesian MAP estimation based on sparse representation. *Signal Processing*, *100*, 132–145. doi:10.1016/j.sigpro.2014.01.022

Tomasi, C., & Manduchi, R. (1998). Bilateral filtering for gray and color images. In *Proceedings of the IEEE Int. Conf. Comput. Vis.* Bombay, India: IEEE. doi:10.1109/ICCV.1998.710815

Tsai, C.-Y., Huang, D.-A., Yang, M.-C., Kang, L.-W., & Wang, Y.-C. F. (2012). Context-aware single image super-resolution using locality-constrained group sparse representation. In *Proceedings of IEEE Visual Commun. Image Process.* San Diego, CA: IEEE. doi:10.1109/VCIP.2012.6410851

Tsai, L.-W., Hsieh, J.-W., Chuang, C.-H., Tseng, Y.-J., Fan, K.-C., & Lee, C.-C. (2008). Road sign detection using eigen colour. *IET Comput. Vis.*, *2*(3), 164–177. doi:10.1049/iet-cvi:20070058

Tzoumas, S., Rosenthal, A., Lutzweiler, C., Razansky, D., & Ntziachristos, V. (2014). Spatio-spectral denoising framework for multispectral optoacoustic imaging based on sparse signal representation. *Medical Physics*, *41*(113301). PMID:25370669

Walha, R., Drira, F., Lebourgeois, F., Garcia, C., & Alimi, A. M. (2015). Resolution enhancement of textual images via multiple coupled dictionaries and adaptive sparse representation selection. *Int. J. Document Analysis and Recognition*, *18*(1), 87–107. doi:10.1007/s10032-014-0235-6

Wright, J., Yang, A., Ganesh, A., Sastry, S., & Ma, Y. (2009). Robust face recognition via sparse representation. *IEEE Transactions on Pattern Analysis and Machine Intelligence*, *31*(2), 210–227. doi:10.1109/TPAMI.2008.79 PMID:19110489

Yang, C.-Y., Huang, J.-B., & Yang, M.-H. (2010). Exploiting self-similarities for single frame super-resolution. In *Proceedings of Asian Conf. Comput. Vis.* (pp. 497–510). Queenstown, New Zealand.

Yang, J., Wang, Z., Lin, Z., Cohen, S., & Huang, T. S. (2012). Coupled dictionary training for image super-resolution. *IEEE Transactions on Image Processing*, *21*(8), 3467–3478. doi:10.1109/TIP.2012.2192127 PMID:22481818

Yang, J., Wright, J., Huang, T. S., & Ma, Y. (2010). Image super-resolution via sparse representation. *IEEE Transactions on Image Processing*, *19*(11), 2861–2873. doi:10.1109/TIP.2010.2050625 PMID:20483687

Yang, M.-C., & Wang, Y.-C. F. (2013). A self-learning approach to single image super-resolution. *IEEE Transactions on Multimedia*, *15*(3), 498–508. doi:10.1109/TMM.2012.2232646

Yeh, C.-H., Kang, L.-W., Chiou, Y.-W., Lin, C.-W., & Fan Jiang, S.-J. (2014). Self-learning-based post-processing for image/video deblocking via sparse representation. *Journal of Visual Communication and Image Representation*, *25*(5), 891–903. doi:10.1016/j.jvcir.2014.02.012

Yeh, C.-H., Kang, L.-W., Lee, M.-S., & Lin, C.-Y. (2013). Haze effect removal from image via haze density estimation in optical model. *Optics Express*, *21*(22), 27127–27141. doi:10.1364/OE.21.027127 PMID:24216937

Yeh, C.-H., Ku, T.-F., Fan Jiang, S.-J., Chen, M.-J., & Jhu, J.-A. (2012). Post-processing deblocking filter algorithm for various video decoders. *IET Image Process.*, *6*(5), 534–547. doi:10.1049/iet-ipr.2010.0545

Yuan, X.-T., Liu, X., & Yan, S. (2012). Visual classification with multitask joint sparse representation. *IEEE Transactions on Image Processing*, *21*(10), 4349–4360. doi:10.1109/TIP.2012.2205006 PMID:22736645

Zhang, D., He, J., Zhao, Y., & Du, M. (2015). MR image super-resolution reconstruction using sparse representation, nonlocal similarity and sparse derivative prior. *Computers in Biology and Medicine*, *58*, 130–145. doi:10.1016/j.compbiomed.2014.12.023 PMID:25638262

Zhang, J., Zhao, D., & Gao, W. (2014). Group-based sparse representation for image restoration. *IEEE Transactions on Image Processing*, *23*(8), 3336–3351. doi:10.1109/TIP.2014.2323127 PMID:24835225

Zhang, R., Ouyang, W., & Cham, W.-K. (2011). Image postprocessing by non-local Kuan's filter. *J. Vis. Commun. Image R.*, *22*(3), 251–262. doi:10.1016/j.jvcir.2010.12.007

Zhang, Y., Liu, J., Yang, W., & Guo, Z. (2015). Image super-resolution based on structure-modulated sparse representation. *IEEE Transactions on Image Processing*, *24*(9), 2797–2810. doi:10.1109/TIP.2015.2431435 PMID:25966473

Zhao, Y., & Yang, J. (2015). Hyperspectral image denoising via sparse representation and low-rank constraint. *IEEE Transactions on Geoscience and Remote Sensing*, *53*(1), 296–308. doi:10.1109/TGRS.2014.2321557

Chapter 2
An Efficient Method for Optimizing Segmentation Parameters

Jacob D'Avy
University of Tennessee, USA

Chung-Hao Chen
Old Dominion University, USA

Wei-Wen Hsu
Old Dominion University, USA

Andreas Koschan
University of Tennessee, USA

Mongi Abidi
University of Tennessee, USA

ABSTRACT

Segmenting an image into meaningful regions is an important step in many computer vision applications such as facial recognition, target tracking and medical image analysis. Because image segmentation is an ill-posed problem, parameters are needed to constrain the solution to one that is suitable for a given application. For a user, setting parameter values is often unintuitive. We present a method for automating segmentation parameter selection using an efficient search method to optimize a segmentation objective function. Efficiency is improved by utilizing prior knowledge about the relationship between a segmentation parameter and the objective function terms. An adaptive sampling of the search space is created which focuses on areas that are more likely to contain a minimum. When compared to parameter optimization approaches based on genetic algorithm, Tabu search, and multi-locus hill climbing the proposed method was able to achieve equivalent optimization results with an average of 25% fewer objective function evaluations.

1. INTRODUCTION

Image segmentation is the process of dividing an image into regions of interest. It is a crucial step in image analysis applications such as facial recognition (Ferrera, Franco & Maio, 2012), target tracking (Heber, Godec, Rüther, Roth & Bischof, 2013), and medical imaging (Chen, Udupa, Bagci, Zhuge & Yao, 2012). Segmentation is a difficult problem which has no general solution. Free parameters are often required to constrain a segmentation problem to produce the desired result. However, the relationship

DOI: 10.4018/978-1-4666-9685-3.ch002

between parameter values and segmentation output is not always clearly defined and finding the best segmentation parameters for an image can be a tedious process. The motivation for parameter optimization is to simplify this process by allowing segmentation methods to work in varying conditions with limited user interaction. There are several challenges associated with optimization in this setting that are described in Crevier (2008).

1. There is no differentiable function to relate segmentation performance with parameters.
2. There are multiple local minima in the parameter space.
3. The process of segmenting and evaluating is time expensive.

These challenges restrict the type of optimization that can be applied to segmentation parameters. The most basic approach to finding optimal parameters is a brute-force search of the possible parameter values (Ilea & Whelan, 2009). This method is straightforward but requires evaluating a very large set of parameter combinations which makes it computationally infeasible. Other approaches have used neural networks to find optimal parameters for segmenting images (Shen, Sandham, Granat & Sterr, 2005). Parameter values were incorporated into network weights and optimized using a set of training data. These approaches are limited to applications where training data is available and a universal segmentation goal can be defined. The most common approach to segmentation parameter optimization has been to use a direct search in the parameter space using methods such as local searches and stochastic searches which do not require differentiation. The typical search process moves through a solution space by making small changes to a candidate solution as it seeks to minimize an objective function. The advantage to direct search methods is that they are relatively efficient in finding local minima in the parameter space and they are also easily adaptable to different segmentation applications.

The main drawback to this type of approach is that the search is trial based which means that every potential solution must be evaluated. In the context of segmentation parameter optimization this means segmenting the original image using the parameter values represented by the potential solution and then evaluating the objective function for the segmentation results. To optimize a segmentation method that uses multiple parameters may require segmenting an image for thousands of parameter combinations. The time required to perform so many segmentations limits the practicality of using this type of parameter search. To overcome this problem we develop a new optimization approach which utilizes knowledge about the segmentation parameter environment. We show that for most segmentation parameters we can assume a monotonic relationship between a parameter value and the uniformity and complexity of the segmentation result. Efficiency is gained by incorporating this basic prior knowledge about the effect of a parameter on the segmentation result into the parameter search. Thus, in this paper we propose a segmentation optimization method that couples an efficient search method with a dual criteria type of segmentation objective function to greatly reduce the computational time required to find optimal segmentation parameters. We utilize a type of segmentation objective function which balances a region uniformity term with a complexity term. The minimum of a weighted sum of these two terms defines an optimal segmentation. Utilizing prior knowledge about the relationship between a segmentation parameter and its effect on the uniformity and complexity terms of the objective function enables our method to shrink the search space by eliminating parameter values that are unable to contain a minimum. Figure 1 shows a simulated example of how the proposed method calculates the best possible objective function score within a region of parameter values. The left image and center image show the values of objective function terms for segmentations of an image created by varying two segmentation parameters.

Figure 1. The left image and center image show simulated objective function data for segmentations of an image that were created by varying two segmentation parameters. The right image shows how the proposed method is able to calculate the best possible objective function score within a region of parameter values. The orange markers represent the nine segmentations that were necessary to determine the best possible objective function score in the four parameter value regions.

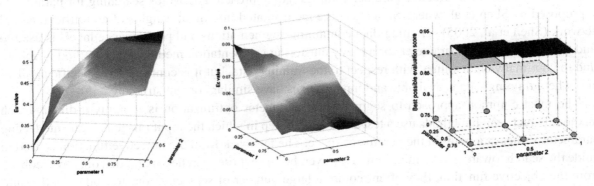

The image on the right shows the best possible objective function score for four parameter regions. The proposed method divides the parameter values into four regions by creating nine segmentations (indicated by orange markers). The best possible objective function score in each region is calculated using prior knowledge about the relationship between the parameter values and the objective function terms. During the proposed parameter search, the best possible objective function score data is used to eliminate parameter regions that cannot contain a minimum.

2. BACKGROUND

There are two components that must be reviewed to give a setting for the work proposed in this paper: segmentation parameter optimization methods and segmentation objective functions. Approaches to segmentation parameter optimization are reviewed first and the motivation for our choice to use a direct search is given. Then segmentation objective functions are reviewed and we describe the function used in our parameter optimization scheme.

2.1 Segmentation Parameter Optimization

Parameters are typically required in segmentation methods to set constraints on the desired segmentation solution. The goal of segmentation parameter optimization is to automate or simplify the process of setting appropriate parameter values for a given image. The function being optimized is a segmentation objective function which is discussed in the next section. Here we assume the existence of an adequate evaluation function which can indicate the performance of a segmentation result. The parameter space is the set of all possible combinations of values for the segmentation parameters. In an exhaustive or brute-force search a grid is created in the parameter space. The input image is segmented for each point in the grid using the combination of parameter values at that point. Each segmentation result is evaluated using the objective function. The parameters that produce the segmentation with the minimal objective function score are considered optimal. An example of this type of search is used by Ilea and Whelan to find the value of a region merging threshold (Ilea & Whelan, 2009). The problem with this type of exhaustive search is that it requires a large number of segmentations to be evaluated even for a parameter grid with moderate resolution. Also, a uniform sampling is not efficient because most parameter spaces contain large areas of ineffective parameter values. An approach that avoids searching for parameters is proposed by Shen et al. where parameters are incorporated into input weights of an artificial neural network (Shen et al, 2005). Training data containing segmentations and performance labels is used to find the best weighting parameter for a fuzzy clustering segmentation method. This method is able to find the optimal weight values with respect to the training data, but it is confined to a specific application where training data is available and input images have similar content structure.

The most common approach to segmentation parameter optimization is to apply a direct search method. Direct search methods use a test and evaluate step in which the input image is segmented using parameter values at a point in the parameter space. The feedback from the objective function is used to guide the search toward a local minimum. However, because these searches are guided only by feedback from the objective function, they often require a large number of segmentations to find a good result. A number of different direct search methods have been used in the literature. A parameter optimization method using Tabu search was proposed by Crevier (Ilea & Whelan, 2009). Tabu search seeks a local minimum by generating potential solutions within a search space using an evolving neighborhood structure (Glover & Laguna, 2013). A short term memory of potential solutions with the best performance is stored. This memory structure is used to create a search window for generating new potential solutions. An ellipsoidal search space is created that encloses the N best parameter values. As the search progresses, the search space shrinks around an area producing better objective function scores which helps create a finer sampling resolution around the minimum. The initial population size, memory size, and new generation size are free parameters which must be set appropriately to get the best performance. A termination criterion must also be defined to stop the search. One possibility is to terminate after a set number of iterations with no change in the N best parameter values. The advantage of Tabu search is that its random generation of new parameter values allows it to explore the parameter space while the memory structure allows the search ellipse to shrink around a minimum. However, it can take a large number of iterations for convergence and each iteration requires segmenting the input image for each new parameter value.

A genetic algorithm (GA) has also been used to search for optimal parameters by Fredrich and Feitosa (Feitosa, Costa, Cazes & Feijo, 2006; Fredrich & Feitosa, 2008), Everingham et al. (2002), and Forouzanfar et al. (2010). Genetic algorithms seek to find an optimal solution by performing a parallel heuristic search (Goldberg, 1989). The process used by Fredrich and Feitosa begins with an initial population that is generated randomly. Each individual in the population is represented by a set of genes. The genes represent the parameter values for the segmentation method. The input image is segmented using the parameters represented by the genes of each individual. The fitness of each individual is evaluated by using the segmentation objective function. Then a new generation is created by reproduction based on the fitness scores. This cycle of fitness evaluation and reproduction is repeated for a designated number of iterations. In each new generation the N individuals with the worst fitness score are replaced by new individuals. New individuals are created using the genetic operations: one point crossover, arithmetic crossover, mutation, and creep mutation. Genetic algorithms have been shown to successfully find optimal segmentation parameters. However, finding the appropriate combination of reproduction operations and populations settings for a particular search problem can be difficult. Also finding a solution often requires many generations of individuals which must be segmented and evaluated. This means it can take a long time to execute.

Min et al. proposed using a multi-locus hill climbing scheme to find optimal parameters for range image segmentation (Min, Powell & Bowyer, 2004). Hill climbing attempts to maximize an objective function by making small adjustments to a potential solution and accepting the new solution if an improvement is made. This method is applied to the parameter search problem by initializing each parameter with G values to make a grid within the useful range. The input image is segmented using the parameter values represented by each point on the grid. For example, for 4 parameters and $G=5$ there would be $5^4=625$ initial segmentations. Each segmentation is evaluated and the images in the top p percent of objective function scores are kept. Then a more refined grid of size r is expanded around each parameter combination that was kept. The new set of refined parameter values is evaluated. This process is repeated until the performance does not improve by a certain threshold, t. The parameters used in the original work are $G=5$, $p=1\%$, $r=3$, and $t=5\%$. The drawback to this type of hill climbing is that evaluating just the original grid of parameter values can take a lot of time and only a fraction of those parameter values end up being used to refine the search. Even more objective function evaluations are required to thoroughly explore the parameter space.

2.2 Segmentation Objective Function

Many evaluation methods have been developed to measure the performance of image segmentation methods (Zhang, Fritts & Goldman, 2008). There are two basic types of segmentation evaluation functions: supervised and unsupervised (Zhang, 2006). Supervised methods evaluate a segmentation based on how well it corresponds to a manually created ground truth segmentation. The score assigned to a test segmentation is based on properties such as region overlap or boundary correspondence between the test segmentation and the ground truth (Dogra, Majumdar & Sural, 2012; Hafiane, Chabrier, Rosenberger & Laurent, 2007; Monteiro & Campilho, 2006; Peng & Zhang, 2012). These methods are straightforward and effective but they are limited to applications where a ground truth is available. In an unsupervised evaluation function a segmented image is judged according to a set of quality criteria (Zhang, 2001). The advantage of unsupervised methods is that they do not require a ground truth. Also they can be used to dynamically adjust segmentation parameters in a self-tunable segmentation algorithm (Zhang et al, 2008). For this reason we use an unsupervised evaluation measure as the objective function in our parameter optimization method. Different types of unsupervised evaluation functions for segmentation have been developed including direct measures, adaptive methods, and machine learning based methods.

A common type of unsupervised evaluation function is based on features calculated within each region (intraregion), features calculated from adjacent regions (interregion), and global features. Many of these features are based on a definition for good segmentation given by Haralick and Shapiro (1985) which states that a segmented region should be uniform with a simple boundary and should be significantly different from adjacent regions. These methods calculate a set of feature values for a segmentation and then combine them to assign a performance score. In one of the first formulations for unsupervised performance evaluation, Levine and Nazif created a set of performance criteria based on a low level general segmentation definition (Levine & Nazif, 1985). The criteria come from four image region properties:

1. Uniformity within a region,
2. Contrast between adjacent regions,

3. Contrast across lines and connectivity,
4. Texture measures.

Liu and Yang (1994) used intraregion variance as a measure of performance quality. A penalty for having too many regions was used to create a balance between over and under segmentation. This measure has a bias toward heavily oversegmented images. This is due to the relatively small penalty for having many regions. Borsotti et al. (1998) adapted Liu and Yang's measure by making a harsher penalty on the total number of regions. The oversegmentation penalty is higher for a segmentation that contains small regions with the same area. In practice, their measure still heavily favors oversegmentations. Heidemann (Heidemann, 2008) used a measure called color saliency(CS) to evaluate segmentation region stability and performance. CS measures the difference between a regions average color and the average color of the bordering regions. This measure tends to prefer undersegmented images. This is due to the fact that it does not penalize large nonhomogeneous regions.

As a result, an image that contains a few large regions can have good saliency scores because there is a big difference between the average colors in adjacent regions. A multiscale evaluation method (MS) was proposed by Philipp-Foliguet and Guigues (2008) that contains a user-set parameter to adjust the desired scale of segmentation. They use a general energy formulation for segmentation evaluation that combines two energies. The first energy represents how well a segmentation region fits an assumed homogeneity model (piecewise constant, Gaussian, etc.). The second energy is a regularizing term which is needed to prevent simplest case segmentations such as one pixel per region. The combined energy term for a segmentation R is given by

$$E(k,R) = \sum_{R_i \in R} E_D(R_i) + k E_C(R_i) \tag{1}$$

where R_i is the ith segmented region, E_D is the fit term, E_C is the complexity term, and k is a scale parameter. The parameter k allows an evaluation method to be adapted to the desired level of segmentation detail. An evaluation method using intra/inter region properties based on visible color difference has been proposed by Chen and Wang (2006). The visible color difference method (VCD) uses the CIE L*a*b* color space because it is perceptually uniform. Intra-region visual error is calculated based on the color difference between every pixel and the average region color. Pixels that have a color difference greater than a threshold are considered erroneous. The inter-region error measures the amount of oversegmentation. Boundary pixels are evaluated to see if the color difference across the boundary is below a threshold. To get a single value for a performance score the inter-region error and intra-region error values are combined using a weighted sum. Zhang et al. (2003) proposed using entropy to evaluate the performance of a segmentation. When applied to segmented images entropy can be used to evaluate the organization of pixels within a region. Uniformity is measured as the bit coding length of the values of a pixel-level feature inside a region. However, a one pixel per region (or complete oversegmentation) segmentation will have very low region entropy. In order to counteract this, a value called the layout entropy is also used. The layout entropy is the bit coding length of the region labels.

The work presented in this paper seeks to create an efficient segmentation parameter optimization method. The objective function should be versatile, fast, and effective in evaluating segmentation quality. Measures such as VCD and MS are flexible, have low computation time, and can work in many segmentation applications. We use this type of evaluation measure as the objective function in our parameter optimization method. In the next section we show how we can exploit additional properties of these objective functions to improve parameter search efficiency.

3. PROPOSED PARAMETER OPTIMIZATION METHOD

The novelty of our segmentation parameter optimization method is that it incorporates knowledge about the segmentation environment into the search process to improve efficiency. The proposed method is able to reduce the search space by eliminating areas that are unable to produce a global minimum. We will first describe how we utilize domain knowledge in the segmentation parameter search. The objective function used in the proposed method is a segmentation evaluation measure composed of two counteracting criteria which balance segmentation complexity and region uniformity. A push-pull type of objective function has a uniformity term E_U, and a complexity term E_C, combined as a weighted sum. The E_U term is a measure of the uniformity within segmented regions. The E_C term is a measure of the segmentation complexity. The weighting value can be used to create a bias toward more oversegmentation or undersegmentation. Domain knowledge is included in our parameter search by defining a basic relationship between parameter values and the terms E_U and E_C. A free segmentation parameter is typically used to control the level of detail or granularity of the segmentation result. A segmentation with finer granularity will have smaller, more uniform regions. It will also have more regions and more intricate region boundaries. The opposite is true for a segmentation with coarse granularity. Consider a parameter which directly or indirectly affects the number of segmented regions. Adjusting that parameter to produce more regions will cause the result to be more uniform and more complex. Based on these observations about parameter effect, we make the assumption that as a segmentation parameter value is increased or decreased it has a monotonic effect on the push-pull terms E_U and E_C. Consider a parameter m which sets the minimum region size allowed for a segmentation. Regions with size less than m are merged with their most similar neighbor. Increasing the value of m can have two possible effects on the segmentation result:

1. If there are no regions with size less than m, there is no change in the segmentation.
2. A region with size less than m is merged with a neighbor.

If regions are merged and they are not identical, then the final merged region will be less uniform than the original regions. Whatever the outcome is, the value of E_U will either stay the same or increase when m is increased. The value of E_C will either stay the same or decrease when m is increased. This indicates a monotonic relationship. The same type of relationship can be extended to almost any type of free parameter used in segmentation. The validity of the monotonic assumption is tested in the experimental results section.

We will now describe how the monotonic relationship between parameter values and the objective function terms is used to develop a parameter optimization method. We begin by looking at a segmentation algorithm with N free parameters. Each parameter $p_1, p_2, \ldots, p_N$ has a range of possible values which create an N-dimensional space of potential parameter values. Within this parameter space there is a point, represented as a parameter vector p, that optimizes a given segmentation objective function. The goal is to efficiently find p. The proposed method divides a parameter space into N-dimensional parameter regions (PR). These regions create the structure that is used to search the parameter space. An important aspect of our search method is the ability to calculate the best possible objective function score that can be achieved within a parameter region. This is made possible using the monotonic relationship assumption between segmentation parameters and push-pull objective function terms E_U and E_C as discussed previously. The best possible score, E_{BPS}, is calculated for a region by using the minimum value for E_U and E_C in the region. Because the values of E_U and E_C change monotonically with the value of a parameter, their minimum value in a region can be calculated by taking their minimum at the region end points.

$$E_{BPS}\left(PR_x\right) = \alpha E_U^{\min} + \left(1 - \alpha\right) E_C^{\min} \tag{2}$$

where

$E_U^{\min} =$ minimum possible value for E_U within the parameter region
$E_C^{\min} =$ minimum possible value for E_C within the parameter region

An example of finding the best possible objective function score is shown in Figure 2. The α is plugged into the parameter vector p to calculate the best possible objective function score that can be achieved within a parameter region. Table 1 has summarized our approach. To calculate E_{BPS} for PR_1 in Figure 2, the minimum of E_U and E_C for $p_1=1$ and $p_1=10000$ is used. See the below equation.

$$E_{BPS}(PR_1)=0.5(\min(0.02, 0.14)) + 0.5(\min(0.07, 0.01))=0.015 \text{ for } \alpha=0.5 \tag{3}$$

Figure 2. The parameter region PR_1 covers the range from $p_1=1$ to $p_1=10000$. The objective function values are shown for a set of segmentations created using parameter values within PR_1. Because the values of E_U and E_C change monotonically as p_1 changes, their minimum values within PR_1 can be found by taking their minimum at the endpoints $p_1=1$ and $p_1=10000$. The best possible objective function score, E_{BPS}, for all parameter values in PR_1 is found by calculating E using the minimum values of E_U and E_C at the parameter region endpoints.

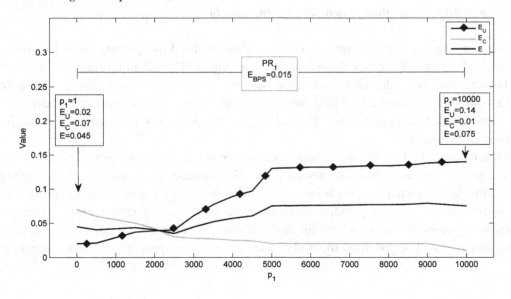

Table 1. The correlation between a segmentation parameter value and the E_U and E_C value of the segmentation result. Spearman's rank correlation coefficient was used to test the monotonic relationship between the segmentation parameter value and the E_U and E_C value of the segmentation result. The 200 training images from the Berkeley Segmentation Dataset were used as test images.

Segmentation Method	Parameter Name	Parameter function	E_U Correlation Coefficient	E_C Correlation Coefficient
Graph Based	σ	Adjust amount of smoothing applied to the input image	0.98	-0.92
Graph Based	k	Defines a merging threshold	0.98	-0.99
Graph Based	m	Sets a minimum area for regions	0.99	-1
Dynamic Region Merging	λ_1	Controls region merging termination	0.99	-0.99
Mean shift	h_r	Kernel bandwidth for range domain	0.98	-0.99

The value of E_{BPS} provides a lower bound for the objective function within a parameter region. As the search progresses, additional parameter regions are created by subdividing the existing regions. Within each new parameter region an exploratory parameter point is evaluated. This exploratory point provides information about the performance of parameter values within the parameter region. The size of the parameter space that must be searched is reduced by eliminating a parameter region if it has an E_{BPS} value that is higher than the E value of the current best p. Figure 3 shows what happens when the parameter region is subdivided. After calculating E_{BPS} for both regions, it can be seen that the exploratory point at $p_1=2500$ has an E value that is less than E_{BPS} for PR_2. At that point PR_2 can be eliminated from the search because it is not possible for any parameter values within the range of PR_2 to produce a minimum for E.

Figure 3. After the parameter region in Figure 2 has been split into two parameter regions, PR_1 and PR_2, an additional exploration point has been created within each parameter range at $p_1=2500$ and $p_1=7500$. The value of E_{BPS} has been calculated for both parameter regions. PR_2 can be eliminated from the search because the value of E for $p_1=2500$ is less than E_{BPS} for PR_2.

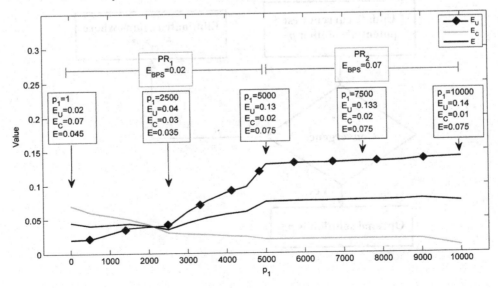

An eliminated region is left out of the search which gives more focus to parameter regions that have potential of containing a minimum. The next parameter region to subdivide is determined by alternating between the largest remaining region (exploration) and the region with the lowest E_{BPS} (exploitation). The exploration step helps to ensure that the search covers the entire parameter space. The exploitation step focuses on regions with more promise for finding a minimum. This creates a finer search resolution around local minima. Combining these two steps creates an adaptive sampling within the parameter space which focuses on more promising parameter regions. Adaptive sampling and region elimination allows the search method to find optimal parameters with relatively few objective function evaluations. The process shown for one free parameter extends to segmentation methods with multiple free parameters. A flow chart showing the search process is shown in Figure 4. The process begins with the whole parameter space contained in one parameter region. Convergence is determined when the current best p does not change for C iterations. A typical value for C is 5.

Figure 4. Flowchart of proposed parameter optimization method. Originally the entire parameter space is considered. On each iteration a parameter region is subdivided and potential solutions are generated within the new regions. Parameter regions can be eliminated if their E_{BPS} value is higher than the E value of the best potential solution. Convergence is determined when there is no improvement in p* after C iterations. The final output of the search is p*, the optimal parameter vector.

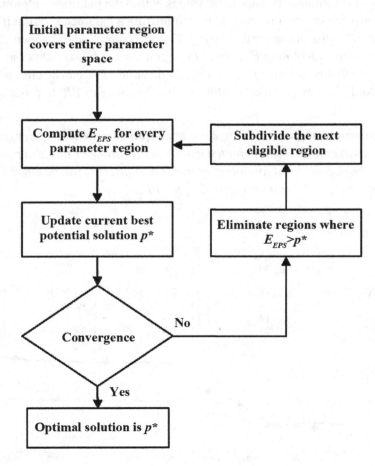

4. EXPERIMENTAL RESULTS

First we show results from experiments that test the assumption of a monotonic relationship between parameter values and the objective function terms. Next, results are shown for experiments that test the ability of the proposed method to find optimal parameters for different segmentation methods. Optimization results for a basic region merging segmentation method are shown and compared to an exhaustive search of parameter values. The results from the proposed method are then compared with three other parameter optimization methods: Tabu search (Crevier, 2008), genetic algorithm (Feitosa et al, 2006), and multilocus hill climbing (Min et al., 2004). Each method was applied to the 200 test images from the Berkeley Segmentation dataset (Arbelaez, Maire, Fowlkes & Malik, 2011). The performance of the optimization methods was measured by comparing the optimized segmentation output to the ground truth images. The methods were also compared based on the total number of objective function evaluations required during optimization. The objective function used for both experiments is the Multiscale method (Philipp-Foliguet & Guigues, 2008) described in Section 2.

4.1 Analysis of Segmentation Parameter Effect on Objective Function Terms

The proposed method is based on a monotonic relationship between segmentation parameter values and the terms of a push-pull objective function. In order to verify this relationship we conducted an experiment where different segmentation parameters were varied and the effect on the objective function terms was recorded. Figure 5 shows an illustrative example of increasing the parameter m for the Efficient Graph Based segmentation method (Felzenszwalb & Huttenlocher, 2004). The plot in Figure 6 shows the monotonic effect of the value of m on the E_U and E_C terms from the push-pull evaluation method used in (Philipp-Foliguet & Guigues, 2008). The E_U and E_C terms represent the error so lower values indicate better fit.

Table 1 shows E_U and E_C data for parameters used in three different types of segmentation methods: graph based (Felzenszwalb & Huttenlocher, 2004), region merging (Peng, Zhang & Zhang, 2011), and clustering (Comaniciu & Meer, 2002). The monotonic assumption was tested experimentally on the 200 training images from the Berkeley Segmentation Dataset (Arbelaez et al, 2011). For each image 10

Figure 5. Segmentations of an image from the Berkeley segmentation set (Arbelaez, Maire, Fowlkes, & Malik, 2011) showing the effect of varying the parameter m. As m is increased to 1000 the small details such as the windows are merged into larger regions which are less uniform. Also, because there are fewer regions and more simple boundaries the complexity is reduced.

Input image   *m*=50   *m*=1000

Figure 6. A plot showing the effect of varying the parameter m for segmentations of the image shown in Figure 5. As m increases, the value of E_U increases monotonically and the value of E_C decreases monotonically. This relationship is used in our proposed parameter optimization method to shrink the range of parameter values that must be searched.

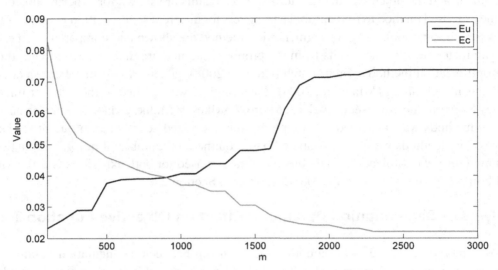

different parameter values were used. For each parameter value the E_U and E_C value of the segmentation result was calculated. The Spearman's rank correlation coefficient (Philipp-Foliguet & Guigues, 2008) was calculated between the parameter value and the E_U and E_C value to test the monotonic relationship. A Spearman correlation value of +1 or -1 indicates a perfect monotonic relationship between the two variables (Chalmer, 1987). The results in Table 1 show that there is strong correlation between the parameter value and the E_U and E_C value. As the segmentation parameter increases, the value of E_U almost always increases and E_C decreases. For some parameters this relationship may be inverted but it is not important as long as the effect is still monotonic.

4.2 Results for Face Image

In this experiment the proposed method is used to find the optimal parameter value for segmenting a clean face image. The segmentations are created using a region growing method. The only parameter used is M which sets a merging threshold. If the difference between the average color in two adjacent regions is less than M the regions are merged. The segmentation evaluation measure in (Philipp-Foliguet & Guigues, 2008) was used as the objective function. The final segmentation result produced after optimizing M is shown in Figure 7. The optimal value of M was searched for within a range between 2 and 200. After 9 iterations the optimal parameter value found was $M=84.2$. The input image was segmented a total of 19 times for this search. The results are compared to an exhaustive search of 396 segmentations where M is varied from 2-200 by steps of 0.5. The optimal parameter value found using the exhaustive search is $M=83.5$. The output segmentations from the exhaustive search and our method are almost identical which shows it was very close to finding the globally optimal parameter value. Figure 8 shows the objective function data for the exhaustive search and our method. The proposed method creates an uneven sampling of the parameter values within the range of M. This is because during the search certain

Figure 7. Parameter optimization results for a face image. The left image is the input image. The image in the center is the optimal segmentation found using an exhaustive search of 396 different parameter values. The right image is the optimal segmentation found using the proposed method. Only 19 different parameter values were evaluated to find the result.

Figure 8. Plot showing the objective function value for segmentations produced with different M values for the face image shown in Figure 7. A minimum value for E indicates an optimal parameter value. The left image is the result from an exhaustive search of 396 segmentations produced using a range of M values from 2-200. The right image shows the E values for the 19 segmentations used by the proposed parameter search method. The concentration of samples around the minimum shows the adaptive sampling which allows the search to concentrate on M values that are more likely to produce a minimum value for E.

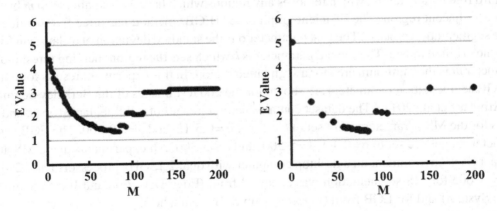

regions of M values were eliminated when it was determined they could not contain a minimum. This allows the search to concentrate on areas more likely to produce a minimum for E.

4.3 Comparison with Other Parameter Optimization Methods

In this section the results from our method are compared with three parameter optimization approaches: multi-locus hill climbing, Tabu search and genetic algorithm. In the experiment each optimization method was used to find the best parameters for segmenting an input image. The segmentation evaluation measure in (Philipp-Foliguet & Guigues, 2008) was used as the objective function for all experiments. The scaling parameter used in the evaluation measure was set to 50. We use the multi-locus hill climbing method as described in (Min et al., 2004). The parameters were adjusted to provide the best performance for the segmentation methods used in this experiment. The initial grid size is 5, the top 3% of results are kept, and the refined grid size is 3. The search was terminated after less than 5% improvement in the top results between iterations. Tabu search was applied using the approach in (Crevier, 2008). There are 3 free parameters that must be set: n_1 - the initial population size, N - the memory size containing points with the best objective function score, and n_2 - the number of additional points generated within the search ellipsoid. The best parameter values for the segmentation methods used in this experiment were found empirically to be $n_1=25$, $N=15$, and $n_2=9$. A convergence criteria was added which terminates after 3 consecutive iterations with no change in the set of N best points. The genetic algorithm used in this experiment was implemented as in (Fredrich & Feitosa, 2008) using a modified version of the genetic algorithm library available from (Janković). Several free parameters must be set to control the search process. The parameters were set empirically to provide the best balance between minimizing the objective function and faster convergence. The population size was set to 30 with half of the population replaced in each generation. The mutation probability was interpolated during the search process from 0.01 initially to a final value of 0.03. The initial crossover probability was 0.7 and the final value was set to 0.6. The maximum number of generations was set to 40 with an additional termination criteria of no improvement in the average population fitness for 3 consecutive generations.

The segmentation methods optimized in this experiment are the Mean Shift method (Comaniciu & Meer, 2002) and the Efficient graph based method (Felzenszwalb & Huttenlocher, 2004). The Mean Shift (MS) segmentation algorithm has two parameters that determine the size of the kernel window, h_s and h_r, and a third free parameter, m, which removes any regions which have area smaller than m by merging them with an adjacent region. The Efficient graph based (EGB) method has three free parameters that control the segmentation process. The first parameter σ is the standard deviation of a Gaussian filter used to smooth the original image. The second parameter is k which sets the region merging threshold and the third parameter m is the minimum area for a segmented region. In this experiment results for optimizing MS and EGB segmentation parameters are shown for the 200 test images of the Berkeley Segmentation Dataset (Arbelaez et al., 2011). The dataset contains natural images of wildlife, landscapes, and people. The ranges for the MS parameters were set to $h_s=1$-15, $h_r=0.5$-15, and $m=10$-500. The EGB segmentation parameter ranges are set to $\sigma=0.4$-1, $k=5$-500, and $m=5$-300. All experiments using MS and EGB were run in a C++ environment on a desktop computer with dual 2.13GHz processors and 12 gigabytes of memory. Code for MS segmentation was acquired from (Edge Detection and Image Segmentation (EDISON) System) and for EGB from (Felzenszwalb & Huttenlocher).

The optimization methods are compared based on how well the segmentation output corresponds to a set of ground truth segmentations. This is done using the Segmentation Covering (SC) method (Arbelaez et al., 2011), Probabilistic Rand Index (PRI) (Unnikrishnan, Pantofaru, & Hebert, 2007), and Variation of Information (VOI) (Meilă, 2005). The SC score is based on overlap between a segmentation and ground truth. PRI scores are based on the number of pixel pairs that have the same label in the segmentation and the ground truth. For SC and PRI a higher score indicates better performance. The VOI score is based on the entropy and mutual information between the regions in the segmentation and the ground truth. A lower score is better for VOI. The methods are also compared based on how many objective function evaluations are required to reach a result. A more efficient optimization will require fewer objective function evaluations.

Figure 9 shows the optimized results for MS and EGB segmentation methods. The two columns on the left show the MS segmentations. The two right-most columns show the EGB segmentations. A sample from the set of ground truths is shown in the second row. There are only small differences between the segmentations created by the proposed method, hill-climbing, and Tabu search. However, each method produced different optimal segmentation parameters. This shows that for these segmentation methods there are multiple parameter value combinations that will produce a local minimum in the objective function. Tables 2 and 3 show the parameter optimization results for MS and EGB segmentation methods on the 200 Berkeley Segmentation Dataset test images. Both of these segmentation methods have three free parameters. There is no significant difference between the average segmentation covering score of the optimization methods. Therefore, segmentation parameter optimizations methods would benefit from focusing on quickly finding a small set of good parameter values. This is the strategy used by the proposed method to efficiently sample the parameter space. In comparison, the genetic algorithm makes

Figure 9. Segmentation results after parameter optimization was applied to MS and EGB segmentation of images from the Berkeley Segmentation Dataset. The top row is the input image. The second row is a sample ground truth from the dataset. The optimized segmentation results for the proposed method, hill climbing, Tabu search, and genetic algorithm are shown in the subsequent rows.

small adjustments in the parameter values as it seeks to find an exact location for the minimum. As seen in Tables 2 and 3, this requires a large number of objective function evaluations and does not always result in a better segmentation. The hill-climbing and Tabu search are able to effectively search the parameter space, but required more objective function evaluations than the proposed method. Overall, the proposed method was able to achieve equivalent segmentation results with approximately 25% less objective function evaluations than the next fastest method.

5. FUTURE RESEARCH DIRECTIONS

The development of many diverse image segmentation methods has led to the need for effective evaluation of segmentation performance. Image segmentation is an important step in many computer vision applications such as facial recognition, target tracking and medical image analysis. Evaluating the ability of a segmentation method to fulfill the goals of a certain application is an important task for benchmarking and parameter optimization. Determining segmentation performance is application-specific; therefore a universal formulation which uses an adaptable push-pull evaluation system is greatly needed. The push-pull evaluation method may be able to shed the light on providing a universal formulation because it parallels the common evaluation task of finding the balance between too much segmentation detail and not enough detail.

Table 2. Results for parameter optimization of Mean shift segmentation of the 200 images in the test set of the Berkeley Segmentation Dataset

Parameter Optimization Method	SC	PRI	VOI	Average Objective Function Evaluations Required to Reach Result	Average Execution Time (s)
Grid search using ground truth	0.58	0.81	1.64	-	-
Proposed method	**0.53**	**0.78**	2.13	186	335
Multi-locus hill climbing	**0.53**	0.77	**2.09**	296	651
Tabu search	**0.53**	0.78	2.13	247	581
Genetic algorithm	**0.53**	0.77	2.13	317	725

Table 3. Results for parameter optimization of Efficient Graph Based segmentation of the 200 images in the test set of the Berkeley Segmentation Dataset

Parameter Optimization Method	SC	PRI	VOI	Average Objective Function Evaluations Required to Reach Result	Average Execution Time (s)
Grid search using ground truth	0.57	0.82	1.87	-	-
Proposed method	**0.50**	**0.8**	**2.3**	182	50
Multi-locus hill climbing	0.49	0.79	2.46	280	89
Tabu search	**0.50**	0.79	2.45	272	85
Genetic algorithm	0.49	0.78	2.47	321	100

6. CONCLUSION

Segmentation parameters create a challenging optimization problem due to factors such as: high cost of objective function evaluations, parameter space redundancy, and unique convergence requirements. We have presented a method which utilizes knowledge about the segmentation parameter environment to improve parameter optimization efficiency. A relationship between parameter values and push-pull objective functions was used to shrink the search space and reduce the total number of objective functions required. Because there are often multiple equally good parameter combinations, the proposed method focuses on quickly finding parameter regions that are most likely to produce good results. Experiments show that the new method is able to adaptively sample the parameter space by eliminating unfeasible parameter regions and focusing on areas more likely to produce a minimum. When compared to other methods, we are able to achieve similar optimization results with approximately 25% fewer objective function evaluations.

REFERENCES

Arbelaez, P., Maire, M., Fowlkes, C., & Malik, J. (2011). Contour detection and hierarchical image segmentation. *Pattern Analysis and Machine Intelligence. IEEE Transactions on, 33*(5), 898–916.

Borsotti, M., Campadelli, P., & Schettini, R. (1998). Quantitative evaluation of color image segmentation results. *Pattern Recognition Letters, 19*(8), 741–747. doi:10.1016/S0167-8655(98)00052-X

Chalmer, B. J. (1987). *Understanding statistics*. New York: Marcel Dekker, Inc.

Chen, H.-C., & Wang, S.-J. (2006). Visible colour difference-based quantitative evaluation of colour segmentation. *Vision, Image and Signal Processing, IEE Proceedings, 153*, 598-609.

Chen, X., Udupa, J. K., Bagci, U., Zhuge, Y., & Yao, J. (2012). Medical image segmentation by combining graph cuts and oriented active appearance models. *Image Processing. IEEE Transactions on, 21*(4), 2035–2046.

Comaniciu, D., & Meer, P. (2002). Mean shift: A robust approach toward feature space analysis. *Pattern Analysis and Machine Intelligence. IEEE Transactions on, 24*(5), 603–619.

Crevier, D. (2008). Image segmentation algorithm development using ground truth image data sets. *Computer Vision and Image Understanding, 112*(2), 143–159. doi:10.1016/j.cviu.2008.02.002

Dogra, D. P., Majumdar, A. K., & Sural, S. (2012). Evaluation of segmentation techniques using region area and boundary matching information. *Journal of Visual Communication and Image Representation, 23*(1), 150–160. doi:10.1016/j.jvcir.2011.09.005

Edge Detection and Image Segmentation (EDISON) System. (n.d.). Retrieved Aug 7, 2013, from https://coewww.rutgers.edu/riul/research/code/EDISON/index.html

Everingham, M., Muller, H., & Thomas, B. (2002). Evaluating image segmentation algorithms using the pareto front. Computer Vision—ECCV 2002, (pp. 34-48).

Feitosa, R., Costa, G., Cazes, T., & Feijo, B. (2006). A genetic approach for the automatic adaptation of segmentation parameters. *Proceedings of the First International Conference on Object-Based Image Analysis*, 4.

Felzenszwalb, P., & Huttenlocher, D. (n.d.). *Efficient Graph-Based Image Segmentation*. Retrieved Aug 7, 2013, from http://cs.brown.edu/~pff/segment/

Felzenszwalb, P. F., & Huttenlocher, D. P. (2004). Efficient graph-based image segmentation. *International Journal of Computer Vision*, *59*(2), 167–181. doi:10.1023/B:VISI.0000022288.19776.77

Ferrara, M., Franco, A., & Maio, D. (2012). A multi-classifier approach to face image segmentation for travel documents. *Expert Systems with Applications*, *39*(9), 8452–8466. doi:10.1016/j.eswa.2012.01.173

Forouzanfar, M., Forghani, N., & Teshnehlab, M. (2010). Parameter optimization of improved fuzzy c-means clustering algorithm for brain MR image segmentation. *Engineering Applications of Artificial Intelligence*, *23*(2), 160–168. doi:10.1016/j.engappai.2009.10.002

Fredrich, C. M., & Feitosa, R. Q. (2008). Automatic adaptation of segmentation parameters applied to inhomogeneous objects detection. *Conference on geographic object-based image analysis held*, (pp. 6-7).

Glover, F., & Laguna, M. (2013). *Tabu Search*. New York: Springer.

Goldberg, D. E. (1989). *Genetic Algorithms in Search, Optimization and Machine Learning*. Boston: Addison-Wesley Longman Publishing Co., Inc.

Hafiane, A., Chabrier, S., Rosenberger, C., & Laurent, H. (2007). *A new supervised evaluation criterion for region based segmentation methods. In Advanced Concepts for Intelligent Vision Systems* (pp. 439–448). Springer. doi:10.1007/978-3-540-74607-2_40

Haralick, R. M., & Shapiro, L. G. (1985). Image segmentation techniques. In *1985 Technical Symposium East* (pp. 2-9). International Society for Optics and Photonics.

Heber, M., Godec, M., Rüther, M., Roth, P. M., & Bischof, H. (2013). 6). Segmentation-based tracking by support fusion. *Computer Vision and Image Understanding*, *117*(6), 573–586. doi:10.1016/j.cviu.2013.02.001

Heidemann, G. (2008). Region saliency as a measure for colour segmentation stability. *Image and Vision Computing*, *26*(2), 211–227. doi:10.1016/j.imavis.2007.05.001

Ilea, D. E., & Whelan, P. F. (2009). Colour saliency-based parameter optimisation for adaptive colour segmentation. *Image Processing (ICIP), 2009 16th IEEE International Conference on*, (pp. 973-976). IEEE.

Janković, M. (n.d.). *Genetic algorithm library*. Retrieved Aug 7, 2013, from http://www.codeproject.com/Articles/26203/Genetic-Algorithm-Library

Levine, M. D., & Nazif, A. M. (1985). Dynamic measurement of computer generated image segmentations. *Pattern Analysis and Machine Intelligence, IEEE Transactions on*, (2), 155-164.

Liu, J., & Yang, Y.-H. (1994). Multiresolution color image segmentation. *Pattern Analysis and Machine Intelligence. IEEE Transactions on*, *16*(7), 689–700.

Meilă, M. (2005). Comparing clusterings: an axiomatic view. *Proceedings of the 22nd international conference on Machine learning* (pp. 577-584). ACM.

Min, J., Powell, M., & Bowyer, K. W. (2004). Automated performance evaluation of range image segmentation algorithms. *Systems, Man, and Cybernetics, Part B: Cybernetics. IEEE Transactions on, 34*(1), 263–271.

Monteiro, F. C., & Campilho, A. C. (2006). *Performance evaluation of image segmentation. In Image Analysis and Recognition* (pp. 248–259). Springer.

Peng, B., & Zhang, L. (2012). Evaluation of image segmentation quality by adaptive ground truth composition. *Computer Vision–ECCV, 2012,* 287–300.

Peng, B., Zhang, L., & Zhang, D. (2011). Automatic image segmentation by dynamic region merging. *Image Processing. IEEE Transactions on, 20*(12), 3592–3605.

Philipp-Foliguet, S., & Guigues, L. (2008). Multi-scale criteria for the evaluation of image segmentation algorithms. *Journal of Multimedia, 3*(5), 42–56. doi:10.4304/jmm.3.5.42-56

Shen, S., Sandham, W., Granat, M., & Sterr, A. (2005). MRI fuzzy segmentation of brain tissue using neighborhood attraction with neural-network optimization. *Information Technology in Biomedicine. IEEE Transactions on, 9*(3), 459–467.

Unnikrishnan, R., Pantofaru, C., & Hebert, M. (2007). Toward objective evaluation of image segmentation algorithms. *Pattern Analysis and Machine Intelligence. IEEE Transactions on, 29*(6), 929–944.

Zhang, H., Fritts, J. E., & Goldman, S. A. (2003). An entropy-based objective evaluation method for image segmentationc. *Electronic Imaging, 2004,* 38–49.

Zhang, H., Fritts, J. E., & Goldman, S. A. (2008). Image segmentation evaluation: A survey of unsupervised methods. *Computer Vision and Image Understanding, 110*(2), 260-280.

Zhang, Y. J. (2001). A review of recent evaluation methods for image segmentation. *Signal Processing and its Applications, Sixth International, Symposium on* (pp. pp. 148-151). IEEE.

Zhang, Y.-J. (2006). A summary of recent progresses for segmentation evaluation. *Advances in Image and Video Segmentation, 423.*

Chapter 3
Study of Noise Removal Techniques for Digital Images

Punyaban Patel
Chhatrapati Shivaji Institute of Technology, India

Bibhudatta Sahoo
National Institute of Technology Rourkela, India

Bibekananda Jena
Purushottam Institute of Engineering and Technology, India

Pritam Patel
National Institute of Technology Agartala, India

Banshidhar Majhi
National Institute of Technology Rourkela, India

ABSTRACT

Images very often get contaminated by different types of noise like impulse noise, Gaussian noise, spackle noise etc. due to malfunctioning of camera sensors during acquisition or transmission using the channel. The noise in the channel affects processing of images in various ways. Hence, the image has to be restored by applying filtration process before the high level image processing. In general the restoration techniques for images are based up on the mathematical and the statistical models of image degradation. Denoising and deblurring are used to recover the image from degraded observations. The researchers have proposed verity of linear and non-linear filters for removal of noise from images. The filtering technique has been used to remove noisy pixels, without changing the uncorrupted pixel values. This chapter presents the metrics used for measurement of noise, and the various schemes for removing of noise from the images.

INTRODUCTION

The processing of visual information by computer has been drawing a very significant attention of the researchers over the last a few decades. The process of receiving and analyzing visual information by the human species is referred to as sight, perception or understanding. Similarly, the process of receiving and analyzing visual information by digital computer is called *digital image processing* (Jain, 1989; Russ, 2002; Gonzalez & Woods, 2009; Sridhar, 2011).

DOI: 10.4018/978-1-4666-9685-3.ch003

Any monochrome image may be described as a two-dimensional function I. (A. Yadav & P. Yadav, 2009).

$$I = f(x, y) \tag{1}$$

where, x and y are spatial coordinates. Amplitude of f at any pair of coordinates $\left(x, y\right)$ is called intensity I or gray value of the image. When spatial co-ordinates and amplitude values are all finite, discrete quantities, the image is called digital image (Chanda & Majumder, 2002). The digital image I is represented by a single 2-dimensional integer array for a gray scale image and a series of three 2-dimensional arrays for each colour bands.

To send visual digital images is a major issue in the modern data communication network. The image sent from sender end may not be the same at the receiving end. The image obtained after transmission is often corrupted with noise. The image received at the receiving end needs processing before it can be used for further applications. Removal of noise is an important step in the image restoration process. The denoising of image remains a challenging problem in current research associate with image processing. The goal of image denoising is to manipulation of the image data to produce a visually high quality image from corrupted image, utilizing prior knowledge on the statistics of natural images, while retaining the edges and other detailed features as much as possible.

There have been several numbers of published algorithms and each target to remove noise from original signal. The problems have been studied intensively with considerable progress made in recent years. However, it seems to that image denoising algorithms are starting to converge and recent algorithms improve over previous one by only fractional dB values. It is thus important to understand, how much can we still improve natural image denoising algorithms? What are the inherent limits imposed by the actual statistics of the data? Those challenges in evaluating such limits that constructing proper models of natural image statistics which is a long standing and yet the problems are unsolved. Noise removal algorithms in spatial domain, as well as other, are finds too much useful in real time noise removal techniques, such as medical imaging and satellite imaging applications. The order of noise and performance measures to be analysed and decides the type of denoising algorithm.

In this chapter the authors tried to explore the different image denoising techniques. Also, the different additive noise models and also multiplicative models such as Gaussian Noise, Salt-and-Pepper Noise, Speckle Noise and Brownian Noise have been discussed. Depending on the noise present in an image a particular algorithm is to be selected. When the image is corrupted with Salt-and-Pepper Noise then it is found that the median filtering approach is the best. In case of Gaussian noise the wavelet based approach is found the best denoising method. For any complex type of noise it is found that the multifractal approach is the best method.

TYPES OF IMAGE

Image can be classified based on many criteria (Sridhar, 2011) as shown in Figure 1.

- Based on attributes

Images can be broadly classified based on attributes, as raster images and vector graphics. Raster images are pixel based however vector graphics use basic geometric attributes such as lines, circle, rectangle etc.

Figure 1. Classification of images

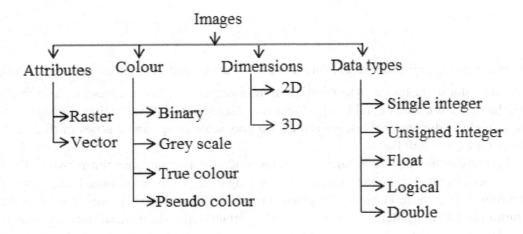

- Based on colour

Based on colour, images can be classified as grey scale, binary, true colour and pseudo colour images. Grey scale and binary images are called monochrome images as there is no colour component in these images. Grey images have many shades of grey between black and white. Most medical images like X-rays, CT images, MRI, and Ultrasound images are belongs to grey scale images. Binary images are called bi-level images whose pixel value is either 0 or 1. Binary images are used for basic shape or line drawing. True colour images represent the full range of available colours and also called three-band images. In true colour images, the pixel has a colour that is obtained by mixing the primary colours (i.e. red, green, and blue). Pseudo colour images are false colour images where the colour is added artificially based on the interpretation of data.

- Based on dimensions

Normally, digital imageis a 2D rectangular array of pixels. If another dimension, of depth or any other characteristic, is considered, then it is called 3D images. A 3D image is a volume image, where pixels are called voxels. In medical imaging, frequently encountered images are CT images, MRIs, and microscopy images.

- Based on data types

Images may be classified based on their data types. A binary image is 1-bit image as one bit is sufficient to represent black and white pixels. Grey scale images are stored as one-byte (8 bit) or two-byte (16-bit) images.

Sometimes image processing operations produce images with negative numbers, decimal fractions, and complex numbers. For example, Fourier transforms produce image involving complex numbers. To handle negative numbers, signed and unsigned integer types are used. In these data types, the first bit is used to encode whether the number is positive or negative.

Floating-point involved storing the data in scientific notation. A number that can be represented exactly is of the following form: $significand \times base^{exponent}$, where,

$$significand \in \mathbb{Z}, base \in \mathbb{N} and\, exponent \in \mathbb{Z}.$$

For example, 1,253 can be represented as 0.1253×10^4, where 0.1253 is called significand and the power called exponent.

IMAGE FILE FORMATS

There is no universal image format that is best for all scenarios. Every type of image format has their own advantages and disadvantages. The simplest way of storing image details by using a 2D array of pixel intensities is referred to as bitmap. The types of image file formats (Sridhar, 2011) have been described. There are two types of image file format i.e. A. Raster Image File Format, and B. Vector Image File Format is as shown in Figure 2.

Some of the popular formats are presented below.

Raster (or Bitmap) Image File Format

Raster images' dimensions are measured in pixels. It depends on the pixel dimension of the image (e.g. 6824 pixels wide by 2345 pixels high) and the pixel resolution i.e. pixels-per-inch (ppi) required by the particular printer(e.g. offset printer 300 ppi or screen printer 240 ppi). It cannot be scaled without losing quality and depending on the complexity; it is time consuming to convert to vector image format. All scanned images, and images from digital cameras are bitmaps.

There are number of different bitmap image formats. Some of the most common include: JPEG, PNG, GIF, BMP, and TIFF. Broadly speaking, they fall into two categories:

Lossy image formats (e.g., JPEG) have smaller file sizes but do not store a perfect copy of the image. They are best suited to photographs and other images where perfect accuracy is not important. They are also commonly used on the web to save bandwidth.

Lossless image formats (e.g., PNG, BMP, and TIFF) store an exact pixel-by-pixel representation of the image, but require more space. They are more suitable for things like logos. Arguably the best of these formats is PNG, which is Vector Magic's recommended bitmap format for logos. It is widely supported and has very good compression.

Figure 2. (A) Raster vs. (B) Vector Image

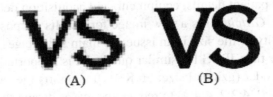

Some of the Raster (or Bitmap) Image File Formats are:

- *JPEG/JPG (Joint Photographic Experts Group)* is the most popular among the image formats used. JPEG files are very 'lossy', meaning so much information is lost from the original image when you save it in JPEG file. This is because JPEG discards most of the information to keep the image file size small; which means some degree of quality is also lost. Almost every digital camera can shoot and save in the JPEG format. JPEG is very web friendly because the file is smaller, which means it occupy less memory space, and requires less time to transfer to a site. It uses RGB-24-bits (8-bit colour) or gray scale - 8-bits, most used and widely accepted image format.
- *BMP (BitMaP)* is an image file format. The Windows and Macintosh have their own formats, both of which are called BMP. Most modern image editing tools are able to read both. In any case, all of the variants of BMP should be avoided when possible, as they use little to no compression and consequently have unnecessarily large file size.
- *PNG (Portable Network Graphics)* is a lossless image file format which is widely supported by web browsers and image viewers/editors. PNG can replace GIF today.
- *PCX (PictureeXchange)* is an image file format. PCX files commonly stored palette-indexed images ranging from 2 or 4 colors to 16 and 256 colors, although the format has been extended to record true-color (24-bit) images as well. PCX image data are stored in rows or scan lines in top-down order.PCX image data are compressed using run-length encoding (RLE).
- *TIFF/TIF (Tagged Image File)* is an image file format has been used to store raw bitmap data by some programs and devices such as scanners. This format comes in a compressed and an uncompressed variant. The former is comparable to PNG, while the latter is more like BMP. Useof uncompressed variant is not advisable.
- *PSD (PhotoShop Document)* is a layered image file format used in Adobe PhotoShop. It is used for saving data. PSD is a proprietary file that allows the user to work with the images' individual layers even after the file has been saved. When an image is complete, Photoshop allows the user to flatten the layers and convert the flat image into a .JPG, .GIF, .TIFF or other non-proprietary file format, so it can be shared. Once a PSD image has been flatten by conversion, however, it cannot be converted back to PSD and the user can no longer work with the image's layers. It is important, therefore, so always save the .PSD file and not overwrite it during conversion.
- *GIF (Graphics Interchange File)* is limited to the 8 bit palette with only 256 colours. GIF is still a popular image format on the internet because image size is relatively small compared to other image compression types. It compresses images in two ways: first, by reducing the number of colour in rich colour images, thus reducing the number of bits per pixel. Second, GIF replaces multiple occurring patterns (large patterns) into one. So instead of storing five kinds of blue, it stores only one blue.GIF is most suitable for graphics, diagrams, cartoons and logos with relatively few colours. GIF is still the chosen format for animation effects.
- *DICON* is a very popular file format in medical imaging. This file format contains image data and also metadata such as patient details, equipment, and acquisition details.
- *BPG (Better Portable Graphics)* is a new image format. Its purpose is to replace the JPEG image format when quality or file size is an issue. Its main advantages are: High compression ratio, files are much smaller than JPEG for similar quality. It is supported by most Web browsers with a small Javascript decoder (gzipped size: 56 KB). It supports the same chroma formats as JPEG (grayscale, YCbCr 4:2:0, 4:2:2, 4:4:4) to reduce the losses during the conversion.

- The *WebP* is a new image file format that provides lossless and lossy compression for images on the web. Its format is based on the RIFF (resource interchange file format) document format. WebP lossless images are 26% smaller in size compared to PNGs. WebPlossy images are 25-34% smaller in size compared to JPEG images at equivalent SSIM index. WebP supports lossless transparency (also known as alpha channel) with just 22% additional bytes. Transparency is also supported with lossy compression and typically provides 3x smaller file sizes compared to PNG when lossy compression is acceptable for the red/green/blue colour channel.

Vector Image File Format

Vector graphics are made of mathematical calculations that form objects or lines - they do not use pixel, therefore, they are resolution-independent. Vector graphics can be scaled to any size without losing quality and can be easily converted to raster image. The number of colours can be easily increased or reduced to adjust printing budget and a large dimension vector graphic can maintain a small file size.

- **EPS (Encapsulated PostScript):** It is a most common vector image format which is used as a standard interchange format in the print industry. It is widely supported as an export format, but due to the complexity of the full format specification, not all programs that claim to support, EPS are able to import all variants of it. Adobe Illustrator and recent versions of CorelDRAW have very good support for reading and writing EPS. Ghostview can read it very well, but does not have any editing capabilities. Inkscape can only export it.
- **AI (Adobe Illustrator):** The native format of Adobe Illustrator is the AI format (Adobe Illustrator Artwork), a modified version of the older EPS format. The AI format is fairly widely supported, but it is less ubiquitous than the EPS format, and most programs that read AI can also read EPS.
- **PDF (Portable Document Format):** Adobe's PDF format is very widely used as a general purpose platform-independent document format. It is a very good vector image format. Adobe gives away the Acrobat PDF reader, but sells the tools required to create PDF files (third party tools that perform the same task are also for sale). Those tools work with any program that is able to print. Support for reading and editing PDF files is much more limited.
- **SVG (Scalable Vector Graphics):** The W3C standard vector image format is called SVG. Inkscape and recent versions of Adobe Illustrator and CorelDRAW have good support for reading and writing SVG. Further information on the SVG format may be found on the official SVG website.
- **DXF (Drawing eXchange Format):** A CAD format from Autodesk, used by CAD tools from many different vendors.

There are numerous other vector formats: CDR is the CorelDRAW native format and XAR is the Xara Xtreme native format, to name a couple. There are different types of noise which affect to image (or image file) will be discussed in the next section.

TYPES OF NOISE

Depending on the model used to characterize the noise, we can encounter Impulse noise, Gaussian noise, Speckle noise, poisons noise and many others. Another possible classification takes into consideration the way the noise affects the image. The additive noises modeled either with a Gaussian, uniform, or Salt-and-Pepper distribution. The speckle noise is multiplicative in nature.

The different types of noise model are explained as below.

Impulsive Noise

Depending on the model used to characterize the noise, we can encounter impulse noise, Gaussian noise and many others. In this chapter, we are giving more importance on impulse noise (Jain, 1989; Wang & Bovik, 2002; Bovik, 2009; Sridhar, 2011; Gonzalez & Woods, 2009) and schemes that are proposed to suppress them. Impulsive noise can be classified as Salt-and-Pepper Noise (SPN) and Random-Valued Impulse Noise (RVIN). (Petrou & Bosdogianni, 2003; Nuruzzaman, 2005; Pratt, 2007)

Salt-and-Pepper Noise (SPN): In Salt-and-Pepper Noise (SPN), noisy pixels take either minimal or maximal values i.e $\left\{ L_{min} \; or \, L_{max} \right\}$, where, L_{min}, L_{max} denote the lowest and the highest pixel luminance values within the dynamic range respectively.

This is also known as fixed value impulse noise, because the pixel substitute in the form of noise may be either of the any two fixed values i.e. $L_{min} = 0$ or $L_{max} = 255$ for 8-bit image. Figure 3 may best describe the SPN. Salt-and-Pepper noise can be described by the following models:

Noise Model 1: Noise is modeled as Salt-and-Pepper Noise (SPN) noise. (Ng & Ma, 2006) The pixels are randomly corrupted by two fixed extremal values, 0 and 255 (for 8-bit monochrome image), generated with the *same probability*. That is, for each image pixel at (i, j) with intensity value $s_{i,j}$, the corresponding pixel of the noisy image will be $x_{i,j}$, in which the probability density function of $x_{i,j}$ is,

$$f(x) = \begin{cases} \dfrac{p}{2} \; , & for \; x = 0 \\ 1 - p \; , & for \, x = s_{i,j} \\ \dfrac{p}{2} \; , & for \, x = 255 \end{cases} \tag{2}$$

where, p is the noise density.

Figure 3. Salt and Pepper Noise with $\left\{ L_{min}, L_{max} \right\}$

Noise Model 2: Noise is modeled as Salt-and-Pepper Noise (SPN) as in model 1. The pixels are randomly corrupted by two fixed extremal values, 0 and 255 (for 8-bit monochrome image), generated with *unequal probabilities*. (Ng & Ma, 2006) That is, for each image pixel at (i, j) with intensity value $s_{i,j}$, the corresponding pixel of the noisy image will be $x_{i,j}$, in which the probability density function of $x_{i,j}$ is,

$$f(x) = \begin{cases} \dfrac{p_1}{2}, & for\ x = 0 \\ 1 - p, & for\ x = s_{i,j} \\ \dfrac{p_2}{2}, & for\ x = 255 \end{cases} \tag{3}$$

where $p = p_1 + p_2$ is the noise density and $p_1 \neq p_2$

Noise Model 3: Instead of two dxed *values*, impulse noise could be more realistically modeled by two dxed *ranges* that appear at both ends with a length of m each, respectively(Ng & Ma, 2006). For example, if m is 10, noise will equal likely be any values in the range of either [0,9] or [246, 255]. That is,

$$f(x) = \begin{cases} \dfrac{p}{2m}, & for & 0 \leq x < m \\ 1 - p, & for & x = s_{i,j} \\ \dfrac{p}{2m}, & for\ 255 - m < x \leq 255 \end{cases} \tag{4}$$

where, p is the noise density.

Noise Model 4: Model 4 is similar to Model 3, except that the densities of low-intensity impulse noise and high-intensity impulse noise are *unequal* (Ng & Ma, 2006). That is,

$$f(x) = \begin{cases} \dfrac{p_1}{2m}, & for & 0 \leq x < m \\ 1 - p, & for & x = s_{i,j} \\ \dfrac{p_2}{2m}, & for\ 255 - m < x \leq 255 \end{cases} \tag{5}$$

where, $p = p_1 + p_2$ is the noise density and $p_1 \neq p_2$.

Random Valued Impulsive Noise (RVIN)

In Random-Valued Impulse Noise (in comparison to SPN), noisy pixel values are distributed uniformly in the range of $\eta\left(i, j\right) \in \left[L_{min}, L_{max}\right]$. where, L_{min}, L_{max} denote the lowest and the highest pixel luminance values within the dynamic range respectively. Figure 4 may best describe the RVIN.

Random-Valued Impulse Noise pixels are very difficult to detect as compare to SPN, because the noisy pixels values are sometimes close to their surrounding pixels. The RVIN can be modeled mathematically as given below.

$$x\left(i, j\right) = \begin{cases} \eta\left(i, j\right) & with\,probability & p \\ \\ y\left(i, j\right) & with\,probability & 1 - p \end{cases} \tag{6}$$

In this case, it is very difficult to detect the noisy pixels due to RVIN. So that, it is a little bit difficult to remove random valued impulse noise rather than salt and pepper noise (Chanda & Majumder, 2002). The preservation of image details faces difficulties due to the attenuation of noise. Figure 4 may best describe the difference between SPN and RVIN. In the case of SPN the pixel substitute in the form of noise may be either $L_{min} = 0$ or $L_{max} = 255$. Whereas in RVIN situation it may range from L_{min} to L_{max}.

Gaussian Noise

Gaussian noise is statistical noise, which has a probability density function of the normal distribution (also known as Gaussian distribution). Here, each pixel in the noisy image is the sum of the true pixel value and a random, Gaussian distributed noise value. It arises in amplifiers and detectors and caused by natural sources such as thermal vibration of atoms and discrete nature of radiation of warm objects. The noise is independent of intensity of pixel value at each point. In this type of noise, the image looks soft and slightly blurry, where each pixel in the image will be changed from its original value by a (usually) small amount. When we plot histogram, then the amount of distortion of a pixel value against the frequency, with which it occurs, shows a normal distribution of noise (Petrou & Bosdogianni, 2003; Gonzalez & Woods, 2009; Bovik, 2009).

The Gaussian (normal) distribution is usually a good model, due to the central limit theorem that says that the sum of independent noises tends to approach a Gaussian distribution. It is most commonly used as additive white noise to yield Additive White Gaussian Noise (AWGN).

A pixel with co-ordinates $\left(x, y\right)$ degraded by additive random noise is modeled as,

Figure 4. Random Valued Impulsive Noise with $y\left(i, j\right) \in \left[L_{min}, L_{max}\right]$

0   [0,255]   255

$$f(x,y) = O(x,y) + \eta(x,y) \tag{7}$$

where, $f(x,y)$ is final image function, $O(x,y)$ is original image function and $\eta(x,y)$ represents the signal independent additive random noise. The Gaussian noise has a normal (Gaussian) probability density function:

$$PDE_{Gaussian} = \frac{1}{\sqrt{2\pi\sigma^2}} e^{-\frac{(g-\mu)^2}{2\sigma^2}} \tag{8}$$

$where, g = gray\,level, \mu = mean, and\,s = standard\,deviation$

Mixed Noise

When more than one type of noise is present in the image, it is called mixed noise. In this type of noise, the image contains dark and white dots and looks soft and slightly blurry, where each pixel in the image is changed from its original value by a (usually) small amount (Gonzalez & Woods, 2009).

Speckle Noise

Speckle noise (Gonzalez & Woods, 2009) is a granular noise that inherently exists in and degrades the quality of images. Speckle noise is a multiplicative noise, i.e. it is in direct proportion to the local grey level in any area. The signal and the noise are statistically independent of each other. This type of noise

Figure 5. Gaussian probability density function

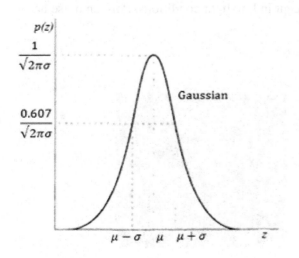

Figure 6. Gaussion Noisy image (a) mean=0, variance = 0.05, (b) mean=1.5, variance =10

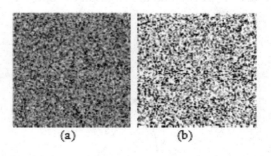

Figure 7. (a) Original Lena image (b) Noisy Image corrupted by Gaussian noise (Mixed noise)

(a)   (b)

occurs in almost all coherent imaging systems such as laser, acoustics and SAR (Synthetic Aperture Radar) imagery. The source of this noise is attributed to random interference between the coherent returns. Fully developed speckle noise has the characteristic of multiplicative noise. Speckle noise can be modelled by random values multiplied by pixel values of an image. Speckle noise follows a gamma distribution and is given as,

$$F\left(g\right) = \frac{g^{\alpha-1}}{\left(\alpha-1\right)! \, a^{\alpha}} \, e^{\frac{-g}{a}}$$

(9)

where variance $= a^2\alpha$ and $g =$ gray level

Poisson Noise (Photon Noise)

Poisson noise, also known as Photon noise (Gonzalez & Woods, 2009), is a basic form of uncertainty associated with the measurement of light; inherent to the quantized nature of light and the independence of photon detections, that is, the noise that can cause, when number of photons sensed by the sensor is not sufficient to provide detectable statistical information. Its expected magnitude is signal dependent and constitutes the dominant source of image noise except in low-light conditions. Poisson noise has a

Figure 8. (a) Gamma distribution (b) Speckle noisy image

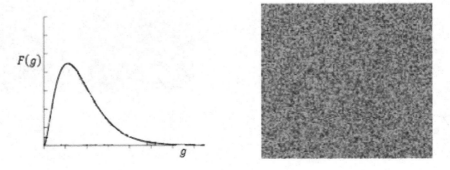

Figure 9. (a) Original Lena image (b) Poisson noisy image

probability density function of a Poisson distribution. This noise has root mean square value proportional to square root intensity of the image.

The Poisson probability density function is

$$f\left(x\,|\,\lambda\right) = \frac{\lambda^x}{x!}e^{-\lambda} \tag{10}$$

where, $x = 0, 1, 2, 3, 4, \ldots, \infty$, e is Euler's number ($e = 2.71828\ldots$), λ = sample mean. As $\lambda > 0$ gets large the Poisson distribution can be approximated by a normal distribution with $\mu = \lambda$ and $\sigma^2 = \lambda$.

Brownian Noise

The brown noise, is one of the many colours of noise, which also include white noise, pink noise and blue noise, called Brownian noise (Véhel, 2000) which is named after botanist Robert Brown, who discovered Brownian motion (random particle motion). It comes under the category of fractal or $1/f$ noises. In Brownian noise, power spectral density is proportional to square of frequency over an octave i.e., its power falls on ¼ th part (6 dB per octave). Brownian noise caused by Brownian motion. The Brownian motion is seen due to the random movement of suspended particles in fluid. The mathematical model for $1/f$ noise is fractional Brownian motion. Fractal Brownian motion is a non-stationary stochastic process that follows a normal distribution. Brownian noise is a special case of $1/f$ noise. It is obtained by integrating white noise. It can be graphically represented as shown in Figure 10(a). On an image, Brownian noise would look like image as shown in Figure 10(b), which is developed from Fraclab (Véhel, 2000).

Now, different denoising algorithms and its classification will be briefly presented in the next section.

IMAGE DENOISING SCHEMES

Noise removal or de-noising is an important task in image processing. Image enhancement is a collection of techniques that improve the quality of the given image, which is making certain features of the image easier to see or reducing the noise.

In general, the results of the noise removal have a strong influence on the quality of the image processing techniques. The spatial filtering methods and transform domain filtering methods are the two fundamental techniques of image denoising as shown in the Figure 11. (Motwani, Gadiya, Motwani & Harris, 2004)

Figure 10. (a) Brownian noise distribution (b) Brownian noise

Figure 11. Classification of image denoising schemes

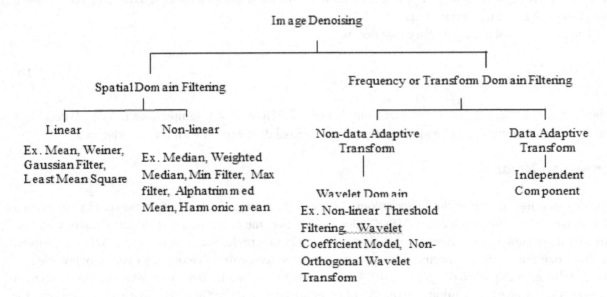

Spatial Filtering

Traditionally, spatial filters are introduced to get rid of noise from image data. The term spatial domain refers to the aggregate of pixels composing an image and spatial domain methods are procedures that operate directly on the pixels. Spatial filters can again be categorized into linear and non-linear filters.

Linear Filters

In linear filtering (Gonzalez & Woods, 2009; Sridhar, 2011), each pixel in the input image is replaced by a linear combination of intensities of neighbouring pixels. That is each pixel value in the output image is weighted sum of the pixels in the neighbouring of the corresponding pixel in the input image. Linear filtering can be used to smoothen as well as sharpen the image. A mean filter is the optimal linear filter for Gaussian noise in the sense of mean square error. The arithmetic mean filtering (AMF) process computes the average value of the corrupted image in the area defined by window. The AMF simply smoothest the image, reduce the noise but blurring is increased. The geometric mean filter (GMF) is better than AMF but loses little image quality during filtering process. The harmonic mean filter (HMF) removes Gaussian noise efficiently. The contra harmonic filter (CHF) is better than HMF. Linear filters too tend to blur sharp edges, destroy lines and other fine image details, and perform poorly in the presence of signal-dependent noise. The wiener filtering (Gonzalez & Woods, 2009) method requires the information about the spectra of the noise and the original signal and it works well only if the underlying signal is smooth. Wiener method implements spatial smoothing and its model complexity control correspond to choosing the window size. To overcome the weakness of the Wiener filtering, the wavelet based denoising scheme have been proposed. (Donoho & Johnstone, 2001).

Non-Linear Filters

With non-linear filters (Gonzalez & Woods, 2009; Sridhar, 2011), the noise is removed without any attempts to explicitly identify it. Spatial filters employ a low pass filtering on groups of pixels with the assumption that the noise occupies the higher region of frequency spectrum. Generally spatial filters remove noise to a reasonable extent but at the cost of blurring images which in turn makes the edges in pictures invisible. In Median Filter (MF), the pixel value is replaced by median value of gray levels of neighbourhood pixels. It is more effective in situation where white spots and black spots appear in the image. Thus, it is better than AMF, GMF, HMF and CHF.

Transform Domain Filtering

The transform domain filtering otherwise known as frequency domain methods (Gonzalez & Woods, 2009; Sridhar, 2011) is based on convolution theorem. It is less complex as compared to spatial domain and the FFT is an efficient implementation of DFT. The DFT and the filter based on DFT generate signals that are approximately uncorrelated (orthogonal). The process of selective frequency inclusion or exclusion is termed as frequency domain filtering. They can be classified as per the selection of basis function. Data adaptive and non-adaptive are further classification of basis function. Let's elaborate on Non-adaptive transforms first owing to its overwhelming popularity.

Non-Data Adaptive Transform

In non-data adaptive (Jung, 2001) representations, the parameters of the transformation remain the same for every time series regardless of its nature. The drst non-data adaptive representations were drawn from spectral decompositions.

- Wavelet Domain

The wavelet transform or wavelet analysis (Gonzalez & Woods, 2009) is the most recent solution to overcome the shortcomings of the Fourier transform. Wavelet image denoising has been widely used in the field of image noise. The wavelet based denoising methods usually rely on thresholding the discrete wavelet transform (DWT) coefficients. Image denoising using DWT consists of three steps namely, image decomposition, followed by thresholding of wavelet coefficients and image reconstruction. Thresholding is a simple nonlinear technique which operates on one wavelet coefficient at a time. This method splits the noise image into varied sub band image. Keeping low frequency wavelet fixed the horizontal, vertical and diagonal wavelet coefficients are brought into comparison with the soft threshold. In the end, it applies the inverse wavelet transform in order to obtain noise free image.

Filtering operations in the wavelet domain can be subdivided into linear and non-linear methods. The linear filter like Wiener filter in wavelet based method gives out maximum outcome. The Non-linear coefficient thresholding based method is the most researched discipline in denoising using wavelet transform. The wavelet based denoising is widely popular because of the properties of sparsity and multi- resolution structure .However, due to the sparsity property of wavelet transform; it maps white noise in signal domain into that of transform domain. Most of the methods are based on choosing the optimal threshold which can be adaptive or non-adaptive to the image in wavelet shrinkage literature.

VISUShrink (Donoho & Johnstone, 2001), a non-adaptive universal threshold, depends merely on a chunk of data points. Because of its large threshold choice, VISUShrink produces abundantly clear image.

SUREShrink (Donoho & Johnstone, 2001), an adaptive universal threshold, employs the combined result of the SURE (Stein's Unbiased Risk Estimator) threshold and universal threshold. It results in better performance than VISUShrink. Bayes Shrink (Ghabel & Amindavar, 2002; Malfait & Roose, 1997; Rajan & Kaimal, 1996) employs Bayesian approach which reduces the Bayes' Risk Estimator function. Most of the time, the performance of Bayes Shrink is better than that of SUREShrink. Cross Validation (Jansen, 2000) gives an replacement to wavelet coefficient with the weighted average of neighbourhood coefficients .It gives rise to minimization of generalized cross validation (GCV) function and provides maximum threshold for every coefficient.

The wavelet coefficient model technique attaches great significance to utilize to the fullest the multi resolution properties of wavelet transform. The modeling of the wavelet coefficients can either be deterministic or statistical. The deterministic method pertains to create tree structure of wavelet coefficients where each node represents the wavelet coefficients and each level in the tree represents scale of transformation (Donoho, 1997).

The statistical modeling of wavelet coefficients is a new statistical model for the relationship of wavelet coefficients and its application to image denoising. The magnitude of a wavelet coefficient usually shows high correlations with the nearby ones. This property has been exploited in many wavelet-based image processing techniques.

The followings are the two techniques that make complete use of statistical properties of the wavelet coefficients guided by the theory of probability (Mihcak, Kozintsev & P, 1999; Moulin & Liu, 1999). A good number of scholars on image denoising techniques have come up with marginal probability models for image in the wavelet domain. In order to model the wavelet coefficients distribution, both the Gaussian Mixture Model and Generalized Gaussian Distribution are usually employed (Lang, Odegard & Burrus, 1995; Cohen, Raj & Malah,1999). The Joint Probabilistic Model is a new method, proposed for image denoising which is based on HMM (hidden Markov modeling) (Buccigrossi & Simoncelli,1999).

- Non-orthogonal Wavelet Transforms

Undecimated Wavelet Transform (UDWT) is based on the idea of no decimation. It applies the wavelet transform and omits both down-sampling in the forward and up-sampling in the inverse transform. The normal hard/soft thresholding was extended to Shift Invariant Discrete Wavelet Transform (SIDWT) (Kaur, Gupta & Chauhan, 2002). After using SIDWT to get number of basis function, the best basis function is selected by the use of Minimum Description Length principle. It, as a result, gives rise to smallest code length so as to describe the given data (Bhoi & Meher, 2008).

Multiwavelets are explored to enhance the performance resulting in the growing computation complexity. When the shift invariance & Multiwavelets are rightly combined, it yields better result for the Lena image in context of MSE (Wu & Ruan, 2006).

Data-Adaptive Transforms

The Data-Adaptive Transforms (Jung, 2001) approach implied that the parameters of a transformation are modified depending on the data available. By adding a data-sensitive selection step, almost all non-data adaptive methods can become data adaptive. Now-a-days the Independent Component Analysis (ICA) as new method of image denoising has grabbed worldwide acceptance. This technique is enormously used (Jung, 2001; Hyvärinen, Oja, Hoyer & J, 1998) to remove the noise in the Non-Gaussian data. The added advantage of using ICA is that it assumes signal to be Non-Gaussian which can denoised images with both Non-Gaussian and Gaussian distribution. However, the ICA based method while comparing to wavelet based methods gives revelation of its limitation of computational cost resulting due to the use of sliding window, sample of noise free data and image frames of the same scene.

The denoising often adds its own noise to an image. Some of the noise artifacts createdby denoising are as follows: (Sridhar, 2011)

- **Blur:** Attenuation of high spatial frequencies may result in smooth edges in the image.
- **Ringing/Gibbs Phenomenon:** Truncation of high frequency transform coefficients may lead to oscillations along the edges or ringing distortions in the image.
- **Staircase Effect:** Aliasing of high frequency components may lead to stair-like structures in the image.
- **Checkerboard Effect:** Denoised images may sometimes carry checkerboard structures.
- **Wavelet Outliers:** These are distinct repeated wavelet-like structures visible in the denoised image and occur in algorithms that work in the wavelet domain.

The metrics used for measuring noise level and the denoising performance of the various algorithms will be presented in the next section.

PERFORMANCE MEASURES

One of the issues of de-noising is the measure of the reconstruction error. In order to separate the noise and image components from a single observation of a degraded image, it is necessary to assume or have knowledge about the statistical properties of the noise. The metrics used for performance comparison of different filters (exists and proposed) are defined below. There are basically two classes through which we can measure the performance and quality of an image. These are Objective quality and the Subjective or Qualitative or Distortion measure. The additional type of metric is used called execution time of the image during image processing.

Objective Quality Measures

The objective quality measures are as follows.

Mean Squared Error (MSE) and Mean Absolute Error (MAE)

In statistics, (Gonzalez & Woods, 2009; Sridhar, 2011) the mean squared error or MSE of an estimator is one of many ways to quantify the amount by which an estimator differs from the true value of the quantity being estimated. Here, it is just used to calculate the difference between an original image and its restored image. Given that original image X of size $(M \times N)$ pixels and as reconstructed image $\hat{X}$, the error can be denoted as, $Error = e(x, y) = \hat{X} - X$

The problem with error is that it may also be negative. To avoid negative numbers, mean square error (MSE) is commonly used and the MSE is defined as:

$$MSE = \frac{1}{M \times N} \sum_{i=0}^{M-1}\sum_{j=0}^{N-1} \left(X_{i,j} - \hat{X}_{i,j} \right)^2 \tag{11}$$

MSE represents the power of noise or the difference between original and tested images.

$$MAE = \frac{1}{M \times N} \sum_{i=0}^{M-1}\sum_{j=0}^{N-1} \left| X_{ij} - \hat{X}_{ij} \right| \tag{12}$$

The goal of de-noising is to find an estimate image such that MAE is minimum.

Signal-to-Noise Ratio (SNR)

The image quality can also be measured as Signal-to-Noise Ratio (SNR) (Gonzalez & Woods, 2009; Sridhar, 2011) which can be defined as

$$SNR = 20 log_{10} \left(\frac{Signal\,Amplitude}{Noise\,Amplitude} \right) dB$$

Normally to calculate SNR, a good quality reference image is required. If such an image is not available, then the SNR of image can be estimated from the given image itself by locating a uniform area which is assumed to be noise free. So, it can be describe as:

$$SNR = 20 log_{10} \left(\frac{\sum_{ij} X^2}{\sum_{ij} \left[X - \hat{X} \right]^2} \right) dB \tag{13}$$

Contrast-to-Noise Ratio (CNR)

Another useful measure is the Contrast-to-Noise Ratio (CNR) (Gonzalez & Woods, 2009; Sridhar, 2011) which is denoted by the formula

$$CNR = 20 \log_{10} \left(\frac{f_{object} - f_{background}}{\sigma_f} \right) \tag{14}$$

where, f_{object} and $f_{background}$ are the average pixel values of the object and background, respectively. σ_f is the standard deviation of the pixel values. CNR can also be defined as the difference between the SNR of the object and the SNR of the background.

Peak Signal to Noise Ratio (PSNR)

PSNR (Gonzalez & Woods, 2009; Sridhar, 2011) analysis uses a standard mathematical model to measure an objective difference between two images. It estimates the quality of a reconstructed image with respect to an original image. Reconstructed images with higher PSNR are judged better. PSNR is the ratio between the maximum possible power of a signal and the power of noise. PSNR is usually expressed in terms of the logarithmic decibel. Given that original image X of size $(M \times N)$ pixels and as reconstructed image $\hat{X}$, the PSNR (dB) is defined as:

$$PSNR(dB) = 10 \ log_{10} \left(\frac{255^2}{MSE} \right) \tag{15}$$

where, 255 is maximum possible amplitude for an 8-bit image.

An improvement in of the PSNR magnitude will increase the visual appearance of the image. PSNR is typically expressed in decibels (dB). For comparison with the noisy image the greater the ratio, the easier it is to identify and subsequently isolate and eliminate the source of noise. A PSNR of zero indicates that the desired signal is virtually indistinguishable from the unwanted noise. PSNR is a good measure for comparing restoration results for the same image, but between images comparison of PSNR are meaningless. One image with 20 dB PSNR may look much better than another image with 30 dB PSNR.

Improved Peak Signal to Noise Ratio (ISNR)

For the purpose of objectively testing the performance of the restored image, Improvement in signal to noise ratio (ISNR) is used as the criteria which is defined by (T & Qu, 2010)

$$ISNR = 10 \ log \frac{\sum_{ij} \left[X_{ij} - Y_{ij} \right]^2}{\sum_{ij} \left[X_{ij} - \hat{X}_{ij} \right]^2} \tag{16}$$

where j and i are the total number of pixels in the horizontal and vertical dimensions of the images X_{ij}, Y_{ij} and $\hat{X}_{ij}$ are the original, degraded and the restored image respectively.

Structural Similarity Index Measure (SSIM)

SSIM is a novel method for measuring the similarity between two images.(Wang, Bovik, Sheikh & Simoncelli, 2004; Wang, Simoncelli & Bovik, 2003; Sheikh & Bovik, 2006) It is computed from three image measurement comparisons: luminance, contrast, and structure. Each of these measures is calculated over an 8×8 local square window, which moves pixel-by-pixel over theentire image. At each step, the local statistics and SSIM index are calculated within the local window. Because the resulting SSIM index map often exhibits undesirable "blocking" artifacts, each window is filtered with a Gaussian weighting function (11×11 pixels). In practice, oneusually requires a single overall quality measure of the entire image; thus, the mean SSIM index is computed to evaluate the overall image quality. The SSIM can be viewed as a quality measure of one of the images being compared, while the other image is regarded as perfect quality. It can give results between 0 and 1, where 1 means excellent quality and 0 means poor quality.

The Structural Similarity Index Measure (SSIM) (Nair & Raju, 2010) between the original image and restored image can be defined by,

$$SSIM\left(X,\hat{X}\right) = L\left(X,\hat{X}\right) * C\left(X,\hat{X}\right) * S\left(X,\hat{X}\right) \tag{17}$$

$$Where, \quad L\left(X,\hat{X}\right) = \left(2\mu_X \mu_{\hat{X}} + C_1\right) / \left(\mu_X^2 + \mu_{\hat{X}}^2 + C_1\right)$$

$$C\left(X,\hat{X}\right) = \left(2\sigma_X \sigma_{\hat{X}} + C_2\right) / \left(\sigma_X^2 + \sigma_{\hat{X}}^2 + C_2\right)$$

$$S\left(X,\hat{X}\right) = \left(\sigma_{X\hat{X}} + C_3\right) / \left(\sigma_X \sigma_{\hat{X}} + C_3\right)$$

$$C_1 = \left(K_1 * G\right)^2, \quad C_2 = \left(K_2 * G\right)^2, \quad C_3 = C_2 / 2$$

$$G = 255\left(\text{for 8 bit image}\right), \quad K_1, \ K_2 \ll 1,$$

$$\left(K_1 = 0.001, K_2 = 0.001\right)$$

where, X is the original Image, $\hat{X}$ is the restored image, Y is the corrupted image, $M \times N$ is the size of the image, L is the luminance comparison, C is the contrast comparison, S is the structure comparison, μ is the mean and σ is the standard deviation.

Similar to SSIM, the Mean SSIM (MSSIM) method is a convenient way to incorporate image details at different resolutions.

$$MSSIM\left(X, \hat{X}\right) = \frac{1}{N} \sum_{k=1}^{N} SSIM\left(X_k, \hat{X}_k\right) \tag{18}$$

where X_k and $\hat{X}_k$ are the image pixels at k^{th} local window, N is number of local windows in the image.

Structural dissimilarity (DSSIM) is a distance metric derived from SSIM (though the triangle inequality is not necessarily satisfied).

$$DSSIM\left(X, \hat{X}\right) = \frac{1 - SSIM\left(X, \hat{X}\right)}{2} \tag{19}$$

(Wang, Simoncelli & Bovik, 2003) This is a novel image synthesis-based approach that helps calibrating the parameters (such as viewing distance) that weight the relative importance between different scales.

Visual Information Fidelity (VIF)

VIF criterion (Sheikh & Bovik, 2006) quantifies the Shannon information that is shared between the reference and distorted images relative to the information contained in the reference image itself. It uses natural scene statistics modeling in conjunction with an image degradation model and an HVS model.

Results of this measure can be between 0 and 1, where 1means perfect quality and near 0 means poor quality.

Visual Signal-To-Noise Ratio (VSNR)

The VSNR (Chandler & Hemami, 2007) operates in two stages. First, the threshold for distortions of a degraded image is determined to decide if it is below or above human sensitivity of error detection. This is computed using wavelet-based models of visual masking. If distortions are below the threshold, then the distorted image is assumed to be perfect (VSNR= ∞). If the distortions are above the threshold, then a second stage is applied. Calculations are made on the low-level visual property of perceived contrast and the midlevel visual property of global precedence. These properties are used to determine Euclidean distances in distortion-contrast space of multiscale wavelet decomposition. Finally, VSNR is calculated from a linear sum of these distances. A higher VSNR means that the tested image is less degraded.

Percentage of Spoiled Pixels (PSP)

PSP (Gonzalez & Woods, 2009; Sridhar, 2011) is a measure of percentage of non-noisy pixels changes their gray scale values in the reconstructed image. In other words it measures the efficiency of noise detectors. Hence, lower the PSPvalue better is the detection, in turn better is the filter performance.

$$PSP = \frac{Number\ of\ Non-noisy\ Pixels\ Changed\ their\ Grey\ Value}{Total\ Number\ of\ Non-noisy\ Pixels} \times 100 \tag{20}$$

Subjective or Qualitative or Distortion Measures

Along with the above performance measures, subjective assessment is also required to measure the image quality. In a subjective assessment measures, the characteristics of human perception become paramount, and image quality is correlated with the preference of an observer or the performance of an operator for some specific task. The qualitative measurement approach does not depend on the image being tested, the viewing conditions or the individual observer.

Image Quality Index (IQI)

In this paper, we also used a qualitative-based performance measure through the metric named image quality index (IQI) to prove the efficiency of our proposed algorithm. It was proposed by (Wang & Bovik, 2002; Nair & Raju, 2010), which is easy to calculate and applicable to various image processing applications. This quality index models any distortion as a combination of three different factors: loss of correlation, luminance distortion, and contrast distortion. IQI can be defined as below:

$$IQI_j = Corr\left(X_w, \hat{X}_w\right) * Lum\left(X_w, \hat{X}_w\right) * Cont\left(X_w, \hat{X}_w\right) \tag{21}$$

$$Where, Corr\left(X_w, \hat{X}_w\right) = \sigma_{X\hat{X}} / \sigma_X \sigma_{\hat{X}}$$

$$Lum\left(X_w, \hat{X}_w\right) = 2\mu_X \mu_{\hat{X}} / \left(\mu_X^2 + \mu_{\hat{X}}^2\right)$$

$$Cont\left(X_w, \hat{X}_w\right) = 2\sigma_X \sigma_{\hat{X}} / \left(\sigma_X^2 + \sigma_{\hat{X}}^2\right)$$

IQI is first applied to local regions using a sliding window approach with size of $w \times w$. The O_w and R_w represents the sliding window of original and restored images, respectively. Here, we have taken $w = 8$. At the jth step, the local quality index IQI_j is computed within the sliding window using the formula given above. If there are total of M steps, then the overall image quality index is given by,

$$IQI = \left(1 / M\right) \sum_j IQI_j \tag{22}$$

where, j varies from 1 to M. The dynamic range of IQI is $[-1,1]$, and the best value 1 is achieved if and only if restored image R is equal to the original image O.

Execution Time

Execution Time (T_E) of a filter, which is used to reduce noise, is defined as the time taken by a Processor to execute that filtering algorithm when no other software, except the operating system (OS), runs on it. Execution Time depends essentially on the system's clock time-period, yet it is not necessarily dependent on the clock, memory-size, the input data size, and the memory access time, etc.

The execution time taken by a filtering algorithm should be low for best online and real-time image processing applications. Hence, when all metrics give the identical values then a filter with lower T_E is better than a filter having higher T_E value.

IMPLEMENTATION OF VARIOUS DENOISING ALGORITHMS

New Adaptive Median Filter (NAMF)

The New Adaptive Median Filter (NAMF) (Patel, Tripathi, Majhi & Tripathy, 2011) scheme uses an improved adaptive median filtering technique that removes salt-and-pepper noise while preserving edges. The filter is designed to reconfigure itself and provide real-time noise reduction. The proposed filter solves the dual purpose of removing noise as well as distortion from the images and capable of removing high density impulse noise (up to 70%). The algorithm of the suggested scheme is given in Algorithm 1.

The simulation has been performed on standard lena.jpg image. The images are subjected to as low as 10% noise density to as high as 90% noise density. The simulation is carried out using MATLAB R2008a. Performance comparisons have been made both through visual results and objective parameters. The MAE, PSNR, SSIM, and IQI parameter comparisons are shown in Tables 1 for Lena.jpg.

The NAMF is better than the existing Median Filtering Technique for Salt and Pepper noise. Here, we introduced a new term- Tolerance value. If we increase the Tolerance value, the PSNR and the qual-

Algorithm 1. New Adaptive Median Filter (NAMF)

Input: The noisy image Y
Output: The filtered image $\hat{X}$

Step 1: Initialize a sub-window size, $W_s = 3$ and maximum window size, $W_{max} = 11$
Step 2: Select a sub-window $W_s \times W_s$ with center pixel $Y_{i,j}$.
Step 3: Find the maximum (Y_{max}) and minimum (Y_{min}) grey values within the window
Step 4: If the $|Y_{max} - Y_{min}| \leq$ Threshold (T), then go to step 9.
Step 5: If the $Y_{min} < Y_{i,j} < Y_{max}$ then go to step 9.
Step 6: Collect the set of pixels $\left(S\right)$ from the sub-window where, $Y_{min} < S_{i,j} < Y_{max}$
Step 7: If the size of $S \geq W$, then replace $Y_{i,j}$ with median of pixels in S.
Go to step 9.
Step 8: $W_s \leftarrow W_s + 2$,
If $W_s \leq W_{max}$, then go to Step 2.
    else
       replace the center pixel by mean of the pixels in sub-window of size W_{max}
Step 9: Shift the test pixel. Go to Step 1
Step 10: Repeat Steps 1 through 9 for image pixels.

Table 1. Simulation results of NAMF in terms of PSNR(dB), SSIM and IQI (Lena image)

% of noise	10	20	30	40	50	60	70	80	90
MAE	2.5606	3.5043	4.0353	4.4467	4.8716	5.4108	6.1545	7.3701	31.995
PSNR	40.437	38.6920	37.0012	35.3524	33.859	32.0523	30.1372	27.7752	12.947
SSIM	0.9987	0.9980	0.9970	0.9957	0.9939	0.9907	0.9855	0.9750	0.5081
IQI	0.9516	0.9397	0.9271	0.9084	0.8810	0.8390	0.7712	0.6570	0.1696

Figure 12. Restored images and image quality map at various noise densities of Lena.jpg image

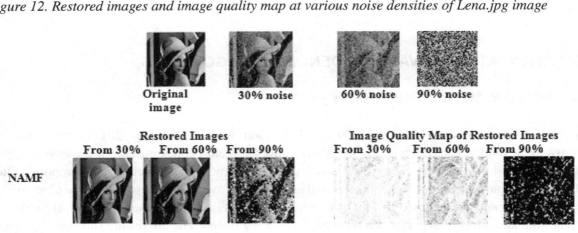

ity of the image increase. This technique gives the best result when the Tolerance value is 40. Greater Tolerance value than this decreases both image quality and the PSNR. Finally, the technique (NAMF) is achieving the filtering operation of an image corrupted with impulse noise up to 70% in the spatial domain. It performs better than that of the traditional median filtering techniques and we hope that our effort will help to improve the future experiments over image processing and performance analysis. In future one can try to explore the effect of other filtering techniques over noisy image and upgrade them so as to achieve the better performance.

Efficient Adaptive Mean Filter (EAMF)

The Efficient Adaptive Mean Filter (Jena, Patel & Tripathy, 2012) contains a simple noise detection stage at the beginning of the filtering operation by inspecting the pixel value. If it is laidbetween the minimum (0) and maximum (255) gray level value, it is considered as a noise free pixel and remain untreated. If the pixel matches with any of the minimum or maximum value, it is considered as a noisy pixel and processed by the proposed filtering method. The filtering stage starts with a 3 × 3 window which is applied on the noisy pixel only. Once a pixel identified as noisy then the mean of the non-noisy neighbours of the current window is used to restore the detected noisy pixel. If the selected window contains all the elements as noisy, the size of window in increased to 5 × 5 and the process is repeated till the window size reaches to a predefined maximum window size. The algorithm automatically chooses the optimal window size. The maximum window size is not allowed to exceed 13×13 which drastically reduced the computation time and preserves the edge details in the case of high-density impulse. The steps of the EAMF algorithm are given in Algorithm 2.

Algorithm 2. Efficient Adaptive Mean Filter (EAMF)

Input: The noisy image Y *Output: The filtered image $\hat{X}$*
Step 1. Initialize a sub-window size, W=3 and maximum window size, W$_{max}$=13 Step 2. Select a sub-window W×W with center pixel X_{ij}. Step 3. If X_{ij} is not equal to 0 or 255, shift the window and go to Step 1 Step 4. Collect the set of pixels (S) from the sub-window ignoring the pixels of intensity value '0' or '255'. Step 5. If the cardinality of set S, |S| ≥ 1, do i. Replace X_{ij} with mean of pixels in S. ii. Shift the window iii. Go to Step 1 Else go to step 6 Step 6. W=W+2; Step 7. If W ≤ W$_{max}$, go to Step 2, else replace the center pixel by mean of all the pixels in the sub-window of size W$_{max}$ Step 8. Repeat Step 2 through Step 7 for all pixels in the image.

The simulation has been performed on standard images. The images are subjected to as low as 10% noise density to as high as 90% noise density. The simulation is carried out using Matlab R2008a. Performance comparisons have been made both through visual results and objective parameters. The PSNR, ISNR, SSIM, and IQI parameters comparison are shown in Tables 2 for Lena.jpg. In addition to the IQI, the image quality maps of restored images of Lena.jpg have also been generated to evaluate the performance of the different algorithms. The restored image of Lena.jpg image at 60% noise densities is shown in Figure 13. The restored images and its corresponding image quality maps at noise level 30%, 60% and 90% are shown in Figures 14 for Boat.jpg image. From the simulations results, it is in general observed that EAMF algorithm outperforms all other noise removal filters in low as well as high density impulse noise.

Wavelet Thresholding Based Image Denoising

The term wavelet thresholding is explained as decomposition of the data or the image into wavelet coefficients, comparing the detail coefficients with a given threshold value, and shrinking these coefficients close to zero to take away the effect of noise in the data. The image is reconstructed from the modified coefficients. This process is also known as the inverse discrete wavelet transform. During thresholding,

Table 2. Simulation results of EAMF in terms of ISNR(dB), PSNR(dB), SSIM and IQI (Lena.jpg image)

% of noise	10	20	30	40	50	60	70	80	90
ISNR	28.6815	28.1760	27.6517	27.1321	26.7030	25.8672	24.6668	23.310	21.2748
PSNR	44.0265	40.5192	38.2512	36.4703	35.0722	33.4347	31.5785	29.650	27.0937
SSIM	0.9994	0.9987	0.9978	0.9966	0.9954	0.9932	0.9896	0.9837	0.9704
IQI	0.9736	0.9616	0.9463	0.9283	0.9070	0.8760	0.8315	0.7562	0.6138

Figure 13. Restored images and image quality map at various noise densities of Lena.jpg image

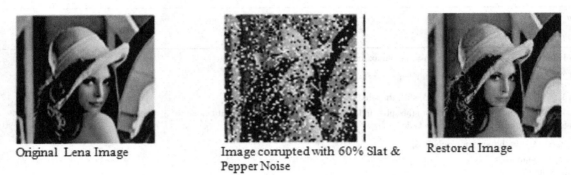

Original Lena Image   Image corrupted with 60% Slat &   Restored Image
Pepper Noise

Figure 14. Performance comparison of filters at different noise densities of Boat.jpg image

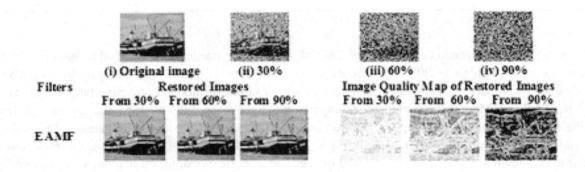

a wavelet coefficient is compared with a given threshold and is set to zero if its magnitude is less than the threshold; otherwise, it is retained or modified depending on the threshold rule. Thresholding distinguishes between the coefficients due to noise and the ones consisting of important signal information. (Kaur, Gupta & Chauhan, 2002)

Algorithm:

- Perform multiscale decomposition the image corrupted by Guassian noise using wavelet transform.
- Estimate the noise variance σ^2 using the formula given below

$$\sigma^2 = \left[\frac{median\left(\left|Y_{ij}\right|\right)}{0.6457} \right]^2 \tag{23}$$

where, Y_{ij} is the diagonal sub-band of first level decomposition.

- For each level, compute the scale parameter β using following equation

$$\beta = \sqrt{\left(\frac{L_k}{J}\right)} \qquad (24)$$

where L_k the length of the sub-band at kth is scale and J is total number of decompositions

- For each sub-band (except the low-pass residual)
  a. Compute the standard deviation σ_y.
  b. Compute threshold T$_N$ using the equation given below

$$T_N = \frac{\beta\sigma^2}{\sigma_y} \qquad (25)$$

where σ_y is the standard deviation of the sub-band

  c. Apply soft thresholding to the noisy coefficients.
- Invert the multiscale decomposition to reconstruct the denoised image.

Independent Component Analysis

A speckle noise reduction scheme for MRI image based on Independent Component Analysis (ICA) is discussed here. Noisy image was first denoised using present Wavelet denoising technique and then the Independent Component Analysis is applied. Image denoising using Independent component analysis is coming under data adaptive transform domain filtering. In ICA an observed random vector is expressed

Figure 15. Restored images of Lena image of wavelet thresholding based image denoising

Original Lena Image   Lena image corrupted with   Restored Image
Gaussian noise $\sigma = 30$

as a linear transformation of another variables that are non-gaussian and statistically independent.(Deokar & Kaushik, 2014) Using vector-matrix notation, the ICA mixing model is written as,

$$X = AS \tag{26}$$

where, $X = \left[x_{1,}x_{2},x_{3}....x_{m}\right]^{T}$ is the observed random vector of size m-dimension; $S = \left[s_{1,}s_{2},s_{3}....s_{n}\right]^{T}$ is the latent (Independent) n-dimensional random vector also called as Source Signal, A is a constant $m \times n$ mixing matrix; The starting point for ICA is the very simple assumption that the components S_{n} are statistically independent and independent component must have non-gaussian distributions. When ICA is performed on data, bivariate non-gaussian distributions are assumed on the sources S. For a given dataset X, ICA estimates the unknown A and S simultaneously. The task of the ICA algorithm is to determine a weight matrix W, Inverse of mixing matrix A, such that

$$S = WX \tag{27}$$

There are three different conditions of ICA:

1. Over complete case when dimension of observed random vector X is greater than the required source vectors s_{i}.
2. Complete case when both are same

Undetermined case when dimension of observed random vector X is less than the required sources vectors

If the number of independent components m is equal to n, the mixing matrix A is the inverse of W, $W = A^{-1}$

There exist some ICA algorithms to find weight matrix W such as the Fast-ICA algorithm, Non-linear PCA algorithm, maximum likelihood estimation algorithm. Fast ICA algorithm which is based on a fixed point iteration scheme for finding a maximum of the non gaussianity of WTX Estimating the independent Components can be accomplished by finding the right linear combinations of the mixture variables. Before applying an ICA algorithm on the data, it is usually very useful to do some pre-processing. The Fast ICA algorithm includes two preprocessing steps, centering and whitening.

*   **Centering:** The most basic and necessary preprocessing is to center X, i.e. subtract its mean vector $m = E\{X\}$ so as to make X a zero-mean variable. This preprocessing is made solely to simplify the ICA algorithms.
*   **Whitening:** Whitening is done after centering and before the application of the ICA algorithm, in which observed vector X is transformed linearly so that we obtain a new vector whose components are uncorrelated.

There are various methods of whitening; one popular method that we are using is Eigen-value decomposition $\left(EVD\right)$ of the covariance of X i.e. $E\{XXT\}$.

From Covariance Matrix we first calculate Eigen values in terms of diagonal Matrix, $D = diag(d1, \ldots, dn)$ and Orthogonal matrix of Eigen vectors E.

When the observed vector is transformed linearly we get m-dimensional whitened vector $\widehat{X}$, such that;

$$\tilde{X} = VX \tag{28}$$

where, $m \times n$ whitening matrix is $V = D^{-\frac{1}{2}}E^T$

After whitening, we seek an orthogonal matrix B which maximizes some given measure of super gaussianity of the components of the vector $= B^{\tilde{X}}$, this may be done by using Fast ICA algorithm.

Now from equation (27)

$$S = WX = BD^{-\frac{1}{2}}E^T X = BD^{-\frac{1}{2}}E^T AS \tag{29}$$

With reference to paper of Hoyer, we first find of $\tilde{A}$ of using A Conventional ICA method and then estimate orthogonal separating matrix by

$$W_{ortho} = W\left(WW^T\right)^{-\frac{1}{2}} \tag{30}$$

This matrix retains the sparseness of the original ICA transformed components and produces acceptable denoising results.

Figure 16. Restored MRI images

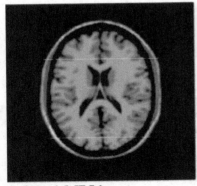 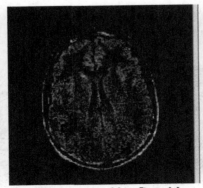 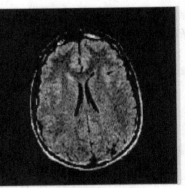

Original MRI image   Image corrupted by Speckl   Denoised image
                            Noise (PSNR=34.02dB)   (PSNR=51.39dB)

Fingerprint Identification and Authentication

Digital Image Processing is an emerging field of research for researchers. It has got wide range of applications areas like face recognition, vein recognition, medical sciences, remote sensing, weather forecasting, robotics etc. Biometrics is one of the popular used techniques for the question of who you are. In general, it can be divided into behavioural-based and physiological based methods (Weaver, 2006). A biometric system is essentially a pattern-recognition system that recognizes a person based on a feature vector derived from specific physiological or behavioural characteristic that the person possesses. Vein pattern detection has been proved to fully comply with this definition and it provides many important biometric features:

- Uniqueness and permanence of the pattern,
- Non-contact detection procedure,
- Almost impossible to forge or copy.

The biometric identification and authentication provides considerable security benefits over token-based or password-based methods. These include identity of theft, cross matching, and the exposure of sensitive private information, as well as trace-ability of individuals. This has stimulated research on the protection of stored biometric data in recent years, primarily focusing on preventing information leakage. Fingerprint recognition is a gifted feature for the Biometric identification and authentication systems. The standard fingerprint image is label as shown in Figure 17.

The field of biometric is still in its formative years, it's unavoidable that biometric systems will play a significant role in the security (Chirillo, John and Blaul, 2003). A biometric system is fundamentally a pattern recognition system that functions by obtaining biometric data from an individual, extracting a feature set from the obtained data, and evaluating this feature set against the template set in the database (Jain, Ross and Prabhakar, 2004). The biometric data comprises of fingerprints (Clancy, Kiyavash and Lin, 2003), facial features (Goh, Ngo, 2003), iris (Wildes, 1997), hand geometry (Polat, Övünç and Yýldýrým, 2008), voice (Monrose, Reiter and Wetzel, 2001), and signature (Pankanti, Prabhakar and Jain, 2002). Biometrics is extensively employed in forensics, in criminal identification and prison security to quote a few of the instances, and has the prospective to be employed in a wide variety of civilian application areas.

Figure 17. (a) Minutiae, (b) Other Fingerprint Characteristics

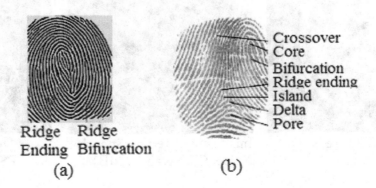

Figure 18. Different stages of the Fingerprint Verification System (Chandra, 2011)

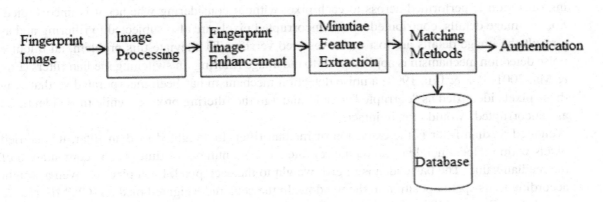

The primary focus is to perform the fingerprint image pre-processing cum image enhancement using the median filter. The different stage of the Fingerprint Verification system is shown in Figure 18.

Fingerprint identification is one of the most well-known and publicized biometrics. Because of their uniqueness and consistency over time, fingerprints have been used for identification for over a century, more recently becoming automated (i.e. a biometric) due to advancements in computing capabilities.

RELATED WORKS

In this section, attempts have been made for detail literature reviews of noise removal schemes on the reported articles. We have classified the schemes based on the characteristics of the filtering schemes and are briefly described as below.

Filtering without Detection

In this type of filtering a window mask is moved across the observed image. The Mask is usually of size $(2N + 1)^2$, where N is a positive integer. Generally, the center element is the pixel of interest. This technique does not detect contaminated pixels. It applies the filtering mechanism throughout the subject without discriminating any pixel.

The Moving Average (Smith & Steven, 1999) is a simple linear filter. Average of all pixels of a sliding window is replaced with the pixel of interest.

$$\hat{Y}_{i,j} = \frac{1}{m \times n} \sum_{(u,v) \in S_{mn}} X_{u,v} \tag{31}$$

where, X is the noisy image, $\hat{Y}$ is the restored image and S_{mn} is the sliding window of size $m \times n$ centered around (i, j). Its performance both in subjective as well as objective way is very poor.

2. In traditional median filtering called standard median filter (SMF) (Han & Lin, 1997) the filtering operation is performed across to each pixel without considering whether it is uncorrupted. So, the image details, contributed by the uncorrupted pixels are also subjected to filtering and as a result the image details are lost in the restored version. To alleviate this problem, an impulse noise detection mechanism is applied prior to the image filtering. In switching median filters (Eng & Ma, 2001; Pok & Liu, 1999) a noise detection mechanism has been incorporated so that only those pixels identified as "corrupted" would undergo the filtering process, while those identified as "uncorrupted" would remain intact.

3. Weighted median filter is the extension of median filter. In weighted median filter, it specified pixels within a local neighbourhood are repeated a given number of times in the computation of the median value. The basic idea is to give weight to the each pixel. Each pixel is given a weight according to its spatial position in the window. In the centered weighted median (CWMF) (Ko & Lee, 1991) filter is giving more weight only to the central value of each window.

Detection Followed by Filtering

This type of filtering involves two steps. In first step it identifies noisy pixels and in second step it filters those pixels. Here also a mask is moved across the image and some arithmetical operations is carried out to detect the noisy pixels. Then filtering operation is performed only on those pixels which are found to be noisy in the previous step, keeping the non-noisy intact. Such filtering schemes differentiate between noisy and non-noisy pixels.

1. The progressive switching median filter (PSMF) (Wang, Zhou & Zhang, 1999) was proposed which achieves the detection and removal of impulse noise in two separate stages. In first stage, it applies impulse detector and then the noise filter is applied progressively in iterative manners in second stage. In this method, impulse pixels located in the middle of large noise blotches can also be properly detected and filtered. The performance of this method is not good for very highly corrupted image.

2. Nonlinear filters such as adaptive median filter (AMF) (Hwang & Haddad, 1995) can be used for discriminating corrupted and uncorrupted pixels and then apply the filtering technique. Noisy pixels will be replaced by the median value, and uncorrupted pixels will be left unchanged. AMF performs well at low noise densities but at higher noise densities, window size has to be increased to get better noise removal which will lead to less correlation between corrupted pixel values and replaced median pixel values.

3. A Minimum-maximum exclusive mean (MMEM) (Han & Lin, 1997) filter to remove impulse noise from highly corrupted images is proposed. This is a simple nonlinear, robust filter that centers around two windows of size 3×3 and 5×5. It checks for a particular range of gray level in the 3×3 windows. If it fails, it goes to 5×5 window. If average of all the pixels of that particular range is more than certain value then that pixel is replaced with the average, otherwise it is left intact. This is one of the good schemes because of its simplicity and easy implementation.

4. An efficient decision-based algorithm (DBA) (Srinivasan & Ebenezer, 2007) was proposed using a fixed window size of 3 × 3, where the corrupted pixels are replaced by either the median pixel or neighborhood pixels. It shows promising results, a smooth transition between the pixels is lost with lower processing time which degrades the visual quality of the image.

5. To overcome the problem in DBA, an improved decision-based algorithm (IDBA) (Madhu, Revathy & Tatavarti, 2008) is proposed where corrupted pixels can be replaced either by the median pixel or, by the mean of processed pixels in the neighborhood. It results in a smooth transition between the pixels with edge preservation and better visual quality for low-density impulse noise. The limitation of this method is that in the case of high-density impulse noise, the fixed window size of 3×3 will result in image quality degradation due to the presence of corrupted pixels in the neighborhood.

6. The Robust Estimation Based Filter (REBF) (Vijaykumar, Vanathi, Kanagasabapathy & Ebenezer, 2008) is proposed for Removal of High Density Impulse Noise from images. The function of the proposed filter is to detect the outlier pixels and restore the original value using robust estimation. In this proposed approach impulses are first detected based on the minimum, median and maximum value in the selected window. If the median pixel and the current pixel lie inside the dynamic range [0,255] then it is considered as noise free pixel. Otherwise it is considered as a noisy pixel and replaced by an estimated value. The visual quality results shows that the proposed filter remove impulse noise completely without any blurring and sinking effect.

7. A novel improved median filtering (NIMF) (Wang, Chen & Qu, 2010) algorithm is proposed for removal of highly corrupted with salt-and-pepper noise from images. Firstly all the pixels are classified into signal pixels and noisy pixels by using the Max-Min noise detector. The noisy pixels are then separated into three classes, which are low-density, moderate-density, and high-density noises, based on the local statistic information. Finally, the weighted 8-neighborhood similarity function filter, the 5×5 median filter and the 4-neighborhood mean filter are adopted to remove the noises for the low, moderate and high level cases, respectively. In experiment, the proposed algorithm is compared with three typical methods, named Standard Median filter, Extremum Median filter and Adaptive Median filter, respectively. The validation results show that the proposed algorithm has better performance for capabilities of noise removal, adaptivity, and detail preservation, especially effective for the cases when the images are extremely highly corrupted.

8. A modified decision based unsymmetrical trimmed median filter (MDBUTMF) (Esakkirajanet, 2011) algorithm is proposed for the restoration of gray scale, and color images that are highly corrupted by salt and pepper noise. The proposed algorithm replaces the noisy pixel by trimmed median value when other pixel values, 0's and 255's are present in the selected window and when all the pixel values are 0's and 255's then the noise pixel is replaced by mean value of all the elements present in the selected window. When this algorithm tested against different gray scale and color images, it gives better Peak Signal-to-Noise Ratio (PSNR) and Image Enhancement Factor (IEF).

9. A Tolerance based Arithmetic Mean Filtering Technique (TSAMFT) (Kaisar, Rijwan, Mahmud, Jubayer & Rahman, 2008) is proposed to remove salt and pepper noise from corrupted images. Arithmetic Mean filtering technique is modified by the introduction of two additional features. In the first phase, to calculate the Arithmetic Mean, only the unaffected pixels are considered. In the second phase, a Tolerance value has been used for the replacement of the pixels. This proposed technique provides much better results than that of the existing mean and median filtering techniques. The Peak Signal to Noise Ratio (PSNR) of the filtered image using the proposed technique is much higher than that of the filtered images obtained by the existing mean filtering techniques.

10. The FBDA (Nair & Raju, 2010) is an improved fuzzy-based switching median filter in which the filtering is applied only to corrupted pixels in the image while the uncorrupted pixels are left un-

changed. During the time of filtering process FBDA selects only uncorrupted pixels in the selected window based on a fuzzy distance membership value.

11. A fuzzy weighted non-local means (FWNLM) filter (Wu & Tang, 2014) has been proposed or removal of random-valued impulse noise. It uses an efficient fuzzy weighting functionfor the NLM algorithm to shutoff the impulsive componentIt has surprisingly good denoising capability.

12. AModified Adaptive Median Filter for Salt & Pepper Noise (Singh & Prakash, 2014) has been proposed which uses ROAD (Rank Order Absolute Difference) statistics to identify the noisy pixels in image corrupted with salt & pepper noise. ROAD statistics that how much different in intensity the particular pixels are from their most similar neighbours. After identify the presence of impulse noise, adaptive window filtering concept is used to filter the salt & pepper noise. The performance of proposed filter, both quantitative and qualitatively performs remarkably well in filtering and preserving the image detail as compared to well-known standard filters.

13. Cluster-based Adaptive Fuzzy Switching Median (CAFSM) (Toh, Kenny & Nor, 2010) is composed of a cascaded easyto-implement impulse detector and a detail preserving noise filter. Initially, the impulse detector classifies any possible impulsive noise pixels. Subsequently, the filtering phase replaces the detected noise pixels. In addition, the filtering phase employs fuzzy reasoning to deal with uncertainties present in local information.The CAFSM filter is capable of filtering all kinds of impulse noise i.e. the random-valued and/or fixed-valued impulse noise under a wide range of noise densities with fast processing times. It outperforms other state-of-the-art impulse noise filters.

Hybrid Filtering

In such filtering schemes, two or more filters are suggested to filter a corrupted location. The decision to apply a particular filter is based on the noise level at the test pixel location or performance of the filter on a filtering mask.

1. A novel and effective median dlter, called tri-state median (TSM) (Chen, Ma & Chen, 1999) dlter, is proposed where noise detection is realized by an impulse detector, which takes the outputs from the Standard Median (SM) filters and Centre Weighted Median (CWM) dlters and compares them with the origin or center pixel value in order to make a tri-state decision. An attractive merit of this dltering scheme is that it provides an adaptive decision to detect local noise simply based on the outputs of these dlters. Given a specided threshold T, the output of our proposed TSM dlter may correspond to one of three possible states, namely the origin pixel value (i.e., the pixel is noise-free), the SM dltered output (i.e., the pixel is corrupted), or the CWM dltered output (i.e., the pixel is probably uncorrupted with $w_c > 1$). As a result, impulse noise can be removed for those corrupted pixels through SM or CWM dltering. For those uncorrupted pixels identided, they remain unchanged in order to preserve the local image details. Consequently, the tradeoff between suppressing noise and preserving detail is well balanced over a wide variety of images.

2. A hybrid algorithm called A Universal Noise Removal Algorithm with an Impulse Detector has been proposed (Garnett, Huegerich, Chui & He, 2005) for removal of both Gaussian and impulse noises from noisy images. It uses a local image statistic for identifying noise pixels in images corrupted with impulse noise of random values. The statistical values quantify how different in intensity the particular pixels are from their most similar neighbors.

3. The proposed method (Umamaheswari & Radhamani, 2012) is used hybrid denoising scheme for removing of Gaussian and impulse noise from medical images. It is based on wavelet transform where soft thresholding is used for suppressing Gaussian noise. Then the center weighted median filter is used to remove impulse noise present in the image during transformation. Results prove that utilization of center weighted median filters in combination with wavelet thresholding filters on DICOM images deteriorates the performance. But, it gives good results in terms of PSNR, MSE, UQI and ET. In addition, the proposed filter gives nearly uniform and consistent results on all the test images.

4. A two-step fuzzy-based filter (Saranya, Porkumaran & Prabakar, 2014) has been proposed for restoring color images corrupted with impulsive and gaussian noise. First step is to identify the noisy pixels by calculating the similarity between the central pixel and its neighborhood in a selected window. The noisy pixels in a selected window are then replaced by its modified value by computing the median around the central pixel. The second step is fuzzy filtering which is carried out by computing the Rank Ordered Logarithmic difference (ROLD) between the central pixel and its neighborhood in a selected window. Depending upon the difference value, a fuzzy membership degree is calculated using a membership function. Computed fuzzy membership values are appropriately utilized as weights for each pixel and then computes the weighted average representing the modified value for the current central pixel. The output of the proposed system is compared with the some of the existing schemes. The experimental analysis shows that the proposed method gives better results even when the mixed noise percentage is above 50%.

5. The authors (Baljozovic, Branko, & Aleksandra, 2013) has been proposed a novel method called mixed noise removal filter for multi-channel images based on halfspace deepest location for removing mixed (mixture of impulse and Gaussian) noise. The multi-channel noise from multi-channel digital images based on a modided version of the algorithm introduced by (Struyf, & Rousseeuw, 2000) for dnding approximate halfspace deepest location (Tukey's median). Denoising results of this new nonlinear spatial domain dltering method applied to images corrupted by multichannel mixed noise outperform currently used spatial domain dlters and state-of-the-art wavelet transform domain dlters in terms of both peak signal-to-noise ratio and visual quality, as well as, eliminates the noise on all channels simultaneously without their separation, thus preserving the spectral correlation between channels in a multi-channel image.

DISCUSSION

The quantitative performance measures and visual quality of the images are taken into consideration to measure the performance of denoising algorithms. However, due to the varied nature and sources of noise, these assumptions may not hold true. An ideal denoising techniques call for apriori knowledge of the noise. On the other hand, the real procedure doesn't require it for the noise model. Most of the researchers have drawn comparison of the performance of various denoising algorithms by assuming the known variance of the noise model.

Performance of denoising algorithms are being is measured using quantitative performance measures such as Mean Squared Error (MSE), Mean Absolute Error (MAE), signal-to-noise ratio (SNR), peak Signal-to-Noise Ratio (PSNR), Improved Peak Signal-to-Noise Ratio(ISNR), Contrast-to-Noise Ratio(CNR), Structural Similarity Index Measure (SSIM), Percentage of Spoiled Pixels (PSP) as well as in terms of visual quality of the images i.e. Image Quality Index(IQI). Many of the current techniques assume the noise model to be Gaussian. In reality, this assumption may not always hold true due to the varied nature and sources of noise. An ideal denoising procedure requires *a priori* knowledge of the noise, whereas a practical procedure may not have the required information about the variance of the noise or the noise model. Thus, most of the algorithms assume known variance of the noise and the noise model to compare the performance with different algorithms. Gaussian Noise with different variance values is added in the natural images to test the performance of the algorithm. Not all researchers use high value of variance to test the performance of the algorithm when the noise is comparable to the signal strength. Use of FFT in filtering has been restricted due to its limitations in providing sparse representation of data. Wavelet Transform is the best suited for performance because of its properties like sparsity, multi-resolution and multiscale nature. In addition to performance, issues of computational complexity must also be considered. Thresholding techniques used with the Discrete Wavelet Transform are the simplest to implement. Non-orthogonal wavelets such as UDWT and Multiwavelets improve the performance at the expense of a large overhead in their computation. HMM based methods seem to be promising but are complex. When using Wavelet Transform, (Nason, 2002) emphasized that issue such as choice of primary resolution (the scale level at which to begin thresholding) and choice of analyzing wavelet also have a large influence on the success of the shrinkage procedure. When comparing algorithms, it is very important that researchers do not omit these comparison details. Several papers did not specify the wavelet used neither the level of decomposition of the wavelet transform was mentioned. It is expected that the future research will focus on building robust statistical models of non-orthogonal wavelet coefficients based on their intra scale and inter scale correlations. Such models can be effectively used for image denoising and compression.

The proposed schemes NAMF, EAMF and FBAMF have been used for suppression of salt-and-pepper noise, the DWT for suppression of Gaussian noise, the ICA for speckle noise reduction for gray scale images. The fuzzy logic has been applied in FBAMF for detecting noisy pixels.

DIRECTIONS FOR FUTURE RESEARCH

From the chapter, it is observed that the performance of any filtering scheme is dependent on the detection mechanism. The better the detector; the superior is the filtering performance. Hence, the performance of a detector plays a vital role. In turn, the detector performance is solely dependent on a threshold value which is compared with a pre-computed numerical value. Mostly the reported schemes use a fixed threshold which does not serve the purpose at various noise conditions as well as in different images. Hence, to improve the detector performance, the need for an adaptive threshold is of utmost necessity which can be automatically determined from the characteristics of an image and the noise present in it.

Also, it shows from the literature survey that the linear filters are often used for the removal of impulse noise which is not efficient. On the other hand, non-linear filters are generally efficient for the removal of impulse noise. However, there exists further scope to improve the performance of these filters.

There are several soft computing techniques available which can be applied more efficiently for detecting noisy pixels present in an image and restored the original one. The research findings made out of this chapter has opened several auxiliary research directions, which can be further investigated. These schemes can be further extended and applied to colour images.

REFERENCES

1fnoise, Brownian Noise. (1999). Retrieved from http://classes.yale.edu/9900/math190a/OneOverF.html

Baljozovic, Kovacevic, & Baljozovic. (2013). Mixed noise removal filter for multi-channel images based on halfspace deepest location. *Image Processing, 7*(4), 310-323.

Bhoi, N., & Meher, D. S. (2008). Total Variation based Wavelet Domain Filter for Image Denoising. *First International Conference on Emerging Trends in Engineering and Technology*. IEEE Computer Society. doi:10.1109/ICETET.2008.6

Bovik, A. C. (2009). *The Essential Guide to Image Processing* (2nd ed.). Academic Press.

Buccigrossi, R. W., & Simoncelli, E. P. (1999, December). Image compression via joint statistical characterization in the wavelet domain. *IEEE Image Process., 8*(12), 1688–1701. doi:10.1109/83.806616 PMID:18267447

Chanda, B., & Majumder, D. (2002). Digital Image Processing and Analysis. Prentice-Hall of India.

Chandler, D. M., & Hemami, S. S. (2007, September). VSNR: A wavelet-based visual signal-to-noise ratio for natural images. *IEEE Transactions on Image Processing, 16*(9), 2284–2298. doi:10.1109/TIP.2007.901820 PMID:17784602

Chen, Ma, & Chen. (1999, December). Tri-State Median Filter for Image Denoising. *IEEE Transactions On Image Processing, 8*(12), 1834-1838.

Chirillo, J., & Blaul, S. (2003). *Implementing Biometric Security*. Wiley Red Books.

Clancy, T. C., Kiyavash, N., & Lin, D. J. (2003). Secure smart cardbased fingerprint authentication. *Proceedings of the 2003 ACM SIGMM Workshop on Biometrics Methods and Application*. doi:10.1145/982507.982516

Cohen, I., Raz, S., & Malah, D. (1999). Translation invariant denoising using the minimum description length criterion. *Signal Processing, 75*(3), 201–223. doi:10.1016/S0165-1684(98)00234-5

Deokar, P. S., & Kaushik, A. R. (2014). Medical Image Denoising using Independent Component Analysis. *International Journal of Advanced Electronics & Communication Systems*.

Donoho, D. L. (1997). CART and best-ortho-basis: A connection. *Annals of Statistics, 25*(5), 1870–1911. doi:10.1214/aos/1069362377

Donoho, D. L., & Johnstone, I. M. (1995, December). Donoho, David L., & Johnstone, Iain M.(2001, July 27). Adapting to unknown smoothness via wavelet shrinkage. *Journal of the American Statistical Association, 90*(432), 1200–1224. doi:10.1080/01621459.1995.10476626

Eng, H.-L., & Ma, K.-K. (2001). Noise adaptive soft-switching median filter. *IEEE Transactions on Image Processing, 10*(2), 242–251. doi:10.1109/83.902289 PMID:18249615

Esakkirajanet, S. (2011, May). Removal of high density salt and pepper noise through modified decision based unsymmetric trimmed median filter. *IEEE Signal Processing Letters, 18*(5), 287–290. doi:10.1109/LSP.2011.2122333

Garnett, Huegerich, Chui, & He. (2005, November). A Universal Noise Removal Algorithm with an Impulse Detector. *IEEE Transactions on Image Processing, 14*(11), 1747-1754.

Ghabel, L., & Amindavar, H. (2002). Image Denoising Using Hidden Markov Models. *Lecture Notes in Computer Science, 2510*, 402–409. doi:10.1007/3-540-36087-5_47

Goh, A., & Ngo, D. C. L. (2003). Computation of cryptographic keys from face biometrics. International Federation for Information Processing. *LNCS, 2828*, 1–13.

Gonzalez, R. C., & Woods, R. E. (2009). *Digital Image Processing* (2nd ed.). Addison Wesley.

Han, & Lin. (1997). Minimum-maximum exclusive mean (MMEM) filter to remove impulse noise from highly corrupted images. *Electronics Letters, 33*(2).

Hwang, H., & Haddad, R. A. (1995). Adaptive median filters: New algorithms and results. *IEEE Transactions on Image Processing, 4*(4), 499–502. doi:10.1109/83.370679 PMID:18289998

Hyvärinen, A., Oja, E., Hoyer, P., & Hurri, J. (1998). Image feature extraction by sparse coding and independent component analysis. In *Proc. Int. Conf. on Pattern Recognition (ICPR'98)*, (pp. 1268-1273). Brisbane, Australia. doi:10.1109/ICPR.1998.711932

Jain, A. K. (1989). *Fundamentals of digital image processing*. Prentice-Hall of India.

Jain, A. K., Ross, A., & Prabhakar, S. (2004). An introduction to biometric recognition. *IEEE Transactions on Circuits and Systems for Video Technology, 14*(1), 4–20. doi:10.1109/TCSVT.2003.818349

Jayaraman, S., Esakkirajan, S., & Veerakumar, T. (2009). *Digital Image Processing*. Tata McGraw Hill Education Private Limited.

Jena, Patel, & Tripathy. (2012, October). An Efficient Adaptive Mean Filtering Technique for Removal of Salt and Pepper Noise from Images. *International Journal of Engineering Research & Technology, 1*(8).

Jung, A. (2001, October). An introduction to a new data analysis tool: Independent Component Analysis. *Proceedings of Workshop GK, Nonlinearity* .

Kaisar, Md. Sakib, Mahmud, & Rahman. (2008, June). Salt and Pepper Noise Detection and Removal by Tolerance based Selectve Arithmatic Mean Filtering Technique for Image Restoration. *International Journal of Computer Science and Network Security, 8*(6), 271-278.

Kaur, Gupta, & Chauhan. (2002, December 22). *Image Denoising using Wavelet Thresholding*. Retrieved from https://www.ee.iitb.ac.in/~icvgip/PAPERS/202.pdf

Ko, & Lee. (1991, September). Center Weighted Median Filters and Their Applications to Image Enhancement. *IEEE Transactions On Circuits And Systems, 38*(9), 984-993.

Lang, M. G., Odegard, H. J. E., & Burrus, C. S. (1995, April). Nonlinear processing of a shift invariant DWT for noise reduction, in Mathematical Imaging: Wavelet Applications for Dual Use. Proc. for Image and Video Database III. *Proceedings of the Society for Photo-Instrumentation Engineers, 2420*, 165–173.

Madhu, N. S., Revathy, K., & Tatavarti, R. (2008). An Improved Decision Based Algorithm for Impulse Noise Removal. In *Proceedings of International Congress on Image and Signal Processing* (CISP 2008), (pp. 426–431). IEEE Computer Society Press.

Malfait, M., & Roose, D. (1997, April). Wavelet-based image denoising using a Markov random field a priori model. *Image Processing, IEEE Transactions on, 6*(4), 549 – 565.

Marteen, J. (2000, April). *Wavelet thresholding and noise reduction.* (Ph. D. Thesis). Katholieke Universiteit Leuven.

Mihcak, M. K. I., & Kozintsev, K. R., & Moulin. (1999, December). Low-Complexity Image Denoising Based On Statistical Modeling of Wavelet Coefficients. *IEEE Signal Processing Letters, 6*(12), ●●●.

Monrose, F., Reiter, M. K., Li, Q., & Wetzel, S. (2001, May).Cryptographic key generation from voice. *Proceedings of the IEEE Symposium on Security and Privacy 2001.* IEEE.

Motwani, Gadiya, Motwani, & Harris. (2004). Survey of Image. Denoising Techniques. *Proc. of GSPx.*

Moulin, P., & Liu, J. (1999, April). Analysis of multiresolution image denoising schemes using generalized Gaussian and complexity priors. *IEEE Infor. Theory, 45*(3), 909–919. doi:10.1109/18.761332

Nair, M. S., & Raju, G. (2010). *A new fuzzy-based decision algorithm for high-density impulse noise removal. Journal of Signal.* Image and Video Processing; doi:10.1007/s11760-010-0186-4

Nason, G. P. (2002). Choice of wavelet smoothness, primary resolution and threshold in wavelet shrinkage. *Journal: Statistics and Computing, 12*, 219–227.

Ng, & Ma. (2006, June). A Switching Median Filter With Boundary Discriminative Noise Detection for Extremely Corrupted Images. *IEEE Transactions on Image Processing, 15*(6), 1506-1516.

Nuruzzaman, M. (2005). *Digital Image Fundamentals in MATLAB.* Author House.

Pandey. (2008, April). An Improved Switching Median filter for Uniformly Distributed Impulse Noise Removal. *Proceedings of World Academy of Science, Engineering and Technology, 28.*

Patel, P., Tripathi, A., Majhi, B., & Tripathy, C.R. (2011, February). *A New Adaptive Median Filtering Technique for Removal of Impulse Noise from Images.* International Conference on Communication, Computing & Security (ICCCS-2011), Department of Computer Science & Engineering, National Institute of Technology, Rourkela, India.

Petrou, M., & Bosdogianni, P. (2003). *Image Processing the Fundamentals* (1st ed.). John Wiley and Sons.

Pok, G., & Liu, J.-C. (1999). Decision based median filter improved by predictions. *Proc. ICIP, 2*, 410–413. doi:10.1109/ICIP.1999.822928

Polat, Ö., & Yýldýrým, T. (2008). Hand geometry identification without feature extraction by general regression neural network. *Expert Systems with Applications, 34*(2), 845–849. doi:10.1016/j.eswa.2006.10.032

Pratt, W. K. (2007). *Digital Image Processing* (4th ed.). John Wiley & Sons, Inc. doi:10.1002/0470097434

Rajan, J., & Kaimal, M.R (1996). Image Denoising Using Wavelet Embedded Anisotropic Diffusion (Wead). In *Proceedings of IEE International Conference on Visual Information Engineering* (VIE), (pp. 589 – 593). IEE.

Romberg, J. K., Choi, H., & Baraniuk, R. G. (2001). Bayesian tree-structured image modeling using wavelet-domain hidden Markov models. *IEEE Image Process.*, *10*(7), 1056–1068. doi:10.1109/83.931100 PMID:18249679

Roy, V., & Shukla, S. (2012). Image Denoising by Data Adaptive and Non-Data Adaptive Transform Domain Denoising Method Using EEG Signal. *Proceedings of All India Seminar on Biomedical Engineering*. Springer.

Russ, J. C. (2002). *The Image Processing Hand Book* (4th ed.). CRC Press.

Saranya, G., Porkumaran, K., & Prabakar, S. (2014, March). Mixed noise removal of a color image using simple fuzzy filter. In *Proceedings of International Conference on Green Computing Communication and Electrical Engineering* (ICGCCEE), (pp. 1-6).

Sheikh, H. R., & Bovik, A. C. (2006). Image information and visual quality. *IEEE Transactions on Image Processing*, *15*(2), 430–434. doi:10.1109/TIP.2005.859378 PMID:16479813

Singh, , & Prakash, . (2014). Modified Adaptive Median Filter for Salt & Pepper Noise. *International Journal of Advanced Research in Computer and Communication Engineerin*, *3*(1), 5067–5071.

Smith, S. W. (1999). *The Scientist and Engineer's Guide to Digital Signal Processing*. San Diego, CA: California Technical Publishing.

Sridhar, S. (2011). *Digital Image Processing*. Oxford University Press.

Srinivasan, K. S., & Ebenezer, D. (2007). A new fast and efficient decision-based algorithm for removal of high-density impulse noises. *Signal Processing Letters, IEEE*, *14*(3), 189-192.

Struyf, & Rousseeuw. (2000). High-dimensional computation of the deepest location. *Computational Statistics & Data Analysis, 34*, 415-426.

Toh, K. K. V., & Nor, A. M. I. (2010). Cluster-based adaptive fuzzy switching median filter for universal impulse noise reduction. *IEEE Transactions on Consumer Electronics*, *56*(4), 2560–2568. doi:10.1109/TCE.2010.5681141

Umamaheswari, J., & Radhamani. (2012). Hybrid Denoising Method for Removal of Mixed Noise in Medical Images. *International Journal of Advanced Computer Science and Applications, 3*(5), 44-47.

Véhel. (2000, May). *Website*. Retrieved from Fraclabwww-rocq.inria.fr/fractales/

Vijaykumar, V.R., Vanathi, P.T., Kanagasabapathy, P., & Ebenezer, D. (2008). High Density Impulse Noise Removal Using Robust Estimation Based Filter. *International Journal of Computer Science, 35*(3).

Wang, C., Chen, T., & Qu, Z. (2010). A Novel Improved Median Filter for Salt-and-Pepper Noise from Highly Corrupted Images. *3rd International Symposium on Systems and Control in Aeronautics and Astronautics (ISSCAA 2010)*. Harbin, China: IEEE.

Wang, Z., & Bovik, A. C. (2002, March). A Universal Image Quality Index. *IEEE Signal Processing Letters, 20*.

Wang, Z., Bovik, A. C., Sheikh, H. R., & Simoncelli, E. P. (2004, April). Image quality assessment: From error visibility to structural similarity. *IEEE Transactions on Image Processing, 13*(4), 600–612. doi:10.1109/TIP.2003.819861 PMID:15376593

Wang, Z., Simoncelli, E. P., & Bovik, A. C. (2003, November). Multi-scale structural similarity for image quality assessment. In *37th Proc. IEEE Asilomar Conf. on Signals, Systems and Computers*. Pacific Grove, CA: IEEE. doi:10.1109/ACSSC.2003.1292216

Wang, Z., & Zhang, D. (1999). Progressive switching median filter for the removal of impulse noise from highly corrupted images. Circuits and Systems II: Analog and Digital Signal Processing. *IEEE Transactions on, 46*(1), 78–80.

Wang, Z., & Zhang, D. (1999, January). Progressive Switching Median Filter for the Removal of Impulse Noise from Highly Corrupted Images. *IEEE Transactions On Circuits And Systems—II: Analog And Digital Signal Processing, 46*(1), 78–80.

Wang, & Qu. (2010, June). A Novel Improved Median Filter for Salt-and-Pepper Noise from Highly Corrupted Images. In *Proceedings of 3rd International Symposium on Systems and Control in Aeronautics and Astronautics* (ISSCAA 2010), (pp. 718-722). IEEE.

Wildes, R. P. (1997, September). Iris recognition: An emerging biometric technology. *Proceedings of the IEEE, 85*(9), 1348–1363. doi:10.1109/5.628669

Wu, J., & Ruan, Q. (2006). Combining Adaptive PDE and Wavelet Shrinkage in Image Denoising with Edge Enhancing Property. In *Proceedings of 18th International Conference on Pattern Recognition* (ICPR'06), (Vol. 3).

Wu, J., & Tang, C. (2014, February). Random-valued impulse noise removal using fuzzy weighted non-local means. *Signal, Image and Video Processing, 8*(2), 349–355. doi:10.1007/s11760-012-0297-1

Yadav, A., & Yadav, P. (2009). *Digital Image Processing* (1st ed.). University Science Press.

Chapter 4

Incorporation of Depth in Two Dimensional Video Captures:
Review of Current Trends and Techniques

Manami Barthakur
Gauhati University, India

Kandarpa Kumar Sarma
Gauhati University, India

ABSTRACT

Stereoscopic vision in cameras is an interesting field of study. This type of vision is important in incorporation of depth in video images which is needed for the ability to measure distances of the object from the camera properly i.e. conversion of two dimensional video image into three dimensional video. In this chapter, some of the basic theoretical aspects of the methods for estimating depth in 2D video and the current state of research have been discussed. These methods are frequently used in the algorithms for estimating depth in the 2D to 3D video techniques. Some of the recent algorithms for incorporation depth in 2D video are also discussed and from the literature review a simple and generic system for incorporation depth in 2D video is presented.

1. INTRODUCTION

Study of stereoscopic vision is receiving wide spread attention. It is primarily due to the fact that it is likely to generate bio-inspired vision capability (Knorr, Smolic & Sikora, 2007). Developments and innovations in stereoscopic vision is an important aspect for creation of artificial vision since it incorporates the third dimension of depth in video images. Conversion of two dimensional (2 D) video images into three dimensional (3 D) form mainly deals with the ability to properly measure and incorporate the depth component. It is related to giving due importance to the distances of the object from the camera while deriving decision regarding object and using the derived inference for some process control. The third dimension of depth can be perceived by the human vision in the form of binocular disparity. Human eyes are located at slightly different positions. The eyes perceive different views from its surroundings and

DOI: 10.4018/978-1-4666-9685-3.ch004

the brain then reconstruct the depth information from these different views. Stereoscopic vision takes advantage of this phenomenon. Two slightly different images of every scene are used and the points in one image are matched with their corresponding points in the other image. Then the disparity i.e. the amount of shift that the corresponding points in the two images is calculated. Now, disparity is inversely proportional to the depth. Therefore, higher the disparity, smaller is the depth and closure is the point to the camera (Wei, 2005). Thus a 3D video can be realized from a 2D video with an appropriate disparity and calibration of parameters.

Three-dimensional video may be the next step in the evolution of motion picture formats. Interest towards 3D video has led to the development of industries to fabricate products like TV, mobile, monitor and various display devices which are capable of displaying 3D images. Common 3D video has several applications in robotics, entertainment world, and in surveillance. A 3D image of a person's face might be used in biometrics instead of fingerprint, iris, face, voice and DNA recognition techniques for identity management and in security. The same technique might also be applied for analysis of security footage from closed-circuit television cameras (CCTV) in crime investigation or in searching for missing persons.

Generation of 3D content is an important step for generation of 3D videos or images. There are several special cameras which have been designed for direct generation of 3D models. A stereoscopic dual camera is such type of camera. In this camera, two separate monoscopic camera in a co-planar configuration is used. Each of the two cameras captures images for each of the eyes. Then using binocular disparity, depth information is achieved. Another example of camera for direct generation of 3D models is depth-range camera which consists of a laser element. The camera captures a normal 2D image and its corresponding depth map is generated. The depth map is a 2D function that gives the depth of an object obtained from the camera as function of image coordinates in the form a grey level image with its pixel value representing the depth. The laser element in the camera is used for the construction of depth map. It emits light towards the object which has been captured by the camera. After hitting the object, the laser light is reflected back and it is subsequently registered for construction of depth map (Wei, 2005). An example is the system designed by Mitsubishi Electrical Research Laboratories (MERL) (Matusik & Pfister, 2004) where the framework had used 16 cameras at different view points, and obtains the 3D video data directly.

Though all the techniques described above, contribute to the prevalence of 3D-TV, but it can be rather expensive and difficult to set up. Moreover, a user may not have an interest in viewing content in 3D that was only captured by one camera. In that case it would be impossible to fill the user's need. On the other hand, there are huge amount of current and past media data in 2D format. These data should be possible to be viewed with a stereoscopic effect. Because of these reasons the 2D to 3D conversion methods are needed. Further, with stereoscopic vision, real time surveillance shall be more reliable. It shall also be an effective addition to process control and in robotic vision. In most case, the video camera's limitation in its 2D presentation can be rectified and the feeds made more effective with the incorporation of 3D vision.

In this chapter, we discuss some of the basic theoretical aspects of the methods for estimating depth in 2D video in next section. These methods are frequently used in the algorithms for estimating depth in the 2D to 3D video techniques. Then in the following section some of the recent algorithms for incorporation depth in 2D video are discussed. From the literature review a simple and generic system for incorporation depth in 2D video is presented in fourth section. Finally, the conclusion is given in the last section.

2. BASIC THEORETICAL ASPECTS

Several algorithms have been developed for conversion of 2D video to 3D. The basic theoretical aspects based on which the researchers have developed these algorithms are discussed here.

2.1 Binocular Disparity

The depth of an object can be recovered by utilizing the binocular disparity from two images of the scene captured from slightly different view point (Trucco & Verri, 1998). Suppose o_1 and o_2 be the centre of the lens for left and right camera respectively, f is the focal length, D is the distance in the Z direction and P_1 and P_2 are the image coordinates in the right and the left image respectively. Since ΔWP_1P_2 and ΔWC_1C_2 are equivalent, therefore,

$$\frac{D+f}{D} = \frac{\left(P_2 - P_1\right)T}{T} \tag{1}$$

or

$$D = \frac{fT}{\left(P_2 - P_1\right)} \tag{2}$$

where $d = P_2 - P_1$ is the disparity. For a given stereo system, the focal length and base line T are known parameters. Also disparity can be calculated from the two images. Therefore, the depth D can be determined from the above equation (2). To find the matching point in the given two images i.e. the stereo correspondence or stereo matching problem is the most time consuming problem in the depth estimation

Figure 1. Disparity (Trucco & Verri, 1998)

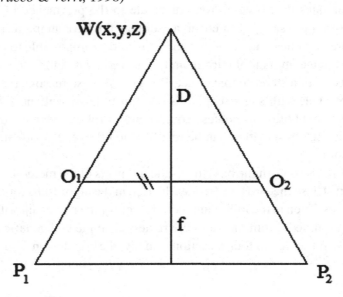

algorithm based on binocular disparity. Several methods such as epipolar geometry, camera calibration, photometric constraint etc. have been introduced by researchers. Normalised cross-correlation (NCC), sum of absolute difference (SAD), sum of squared differences (SSD) are the current stereo algorithm which are based on correlation of local windows on the matching of a set of image features.

2.2 Motion

The depth estimation algorithms based on relative motion between the viewing camera and the observed scene are the most recent and frequently used techniques. The objects near the retina moves faster than the objects which are far away from the retina. The 2D velocity vectors of the image points due to relative motion between the observed camera and the observed scene is called the motion field which can be represented as disparity over time. The extraction of 3D structure and the camera motion from image sequence is termed as structure from motion (SFM). The relative motion v between the camera and a 3D point $P = \begin{bmatrix} XYZ \end{bmatrix}^T$ the camera reference frame is given by (Trucco & Verri, 1998),

$$v = -v_T - w \times p \tag{3}$$

where v_T and w are the translational velocity and the angular velocity of the camera respectively. The relation between the depth of the of 3D point and its 2D motion field is given by (Han & Kanade, 2003),

$$v_x = v_{T_z} x - v_{T_z} f - w_y f + w_z y + \frac{w_x xy}{f} - \frac{w_x x^2}{f} \tag{4}$$

$$v_y = \frac{v_{T_z} x - v_{T_y} f}{D} - w_x f + w_z y + \frac{w_y xy}{f} - \frac{w_x y^2}{f} \tag{5}$$

where v_x and v_y are the motion field component in x and y direction respectively, v_{T_z} is the translational velocity in the direction of z, w_x w_y and w_z are angular velocity component in x, y and z direction respectively, f is the focal length of the lens and D is the depth of the 3D point. Thus in the algorithms for depth estimation, motion field is computed before recovering in the depth. But in algorithms like factorization algorithm (Han & Kanade, 2003) 3D structure is directly computed with the motion field in the estimation process. The algorithm based on optical flow method is an example of motion estimation algorithm. But this method yield less accurate depth map. Most recent algorithms for estimation of motion is based on tracking separate features in the image sequence to generate depth map. Kalmar filter (Matsuyama, 2004), and Kanade – Lucas –Tomashi (KLT) (Wu, Er, Xie, Li, Cao & Dai, 2008) are the most frequently used techniques.

2.3 Depth from Defocus

The objects near to the camera are clearly focused and the objects which are at far distances are blurred i.e. defocused. Thus the amount of blurring in a image can be used to generate depth map. In Figure 2,

Figure 2. Thin lens system (Wei, 2005)

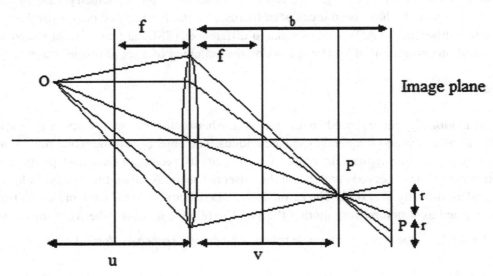

a thin lens system is shown (Wei, (2005). The point O is projected on the image plane. The projection of O on the image plane is a circular blur patch centred at P with blur radius r The blur is caused by the convolution of the projected image and the camera point spread function (PSF). The relation between the depth u and blur r is given by (Wei, 2005).

$$u = \begin{cases} \frac{fb}{b-f-ar} & \text{if } u \succ v \\ \frac{fb}{b-f+ar} & \text{if } u \prec v \end{cases} \qquad (6)$$

where u is the depth, v is distance between the lens and the image plane, f is the focal length of the lens and a is a constant determined by camera calibration. Thus from equation (6), it is seen that depth u can be determined by computing the camera parameters and blur radius r. Since camera parameters can be found from the camera calibration, therefore, the depth from defocus algorithms mainly focus on the blur radius estimation techniques. Inverse filtering, S-transform etc. are example techniques based on which the blur radius is estimated.

2.4 Depth from Focus

Depth from focus approach uses a series of images with different focal setting. The focal setting of these images is changed gradually and the distance between the camera and scene is registered. The focal setting with the highest focal level is marked as local depth. Therefore, the main task in this method is to define the focal criterion (Lin, Suo, & Dai, 2014). Suppose an object with arbitrary surface is placed at the translational stage, which moves towards the camera starting from the reference plane as shown in the Figure 3. The focused plane called optics is located at the position where all points on it are focused on the camera sensor plane. Let 's' be a surface point on the object. When moving the stage towards the focused plane, the images of 's' become more and more focused and will obtain its maximum sharp-

Figure 3. Depth from focus (Lin, Suo, & Dai, 2014)

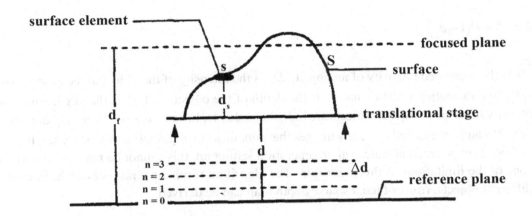

ness when ' s ' reaches the focused plane. After this, moving ' s ' furthermore makes its image defocused again. During this process, the displacements of the translational stage are registered. If the displacement is d_m when ' s ' is maximally focused and the distance between the 'focused plane' and the reference plane is d_r then the depth value of ' s ' relative to the stage will be $d_s = d_m - d_r$. Applying this same procedure for all surface elements and interpolating the focus measures, a dense depth map can be constructed.

2.5 Linear Perspective

With distance, parallel lines such as railroad tracks appear to converge and at horizon they reach a vanishing point. The more the lines converges, they appear farther away from the person. This fact can be used to estimate the depth in an image. Battiato, Curti, Cascia, Tortora, & Scordato (2004) proposed a gradient plane assignment approach. At first edge detection is performed to locate the predominant lines in the image. Then the point of intersection of these lines is considered to be the vanishing point. The major lines close to the vanishing point are marked as the vanishing lines and in between two neighbouring vanishing lines a gradient plan is assigned. The pixel closure to the vanishing points is assigned a larger dept value.

2.6 Atmosphere Scattering

Atmosphere scattering refers to the fact that the atmosphere produces a bluish tint by scattering of light rays. It provides less contrast to objects that are far away distance and better contrast to objects which are at near distance. A large number of outdoor images are used and semantic region detection is performed by Yamada, Suehiro, & Nakamura (2005) to divide the images into six regions such as sky, farthest mountain, far mountain, near mountain, land and other. Then a depth value is assigned to each region so that sky region will be the farthest one and the other region will be the closer one. Colour dependent information is also used by Vázquez & Tam (2010), where Cr component in YCbCr- colour space is used to substitute for actual depth in a scene.

The relationship between the radiance of an image and the distance between the object and the viewer is given by,

$$\overline{D} = D_0 e^{-\beta z} + P(1 - e^{-\beta z})$$ (7)

where $\overline{D}$ is the measured intensity of an object, D_0 is the intensity of the object in the absence of scattering, β is the extinction coefficients, z is the depth of the object, and P is the sky intensity which is the intensity of an area in which objects are indistinguishable. In some cases, β and D_0 are unknown. Therefore, P can be measured from any images that contain a sky region. For indoor scenes, the estimation of P needs experimental water vapor generation setting up, this cannot be realized automatically. This is one of the limitations of this algorithm. The algorithm results in a ratio of depth difference between different objects, from which a sparse depth map can be derived.

2.7 Shape from Shading

Shape from shading method is used to reconstruct 3D shape by using the relationship between the surface geometry and image brightness. Suppose $o = \begin{bmatrix} x & y \end{bmatrix}^T$ is the image of a 3D point $O = \begin{bmatrix} X & Y & Z \end{bmatrix}^T$, where Z is depth of the 3D point O and can be described as $Z = (x, y)$. Then the surface slope h and g can be calculated by taking x and y partial derivative of the vector $[x, y, Z(x,y)]$ i.e. $h = \begin{bmatrix} 1, 0, \dfrac{dz}{dx} \end{bmatrix}^T$ and $h = \begin{bmatrix} 0, 1, \dfrac{dz}{dx} \end{bmatrix}^T$. The relationship between the estimated reflectance map $r(g, h)$ and the surface slope is given by (Wei, 2005),

$$(h, g) = \frac{\rho}{\sqrt{1 + h^2 + g^2}} i^T [-h, -g, 1] r(h, g) = \frac{\rho}{\sqrt{1 + h^2 + g^2}} i^T [-h, -g, 1]$$ (8)

where ρ is the parameter of surface material which is called surface albedo and i is the direction and amount of light incident. After estimating ρ and i and solving equation (8) the depth Z can be achieved.

2.8 Interposition

This method is also known as depth from occlusion. The algorithms based on this method offer much information in relative depth ordering of the objects. The principle of depth from occlusion method is that an object which overlaps or partly obscures the view of another object is considered to be closer (Zhang, Vázquez & Knorr, 2011).

Curvature is one of the depth cues which might be grouped under the header of occlusion due to its inherent characteristics related to occlusion. Curvature is a depth cue based on the geometry and topology of the objects in an image. The majority of objects in 2D images contain no holes i.e. they have a sphere topology, for example, closed grounds, humans, telephones etc. It is observed that the curvature of object outline is proportional to the depth derivative and can thus be used to retrieve the depth information. The curvature of points on a curve can be computed from the segmentation of the image. A circle has a constant curvature and thus a constant depth derivative along its boundary, which indicates that it has a uniform depth value. Similarly, a non-circle curve such as a square does not have a constant curvature. A smoothening procedure is needed in order to obtain a uniform curvature/depth profile. After the smoothing process, each object with an outline of uniform curvature is assigned one depth value.

Some of the methods which are frequently used in estimating depth information have been presented in this section. In the next section, the detailed review of recent methods for converting 2D video to 3D will be presented.

3. REVIEW OF RECENT METHODS OF 2D TO 3D VIDEO CONVERSION

Several algorithms have been developed for incorporating the depth information in 2-D images and video. These algorithms can roughly be divided into two categories. The first one that tends to directly produce stereoscopic videos from the captured scenes (Knorr, Smolic & Sikora, 2007) is called image based rendering. The second category, discussed below, produces 3D effect using only one monoscopic video with an associated depth map. Knorr, Imre, Özkalayci, Alatan, & Sikora (2006) proposed a modular system which is capable of efficiently reconstructing 3D scenes from 2D video. Their system consists of four constitutive modules such as tracking and segmentation, self-calibration, sparse reconstruction and dense reconstruction.

Cao, Bovik, Wang & Dai (2011) discussed some common 3D content-creation processes. They also presented the key elements that affect quality. The proposed approach that converts 2D content to 3D content is an efficient path to a 3D multimedia experience.

Rotem, Wolowelsky & Pelz (2005) derived an automatic 2D to 3D conversion algorithm. It is based on a planar transformation between the images in a sequence. The system generates stereoscopic image pairs and each pair consists of the original image and a transformed image. The transformed image is generated from another image of the original sequence. That image is selected by the algorithm such that a parallax is developed between the two original frames. The chosen image is then warped using the planar transformation.

Han & Kanade (2003) estimated the 3D model directly with motion field which is integrated in estimation process. They developed the factorization algorithm, where the registered measurement matrix, containing entries of the normalized image point coordinates over several video frames, is converted into a product of a shape matrix and motion matrix. The shape matrix registers the coordinates of the 3D object, and the motion matrix describes the rotation of a set of 3D points with respect to the camera.

Watanabe, Kitahara, Kameda & Ohta (2003) proposed an interface for capturing the 3D free view point video using bimanual operation. The work used a 3D tracker to input the 3D position and the orientation of a virtual camera which captures the 3D free-viewpoint video. The system displays the overhead-view where a user manipulates the virtual camera. By browsing this overhead-view, the context can be easily understood in a virtualized scene.

The above algorithms are the examples of the first category (directly provide stereoscopic videos from the captured scenes) which we have discussed earlier. The more widely used methods in recent years fall in the second category. It shows 3D effect using only one monoscopic video with an associated depth map sequence. These method of synthesising a 3D view from a depth map sequence and from the geometry of the scene in the images can be roughly divided into three category, e.g., depth image based rendering (IDBR), layered depth images (LDI) and intermediate view reconstruction (IVR). Some of the example of this kind and depth estimation algorithms are presented below.

Han & Hsiao (2014) presented an algorithm where two transformation models for stationary scenes and non-stationary objects is used. The transformation model for stationary scenes to estimate the depth information is based on the information of the vanishing point and vanishing lines of the given video. The transformation model for non-stationary regions is the result of combining the motion analysis of the non-stationary regions and the transformation model for stationary scenes to estimate the depth information. The model for the non stationary objects is to link the position of an object to its foothold on the stationary background, and the model for stationary scene is utilized for updating the depth of moving objects with the consideration of motion information. The block diagram in Figure 4 illustrates their steps for conversion of 2D monocular video to 3D video.

Li, Xie, & Liu (2009) proposed an algorithm on 2D to 3D conversion by skeleton line tracking. At firs the foreground objects and the background objects are segmented. Then a grass-fire algorithm is used to obtain the skeleton lines of the object. At the same time, optical flow is used to determine the motion vectors of the object and optical flow method is used to estimate motion vectors of the objects. The skeleton lines and motion vectors are used to determine new skeleton lines of the objects for the next frame. After obtaining the new skeleton lines, the lazy snapping method is used to recover the object. Then depths are assigned so that the foreground is given a depth of intensity 255 (near), and the background a depth of intensity 0 (far). The rest of the depths are determined using a combination of the motion vectors and skeleton lines. Figure 5 illustrates a block diagram of this approach.

Liao, Gao, Yang & Gong (2012) presented a semiautomatic system that converts conventional videos into stereoscopic videos by combining motion analysis with user interaction and to transfer as much as

Figure 4. Steps for conversion of monocular video to 3D (Han & Hsiao, 2014)

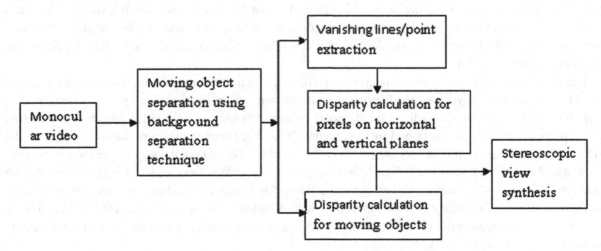

Figure 5. 2D to 3D conversion using skeleton line tracking (Li, Xie, & Liu, 2009)

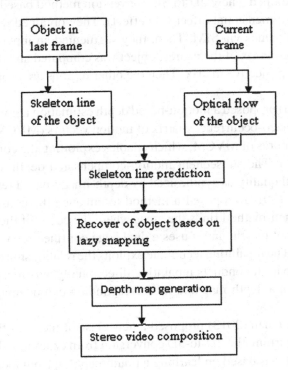

possible labelling work from the user to the computer., They developed two new methods that analyze the optical flow to provide additional qualitative depth constraints in addition to the widely used structure from motion (SFM) techniques. Their method remove the camera movement restriction imposed by SFM so that general motions can be used in scene depth estimation. They further developed a quadratic programming approach to incorporate both quantitative depth and qualitative depth to recover dense depth maps for all frames, from which stereoscopic view can be synthesized.

Yan, Yang, Guihua & Dai (2011) proposed an efficient semi-automatic depth map generation scheme. It is based on limited user inputs and depth propagation. The original image is over-segmented and then, the depth values of selected pixels and the approximate locations of T-junctions are specified by user inputs. The final depth map is obtained by depth propagation combining user inputs, colour and edge information.

Wang, Yang, Zhang & Yang (2011) summarized different transformation methods based on the characteristics of 2D to 3D technology. They presented a semi-automatic depth extraction scheme from motion estimation.

Huang, Cao, Lu & Dai (2013) proposed a two-stage depth propagation algorithm for semi-automatic 2D-to-3D video conversion. Both forward and backward motion vectors are estimated at first. Then the motion vectors are compared to decide initial depth values. Then a compensation process was adopted to further improve the depth initialization. The luminance and initial depth was then decomposed into a wavelet pyramid. Each sub-band of depth was inferred using a Bayesian formulation under a natural scene statistic prior assumption. This was incorporated into a propagation target function as a prior regularizing term. The final depth map associated with each frame of the input 2D video is optimized by composing all the sub-bands.

Kim & Song (2013) developed a new 2D-to-3D conversion method based on structure from motion (SfM) to improve the three-dimensional effect (3D effect). They obtained the 3D information such as camera positions and depth values via SfM. Then, they segmented an input image to find the nearest object region. The projective matrix of the nearest object was computed and then the nearest object was warped using the computed projective matrix. Then the other regions are properly warped according to their depth values.

Wang, Chen & Lee (2013) proposed a motion-based depth estimation algorithm for automatic 2D-to-3D video. They employed the co-occurrence matrix of motion vectors (MVCM) in the algorithm. Video scenes possess distinct signatures of MVCM, which enables exploiting the corresponding motion-depth relation for depth generation. The subsequent motion-compensated depth updating scheme provides stable and comfort 3D visual quality as synthesized by depth-image-based rendering.

Hung, Miaou & Chiang (2013) proposed a method to enhance the consistency between a colour image and its depth map. Their method finds the areas where the edges of the 2D colour image and the edges of the depth map do not match, and it uses a dual edge confined inpainting technique to inpaint the edge-mismatched areas. The inpainting technique exploits the relationship between edges and objects in colour image and depth map. It conducts inpainting directionally, where a depth map is inpainted at the inconsistent part between a depth map and its corresponding colour image to improve the quality of the depth map.

Konrad, Wang, Ishwar & Chen (2013) proposed a new class of methods that are based on the radically different approach of learning the 2D-to-3D conversion from examples. They developed two types of methods in which the first was based on learning a point mapping from local image/video attributes, such as color, spatial position, and, in the case of video, motion at each pixel, to scene-depth at that pixel using a regression type idea. The second method was based on globally estimating the entire depth map of a query image directly from a repository of 3D images (image+depth pairs or stereopairs) using a nearest-neighbor regression type idea.

Han, Lee, Lee, Kim & Lee (2013) presented a new method for depth estimation for 2D/3D conversion. The distance between objects was determined by the distances between objects and light source position. The light source position was estimated by the analysis of the image. The estimated lighting value was used to normalize the image. A threshold value was determined by some weighted operation between the original image and the normalized image. Then the background area is removed by applying the threshold value to the original image. Depth information of interested area is calculated from the lighting changes.

Ayatollahi, Masoud, Moghadam, Hosseini (2013) proposed a taxonomy of depth map creation methods which was used in multiview video compression. Their focus was on investigation of approaches that used in 3D video compression. They proposed the taxonomy by classifying depth map based methods into three categories which are hardware or software based depth estimation methods, level of algorithms and 2D/3D depth map production. Finally, a comparison was performed on software-based methods based on video quality measure to evaluate the performance of some well-known approaches in this area.

Guo, Tang & Peng (2014) proposed a novel method for estimating a depth map for stereoscopic conversion. A simulated haze image generated by adding a haze veil on the input image is used to represent salient region segmentation. Based on the depth map estimated by the haze removal algorithm without any user interaction, the 3D stereoscopic image is generated.

Liu, Wu, Guo & Hu (2013) presented an approach for 2D to 3D video conversion based on structure from motion (SFM). The key contributions include a piecewise SFM approach and a novel nonlinear depth warping considering the characteristics of stereoscopic 3D. The dense depth maps are generated and further refined with color segmentation.

Beyang, Gould & Koller (2010) performed a semantic segmentation of the scene and used the semantic labels to guide the 3D reconstruction. By knowing the semantic class of a pixel or region, depth and geometry constraints can be easily enforced (e.g., "sky" is far away and "ground" is horizontal). In addition to that depth was more readily predicted by measuring the difference in appearance with respect to a given semantic class. For example, a tree will have more uniform appearance in the distance than it does close up.

Tam & Zhang (2006) provide an overview of the fundamental principle of 2D to 3D conversion techniques. A number of approaches for depth extraction using a single image is presented. A highlight of the potential use of depth maps in depth image based rendering for 2D-to-3D conversion is also discussed.

Ko, Kim & Kim (2007) generated a stereoscopic image, using the degree of focus of segmented regions. To extract foreground objects, a customized image segmentation algorithm was used. This algorithm is also used to partition the image into homogeneous regions. Then a higher-order statistics map is used to represent the spatial distribution of high-frequency components of the input image. Since it can suppress Gaussian noise and preserve some of the non- Gaussian information, the map is well suited for detection and classification problems. The relative depth map is calculated with these two cues. Then it is refined by post processing.

Tam, Vazquez & Speranza (2009) decomposed the video sequence into the YCbCr colour space. They used the Cr color channel as a measure of depth. The reasoning is that different objects have different hues, and thus the Cr channel provides an approximate segmentation of the objects, which are characterized by different intensities in the Cr component image. Each intensity should belong to the same kind of objects, and thus the same depth value.

Wu, Er, Xie, Li, Cao & Dai (2008) proposed a novel semi-automatic method for converting monoscopic video to stereoscopic video. To segment the object of interest in the key frames an efficient interactive image cutout tool is used. Then, the initial depth information is assigned to the segmented objects. These objects are tracked in the whole video sequence through a bi-directional Kanade-Lucas- Tomashi (KLT) algorithm. Depth interpolation is employed to produce the depth information in the non-key frames. Finally, stereoscopic video is synthesized in consideration of different 3D display types.

Tsai, Chang & Chen (2009) presented a robust and reliable block-based method for vanishing line and vanishing point detection which provides assistance in construction of a depth map. The method also focused on the fundamental image structural element analysis which was divided into six successive steps. The authors also replaced the complicated mathematic calculation and approximation by six block-based estimation algorithms.

Lizuka, Endo, Kanamori, Mitani & Fukui (2014) proposed an interactive technique for constructing a 3D scene via sparse user inputs. They represented a 3D scene in the form of a Layered Depth Image (LDI) which was composed of a foreground layer and a background layer, and each layer has a corresponding texture and depth map. Given user-specified sparse depth inputs, depth maps were computed based on superpixels using interpolation with geodesic-distance weighting and an optimization framework. This computation was done immediately, which allowed the user to edit the LDI interactively. Their technique also automatically estimates depth and texture in occluded regions using the depth discontinuity. The user paints strokes on the 3D model directly. The drawn strokes serve as 3D handles with which the user could pull out or push the 3D surface easily and intuitively with real-time feedback.

Karlsson & Sjostrom (2011) presented a scheme that combines scalability based on the position in depth of the data and the distance to the centre view. The scheme preserved the centre view data, whereas the data of the remaining views was extracted in enhancement layers depending on distance to the viewer and to the center camera. The data was assigned into enhancement layers within a view based on depth data distribution. Strategies concerning the layer assignment between adjacent views were proposed.

Niebner, Schafer & Stamminger (2011) presented a novel hybrid rendering method for diffuse and glossy indirect illumination. A scene was rendered using standard rasterization on a GPU. In a shader, secondary ray queries were used to sample incident light and to compute indirect lighting. They observed that it is more important to cast many rays than to have precise results for each ray. They approximate secondary rays by intersecting them with pre computed layered depth images of the scene. They achieved interactive to real-time frame rates including indirect diffuse and glossy effects.

Cheng, Sun & Yang (2007) proposed an approach which refines colours of the depth pixels by choosing proper candidate depth pixels, removes matting effects by projecting LDI backward to reference views, and eliminate the gaps or holes due to disocclusion and undersample by local background interpolation during generation of LDI.

Zhang, Li, Guo, Wang & Huang (2015) proposed a novel depth map refinement method based on by GMM and CS theory which enable the kinect sensor to generate a dense depth map. The background large holes were filled without blurring, and the edges of the objects were sharpened. Median filter is used to remove noise.

Devernay, Duchene & Peon (2011) proposed a method to generate new views in which perceived depth is similar to the original scene depth. They developed the method to detect and reduce artifacts in the process where the artifacts were created by errors contained in the disparity.

Ince & Kornad (2008) identified challenges related to disparity estimation and view interpolation in presence of occlusions. They then proposed an occlusion-aware intermediate view interpolation algorithm that uses four input images to handle the disappearing areas. The algorithm was consisted of three steps. First, all pixels in view to be computed were classified in terms of their visibility in the input images. Then, disparity for each pixel was estimated from different image pairs depending on the computed visibility map. Finally, luminance/color of each pixel was adaptively interpolated from an image pair selected by its visibility label.

On the basis of different mechanism of view synthesis such as image based rendering (IBR), depth image based rendering (DIBR), layered depth images (LDI) and intermediate view reconstruction (IVR), the above literatures are summarised in the following tables.

In the literature cited above, some of the recent algorithms for estimating depth in 2D video for conversion of 2D to 3D are discussed. These works have covered certain methods which have their respective strengths and weaknesses. Now, from this review a general system for conversion of 2D to 3D is presented in the next section.

Table 1. Summary of algorithms related to DIBR view synthesis

Sl. No	References	Depth Cues	Method Used
1	(Han & Hsiao 2014)	Linear perspective	Vanishing line and vanishing point detection
2	(Li, Xie, & Liu 2009)	Motion	Optical flow method, Grass fire algorithm.
3	(Liao, Gao, Yang, 2012)	Motion	Structure from Motion
4	(Yan, Yang, Guihua & Dai, 2011)	Interposition	Edge information based and colour based
5	(Hung, Miaou & Chiang, 2013)	Shape from shading	Dual edge confined inpainting technique
6	(Huang, Cao, Lu & Dai, 2013)	Motion	Structure from motion
7	(Kim & Song,2013)	Motion	Structure from motion
8	(Konrad, Wang, Ishwar & Chen, 2013)	Binocular disparity	Nearest neighbor regression method
9	(Han, Lee, Lee, Kim & Lee, 2013)	Atmospheric scattering	Light scattering
10	(Liu, Wu, Guo & Hu, 2013)	Motion	Structure from motion
11	(Beyang, Gould & Koller, 2010)	Atmospheric scattering	Semantic segmentation method
12	(Ko, Kim & Kim, 2007)	Depth from focus	A set of segmented region of different focus level is used
13	(Tam, Vazquez & Speranza, 2009)	Atmospheric scattering	Color based method
14	(Wu, Er, Xie, Li, Cao & Dai, 2008)	Motion	Kanade- Lucas- Tomashi (KLT) method
15	(Finally, Tsai, Chang & Chen, 2009)	Linear perspective	Vanishing line and vanishing point detection

Table 2. Summary of algorithms as part of LDI for view synthesis

Sl. No	References	Depth Cues	Method Used
1	(Lizuka, Endo, Kanamori, Mitani & Fukui, 2014)	Linear perspective	Interpolation with geodesic distance weighing and an optimization framwork
2	(Karlsson & Sjostrom, 2011)	Motion	MPEG-4 Motion vector
3	(Niebner, Schafer & Stamminger, 2011)	Atmospheric scattering	Light scattering
4	(Cheng, Sun & Yang, 2007)	Atmospheric scattering	Color based method

Table 3. Summary of algorithms as part of IVR for view synthesis

Sl. No	References	Depth Cues	Method Used
1	(Zhang, Li, Guo, Wang & Huang, 2015)	-	Depth range camera is used
2	(Devernay, Duchene & Peon, 2011)	Depth from occlusion	Images are classified according to their visibility level
3	(Ince & Kornad, 2008)	Symmetric patterns	Geometric constrains

Table 4. Summary of algorithms as part of IBR for view synthesis

Sl. No.	References	Methods Used
1	(Rotem, Wolowelsky & Pelz, 2005)	Plannar transformation method
2	(Han & Kanade, 2003)	Factorization algorithm
3	(Watanabe, Kitahara, Kameda & Ohta, 2003)	Bimanual operation method

4. GENERIC SYSTEM FOR INCORPORATION OF DEPTH INFORMATION IN 2D VIDEO

A generic system for incorporation depth in 2D video i.e. to convert a 2D video to 3D video is presented in Figure 5. The different blocks are also discussed below.

4.1 Input

The first stage of any vision system is the image acquisition. The characteristics such as that of the 2D input image or video depend on the algorithm used in order to work reliably. In case video, it is first divided into frames of images depending upon the Frames Per Second (FPS) rate of the monocular camera or any other device that captures video because processing will be done on these images.

4.2 Pre-Processing

The pre-processing step in 2D to 3D conversion depends upon the algorithm used to estimate depth. Background and foreground segmentation, tracking of different objects in the image, converting the image into other colour space etc. are processes which are included in the in the pre-processing step. Depending on the algorithm used, proper pre-processing method is selected for further processing of the image.

4.3 Depth Estimation

Several methods for estimating the depth have already been discussed in the section above. Binocular disparity, motion based depth estimation, defocus/focus based method, linear perspective, interposition etc. are the methods which are used to estimate the depth map. Depending on the method, motion estimation, degree of blur estimation, vanishing point/line detection etc several algorithms have been proposed which was discussed in the third section. By employing a proper algorithm depth of different objects in the image is estimated and the depth map is created in this step.

Figure 6. Generic system for incorporation of depth information in 2D image/video

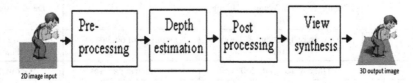

4.4 Post-Processing

The depth map estimated in previous step should be scaled up to the pixel level and aligned to conform to the colour edges for better 3D perception. To generate a smooth depth map inside the smooth region with similar pixel values and to preserve sharp depth discontinuity on the object boundary some post-processing should be done. Bilateral filter (Bharathi & Vasuki, 2012), median filter, temporal filter (Lin, Huang, Chen, Yeh, Liu & Lie 2012) etc. are the filters which are used in the algorithms of these purposes.

4.5 View Synthesis

Two or more images of the same scene with slightly different view (left and right view) is required to get a 3D perception of the image. Depending on known geometric properties, different approaches exist in the literature for this purpose, e.g., image-based rendering (IBR), depth image based rendering (DIBR), layered-depth images (LDI), and intermediate view reconstruction (IVR). The most commonly and frequently used method is depth image based rendering. The algorithm based on this method mainly consists of three parts which are described below (Lin, Huang, Chen, Yeh, Liu & Lie 2012).

1. **Pre-Processing of Depth Map:** Pre-Processing of depth map is usually a smoothing filter. Smoothing filter is applied to smooth sharp transition to reduce the number of big hole. which might be appear after warping.
2. **3D Image Warping:** 3D image warping transforms the location of pixels according to depth value by mapping the intermediate view pixel by pixel to left or right view according to the pixel depth value.
3. **Hole-Filling:** The most significant problem in 3D warping is to deal with holes generated in the warped image. Holes are due to the difference of sampling resolution between the input and output images and the disocclusion where part of the scene is seen by the output image but not by the input images. To fill in holes, the most commonly used method is to splat a pixel in the input image to several pixels size in the output image

4.6 Output

The output will be a red-cyan stereoscopic image. Red/cyan glasses or 3D display systems are recommended to view the image correctly.

The generic system discussed above is presented on the basis of the literature. The system is general system for 2D to 3D conversion methods where DIBR method of view synthesis, which is a popular method, is used. A compassion two such method 2D to 3D conversion system is presented in Table 5. In the first system, Wang, Lang, Frei, Hornung, Smolic & Gross (2011) proposed a novel workflow, called Stereobrush, for stereoscopic 2D to 3D conversion in which the user "paints" depth onto a 2D image via sparse scribbles. The approach was enabled by the introduction of a discontinuous warping technique that creates stereoscopic pairs from sparse, possibly erroneous user input. The method assumed a piecewise continuous depth representation by preserving visual continuity in most areas and by creating sharp depth discontinuities at important object boundaries. Their scribbles are processed as soft constraints in a global solve and operate entirely on image domain disparity, allowing for relaxed input requirements. This formulation also allowed the authors to simultaneously compute a disparity-

and-content-aware stretching of background areas to automatically fill disoccluded regions with valid stereo information. The tightly integrated all steps of stereo content conversion into a single optimization framework, which can then be solved on a GPU at interactive rates.

In the second method Fan, Chen & Chou (2014) proposed a system which processes 2D images to capture a depth map of the intermediate view image during 3D contents capturing. In their approach, they utilized the vanishing point detection and color image segmentation technique to find the objects and deepest point (i.e., vanishing point) in the image, and then they assigned depth value by comparing the vanishing point of object with image. After depth map generation, they proposed the Vivid-DIBR system to imitate how human eyes see things. Their system solved the holes (warping error points) problem by redistributing corresponding depth map. The design aimed to convert 2D images into multi-view images which will be suitable for any interlacing 3D display by adjusting the focal plane location.

A comparison of the above two system is presented based on their performance, method used, types of inputs, limitation etc. in Table 5.

5. CONCLUSION

In this chapter, we have discussed some of the basic theoretical aspects of the methods for estimating depth in 2D video. These methods are frequently used in the algorithms for estimating depth in the 2D to 3D video techniques. Then some of the recent algorithms for incorporation of depth in 2D video is

Table 5. Comparison between the two methods (Wang, Lang, Frei, Hornung, Smolic & Gross, 2011) and (Fan, Chen & Chou, 2014) based on their performance.

Sl No	Qualitative Aspects	References	
		(Wang, Lang, Frei, Hornung, Smolic & Gross, 2011)	**(Fan, Chen & Chou, 2014)**
1	No of input Images	One single image	One single image
2	Image acquisition	2D image of stationary scene or per key frame level for 2D video	2D images containing geometric appearance
3	Depth cues	A sparse and rough scribble map where higher intensity represents closer obects	Vanishing point detection method is used.
4	View synthesis method	A hole filling DIBR method is used where a hardware accelerated method of rendering is used	Vivid DIBR based on Non hole filling DIBR system
5	Display system required	High quality 3D display is required	Suitable for any interfacing 3D device
6	Time required	Rough 3D shape become visible within a few second and final version completed under 5 minutes	Not Mentioned
7	Limitations	1. Could not detect edge when the scene contain too much visually salient content. 2. Transparent objects, were multiple depth exist per pixel are not correctly modelled by the approach	The approach is tested for 2D video images

discussed in the literature review section. From the literature review a simple and generic system for incorporation depth in 2D video is also presented.

Most 2D to 3D conversion algorithms for generating stereoscopic videos are based on the generation of a depth map. But a depth map has a disadvantage. The depth map should be very dense and accurate. Otherwise there will be some local deformations in the stereo pairs which are derived in the algorithm. Each method for estimation of depth has some advantages and disadvantages. To achieve a robust 2D to 3D conversion algorithm two or more the depth estimation methods are combined in the algorithms. Some of the depth estimation methods offers less detailed surface information (low frequency) due to reasons such as smoothness constraints. On the other hand some of the methods produce a better detailed surface (high frequency).Thus combining such methods them a better result may be achieved.

In the literature review, we found that many researchers have used motion based depth estimation algorithm for 2D to 3D video conversion. The relative motion experienced throughout the frames of a 2D video can be used to determine the depth in a scene, by fact that higher motion denotes that objects are closer to the camera, and smaller motion denotes the objects are away from the camera. But there can be several disadvantages in estimating depth using motion. In the video there may be a object which is far away from the camera but it may move with very high speed and there may be another objects which are closer to the camera and moving with same speed as the far object. In that case the estimated depth of both objects will be same which is wrong. Again for very fast moving in video there may be error in the motion estimation. In that case estimation of depth for tat particular object there will be some error. Though there are several disadvantage of this method, it is a very popular method, as motion is already available in the encoded video itself as discussed in the literature review.

In the literature review there are algorithms for conversion of 2D to 3D video using scene features such as edge, colour, shape and texture etc. In these algorithms the main disadvantage is that the accuracy of the estimation of depth value depend the accuracy of the selection of these features. For example if segmentation is performed for selection of an object or features, the accuracy of the depth value estimation will depend on the accuracy the segmentation method.

Despite the disadvantages these algorithms these are very important topic for realizing a sense of depth in 2D video. These methods are very useful since these are the alternative solution for producing 3D content in 2D video. These algorithms are also very cost effective.

The trend is towards incorporation of small scale 3D video capability in robotic systems and generation of depth aspect in the bio-inspired designs of eye-like systems.

REFERENCES

Ayatollahi, S. M., Masoud, A., Moghadam, E., & Hosseini, M. S. (2013). A taxonomy of depth map creation methods used in multiview video compression. Springer Science and Business Media.

Battiato, S., Curti, S., Cascia, M. L., Tortora, M., & Scordato, E. (2004). Depth map generation by image classification. In *Proceedings on SPIE conference on Three Dimensional Image Capture and Applications* (vol. 5302-95). SPIE. doi:10.1117/12.526634

Bharathi, S., & Vasuki, A. (2012). 2D-To-3D Conversion of Images using Edge Information. In *Proceedings of International Conference on Recent Trends in Computational Methods, Communication and Controls*.

Cao, X., Bovik, A. C., Wang, Y., & Dai, Q. (2011). Converting 2D Video to 3D: An Efficient Path to a 3D Experience. *IEEE MultiMedia, 18*(4), 12–17. doi:10.1109/MMUL.2011.65

Chang, Y. L., Fang, C. Y., Ding, L. F., & Chen, S. Y. (2007). Depth Map Generation for 2D-to-3D Conversion by Short-Term Motion Assisted Color Segmentation. In *Proceedings of IEEE International Conference on Multimedia and Expo* (pp-1958-1961). IEEE. doi:10.1109/ICME.2007.4285061

Cheng, X., Sun, L., & Yang, S. (2007). Generation of Layered Depth Images from Multi-View Video. In *Proceedings of IEEE International Conference on Image Processing* (*Vol. 5*, pp. V - 225 - V – 228). IEEE. doi:10.1109/ICIP.2007.4379806

Devernay, F., Duchene, S., & Peon, A. R. (2011). Adapting stereoscopic movies to the viewing conditions using depth-preserving and artifact-free novel view synthesis. In *Proceedings of SPIE 7863*. Stereoscopic Displays and Applications XXII. doi:10.1117/12.872883

Fan, Y. C., Chen, Y. C., & Chou, S. Y. (2014). Vivid-DIBR Based 2D–3D Image Conversion System for 3D Display. *Journal of Display Technology, 10*(10), 887–898. doi:10.1109/JDT.2014.2331064

Guo, F., Tang, J., & Peng, H. (2014). Adaptive Estimation of Depth Map for Two-Dimensional to Three-Dimensional Stereoscopic Conversion. Journal of Optical Review, 21(1), 60–73.

Han, C. C., & Hsiao, H. F. (2014). Depth Estimation and Video Synthesis for 2D to 3D Video Conversion. Journal of Signal Processing System, 76, 33-46.

Han, H., Lee, G., Lee, J., Kim, J., & Lee, S. (2013). A new method to create depth information based on lighting analysis for 2D/3D conversion. *Journal of Central South University, 20*(10), 2715–2719.

Han, M., & Kanade, T. (2003). Multiple Motion Scene Reconstruction with Uncalibrated Cameras. *IEEE Transactions on Pattern Analysis and Machine Intelligence, 25*(7), 884–894. doi:10.1109/TPAMI.2003.1206517

Han, M., & Kanade, T. (2003). Multiple Motion Scene Reconstruction with Uncalibrated Cameras. *IEEE Transactions on Pattern Analysis and Machine Intelligence, 25*(7), 884–894. doi:10.1109/TPAMI.2003.1206517

Huang, W., Cao, X., Lu, K., & Dai, Q. (2013). Towards naturalistic depth propagation. In *Proceedings of 11th IEEE IVMSP Workshop* (pp.-1-4). IEEE.

Hung, M. F., Miaou, S. G., & Chiang, C. Y. (2013).Dual edge-confined inpainting of 3D depth map using color image's edges and depth image's edges. In *Proceedings of IEEE International Conference on Signal and Information Processing* (pp.-1-9). doi:10.1109/APSIPA.2013.6694295

Ince, S., & Kornad, J. (2008). Occlusion-aware view interpolation. *Journal on Image and Video Processing, 21*(1), 60–73.

Karlsson, L., & Sjostrom, M. (2011). Layer assignment based on depthdata distribution for multiview-plus-depth scalable video coding. *IEEE Transaction of Circuits System and Video Technology, 21*(6), 742–754. doi:10.1109/TCSVT.2011.2130350

Kim, H. G., & Song, B. C. (2013). Automatic object-based 2D-to-3D conversion. In *Proceedings of 11th IEEE IVMSP Workshop* (pp.-1-4). IEEE. doi:10.1109/MEC.2011.6025855

Knorr, S., Imre, E., Özkalayci, B. A., Alatan, A., & Sikora, T. (2006). A modular scheme for 2D/3D conversion of TV broadcast. *Third International Symposium on 3D Data Processing, Visualization, and Transmission* (3DPVT). doi:10.1109/3DPVT.2006.15

Knorr, S., Smolic, A., & Sikora, T. (2007). From 2D-to stereo-to multi-view video. In *Proceedings of 3DTV Conference* (pp. 1–4).

Ko, J., Kim, M., & Kim, C. (2007). Depth-map estimation in a 2D single-view image. In *Proceedings of SPIE Electronic Imaging, Applications of Digital Image Processing* (Vol. 6696, pp. 66962A-1–66962A-9). doi:10.1117/12.736131

Ko, J., Kim, M., & Kim, C. (2007). Depth-map estimation in a 2D single-view image. In *Proceedings of SPIE Electronic Imaging—Applications of Digital Image Processing* (Vol. 6696, pp. 66962A-1–66962A-9). SPIE.

Konrad, J., Wang, M., Ishwar, P., Wu, C., & Mukherjee, D. (2013). Learning-Based, Automatic 2D-to-3D Image and Video Conversion. *IEEE Transactions on Image Processing, 22*(9), 3485–3496. doi:10.1109/TIP.2013.2270375 PMID:23799697

Li, Z., Xie, X., & Liu, X. (2009). An efficient 2D to 3D video conversion method based on skeleton line tracking. In Proceedings of IEEE 3DTVCON (pp. 1–4). IEEE.

Liao, M., Gao, J., Yang, R., & Gong, M. (2012). Video stereolization: Combining motion analysis with user interaction. *IEEE Transactions on Visualization and Computer Graphics, 18*(7), 1079–1088. doi:10.1109/TVCG.2011.114 PMID:21690648

Lin, G. S., Huang, H. Y., Chen, W. C., Yeh, C. Y., Liu, K. C., & Lie, W. N. (2012). *A stereoscopic video conversion scheme based on spatio-temporal analysis of MPEG videos. EURASIP Journal on Advances in Signal Processing*.

Lin, X., Suo, J., & Dai, Q. (2014). Extracting Depth and Radiance from a Defocused Video Pair. *IEEE Transactions on Circuits and Systems for Video Technology*.

Liu, B., Gould, S., & Koller, D. (2010). Single image depth estimation from predicted semantic labels. In *Proceedings of IEEE International Conference on Computer Vision and Pattern Recognition (CVPR)* (pp. 1253 – 1260). IEEE. doi:10.1109/CVPR.2010.5539823

Liu, W., Wu, Y., Guo, F. & Hu, Z. (2013). An efficient approach for 2D to 3D video conversion based on structure from motion. *Journal of the Visual Computer*.

Lizuka, S., Endo, Y., Kanamori, Y., Mitani, J., & Fukui, Y. (2014). Efficient Depth Propagation for Constructing a Layered Depth Image from a Single Image. In *Proceedings of Computer Graphics Forum* (Vol.33, No.7, pp. 279-288). doi:10.1111/cgf.12496

Matsuyama, T. (2004), Exploitation of 3D video technologies. In *International Conference on Informatics Research for Development of Knowledge Society Infrastructure*, (pp. 7-14). doi:10.1109/ICKS.2004.1313403

Matusik, W., & Pfister, H. (2004). 3D TV: A scalable system for real-time acquisition, transmission, and autostereoscopic display of dynamic scenes. *ACM Transactions on Graphics, 24*(3), 811–821.

Niebner, M., Henry, S., & Marc, S. (2010). Fast indirect illumination using Layered Depth Images. *Journal of The Visual Computer, 26*, 679–686.

Rotem, E., Wolowelsky, K., & Pelz, D. (2005). Automatic video to stereoscopic video conversion. In *Proceedings of SPIE Electronic Imaging—Stereoscopic Displays and Virtual Reality Systems XII* (Vol. 5664, pp. 198– 206). doi:10.1117/12.586599

Tam, W. J., Vazquez, C., & Speranza, F. (2009). Three-dimensional TV: A novel method for generating surrogate depth maps using colour information. In *Proceedings of SPIE Electronic Imaging—Stereoscopic Displays and Applications XX* (Vol. 7237, pp. 72371A-1–72371A-9). SPIE. doi:10.1117/12.807147

Tam, W. J., & Zhang, L. (2006). 3D-TV Content Generation: 2D-to-3D Conversion. In *Proceedings of IEEE International Conference on Multimedia and Expo* (pp. 1869 – 1872). IEEE.

Trucco, E., & Verri, A. (1998). Stereopsis. In Introductory Techniques for 3-D Computer Vision (1st ed.). Prentice Hall.

Tsai, Y. M., Chang, Y. L., & Chen, L. G. (2009), Block-based Vanishing Line and Vanishing Point Detection for 3D Scene Reconstruction. In Proceedings of IEEE 3DTVCON (pp. 1–4). IEEE.

Vázquez, C., & Tam, W. J. (2010). 2D to 3D conversion using colour-based surrogate depth maps. In *Proceedings of International Conference on 3D System and. Application (3DSA)*.

Wang, H., Yang, Y., Zhang, L., & Yang, Y. (2011). 2D-to-3D conversion based on depth from motion. In Proceedings of International Conference on Mechatronic Science, Electric Engineering and Computer (MEC) (pp.-1892-1895).

Wang, M. J., Chen, C. F., & Lee, G. G. (2013). Motion-based depth estimation for 2D-to-3D video conversion. In *Proceedings of IEEE Conference on Visual Communications and Image Processing (VCIP)* (pp.1-6). doi:10.1109/VCIP.2013.6706329

Wang, O., Lang, M., Frei, M., Hornung, A., Smolic, A., & Gross, M. (2011). StereoBrush: Interactive 2D to 3D Conversion Using Discontinuous Warps. *EUROGRAPHICS Symposium on Sketch-Based Interfaces and Modeling*. doi:10.1145/2021164.2021173

Watanabe, T., Kitahara, I., Kameda, Y., & Ohta, Y. (2003). 3D Free-Viewpoint Video Capturing Interface by using Bimanual Operation. *ACM Transactions on Graphics, 22*(3), 569–577.

Wei, Q. (2005). *Converting 2D to 3D: A survey. In Project Report* (pp. 1–34). Delft University of Technology.

Wu, C., Er, G., Xie, X., Li, T., Cao, X., & Dai, Q. (2008). A novel method for semi-automatic 2D to 3D video Conversion. In Proceedings of IEEE 3DTVCON (pp. 65–68). IEEE.

Yamada, K., Suehiro, K., & Nakamura, H. (2005). Pseudo 3D image generation with simple depth models. In *Proceedings of International Conference on Consumer Electronics, Digest of Technical Papers* (pp. 277–278). doi:10.1109/ICCE.2005.1429825

Yan, X., Yang, Y., Guihua, E., & Dai, Q. (2011). Depth map generation for 2D-to-3D conversion by limited user inputs and depth propagation. In *Proceedings of 3DTV Conference: The True Vision - Capture, Transmission and Display of 3D Video (3DTV-CON)* (pp. 1-4).

Zhang, L., Vázquez, C., & Knorr, S. (2011). *3D*-TV Content Creation: Automatic 2D-to-3D Video Conversion. *IEEE Transactions on Broadcasting*, *57*(2).

Zhang, Q., Li, S., Guo, W., Wang, P., & Huang, J. (2015). Refinement of Kinect Sensor's Depth Maps Based on GMM and CS Theory. *International Journal of Signal Processing*, *Image Processing and Pattern Recognition*, *8*(5), 87–92.

Section 2
Image and Video Compression, Indexing, and Retrieval

Chapter 5
Wavelets with Application in Image Compression

Piyush Kumar Singh
DST- Centre for Interdisciplinary Mathematical Sciences, Banaras Hindu University, India

Ravi Shankar Singh
Department of Computer Science and Engineering, IIT Banaras Hindu University, India

Kabindra Nath Rai
Department of Mathematical Sciences, IIT Banaras Hindu University, India

ABSTRACT

This chapter focus mainly on different wavelet transform algorithms as Burt's Pyramid, Mallat's Pyramidal Algorithm, Feauveau's non dyadic structure and its application in Image compression.This chapter focus on mathematical concepts involved in wavelet transform like convolution, scaling function, wavelet function, Multiresolution analysis, inner product etc, and how these mathematical concepts are liked to image transform application. This chapter gives an idea towards wavelets and wavelet transforms. Image compression based on wavelet transform consists of transform, quantization and encoding. Basic focus is not only on transform step, selection of particular wavelet, wavelets involved in new standard of image compression but also on quantization and encoding, Huffman code, run length code. Difference in between JPEG and JPEG2000, Quantization and sampling, wavelet function and wavelet transform are also given. This chapter is also giving some basic idea of MATLAB to assist readers in understanding MATLAB Programming in terms of image processing.

INTRODUCTION

History of Wavelets

Wavelet is a mathematical tool having a wide application in many areas. Wavelet transform allow time frequency localization. It was firstly introduced as Haar function in 1909 by Hungarian mathematician named Alfred Haar which consists of short positive pulse followed by short negative pulse. In 1930

DOI: 10.4018/978-1-4666-9685-3.ch005

English Mathematician Jhon Littlewood and R.E.A.C. Paley developed method of creating a signal well localized in frequency and relatively well localized in time. In 1946 Gabor Transform having greatest possible localization in time and frequency developed by a British Hungarian physicist Dennis Gabor. But new milestone was held by Morlet, who was an engineer developed his own way of analysing seismic signals by creating component localized in space known as "wavelet of constant shape" later named as "Morlet wavelets". He proceed his work with Alex Grossmann, a physicist to confirm that waves could be reconstructed from its wavelet decompositions also wavelet transforms turned out better than Fourier transform. Morlet and Grossmann firstly introduced word "wavelet" in their paper published in 1984. Later Mayer discovered orthogonal wavelets. In 1986, Stephane Mallat, a former student of Mayer linked wavelet theory with subband coding and quadrature mirror filter. In 1987 Indrid Daubechies discovered a whole new class of wavelet which were orthogonal and without jumps, smooth wavelet which become an important tool in signal processing area used to break up digital data into contribution of various scales (Soman, Ramchandran & Resmi, 2011, p 1-15).

Wavelets have a wide applications in many areas as many of books are written in different areas some of them are "Wavelet in medicine and biology" by Akram Aldroubi and Michal Unser, CRC Press, 1996, "Wavelet in chemistry", editor Beata Walczak, Elsevier, 2000, "Wavelets for sensing technologies" by K. Chan, Chen Peng, Artech House Publisher, 2003, "Wavelet and wave analysis as applied to materials with micro and nano structures" by C. Cattani and J. Rushchitsky, World Scientific Publishing Co., 2007, "Ultra-low biomedical signal processing: An analog wavelet filter approach for pacemakers" by Haddad and Serdijn, Springer, 2008 (Soman, Ramchandran & Resmi, 2011, p 1-15).

PRELIMINARIES

Fourier Transform

If $\hat{\psi}$ represents Fourier transform given by

$$\hat{f}(\omega) = \frac{1}{\sqrt{2\pi}} \int\limits_{-\infty}^{+\infty} f(t)e^{-it\omega}dt. \tag{1}$$

where ω frequency and t is time parameter and inverse Fourier transform can be given by (Soman, Ramchandran & Resmi, 2011, p 33-48)

$$f(t) = \frac{1}{\sqrt{2\pi}} \int\limits_{-\infty}^{+\infty} \hat{f}(\omega)e^{-it\omega}d\omega \tag{2}$$

Wavelets

Mathematically if $\psi \in L^2(\mathbb{R})$ and a is scaling and b is translation parameter satisfy following admissibility criterion (Chui, 1992, p 60-65; Soman, Ramchandran & Resmi, 2011, p 33-37)

$$C_\psi = \int\limits_{-\infty}^{+\infty} \frac{\left|\hat{\psi}(\omega)\right|}{|\omega|} d\omega < \infty, \tag{3}$$

then ψ is called basic wavelet and given by

$$\psi_{(a,b)}(t) = \psi(\frac{t-b}{a})\frac{1}{\sqrt{|a|}}. \tag{4}$$

Integral Wavelets Transform

Relative to every basic wavelet ψ the integral wavelets transform on $L^2(\mathbb{R})$ is defined by

$$(W_\psi f)_{(a,b)} = |a|^{(-1/2)} \int\limits_{-\infty}^{+\infty} f(t)\overline{\psi(\frac{t-b}{a})}dt \tag{5}$$

where $f \in L^2(\mathbb{R})$, $a, b \in \mathbb{R}$ and $a \neq 0$ (Chui, 1992,p 60-65; Soman, Ramchandran & Resmi, 2011, p 33-37).

Discrete Wavelets Transform

By changing scaling coefficient $a = a_0^m$ such that $a \neq 0,1$ and $b = nb_0 a_0^m$ such that $b \neq 0$ in $\psi_{(a,b)}$ we get discrete wavelet as (Lokenath Debnath, 2002, p 382-383)

$$\psi_{(m,n)}(t) = a_0^{(-m/2)}\psi(a_0^{-m}t - nb_0) \tag{6}$$

and discrete wavelet transform of function $f \in L^2(\mathbb{R})$ can be given by inner product of function f with wavelet function ψ

$$(W_\psi f)_{(m,n)} = |a|^{(-1/2)} \int\limits_{-\infty}^{+\infty} f(t)\overline{a_0^{(-m/2)}\psi(a_0^{-m}t - nb_0)}dt. \tag{7}$$

Image Processing

Digital image processing is highly interdisciplinary area having its component tools as mathematical transforms, matrix theory, estimation theory and information theory (Jain, 2012, p 11-47). Mathematically digital image is a matrix. A digital image is an array of numbers (termed as pixels) either real or complex represented by finite number of bits. It has a wide application in remote sensing, image transmission and storage, radar, robotics and automated inspection of industrial parts. Many operations are done in image processing this consists of image enhancement, image restoration, image analysis, image compression, image denoising, image watermarking . Image enhancement, means enhancement of certain image features like contrast stretching. Image restoration, which refers to minimization of known degradation in image. Image analysis, means quantitative measurements from image (Jain, 2012, p 1-10). Image compression mainly consists of removal of coding redundancy, spatial or temporal redundancies and irrelevant information. Removal of coding redundancy means less optimal code is used. Spatial or temporal redundancies occur as a result of pixel correlations. Irrelevant informations are those that are visually non essential information. Image denoising consists of recovery original image by removing undesired added noise. Image watermarking consists of embedding watermark within digital image before publishing it to stop piracy (Gonzalez,Woods & Eddins, 2011, p 374-439; Toufik & Mokhtar, 2012).

As in 1970 and 1980, the signal and image processing communities introduced wavelet analysis by names as "subband coding", "quadrature mirror filters" and "pyramidal algorithm" and wavelet become a dream tool for this area after Daubechies work (Soman, Ramchandran & Resmi, 2011, p 1-15). It is widely used in digital image processing, that refers to processing of two dimensional picture by digital computer (Jain, 2012, p 1-10).

If signal, scaling function and wavelet function are discrete in time then wavelet series expansion of signal is discrete in time known as discrete wavelet transforms (Thyagarajan, 2011, P 99-105). In digital image processing, discrete wavelet transform provides vision in both frequency and spatial component of digital image. The kernels used in wavelet transform of images have useful properties of separability, scalability, translatability, Multiresolution compatibility and orthogonality. Convolution based fast wavelet transform are developed using scaling and wavelet vectors that generates approximation, horizontal, vertical and diagonal components of image. Basic steps in wavelet transform based digital image processing consists of computing two dimensional discrete wavelet transform of image, alter the wavelet coefficient then find inverse transform (Gonzalez,Woods & Eddins, 2011, p 331-373).

BACKGROUND

As given in introduction section "Wavelets" introduced in 1984. Wavelets are soon analysed as a powerful tool in signal analysis as it can break a function f in different time frequency bands. The translation and dilation parameter a and b given above have an exciting property of analysing signals or in mathematical term the function f can be analysed by wavelet transform as wavelets are time frequency localized function.

Time Frequency Localization of Fourier and Wavelet Transform

Let us consider a signal $f(t)$ or a continuous mathematical function of time t. If $f \in L^2(\mathbb{R})$ means f have finite energy given by its L²-norm. In signal processing generally signals are studied in time domain and corresponding spectral information is studied in frequency domain. Then its Fourier transform gives power spectrum of the signal. But frequency information on a particular localized time is not easy to read. This problem leads to short time Fourier transform which causes windowing the signal to take well localized size of f. The time frequency window provided in short time Fourier transform have limitation that it have rigid window means a window whose width remain unchanged while analysing frequency bands. Wavelet transform also provides time frequency localization but having flexible window. That is, wavelet transform is mare suitable for analysing signals using time interval window for higher frequency bands and wide time interval window for low frequency band.

Since this chapter is mainly concentrates on digital images hence the two parameters are in spatial domain and corresponding frequency domain (Chui, 1992,p 6-7).

SCALING AND WAVELET FUNCTIONS

- Since admissibility condition

$$C_{\psi} = \int_{-\infty}^{+\infty} \frac{|\hat{\psi}(\omega)|}{|\omega|} d\omega < \infty \qquad (8)$$

suggests that $\hat{\psi}(\omega) \to 0$ as $\omega \to 0$. Where $\hat{\psi}$ represents Fourier transform, which ultimately gives (Soman, Ramchandran & Resmi, 2011, p 33-48)

$$\int_{-\infty}^{+\infty} \psi(t)dt = 0. \qquad (9)$$

- Putting m=j, n=k, a_0=2 and b_0=1 in discrete wavelet transform equation we get

$$\psi_{(j,k)}(t) = 2^{\left(-j/2\right)} \psi(2^{-j}t - k) \text{ where } j,k \in \mathbb{Z}. \qquad (10)$$

Here a_0=2 and b_0=1 is taken for computational simplicity. This also indicates a nice property that is the wavelet is not working on single frequency but set of frequency bands or octaves. This also indicates that single $\psi(t)$ can be translated by 2^{-j} and dilated by $\dfrac{k}{2^{-j}}$ to get $\psi(2^{-j}t - k)$.

- **Multiresolution Analysis:** Multiresolution analysis provides analysis of signal in time frequency terms. This can be used by orthonormal wavelets. Consider whole space $L^2(\mathbb{R})$ have set of nested closed subspaces V_i such that

1. $V_{-\infty} \subset ... \subset V_{i-1} \subset V_i \subset V_{i+1} \subset ... \subset V_{\infty}$
2. $(\bigcup_{j \in \mathbb{Z}} V_j) = L^2(\mathbb{R})$ where each V_j is closed subspace of $L^2(\mathbb{R})$
3. $(\bigcap_{j \in \mathbb{Z}} V_j) = \{0\}$
4. $V_{j+1} = V_j \oplus W_j$ where $j \in \mathbb{Z}$ and $\oplus$ denotes direct sum.
5. Let some $f(x)$ exists Such that if $f(x) \in V_j$ then $f(2x) \in V_{j+1}$, $j \in \mathbb{Z}$

Also each W subspace is disjoint to any other W subspace. In more clear way it can be stated that $W_j \cap W_k = \{0\}$ where $j \neq k$ (Chui, 1992, p 9-20).

- **Scaling Function:** As a benefit of Multiresolution analysis there exists ϕ function belonging to $L^2(\mathbb{R})$ space termed as scaling function defined by following equation

$$\phi_k(t) = \phi(t-k) \text{ where } k \in \mathbb{Z} \tag{11}$$

Also,

$$V_0 = \underset{k}{span}\{\phi_k(t)\} \tag{12}$$

The above equations states that $\phi_k(t)$ is translates of $\phi(t)$ and $\phi_k(t)$ can be spanned to generate space V_0. If whose space can be generated by $\phi(t)$ then any function belonging in space V_0 can be generated by linear combination of $\phi_k(t)$ as $\phi_k(t)$ generates whole space V_0 so $\phi_k(t)$ becomes basis for V_0. So any function defined in space V_0 can be represented by linear span of its basis $\phi_k(t)$. Further the coefficient of linear span can be calculated by inner product of given function with ϕ_k. The two dimensional scaling function with translates and dilates can be given by

$$\phi_{(a,b)}(t) = \phi(\frac{t-b}{a})\frac{1}{\left|\sqrt{a}\right|} \tag{13}$$

By replacing a=2^{-j} and b=2^{-j}.k we get discrete version of scaling function given by following formula

$$\phi_{j,k}(t) = 2^{j/2}\phi(2^j t - k) \tag{14}$$

Since $\phi(t) \in V_0$ and by property (4) of Multiresolution analysis, $V_1 = V_0 \oplus W_0$ this means that V$_0$ is a subset of V$_1$ and using property (5) of Multiresolution analysis stated above we can say that

$$\phi(t) = \sum_k h_\phi(k)\sqrt{2}\phi(2t - k) \tag{15}$$

Here $h_\phi(k)$ is coefficient of expansion. The above equation state that $\phi(t)$ can be expressed by next higher level scaling function as $V_0 \subset V_1$ (Toufik & Mokhtar, 2012).

- **Wavelet Function:** Wavelet function $\psi(t)$ can be defined in similar way as scaling function. Wavelet function $\psi(t)$ is basis for W$_0$ space. It is not very difficult to understand that W space is an orthogonal complement of corresponding V space and jointly direct sum of both space generates next level V space. Since $\phi(t)$ is a scaling function which can span V space. Corresponding W space be generated by $\psi(t)$. As $V_{j+1} = V_j \oplus W_j$ this implies that $V_j \subset V_{j+1}$ so $V_0 \subset V_1$, using property (5) of MRA this wavelet function can be expressed by next higher level scaling function. Using similar argument as in scaling function we can express wavelet function $\psi(t) \in W_0$ can be expressed by next level higher scaling function by given equation (Toufik & Mokhtar, 2012).

$$\psi(t) = \sum_k h_\psi(k)\sqrt{2}\phi(2t-k) \tag{16}$$

WAVELET TRANSFORM ALGORITHM FOR DIGITAL IMAGE

Wavelet transform is becoming a powerful tool in image compression. Wavelet transform formula discussed above is termed in term of time and frequency. This chapter is focussed on digital image processing and image compression of digital images. The two components used repetitively in digital image transform are spatial and frequency domain unlike the above section in this section the variable used is 'x' denoting space rather than 't'. Beside the property of scaling, translation and multiresolution analysis as discussed above wavelets have property of separability and orthogonality which make it easy to apply on two dimensional digital images. The separability property states that wavelet and scaling both are separable such that $\psi^H(x,y) = \psi(x)\phi(y)$, $\psi^V(x,y) = \phi(x)\psi(y)$, $\psi^D(x,y) = \psi(x)\psi(y)$ and $\phi(x,y) = \phi(x)\phi(y)$ known as horizontal, vertical, diagonal wavelets and scaling function of next space.

Mallat's Pyramidal Algorithm Based Fast Wavelet Transform

The algorithm given here is based on Mallat's Pyramidal Algorithm is termed as Fast Wavelet Transform in short FWT because it used convolution theorem to make wavelet transform fast. The wavelet transform method does not need the whole structure of wavelets rather than the corresponding peak value of wavelet (wavelet tap) can be convolved in time reversed manner on the digital image and it is applied on row wise and column wise manner respectively. The below two equation discussed in scaling and wavelet function can be used (Gonzalez,Woods & Eddins, 2011, p 374-439; Gonzalez,Woods & Eddins, 2011, p 331-373).

$$\phi(x) = \sum_k h_\phi(k)\sqrt{2}\phi(2x-k) \tag{17}$$

$$\psi(x) = \sum_k h_\psi(k)\sqrt{2}\phi(2x-k) \tag{18}$$

Using convolution theorem if there is a digital image of n rows and m columns then time reversed convolution of the expansion coefficients 'h' for phi and psi are known as scaling and wavelet vectors in spatial domain gives transformed coefficients. In digital image processing it is also known as low pass and high pass decomposition filters. Then after decomposition it gets downsampled by two. Downsampling by 2 reduces the number of pixels required to represent image data by half. This process is applied on digital image in row wise and column wise resulting in generation of four component of digital image with same dimension as original image dimension. This scheme stated here is termed as subband coding and also termed as analysis filter bank. This type of wavelet transform generates four components of images known as horizontal, vertical, diagonal and approximation component (Gonzalez, Woods & Eddins, 2011, p 374-439; Gonzalez, Woods & Eddins, 2011, p 331-373).

Algorithm for Fast Wavelet Transform of Digital Image

1. Take an image I(m,n) with m rows and n columns.
2. It is set of two steps
   a.   Convolve the image with $h_\psi(-n)$ that is time reversed coefficients and downsample the result obtained by 2 along the columns.
   b.   Convolve the image with $h_\phi(-n)$ that is time reversed coefficients and downsample the result obtained by 2 along the columns.
3. It is set of four steps
   a.   The result obtained from step (2.a) is again convolved with $h_\psi(-m)$ and result obtained is down sampled along rows by 2 to get diagonal component of transformed image.
   b.   The result obtained from step (2.a) is again convolved with $h_\phi(-m)$ and result obtained is down sampled along rows by 2 to get vertical component of transformed image.
   c.   The result obtained from step (2.b) is again convolved with and result obtained is down sampled along rows by 2 to get horizontal component of transformed image.
   d.   The result obtained from step (2.b) is again convolved with $h_\phi(-m)$ and result obtained is down sampled along rows by 2 to get approximation component of transformed image.
4. For next level wavelet transform take approximation component as original image I(m1,n1) and repeat whole process from step 1 to 3.

The reverse of this means synthesis filter bank convolves each subband with in time peaks of wavelet h-psi and h-phi in same reverse order of analysis filter bank. Before applying convolution it is needed to upsample each subband. Upsampling is a reverse process of down sampling process (Gonzalez,Woods & Eddins, 2011, p 374-439; Gonzalez,Woods & Eddins, 2011, p 331-373).

Algorithm for Inverse Fast Wavelet Transform of Digital Image

1. It is set of following four steps
   a.   The diagonal component is upsampled by 2 along rows by inserting zeros between two pixels then convoluted with $h_\psi(m)$.
   b.   The vertical component is upsampled by 2 along rows by inserting zeros between two pixels then convoluted with $h_\phi(m)$.

    c.   The horizontal component is upsampled by 2 along rows by inserting zeros between two pixels then convoluted with $h_\psi(m)$.

    d.   The diagonal component is upsampled by 2 along rows by inserting zeros between two pixels then convoluted with $h_\phi(m)$.

2.   It is set of following two steps

    a.   Result obtained from (1.a) and (1.b) are added and result is upsampled along column then convoluted with $h_\psi(n)$.

    b.   Result obtained from (1.c) and (1.d) are added and result is upsampled along column then convoluted with $h_\phi(n)$.

3.   Obtain result by adding the results from (2.a) and (2.b).

4.   Result obtained from step (3) denotes original image or approximation component depending on more number of inverse transform is needed or not. If further inverse transform is needed then taking result obtained from step (3) as approximation component and given horizontal, vertical and diagonal component of corresponding level repeat step (1)-(3) (Gonzalez,Woods & Eddins, 2011, p 374-439; Gonzalez,Woods & Eddins, 2011, p 331-373).

Feauveau's Algorithm

This algorithm was proposed by Feauveau in 1990 based on Aldenson's work. This is similar to mallat's algorithm with a difference. In analysis filter bank design the original image is transformed through scaling and wavelet function. After transformation the result generated is downsampled along the rows. The scaling function transformed part is taken over for next step and again transformation applied where as the wavelet function transformed part remains unchanged (Toufik & Mokhtar, 2012).

In synthesis filter bank of this approach is a reverse process of analysis filter bank. The last level transformed component (one of them is scaling function transformed component and one is wavelet function transformed component) the two component are firstly upsampled by 2 along rows is inverse transformed by their corresponding scaling and wavelet function. The two components are added to generate next scaling function transformed component which is upsampled by 2 and again inverse transformed with scaling function. The corresponding level wavelet transformed component which is transported without change is upsampled by 2 and inverse transformed by wavelet function and added to scaling function inverse transformed component of same level. This process is repeated again and again until all wavelet transformed component become used up. The final output will be inverse wavelet transformation of original image. For calculating inverse and direct wavelet transform convolution technique can be used (Toufik & Mokhtar, 2012).

Lifting Scheme

Lifting scheme links both Fourier with wavelet transformation in digital image processing. Lifting scheme is proposed by Swelden. Lifting scheme in transformation step is a set of three subparts split, Predict and update. First image data splits in even and odd parts and transformation is taken up using lazy wavelet transform. Then difference of two is calculated using predicator and finally updating of data is done using updater. In synthesis filter bank using lifting scheme the reverse process takes place that is predict then update. After updating both odd and even parts are get merged (Toufik & Mokhtar, 2012).

Burt's Pyramidal Algorithm

Burt's Pyramidal algorithm is basically dedicated towards lossless image coding. It is basically splitting the signal in low resolution and high resolution component. This splitting can be done by application of reduction and expansion process (Toufik & Mokhtar, 2012).

IMAGE COMPRESSION

Image compression is a part of image processing dedicated to represent image in lower number of bits. As we know that digital images are of very large dimension. As the technology increases very high resolution cameras are coming in the market. The digital image produced by these cameras is of very large dimension. This means that those images have very large number of pixels and each pixel require some finite number of bits to represent its value. Normally a gray scale image require 8 bit for each pixel value. Colour images however require three components namely red, green and blue and each colour component require 8 bit hence total 24 bits are required. Hence it is easy to understand that what amount of data storage is required for storing an digital image in ram. If an image is of rgb type having dimension $n \times m$ implies that there is $n \times m$ number of pixels, since each pixel requires 24 bit for single pixel storage hence total of $n \times m \times 24$ bits are required for single rgb image storage in computer memory. Hence it is very essential task to compress image. For example if an image is of dimension 100×400 then it have 40000 pixels in image and total bits required to store data of a grayscale image is 40000×8 bits that is 320000 bits. If the image is a rgb colour image then every pixel will require 8 bits for each red, green and blue component so a total of 24 bits is required for every pixel representation so a total of 40000×24 bits will be required that is 960000 bits will be required (Gonzalez, Woods & Eddins, 2011, p 374-439). How vast data storage requirement ?

Image compression is required as this is era of internet and we know that in this internet era many of multimedia works are happening. Videos are sequence of images coming at a very fast rate. Due to all these fact image compression is required. Image compression is actually representation of same image with less number of bits. This can be done by removing redundant information from image. Redundant information is three types found in images namely coding redundancy, spatial and temporal redundancy and irrelevant information. Removal of coding redundancy means less number of code words or in other words more optimal code words should be used at place of less optimal code words. Spatial or temporal redundancy lies in images or sequence of images. Spatial correlation is as a result of pixel correlation of each pixel with its neighbouring pixels. Temporal correlation is in case of sequence of images (video is a sequence of images). Temporal redundancy is due to pixel correlation of pixels with neighbouring image pixels. Some of information in image have no relevance for human visual system. As these information are ignored by human visual system these are known as irrelevant information. Removal of irrelevant information can also be used in image compression (Gonzalez, Woods & Eddins, 2011, p 374-439).

Normally there is two types of compression schemes one is lossy and other is lossless compression.

Lossy compression loses some of information from the image. Lossy compression generally removes irrelevant information. Whereas in lossless compression data is not lost. Lossless compression is generally very important in sensitive images like medical image processing. Lossless images are information preserving and error free. The decompressed image of lossless image compression has either no distortion or has same level of distortion as original image. Lossless image compression algorithms the original data can be reconstructed from the compressed data (Gonzalez,Woods & Eddins, 2011, p 374-439).

Compression Ratio

Compression ratio is a numerical quantity which is used to find extent of compression. Mathematically compression ratio is ratio of size of original image with size of compressed image. Usually size of original and compressed image expressed in bits. If an compressed image have compression ratio 5 means original image is 5 times larger than its compressed image means if original image is of 2000 bits then its compressed image will be of 400 bits only. Let if original image is of size s1 and compressed image be of size s2 then compression ratio can be expressed as (Gonzalez,Woods & Eddins, 2011, p 374-439).

$$C_R = \frac{s1}{s2} \qquad (19)$$

Mean Square Error Method

After compression of image it is needed to decompress image. As compressed image can be send via network but at other end it is needed to decompress image. The loss in image information can be taken through mean square error. Mean square error method takes square of absolute value difference of each pixel in original image and corresponding pixel in corresponding decompressed image. The it take square root of mean of square of such value over whole image. If original image is I(x,y) and decompressed image is I'(x,y) and image is with dimension m and n then total number of pixels will be mn. Then mean square error can be defined as (Gonzalez,Woods & Eddins, 2011, p 374-439).

$$mse = [\frac{1}{mn} \sum_{x=0}^{m-1} \sum_{y=0}^{n-1} \{I'(x,y) - I(x,y)\}^2]^{\frac{1}{2}} \qquad (20)$$

APPLICATION OF WAVELETS IN IMAGE COMPRESSION

Wavelets have very wide application in image processing. As images have pixels whose values are highly correlated with neighbouring pixels. Wavelet transform of images generates subbands of images. These images are decorrelated. This is easier to encode these decorrelated subband images more efficiently. Wavelet transform coding is different from other coding scheme as in any other coding scheme transform is applied on sub blocks of image where as in wavelet transform based coding scheme transform is applied on whole image. For example in discrete cosine transform based coding scheme there is concept of energy compaction. In DCT discrete cosine functions are used and major concept is the more energy is concentrated in higher coefficients. In DCT 8×8 pixel block is taken for transformation. Note that DCT based image compression is a popular technique for image compression used in JPEG technique. Wavelet transform in image processing is performed by choosing suitable wavelet or commonly referred as kernel which should be capable of representing four 2-D scalable and separable function generated from 1-D scaling and wavelet function. Each of four 2-D functions represents vertical component, horizontal component, diagonal component and coarse scale approximation component. These three vertical, horizontal and diagonal components are jointly known as detail component and also known as fine scale component. The one coarse scale component is known as approximation component. In each transform step four components of image is generated. In every next step the approximation component get transformed as four new component containing next detail and approximation component. Wavelet based image compression is basically consists of three steps. The first step is transform step. Second is quantization and the third one is encoding step (Gonzalez,Woods & Eddins, 2011, p 374-439; Gonzalez,Woods & Eddins, 2011, p 331-373; Singh, Singh, Rai & Jaiswal, 2014).

There are various parts of the JPEG2000 (wavelet based) which is now using as the standard in the image compression schemes, the baseline system and core coding system. The part third of JPEG2000 is for the motion pictures MJP2 which is particularly adopted by Hollywood as in this technology the image sequences are encoded by JPEG2000 and random access to particular frame is also possible. The MPEG (Moving Pictures Expert Group) is international organization setting standard in moving pictures. It has various versions MPEG-1, MPEG-2, MPEG-3, MPEG-4. MPEG-4 is based on the wavelet transform based image compression using JPEG2000 on sequences of the images. The MPEG visual part 2 deals with visual objects, video conferences, animated faces etc. (Richardson, 2003, pp 85-98; Shi and Sun, 2008, Chapter 8, Wavelet transform for image coding: JPEG2000).

Steps Involved in Wavelet Based Image Compression

1. Transform Step

In wavelet transform of image following two equation are used

$$\phi(x) = \sum_k h_\phi(k)\sqrt{2}\phi(2x-k) \tag{21}$$

$$\psi(x) = \sum_k h_\psi(k)\sqrt{2}\phi(2x-k) \tag{22}$$

The details of above two equations are already discussed. These two equation applied on a digital image generate four component as stated above as horizontal component, vertical component, diagonal component and detail component. These two equation are applied firstly row wise then column wise over whole image. It generates four components (see Figure 1). Notice that in next level wavelet transform of figure only approximation component is taken into consideration for further transform in next level as that is courser scale and contain most of information (Gonzalez,Woods & Eddins, 2011, p 374-439; Gonzalez,Woods & Eddins, 2011, p 331-373) (see Figure 2).

Figure 1. Wavelet transform of an image at the first level

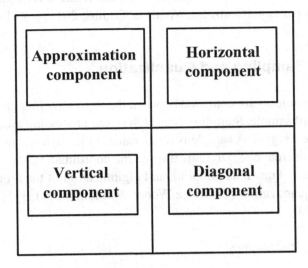

In Figure 2, 1h component, 1d component, 1v component represents respectively first level horizontal component, diagonal component and vertical component and 2h component, 2d component, 2v component represents respectively second level horizontal component, diagonal component and vertical component.

2. Quantization

Elimination of psychovisually redundant data which result in loss of some data is known as quantization. In other words we can say that representation of same pixel information in lesser number of bits than in original one. For example if an image have each pixel information in 8 bits than if we represent

Figure 2. Wavelet transform structure at the second level wavelet transforms application

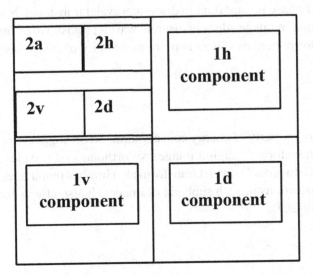

each bit information in only 6 bits then it is known as 8 bit information is quantized into 6 bits. And this result in loss of some information (Gonzalez,Woods & Eddins, 2011, p 374-439; Gonzalez,Woods & Eddins, 2011, p 331-373).

Difference between Sampling and Quantization

It is often seen that many students are confused between the term sampling and quantization. Sampling is a term derived from word sample. Sampling is used in signal processing area when continuous signal is need to convert in discrete signal. A sample is set of values or a single value taken at a particular time form function to make it discrete one. Digitalization of the coordinate value in an continuous image to convert it into discrete one is known as sampling and digitalization of the amplitude valu in the signal or in image is known as quantization (Gonzalez,Woods & Eddins, 2011, p 374-439; Gonzalez,Woods & Eddins, 2011, p 331-373).

3.   Reduction of Coding Redundancy

Reduction in coding redundancy means representation of data with more optimal code. It means that that coding scheme that reduces the average length of representation of pixel values. There are various coding scheme like Huffman coding, run length coding etc can be used in encoding of wavelet transform of image.

So, basics in wavelet based image processing or more specific in image compression consists of three basic steps one is calculation of wavelet transform of image then in next step we can apply some mechanism on the transformed coefficients like entropy based filtering of image coefficient then inverse wavelet transform (Gonzalez,Woods & Eddins, 2011, p 374-439; Gonzalez,Woods & Eddins, 2011, p 331-373).

Choosing Wavelet for Wavelet Transform of Image

Linear Phase

Wavelet function of linear phase is important in discrete wavelet transform. Non-linear phase of wavelet function produces distortion in image edges in discrete wavelet transform of image. As number of levels of discrete wavelet transform increases there is more probability of image distortion at edges (Thyagarajan, 2011, P 259-267).

Orthogonality

Orthogonal transform have property of energy conservation. So orthogonal or orthonormal wavelets are used in discrete wavelet transform of digital image. An orthonormal wavelet is an orthogonal wavelet function with unit norm. Orthogonal wavelet transform also implies that it have distortion due to quantization id due to sum of distortions in each subband of images. It also effects like unitary transformation (Thyagarajan, 2011, P 259-267).

Filter Length

Higher order filter length is found to be useful however filter of very long length is have some ringing effect on the inversed discrete wavelet transformed image. Ringing effect causes some band like structure at edges of image (Thyagarajan, 2011, P 259-267).

Regularity

Regularity of wavelet function means iteration of wavelet function is continuous in nature. In discrete wavelet transform of image if wavelet function is of regular and orthogonal it produces better results for higher level of transforms. The term ringing effect is used as the distortion is caused due to oscillation of the function (Thyagarajan, 2011, P 259-267).

Encoding Schemes

Huffman Algorithm

Huffman codes are a scheme of providing smallest possible number of code symbols on the basis of probabilities of occurring source symbol. It is have constraint that source symbol are encoded once at a time. The mechanism involved in Huffman based coding scheme is taking lowest probability symbols in a single symbol and then replaces it to next source reduction. Huffman codes generate instantaneous decidable code blocks and very widely used (Gonzalez,Woods & Eddins, 2011, p 374-439).

Run Length Encoding

In many of image schemes we have runs of several runs of a single pixel value. Consider a binary image consisting of only 0 and 1 such an image may be easily represented by such runs of a single string. Giving you some rough idea let us consider a long run of 0. As in binary images it is possible as binary image contain only zero and one (Jain, 2012, p 375-376).

JPEG and JPEG2000

JPEG stands for joint photographic experts group is an international agency and joint committee between ISO/IEC JTC1 and ITU-T (formerly CCITT) that created the JPEG and JPEG-2000 standards. Both JPEG and JPEG-2000 standards are set by this committee. JPEG standard is some old one and JPEG-2000 is newer one. JPEG is based on discrete cosine transform of image by taking image in blocks of eight cross eight means taking 64 pixels at a time. The concept behind JPEG compression scheme is concept of energy compaction in higher coefficient generated in discrete cosine transform and considering that lower order coefficient has very low energy retained. In JPEG-2000 the concept is wavelet transform of image. The wavelet transform of image is then quantized and encoded by some suitable encoding scheme. The wavelet used in JPEG-2000 encoding is jpg9.7 for lossy image compression. The encoding scheme use in JPEG-2000 is EBCOT also known as Embedded Block Coding with Optimal Truncation. Note that in JPEG there is always some loss of information as some of lower order coefficients are drloped out where as there is possibility of lossless image compression in JPEG-2000 by lossless wavelet transform. The quantization is however always lossy step (Gonzalez,Woods & Eddins, 2011, p 374-439; Gonzalez,Woods & Eddins, 2011, p 331-373)..

SOME MATLAB COMMANDS AND USER DEFINED FUNCTIONS

MATLAB is one of the popular programming environment and language used in image processing area. MATLAB stand for matrix laboratory and all data type is treated as matrix. Here we are giving some programs regarding some basic operation on image processing. MATLAB consists of four parts in its editor one is command window others are command history, workspace and current folder. Command window provides environment for putting command. The output is also shown on command window. Command history keeps record of previously written command. That is all the commands are available on command history. Workspace keeps all current variables available at current time inside memory. The current folder shows current folder where the operations are being done. Now script and functions can be written at their provided area. The main point to be noted in writing functions in MATLAB as we are giving some examples of some basic operations on functions that is the function should be saves with their function name (Gonzalez,Woods & Eddins, 2011).

Here we are giving some common function used in image processing and in basics of Matlab. We are also given some functions below using some of system defined function. This is to make clear meaning of some of the function used in user defined functions given below (Gonzalez,Woods & Eddins, 2011).

- clc: It is used to clear up command window area.
- clear: It is used to clear the workspace area. That is it clears all the previously allocated variables available in workspace area.
- imshow(): To show an image.
- imread(): To read an image matrix.
- imwrite(): It writes image in current folder.
- imrotate(): Rotates an given image at a specified angle.

Some MATLAB User Defined Functions

1. Program for creating black and white image of integer and double type

```
img_black_int = uint8(zeros(512,1024));
figure(1);
imshow(img_black_int);
img_black_double = double(zeros(512,1024));
figure(2);
imshow(img_black_double);
img_white_int=uint8(255*ones(512,1024));
```

```
figure(3);
imshow(img_white_int);
img_white_double=double(ones(512,1024));
figure(4);
imshow(img_white_double);
whos img_white_double;
```

2. Function generating colour components in an rgb image

```
function y = colorcompo(x)
f = imread(x);
imshow(f)
figure(1);
red = f(:,:,1);
figure(2)
imshow(red);
green = f(:,:,2);
figure(3)
imshow(green);
blue = f(:,:,3);
figure(4)
imshow(blue);
end
```

3. Function generating colour components in an rgb image and swapping red and blue plane

```
function y = colorcompoplus(x)
f = imread(x);
imshow(f)
figure(1);
red  =  f(:,:,1);
figure(2)
imshow(red);
green = f(:,:,2);
figure(3)
imshow(green);
blue = f(:,:,3);
figure(4)
imshow(blue);
%swapping of green and red plane
```

```
g(:,:,1) = f(:,:,2);
g(:,:,2) = red;
g(:,:,3) = f(:,:,3);
figure(5);
imshow(g);
end
```

4.   Function converting an image in jpeg format

```
function y = jpgformat(img)
f  =  imread(img);
imshow(f)
figure(1);
dim = size(img);
figure;
imshow(img);
imwrite(img,'output.jpg','jpg');
imtool(img);
end
```

5.   Function converting an image in bmp format

```
function y = bmpformat(img)
f  =  imread(img);
imshow(f)
figure(1);
dim  =  size(img);
figure;
imshow(img);
imwrite(img,'output.bmp','bmp');
imtool(img);
end
```

6.   Function converting an image in tif format

```
function y = tifformat(img)
f  =  imread(img);
imshow(f)
```

```
figure(1);
dim = size(img);
figure;
imshow(img);
imwrite(img,'output.tif','tif');
imtool(img);
end
```

7.   Function to rotate an image at specified angle

```
function y = rotateformat(img)
f = imread(img);
img2 = imrotate(img,65);  % rotate image img by 65 degrees
figure(1);
imshow(img2);
imshow(f)
figure(1);
end
```

FUTURE RESEARCH DIRECTIONS

Recently many parallel algorithms are developed for fast wavelet transform using CUDA which is GPU based computing that are used for large scale image processing (Franco, Bernab, Fernndez & Acacio, 2009; Prajapati & Vij, 2011). The generalization of wavelet transform is Wavelet packet transform. In wavelet packet transform each of the detail component is also analysed by recursive wavelet transform as like in approximation component. Threshold entropy based wavelet packet best tree algorithms are developed for better image compression using wavelet packet which is extension of wavelets with basis function having better frequency localization (Kharate, 2010; Sethi, Mishra, Dash, Mishra & Meher, 2011; Singh, Singh, Rai & Jaiswal, 2014; Soman, Ramchandran & Resmi, 2011, p 1-15). Using finite number of wavelet functions instead of one fixed function is known as multiwavelets. Image compression research are carrying on based on multiwavelets and multiwavelet packets which produces better result that wavelet filters (Martin & Bell, 2001; Soman, Ramchandran & Resmi, 2011, p 1-15).

CONCLUSION

Wavelet transform have wide application in image compression. Algorithms of wavelet transform like Burt's Pyramid, Mallat's Pyramidal Algorithm, Feauveau's non dyadic structure and Swelden's lifting scheme have applications in image compression and in new standard of image compression that is JPEG2000 (Gonzalez,Woods & Eddins, 2011, p 374-439; Toufik & Mokhtar, 2012; Rehna & Jaya,

2012). The fast wavelet transform algorithm for image processing is also illustrated on Mallat's Pyramidal Algorithm and inverses is also given is most widely used in image compression. Yet this chapter is not giving MATLAB codes for image transforms but some of introductory image application codes are given in this chapter to have a start up in MATLAB coding language.

REFERENCES

Chui, C. K. (1992). *An Introduction to Wavelets*. London, UK: Academic Press.

Debnath. (2002). *Wavelet Transforms and Their Applications. In Wavelet Transforms and Basic Properties* (pp. 382–383). Boston: Birkhauser.

Franco, J., Bernab, G., Fernndez, J., & Acacio, M. E. (2009). A parallel implementation of the 2d wavelet transform using cuda. IEEE Computer Society.

Gonzalez, R. C., Woods, R. E., & Eddins, S. L. (2011). *Digital Image Processing Using MATLAB. In Image Compression* (2nd ed.; pp. 374–439). New Delhi: Tata McGraw Hill Education Private Limited.

Jain, A. K. (2012). Fundamentals of Digital Image Processing. New Delhi: Academic Press.

Kharate, G. K. (2010, March). Colour image compression based on wavelet packet best tree. *IJCSI International Journal of Computer Science Issues*, 7, 31–35.

Martin, M. B., & Bell, A. E. (2001, April). New image compression techniques using multiwavelets and multiwavelet packets. *IEEE Transactions on Image Processing*, 10(4), 500–510. doi:10.1109/83.913585 PMID:18249640

Prajapati, H. B., & Vij, S. K. (2011). Analytical study of parallel and distributed image processing. In *Proceedings of the 2011 International conference on Image Information Processing*. doi:10.1109/ICIIP.2011.6108870

Rehna, V. J., & Jaya Kumar, M. K. (2012, August). Wavelet Based Image Coding Schemes: A Recent Survey. *International Journal on Soft Computing*, 3(3), 101–118. doi:10.5121/ijsc.2012.3308

Richardson, I. E. G. (2003). *H.264 and MPEG-4 Video Compression. In The MPEG-4 and H.264 Standards* (pp. 85–98). Jhon Wiley and Sons, Ltd. doi:10.1002/0470869615.ch4

Sethi, J., Mishra, S., Dash, P. P., Mishra, S. K., & Meher, S. (2011, January). Image compression using wavelet packet tree. *ACEEE Int. J. on Signal and Image Processing*, 2(1), 41–43.

Shi, Y. Q., & Sun, H. (2008). Image and Video Compression for Mutimedia Engineering Fundamental Algorithm and Standards. CRC Press Taylor & Francis Group. doi:10.1201/9781420007268

Singh, P. K., Singh, R. S., Rai, K. N., & Jaiswal, S. (February, 2014). *Comparative study of Image Compression Technique based on Wavelet Transform and Wavelet Packet Transfor*. Paper Presented at International Conference on Recent Trends in Computer Science and Engineering, Bihar, India.

Soman, K. P., Ramachandran, K. I., & Resmi, N. G. (2011). *Insight into Wavelets – From Theory to Practice*. PHI Learning Private Limited.

Thyagarajan, K. S. (2011). *Still Image and Video Compression with MATLAB*. Wiley. doi:10.1002/9780470886922.ch4

Toufik, B., & Mokhtar, N. (2012). Advances in Wavelet Theory and Their Applications in Engineering, Physics and Technology. In The Wavelet Transform for Image Processing Applications, (pp 395-422). In Tech.

KEY TERMS AND DEFINITIONS

Convolution: Convolution operation between two function f and g belonging to $L^1(\mathbb{R})$ space is denoted by * and defined as $(f*g)(x) = \int_{-\infty}^{+\infty} f(x-y)g(y)dy$. x should exist almost everywhere in R.

Convolution Theorem: Convolution theorem states that the convolution of two functions in one domain is equivalent to product of Fourier transform of that function in other domain and vice versa. For example convolution of two functions f and g in time domain can be obtained by taking inverse Fourier transform of product of Fourier transforms of two function f and g in frequency domain. Conversely convolution of Fourier transforms of two functions f and g can be computed by taking Fourier transforms of product of f and g in time domain.

Entropy: The average information generated by a source is known as entropy of that source. More clearly, Entropy is amount of uncertainty. In information science it is amount of uncertainty in output. For any source symbol A possible output be ranges from 1 to n. If a_i denote the possible output and $P(a_i)$ denote probability of output as a_i then entropy of A is defined as $H(A) = -\sum_{i=1}^{n} P(a_i)\log_2(P(a_i))$.

Estimation Theory: Estimation theory is from statistical fields have wide application in image processing as the data set in image processing are very large so estimates are usually taken like mean square estimate.

Functions in L^2 Space: Set of square integarable function is in L^2 space.

Information Theory: Information theory have very wide application in image processing as the image transforms, quantization and data compression all comes under information theory.

Inner Product: Inner Product can be defined in terms of inner product space as if V is a vector space and F is a field then inner product space is defined as $< \cdot, \cdot > = V \times V \to F$ such that it holds three properties that is conjugate symmetry, linearity and positive definiteness. The term conjugate symmetry implies that inner product of x and y will be equal to conjugate of inner product of y with x. The term linearity states that inner product is a linear operation. Positive definiteness states that inner product of x with x will be always greater than zero but it can be zero if x itself is equal to zero.

Matrix Theory: The term matrix theory in this chapter is focussed on the fact that image processing has wide application of matrix algebra. Operations like orthogonal and unitary matrix, circulant and toeplitz matrices, transposition etc are under matrix theory.

Orthogonal: Two vectors in inner product space are said to be orthogonal if their inner product is zero.

Signal: A signal can be said as a mathematical function which carries some information regarding some phenomenon.

Chapter 6
An Efficient Algorithm for Fast Block Motion Estimation in High Efficiency Video Coding

Murugesan Ezhilarasan
Pondicherry Engineering College, India

Kumar K. Nirmal
Pondicherry Engineering College, India

P. Thambidurai
Perunthalaivar Kamarajar Institute of Engineering and Technology, India

ABSTRACT

The Motion Estimation is an indispensable module in the design of video encoder. It employs Block Matching algorithm which involves searching a candidate block in the entire search window of the reference frame taking up to 80% of the total video encoding time. In order to increase the efficiency, several Block Matching Algorithms are employed to minimize the computational time involved in block matching. The chapter throws light on an efficient approach to be applied to the existing Block Matching Search techniques in HEVC which outperforms the various Block Matching algorithms. It involves two steps namely – Prediction and Refinement. The prediction step considers two parameters such as the temporal correlation and the direction to predict the MV of the candidate block. Several combinations of the search points are formulated in the refinement step of the algorithm to minimize the search time. The results depict that the Efficient Motion Estimation schemes provide a faster search minimizing the computational time upon comparison with the existing Motion Estimation algorithms.

INTRODUCTION

The rapid advancements in the field of Video Coding lead to the evolution of video coding standards. With H.261 and H.263 developed by ITU-T and MPEG-1 and MPEG-4 Visual developed by ISO/IEC, the experts of ITU-T Video Coding Experts Group (VCEG) and ISO/IEC Moving Pictures Experts Group

DOI: 10.4018/978-1-4666-9685-3.ch006

(MPEG) standardization organizations come up with a Joint Collaborative Team on Video Coding (JCT-VC) which prepared the H.265. Taking into account the demands of the market, which expects Ubiquitous HD in all real-time applications, all the Video CODECs fail to meet up with the requirements. H.265 also known as HEVC, the successor of H.264/MPEG-4 AVC, helps to provide the video of same perceptual quality in half the bit rate of AVC. In addition, HEVC also provides support for Ultra HD format and can also help to achieve Ubiquitous HD. A few notable applications of HEVC includes Broadcasting of High Definition (HD) TV signals over the satellite, cable and other terrestrial transmission systems, Video Content Acquisition system, Security Applications, Blue-Ray Discs, Real-time applications, Video Conferencing and Telepresence systems. The development of HEVC is to essentially address all existing H.264/MPEG-4 AVC applications and focus on two important attributes: Increased usage of parallel processing structures and increased resolution of the video sequences (Sullivan, 2012).

The block based video coding merely involves two important processes namely, the Motion Estimation and the Motion Compensation. The Motion Estimation (ME) module compares two frames namely; the reference frame and the current frame and identify the best matched block position depicting the Motion Vector. The Motion Compensation (MC) module is used to generate the compensated frames through the Motion Vectors. Upon comparison, it has been identified that the ME module is very challenging and time consuming than the MC module. The ME module involves division of the frames into variable sized non-overlapping blocks and computation of the displacement of the best matched block from the reference frame. It includes search techniques which play a vital role in eliminating the temporal redundancy of a video sequence (see Figure 1 and 2).

The problem of Temporal Redundancy can be mitigated to a greater extent by the employment of efficient algorithms in the ME module. For specific applications like the Distributed Video Coding, the complexity of the ME module can be shifted to the side of the decoder, but, the overall complexity remains unaffected (Purnachand et al., 2012; Dufaux et al., 2009). A few other techniques that can be employed by the ME module apart from the video compression is the Frame Interpolation which is primarily used to Frame Rate up-conversion (Asencenso et al., 2005; Hong et al., 2010). Block Matching is the process of comparing each target block of the current frame with that of the previous (reference frame) so as to identify the best matching block. The best match can be calculated using Mean Absolute Difference (MAD) (Cafforio. C & Rocca. F, 1976) (see Figure 3).

Figure 1. Quad-Tree Coding Structure in HEVC

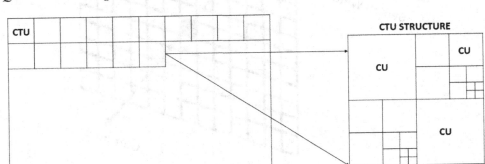

Figure 2. Quad-Tree Structure

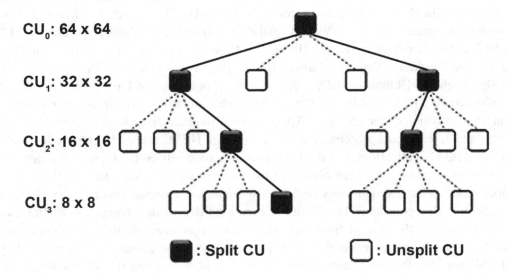

Figure 3. Illustration of ME process

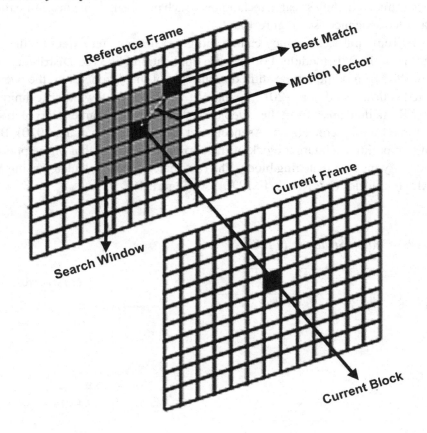

The full or exhaustive search algorithm delivers the optimal solution by traversing all possible blocks within the search window. However, it has a bottleneck of high computational time which needs to be reduced significantly to improve the efficiency. A number of fast block motion estimation algorithms were considered such as Diamond Search (DS) (Shan Zhu & Kai-Kuang Ma, 2000), Cross-Diamond Search (CSD) (Chun-Ho Cheng & Lai-Man Po, 2002), Novel Hexagon-based Search (NHS) (Ce Zhu et al., 2004) and Efficient Three Step Search (E3SS) (Xuan Jung & Lappui Chau, 2004). The Diamond Search Motion Estimation Algorithm has been incorporated in the recently developed H.265/HEVC video coding standard. All these algorithms primarily concentrate upon minimizing the search time which is accomplished in two ways; having different search patterns or reduced number of search points. To effectively minimize the search time involved in ME module, an Efficient Motion Estimation Algorithm is employed.

The second section will give a brief overview on the motion estimation methods employed in HEVC and its predecessors. The third section will provide a detailed discussion of the efficient and simple Efficient Motion Estimation algorithms and its integration within the motion estimation algorithms. The experiments are performed on various SIF (Source Input Format) and CIF (Common Intermediate Format) video sequences and a comparison is drawn between the existing and the Efficient Motion Estimation algorithm and is discussed in the fourth section.

EXISTING METHODS

As far as the predictive coding (Netravali. A.N. & Robbins. J.D., 2004; Netravali. A.N. & Limb. J.O., 1985; Kappagantula. S. & Rao. K.R., 1985) is concerned, the prediction is carried out by adopting any one of the Block Matching Algorithms and the difference between the current and the predicted frame is encoded. Generally, BMA are employed to estimate the Motion Vectors.

A video sequence consists of many frames. Upon considering an individual frame, a rectangular region is considered and the search operations are performed. This region denotes the Search Area of that particular frame. The basic assumption made is that Turbulence is a very rare phenomenon expected in a video sequence consisting of a number of frames where an object in one frame tends to move between the adjacent frames by a particular distance called the Maximum Displacement. The thumb rule employed here is that when the value assumed for the maximum displacement is larger, then the accuracy of reconstruction will tend to be greater i.e., the accuracy of reconstruction of the objects in a particular frame is directly proportional to the value of the maximum displacement.

In the full or exhaustive search technique, block matching is performed on all the blocks in the search area of that frame. The Motion Vector (MV) depict the location of the matching block from the reference frame taking into consideration the position of the target block in the current frame. The parameter used to denote the distortion that occurs between the current and the reference blocks is Mean Squared Error (MSE) or the Mean Absolute Difference (MAD). As the computational complexity of MSE is high when compared to MAD, MAD will serve as the efficient measure for distortion. Let us consider a macro block A of size M x N located at the coordinates (x, y) of the current frame and another block B present in the previous or reference frame. The Mean Absolute Difference (MAD) can be depicted symbolically as:

$$MAD = \frac{1}{MN} \Sigma_{i=0}^{M-1} \Sigma_{j=0}^{N-1} \left| C_{ij} - R_{ij} \right| \tag{1}$$

where, C_{ij} and R_{ij} represent the pixel intensity in the current and previously processed frames respectively. After the computation of MAD value, the macro block in location (x, y) with minimum Mean Absolute Difference (m-MAD) is identified. The magnitude of MAD is indirectly proportional to the accuracy of the prediction. The Bit sequences are set after the determination of Motion Vectors and the difference between the predicted and original frame are encoded along with them. However, the time complexity is very high for the above mentioned procedure. To mitigate this problem, several fast block matching motion estimation algorithms are introduced to minimize the search time (Ohm et al., 2012). A few notable fast BMA are considered for evaluation and full or exhaustive search serves as the benchmark for comparison. Some of the search patterns employed in HEVC include the square and diamond search patterns (see Figure 4).

Cross Diamond Search (CDS) Algorithm

In the CDS algorithm, the initial step involves a cross-shaped search pattern and the subsequent steps involve small/large diamond search patterns. The initial cross-search pattern involves nine probable locations for which possess relatively high probable candidates that are located both horizontally and vertically at the center of the search window. This design fits the cross-center biased MV distribution characteristics of the frames in the video sequence. It also speeds up the motion estimation of both stationary and quasi-stationary macro blocks.

Figure 4. Square Search Pattern

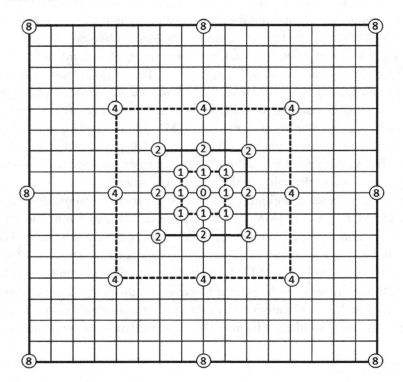

Efficient Three Step Search (E3SS) Algorithm

The E3SS algorithm provides better computational complexity and decent distortion to other fast BMAs. The initial step involves a small diamond search pattern at the center of the search window. If at any one of the points of the 9x9 grid lies in the minimum block distortion measure point, and if it is one of the four points of the small diamond search pattern, then, the small diamond pattern is marked as the minimum point and the rest three points will be traversed.

Novel Hexagon-Based Search (NHS) Algorithm

The NHS algorithm is specifically designed to drastically minimize the search time i.e., achieve faster search speed. To match this characteristic, it employs a circle-shaped search pattern in the initial step. The circle shaped pattern comprises of uniformly distributed minimum number of search points each of which can be equally utilized with efficiency rooting up to the maximum. Two versions of Hexagon-Search exist namely Horizontal and Vertical Hexagon Pattern (see Figure 5 and 6).

Figure 5. Horizontal Hexagon Pattern

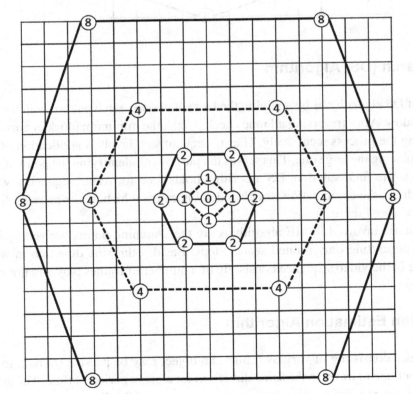

Figure 6. Vertical Hexagon Pattern

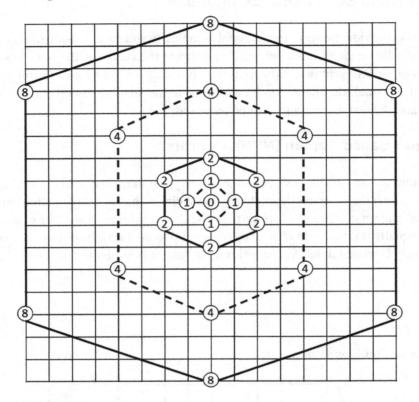

Diamond Search (DS) Algorithm

The initial step of DS algorithm is by applying the large diamond search pattern which is centered origin of the search window. After traversing all nine check points, the minimum block distortion point is identified by repeating the process recursively. The subsequent step involves application of small diamond search pattern replacing the large one. This serves the purpose of identifying the point of minimum block distortion which is the final solution. DS algorithm holds food for frame sequences with wide distortions and also reduces the computation to a considerable extent which marks a reason for DS algorithm included in HEVC (see Figure 7).

The major criteria involved in ME algorithms are the searching points derived by different search patterns thereby permitting only limited search steps. Besides this, the direction in which the object proceeds to move in the video sequence consisting of a number of frames play a major role in minimizing the search time.

Efficient Motion Estimation Algorithm

In a video sequence consisting of various frames, an object may be passive (remain in the same position) or active (continue to travel in the same direction) for a given period of time. The assumption made here is that the object present in the reference frame do not exhibit Turbulence phenomenon. Hence,

Figure 7. Diamond Search Pattern

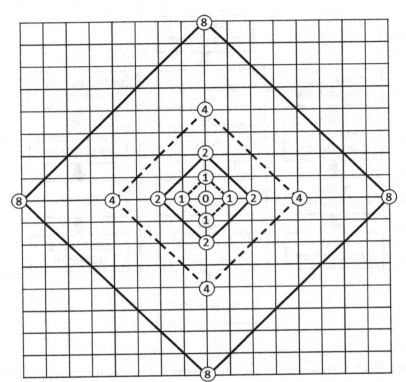

the entire set of candidate blocks need not be searched (as in full or exhaustive search) for comparing the matching and the target block. To avoid this, prediction of the candidate block that is to be searched has to be carried out with a high degree of accuracy with the Motion Vectors (MV) computed from the reference frame. If any degree of coincidence exists in predicting the matching block, then, the MVs computed for the reference frame can be considered as the MVs of the target block. On the other hand, if no coincidence exists, the MVs require Refinement which can be fulfilled by employing any one of the existing fast Block Matching algorithms with a very small search area thereby minimizing the search time (see Figure 8).

The Efficient Motion Estimation (EME) algorithm drastically reduces the search time by adopting the Motion Vector utilizing the relationship that exists between the frames. The algorithm involves two important steps namely: Prediction and Refinement.

Prediction

The EME algorithm predicts the MVs of the current frame using the MVs of the reference frame. The Predicted Motion Vectors (PMVs) for all macro blocks in the current frame are initialized to (0,0) well before the execution of the Prediction step.

Figure 8. Flow Chart of Motion Estimation module

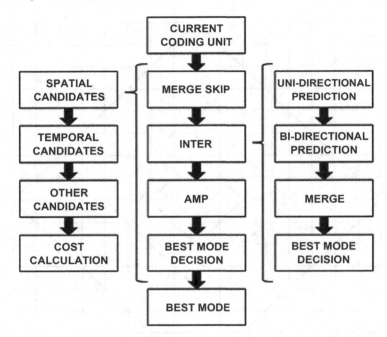

Let us consider a block represented by the coordinates (i, j) of both reference frame I_{k-1} and the current frame I_k. As stated earlier, the values of MVs of I_{k-1} are employed to predict the values of MVs of l_k. Let us assume that the MV of the (k-1)th frame to be (m, n). Symbolically,

$$(PMV_{k-1}(i, j)) = (m, n) \tag{2}$$

Then, the PMV of kth frame will eventually be,

$$(PMV_k(i + \psi, j + \phi)) = (m, n) \tag{3}$$

where, (i, j) is the position of the object, $\varphi = \left(\frac{m}{M}\right)$ represent the number of blocks in the vertical direction and $\psi = \left(\frac{n}{N}\right)$ represent the number of blocks in the horizontal direction. The above equation follows the principle that the object at block (i, j) in the frame I_{k-1} can be computed by traversing the block $(i - \psi, \ j - \varphi)$ back from the frame I_{k-2} by the distance (m, n).

For all those macro blocks that were not referred during the prediction step, the PMVs will be initialized to (0, 0). During the refinement step, their MVs are computed by searching the corresponding matches. There occurs a probability that the same macro block can possess more than one PMV. In such cases, the MV that contributes to minimum or least Mean Absolute Difference (MAD) will be taken into consideration.

Refinement

The refinement step is generally carried out to improvise the accuracy of the PMV (see Figure 9 and Table 1).

Let us consider the block (i, j) in the current frame and its Predicted Motion Vector (PMV) to be (m, n). The block (i, j) possesses two PMV namely (0, 0) and (m, n). In this case, the Mean Absolute Differences MAD $_{(i, j)}$ (0, 0) and MAD $_{(i, j)}$ (m, n) are calculated and is compared to identify which of the MAD value is minimum. There exist two possibilities in this case namely:

- MAD $_{(i, j)}$ (0,0) is minimum: Refinement is centered on the block (i, j)

  MAD $_{(i, j)}$ (m, n) is minimum: Refinement is done around the block $(i + \Psi, \ j + \varphi)$

Figure 9. Search patterns

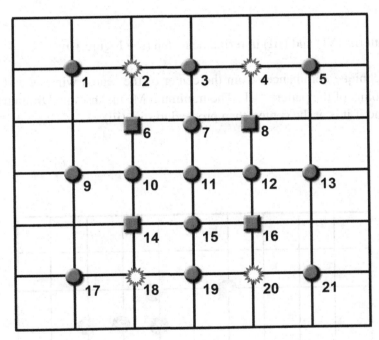

Table 1. Search patterns

Pattern Name	No. of Search Points (NOP)	Search Points
Pattern 'I'	8 Search points	1, 9, 17, 19, 21, 13, 5, 3, 11
Pattern 'II'	8 Search Points	3, 7, 15, 19, 9, 10, 12, 13, 11
Pattern 'III'	8 Search Points	6, 10, 14, 15, 16, 12, 8, 7, 11
Pattern 'IV'	4 Search Points	7, 12, 15, 10, 11
Pattern 'V'	8 Search Points	9, 6, 3, 8, 13, 16, 19, 14, 11
Pattern 'VI'	6 Search Points	2, 4, 13, 20, 18, 9

EME Schemes

EME algorithm is extended with its incremental versions namely, EME1, EME2, EME3, EME4 and EME5 which are referred to as EME Schemes. Different search patterns have been identified and have been employed in each of these schemes. This is to identify which scheme is best suited for specific video sequence. Moreover, the average number of search points in the EME schemes varies from one scheme to another. The most predominantly employed search patterns are identified and are made use of in the Refinement step of the EME Schemes. The following are the various EME schemes formulated using the search patterns:

EME1

All pixels in the small search window centered around the $MAD_{(i,j)}$ (m, n) region are searched with (i + m/M, j + n/N) displacements to locate the best match block.

EME2

Apply searching patterns (VI) and (III) in refinement step (see Figure 10):

- The search technique commences from the center of the search window and it traverses all the eight search points of the pattern 'VI'. The minimum Mean Absolute Difference (m-MAD) point is identified and if it is at the center, then proceed to step (iii)

Figure 10. EME2

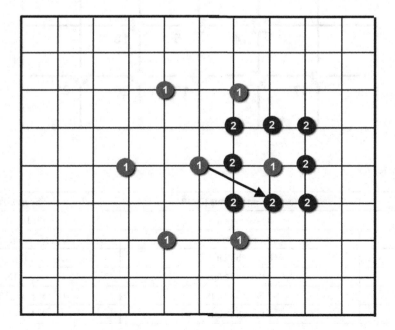

- The m-MAD computed in step (i) is taken up as the center for the new search with pattern 'VI'. Repeat this step recursively until the m-MAD is at the center position
- The pattern 'III' is applied to the new center with m-MAD and the best matching block is spotted for all four search points.

EME3

The EME3 approach involves application of three search patterns 'II', 'V' and 'IV' in the Refinement step (see Figure 11):

- The search technique commences from the center of the search window and it traverses all the eight search points of the pattern 'II'. The minimum Mean Absolute Difference (m-MAD) point is identified and if it is at the center, then proceed to step (iii)
- The m-MAD computed in step (i) is taken up as the center for the new search with pattern 'V'. Repeat this step until the m-MAD is at the center position
- The pattern 'IV' is applied to the new center with m-MAD and the best matching block is spotted for all four search points

EME4

The EME4 approach involves application of two search patterns 'V' and 'IV' in the Refinement step (see Figure 12):

Figure 11. EME3

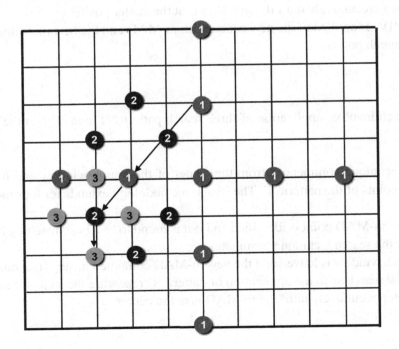

Figure 12. EME4

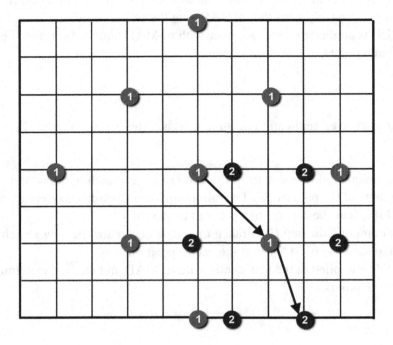

- The search technique commences from the center of the search window and it traverses all the eight search points of the pattern 'V'. The minimum Mean Absolute Difference (m-MAD) point is identified and if it is at the center, then proceed to step (iii)
- The m-MAD computed in step (i) is taken up as the center for the new search with pattern 'V'. Repeat this step recursively until the m-MAD is at the center position
- The pattern 'IV' is applied to the new center with m-MAD and the best matching block is spotted for all four search points.

EME5

The EME5 approach involves application of three search patterns 'I' and 'IV' in the Refinement step (see Figure 13):

- The search technique commences from the center of the search window and it traverses all the eight search points of the pattern 'I'. The search methodology extends for four more points in pattern 'IV'.
- The minimum m-MAD point is identified and if it is found to be a best matching block and located at the center, the search technique terminates.
- The 9x9 search window is halved and the new m-MAD computed in step (i) is taken up as the center for the new search with the application of pattern 'I' repeating the steps for eight other points. Repeat this step recursively until the m-MAD is at the center

Figure 13. EME5

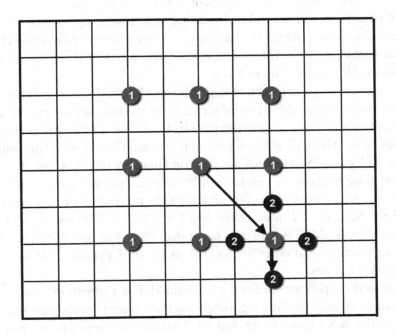

- The newly computed m-MAD search point is considered as the center of the search window with the application of pattern 'VI' repeating the steps for the other four search points.

The refinement step is carried out by adopting any one of the above mentioned procedures at the position of minimum distortion ((m, n) or (0, 0)) as the center. However, the constraint is to maintain the minimum number of search points so as to minimizing the search time consistently.

EXPERIMENTAL RESULTS AND DISCUSSION

This section throws light on the efficiency of the proposed Efficient Motion Estimation (EME) Algorithm in comparison with the existing optimal and sub-optimal fast BMA. Mean Absolute Difference and Average Number of Search Points are the parameters that are commonly employed measures to analyze the performance of the Motion Estimation Module in H.265.

Three different SIF (Source Input Format) of size (352 x 240) and parameters (30 fps, 24 bpp) and a CIF (Common Intermediate Format) of size (352 x 288) and parameters (50 frames, 25 fps, 24 bpp) video sequences were used for carrying out the experiments. The SIF sequences used were Aircraft Sequence (241 frames), Bike sequence and Flower Garden sequence having 147 frames each and the CIF sequence used is the Football video sequence.

The Bike sequence is typically slow varying because the bike is the only object that is in motion and the objects in background remain to be stationary or quasi - stationary and there is no intervention by foreign objects. The Flower Garden sequence opts for faster panning motion of the camera while most of the objects remain stationary. The introduction of foreign objects in the middle of the sequence accounts for a number of interventions that are present. The Air Craft sequence possesses a combination of faster motion of objects with slow, still and panning motion accompanied by a camera zoom. The Football Video Sequence involves large displacement and involvement of local object motion in a swift manner. In addition to this, it also involves different combinations of slow, still, panning motion and faster motion of objects along with camera zoom.

The Table 2 represents the performance of the Efficient Motion Estimation Schemes with the existing optimal and sub-optimal Block Matching algorithms for the Bike sequence. The analysis is carried out by measures like Mean Absolute Difference per pixel and Average Search points where there exists a trade-off between them. The typical High Efficiency Video Coding standard utilize the searching patterns in its Motion Estimation modules are the combinations of DS, CDS, NHS and E3SS only. Hence in this paper, these patterns are compared with different combinations of the proposed Motion Estimation algorithms. As far as the speed of searching the desired block is concerned, EME1 is 4.8 times faster than FS, EME2 is 12.2 times faster than FS, EME3 is 5.8 times faster than FS, EME4 is 9.2 times faster than FS and EME5 is 7.1 times faster than FS. It can be inferred for the Bike sequence that EME2 proves to be faster than other BMAs such as DS by 3.1 times, CDS by 2.4 times, NHS by 1.3 times and E3SS by 2.8 times.

The Table 3 represents the performance of the Efficient Motion Estimation Schemes with the existing optimal and sub-optimal Block Matching algorithms for the Flower Garden sequence. Clearly, it can be demonstrated that EME1 is 5.1 times faster than FS, EME2 is 16.7 times faster than FS, EME3 is 9.1 times faster than FS, EME4 is 11.9 times faster than FS and EME5 is 7.8 times faster than FS. Therefore, EME2 algorithm finds itself to be more efficient as the fastest scheme upon comparison with other BMAs for the Flower Garden sequence. It can be inferred for the Bike sequence that EME2 proves to be faster than other BMAs such as DS by 3.1 times, CDS by 2.4 times, NHS by 1.3 times and E3SS by 2.8 times.

The Table 4 represents the performance of the Efficient Motion Estimation Schemes with the existing optimal and sub-optimal Block Matching algorithms for the Air Craft sequence. Clearly, it can be demonstrated that EME1 is 6.5 times faster than FS, EME2 is 7.68 times faster than FS, EME3 is 6.68

Table 2. Performance evaluation for bike sequence

BMA	MAD per Pixel	Avg. NOP
FS	4.05	225.00
DS	5.02`	45.90
CDS	4.74	47.10
NHS	4.80	33.23
E3SS	5.04	39.54
EME1	4.58	48.02
EME2	5.19	19.32
EME3	4.76	34.81
EME4	5.17	27.67
EME5	5.41	33.07

Table 3. Performance evaluation for flower garden sequence

BMA	MAD per Pixel	Avg. NOP
FS	12.95	225.00
DS	16.30	35.10
CDS	15.00	27.70
NHS	14.00	21.26
E3SS	14.89	27.63
EME1	13.59	43.19
EME2	20.56	17.96
EME3	13.73	25.78
EME4	20.50	12.59
EME5	14.01	29.62

times faster than FS, EME4 is 9.04 times faster than FS and EME5 is 10.75 times faster than FS. The inference from Table 3 is that EME5 clearly outperforms all fast Block Matching Algorithms and other EME schemes considering the measures like Average Search Points and MAD per pixel.

The Table 5 represents the performance of the Efficient Motion Estimation Schemes with the existing optimal and sub-optimal Block Matching algorithms for the Football sequence. The analysis is carried out by measures like Mean Absolute Difference per pixel and Average Search points where there exists a trade-off between them. As far as the speed of searching the desired block is concerned, EME1 is 4.9 times faster than FS, EME2 is 13.9 times faster than FS, EME3 is 9.1 times faster than FS, EME4 is 13.2 times faster than FS and EME5 is 8.6 times faster than FS. It can be inferred for the Bike sequence that EME4 proves to be faster than other BMAs such as DS by 2.7 times, CDS by 2.4 times, NHS by 1.3 times and E3SS by 2.8 times.

The graphs are plotted frame by frame to compare the performances of the EME schemes with the other fast BMAs. The statistical comparisons illustrates that the EME schemes outperform the existing optimal and sub-optimal fast BMAs in terms of average search points per block and MAD per pixel.

The Figures 14, 15 and 16 represent the performance comparison of the proposed EME schemes and existing algorithm with respect to the average number of search points against the frame number. For a video sequence with given number of frames, the lesser the average number of search points and more the Mean Absolute Difference per pixel, reduces the search time to a considerable extent; hence proving to be the most efficient algorithm. The statistical comparisons illustrate that the proposed EME algorithm outperforms the existing optimal and sub-optimal fast Block Matching Algorithms in terms of average search points per block and MAD per pixel. Several other SIF and CIF standard video sequences were also considered for evaluating the performance of the proposed EME algorithm and the results were promising.

Table 4. Performance evaluation for air craft sequence

BMA	MAD per Pixel	Avg. NOP
FS	5.70	225.00
DS	6.73	28.61
CDS	6.98	27.33
NHS	7.23	31.65
E3SS	7.12	24.64
EME1	6.33	34.63
EME2	7.39	24.90
EME3	6.54	33.67
EME4	7.39	29.30
EME5	6.62	20.94

Table 5. Performance evaluation for football sequence

BMA	MAD per Pixel	Avg. NOP
FS	4.09	225.00
DS	4.59	33.84
CDS	5.21	29.80
NHS	4.92	21.20
E3SS	4.78	34.08
EME1	4.91	45.92
EME2	6.15	17.18
EME3	4.89	24.73
EME4	5.18	14.56
EME5	5.97	26.16

Figure 14. Frame by Frame average number of search point's performance evaluation among EME2 and fast BMAs for Flower Garden Sequence

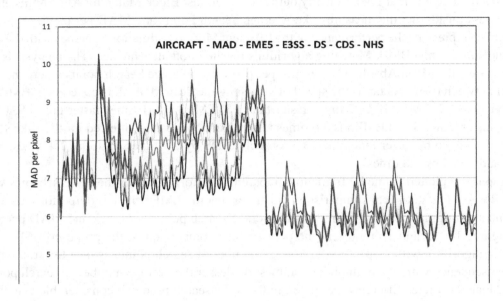

Figure 15. Frame by Frame average number of search point's performance evaluation among EME2 and fast BMAs for Air Craft Sequence

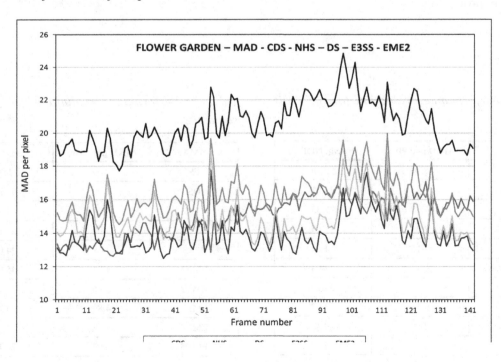

Figure 16. Frame by Frame average number of search point's performance evaluation among EME2 and fast BMAs for Football Sequence

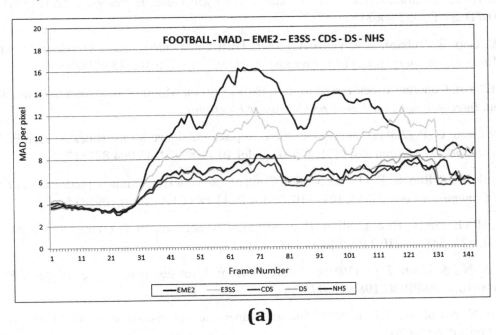

(a)

CONCLUSION

The Efficient Motion Estimation Algorithm for Fast Motion Estimation delivers desirable results in increasing the efficiency of High Efficiency Video Coding Standard encoder. The direction of the reference frame is used for predicting the MV of the candidate block. The different Data Schemes play a major role in the refinement step of the algorithm hence minimizing the search time. The performance of the EME algorithm is compared with the bench-mark Full or Exhaustive Search and well known Fast Block Motion Estimation algorithm like the DS, CDS, E3SS and NHS. The simulation results obtained from the experiments on different SIF and CIF video sequences clearly illustrate that; in terms of search points, the EME algorithms outperform the benchmark FS algorithm and in terms of average search points per block and MAD per pixel, the different versions of EME simulated in this work proves efficient over the fast BMAs used in High Efficiency Video Coding for different set of video sequences.

REFERENCES

Ascenso, J., Brites, C., & Pereira, F. (2005). Improving Frame Interpolation with Spatial Motion Smoothing for Pixel Domain Distributed Video Coding. *Proc. EURASIP Conference on Speech and Image Processing, Multimedia Communications and Services.*

Cafforio, C., & Rocca, F. (1976). Methods for measuring small displacements of television images. *IEEE Transactions on Information Theory, 22*(5), 573–579. doi:10.1109/TIT.1976.1055602

Cheung, C.-H., & Po, L.-M. (2002). A novel cross-diamond search algorithm for fast block motion estimation. *IEEE Transactions on Circuits and Systems for Video Technology*, *12*(12), 1168–1177. doi:10.1109/TCSVT.2002.806815

Dufaux, W., Gao, W., Tubaro, S., & Vetro, A. (2009). Distributed video coding: Trends and perspectives. *EURASIP Journal on Image and Video Processing*, *2009*, 1–13. doi:10.1155/2009/508167

Hong, H. (2010). Coherent Block-Based Motion Estimation for Motion-Compensated Frame Rate Up-Conversion. *International Conference on Consumer Electronics*.

Jing, X., & Chau, L.-P. (2004). An efficient three-step search algorithm for Block Motion Estimation. *IEEE Transactions on Multimedia*, *6*(3), 435–438. doi:10.1109/TMM.2004.827517

Kappagantula, S., & Rao, K. R. (1985). Motion Compensated interframe image prediction. *IEEE Transactions on Communications*, *33*(9), 1011–1015. doi:10.1109/TCOM.1985.1096415

Musmann, H. G., Pirsch, P., & Grallert, H.-J. (1985). Advances in picture coding. *Proceedings of the IEEE*, *73*(4), 523–548. doi:10.1109/PROC.1985.13183

Netravali, A. N., & Limb, J. O. (1980). Picture Coding: A review. *Proceedings of the IEEE*, *68*(3), 366–406. doi:10.1109/PROC.1980.11647

Netravali, A. N., & Robbins, J. D. (2004). Motion Compensated television coding: Part I. *The Bell System Technical Journal*, 631–670.

Ohm, J. R., Sullivan, G. J., Schwarz, H., Tan, T. K., & Wiegand, T. (2012). Comparison of the coding efficiency of video coding standards – Including High Efficiency Video Coding (HEVC). *IEEE Transactions on Circuits and Systems for Video Technology*, *22*(12), 1668–1683. doi:10.1109/TCSVT.2012.2221192

Purnachand, N., Alves, & Navarro. (2012). Fast Motion Estimation Algorithm for HEVC. *Proc. IEEE Second International Conference on Consumer Electronics (ICCE)*.

Sullivan, G. J., Ohm, J. R., Han, W. J., & Wiegand, T. (2012). Overview of high efficiency video coding (HEVC) standard. *IEEE Transactions on Circuits and Systems for Video Technology*, *12*(12), 1649–1668. doi:10.1109/TCSVT.2012.2221191

Zhu, C., Lin, X., Chau, L., & Po, L.-M. (2004). Enhanced Hexagonal search for fast block motion estimation. *IEEE Transactions on Circuits and Systems for Video Technology*, *14*(10), 1210–1214. doi:10.1109/TCSVT.2004.833166

Zhu, S., & Ma, K.-K. (2000). A new diamond search algorithm for fast block-matching motion estimation. *IEEE Transactions on Image Processing*, *9*(3), 287–290. doi:10.1109/TIP.2000.826791 PMID:18255398

Chapter 7
Multi–Modal Fusion Schemes for Image Retrieval Systems to Bridge the Semantic Gap

Nidhi Goel
University of Delhi, India

Priti Sehgal
University of Delhi, India

ABSTRACT

Image retrieval (IR) systems are used for searching of images by means of diverse modes such as text, sample image, or both. They suffer with the problem of semantic gap which is the mismatch between the user requirement and the capabilities of the IR system. The image data is generally stored in the form of statistics of the value of the pixels which has very little to do with the semantic interpretation of the image. Therefore, it is necessary to understand the mapping between the two modalities i.e. content and context. Research indicates that the combination of the two can be a worthwhile approach to improve the quality of image search results. Hence, multimodal retrieval (MMR) is an expected way of searching which attracts substantial research consideration. The main challenges include discriminatory feature extraction and selection, redundancy identification and elimination, information preserving fusion and computational complexity. Based on these challenges, in this chapter, authors focus on comparison of various MMR systems that have been used to improve the retrieval results.

INTRODUCTION

We are living in the age of information where the amount of accessible data from science and culture is almost limitless. Multimedia is one of the most interesting and exciting aspects of this information era (Guan et al., 2010). By name, it represents a combination of information content from different media sources in various forms. Examples are audio, video, image, and text each of which can be considered as a modality in multimodal multimedia representation. Development in the data storage media and acquisition techniques has led to the availability of huge amount of multimedia information/data, from

DOI: 10.4018/978-1-4666-9685-3.ch007

medical domain to web to personal data collection. However, finding an item of interest is increasingly difficult. In area of search, the greatest societal impact has been in WWW image search engines and recommendation systems. Google, Yahoo!, and Bing are the image search engines used by millions of people daily. Recommendation systems such as Amazon (Linden, Smith, & York, 2003), napster (Napster, 2001) recommend from books to clothing, movies to music based on priorities selected by user. Another worthy example is Getty images (Machin, 2004) where user is assumed knowledgeable which is reflected by image search engine through multimodal interactive search by content, context, style, composition, and user feedback. All the systems mentioned above fall under one category i.e. image retrieval systems.

So, what is an image retrieval system? Image retrieval (IR) system is a computerized system for browsing, searching, and retrieving images from a large database of digital images. Apart from personal albums (e.g., Flickr, photo bucket, Picasa web album and photo.net) and general-purpose image collections (e.g., Google Images and Yahoo! Images), IR systems are used in various applications like face matching, fingerprint matching in biometrics, X-rays and tumors matching in medical applications, tattoo and scar matching in crime detection, scene matching in surveillance, satellite image matching in GIS and remote sensing, sketch matching in archeological, art and fashion application, disease detection in crops, food quality evaluation, defect detection for machines in industry and the list goes on. As processing has now become increasingly powerful and memory has become cheaper, the deployment of large multimedia datasets for various applications has relatively become easier and efficient.

Till date, there have been various research techniques for indexing and searching the multimedia data (Datta, Joshi, Li, & Wang, 2008). Co-existence of multimodal information demands a retrieval system to search results across various multimedia objects (J. Liu, Xu, & Lu, 2010). Therefore, cross-media retrieval is an expected way of searching which has become increasingly important and attracts substantial research consideration. It enables users to query in more than one mode. Typically, for image retrieval systems, text and content are the two most common modes of query. For decades, image retrieval has evolved from text based (1980s) to content based (1990s) to fuzzy image retrieval (2004) (Singhai & Shandilya, 2010).

Text-Based Image Retrieval (TBIR) Systems

In TBIR systems, the images are retrieved from the database based upon the text annotations (or metadata) associated with the images (H. Zhang, Jiang, & Zhang, 2009). Apache Lucene is amongst the initial TBIR systems that requires full-text search (Jakarta, 2004). Chang et al. (N.-S. Chang & K. S. Fu, 1980) have used an approach in which they first annotate the image with text and then use text-based database management system for IR. Enhancements in data modeling, multidimensional indexing, and query evaluation has generated many new retrieval systems. One representative of such system is QPE (N.-S. Chang & K.-S. Fu, 1980) in which queries were specified in terms of only the defined vocabulary of the database. The user selects from those predefined queries only and the corresponding results are displayed. PICQUERY (Joseph & Cardenas, 1988) is another text-based IR system which provides a high-level query language for specifying the textual-query for pictorial database management system (PDBMS). TBIR is beneficial due to two reasons, first is the user-friendliness as user can easily compose queries using their natural language. Second, it provides better results and is useful in applications where more semantic relationships are involved (Jain & Sinha, 2010). However nowadays TBIR is considered to be laborious and time consuming task of manual annotations (Alemu, Koh, Ikram, & Kim, 2009). Additionally, text-annotations are user-biased i.e. in what context the user is annotating an image differs from user to user. For example: "an image of red car" userA may annotate it as car.jpg, userB can annotate it with redcar.jpg or userC can name it like DSC_103.jpg. This may lead to inconsistency (Pavlidis, 2008). Another disadvantage associated with TBIR is that it provides hit-miss type searching of images. If keyword provided matches with annotated text then only image is retrieved otherwise the desired image is unreachable. On the other side, if erroneously some image is not annotated properly it may result in garbage data also. So a method was required to produce results that are more accurate. Then the content-based image retrieval (CBIR) systems came into existence.

Content-Based Image Retrieval (CBIR) Systems

CBIR is an IR technique which is based on visual content (Color, shape, texture and spatial layout) (Long, Zhang, & Feng, 2003; Gudivada & Raghavan, 1995) to search images from large image databases. Xu et al.(Xu, Xu, & Men, 2010) says that image retrieval based on feature similarity matching extracted from the rich content of an image performs better than the text query provided for the same. It has been observed that most CBIR approaches are based on the color visual content. However the selection and criteria for choosing visual content changes with application. A CBIR system for iris matching uses color texture and shape as feature descriptor (Choras, 2007). Another system Sketch4Match uses color as the feature descriptor for matching of a sketch with the corresponding image (Szántó, Pozsegovics, Vámossy, & Sergyán, 2011). A clip art retrieval system (Mourato & Jesus, 2014) used color moments as the feature descriptor for extracting the color information. Authors (Yue, Li, Liu, & Fu, 2011) developed a CBIR system in which they used color and texture feature for image similarity matching. In stock photography, color has been the most effective feature, however for medical applications texture and shape feature are important than color feature (Müller, Michoux, Bandon, & Geissbuhler, 2004). Authors (Kannan, Mohan, & Anbazhagan, 2010) in their work proposed a CBIR system which was based on entropy texture feature. CBIR gives better result where application contains more of visual content rather than semantic content. For e.g.:- CBIR is suitable for queries in medical diagnosis involving comparison of an X-ray picture with previous cases. However, suppose, if a query demands retrieval of images of "cancerous tissues/ cells", or "A man holding shooting camera". In these examples, text outweighs visual content (Hartvedt, 2010) and it is not clear what kind of image should be retrieved . Now here CBIR fails because of the fact that visual features cannot fully represent the semantic concepts.

Hybrid Systems

As discussed above, we can conclude that both TBIR systems and CBIR systems have their own individu- alities and pros and cons. Efforts have been made by the researchers to combine these two approaches to provide us with satisfactory results (N. Zhang & Song, 2008). In 1999 an important research work was done focusing on Content based retrieval inspired from text retrieval (Squire, Müller, Müller, & Raki, 1998). Abbas et al. (Abbas, Qadri, Idrees, Awan, & Khan, 2010) suggests that combination of both text and content could better the performance of search systems benefitting both the approaches. It is based upon the idea if ability to examine the image content does not exist, and then search depends upon meta- data like captions/keywords. It says that TBIR is as fast as CBIR. An effort has been made to combine content and semantics in medical domain also. Authors Jin et al., proposed a scheme *MedImGrid* to combine CBIR and semantics using grid computing. Shape, color and texture features of every medical image was extracted and Euclidean distance metric was used for the similarity matching of visual content of the image (Jin et al., 2007). Semantic context information extracted was used as clue to improve efficiency. The Authors (Luo, Wang, & Tang, 2003) developed a hybrid image retrieval system for World Wide Web using both text and image content features. They first used a text-based image meta-search engine to retrieve images from the Web based on the text information. Text-based approach was used by authors due to its high speed and low cost nature. An image content based ordering was then performed on the initial image set. In addition, user feedback was used to rerank the ordered set of images. In the paper (Gao et al., 2013), an approach was proposed that simultaneously utilizes both visual and textual information for social image search. Both visual content and tags were used to generate the hyperedges of a hypergraph, and a relevance learning procedure was performed on the hypergraph structure where a set of pseudo-relevant samples were employed. It has been pointed out that diversity is also important for improving the search results.

Underlying hypothesis is that such approaches will make it easier for an IR system to understand the user's intention behind a search. However, finding the correlation between low-level features and high-level concepts to bridge the gap between visual features and semantic content has been a major challenge in this research field.

Semantic Gap

The main challenge that persists today also is the problem of semantic gap. According to Smeulders et al. (Smeulders, Worring, Santini, Gupta, & Jain, 2000), semantic gap is the mismatch between the user requirement and the capabilities of the image retrieval (IR) system. Semantic gap is the gap between human impressions ("semantics") and quantities that can be computed ("features") (Pavlidis, 2008). The semantic interpretation of an image has very little to do with the statistics of the value of the pixels. The image data is generally stored in systems in the form of value of the pixels. On the contrary, the humans who need to search these large image datasets express their query by using the text (context) in the form of keywords. Therefore, it is necessary to understand the mapping between the two modalities i.e. content and context. Content is the statistical interpretation of image in terms of color, texture, shape, spatial relationships. It corresponds to low-level features. Context is highly subjective i.e. it differs from one user to another in how he/she interprets the image. Two different persons can interpret the same image in their own different ways. Context can be retrieved from the text or by applying extreme algorithms and mathematics on low-level features. Context refers to high-level concepts. Two important factors contribute to semantic gap. Firstly, users are unable to formulate the query properly i.e. there may be a difference between the image query and textual query provided by them. Secondly, IR systems lack the understanding of user intention behind the query. Later is known as intention gap (H. Zhang et al., 2009), (Hua, Worring, & Chua, 2013). Over the years, it has been realized that both text and content are necessary for retrieving good results. Their combination helps in reducing the semantic gap. Research results by (Zhou, Eggel, & Müller, 2010) and (Müller, Ruch, & Geissbühler, 2004) indicate that a combination of text and image contents can be a worthwhile approach to improve the quality of image result sets. The experiments conducted by (Christel, 2007) show that using multiple access strategies on CBIR reveal good results rather than using CBIR alone. Four access strategies are used namely query-by-text, query-by-image, query-by-bestoftopic, and query-by-concept. Grosky et al., (Grosky, Agrawal, & Fotouchi, 2008) have emphasized that there is need for finding and managing the correlation between low-level features and high-level semantics information. (Westman, Lustila, & Oittinen, 2008) demonstrated the search strategies in multimodal retrieval systems and it was observed that text was the main query mode amongst the text, color, sketch, and category modes. Zhang et al., (N. Zhang & Song, 2008) have also combined the two approaches to overcome the drawbacks of pure content-based approach and pure text based approach. For text matching, full-text index created using SQL was used. For content retrieval, the weighted combination of color layout, edge histogram, and auto-correlogram was used. Authors (Jain & Sinha, 2010) say that content without context is meaningless. They give four reasons to support their study and present approaches that appropriately combine content with context to bridge the semantic gap. A web image search engine Extended CBIR (ExCBIR) was proposed (Gui, Liu, Xu, & Lu, 2010), which learns the semantics of query image. It weightily combines the two vectors (text and image) into semantic representation of query image according to different confidence of each feature. In the proposed system (Seetharaman & Sathiamoorthy, 2014), the semantic gap between the low-level visual features and high-level semantic concepts perceived by the users was reduced by adopting the query refinement approach of short-term learning based relevance feedback (RF) mechanism. Here, user marks the retrieved images as relevant, highly relevant, and irrelevant to the query image. Author in (Hartvedt, 2010) discusses how combining existing techniques may help improve the understanding of user intentions in IR. Liu et al., (Y. Liu, Zhang, Lu, & Ma, 2007) identified five major categories of the state-of-the-art techniques in narrowing down the 'semantic gap': (1) using object ontology to define high-level concepts; (2) using machine learning methods to associate low-level features with query concepts; (3) using relevance feedback to learn users' intention; (4) generating semantic template to support high-level image retrieval; (5) fusing the evidences from HTML text and the visual content of images for WWW image retrieval. Abbas et al., suggest that combination of both text and content improves the performance of search systems gaining from both the approaches (Abbas et al., 2010). Moreover, it is shown that multimodal information is capable of providing a more complete and effective description of the features, producing improved system performance than single modality only (Guan et al., 2010). Therefore, the major task of the image retrieval system is to help the users in the retrieval of images in the efficient manner using the depicted keyword query or image content query.

The main challenges in multi-media retrieval include discriminatory feature extraction and selection, redundancy identification and elimination, information preserving fusion and computational complexity (Guan et al., 2010). In this chapter, we discuss our contribution to the related areas. Specifically, fusion of text and content for image retrieval is discussed based on semantics and user's intention. Rest of the chapter is organized as, first the overview of the commonly used feature extraction and representation techniques in TBIR, CBIR are discussed. Then the fusion techniques are reviewed in detail and how they play an important role in depicting the user's intention thereby improving the retrieval results.

OVERVIEW

Feature Representation

How to describe the image is always one of imperative issues in computer vision. An effective feature representation is indeed the first step to achieve a satisfied multimedia retrieval. Further details intricate a few of the common feature representations for both text and content. For content representation, specifically color feature representations are discussed.

Textual Feature Representation

Typically textual information is represented with TF-IDF (term frequency-inverse document frequency) based word vector weighting (Salton, Wong, & Yang, 1975). Other popular techniques used for textual information representation includes document clustering (Griffiths, Luckhurst, & Willett, 1997), latent semantic indexing (LSI) (Manning, Raghavan, & Schütze, 2008), natural language processing (NLP) (Strzalkowski, 1995).

Tf-idf

Tf-idf is a vector space model where text is represented by a vector of terms. Before applying tf-idf weighting to the words, preprocessing of the documents (images) is done. Pre-processing functions for tokenization and stopword removal are applied on the processed metadata (title, description, notes, location etc.). These words are then tokenized using Porter Stemmer Algorithm (Van Rijsbergen, Robertson, & Porter, 1980). After stemming, words are known as tokens and set of these tokens is known as vocabulary. An inverted index is built with an entry for each token in the vocabulary obtained. Hash tables are used for creating the inverted index as they permit the fast access of the data (Stata, Bharat, & Maghoul, 2000). After creating inverted index, weights are assigned to the indexed terms/tokens. The term frequency-inverse document frequency (tf-idf) weight of a term is the product of its term frequency (tf) weight and its inverse document frequency (idf) weight. The tf(t,d) of term t in document d is defined as the number of times term 't' occurs in document 'd' and idf is a measure of whether the term is common or rare across all documents. The weight, $W_{t,d}$ assigned to the tokens is calculated using Equation (1).

$$w_{t,d} = \log(1 + \mathrm{tf}_{t,d}) \times \log_{10}(N \,/\, \mathrm{df}_t) \tag{1}$$

where:

N represents the total number of documents.
$\mathrm{tf}_{t,d}$ is the term-frequency.
df_t is the document frequency of term 't' i.e. the number of documents that contain 't'.

Advantage of tf-idf weighting scheme is that the documents and the query are represented as vectors. The key idea behind this representation is that we can easily rank documents according to their proximity (similarity of vectors) to the query in the vector space.

Text Retrieval and Ranking

For ranking of the documents based on textual similarity, euclidean distance, cosine similarity are the common methods. Euclidean distance/metric gives the distance between the two documents that can be quite large for vectors of different lengths. Whereas, cosine similarity tells the angle between two vectors (Salton et al., 1975). The angle between two most similar documents is zero. Hence, the cosine similarity scores are calculated between a query and each document using the Equation (2).

$$\cos(\vec{q}, \vec{d}) = \frac{\vec{q} \bullet \vec{d}}{|\vec{q}||\vec{d}|} = \frac{\vec{q}}{|\vec{q}|} \bullet \frac{\vec{d}}{|\vec{d}|} = \frac{\sum_{i=1}^{|V|} q_i d_i}{\sqrt{\sum_{i=1}^{|V|} q_i^2} \sqrt{\sum_{i=1}^{|V|} d_i^2}} \qquad (2)$$

where:

q_i is the tf-idf weight of term i in the query.
d_i is the tf-idf weight of term i in the document.
cos(q,d) is the cosine similarity of q and d or equivalently, the cosine of the angle between q and d.

Since cosine function is monotonically decreasing function, value of 1 represents the perfect match and 0 means the worst match.

Levenshtein Distance Approach: Fuzzy String Matching

Levenshtein (Levenshtein, 1966) approach is used for fuzzy string matching. Fuzzy string matching means matching the pattern in words approximately rather than exactly (Navarro, 2001). It calculates the number of edits i.e. insertion and deletions required to match the two strings. The distance of a match is measured in terms of the number of basic operations are required to convert the string into an exact match. This number is called the edit distance. The usual basic operations are:

- **Insertion:** e.g. gren → green
- **Deletion:** e.g. waters → water

The number of edits obtained from fuzzy string matching is converted to match percentage using Equation (3).

$$strDist = 1.0 - (LevenshteinDist(s1, s2)) \, / \, \max(s1, s2) \qquad (3)$$

where, LevenshteinDist (s1, s2) = edit distance between s1, s2, s1 = length of string1, s2 = length of string2

The subsequent example demonstrates how the match percentage is obtained using the edit distance between two strings.

Example: To match "building" with "buildings."

n = 1 using Levenshtein distance, s1 = 8, s2 = 9

max(s1,s2) = 9

strDist = 1- 1/9

strDist = 0.88 or we can say 88.8% which is good enough.

Fuzzy string matching approach overcomes the hit/miss type search. Suppose the text query entered by user is "cherry" but the annotations available in dB do not have word cherry but instead they have "cherries". Using tf-idf approach, the result is based on exact search and no match for the query will be returned. The images with annotation "cherries" would be missed although the word is just the plural of the word in query. Now on other hand, if we use fuzzy string matching then the search will return 0.5 (50% match) for the query which is good enough to match the results. So we will not at least miss the images which are tagged "cherries" and not exactly "cherry". Therefore, fuzzy string matching approach helps to overcome the disadvantage of hit/miss type search for TBIR systems.

Content Representation

Color

One of the most important features a human uses for visual communication is color. It is the most prominent perceptual features of an image. Color is a property that depends on the reflection of light to the eye and the processing of that information(reflection) in the brain (Wang, 2001). Usually colors are defined in three dimensional color spaces. These could be RGB (Red, Green, and Blue), HSV (Hue, Saturation, and Value), or HSB (Hue, Saturation, and Brightness). RGB is the simpler color space in terms of computation but it not used because the values changes with illumination change in the image. The last two are dependent on the human perception of hue, saturation, and brightness. Several approaches such as color histogram, color moments, color correlogram, color autocorrelogram and MPEG-7 based scalable color descriptor (SCD), dominant color descriptor (DCD), color layout descriptor (CLD), and color structure descriptor (CSD) have been used in the literature to represent the color information of an image. In brief, color histogram and color moments and fuzzy color histogram techniques are elaborated.

- *Color Histogram*

Conventional color histogram (CCH) is the approach more frequently adopted for CBIR systems (Suhasini, Krishna, & KRISHNA IV, 2009). A color histogram describes the frequency of colors in images. CCH has advantage of simplicity, ease of calculation (Patil & Dalal, 2011) and low demand of memory space (Jin et al., 2007). A color histogram does not change with the variations of pictures' geometry, so it is a widely used feature for image indexing although it has some disadvantages associated with it. CCH is sensitive to noisy interferences. Small change in image might result in large change in histogram values. Since CCH is three-Dimensional (3-D), similarity matching for CCH proves to be computationally expensive.

- *Color Moments*

Color moments have proven to be a successful technique for indexing images based on color (Kodituwakku & Selvarajah, 2004). Their correctness outweighs classic color indexing techniques such as cumulative color indexing (Stricker & Orengo, 1995). The three color moments namely the first order (mean), the second (standard deviation) and the third order (skewness) values can be calculated for any number of color channels in any of the color space like RGB, HSV, etc. For instance, color channels in

RGB space are Red, Green Blue, and HSV are Hue, Saturation, and Value. Equations (4), (5), and (6) gives the formula for the three moments respectively.

1st Moment – Mean:

$$E_i = \frac{1}{n} \sum_{j=1}^{n} p_{ij} \tag{4}$$

2nd Moment – Standard Deviation:

$$\sigma_i = \sqrt{\frac{1}{n} \sum_{j=1}^{n} (p_{ij} - E_i)^2} \tag{5}$$

3rd Moment – Skewness:

$$S_i = \sqrt[3]{\frac{1}{n} \sum_{j=1}^{n} (p_{ij} - E_i)^3} \tag{6}$$

where:

p_{ij} = value of ith color channel for jth pixel of image
n – Number of pixels in the image
E_i – mean of image for ith color channel
σ_i – standard deviation of image for ith color channel
S_i – skewness of image for ith color channel
i – Color channel index

For instance, if color moments are to be calculated in HSV color space, then variable 'i', can take values from 1-3 (i.e. 1 = H, 2 = S, 3 = V).Hence the feature vector for the image contains 9 values in the form of 3X3 matrix of the following format:-

$$\begin{bmatrix} E_{11} & E_{12} & E_{13} \\ \sigma_{11} & \sigma_{12} & \sigma_{13} \\ S_{11} & S_{12} & S_{13} \end{bmatrix}$$

where:

$E_{11} \, E_{12} \, E_{13}$ represents Mean value for HSV components.
$\sigma_{11} \, \sigma_{12} \, \sigma_{13}$ represents Standard deviation value for HSV.
$S_{11} \, S_{12} \, S_{13}$ represents Skewness value for HSV.
   ◦ *Fuzzy Color Histogram (FCH)*

As discussed, CCH is the approach more frequently adopted for CBIR systems but it has some short-comings. Those shortcomings can be resolved by using fuzzy color histogram (FCH) (Konstantinidis, Gasteratos, & Andreadis, 2005). FCH is computed using fuzzy histogram linking approach. It computes the color similarity information by spreading each pixel's total membership value to all the histogram bins, in contrary to CCH, which calculates the color similarity by finding the probability of each pixel value. Besides CCH is 3-Dimensional (3D), so they are computationally expensive. Fuzzy histogram linking projects 3D to 1D histogram and makes resulting FCH computationally less intensive and much less sensitive to noisy interferences. We can say that fuzzy histogram linking approach has 2-fold advantages. Firstly, it acquires the benefits of CCH and secondly resolves the sensitivity and computational complexity issue of CCH. Further, Fuzzy histogram linking approach is elaborated.

Fuzzy Histogram Linking Approach

Fuzzy histogram linking approach (Konstantinidis et al., 2005) is based on the L*a*b color space as it is perceptually more uniform color space. The a* and b* components are subdivided into five regions representing green, greenish, the middle of the component, reddish, red for a*, blue, bluish, the middle of the component, yellowish and yellow for b*, whereas L* is divided into three regions: black, grey and white. The fuzzification is done using triangular shaped built in membership functions (MF) for L*, a*, b*. The fuzzy linking of three components (L*, a*, b*) is made according to 27 fuzzy rules, which lead to the output of the system. The a* and b* components are given more weightage than L* as they provide most color information of the image. The defuzzification process is done along the 10 MFs that lead to 10 bin final fuzzy histogram. Since only 10 bins are used to describe the color distribution of image and 3-D histogram is projected to 1-D histogram, comparison of histograms becomes faster.

Similarity Measure and Image Matching

Different similarity measures affect the performance of IR systems considerably. Good integration of similarity measure and the image feature should be used to calculate the similarity between the two images (Bugatti, Traina, & Traina Jr, 2008). L1 distance metric, quadratic form distance (QFD), Canberra distance, Mahalanobis distance, L2 distance, and L∞ distance metric are some of the commonly used distance metrics for image retrieval. Further, QFD, euclidean or L1 distance metric are introduced in brief.

- *QFD*

This similarity measure is used to find out the distance between the histogram bins. It can lead to perceptually more desirable results than euclidean distance and histogram intersection method as it considers the cross similarity between colors. However, QFD has a disadvantage of being computational expensive. Suppose if a histogram has 'n' number of bins, then it requires 'n x n' calculations for cross similarity matching. Therefore, the complexity is $O(n^2)$. This makes the method computationally very expensive but provides good visually similar results. The formula for QFD is given by Equation (7).

$$D_{QI} = \sqrt{(H_Q - H_I)^T * A * (H_Q - H_I)} \qquad (7)$$

where:

D_{QI} = distance between the query image Q and database image I.
A = [aij] is a similarity matrix, and aij denotes the similarity between bin i and j.
HQ = histogram bins of the Query Image Q
HI = Histogram bins of the database Image I

   ◦   *Euclidean Distance or L1 Distance*

Euclidean or L1 distance performs well among all the distance metric (Bugatti et al., 2008). L1 distance is calculated using Equation (8).

$$d(I,J) = \sum_{k=1}^{n} \left| x_k(I) - x_k(J) \right| \qquad (8)$$

where, d(I,J) is the distance between image I and image J, k is dimension of the feature vector x, x_k is the kth dimension of feature vector x for image, k = 1,2,.....,n and n is the number of dimensions of the feature.

Understanding Semantic Gap

To lessen the semantic gap, we need to understand the mapping between textual and visual query to exploit both the modalities to their utmost. At querying time, retrieval methods based on text mode and content mode returns a list of images tentatively relevant to a given query. The output of the different retrieval methods is then combined for obtaining a single list of ranked images. As discussed earlier in literature survey, accuracy of the combined approach is higher than the individual system. Tremendous amount of work is done in reducing the semantic gap.

Semantic Similarity

Semantic similarity or semantic relatedness is a metric defined over a set terms, where the notion of distance between them is based on the similarity of their meaning or semantic content as opposed to similarity which can be estimated using their syntactical representation (e.g. their string / word format) (Harispe, Ranwez, Janaqi, & Montmain, 2013). Mathematically, it is a numerical description used to estimate the strength of the semantic relationship between units of language, concepts, or instances. Several similarity measures have been proposed to find out the semantic similarity in taxonomy such as WordNet.

●   *WordNet*

WordNet (Patwardhan & Pedersen, 2006) is a large lexical database of english words consisting of nouns, verbs, adjectives, and adverbs. English words are organized into synonym sets called as synsets. Synsets are interlinked by means of conceptual-semantic and lexical relations. The most frequently encoded relation among synsets is the super-subordinate relation (also called IS-A relation). Broadly, most of the semantic similarity measures fall under four categories namely edge-based, information content-based (IC-based), feature-based and hybrid. All the approaches have inherent strength and weakness. Subsequently, we are focusing on the IC based technique as IC based technique avoids the unreliability of edge counting and expresses the relations among the features in a better manner (Resnik, 1999). Information content (IC) based methods assumes that the nodes highest in the hierarchy have a smallest IC. The information shared by two nodes is represented by their least common subsume (common ancestors). The more information two terms share, the more similar they are considered. Resnik (Resnik, 2011) approach is an IC-based approach that deals with nouns only and is based on the IS-A hierarchy of WordNet. Lin (Lin, 1998) used information content technique similar to Resnik, but added normalization factor based on IC of the two input concepts. Lord (Lord, Stevens, Brass, & Goble, 2003) compared two terms by using a measure that simply uses the probability of the most specific shared parent. To decide the similarity method, correlation coefficient is used between comparable similarity methods and Miller and Charles (Miller & Charles, 1991). Highest correlation value has been reported for Lin similarity measure approach.

- *Lin Similarity Measure*

Lin computes the semantic relatedness of word senses using the information content of the concepts in WordNet and the 'Similarity Theorem'. The measure assumes that the taxonomy is a tree. The relatedness value returned by the Lin measure is given by Equation (9).

$$\text{Lin}(w_1, w_2) = \frac{2\ X \log P(C_0)}{logP(C_1) + logP(C_2)} \tag{9}$$

where,

w_1 – word1, w_2 – word2
C_0, C_1, C_2 – classes to which a particular word belongs
$w_1 \epsilon\ C_1$, $w_2 \epsilon\ C_2$
C_0 is the most specific class that subsumes both C_1 and C_2.
P(C) is the probability that a randomly selected object belongs to class C.

The relatedness value lies between 0 and 1.

Fusion Techniques

Multiple modalities influence the way the fusion process is carried out. Most of the research work (Christel, 2007), (Westman et al., 2008) shows that combining the two modalities i.e. text and content even with simple fusion techniques such as linear combination helps in alleviating the retrieved results. Further, we elaborate the levels of fusion and how to fuse the two modalities and what are the problems faced during fusion process.

- *Levels of fusion*

The fusion techniques fall in two categories early fusion or feature level fusion and late or decision level fusion. The *early fusion* approach combines the textual and visual attributes at the feature space level itself into a single vector. This vector uniquely represents the feature space and the similarity is measured using that single vector only. Researchers (Cheng, Yeh, Ke, Chien, & Yang, 2004; Deselaers, Gass, Weyand, & Ney, 2007) have examined various feature weighting schemes used for early fusion. The advantage of early fusion strategy is that it utilizes the inherent interaction across modalities but suffers with well-known "curse of dimensionality" drawback.

On contrary, *late fusion* approach works at similarity level or decision level rather than the feature level. The late fusion techniques combine the similarities of the two modalities (text, image) by means of some aggregating functions. The simplest late fusion technique is the linear combination technique that linearly combines the two modalities. Zhang et al. (D. Zhang, Islam, Lu, & Hou, 2009) proposed a novel technique which combines the text data and content data of the image. This technique translates the images into textual documents using region based inverted files. The weights are assigned to the semantic keywords associated with image based on the region size. A system was proposed called Extended CBIR, ExCBIR (Gui et al., 2010) that first performs CBIR to obtain visually similar results, then the semantics of the obtained images were learned from the associated text (url, title, keyword) in the images using tf-idf strategy. According to the semantics learned, the images are assigned weights and the two similarity lists are combined using late fusion technique. Mean Average Precision (MAP) of 0.27 was achieved by the system. Goel et al. also used late fusion technique (linear combination) for combining text and content (color) but assigned weights to the modalities based on the correlation between text similarity list and color similarity list (Goel & Sehgal, 2014a). In the paper by Rahman et al. (Rahman, Desai, & Bhattacharya, 2007), the weights are updated dynamically based on user's relevance feedback. Document–specific weighting is used in (Granados, Benavent, García-Serrano, & Goñi, 2008) where weight of a document is divided by its rank. Many researchers (Stephane Clinchant, Renders, & Csurka, 2007; Zhou et al., 2010) used the simple linear combination only by assigning equal weights to both modalities.

Image Reranking/Reordering (Depeursinge & Müller, 2010) is one of the late fusion techniques that works at decision level. The technique has two phases. In the first phase, the similarity is calculated using one of the modalities (text/content). In the second phase, the results obtained in the first phase are re-ranked based on other modality. Authors (Simpson, Rahman, Demner-Fushman, Antani, & Thoma, 2009; Mulhem, Chevallet, Quenon, & Al Batal, 2009) reordered the textually retrieved documents based on their visual scores. Inversely, the authors(Granados et al., 2008; Ah-Pine, Cifarelli, Clinchant, Csurka, & Renders, 2009) have shown the results using reordering of visually retrieved documents based on their corresponding textual scores. Advantage of this technique is that it filters out result in the first phase, which reduces the size of dataset for further computations.

Transmedia fusion is another decision level fusion technique. It can be said that this method in itself is the fusion of two different fusion strategies. The main idea is to use first one of the modalities (say text) to gather relevant documents (nearest neighbors from a conceptual point of view) and then to use the both modalities (visual representations of the textually nearest neighbors) to perform the final retrieval. Clinchant et al. used transmedia fusion technique and called it as late semantic combination that combines the image reranking with late fusion strategy(Stéphane Clinchant, Ah-Pine, & Csurka, 2011). They have tested it on four benchmark datasets and achieved a maximum Mean Average Precision (MAP) of 0.396. Authors (Goel & Sehgal, 2013) first discovered semantically similar images and reranked based on their visual similarity. After that, both the modalities were combined linearly to obtain the final retrieval results.

- *Fusion Process*

It includes how the fusion process employs the feature and decision level correlation among the modalities and how it affects the overall fusion process (Poh & Bengio, 2005), (Goel & Sehgal, 2014a). The correlation among different modalities represents how they are allied with each other. Correlation between them can provide additional hints that are very helpful in fusing them. Therefore, it is important to know different methods of computing correlations and to analyze them from the perspective of how they affect fusion. The correlation can be known at low-level features and the semantic-level decisions also. Moreover, there are different forms of correlation that have been utilized by the researchers in the multimodal fusion process. The correlation between features has been computed in the forms of correlation coefficient, mutual information (Li, Dimitrova, Li, & Sethi, 2003), latent semantic analysis (also called lament semantic indexing) (Dumais, 2004), canonical correlation analysis, and cross-modal factor analysis (Li et al., 2003). Causal link analysis, causal strength and agreement coefficient (Atrey, Hossain, El Saddik, & Kankanhalli, 2010) are the methods for estimating the decision level correlation. Correlation coefficient technique is elaborated further.

Correlation Coefficient

The correlation coefficient is a measure of the strength and direction of a linear relationship between any two modalities. One of the most simple and widely used forms of the correlation coefficient is the Pearson's product-moment coefficient. The correlation is calculated using Equation (10).

$$R_{tv} = \frac{\sum tv}{\sqrt{\sum tt \sum vv}} \tag{10}$$

R_{tv} is the Correlation between the distance $d_t(q,X)$ obtained for textual similarity and distance $d_v(q,X)$ obtained for visual similarity of each of the image X from the database given a query q.

$$\sum tv = \frac{1}{N} \sum_{n=1}^{N} \left(d_t\left(q, X_n\right) - \mu_t \right) \cdot \left(d_v\left(q, X_n\right) - \mu_v \right) \tag{11}$$

$\sum tv$ is the covariance matrix of d_t and d_v and is calculated using Equations (11) and (14)

$$\sum tt = \frac{1}{N} \sum_{n=1}^{N} \left(d_t\left(q, X_n\right) - \mu_t \right)^2 \tag{12}$$

$\sum tt$ is the covariance matrix of d_t and d_t and is calculated using Equations (12) and (14)

$$\sum vv = \frac{1}{N} \sum_{n=1}^{N} \left(d_v\left(q, X_n\right) - \mu_v \right)^2 \tag{13}$$

$\sum vv$ is the covariance matrix of d_v and d_v and is calculated using Equations (13) and (14)

$$\mu_i = \frac{1}{N} \sum_{n=1}^{N} d_i(q, X_n) \qquad (14)$$

Here, $\mu_i = \{\mu_t, \mu_v\}$, $X \in (X_1, X_2, X_3 \ldots X_N)$ and N is the number of database images.

The value of correlation coefficient R ranges from 0 to 1. Value 0 represents that the two modalities are completely uncorrelated. As the value move towards 1, it represents the increase in strength of the correlation between two modalities.

Performance Measures

Two traditional information retrieval methods to evaluate the performance of retrieval system are recall and precision [87]. Precision evaluates the fraction of retrieved images that are relevant; recall evaluates the fraction of relevant images retrieved out of the total relevant images available in the database. Precision and recall are calculated by the following Equations (15) and (16) respectively.

$$Precision = \frac{\text{No. of Relevant images retrieved}}{\text{No. of images retrieved}} \qquad (15)$$

$$Recall = \frac{\text{No. of Relevant images retrieved}}{\text{No. of relevant images in database}} \qquad (16)$$

Generally, a tradeoff is there between these two measures, as improving one will sacrifice the other. In typical retrieval systems, with increase in precision, recall value tends to decreases or vice-versa. In addition, selecting a relevant data set is much less stable due to various interpretations of the images. For the reason, performance metrics for evaluating IR systems are adapted to be based upon ranked outputs. These metrics order the retrieved documents based on a score specifying the similarity of each document to the user's query. Density of relevant documents typically reduces as one move from the top of a ranking to downwards.

- *Averaged 11-point interpolated Precision-Recall Graph*

Here precision is measured at a set of standard recall points for each query in a test collection and the mean of precision values at each point is taken. 11 points are fixed starting at 0% recall value incrementing by 10% up to recall of 100%. Interpolation functions were used to measure the precision at these fixed points. Lesser fall in the precision value with the increase in recall value is desirable for good IR system.

- *Mean Average Precision (MAP)*

It is a rank based performance measure. Among evaluation measures, Mean average precision (MAP) is considered to be a suitable, discriminative, stable and, single-figure measure of quality. MAP is calculated for a batch of queries. It is the mean of Average Precision (AP) scores over the batch of queries. Where, AP is the mean of precision scores after each retrieved relevant image. MAP is given by the formula in Equation (17).

$$\mathbf{MAP} = \left(\sum_{i=1}^{Q} AP \right) / Q \tag{17}$$

$$AP = \left(\sum_{i=1}^{R} \frac{i}{Rank_i} \right) / R \tag{18}$$

where

Q = number of queries in a batch
AP = Average Precision
R = number of relevant docs for that query and $i/rank_i = 0$ if document i was not retrieved

- ○ *F-Measure*

F-measure is the weighted harmonic mean of precision and recall. It can be interpreted as the measure of effectiveness of retrieval while giving equal weightage to both precision and recall.

VARIOUS METHODOLOGIES FOR FUSION OF CONTENT AND TEXT FOR IMAGE RETRIEVAL

An image retrieval system can be viewed as a three-phase process. First phase deals with the input from the user in the form of text /image. Second phase deals with finding out the similarity between the user's input and the data available in the database. At the last level, the results are ranked according to their similarity with the users input and are displayed. Further, in this chapter, we discuss our contribution to the related areas. Specifically, IR systems are conversed keeping in focus the fusion of two modalities text and content (color) and how fusion can help in reducing the semantic gap. Moreover, understanding the user's intention at the querying time instead of decision time is focused upon. Here in, IR system are considered that uses both the visual content and text (metadata) associated with the image. The system has user interface where user can enter the query in the form of text and/or a query image.

Fusion of Content (Color) and Text (Word Similarity) Using Equal Weightage

An IR system (Goel & Sehgal, 2012) was developed which uses both the visual content and text (metadata) associated with the image. In this system, the fusion method deployed was combination of two fusion techniques viz. late fusion and reordering. First, the two modalities were fused together using late fusion with linear combination. Further, the list obtained after fusion was reordered based on visual similarity. Tf-idf weighting was used for feature vector generation to represent the text modality and cosine similarity measure for text matching. The feature vector for content was represented using color in HSV space model. Color was extracted in terms of three moments: 1st moment (mean), 2nd moment (variance), and 3rd moment (skewness). The similarity-matching algorithm as executed on the color descriptors vector. Two independent similarity lists of score were generated for both the modalities. Now these two similarity lists were fused using linear combination to generate a combined similarity score list for the images. The default weight given to both the methods is 0.5(50%). Scores were combined using summation. Color moments were used as first pass for visual similarity due to their compactness and ease of calculations. This may result in some unwanted results. List obtained after fusion was reordered based on visual similarity. For second pass of visual similarity, CCH and QFD metric were used to re-order the results from the initial set of similar images obtained. CCH was used in second pass because it provides better visually similar results but is computationally expensive. So, CCH was used when the images were filtered and lesser number of images was left. This reduced the computational complexity and the same time gave better visually similar results. Figure 1 shows the flowchart for the system.

Experimental results in the work shows that the system achieved good precision and recall for the queries. The drop in fall-out value shows that the image reordering done in the second phase removes the unwanted results and displays more visually similar results.

Figure 1. Flowchart for system based on fusion of content (color) and text (word similarity) using equal weightage

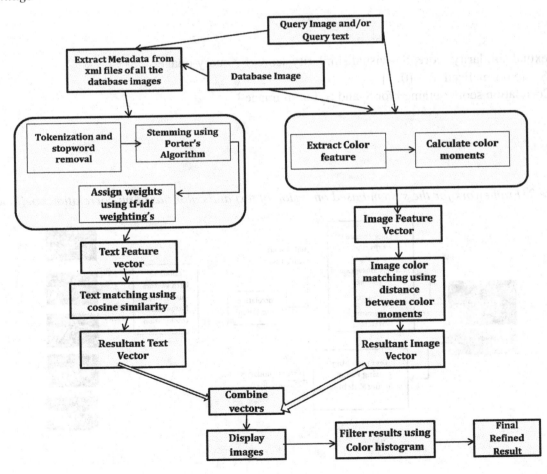

Fusion of Content (Color) and Text (Fuzzy String Similarity) Based on Correlation among Them

The idea behind this system (Goel & Sehgal, 2014a) is based upon the correlation between the two modalities, text and color. In comparison to the system discussed above, here textual similarity is measured using fuzzy string matching rather than exact word matching. For color matching, fuzzy color histograms were deployed. Individual similarity list are created for textual similarity as well as the visual similarity. Correlation is found out at the feature level itself using Pearson's correlation coefficient that is used to fuse the two modalities at the decision level. The correlation coefficient tells measure of the strength and direction of a linear relationship between these two modalities. The value of correlation coefficient helped in understanding the gap between the textual query and visual query entered by the user. If the query image and textual query are highly correlated then equal weightage is given to text and content for image retrieval but if they are weakly correlated or uncorrelated more weightage is given to content. Weightage is equal to the value of the correlation coefficient obtained. Final combined similarity score list S_{com} is attained using late fusion with linear combination technique using Equation (19). Figure 2 shows the framework for this algorithm.

$$S_{com}(I) = R * (1 - S_t(I)) + (1 - R) * S_v(I) \tag{19}$$

where:

S_t – textual similarity score, S_v – visual similarity score, I – query image
S_t & S_v are normalized, R ϵ [0, 1]
R – Correlation score obtained for S_t and S_v for an image I.

Figure 2. Framework for the system based on fusion of text and color based on correlation coefficient

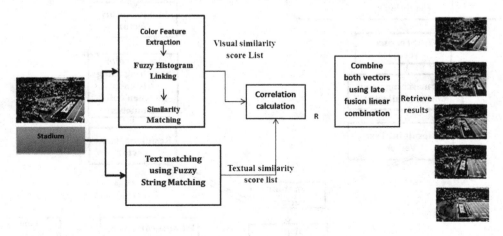

Cross-Media Fusion of Content (Color) and Semantic Similarity: Understanding User's Intention at Querying Time

Moving from exact word matching to fuzzy string matching, the system (Goel & Sehgal, 2015) is adapted to finding out semantic similarity of words. As stated earlier, a typical IR system has three levels. Most of the research work focuses on finding out the semantics at the second level or the third level. At the second level, semantics are deduced either by finding out the word (textual or semantic) similarity between the annotations of query images and database images or by assessing the high-level concepts from low level features. At the third level, various fusion techniques are applied on different modalities to produce semantically better results. However, none of the work focuses on the finding out the semantics at the first level itself i.e. when user provides input to the system. A weighted semantic similarity approach is put forward in the paper (Goel & Sehgal, 2013) which focuses on the learning of the user's intentions by finding out the semantics at the very first level of image retrieval where user provides the input in form of textual query and the query image. Further, parallel computing is introduced in weighted semantic similarity technique for IR. This technique gives the weightage to the annotations associated with the query image based upon their semantic similarity with user's query and then establishes the semantics with database images. Figure 3 displays the framework for this system.

Figure 3. Semantic Based Image Retrieval with parallelization

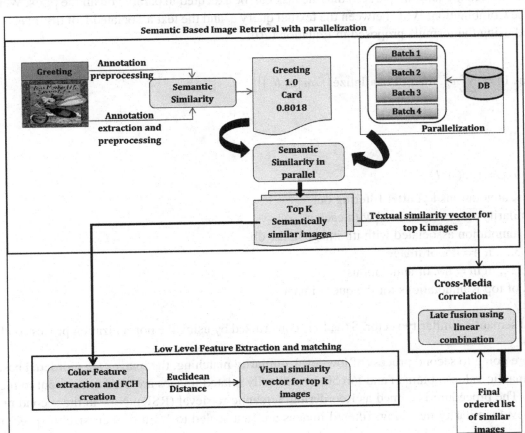

The system developed consists of three processes namely semantic based image retrieval with parallelization, low-level similarity matching and cross-media correlation. In the first process semantics are established first between the two modes of query i.e. image, q_c and text, q_t itself. This is done by finding out the semantic similarity between query text qt and the annotations associated with the query images a1, a2, a3, …,an. Semantic similarity between the words is calculated using WordNet and Lin similarity measure. Semantic similarity value ranges from 0 to 1 where 0 represents the least similarity and 1 represents the highest similarity. Similarity values falling in the range of 0 to 0.5 are considered as the lowest and are discarded. Whereas, those falling in the range of 0.5 to 1 will be considered as good values and will be kept. Finding out the annotations, which are semantically similar to the query text, will help in understanding the user's intention behind the search and in turn will lead to better retrieval of the results. Semantic filtering helps in eliminating the annotations that are not related with user's query. Even if the annotations of database images do not contain the query text as it is, the system is still able to find the images in database having annotations similar to the ones that are semantically similar to the query text.

It can be said that user's search query is expanded by finding out the semantically similar words from the annotation of query image itself. The semantically similar words are assigned the weights according to their relatedness with the query word provided by the user. After this, the semantics are established between the query image and the database images. Since number of images in the database can be large enough, the parallelization was done here. Parallel processing is done at data level using the SPMD (Single Program Multiple Data) programming model. The system is implemented in Matlab. The dataset is divided into four equal sub parts so that the task can be executed in parallel on all the parts. Weighted Semantic Combination, WSC between the textual query q_t and the text associated I_t of dB images $I_i \forall i$ is obtained using the formula proposed in Equation (20).

$$\text{WSC}\,(q_t, I_t) = \sum_{k=1}^{K} w_k \cdot \max\left\{ \textbf{Parallelize}\left(sim\left(a_k, b_{ij} \right) \right) \right\} \tag{20}$$

where,

$$sim\left(a_k, b_{ij} \right) = \text{Lin}(a_k, b_{ij})$$

a_k - top K annotations left after filtering out
w_k – similarity values associated with each a_k
b_{ij} = jth annotation associated with ith image in the db.
i = 1,2, 3,. ., n n= no. of images
j = 1,2,3,. ., m m = no. of annotations
K = no. of top K annotations for the query image.

Final semantic similarity vector, $S_t(q_t, I_t)$ is constructed by using the normalization process on Equation (20).

Before going to second process of low-level similarity matching, the images are reordered based on their semantic values obtained and top 50 semantically related images are used as an input to the next process. The procedure is named as Reordering Semantic retrieval (RSR). Now in the second process of low-level similarity matching, filtered images are first scaled to 1/4th of their size to speed up the calculations. This helps in avoiding the normalization of histogram bins, since normalization lead to loss of color quantity information. FCH for the database images and query images using histogram-linking approach is calculated. Using L1 similarity measure the distance between query image and the database images is calculated. Thus, a list of score for visual similarity, S_v for filtered images is obtained.

The third process is cross-media correlation. Here, both the medias are exploited and the two lists are combined in linear manner with each having equal weightage of 0.5. Final similarity score list is obtained using Equation (21). The idea behind the method is that the system considers both textual similarity scores and visual similarity scores for the top K images that were retrieved by the semantic matching.

$$S(I) = \alpha * N(RSR(q_t, I_t)) + (1 - \alpha) * N(S_v(q_c, I_c)) \qquad (21)$$

$$RSR\ (Q,\ I) = \begin{cases} = 1, if\ I\ belong\ to\ top\ K\ images \\ = 0\ , if\ I\ does\ not \end{cases} \qquad (22)$$

where,

Q is the bimodal Query applied on image I.
α is the weightage, $\alpha = 0.5$
$Q = \{q_t, q_c\}$ qt represents the textual query and q_c is query image.
RSR is the reordered similarity score list of top- k semantically similar images.
$S_v(q_c, I_c)$ is the content similarity vector between q_c and I_c.

Finding out semantics at input level with parallelization has several advantages. Experimental results show that this strategy allows us to establish the semantics at the first step only which helps in understanding the user's intention and providing good retrieval results. The filtered list of top k semantically similar results and elimination of non-semantic results, addresses the issue of redundancy identification and elimination in multimedia fusion. On the other hand, the visual similarity that requires most of the computations is computed between the query and the filtered images only, resulting in a reduced number of computations. Parallel processing employed helps in achieving good response time of the system. Both semantic filtering and parallel processing makes the approach scalable to very large datasets. Combining the results from both the modalities for semantically related results ensures information preserving fusion.

EXPERIMENTAL RESULTS AND DISCUSSIONS

Experimental Setup

The system is tested using two standard datasets UW annotated database and ESPgame dataset. UW database is created at the University of Washington and consists of categorized collection of approximately 1109 images. These images are annotated using keywords. There are 18 categories, for example "spring flowers", "Swiss mountains", "Iraq", "cherries" etc. On an average, each image has about 6 words of annotation. Minimum number of keywords per image is 1 and maximum is 26. ESPgame dataset is quite large with approximately 67000 images with 358,000 labels. On an average, 5 labels are there in one image. Minimum number of label per image is 1 and maximum is 19. The dataset is also very 'natural', consisting of images inspired from the internet. Annotations for both the datasets are available in the form of text files. Implementation is done on system with INTEL core i3 processor having 2 cores/4threads with clock speed of 2.27 GHz. Matlab 7.0 is used for developing the algorithms.

During experiments, it was observed that on an average the annotations are evenly distributed for the database. If load balancing is implemented, then the system has to bear the overhead and the response time of the system is affected. Therefore, the experiments have been performed without load balancing to have the good response time of the system.

Comparing System Based on Fusion Using equal Weightage and System Based on Fusion Using Correlation Coefficient

The results of the system (Goel & Sehgal, 2012) based on fusion of text and color using equal weightage are compared with the system (Goel & Sehgal, 2014a) based on fusion of text and color using correlation coefficient. As discussed earlier, in the first system tf-idf weighting was used for feature vector generation of text. The feature vectors for images were created using color moments in the first pass and CCH in the second pass. The two modalities were fused together using late fusion technique and gives equal weightage to the both. Whereas in the later, FCH is deployed instead of CCH and fuzzy string matching is used instead of tf-idf approach. Additionally, the correlation coefficient is employed to fuse the two modalities. Figure 4 shows the F-measure values for the ten categories of UW annotated database obtained using the mentioned approaches. The higher value of F-measure for the system 2 shows that correlation coefficient helps in better understanding of the user's intention and thus improving the retrieval results.

Figure 4. Comparison of F-measure values

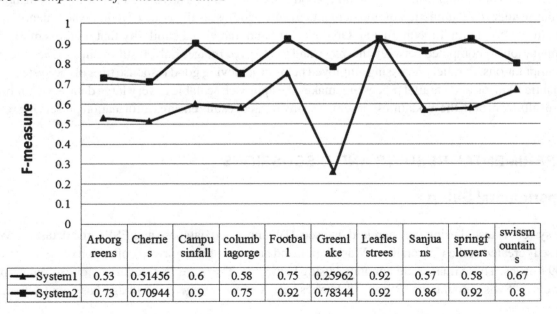

	Arborg reens	Cherries	Campu sinfall	columb iagorge	Football	Greenl ake	Leafles strees	Sanjua ns	springf lowers	swissm ountain s
System1	0.53	0.51456	0.6	0.58	0.75	0.25962	0.92	0.57	0.58	0.67
System2	0.73	0.70944	0.9	0.75	0.92	0.78344	0.92	0.86	0.92	0.8

Comparison of Performance of the Semantic-Based System for Two Datasets

For comparison purpose, set of around 1000 images is selected at random from the ESPgame dataset. The performance of the semantic-based approach (Goel & Sehgal, 2014b) is evaluated using 11-point interpolated average precision. For each of the query from the set of 50 queries, the interpolated precision is measured at the 11 recall levels of 0.0, 0.1, 0.2, 0.3, 0.4, 0.5, 0.6, 0.7, 0.8, 0.9, and 1.0. We then, calculate the arithmetic mean of the interpolated precision at each recall level for each of the 50 queries. Figure 5 displays the average precision-recall graph for both UW and ESPgame dataset. From the graph, we can depict that with increasing recall values, precision values fall but at relatively slow rate. The system is able to achieve good precision at higher recall values also, which is desirable for any good retrieval system. The MAP value is evaluated over a batch of 50 queries. System achieved the MAP of 0.533 for UW dataset and 0.594 for ESPgame dataset.

Figure 5. Averaged 11-point precision/recall graph across 50 queries for UW and ESPgame datasets

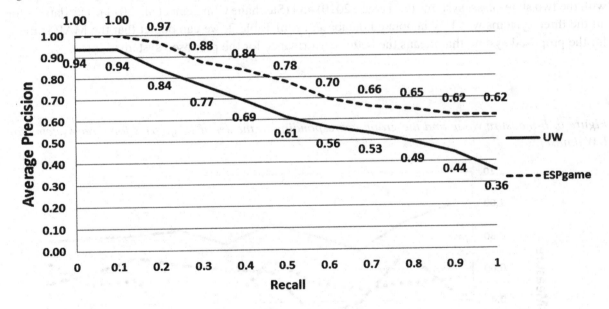

Table 1. MAP for UW dataset and ESPgame dataset

Dataset	MAP
UW	0.533
ESPgame	0.594

Comparison of Combined Semantic Based Approach with Only CBIR and Combined CBIR and TBIR Approach

The approach based on semantics is compared with the approach based only on visual similarity (CBIR) and combined (CBIR + TBIR) approach. The performances of these are evaluated using F-measure over the set of 10 queries for UW dataset as well as ESPgame dataset. F-measure is the weighted harmonic mean of precision and recall. It can be interpreted as the measure of effectiveness of retrieval while giving equal weightage to both precision and recall. Figure 6 displays the F-measure value and the graph corresponding to the set of 10 queries for three systems for UW dataset. Figure 7 displays the F-measure value and the graph corresponding to the set of 10 queries for three systems for ESPgame dataset. We can observe that semantic-based approach has a higher F-measure than both of the two other approaches do. This indicates that the semantic-based approach has higher retrieval quality, whereas other two approaches perform almost equivalently.

Comparisons with State-of-Art Results

System (Goel & Sehgal, 2015) based on semantic understanding of the user's intention system is compared with the two state-of-art systems (Gui et al., 2010) and (Stéphane Clinchant et al., 2011). The dataset for all the three systems was UW annotated database. From Table 2, we can depict that the MAP is more for the proposed system that means the better performance for the proposed system.

Figure 6. F-measure value and the graph corresponding to the set of 10 queries for three systems for UW dataset

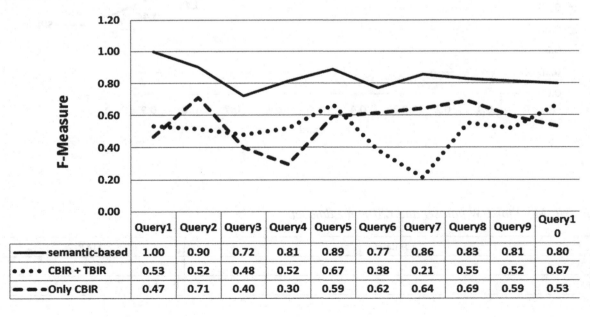

	Query1	Query2	Query3	Query4	Query5	Query6	Query7	Query8	Query9	Query10
——— semantic-based	1.00	0.90	0.72	0.81	0.89	0.77	0.86	0.83	0.81	0.80
• • • • CBIR + TBIR	0.53	0.52	0.48	0.52	0.67	0.38	0.21	0.55	0.52	0.67
— — •Only CBIR	0.47	0.71	0.40	0.30	0.59	0.62	0.64	0.69	0.59	0.53

Figure 7. F-measure value and the graph corresponding to the set of 10 queries for three systems for ESPgame dataset

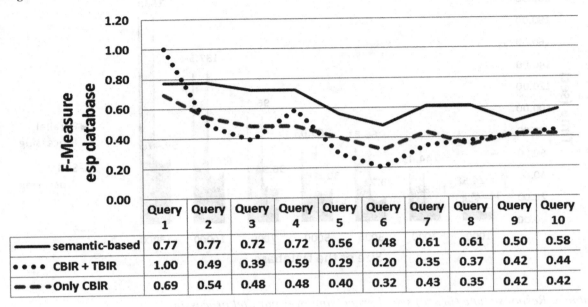

	Query 1	Query 2	Query 3	Query 4	Query 5	Query 6	Query 7	Query 8	Query 9	Query 10
—— semantic-based	0.77	0.77	0.72	0.72	0.56	0.48	0.61	0.61	0.50	0.58
•••• CBIR + TBIR	1.00	0.49	0.39	0.59	0.29	0.20	0.35	0.37	0.42	0.44
— — •Only CBIR	0.69	0.54	0.48	0.48	0.40	0.32	0.43	0.35	0.42	0.42

Table 2. Comparisons with state-of-art results

	Gui et al.(2010)	Clinchant et al.(2011)	Proposed Semantic-Based System (Goel & Sehgal, 2015)
MAP	0.27	0.396	0.533

Running Time Comparison between Parallel and Serial Processing

Response time is measured for several sets containing different number of images to evaluate the efficiency of the system. For the same purpose, ESPgame dataset with a huge collection of 67,000 is used. Each imageset contains increasing number of images. All the image sets are tested against parallel processing as well as serial processing and the response time is measured. Figure 8 displays the response time graph for the each of the seven image sets. From the graph, we can observe that with increasing number of images the serial processing time increases at very fast rate. Whereas, for parallel processing response time increases at much slower rate. The comparison of serial implementation over parallel implementation is shown in Table 3. This Table reports the speedup for varying problem sizes and the speedup average. On an average, speedup of 2.67 is achieved. From the table we can observe that as the size of the database increases, the time difference between the serial and parallel processing increases. This shows that parallel computing makes the system scalable to large datasets.

Figure 8. Response time graph for different sizes of image sets8

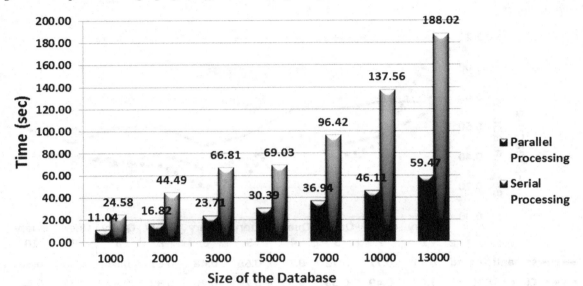

Table 3. Response time (in sec) serial processing over parallel processing

Size of dB	Serial Processing	Parallel Processing	Speedup	Average Speedup
1000	24.58	11.04	2.23	
2000	44.49	16.82	2.64	
3000	66.81	23.71	2.82	
5000	69.03	30.39	2.27	2.67
7000	96.42	36.94	2.61	
10000	137.56	46.11	2.98	
13000	188.02	59.47	3.16	

Comparison of Retrieval Results

The retrieval results displayed in Figure 9 will help us to better illustrate the difference between the three systems viz. only CBIR, CBIR+TBIR and the system based on combined semantic approach.

The first row in Figure 9 displays the images retrieved using only Content. Color feature is extracted and FCH is used for feature vector creation. The similarity measure used is Euclidean distance. We can clearly see that the among the images retrieved using only visual similarity two images which are completely uncorrelated with the query image are also retrieved since their content (i.e. color) information is almost equivalent. Moreover, the computations are done on the whole dataset, so it is difficult to scale the technique to large datasets. The second row in Figure 9 displays the images retrieved using the technique described in (Goel et al., 2013(a)). The technique uses FCH for visual similarity and fuzzy string matching for text-similarity. It then calculates the correlation between the two similarities obtained and further uses it to combine the two modalities. Here the text-based search will be done using query

Figure 9. Bimodal query and results on the UW annotated Dataset. Top most image displays the query text and query image provided by the user as an input. First row shows the result using only visual similarity. Second row displays the results of combined (text + image) approach. Last row shows the result of parallel weighted semantic combination of text and content.

Query : "flower"

text only i.e. "flower". Results in second row shows that combination of two modalities definitely helps in alleviating the results but the images retrieved are not similar to the query image except the first two. Now the last row displays the result using the parallel weighted semantic combination. Here the semantics are established between the query text and image before the retrieval. Here, the text-based search is done not only with "flower" but also with the combination of "flower tree bush", which are retrieved as semantically similar words corresponding to the query image. This combination helps in uniquely identifying the similar images in the database. After filtering out the top semantically similar images, the CBIR is performed and the images are reranked.

Using reordering fusion technique based on weighted semantic combination (WSC) with parallelization approach offers multiple advantages. Firstly, the results are better than both the pure visual approach and the combined approach. Secondly, the semantics learned earlier helps in better retrieval of results and largely reduces the computations done at the later stages of fusion. Thirdly, weighted semantic combination helps in better establishment of the semantics rather just using the query text itself. Fourthly, parallel computation resulted in better performance of the system making the approach scalable to large datasets also. Lastly, the approach is based on semantic filtering and the images are filtered out before visual matching thus reducing the computational complexity of the system.

CONCLUSION

A CBIR system that only depends on extraction and matching of low-level features has no understanding of user's need. Consequently, multi-media retrieval (text and image) has been used to improve the retrieval results. Establishing the semantics at the input level helped in understanding the user's intention behind the search prior to retrieval. The semantic-based approach expands the user's search query by finding out the semantically similar words from the annotation of query image itself. The semantically similar words are assigned the weights according to their relatedness with the query word provided by the user. This helps in enhanced creation of the semantics and only the top semantically similar images are filtered for visual matching reducing the computations largely. Parallel processing implemented helps in reducing the response time of the system up to a large extent. Henceforth, both semantic filtering and parallel processing reduces the complexity of the retrieval system while preserving the information during fusion. Mean average precision achieved by the semantic-based system for two different datasets proves the effectiveness of the algorithm and response time measured shows the efficiency of the algorithm

FUTURE PERSPECTIVES

Concluding, we want to draw the attention towards two directions. First is that rather than working on generic CBIR, one should focus on retrieval of images in specific applications where it is feasible to derive the semantic relationships and features. In this chapter, for content feature representation color is extracted, however, depending on the application other depiction of content i.e. shape or texture can also be extracted. Secondly, algorithms should not only rely on the text that is based on linguistic expressions of human concepts for understanding the context of the image. Rather context can also be derived using other disciplines and instilled into the system using computer vision techniques. Cognitive neuroscience can be used to understand how brain "sees" and "retrieves." Psychology can provide the knowledge of attentive processing. Combing these disciplines for deriving the context will help in better understanding and will improve the CBIR systems well beyond the current approaches.

REFERENCES

Abbas, J., Qadri, S., Idrees, M., Awan, S., & Khan, N. A. (2010). Frame work for content based image retrieval (Textual Based) system. *Journal of American Science*, 6(9), 704–707.

Ah-Pine, J., Cifarelli, C., Clinchant, S., Csurka, G., & Renders, J. (2009). *XRCE's participation to ImageCLEF 2008*. Academic Press.

Alemu, Y., Koh, J.-b., Ikram, M., & Kim, D.-K. (2009). *Image retrieval in multimedia databases: A survey*. Paper presented at the Intelligent Information Hiding and Multimedia Signal Processing, 2009. IIH-MSP'09. Fifth International Conference on. doi:10.1109/IIH-MSP.2009.159

Atrey, P. K., Hossain, M. A., El Saddik, A., & Kankanhalli, M. S. (2010). Multimodal fusion for multimedia analysis: A survey. *Multimedia Systems*, 16(6), 345–379. doi:10.1007/s00530-010-0182-0

Bugatti, P. H., Traina, A. J., & Traina, C., Jr. (2008). *Assessing the best integration between distance-function and image-feature to answer similarity queries*. Paper presented at the 2008 ACM Symposium on Applied Computing. doi:10.1145/1363686.1363969

Chang, N.-S., & Fu, K.-S. (1980). Query-by-pictorial-example. *Software Engineering, IEEE Transactions on,* (6), 519-524.

Chang, N.-S., & Fu, K. S. (1980). *A relational database system for images.* Springer. doi:10.1007/3-540-09757-0_11

Cheng, P.-C., Yeh, J.-Y., Ke, H.-R., Chien, B.-C., & Yang, W.-P. (2004). *NCTU-ISU's Evaluation for the User-Centered Search Task at ImageCLEF 2004.* Paper presented at the Working notes of the 2004 CLEF workshop, Bath, UK.

Choras, R. S. (2007). Image feature extraction techniques and their applications for CBIR and biometrics systems. *International Journal of Biology and Biomedical Engineering, 1*(1), 6-16.

Christel, M. G. (2007). *Examining user interactions with video retrieval systems.* Paper presented at the Electronic Imaging 2007.

Clinchant, S., Ah-Pine, J., & Csurka, G. (2011). *Semantic combination of textual and visual information in multimedia retrieval.* Paper presented at the 1st ACM International Conference on Multimedia Retrieval. doi:10.1145/1991996.1992040

Clinchant, S., Renders, J.-M., & Csurka, G. (2007). XRCE's Participation to ImageCLEFphoto 2007. *Working Notes of the CLEFWorkshop.*

Datta, R., Joshi, D., Li, J., & Wang, J. Z. (2008). Image retrieval: Ideas, influences, and trends of the new age. *ACM Computing Surveys, 40*(2), 5. doi:10.1145/1348246.1348248

Depeursinge, A., & Müller, H. (2010). *Fusion techniques for combining textual and visual information retrieval. In ImageCLEF* (pp. 95–114). Springer.

Deselaers, T., Gass, T., Weyand, T., & Ney, H. (2007). *FIRE in ImageCLEF 2007.* Paper presented at the Working Notes for the CLEF 2007 Workshop, Budapest, Hungary.

Dumais, S. T. (2004). Latent semantic analysis. *Annual Review of Information Science & Technology, 38*(1), 188–230. doi:10.1002/aris.1440380105

Gao, Y., Wang, M., Zha, Z.-J., Shen, J., Li, X., & Wu, X. (2013). Visual-textual joint relevance learning for tag-based social image search. *Image Processing. IEEE Transactions on, 22*(1), 363–376.

Goel, N., & Sehgal, P. (2012). A refined hybrid image retrieval system using text and color. *Int. J. Comput. Sci,* (9), 4.

Goel, N., & Sehgal, P. (2013). *Weighted semantic fusion of text and content for image retrieval.* Paper presented at the Advances in Computing, Communications and Informatics (ICACCI), 2013 International Conference on. doi:10.1109/ICACCI.2013.6637255

Goel, N., & Sehgal, P. (2014a). Image Retrieval Using Fuzzy Color Histogram and Fuzzy String Matching: A Correlation-Based Scheme to Reduce the Semantic Gap. In D. P. Mohapatra & S. Patnaik (Eds.), *Intelligent Computing, Networking, and Informatics* (Vol. 243, pp. 327–341). Springer India. doi:10.1007/978-81-322-1665-0_31

Goel, N., & Sehgal, P. (2014b). Parallel Weighted Semantic Fusion for Cross-Media Retrieval. *International Journal of Computational Intelligence Studies*.

Goel, N., & Sehgal, P. (2015). Parallel weighted semantic fusion for cross-media retrieval. *International Journal of Computational Intelligence Studies*, *4*(1), 50–71. doi:10.1504/IJCISTUDIES.2015.069832

Granados, R., Benavent, X., García-Serrano, A., & Goñi, J. (2008). *MIRACLE-FI at ImageCLEFphoto 2008: Experiences in merging text-based and content-based retrievals.* Paper presented at the Working Notes of the 2008 CLEF Workshop, Aarhust, Denmark.

Griffiths, A., Luckhurst, H. C., & Willett, P. (1997). *Using interdocument similarity information in document retrieval systems. In Readings in Information Retrieval* (pp. 365–373). San Francisco, CA: Morgan Kaufmann Publishers.

Grosky, W. I., Agrawal, R., & Fotouchi, F. (2008). *Mind the gaps-finding the appropriate dimensional representation for semantic retrieval of multimedia assets. In Semantic Multimedia and Ontologies* (pp. 229–252). Springer.

Guan, L., Wang, Y., Zhang, R., Tie, Y., Bulzacki, A., & Ibrahim, M. (2010). Multimodal information fusion for selected multimedia applications. *International Journal of Multimedia Intelligence and Security*, *1*(1), 5–32. doi:10.1504/IJMIS.2010.035969

Gudivada, V. N., & Raghavan, V. V. (1995). Content based image retrieval systems. *Computer*, *28*(9), 18–22. doi:10.1109/2.410145

Gui, C., Liu, J., Xu, C., & Lu, H. (2010). *Extended CBIR via learning semantics of query image. In Advances in Multimedia Modeling* (pp. 782–785). Springer.

Harispe, S., Ranwez, S., Janaqi, S., & Montmain, J. (2013). *Semantic Measures for the Comparison of Units of Language, Concepts or Instances from Text and Knowledge Base Analysis.* arXiv preprint arXiv:1310.1285

Hartvedt, C. (2010). *Using context to understand user intentions in Image retrieval.* Paper presented at the Advances in Multimedia (MMEDIA), 2010 Second International Conferences on. doi:10.1109/MMEDIA.2010.35

Hua, X.-S., Worring, M., & Chua, T.-S. (2013). *Internet Multimedia and Search Mining.* Citeseer. doi:10.2174/97816080521581130101

Jain, R., & Sinha, P. (2010). *Content without context is meaningless.* Paper presented at the International Conference on Multimedia.

Jakarta, A. (2004). *Apache Lucene-a high-performance, full-featured text search engine library.* Apache Lucene.

Jin, H., Sun, A., Zheng, R., He, R., Zhang, Q., Shi, Y., & Yang, W. (2007). *Content and semantic context based image retrieval for medical image grid.* Paper presented at the 8th IEEE/ACM International Conference on Grid Computing. doi:10.1109/GRID.2007.4354122

Joseph, T., & Cardenas, A. F. (1988). PICQUERY: A high level query language for pictorial database management. *Software Engineering. IEEE Transactions on, 14*(5), 630–638.

Kannan, A., Mohan, V., & Anbazhagan, N. (2010). *Image clustering and retrieval using image mining techniques.* Paper presented at the IEEE International Conference on Computational Intelligence and Computing Research.

Kodituwakku, S., & Selvarajah, S. (2004). Comparison of color features for image retrieval. *Indian Journal of Computer Science and Engineering, 1*(3), 207–211.

Konstantinidis, K., Gasteratos, A., & Andreadis, I. (2005). Image retrieval based on fuzzy color histogram processing. *Optics Communications, 248*(4), 375–386. doi:10.1016/j.optcom.2004.12.029

Levenshtein, V. I. (1966). *Binary codes capable of correcting deletions, insertions, and reversals.* Paper presented at the Soviet Physics Doklady.

Li, D., Dimitrova, N., Li, M., & Sethi, I. K. (2003). *Multimedia content processing through cross-modal association.* Paper presented at the Eleventh ACM International Conference on Multimedia. doi:10.1145/957013.957143

Lin, D. (1998). *An information-theoretic definition of similarity.* Paper presented at the ICML.

Linden, G., Smith, B., & York, J. (2003). Amazon. com recommendations: Item-to-item collaborative filtering. *IEEE Internet Computing, 7*(1), 76–80. doi:10.1109/MIC.2003.1167344

Liu, J., Xu, C., & Lu, H. (2010). Cross-media retrieval: State-of-the-art and open issues. *International Journal of Multimedia Intelligence and Security, 1*(1), 33–52. doi:10.1504/IJMIS.2010.035970

Liu, Y., Zhang, D., Lu, G., & Ma, W.-Y. (2007). A survey of content-based image retrieval with high-level semantics. *Pattern Recognition, 40*(1), 262–282. doi:10.1016/j.patcog.2006.04.045

Long, F., Zhang, H., & Feng, D. D. (2003). *Fundamentals of content-based image retrieval. In Multimedia Information Retrieval and Management* (pp. 1–26). Springer. doi:10.1007/978-3-662-05300-3_1

Lord, P. W., Stevens, R. D., Brass, A., & Goble, C. A. (2003). Investigating semantic similarity measures across the Gene Ontology: The relationship between sequence and annotation. *Bioinformatics (Oxford, England), 19*(10), 1275–1283. doi:10.1093/bioinformatics/btg153 PMID:12835272

Luo, B., Wang, X., & Tang, X. (2003). *World Wide Web Based Image Search Engine Using Text and Image Content Features.* Academic Press.

Machin, D. (2004). Building the world's visual language: The increasing global importance of image banks in corporate media. *Visual Communication, 3*(3), 316-336.

Manning, C. D., Raghavan, P., & Schütze, H. (2008). *Introduction to information retrieval* (Vol. 1). Cambridge University Press.

Miller, G. A., & Charles, W. G. (1991). Contextual correlates of semantic similarity. *Language and Cognitive Processes, 6*(1), 1–28. doi:10.1080/01690969108406936

Mourato, A. S., & Jesus, R. (2014). Clip Art Retrieval Using a Sketch Tablet Application. *Procedia Technology*, *17*, 368–375. doi:10.1016/j.protcy.2014.10.246

Mulhem, P., Chevallet, J.-P., Quenon, G., & Al Batal, R. (2009). MRIM-LIG at ImageCLEF 2009: Photo Retrieval and Photo Annotation tasks. *CLEF Working Notes*.

Müller, H., Michoux, N., Bandon, D., & Geissbuhler, A. (2004). A review of content-based image retrieval systems in medical applications—clinical benefits and future directions. *International Journal of Medical Informatics*, *73*(1), 1–23. doi:10.1016/j.ijmedinf.2003.11.024 PMID:15036075

Müller, H., Ruch, P., & Geissbühler, A. (2004). Enriching content-based image retrieval with multilingual search terms. *Swiss Medical Informatics*, *21*(54), 6–11.

Napster. (2001). *Napster*. Retrieved from http://www. napster. com

Navarro, G. (2001). A guided tour to approximate string matching. *ACM Computing Surveys*, *33*(1), 31–88. doi:10.1145/375360.375365

Patil, C., & Dalal, V. (2011). *Content based image retrieval using combined features*. Paper presented at the International Conference & Workshop on Emerging Trends in Technology. doi:10.1145/1980022.1980043

Patwardhan, S., & Pedersen, T. (2006). *Using WordNet-based context vectors to estimate the semantic relatedness of concepts*. Paper presented at the EACL 2006 Workshop Making Sense of Sense-Bringing Computational Linguistics and Psycholinguistics Together.

Pavlidis, T. (2008). *Limitations of content-based image retrieval*. Paper presented at the Invited Plenary Talk at the 19th Internat. Conf. on Pattern Recognition, Tampa, FL.

Poh, N., & Bengio, S. (2005). How do correlation and variance of base-experts affect fusion in biometric authentication tasks? *Signal Processing. IEEE Transactions on*, *53*(11), 4384–4396. doi:10.1109/TSP.2005.857006

Rahman, M., Desai, B. C., & Bhattacharya, P. (2007). Multi-modal interactive approach to imageCLEF 2007 photographic and medical retrieval tasks by CINDI. *Working Notes of CLEF, 7*.

Resnik, P. (1999). Semantic Similarity in a Taxonomy: An Information-Based Measure and its Application to Problems of Ambiguity in Natural Language. *Journal of Artificial Intelligence Research*, *11*, 95–130.

Resnik, P. (2011). *Semantic similarity in a taxonomy: An information-based measure and its application to problems of ambiguity in natural language*. arXiv preprint arXiv:1105.5444

Salton, G., Wong, A., & Yang, C.-S. (1975). A vector space model for automatic indexing. *Communications of the ACM*, *18*(11), 613–620. doi:10.1145/361219.361220

Seetharaman, K., & Sathiamoorthy, S. (2014). Color image retrieval using statistical model and radial basis function neural network. *Egyptian Informatics Journal*, *15*(1), 59–68. doi:10.1016/j.eij.2014.02.001

Simpson, M., Rahman, M. M., Demner-Fushman, D., Antani, S., & Thoma, G. R. (2009). *Text-and content-based approaches to image retrieval for the ImageCLEF 2009 medical retrieval track*. Paper presented at the CLEF2009 Working Notes. CLEF 2009 Workshop.

Singhai, N., & Shandilya, S. K. (2010). A Survey On: Content Based Image Retrieval Systems. *International Journal of Computers and Applications*, *4*(2), 22–26. doi:10.5120/802-1139

Smeulders, A. W., Worring, M., Santini, S., Gupta, A., & Jain, R. (2000). Content-based image retrieval at the end of the early years. *Pattern Analysis and Machine Intelligence. IEEE Transactions on*, *22*(12), 1349–1380.

Squire, D. M., Müller, W., Müller, H., & Raki, J. (1998). *Content-based query of image databases, inspirations from text retrieval: inverted files, frequency-based weights and relevance feedback*. Academic Press.

Stata, R., Bharat, K., & Maghoul, F. (2000). The term vector database: Fast access to indexing terms for web pages. *Computer Networks*, *33*(1), 247–255. doi:10.1016/S1389-1286(00)00046-3

Stricker, M. A., & Orengo, M. (1995). *Similarity of color images*. Paper presented at the IS&T/SPIE's Symposium on Electronic Imaging: Science & Technology.

Strzalkowski, T. (1995). Natural language information retrieval. *Information Processing & Management*, *31*(3), 397–417. doi:10.1016/0306-4573(94)00055-8

Suhasini, P., & Krishna, K., & Krishna, M. (2009). CBIR using color histogram processing. *Journal of Theoretical & Applied Information Technology*, *6*(1).

Szántó, B., Pozsegovics, P., Vámossy, Z., & Sergyán, S. (2011). *Sketch4match—Content-based image retrieval system using sketches*. Paper presented at the Applied Machine Intelligence and Informatics (SAMI), 2011 IEEE 9th International Symposium on.

Van Rijsbergen, C. J., Robertson, S. E., & Porter, M. F. (1980). *New models in probabilistic information retrieval*. Computer Laboratory, University of Cambridge.

Wang, S. (2001). *A robust CBIR approach using local color histograms*. University of Alberta.

Westman, S., Lustila, A., & Oittinen, P. (2008). *Search strategies in multimodal image retrieval*. Paper presented at the Second International Symposium on Information Interaction in Context. doi:10.1145/1414694.1414700

Xu, J., Xu, B., & Men, S. (2010). *Feature-based Similarity Retrieval in Content-based Image Retrieval*. Paper presented at the Web Information Systems and Applications Conference (WISA), 2010 7th. doi:10.1109/WISA.2010.46

Yue, J., Li, Z., Liu, L., & Fu, Z. (2011). Content-based image retrieval using color and texture fused features. *Mathematical and Computer Modelling*, *54*(3), 1121–1127. doi:10.1016/j.mcm.2010.11.044

Zhang, D., Islam, M. M., Lu, G., & Hou, J. (2009). *Semantic image retrieval using region based inverted file*. Paper presented at the Digital Image Computing: Techniques and Applications, 2009. DICTA'09. doi:10.1109/DICTA.2009.48

Zhang, H., Jiang, M., & Zhang, X. (2009). *Exploring image context for semantic understanding and retrieval*. Paper presented at the Computational Intelligence and Software Engineering, 2009. CiSE 2009. International Conference on. doi:10.1109/CISE.2009.5364019

Zhang, N., & Song, Y. (2008). *An image indexing and searching system based both on keyword and content. In Advanced Intelligent Computing Theories and Applications. With Aspects of Theoretical and Methodological Issues* (pp. 1032–1039). Springer.

Zhou, X., Eggel, I., & Müller, H. (2010). *The MedGIFT group at ImageCLEF 2009. In Multilingual Information Access Evaluation II. Multimedia Experiments* (pp. 211–218). Springer.

Chapter 8
Indexing of Image Features Using Quadtree

N. Puviarasan
Annamalai University, India

R. Bhavani
Annamalai University, India

ABSTRACT

In Content based image retrieval (CBIR) applications, the idea of indexing is mapping the extracted descriptors from images into a high-dimensional space. In this paper, visual features like color, texture and shape are considered. The color features are extracted using color coherence vector (CCV), texture features are obtained from Segmentation based Fractal Texture Analysis (SFTA). The shape features of an image are extracted using the Fourier Descriptors (FD) which is the contour based feature extraction method. All features of an image are then combined. After combining the color, texture and shape features using appropriate weights, the quadtree is used for indexing the images. It is experimentally found that the proposed indexing method using quadtree gives better performance than the other existing indexing methods.

INTRODUCTION

With the development of digital image processing technology, it has become essential to find a method to efficiently and effectively search and browse images from large image database. The visual information system provides the content-based access to images. The content based image retrieval (CBIR) is a technique uses visual contents to index and retrieve the images from the large image database according to user's interest. The most widely used visual features are color, texture and shape features of images. The images in the database are represented by feature vectors in medium or high dimensional space. The similarity between query image and images in the database is measured using distance or indexing methods in feature space by Te-Wei Chian et.al (2007). Some of the examples for CBIR systems are IBM's QBIC discussed by Niblack et.al (1993) and MIT's Photobook in Pentland et.al(1994). When the number of images used is small (100-10,000), the simple linear searching technique is used to retrieve

DOI: 10.4018/978-1-4666-9685-3.ch008

the images. The authors of Manjunath et.al (1998) and Ogle et.al (1995) discussed in their research paper that if the number of images in the database is very large(100,000-10,000,000), like digital libraries and other information systems where indexing the image features becomes inevitable.

The main components of CBIR are features. They are classified into local features and global features. Object recognition can be done easily using the local features. This paper focuses on retrieving the relevant images using global features. The color, texture and shape features are extracted from the images and they are combined using proposed weighted features. Then, the quadtree indexing is used to index all the images available in the large database.

RELATED WORK

Many approaches are devised to index the large databases. In spatial access indexing method, an image is represented using image features and different distances are used to find the similarity between the query image and database images. KD-Tree by Bentley et.al (1975) and R-Tree by Guttman et.al (1984) are the examples of spatial access method. An R-tree is a height-balanced tree similar to B-tree with index records are in its leaf nodes containing pointers to data objects. The structure of R tree which is designed so that a spatial search requires visiting only a small number of nodes, the index is completely dynamic. Then, R* Tree discussed by Beckmann et.al (1990) gives better performance than the R-Tree. R*-tree incorporates a combined optimization of area, margin and overlap of each enclosing rectangle in the directory. Rb-Tree was introduced by Sellis et.al (1987) used a method called 'forced reinstart'.

The nearest neighbour search algorithms based on kd-trees, have been applied to large scale indexing and searching was found by Arya et.al (1998) and Lowe et.al (2004). Octavian et.al (2003) proposed Bkd- tree which is the extension of kd-tree is proposed to make static structure of tree to be dynamic. Complete survey of multi-dimensional indexing are found by Gaede et.al (1998) and Arge et.al (2002). The authors Berg et.al (2008) and Shakhnarovich et.al (2006) discussed that the nearest neighbour (NN) search is a fundamental problem in the research communities of computational geometry and machine learning. The k-D-B Tree is proposed by Robinson (1981). It is a height-balanced tree similar to the B+tree and its tree structure is constructed by dividing the search space into sub regions with coordinate planes recursively.

The TV-Tree using telescope vectors is devised by Lin et.al (1994). It organises the data in hierarchical structure. Berchtold et.al (1996) introduced X-Tree for indexing high-dimensional data. It uses the split algorithm minimizing overlap and additionally utilizes the concept of supernodes. It performs better than TV-Tree and R* Tree. RP-KD Tree is proposed by Pengcheng et.al (2011) in which multiple KD trees are used to present the data points in CBIR system into a lower-dimensional space. Space partitioning structures like quadtree by Samet (1984) and LSD Tree by Andreas et.al (1989) are used for high-dimensional feature space. A variant optimized k-d tree called VAM k-d tree is presented by White et.al (1997). A new dynamic index structure called GC-tree is proposed by Guang-Ho Cha et.al (2002). It is based on subspace partitioning method optimized for high-dimensional image dataset.

Norio Katayama et.al (1997) proposed SR-tree which is the integration of bounding spheres and bounding rectangles. White et.al (1996) introduced SS-Tree which uses minimum bounding spheres instead of rectangles. The author Xing Tong et.al (2013) a new type of index structure called SR tree based on R-Tree and inverted table is proposed. There are several tree approaches like S^2-Tree by Haixun Wang et.al (2001) which is a combination of two trees like X tree, which provides the clustering methods of spatial objects and suffix tree which implements subsequence matching on the binary sequences. The Hybrid Tree by K.Chakrabarti (1999), high dimensional large size feature databases demonstrate that the hybrid tree scales well to high dimensionality and large database sizes. Sakurai et.al (2000) proposed A-Tree includes the virtual bounding rectangles and contains approximate minimum bounding rectangles and data objects.

The quad tree structure is introduced by Aouat (2010) to specify block-oriented decomposition of database images. 3D objects are represented by their silhouettes and codified following the filling rate of each quadrant at different levels of the quad-tree subdivision. It is found that the three decomposition levels are sufficient to efficiently index all the images of the database. Eyas El-Qawasmeh (2003) used the quadtrees to splits the database into multi-subsets by adding some extra fields to facilitate the image search. A centroid partial match algorithm is suggested to process the search query. The algorithm selects random points from an image in a circular uniform movement to check for image match. It searches a subset of the image database rather than the whole database. John R.Smith et al (1994) proposed the quad-tree method for iteratively testing conditions for splitting parent blocks based on texture content of children blocks. The proposed method is used to extract the homogeneous blocks of texture which can be used in a database index.

As a result, quadtree is picked as the preferred representation method of multi-dimensional indexing in this chapter. The proposed indexing method using quadtree with weighted features of the combination of color, texture and shape feature and is not discussed in any of the literature discussed above.

PROPOSED WORK

Content Based Image Retrieval system is used to search digital images in large databases and retrieve the relevant ones based on the actual content of the given query image. Content can be in the form of low-level features or any other information from the image. Figure 1 shows the block diagram of the proposed CBIR system using the quadtree indexing method. The steps involved in the proposed process are shown as the following:

1. Color features of an image are obtained using color coherence vector.
2. Texture features are extracted using segmentation based fractal texture analysis.
3. Shape features are retrieved using Fourier descriptors.
4. All features are combined to get a single feature vector with appropriate weights.
5. The proposed quadtree algorithm is used to index each image using its corresponding feature vector after applying step 1 to step 4 to all images in the database.
6. The proposed quadtree indexing method is compared with other indexing methods.

COLOR COHERENCE VECTOR (CCV)

Color coherence vector classifies each pixel as either coherent or incoherent. Coherent pixel is part of a big connected component (CC) while incoherent pixel is part of a small connected component. Of course, defining the criteria to measure whether a connected component is big or not, is an initial task.

Figure 1. Block diagram of the proposed CBIR system

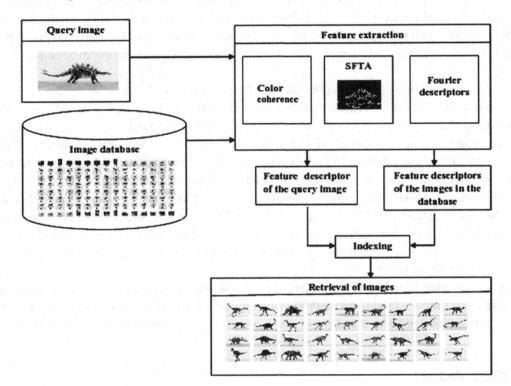

Computing CCV

At first, blur the image slightly by replacing pixel values with the average value in a small local neighbourhoods currently including 8 adjacent pixels. It eliminates small variations between neighboring pixels.

The next step is classifying the pixels within a given color bucket as either coherent or incoherent. A coherent pixel is part of a large group of pixels of the same color, while an incoherent pixel is not. Then, determine the pixel groups by computing connected components. A connected component C is a maximal set of pixels such that for any two pixels $p, p' \in C$, there is a path in C between p and p'. As connected components within a given discretized color bucket are only computed, segmenting the image based on the discretized colorspace becomes more effective.

Connected components can be computed in linear time. When this is complete, each pixel will belong to exactly one connected component. Then, classify the pixels as either coherent or incoherent depending on the size in pixels of its connected component. A pixel is coherent if the size of its connected component exceeds a fixed value ; otherwise, the pixel is incoherent.

For a given discretized color, some of the pixels with that color will be coherent and some will be incoherent. Let us call the number of coherent pixels of the jth discretized color is $\propto_j$ and the number of incoherent pixels is β_j. Clearly, the total number of pixels with that color is $\propto_j + \beta_j$, and so a color histogram would summarize an image as

$$< \alpha_j + \beta_j, ..., \alpha_n + \beta_n > \tag{1}$$

Instead, for each color, compute the pair

$$(\alpha_j, \beta_j) \tag{2}$$

which is called as the coherence pair for the jth color. The color coherence vector for the image consists of

$$< \alpha_j + \beta_j, ..., \alpha_n + \beta_n > \tag{3}$$

This is a vector of coherence pairs, one for each discretized color. (Alaa Al-Hamami et.al, 2010)

SEGMENTATION BASED FRACTAL TEXTURE ANALYSIS

The texture feature extraction technique used here is Segmentation based Fractal Texture Analysis(SFTA). It can be divided into two main parts: First, the input color image is converted into a gray scale image. Second, the gray scale image is decomposed into a set of binary images by employing a new technique named Two-Threshold Binary Decomposition (TTBD). Then, for each resulting binary image, the fractal dimension from its region's boundaries is calculated. The mean gray level and size of each region are also calculated.

Two-Threshold Binary Decomposition

The Two-Threshold Binary Decomposition takes a gray scale image $I(x, y)$ as input, and returns a set of binary images. The first step of TTBD is computing a set T of threshold values. The set T is obtained by selecting equally spaced gray level values by employing the multi-level Otsu algorithm. This algorithm finds the threshold that minimizes the input image intra-class variance. Then, recursively, the algorithm is applied to each image region until the desired number of thresholds n_t is obtained, where n_t is a user defined parameter.

The next step of the TTBD algorithm is decomposing the input gray scale image $I(x,y)$ into a set of binary images. This is achieved by selecting pairs of thresholds from T and applying two-threshold segmentation as follows:

$$I_b(x, y) = \begin{cases} 1, & if \ t_e < I(x, y) \le t_u \\ 0, otherwise \end{cases} \tag{4}$$

where t_e and t_u denote lower and upper threshold value respectively. The segmentation is applied on the input image using all pairs of contiguous thresholds from $T \bigcup \{n_l\}$ and all pairs of thresholds

$\{t, n_l\}$, $t \in T$, where n_l corresponds to the maximum possible gray level in $I(x, y)$. Thus, the number of resulting binary images obtained is $2n_t$, where $n_t = 8$.

An important property of the TTBD is that the set of binary images obtained is a superset of all binary images that would be obtained by applying a threshold segmentation using the thresholds computed with the multilevel Otsu algorithm. The rationale for using pairs of thresholds to compute the set of binary images is to segment objects that otherwise would not be segmented by regular threshold segmentation. It is especially true for objects and structures whose gray level lies in the middle range of the input image histogram.

Segmentation Based Fractal Texture Analysis (SFTA)

After applying the Two Threshold Binary Decomposition on the input gray level image, the fractal dimension from its regional boundaries, mean gray level and size of the resulting set of binary images are used to construct the SFTA feature vector. The elements of feature vector are calculated as follows:

The fractal measurements are employed to describe the boundary complexity of objects and structures segmented in the input image. The region boundaries of a binary image $I_b(x, y)$ are represented as a border image denoted by $\Delta(x, y)$ and computed as follows:

$$\Delta(x, y) = \begin{cases} 1, & if \quad \exists(x', y') \in N_8\big[(x, y)\big]: \\ & \quad I_b(x', y') = 0 \text{ } ^\wedge \\ & \quad I_b(x, y) = 1 \\ 0, & otherwise \end{cases} \qquad (5)$$

where $N_8\big[(x, y)\big]$ is the set of pixels that are 8-connected to (x, y). $\Delta(x, y)$ takes the value 1 if the pixel at position (x, y) in the corresponding binary image $I_b(x, y)$ has the value 1 and having at least one neighboring pixel with value 0. Otherwise, $\Delta(x, y)$ takes the value 0. Hence, one can realize that the resulting borders are one-pixel wide. The fractal dimension D is computed from each border image using the box counting algorithm. (A.F.Costa et.al, 2012)

The features extracted from the resulting binary images are three. They are fractal dimensions, mean gray levels and sizes. As each feature has four values, totally 12 feature values are used to represent the texture features of the given image. Figure 2 shows the sample input images of Corel-1K database and Figure 3 presents the sample images after applying the two-threshold binary decomposition on the Corel-1K database.

FOURIER DESCRIPTORS

In order to achieve an efficient content based image retrieval, extracting an appropriate shape signature of an image is essential. In this work, Fourier descriptors of image are considered as shape signature. Fourier descriptors are obtained by applying Fourier transform on the shape boundary. The Fourier transformed coefficients are called as Fourier descriptors. The method for calculating the Fourier coefficients are given as follows:

Figure 2. Sample input images of Corel-1K database

Figure 3. The images after applying two threshold binary decomposition on Corel-1K database

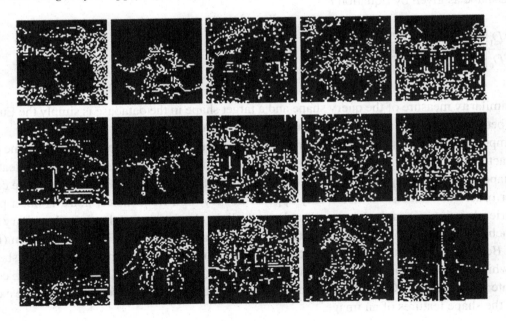

At first, shape boundary is a set of coordinates (x_i, y_i), $i = 1, 2, \ldots, L$, which are extracted out in the preprocessing stage by contour tracing technique. The centroid distance function is expressed by the distance of the boundary points from the centroid (x_c, y_c) of the shape as

$$r_i = \sqrt{([x_i - x_c]^2 + [y_i - y_c]^2)}, i = 1, 2, \ldots, L \tag{6}$$

where (x_c, y_c) are averages of x coordinates and y coordinates respectively. Due to the subtraction of centroid from boundary coordinates, the centroid distance representation is invariant to shape translation.

In order to apply Fourier transform, all the shapes in the database are normalized to the same number of boundary points (N). In this normalisation process, N is fixed to 128 since it provides optimal results. The discrete Fourier transform of $r_i, i = 0, 1, \ldots, N-1$ is then given by

$$u_n = \frac{1}{N} \sum_{i=0}^{N-1} r_i^{\left(\frac{-j2\pi ni}{N}\right)}, n = 0, 1, \ldots, N-1 \tag{7}$$

The coefficients $u_n, n = 0, 1, \ldots, N-1$, are called as Fourier descriptors (*FD*) of the shape, denoted as FD_n, $n = 0, 1, \ldots, N-1$.

The *FD*s acquired in this way are translation invariant due to the translation invariance of centroid distance. To achieve rotation invariance, phase information of the *FD*s are ignored and only the magnitudes $|FD_n|$ are used. Scale invariance is achieved by dividing the magnitudes by the discrete component(DC), i.e., $|FD_0|$. Since, centroid distance is a real value function, only half of the *FD*s are needed to index the shapes. Finally, the following feature vector is used as the Fourier descriptors to index the shape as given by Equation 8.

$$f = \left[\frac{|FD_1|}{|FD_0|}, \frac{|FD_2|}{|FD_0|}, \ldots, \frac{|FD_{N/2}|}{|FD_0|} \right] \tag{8}$$

The similarity measure of the query shape and a target shape in the database is simply the Euclidean distance between the query and the target shape feature vectors.

The important properties of Fourier descriptors are its robustness, being able to capture some perceptual characteristics of the shape and easy to derive. With Fourier descriptors, coarse shape features or global shape features are captured by lower order coefficients and the finer shape features are captured by higher order coefficients. As noise only appears in very high frequencies, noise is not a problem with Fourier descriptors and they are truncated out. A slight change around the shape boundary doesn't cause much difference in the final representation. The computation of fast Fourier transform (FFT) is efficient. Because a small number of low order coefficients are enough to capture the overall shape features in which, the representation of shape is also compact (Zhang et.al, 2001). In this work, complex co-ordinate value is 20 and Cumulative angular function value is 20. So, 40 feature values are extracted to define the shape features of an image.

COMBINING THE FEATURES

The color feature of an image is extracted using the Color coherent vector. The feature vector is represented as f. The texture features are retrieved using Segmentation based Fractal Texture Analysis (SFTA). Its feature vector is written as f_t. The shape features of an image are retrieved using Fourier descriptors. The feature vector of shape features is represented as f_s. Weights such as w_c, w_t and w_s are assigned to color, texture and shape features respectively. Initially, random values between 0 and 1 are assigned to w_c, w_t and w_s. Then, based on experimental results optimal weights are found. The sum of weights of the features is 1. The combined feature vector is given as

$$f_{com} = w_c f_c + w_t f_t + w_s f_s \qquad (9)$$

The combined feature vector f_{com} has 60 values. The mean and median of combined feature vector are considered for constructing the quadtree and searching of the relevant images.

INDEXING

The feature vectors of images tend to have high dimensionality and therefore are not well suited to traditional indexing structures like distance based similarity measurement. To make the content-based image retrieval truly scalable to large size image collections, efficient multidimensional indexing techniques need to be explored. In this chapter, one of the tree indexing methods, quadtree indexing is used to index the features of the images in the large image database.

Point Region Quadtree Creation

One of the most famous space partitioning structures is the quadtree. In general, the quadtree is used to organize two dimensional data in a tree structure by recursively subdividing the space into four quadrants or cells, each of which corresponding to a rectangle. Here, Point region(PR) quadtree is used. PR quadtree always split regions into four parts. In a 2-d tree, node N splits a region into two by drawing one line through the point (N.xval, N.yval). In a PR quadtree, node N splits the region into four by drawing both horizontal and a vertical line through the point (N.xval, N.yval). These four parts are called northwest (NW), southwest (SW), northeast (NE) and southeast (SE) quadrants. Each of these quadrants corresponds to a child of node N. In binary search trees, the structure of the tree depends upon not only what data values are inserted, but also in what order they are inserted. In contrast, the structure of a Point-Region quadtree is determined entirely by the data values it contains, and is independent of the order of their insertion (C.W.Emerson et.al, 2006). Figure 4 depicts the structure of the PR-Quadtree after the insertion of data into leaf nodes.

. In effect, each node of a PR quadtree represents a particular region in a 2D coordinate space. Internal nodes have exactly four children of which some of them may be empty. Each node represents a different, congruent quadrant of the region represented by their parent node. Internal nodes do not store data. Leaf nodes hold a single data value. Therefore, as insertions are performed, the coordinate space is partitioned so that no region contains more than a single point. PR quadtrees represent points in a finite bounded coordinate space.

Figure 4. Structure of the PR-Quadtree after the insertion of data into leaf nodes

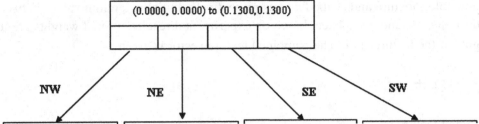

PR Quadtree Insertion

Inserting the first node in a PR quadtree results in the creation of a leaf node (root node) holding the first data node. Inserting next node causes the partitioning of the original coordinate space into four quadrants, and the replacement of the root to an internal node with two nonempty children: The Algorithm 1 presents the process for inserting a new node in PR-quadtree and Algorithm 2 depicts the steps involved in searching the relevant images from the PR-quadtree.

PR-Quadtree Searching Method

In this method, the searching algorithm finds the optimal range in the tree in the direction of NW, NE, SE and SW respectively. If the optimal region is found, and in that region if the leaf contains the mean and median values closer to the query image's mean and median values, then it is added to the relevant image list. The process is repeated in all 4 directions and the relevant images are displayed.

Algorithm 1. Insertion of new node into PR- Quadtree

Input   : Mean and median feature vectors fm_i and fmd_i in feature database.
(Mean and median feature vector f_d ($f_{d_i} \rightarrow [fm_i ; fmd_i]$)

Output : Created tree structure
Method:

Step 1: **for** each feature vectors in the feature database f_d
Step 2:   **Read**   [fm_i;fmd_i] and
Step 3:   Check for the empty tree.   // (t == null)
             if the tree is empty
Step 4:   Create a root which contains the range ($fm_{\_min}$;$fmd_{\_min}$) to ($fm_{\_max}$;$fmd_{\_max}$)
Step 5:   Place [fm_i;fmd_i] in the root
Step 6:   **else**
                   Check for the leaf
Step 7:   **if** the current node is leaf   // to move in the correct direction

Continued on following page

Algorithm 1. continued

```
Step 8:                              Call the split_function() by passing the new
node [fm_i; fmd_i]
Step 9:                                else
                                 Move down towards one of the splitted node
                        if the node lies in the (fm_min; fmd_mid) to (fm_mid; fmd_max)
Step 10:                               Move towards North West node
Step 11:                               Repeat the steps from 7
Step 12:                    else if the node lies in the (fm_mid; fmd_mid) to
(fm_max; fmd_max)
Step 13:                               Move towards North East
Step 14:                               Repeat the steps from 7
Step 15:                    else if the node lies in the (fm_min; fmd_min) to
(fm_mid; fmd_mid)
Step 16:                               Move towards South West
Step 17:                               Repeat the steps from 7
Step 18:                    else if the node lies in the (fm_min; fmd_min) to
(fm_mid; fmd_mid)
Step 19:                               Move towards South East
Step 20:                               Repeat the steps from 7
Step 21: end
```

```
Split_ function()
Step 1: create four child node for the node under consideration [fm_c; fmd_c]
Step 2: Node NW is created for the range (fm_min; fmd_mid) to (fm_mid; fmd_max)
Step 3: Node NE is created for the range (fm_mid; fmd_mid) to (fm_max; fmd_max)
Step 4: Node SW is created for the range (fm_min; fmd_min) to (fm_mid; fmd_mid)
Step 5: Node SE is created for the range (fm_min; fmd_min) to (fm_mid; fmd_mid)
Step 6: Bring down the current node [fm_c; fmd_c] to either NW, NE, SW, SE
Step 7: For the new node [fm_i; fmd_i] repeat from step 7 in insertin().
```

EXPERIMENTAL RESULTS

Experiment 1

The proposed work is experimented on Corel-1K database. The database has 10 categories. In each category, there are 100 images. The total number of images in the database is 1000. The size of images in the database is 384 x 256 or 256 x 384. Table 1 shows the categories of images in Corel-1K database.

Algorithm 2. Searching of relevant node from PR- Quadtree

Input   :   Created PR-tree
Output :   Retrieving of relevant node

Method:

Step1:   **While** (!tree empty)
Step 2:   **if** the optimal region falls inside the root region then
move down
Step 3:   **if** the optimal region falls on the NW's region
Step 4:   **if** NW is a leaf
Step 5:   Add it to relevant image array
Step 6:   **else**
Step 7:   Go to step 3
Step 8:   **else if**
Step 9:   Check NE's region
Step 10:   **if** NE is a leaf
Step 11   :   Add it to relevant image array
Step 12   :   **else**
Step 13   :   Go to step 3
Step 14   :   **else if**
Step 15   :   Check SE's region
Step 16   :   **if** SE is a leaf
Step 17   :   Add it to relevant image array
Step 18   :   **else**
Step 19   :   Go to step 3
Step 20   :   **else if**
Step 21   :   Check SW's region
Step 22   :   **if** SW is a leaf
Step 23   :   Add it to relevant image array
Step 24   :   **else**
Step 25:   Go to step 3
Step 26   :   else if
Step 27   :   add all the leaf nodes to node under
consideration
Step 28: **end**

Table 1. Categories in the Corel image database

African people and villages
Beach
Buildings
Buses
Dinosaurs
Elephants
Flowers
Horses
Mountains and Glaciers
Food

Experiment 2

The experiment is done on Caltech-101 database. It has 101 categories of images. The total number of images in the database is 9146. The size of images in the database is 300 x 200. It has different objects such as Butterflies, Pigeon, Emu, Buddha, Fish, Rooster, Water lily, Sunflower, Kangaroo, etc.

Performance Evaluation

Let N_{rr} be the number of relevant images retrieved and N_r be the number of images retrieved, then the precision is defined as the ratio of N_{rr} to N_r. Let N_{rd} be the number of relevant images in the database. Recall is defined as the ratio of the N_{rr} to N_{rd}

$$Precision = \frac{N_{rr}}{N_r}$$

$$Recall = \frac{N_{rr}}{N_{rd}}$$

The experiment is done for different values of w_c, w_t and w_s. It is found that the best results are obtained when $w_c = 0.3$, $w_t = 0.3$ and $w_s = 0.4$ respectively.

Figure 5 and Figure 6 represent the relationship between precision and recall of the proposed PR-quadtree with other indexing methods like Rb tree, Bkd tree and TV tree. It is found that the proposed PR-quadtree indexing method with the fusion of weighted features gives better results than the other indexing methods with average precision of 0.83 value on Corel-1K database and average precision of 0.76 value on Caltech-101 database. Figure 7 and Figure 8 show the comparison of retrieved results of proposed indexing method and other indexing methods on Corel-1K database and Caltech-101 database respectively.

Figure 5. Precision-recall graph of different indexing methods on Corel-1K database

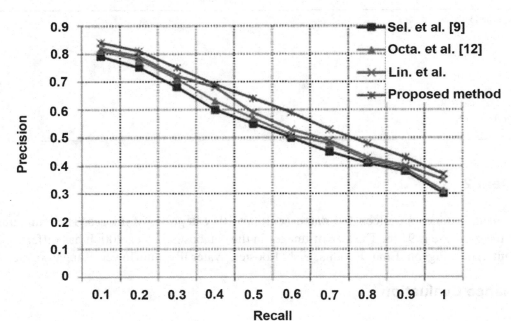

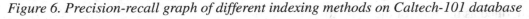

Figure 6. Precision-recall graph of different indexing methods on Caltech-101 database

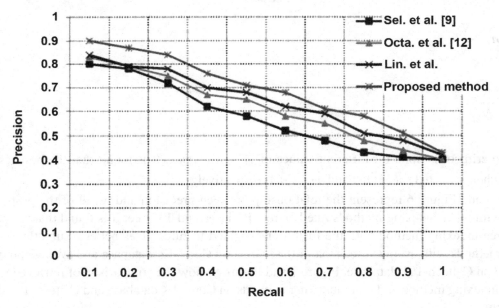

Figure 7. (a) Query image (b) Retrieved results of Sel.et.al [9] (c) Retrieved results of Octa.et.al[12] (d) Retrieved results of Lin.et.al[18] (e) Retrieved results of proposed PR-quadtree of Corel-1K database

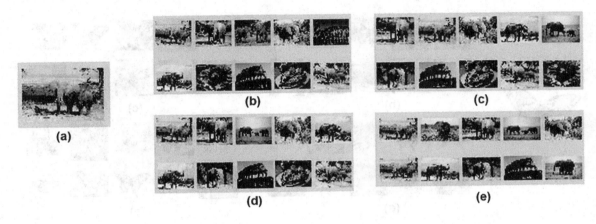

Figure 8. (a) Query image (b) Retrieved results of Sel.et.al [9] (c) Retrieved results of Octa.et.al[12] (d) Retrieved results of Lin.et.al[18] (e) Retrieved results of proposed PR-quadtree of Corel-1K database

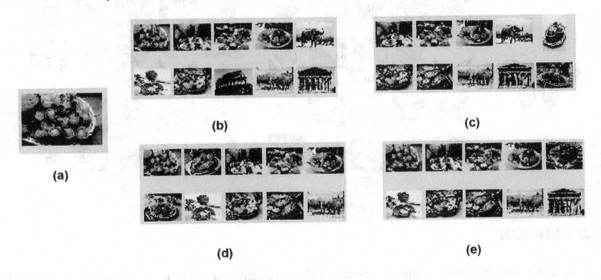

Figure 9. (a) Query image (b) Retrieved results of Sel.et.al [9] (c) Retrieved results of Octa.et.al[12] (d) Retrieved results of Lin.et.al[18] (e) Retrieved results of proposed PR-quadtree of Caltech-101 database

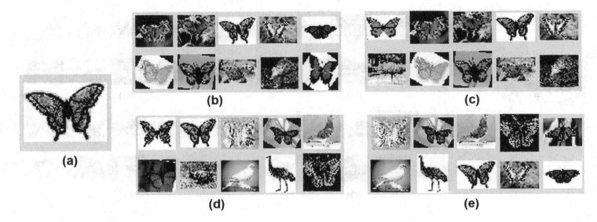

Figure 10. (a) Query image (b) Retrieved results of Sel.et.al [9] (c) Retrieved results of Octa.et.al[12] (d) Retrieved results of Lin.et.al[18] (e) Retrieved results of proposed PR-quadtree of Caltech-101 database

CONCLUSION

In this chapter, the color features are extracted by Color coherent vector. The texture features are obtained by applying Segmentation based Fractal Texture Analysis. The shape features are extracted by Fourier descriptors. The extracted features are combined using appropriate weights assigned to the features. The PR-quadtree is proposed as the indexing method to index all images in the database. The relevant images are retrieved using the proposed PR-quadtree indexing method and compared with the existing indexing methods like Rb tree, Bkd tree and TV tree. The experiment is conducted on benchmark databases like Corel-1K database and Caltech-101 database. It is found experimentally that the proposed PR-quadtree with weighted features gives average precision of 0.83 value on Corel-1K database and average precision of 0.76 value on Caltech-101 database. It is observed that PR quadtree outperforms than other existing indexing methods for image retrieval from large image database. In future, integrated image retrieval based on the low-level features and high-level semantic features of images will be considered to reduce the semantic gap. Further research will develop and test the combination of quadtree with any other tree for indexing to minimize the image retrieval time.

REFERENCES

Al-Hamami, A., & Al-Rashdan, H. (2010). Improving the Effectiveness of Color Coherehence Vector. Histogram. *The International Arab Journal of Information Technology, 7*(3), 324–332.

Aouat. (2010). Indexing binary images using quad-tree decomposition. In *Proceedings of IEEE International Conference on Systems Man & Cybernetics,* (pp. 3074-3080). IEEE.

Arge, L. (2002), External memory data structures. In J. Abello, P. M. Pardalos, & M. G. C. Resende (Eds.), Handbook of Massive Data Sets, (pp. 313–358). doi:10.1007/978-1-4615-0005-6_9

Arya, S., Mount, D. M., Netanyahu, N. S., Silverman, R., & Wu, A. Y. (1998). An optimal algorithm for approximate nearest neighbor searching fixed dimensions. *Journal of the ACM, 45*(6), 891–923. doi:10.1145/293347.293348

Beckmann, N., Kriegel, H. P., Schneider, R., & Seeger, B. (1990). The R*-Tree: An efficient and robust access method for points and rectangles. *Proceedings of the ACM SIGMOD International Conference on Management of Data*. ACM. doi:10.1145/93597.98741

Bentley, J. L. (1975). Multi dimensional binary search trees used for associative searching. *Communications of the ACM, 18*(9), 509–517. doi:10.1145/361002.361007

Berchtold, S., Keim, D., & Kriegel, H. P. (1996). The X-Tree: An index structure for high-dimensional data. *Proceedings of the International Conference on Very Large Databases*, (pp. 28–39).

Cha, G.-H., & Chung, C.-W. (2002). The GC-Tree: A High-Dimensional Index Structure for Similarity Search in Image Databases. *IEEE Transactions on Multimedia, 4*(2), 235–247. doi:10.1109/TMM.2002.1017736

Chakrabarti, K., & Mehrotra, S. (1999). The hybrid Tree: An index structure for high dimensional feature spaces. *Proceedings of the International Conference on Data Engineering*, (pp. 440–447). doi:10.1109/ICDE.1999.754960

Chiang, Tsai, & Huang. (2007). An Efficient Indexing Method for Content-Based Image Retrieval. *Proceedings of IEEE International Conference on Innovative Computing, Information and Control*, (pp. 222-225). IEEE.

Costa, Humpire-Mamani, & Machado Traina. (2012). An Efficient Algorithm for Fractal Analysis of Textures. In *Proceedings of IEEE 25th SIBGRAPI Conference on Graphics, Patterns and Images*, (pp. 39-46). IEEE.

de Berg, M., Eindhoven, T., Cheong, O., Van Kreveld, M., & Overmars, M. (2008). Computational Geometry: Algorithms and Applications. Springer-Verlag.

El-Qawasmeh, E. (2003). A quadtree-based representation technique for indexing and retrieval of image databases. *Journal of Visual Communication and Image Representation, 14*(3), 340–357. doi:10.1016/S1047-3203(03)00034-8

Emerson, C. W., & Chinniah, S. (2006) A Region Quadtree Approach To Content Based Image Retrieval. *Proceedings of ASPRS*, (pp. 1-11).

Gaede, V., & Gunther, O. (1998). Multidimensional access methods. *ACM Computing Surveys, 30*(2), 170–231. doi:10.1145/280277.280279

Guttman, A. (1984). R-Trees: a dynamic index structure for spatial searching. *Proceedings of the ACM SIGMOD International Conference on Management of Data*. Boston, MA: ACM. doi:10.1145/602259.602266

Henrich, A., Six, H.-W., & Widmaye, P. (1989). The LSD tree: Spatial access to multidimensional point and non-point objects. In *Proceedings of the Fifteenth International Conference on Very Large Data Bases* (pp. 45–53).

Katayama, N., & Satoh. (1997). The SR-tree: An Index Structure for High-Dimensional Nearest Neighbor Queries. *Proceedings of ACM SIGMOD, International Conference on Data, 26*(2), 369-380. doi:10.1145/253260.253347

Lin, K., Jagadish, H. V., & Faloutsos, C. (1994). The TV-Tree: An index for high dimensional data. *The VLDB Journal, 3*(4), 517–543. doi:10.1007/BF01231606

Lowe, D. G. (2004). Distinctive image features from scale-invariant key points. *International Journal of Computer Vision, 60*(2), 91–110. doi:10.1023/B:VISI.0000029664.99615.94

Manjunath, B. S. (1998). Image Browsing in the Alexandria Digital Library (ADL) Project. *Proceedings of IEEE International Forum on Research and Technology Advances in Digital Libraries*, (pp. 180-187). IEEE. doi:10.1109/ADL.1998.670393

Niblack, W., Barber, R., Equitz, W., Flickner, M., Glasman, E. H., Petkovic, D., & Taubin, G. et al. (1993). The QBIC project: Querying images by content using color, texture, and shape. *Proceedings of the SPIE: Storage and Retrieval for Image and Video Databases, 1908*, 173–187. doi:10.1117/12.143648

Ogle, V. E., Stonebraker, M., & Chabot. (1995). Retrieval from a relational database of images. *IEEE Computer, 28*(9), 40–48.

Pengcheng, W., Hoi, Nguyen, & He. (2011). Randomly Projected KD-Trees with Distance Metric Learning for Image Retrieval. *The 17th International Conference on Multi Media Modeling*, 1-11.

Pentland, A. P., Picard, R., & Sclaroff, S. (1994). Photobook: Tools for Content-Based Manipulation of Image databases. In *Proceedings of the SPIE: Storage and Retrieval for Image and Video Databases II*. doi:10.1117/12.171786

Procopiuc, & Agarwal, P. K. (2003). Bkd-Tree: A Dynamic Scalable kd-Tree. *LNCS, 2750*, 46–65.

Robinson, J. T. (1981) The k-D-B-Tree: A Search Structure for Large Multidimensional Dynamic Indexes. *Proc. ACM SIGMOD*, 10-18. doi:10.1145/582318.582321

Sakurai, Y., Yoshikawa, M., Uemura, S., & Kojima, H. (2000). The A-tree: An index Structure for High-Dimensional Spaces Using Relative Approximation. *Proceedings of the 26th VLDB Conference.*

Samet, H. (1984). The quadtree and related hierarchical data structure. *ACM Computing Surveys, 16*(2), 187–260. doi:10.1145/356924.356930

Sellis, T. K., Roussopoulos, N., & Faloutsos, C. (1987). The Rb-Tree: A dynamic index for multi-dimensional objects. *Proceedings of the 13th International Conference on Very Large Data Bases*, (pp. 507–518).

Shakhnarovich, G., Darrell, T., & Indyk, P. (2006). *Nearest-Neighbor Methods in Learning and Vision: Theory and Practice.* The MIT Press.

Smith, J. R., & Chung, S.-F. (1994). Quad-tree segmentation for texture-based image query. *Proceedings of ACM second International Conference on Multimedia*, (pp. 1-9). ACM.

Tong, X., Liu, Y., Shi, Z., Zeng, B., & Yu, H. B. (2013). SR-Tree: An index structure of sensor management system for spatial approximate query. *Advanced Materials Research, 756*, 885–889. doi:10.4028/www.scientific.net/AMR.756-759.885

Wang, H., & Perng. (2001). The S2-Tree: An index structure for subsequence matching of spatial objects. *Fifth Pacific-Asic Conference on Knowledge Discovery and Data Mining(PAKDD)*, (LNAI), (vol. 2035, pp. 312-323). Springer.

White, D. A., & Jain, R. (1997). *Similarity Indexing: Algorithms and Performance. In Visual Computing Laboratory* (pp. 1–7). San Diego, CA: University of California.

Zhang, D., & Lu, G. (2001). Content-Based Shape Retrieval Using Different Shape Descriptors: A Comparative Study. *Proceedings of IEEE Conference on Multimedia and Expo*, (pp. 1139-1142).

Section 3
Image and Video Processing in Public Safety

Chapter 9
Early Recognition of Suspicious Activity for Crime Prevention

M. Kalaiselvi Geetha
Annamalai University, India

J. Arunnehru
Annamalai University, India

A. Geetha
Annamalai University, India

ABSTRACT

Automatic identification and early prediction of suspicious human activities are of significant importance in video surveillance research. By recognizing and predicting a criminal activity at an early stage, regrettable incidents can be avoided. Initially, an action recognition framework is developed for identifying the suspicious actions using interest point based 2D and 3D features and transform based approaches. This is subsequently followed by a novel approach for predicting the suspicious actions for crime prevention in real-world scenario. The prediction problem is formulated probabilistically and a novel approach that employs the mixture models for prediction is introduced. The developed system yields promising results for predicting the actions in real-time.

1. INTRODUCTION

Video surveillance is attracting much of the researchers' attention since it is a crucial tool for protecting people and public property and finds most promising application in computer vision. The recent acts of terrorism have necessitated the vital need for well-organized surveillance of suspicious human behaviors at important public places. Suspicious behavior in general incorporates an event that builds a disbelief or mistrust. These events have to be reported for further critical examinations. Currently the surveillance cameras are used extensively and the purpose of these cameras are primarily for security monitoring and identifying illegal actions and events. It is unfeasible for a human supervisor to inspect a huge volume of video recordings, since security personnel are also required to manage other tasks, such as access control, handling emergency calls, following up on fire alarms, radio communications control,

DOI: 10.4018/978-1-4666-9685-3.ch009

etc. However, this is still a novel technology with many practical restrictions. How can one differentiate among an individual running because he/she is delayed or because he/she has just committed a crime? Under such scenario, activity detection alone is not sufficed; prevention of such crime becomes necessary. Current researches on video analysis for surveillance system are post investigation methods and necessitate real-time processing. For example, recognizing missing objects after they have been stolen is of no use. Hence, it is enviable to predict the intension of a person, before the complete happening of the suspicious event. This prediction will possibly prevent a criminal activity, thus providing enough time to the security person to react upon the critical condition to ensure public safety. Hence an automatic activity recognition methodology is necessary.

A greater part of the present surveillance systems only record the events and act as a post event investigation tool which is not preferred. Other systems still submissively observe the surroundings and raise the alarm once a suspicious action is detected. Such an alarm will not help to prevent an unwanted event. Predicting a person's action before it is executed has an ample choice of applications in autonomous robots, surveillance and health care. While comparing the action recognition using full length video, action prediction with unfinished video observations requires identifying the well-grained factors intrinsic to the existing observations that would direct to the future action. For example, a person with stretched open arms indicates that he/she is going to hug. Although, traditional models like hidden markov models are used to approximate the prediction problem, they are found to be inappropriate for the sparse discontinuous features of the video. Thus it is indispensable to develop a novel prediction methodology for recognizing/predicting an incomplete activity from a video.

Activity recognition can be sensor-based or vision-based and this chapter addresses the problem of activity recognition using the later approach. In vision-based activity recognition, the computational procedure is done at four steps viz. human detection, tracking, activity recognition and then a complex activity evaluation.

Latest enhancement in the digital media makes people to produce their own digital video information. This creates the problem of categorizing the new video sequences based on the action categories. Apparently classifying this information for future reference manually is challenging and requires automated techniques. An effective approach to the detection of small objects is seen in (Hsieh, Han, Wu, Chuang & Fan, 2006) by employing watershed-based transformation. The proposed detection system comprises of two main modules, locating region of interest (ROI) and contour extraction. An image differencing technique is first employed on two neighboring image frames to produce rough candidate objects appearing in the images. A novel framework for contour based object detection from cluttered environments is discussed in (Lu, Adluru, Ling, Zhu & Latecki, 2010). The contour model for a class of objects is hierarchically decomposed into portions. Then, they are combined into part bundles, where a part bundle can contain overlapping portions. A background modeling that is appropriate to any spatio-temporal non-parametric moving object recognition strategy is proposed in (Cuevas & García, 2013). Through a proficient and strong method to dynamically estimate the bandwidth of the kernels used in the modeling, the efficiency of previous approaches are improved. Furthermore, by adding a novel mechanism to selectively revise the background model, the number of misdetections is decreased significantly, thus attaining improved performance. (Grabner, Leistner & Bischof, 2008) built a tracking method that utilizes variation in the appearance of the object due to lighting and rotation variations. To track the object using selected distinguishable low-level color features is suggested by (Collins, Liu & Leordeanu, 2005). Labeled information that exploits the underlying structure for selecting positive and negative samples for update is seen in (Kalal, Matas & Mikolajczyk, 2010). Multiple instances learning (MIL) is utilized by (Babenko, Yang & Belongie, 2009) handling ambiguously labeled positive and negative data.

Robustness of object detection is affected by occlusion in the presence of multiple objects. Occlusion is the main cause for performance degradation in surveillance systems. Under occlusion, the objects will become overlapped and may be found moving together in a scene. Occlusion can be classified as complete, partial and non-occlusion. Handling occlusion is an imperative issue in object tracking and is required all through the occlusion and subsequent to the occlusion. During occlusion, two forms of challenges arise. Initially, while two foreground objects occlude each other, the foreground blob of both the objects will form a single blob and become a challenging issue to differentiate the pixels of both the objects precisely. Secondly, at the time of occlusion, the real position of a traced object becomes hard to decide due to the visibility of the object absolutely missing. Further, it is difficult to identify the reappearing object after occlusion. The issue becomes more confusing particularly while tracking multiple objects having identical appearance. Complete occlusion during tracking is normally handled by fusing the object motion with the appearance model by linear dynamic or nonlinear dynamic models for predicting the location of the reappearing object after occlusion. Kalman filter is used for estimating the moving object location in (Ali & Terada, 2009) and (Ren & Hao, 2012). Recently, abundant research have been done in human action recognition field (Poppe, 2010) and (Aggarwal & Ryoo, 2011). Body parts are tracked (Yilma & Shah, 2005) and (Song, Goncalves & Perona, 2003) using the motion trajectories to identify the actions. Feature points are identified in frame-by-frame manner and these points are tracked. These approaches are computation intensive, since they utilize redundant information. Thus, part-based approaches that use the space-time interest points are proposed by I. Laptev (2005).

Derpanis, Sizintsev, Cannons & Wildes (2013) propose to represent actions by shape-motion paradigm trees using hierarchical k-means clustering and then recognition obtained by matching the combined likelihood of the actor location and action paradigm sequences. Wang, Wang, Jiang, Zhao & Gao (2013) proposed a technique for fast frame-based action recognition by combining the optical flow and edge features to discriminate one action from another. Wu & Shao (2013) uses a method based on an extended motion model from human silhouettes. The holistic structural features were extracted from motion templates to discriminate the human activity, which represents local and global information. Lu & Kudo (2014) proposed a novel framework for action representation based on Local Temporal Self-Similarities (LTSSs) pattern is directly derived from the difference images (temporal difference) and does not require location of the human body in each frame. In the frequency domain, well known transform based techniques are Discrete Cosine Transform (DCT) and Discrete Wavelet Transform (DWT). DCT uses real data that concentrates the large DCT coefficients into low frequency region. It has fine energy compactness characteristics. DWT is an orthogonal function that decomposes a discrete signal into a set of discrete wavelets instead of sine and cosine waveforms. It captures both frequency and space information.

Recognizing complex activity and extracting semantic information remains a challenging and active area of research. Environmental variations such as moving backgrounds like trees and handling moving camera is a serious issue. Further, people will execute an activity in their own style. For example walking style of people varies from person to person. A huge number of actions, interactions and group activities create another complication; the ultimate goal is to make a system to recognize the actions with reliability. The bottleneck behind this goal is insufficient amount of training data. In addition, one of the toughest challenges comes from occlusion where the object is covered by a different object for some time. Unfortunately, another object may occlude the target for a long time or might be analogous to the objects' color.

The purpose of this chapter is to investigate the possibilities to predict the actions that a person is going to execute by observing a short video or with a single frame while discussing the techniques for human action prediction problem. It starts with introduction followed by the visual information representation. This is followed by the framework of proposed action recognition approach. Further, activity prediction problem is formulated probabilistically and the novel methodology is explained to solve the problem by effectively estimating the activity in real-time. This is followed by directions for future research and conclusions. Finally, references are listed at the end of the chapter.

VISUAL INFORMATION REPRESENTATION AND ACTIVITY RECOGNITION APPROACHES

Conventionally, activity recognition techniques have centered on the branch of pattern recognition and machine learning. The literature classifies the approaches as sensor based, vision based, data-driven and knowledge-driven. In sensor-based techniques, the wearable sensors are attached to an object under surveillance. These techniques employ the sensor network technology for activity sensing and monitoring. The vision-based approaches use video cameras to monitor the behavior. The data will be in the form of digitized video sequences. These approaches make use of computer vision procedures to analyze the visual patterns for recognition. Data-driven approaches are based on probabilistic classification and are competent of managing uncertain information. However, this approach requires huge datasets for training. Activity models constructed using the knowledge based approaches are generally utilized for activity prediction through formal reasoning. These approaches are easy to start, semantically understandable and logically well-designed but cannot handle uncertainty.

For recognizing an action, still certain improvements are to be done in the existing approaches, particularly to deal with the posture and clothes, moving background, imperfect occlusion, camera motion, zooming, etc. In order to overcome these difficulties, researchers concentrate on part-based approaches where only the 'interesting' parts of the video are examined instead of the complete video. These 'interesting' parts can be corners, contours generated from silhouettes and spatio-temporal interest points. A recognition method that employs spatio-temporal interest points, which are robust to moving background, viewpoint variations and zooming is proposed in this chapter. A video sequence v is given as a function $v : \mathbb{R}^2 \times \mathbb{R} \to \mathbb{R}$. A sampling point $(x, y, t, \sigma, \tau)^{\mathrm{T}}$ is located in the video sequence at $(x, y, t, \sigma, \tau)^{\mathrm{T}}$. The characteristic spatial and temporal scales are σ and τ respectively. The spatial scale (σ) describes the similar structure seen in the image plane. The temporal scale (τ) models similar motion seen over a different length of time. σ and τ establish the spatial and temporal neighborhood size of the descriptor at position (x, y, t). Plenty of research is seen in extracting the 'interesting' regions from the image sequences. These regions can be extracted either inclusive of other details or confined only to the local patches. The earlier approach is more influential since it includes more information but is more sensitive to noise, viewpoint and occlusions and hence the proposed work is confined only to the extraction of local patches.

Figure 1. General architecture of surveillance system for action prediction

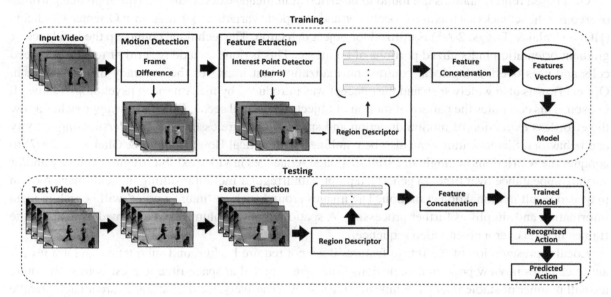

The general architecture of the surveillance system is shown in Figure 1. Activity recognition approaches are normally based on motion identification from video. The following discussions briefly explain the approaches for motion detection and image feature representation approaches.

Before embarking an in-depth discussion on human activity, it is helpful to discriminate human behaviors in various levels of granularity. Activity refers to the intricate sequence of motion patterns performed in a restricted style. For example, the behavior for the phrase 'take the book', indicates the sequence of motion patterns such as going near the table, and taking the book. Similarly, recognizing a suspicious activity originally involves classifying the normal and suspicious events and then identifying the particular suspicious activity. Thus the activity recognition approaches naturally follows a hierarchical pattern. Lower level involves detection, tracking and recognition. Higher level semantics of the recognized activities are encoded based on the lower level primitive information.

Median filter is a technique for background subtraction. The applications on median operations are limited due to their time consumption. Recently (Hung, Pan & Hsieh, 2014) uses temporal median filters for background subtraction. Temporal median computes the preceding frames median in a video sequence and set up a numerical background model. It is one among the most largely used background subtraction approach. Conversely, the time consumption of the same limits its applications. A fast temporal median can be computed by using the properties of high correlation of contiguous frames. The method checks whether the median of the current frame is equal to that of the previous frame. However it requires relatively high memory requirements. In background mixture model, every pixel's intensity values in the video are modeled using a Gaussian Mixture Model. The Gaussians that provide the supporting evidence and least variance correspond probably to the background. The pixels that do not satisfy this criterion are grouped using 2D connected component analysis and are considered to be foreground pixels. Initializing the Gaussians, too many parameters and sudden, drastic lighting changes are a few of the shortcomings of this approach. Further low-level features are also extracted using the global distribution of color (Yanagawa, Hsu & Chang, 2006), texture (Manjunath & Ma, 1996) and edges.

Grid based representations are found to be efficient in image/video analysis. This approach partially overcomes the setbacks such as noise, occlusion and viewpoint variations. Histogram of Oriented Gradients (HOG) (Dalal & Triggs, 2005) is utilized for object detection. The technique counts up the incidence of gradient orientation in localized portions of an image. This is done on a dense grid of regularly spaced cells and uses overlapping local contrast normalization that improves the accuracy of the approach. Optical flow is also widely seen and the concept was introduced by the American psychologist James J. Gibson. This computes the pattern of motion of objects in a visual scene. Optical flow approaches allow the effortless extraction of motion direction and speed, which are essential for understanding activity and behaviors. Shape features can also be combined with optical flow (Danafar & Gheissari, 2007) to conquer the restrictions of single illustration. Image sequences in video exhibit irregular velocity and/or varying appearance over time. In general, a point with irregular motion resulting in local image motion may also result in global object motion. The images around such an 'interest point' will be rich in local information and simplifies further processing. A spatio-temporal volume can be formed by heaping the frames in time over a given video sequence.

Local representation of the image features does not require background subtraction and are invariant to changes in view point and occlusions. They are sampled at space-time interest points. But quite a small number of stable interest points are an issue. Alternatively, local descriptors are ideal to handle background clutter and invariant to rotation, scale and are decided by the interest point scale. Further, they are robust to viewpoint, scale changes and are capable of capturing appearance and motion. They are easy to implement and show good performance for action classification in videos. A transform based action recognition framework is proposed by Shao, Gao, Liu & Zhang (2011) using cuboids constructed around interest points. The proposed work presents a novel method that uses the local motion information for detecting the interest points from the video. Initially, the approach extracts the structural information by locating the maximum moving regions and then identifies the cuboids in neighborhoods having a higher probability of relevant information for recognizing the actions.

HUMAN ACTION RECOGNITION FRAMEWORK - OVERVIEW

For better understanding of the underlying study of this chapter, a real life scenario for human action recognition is experimented. The actions such as handshake, hug, kick, point, punch, push etc., between two persons meeting each other are to be predicted in the scenario. The proposed work employs ideal feature extraction approaches and classifiers which reveal promising outcomes.

The overview of the proposed approach is in the Figure 2. Frame difference is applied to extract the motion information. 2D/3D cuboids are constructed from the spatio-temporal interest points that exploit the structural and motion information. Support vector machines and random forest classifiers are employed to classify the test video to the most feasible action type based on the trained model.

Feature Description

Background subtraction or foreground detection is a technique in which region of interest or objects (human, vehicle etc) are extracted from image sequences. Frame differencing is a popular approach to identify motion patterns in a scene by subtracting the consecutive frames in a video on a pixel by pixel

Figure 2. Overview of the proposed Action Recognition Framework

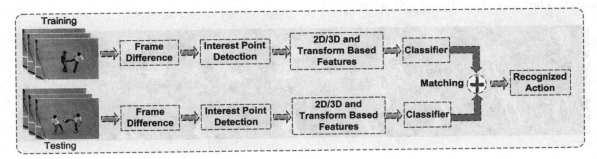

basis. As seen in Figure 3, the punching action can be easily perceived. The shape of the human silhouette plays a major role in recognizing human actions, and it can be extracted by frame differencing.

Difference image is given by,

$$D_k(i,j) = |I_k(i,j) - I_{k+1}(i,j)| \qquad (1)$$
$$1 \le i \le w, \ 1 \le j \le h$$

where, $I_k(i,j)$ is the intensity of the pixel (i,j) in the kth frame, w and h are the width and height of the image respectively.

Motion information T_k is calculated using:

$$T_k(i,j) = \begin{cases} 1, & \text{if } D_k(i,j) > t; \\ 0, & \text{Otherwise;} \end{cases} \qquad (2)$$

where t is the threshold. The value of $t = 30$ is used in the experiments. The dynamic information is extracted from the difference image D_k as in Eq. (1) and Eq. (2). The major aim of frame differencing is to identify the maximum motion region while performing the action. But, the efficiency depends on object speed and frame rate.

Two dominant and different edge directions in a local region are defined as a corner. An interest point has a well-defined position in an image having local intensity maximum or minimum or where the cur-

Figure 3. Computing difference image from two consecutive frames

(a) Frame at '(t-1)'   (b) Frame at 't'   (c) Difference Image

Figure 4. Extracted spatial-temporal interest points for action 'hug'. The highlighted points indicate the local patches placed on the interest points.

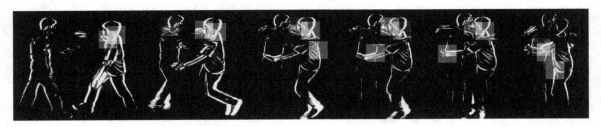

vature is locally maximal. Harris 2D (Laptev, Marszalek, Schmid, & Rozenfeld, 2008) and 3D (Harris & Stephens, 1988) are utilized and the features extracted improve the performance of the activity recognition approach. 3D Harris corner detector uses 2D Gaussian filter and 1D Gabor filters in spatial and temporal directions respectively. A response value is given at every position (x, y, t). Initially, various experiments are performed to fix the number of interest points for computation purpose. The number of interest points is varied as $n = 2, 3, 5$ and 7. Good performance is obtained with $n = 3$ and increasing the number of interest points increases the computational complexity. Thus for further analysis the number of interest points is fixed as 3. The interest points are selected at the locations of local maximal responses. A local patch of size (49×49) is placed on the interest point along the spatial domain. The highlighted spatial temporal interest points correspond to local maxima of response function as shown in Figure 4 for the local patches placed on the detected interest points in a 'hug' sequence. 2D features are extracted from these patches.

Secondly, 3D features are extracted by constructing cuboids as follows. For each local patch placed on each interest point, another dimension is included along the time scale t, where t corresponds to number of frames considered for constructing the cuboids and $t = 14, 21, 28, 35$. The regions enclosed by the cuboids are encoded into feature vectors to build the valid model for action recognition. The 3D feature extraction procedure is shown in Figure 5.

Figure 6 shows the cuboids extracted for the individual actions and the features extracted from these cuboids exhibit significant performance in discriminating the different action types. Finally, a new discriminative feature descriptor method based on time frequency transformation technique to make features more reliable in action representation and further to enhance the recognition rate, which have the wide

Figure 5. 3D Feature Extraction from video patches - cuboids

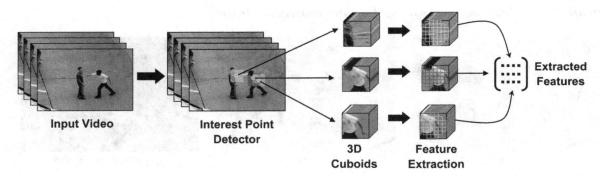

Figure 6. The view of cuboids extracted around each spatial temporal interest point for kick, punch and push actions. For simplicity, only five frames are shown for each action. Different distribution of interest points for these three actions is shown as colored representation of patches that indicates the discriminative capability of the proposed 3D – features.

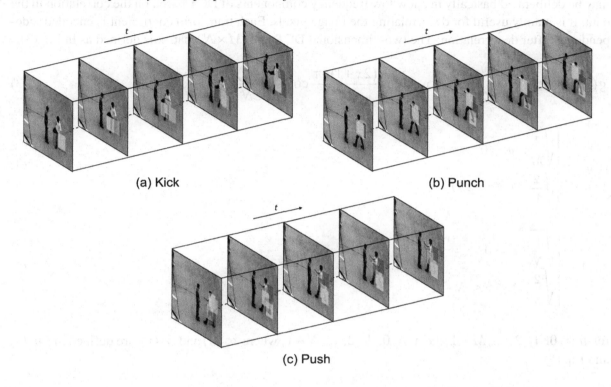

(a) Kick

(b) Punch

(c) Push

usage in the image processing area are adopted as follows. Transform based approaches such as Discrete Cosine Transform (DCT) and Discrete Wavelet Transform (DWT) are utilized in order to achieve the human action recognition due to their good performance in image and video processing. Further, recognition performance can be improved by combining DWT and DCT. The combined transforms could pay off the drawbacks of each other, resulting in efficient recognition. This is done by adjusting the wavelet coefficients of DWT sub-bands and then by applying DCT on the selected sub-bands denoted as Hybrid DWT+DCT. These transform based descriptors are utilized to represent the information inside the cuboids. The transformed features carry discriminative information for distinguishing the actions more reliably. F-score $\left(2PR/\left(P+R\right)\right)$, a statistical method for determining accuracy that employs both precision (P) and recall (R) is utilized for experimental evaluation to compute the accuracy.

Discrete Cosine Transform

Discrete cosine transform (DCT) can transform the data linearly into the frequency domain, where the data is characterized by a set of coefficients. Time frequency transformation technique converts a signal to different frequency components which make features more reliable in action representation and further enhance the recognition rate, which has the wide usage in the image processing area. Transform coding relies on the principle that the image pixels exhibit a certain level of correlation with their neighboring pixels. The discrete cosine transform (DCT) (Khayam, 2003) represents an image data by means of sum of sinusoids of varying frequencies. One of the major benefits of DCT is, the energy of the original data may be deliberated basically in a few low frequency components of DCT based on the correlation in the data. It is mainly useful for decorrelating the image pixels. Each transform coefficient is encoded independently after decorrelation. The two-dimensional DCT of a $M \times N$ matrix is defined as in Eq. (3).

$$g(u,v) = \alpha(u)\alpha(v)\sum_{x=0}^{M-1}\sum_{y=0}^{N-1} f(x,y)\cos\frac{(2x+1)u\pi}{2M}\cos\frac{(2y+1)v\pi}{2N} \tag{3}$$

$$\alpha(u) = \begin{cases} \sqrt{\dfrac{1}{M}}, & u = 0 \\ \sqrt{\dfrac{2}{M}}, & 1 \le u \le M-1 \end{cases} \tag{4}$$

$$\alpha(v) = \begin{cases} \sqrt{\dfrac{1}{N}}, & v = 0 \\ \sqrt{\dfrac{2}{N}}, & 1 \le v \le N-1 \end{cases} \tag{5}$$

for $u = 0, 1, 2, ..., M-1$ and $v = 0, 1, 2, ..., N-1$, where $\propto(u)$ and $\propto(v)$ are defined in Eq. (4) and Eq. (5).

Discrete Wavelet Transform

Discrete wavelet transform (DWT) is discretely sampled. Its key advantage is temporal resolution. It captures both frequency and location information in time. It splits data into diverse frequency components and then learns them with resolution matched to its scale. It is part of harmonic analysis of the family of wavelets, which decomposes a signal into a set of basic functions and efficiently used to model complex phenomena. The wavelet transform (WT) is widely used in signal processing and image compression. The 'wavelets' did not use sine and cosine curves. It is calculated separately for various segments of the time-domain signal at different frequencies. Multi-resolution analysis is designed to give good time resolution and poor frequency resolution at high frequencies and good frequency resolution and poor time resolution at low frequencies which have a good signal with high frequency components for small durations and low frequency components for lengthy duration. Wavelets are acquired from a distinct prototype wavelet $y(t)$ called mother wavelet by dilations and shifting. A set of wavelets derived from (x) as in Eq. (6).

$$\gamma_{a,b}(x) = \frac{1}{\sqrt{a}}\gamma(\frac{x-b}{a}), (a,b \in \mathbb{R}, a > 0) \tag{6}$$

where a is the scaling parameter and b is the shifting parameter

The Discrete Wavelet Transform is a mapping $T : L^2(\mathbb{R}) \to l^2(\mathbb{Z}^2)$

$$(Tf)_{a,b} = \int f(x)\gamma_{a,c}(x)dx \qquad (7)$$

where the mother wavelet $\gamma_{a,b}(x)$ satisfies

$$\int \gamma(x)dx = 0$$

Principal Component Analysis (PCA)

'Curse of dimensionality' refers to the issues related to the multivariate data analysis as the dimensionality increases. In practice, it means that there is maximum number of features, above which the performance of the classifier degrades rather than improving. Further, in some cases, not all the variables are 'significant' for understanding the implication of the data. 'Curse of dimensionality' can be handled by incorporating prior knowledge or by reducing the dimension of the feature vectors. Principal Component Analysis (PCA) in the mean-square error sense, is the linear dimension reduction technique. It is also known as the singular value decomposition (SVD), the Karhunen-Lo`eve transform, the Hotelling transform, and the empirical orthogonal function (EOF) method. PCA is a valuable statistical procedure that has found significance in many fields, and is a well-known method for finding patterns in data of high-ceilinged dimension. PCA 'combines' the essence of attributes by generating another smaller set of variables (Person, 1901) and (Hotelling, 1933). The initial data can subsequently be projected onto this lesser set of variables. Suppose that $x_1, x_2, ..., x_p$ are P training vectors, each belonging to one of N classes $\{\zeta_1, \zeta_2, ..., \zeta_N\}$. Then, the training vector, x_p, can be projected to lower dimension vector y_p, using an orthonormal linear transform given by $y_p = W^T x_p$. The transformation matrix $(\mathbf{W})$ can be obtained from the eigenvalues and eigenvectors of the covariance matrix $(\sum)$ of the input data. By definition, the covariance of the input data can be estimated as in Eq. (8).

$$\sum = \frac{1}{P} \sum_{p=1}^{P} (x_p - \mu)(x_p - \mu)^T \qquad (8)$$

where μ is the mean vector of all the training images.

The eigenvectors of the covariance matrix are $\mathbf{e}_1, \mathbf{e}_2, ..., \mathbf{e}_K$ associated with eigen values $\lambda_1 \geq \lambda_2 \geq ... \lambda_K$ respectively, where K is the feature vector dimension. The transformation matrix $(\mathbf{W})$ can be obtained by retaining $D(D \ll K)$ eigenvectors corresponding to D maximum eigenvalues, i.e., $(\mathbf{W}) = [\mathbf{e}_1 \ \mathbf{e}_2...\mathbf{e}_D]$. Since the spread (variance) of the feature population along the direction $(\mathbf{e}_i)$, and the amount of information in a population increases with the spread, feature $[\mathbf{e}_1 \ \mathbf{e}_2...\mathbf{e}_D]$ retain, for any D, which is the significant part of information in the feature population.

A given test data is also projected to the lower dimension space (say vector *t*). Then, by minimum distance matching, the test data can be assigned to the class corresponding to the training feature vector $\mathbf{x}_{i_o}$, where $i_o = \arg\min_{1 \le i \le p} \|\mathbf{t} - \mathbf{y}_i\|$, where $\| . \|$ represents the Euclidean distance in $\mathbb{R}^D$. The first eigenvector corresponds to the direction of maximum variance of the zero mean two dimensional data. The second eigenvector is orthogonal to the first eigenvector and it corresponds to the direction of next maximum variance.

Support Vector Machine (SVM)

Support Vector Machine (SVM) is a popular technique for classification in visual pattern recognition (Cristianini & Shawe-Taylor, 2000) and (Mitchell, 1997). It achieves reasonably vital pattern recognition performance in optimization theory. Classification tasks are typically involved with training and testing data. The training data are separated by $(x_1, y_1), (x_2, y_2), ...(x_m, y_m)$ into two classes, where $x_i \in \mathbb{R}_N$ contains $n-$ dimensional feature vector and $y_i \in \{+1, -1\}$ are the class labels. The aim of SVM is to generate a model which predicts the target value from testing set. In binary classification the hyper plane $w.x + b = 0$, where $w \in \mathbb{R}^n, b \in \mathbb{R}$ is used to separate the two classes in some space $\mathbb{Z}$. The maximum margin is given by $M = 2/ \| w \|$ as shown in Figure 7.

Figure 7. Hyperplane in linear SVM

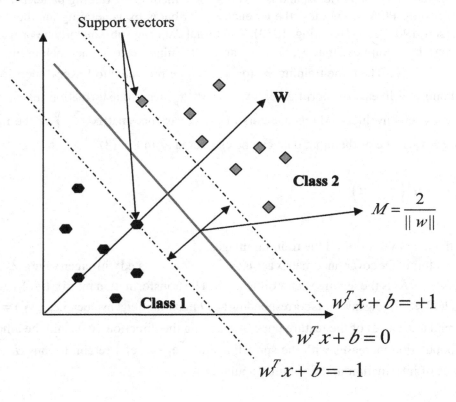

The minimization problem is solved by using Lagrange multipliers $\alpha_i (i = 1, ... m)$ where w and b are optimal values obtained from Eq. (9).

$$f(x) = sgn\left(\sum_{i=1}^{m} \alpha_i y_i K(x_i, x) + b\right) \tag{9}$$

The non-negative slack variables ξ_i are used to maximize margin and minimize the training error. The soft margin classifier obtained by optimizing the Eq. (10) and Eq. (11).

$$\min_{w,b,\xi} \frac{1}{2} w^T w + C \sum_{i=1}^{l} \xi_i \tag{10}$$

$$y_i(w^T \phi(x_i) + b \geq 1 - \xi_i, \xi_i \geq 0 \tag{11}$$

If the training data is not linearly separable, the input space is mapped into high dimensional space with kernel function $K(x_i, x_j) = \phi(x_i).\phi(x_j)$. The typical kernel functions are shown in Table 1.

In multiclass SVM, N-binary classifiers were constructed and one class was separated from all the rest. The training sets of the ith class are with positive labels and all others are with negative labels. The ith SVM solves i^{th} decision function given in Eq. (9).

In RBF kernel, a grid search strategy has been carried out to estimate the best parameter for C and γ in parameter space using LIBSVM (Chang & Lin, 2011). The optimal parameters C and γ are not known before hand, where C is the slack variable or error weight and γ is the curvature of the decision boundary or penalty parameter, where these two parameters are used to obtain the optimal classifier performance.

Table 1. Types of SVM inner product kernels

Types of Kernels	Inner Product Kernel
Linear	$K(x_i, x_j) = x^T_i x_j$
Polynomial	$K(x_i, x_j) = (\gamma x^T_i x_j + \gamma)^d, \gamma > 0$
Radial Basis Function (RBF)	$K(x_i, x_j) = \exp(-\gamma \| x_i - x_j \|^2), \gamma > 0$
Sigmoid	$K(x_i, x_j) = \tanh(\gamma x^T_i - x_j + r)$

where, $\gamma, r,$ and d are kernel parameters.

Random Forest (RF)

RF as defined by L. Breiman (2001) is a combination of classifiers that uses K tree-structured base classifier $\{h(\mathrm{I}, \Phi_n), N = 1, 2, 3, ...K\}$, where I indicates the input information and $\{\Phi_n\}$ is a family of similar and dependent random vectors. Each decision tree is constructed by randomly selecting the data. In computer vision, RF was introduced by Lepetit & Fua (2006) and Ozuysal, Fua & Lepetit (2007). It is an ensemble of decision trees that will generate a prediction value. Each decision tree is built with the random subset of the training samples. It is a famous supervised classification and regression technique that uses the notion of random feature selection. In a RF, the features are randomly chosen in each split. The correlation between the trees is minimized by randomly selecting the features to facilitate the prediction ability that generates very good efficiency. It is appropriate for high dimensional data, since it can handle missing and continuous information. The random tree implementation of WEKA (open source software) (Witten & Frank, 2005) is utilized for experimental purpose. The number of trees is set to 100 and the depth is set to 50 after analysis.

UT - Interaction Dataset

The UT-Interaction (Ryoo, Chen, Aggarwal & Roy-Chowdhury, 2010) dataset contains a video sequence of 6 classes of human interactions: like shake-hands, hug, kick, point, punch and push. The proposed work considers all 6 classes of actions for experimental purpose. There is a total of 20 video sequences whose lengths are around 60 seconds. Each video contains interaction between two persons, providing 8 executions of human activities for each video on an average.

Several participants with various clothing conditions, more than 15 different types appear in the videos. The videos are captured with the resolution of 720×480, at 30fps, and the height of a person in the video is about 200 pixels. The video is divided into two sets. Example frames of UT- Interaction dataset is shown in Figure 8. In UT-Interaction dataset, #1 consists of 10 video sequences taken in a parking lot with slightly different zoom rates and their backgrounds are almost static with little camera jitter. #2 (i.e. other 10 sequences) are taken on a lawn in a windy day with slight moving background and contain more camera jitters. Each set has a different background, scale, and illumination.

2D- Features

Initially 2D features are extracted from the patches built from each spatio-temporal interest points as explained earlier in feature description section. PCA is applied for dimension reduction. The projected features are fed to SVM and RF classifier to evaluate the performance of the extracted feature vectors. The confusion matrix for the best performance obtained with 2D features using SVM classifier for the actions handshake, hug, kick, point, punch and push in #1 and #2 are shown in Table 2(a) and Table 2(b) respectively. Similarly, the confusion matrix for the performance obtained with 2D features using random forest classifier for the actions handshake, hug, kick, point, punch and push in #1 and #2 are shown in Table 3(a) and Table 3(b) respectively. The performance of the SVM classifier is found to be comparable with the random forest classifier.

Figure 8. Example frames of each action of UT-Interaction dataset

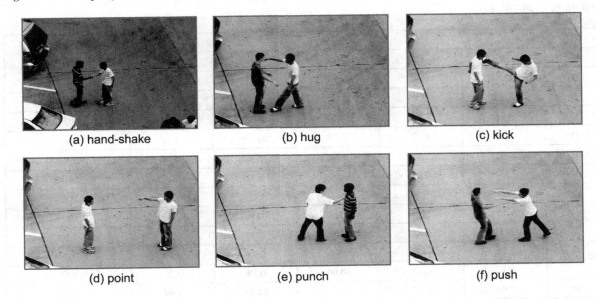

(a) hand-shake   (b) hug   (c) kick

(d) point   (e) punch   (f) push

Table 2. Confusion matrix of projected 2D - features in (%), A-hand-shake, B-hug, C-kick, D-point, E-punch, F-push

(a) SVM - #1					
	A	**B**	**C**	**D**	**E**	**F**
A	**92.66**	1.68	1.68	1.22	0.61	2.14
B	1.21	**91.68**	2.05	1.57	0.72	2.77
C	2.23	2.75	**88.73**	1.83	1.83	2.62
D	2.48	3.73	1.45	**90.06**	1.04	1.24
E	2.61	2.43	2.43	0.93	**84.89**	6.72
F	1.57	3.13	1.72	0.63	1.72	**91.22**
(b) SVM - #2					
	A	**B**	**C**	**D**	**E**	**F**
A	**90.06**	5.25	0.55	0.14	1.52	2.49
B	2.78	**89.52**	1.26	0.76	1.89	3.79
C	3.37	4.16	**85.94**	0.59	1.39	4.55
D	1.99	1.99	2.33	**83.72**	2.66	7.31
E	2.73	4.92	0.36	0.36	**85.79**	5.83
F	1.69	3.38	1.52	0.34	2.54	**90.52**

Table 3. Confusion matrix of projected 2D - features in (%), A-hand-shake, B-hug, C-kick, D-point, E-punch, F-push

(a) RF - #1						
	A	**B**	**C**	**D**	**E**	**F**
A	**90.83**	4.59	1.99	0.61	0.92	1.07
B	2.90	**90.83**	2.65	0.60	0.97	2.05
C	2.23	3.93	**89.91**	0.92	0.79	2.23
D	5.18	4.97	2.69	**85.09**	0.62	1.45
E	2.61	8.02	1.87	1.68	**81.90**	3.92
F	2.04	6.11	2.66	0.31	0.47	**88.40**
(b) RF - #2						
	A	**B**	**C**	**D**	**E**	**F**
A	**90.19**	6.35	1.10	0.00	1.24	1.10
B	6.06	**88.51**	1.01	0.13	1.64	2.65
C	3.17	6.93	**80.00**	0.79	3.76	5.35
D	2.99	3.32	1.99	**84.72**	1.99	4.98
E	1.09	6.74	0.73	0.18	**86.70**	4.55
F	1.52	6.09	2.03	0.51	2.88	**86.97**

3D - Features

As explained in feature extraction section, 3D features are extracted from the cuboids built from each spatio-temporal interest points. The length of the cuboid is varied as 14, 21, 28 and 35 to extract the features along the time scale. PCA is employed for dimension reduction. The projected features are fed to SVM and RF classifier to evaluate the performance of the extracted feature vectors. The projected feature for the cuboid length of 28 gives good performance. Figure 10 shows the results of SVM classifier on UT Interaction dataset #1 and #2 for various projected 3D feature dimensions. The confusion matrix obtained for the 3D-features for the cuboid length of 28 on #1 and #2 using the SVM classifier is shown in Table 4(a) and Table 4(b) respectively. The confusion matrix obtained using RF classifier is shown in Table 5(a) and Table 5(b) for #1 and #2 respectively. The performance of 3D – features of various projected dimensions on #1 and #2 is shown in Figure 9.

In transform based feature extraction step, DCT coefficients are extracted in zigzag fashion from the spatio-temporal patches. For each interest point, the approach applies DCT on each of the 7x7 block and retains only 20 significant coefficients in a zigzag fashion. These coefficients from each interest point are concatenated to form the feature vector.

The DWT features are extracted from the spatio-temporal patches. Single level decomposition is adopted for extracting the features from the sub-band LL which retains more details. 16 dimensional features are extracted from each interest points and they are concatenated to form the feature vector. Further, to evaluate the performance of the proposed approach, DWT is combined with DCT, where resultant coefficients are given as input to DCT in order to reduce the redundancy to discriminate the action in more efficient manner.

Figure 10. Results of transform based features on SVM and RF

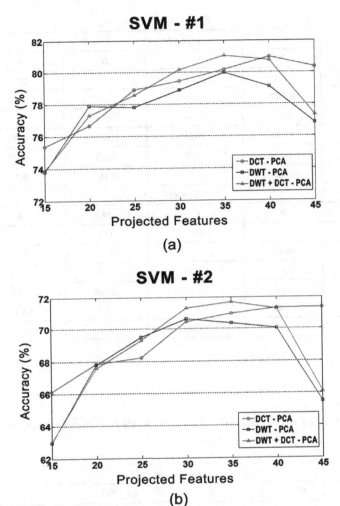

Finally, in the classification phase, the SVM with RBF kernel and RF classifier are adopted by leave one-out-cross validation (LOOCV) approach. Best parameters are selected by 10 fold cross validation. Figure 10 illustrates the performance comparisons among transform based descriptor methods, using SVM classifiers. Apparently, the hybrid DWT+DCT outperforms both the DCT and DWT methods. A comparison of the average performance obtained by the proposed features on SVM and RF classifiers are tabulated in Table 6. It is seen that the proposed 3D-features outperforms all other features. Since, in 3D-features one more additional dimension along the time scale is considered for extracting features.

Further, a comparison of the performance of proposed 3D – features with the present state of the art techniques is shown in Table 7. It is seen that the proposed feature shows good results.

Table 4. Confusion matrix of projected 3D - features for in (%), A-hand-shake, B-hug, C-kick, D-point, E-punch, F-push

(a) SVM - #1						
	A	**B**	**C**	**D**	**E**	**F**
A	**94.66**	0.76	1.27	1.02	2.29	0.00
B	0.21	**95.47**	1.03	0.41	2.88	0.00
C	2.22	0.49	**92.84**	0.74	3.46	0.25
D	0.00	0.00	0.00	**100.00**	0.00	0.00
E	0.65	0.86	1.29	0.22	**96.77**	0.22
F	0.46	0.23	0.92	0.00	0.23	**98.16**
(b) SVM - #2						
	A	**B**	**C**	**D**	**E**	**F**
A	**91.51**	0.63	0.94	0.63	1.57	4.72
B	1.33	**88.67**	1.67	0.67	3.33	4.33
C	1.37	2.73	**82.24**	0.55	2.46	10.66
D	0.00	0.00	0.00	**100.00**	0.00	0.00
E	0.68	0.46	0.91	1.14	**93.15**	3.65
F	1.57	0.79	0.26	0.00	0.79	**96.59**

Table 5. Confusion matrix of projected 3D - features in (%), A-hand-shake, B-hug, C-kick, D-point, E-punch, F-push

(a) RF - #1						
	A	**B**	**C**	**D**	**E**	**F**
A	**89.57**	2.54	5.34	0.51	1.27	0.76
B	1.03	**93.21**	3.50	0.41	1.23	0.62
C	7.16	7.16	**79.01**	0.99	2.72	2.96
D	0.00	0.62	0.00	**99.38**	0.00	0.00
E	0.86	1.72	2.15	0.86	**91.83**	2.58
F	1.84	1.84	2.53	0.00	1.61	**92.18**
(b) RF - #2						
	A	**B**	**C**	**D**	**E**	**F**
A	**77.67**	2.20	1.26	0.63	8.81	9.43
B	6.33	**67.67**	2.33	0.33	14.67	8.67
C	3.28	3.28	**75.96**	0.82	13.11	3.55
D	0.00	0.00	0.00	**100.00**	0.00	0.00
E	1.14	1.37	3.65	0.68	**89.50**	3.65
F	2.62	2.36	2.36	0.00	7.87	**84.78**

Figure 9. Performance of 3D - projected features of various dimensions

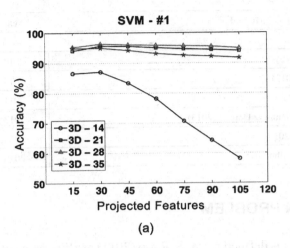

(a)

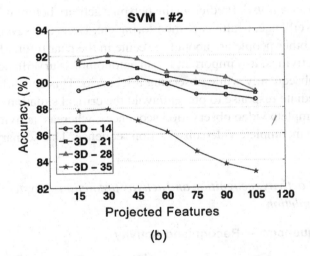

(b)

Table 6. Comparison of performance of the proposed features

Classifiers	Proposed Feature	#1 Accuracy (%)	#2 Accuracy (%)
SVM	3D - Feature	**96.32**	**92.03**
	2D - Feature	89.87	87.59
	DCT - PCA	80.96	71.34
	DWT - PCA	79.96	70.62
	DWT + DCT - PCA	81.04	71.69
Random Forest	3D - Feature	90.86	82.60
	2D - Feature	87.83	86.18
	DCT - PCA	64.30	52.72
	DWT - PCA	63.08	51.44
	DWT + DCT - PCA	63.21	51.76

Table 7. State-of-the-art recognition accuracy (%) for the UT: Interaction dataset

Method	Year	#1	#2
Proposed	-	**96.32**	**92.03**
Zhang, Liu, Chang, Ge & Chen (2012)	2012	95.00	90.00
Peng, Wu, Peng, Qi, Qiao & Liu (2013)	2013	94.50	91.70
Vahdat, Gao, Ranjbar & Mori (2011)	2011	93.00	90.00
Motiian, Feng, Bharthavarapu, Sharlemin & Doretto (2013)	2013	91.80	87.87
Waltisberg, Yao, Gall & Van Gool (2010)	2010	88.00	77.00
Ryoo, Chen, Aggarwal & Roy-Chowdhury (2010)	2010	85.00	70.00

ACTION PREDICTION PROBLEM

Predicting the future activity is defined by M. S. Ryoo (2011) as: *'inference of the ongoing activity given temporally incomplete observations'*. Predicting the person's activity before it is actually performed has broad applications in surveillance, health care monitoring etc. Everyday several conditions require the prediction of actions that other people are about to execute in the near future. Especially for preventing the crimes and terrorist activities, it is important for an autonomous surveillance system to predict what people are about to do subsequently while observing a scenario. This capability enables the system to plan in advance for immediate response to prevent/avoid the critical situations. In general, activity recognition considers the complete video observation sequences, whereas, activity prediction predicts the ongoing activity, given an incomplete video observation sequence. This scenario is shown in Figure 11.

Figure 11. Comparison of activity recognition and activity prediction. A system should predict the ongoing activity before its completion

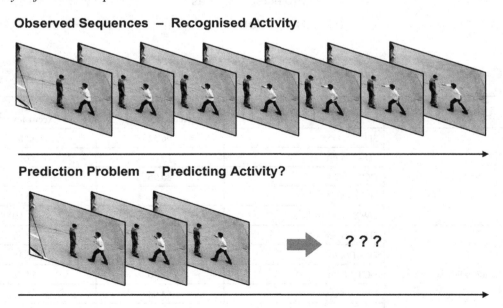

This work considers the future action prediction problem in normal scenario. Given a training video collections that contains human performing normal and suspicious actions, the system learns how the human actions tend to progress next, while observing the short video clip. Predicting the future actions entail identifying the fine-grained details intrinsic to the ongoing observations that would direct to a future action. It is imperative for an automatic surveillance system to raise an alarm while observing a stealing activity before the completion of such action.

Mixture models are habitually used for density approximation because of their excellent approximation characteristics. They are probabilistic models capable of identifying analogous data. In machine learning terminology, a mixture model is an unsupervised learning paradigm. Mixture models have a wide range of applications. It is a probability density function, and hence the tasks that can be performed with other probability distributions such as Gaussian can be done using the mixture models. Actually, most mixture models are a mixture of multivariate Gaussians. Even though mixture models are unsupervised techniques, they can be used for prediction. The learning process does not create a model, rather it simply finds the natural clusters in the data. Thus the mixture models are surprisingly good at predictions and the predictions are done without the assumptions made by the model.

In this work, Future actions are predicted by calculating the statistical mean and covariance of conditional probability distribution $p(a_f \mid a_h)$, where a_f is the approximated future action and a_h is the past observed action sequences. The probabilistic action prediction for a particular probability density function, $p(a_f, a_o)$ can be defined. Gaussian Mixture Model (GMM) is a parametric probability density function which is represented as a sum of Gaussian component densities. Gaussian density function is defined as,

$$p(a) = \sum_{j=1}^{k} w_j N(a \mid \mu_j, \Sigma_j) \tag{12}$$

where a is a $d-$ dimensional feature vector $a = (a^1, a^2, \ldots a^d)^T$ defined by,

$$N(a \mid \mu, \Sigma) = \frac{1}{(2\pi)^{d/2} \sqrt{|\Sigma|}} \exp\left[-\frac{1}{2}(x-\mu)^T \sum{}^{-1} (x-\mu) \right] \tag{13}$$

and $N(a \mid \mu_j, \Sigma_j)$ is the multivariate normal distribution with mean μ_j and covariance matrix Σ_j and w_j is the prior probability of the jth Gaussian that satisfy

$$\sum_{j=1}^{k} w_j = 1 \quad 0 \leq w_j \leq 1 \tag{14}$$

The iterative two-step Expectation- Maximization (EM) algorithm is utilised to derive the model parameters of the observed training data X which maximize the likelihood $p(x \mid \theta)$ with regard to the model parameters θ.

$$\theta^* = \underset{\theta}{\mathrm{argmax}}\, p(x \mid \theta) = \underset{\theta}{\mathrm{argmax}} \prod_{j=1}^{k} p(x_j \mid \theta) \tag{15}$$

For action prediction, a joint Gaussian mixture distribution is inferred as,

$$p(a_f, a_o) = \sum_{j=1}^{k} w_j N(a_o, a_f \mid \mu_j, \Sigma_j) \tag{16}$$

over the approximated past observed action sequences and future action predictions a_o and a_f. Finally action prediction is done by calculating the conditional mixture density.

Results on Action Prediction

Prediction problem is concerned with making a decision on the activity in the middle of the activity execution. Hence the prediction approach must estimate the evolution of each activity automatically and must decide the most probable action likely to occur in future based on the video observation. The experiments are conducted on 6 different observation ratio settings. The results obtained with the proposed probabilistic GMM based approach is shown in Figure. 12. X axis corresponds to the observation ratio of the test video and Y axis indicates the accuracy obtained. It is observed that the proposed system is able to predict the action even with an observation ratio of 0.2 of the test video and the prediction accuracy is improved by increasing the observed samples. In the proposed prediction problem, prediction is done in real-time except for the feature extraction step. Provided the suitable features to the system in real-time, the approach is able to predict the ongoing activities in real-time. It is fascinating to notice that the proposed approach is able to predict the on going activity at an early stage (approximately 0.15 seconds). The fine-grained semantics of an activity is likely to appear around 5 to 7 frames before the actual intended action is initiated. The visual demonstration of the activity prediction is shown in Figure

Figure 13. Prediction results at different stages of an ongoing activity, (a) - (c) indicates correct prediction. (d) Shows initial misprediction and this action require additional frames for correct prediction.

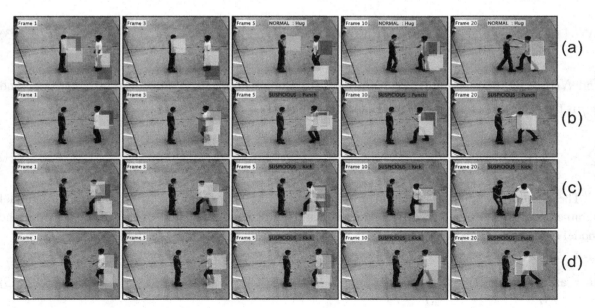

Figure 12. Prediction results for various actions on #1 and #2

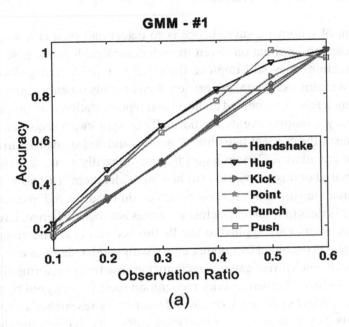

(a)

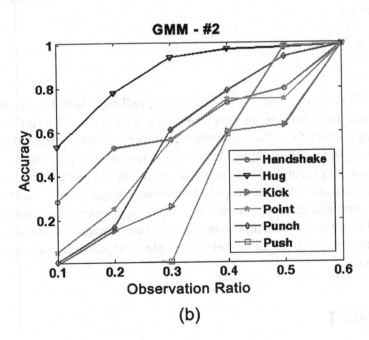

(b)

13. Figure 13(a) is a normal 'hug' action. Figure 13(b) - 13(d) are suspicious events. The aim is to raise an alarm once the system predicts an activity as suspicious. It is seen that the system correctly predicts the actions punch and kick at an early stage than the push action.

FUTURE RESEARCH DIRECTIONS

The major application of automatic surveillance is to detect and predict a suspicious event to avoid some remorseful or dangerous situation. Even though considerable work is seen in the field, several potential research directions may still improve the efficiency of the recognition system appreciably. Video information is a multimodal data, researchers focus mainly on either audio or visual information for their analysis except a few. A combined audio-visual representation may produce an immense rise in the recognition accuracy. Complex events can normally be split into a sequence of concepts that make up that event. Each one of the concept like objects, actions and audio involved in the incident have their own distinct semantic granularity. Certain issues that are normally seen are (i) how to define/combine these concepts (supervised or unsupervised)? (ii) how to model them? (iii) how to reliably detect them? (iv) how to handle semantic similarity. If these issues could be answered, recognizing complex events would ultimately be effortless to resolve. Occlusion creates another challenge. Even though optical flow and spatio-temporal techniques are applied to handle this issue, it is always complicated to handle this problem when the object is occluded by another entity with similar shape and motion. In particular, an aspect which has not been much investigated is, recognizing an activity performed by different individuals in various manners. Moreover, human activity recognition must be analyzed from the domain expert's perspective. From the context of military or law enforcement a researcher's expressive language may be misinterpreted. This may in turn lead to significant ambiguity in operating the commands that will lead to operational failure.

CONCLUSION

This chapter introduced a new exemplar for human action prediction. Initially, a novel feature extraction procedure was discussed for action recognition framework. This is extended further to build an activity prediction methodology. Given the initial observation, the motivation is to detect the incomplete activity to enable crime prevention by activating an alarm to alert the security personal for appropriate action. The problem is formulated probabilistically and a novel action recognition methodology is presented using the proposed feature extraction from space-time interest points by constructing the cuboids. Experimental results demonstrate that the proposed approach outperforms the existing techniques of action prediction problem. Few of the promising future research directions are discussed towards the end. The authors believe that this effort could afford helpful insights and valuable assistance to the researchers for exploring this topic.

ACKNOWLEDGMENT

The authors gratefully acknowledge the support of *University Grants Commission of India,* for supporting this work. [F. No. 41-636/2012 (SR)].

REFERENCES

Aggarwal, J. K., & Ryoo, M. S. (2011). Human activity analysis: A review. *ACM Computing Surveys*, *43*(3), 16. doi:10.1145/1922649.1922653

Ali, A., & Terada, K. (2009, September). A framework for human tracking using kalman filter and fast mean shift algorithms. In *Computer Vision Workshops (ICCV Workshops), 2009 IEEE 12th International Conference on* (pp. 1028-1033). IEEE.

Babenko, B., Yang, M. H., & Belongie, S. (2009, June). Visual tracking with online multiple instance learning. In *Computer Vision and Pattern Recognition, 2009. CVPR 2009. IEEE Conference on* (pp. 983-990). IEEE.

Breiman, L. (2001). Random forests. *Machine Learning*, *45*(1), 5–32. doi:10.1023/A:1010933404324

Chang, C. C., & Lin, C. J. (2011). LIBSVM: A library for support vector machines. *ACM Transactions on Intelligent Systems and Technology*, *2*(3), 27. doi:10.1145/1961189.1961199

Collins, R. T., Liu, Y., & Leordeanu, M. (2005). Online selection of discriminative tracking features. *Pattern Analysis and Machine Intelligence. IEEE Transactions on*, *27*(10), 1631–1643.

Cristianini, N., & Shawe-Taylor, J. (2000). *An introduction to support vector machines and other kernel-based learning methods*. Cambridge University Press. doi:10.1017/CBO9780511801389

Cuevas, C., & García, N. (2013). Improved background modeling for real-time spatio-temporal non-parametric moving object detection strategies. *Image and Vision Computing*, *31*(9), 616–630. doi:10.1016/j.imavis.2013.06.003

Dalal, N., & Triggs, B. (2005, June). Histograms of oriented gradients for human detection. In *Computer Vision and Pattern Recognition, 2005. CVPR 2005. IEEE Computer Society Conference on*, (pp. 886-893). IEEE.

Danafar, S., & Gheissari, N. (2007). Action recognition for surveillance applications using optic flow and SVM. In *Computer Vision–ACCV 2007* (pp. 457–466). Springer Berlin Heidelberg. doi:10.1007/978-3-540-76390-1_45

Derpanis, K. G., Sizintsev, M., Cannons, K. J., & Wildes, R. P. (2013). Action spotting and recognition based on a spatiotemporal orientation analysis. *Pattern Analysis and Machine Intelligence. IEEE Transactions on*, *35*(3), 527–540.

Grabner, H., Leistner, C., & Bischof, H. (2008). Semi-supervised on-line boosting for robust tracking. In *Computer Vision–ECCV 2008* (pp. 234–247). Springer Berlin Heidelberg. doi:10.1007/978-3-540-88682-2_19

Harris, C., & Stephens, M. (1988, August). A combined corner and edge detector. Alvey Vision Conference, 15, 50. doi:10.5244/C.2.23

Hotelling, H. (1933). Analysis of a complex of statistical variables into principal components. *Journal of Educational Psychology*, *24*(6), 417–441. doi:10.1037/h0071325

Hsieh, F. Y., Han, C. C., Wu, N. S., Chuang, T. C., & Fan, K. C. (2006). A novel approach to the detection of small objects with low contrast. *Signal Processing, 86*(1), 71–83. doi:10.1016/j.sigpro.2005.03.020

Hung, M. H., Pan, J. S., & Hsieh, C. H. (2014). A Fast Algorithm of Temporal Median Filter for Background Subtraction. *Journal of Information Hiding and Multimedia Signal Processing, 5*(1), 33–40.

Kalal, Z., Matas, J., & Mikolajczyk, K. (2010, June). Pn learning: Bootstrapping binary classifiers by structural constraints. In *Computer Vision and Pattern Recognition (CVPR), 2010 IEEE Conference on* (pp. 49-56). IEEE.

Khayam, S. A. (2003). *The discrete cosine transform (DCT): theory and application.* Michigan State University.

Laptev, I. (2005). On space-time interest points. *International Journal of Computer Vision, 64*(2-3), 107–123. doi:10.1007/s11263-005-1838-7

Laptev, I., Marszalek, M., Schmid, C., & Rozenfeld, B. (2008, June). Learning realistic human actions from movies. In *Computer Vision and Pattern Recognition, 2008. CVPR 2008. IEEE Conference on* (pp. 1-8). IEEE.

Lepetit, V., & Fua, P. (2006). Keypoint recognition using randomized trees. *Pattern Analysis and Machine Intelligence. IEEE Transactions on, 28*(9), 1465–1479.

Lu, C., Adluru, N., Ling, H., Zhu, G., & Latecki, L. J. (2010). Contour based object detection using part bundles. *Computer Vision and Image Understanding, 114*(7), 827–834. doi:10.1016/j.cviu.2010.03.009

Lu, G., & Kudo, M. (2014). Learning action patterns in difference images for efficient action recognition. *Neurocomputing, 123*, 328–336. doi:10.1016/j.neucom.2013.06.042

Manjunath, B. S., & Ma, W. Y. (1996). Texture features for browsing and retrieval of image data. *Pattern Analysis and Machine Intelligence. IEEE Transactions on, 18*(8), 837–842.

Mitchell, T. M. (1997). *Machine learning.* WCB.

Motiian, S., Feng, K., Bharthavarapu, H., Sharlemin, S., & Doretto, G. (2013). Pairwise kernels for human interaction recognition. In *Advances in Visual Computing* (pp. 210–221). Springer Berlin Heidelberg. doi:10.1007/978-3-642-41939-3_21

Ozuysal, M., Fua, P., & Lepetit, V. (2007, June). Fast keypoint recognition in ten lines of code. In *Computer Vision and Pattern Recognition, 2007. CVPR'07. IEEE Conference on* (pp. 1-8). IEEE.

Peng, X., Wu, X., Peng, Q., Qi, X., Qiao, Y., & Liu, Y. (2013, August). Exploring dense trajectory feature and encoding methods for human interaction recognition. In *Proceedings of the Fifth International Conference on Internet Multimedia Computing and Service* (pp. 23-27). ACM. doi:10.1145/2499788.2499795

Person, K. (1901). On lines and planes of closest fit to systems of points in space. *Philosophical Magazine, 2*(6), 559–572. doi:10.1080/14786440109462720

Poppe, R. (2010). A survey on vision-based human action recognition. *Image and Vision Computing, 28*(6), 976–990. doi:10.1016/j.imavis.2009.11.014

Ren, J., & Hao, J. (2012, October). Mean shift tracking algorithm combined with Kalman Filter. In *Image and Signal Processing (CISP), 2012 5th International Congress on* (pp. 727-730). IEEE.

Ryoo, M. S. (2011, November). Human activity prediction: Early recognition of ongoing activities from streaming videos. In *Computer Vision (ICCV), 2011 IEEE International Conference on* (pp. 1036-1043). IEEE.

Ryoo, M. S., Chen, C. C., Aggarwal, J. K., & Roy-Chowdhury, A. (2010). An overview of contest on semantic description of human activities (SDHA) 2010. In *Recognizing Patterns in Signals, Speech, Images and Videos* (pp. 270–285). Springer Berlin Heidelberg. doi:10.1007/978-3-642-17711-8_28

Shao, L., Gao, R., Liu, Y., & Zhang, H. (2011). Transform based spatio-temporal descriptors for human action recognition. *Neurocomputing, 74*(6), 962–973. doi:10.1016/j.neucom.2010.11.013

Song, Y., Goncalves, L., & Perona, P. (2003). Unsupervised learning of human motion. *Pattern Analysis and Machine Intelligence. IEEE Transactions on, 25*(7), 814–827.

Vahdat, A., Gao, B., Ranjbar, M., & Mori, G. (2011, November). A discriminative key pose sequence model for recognizing human interactions. In *Computer Vision Workshops (ICCV Workshops), 2011 IEEE International Conference on* (pp. 1729-1736). IEEE.

Waltisberg, D., Yao, A., Gall, J., & Van Gool, L. (2010). Variations of a hough-voting action recognition system. In *Recognizing Patterns in Signals, Speech, Images and Videos* (pp. 306–312). Springer Berlin Heidelberg. doi:10.1007/978-3-642-17711-8_31

Wang, L., Wang, Y., Jiang, T., Zhao, D., & Gao, W. (2013). Learning discriminative features for fast frame-based action recognition. *Pattern Recognition, 46*(7), 1832–1840. doi:10.1016/j.patcog.2012.08.016

Witten, I. H., & Frank, E. (2005). *Data Mining: Practical machine learning tools and techniques.* Morgan Kaufmann.

Wu, D., & Shao, L. (2013). Silhouette analysis-based action recognition via exploiting human poses. *Circuits and Systems for Video Technology. IEEE Transactions on, 23*(2), 236–243.

Yanagawa, A., Hsu, W., & Chang, S. F. (2006). Brief descriptions of visual features for baseline trecvid concept detectors. *Columbia University ADVENT Technical Report*, 219-2006.

Yilma, A., & Shah, M. (2005, October). Recognizing human actions in videos acquired by uncalibrated moving cameras. In *Computer Vision, 2005. ICCV 2005. Tenth IEEE International Conference on,* (pp. 150-157). IEEE. doi:10.1109/ICCV.2005.201

Zhang, Y., Liu, X., Chang, M. C., Ge, W., & Chen, T. (2012). Spatio-temporal phrases for activity recognition. In *Computer Vision–ECCV 2012* (pp. 707–721). Springer Berlin Heidelberg. doi:10.1007/978-3-642-33712-3_51

Chapter 10
Iris Identification System:
A New Perspective

N. Poonguzhali
Pondicherry Engineering College, India

M. Ezhilarasan
Pondicherry Engineering College, India

ABSTRACT

Recent research on iris is not only on recognition; emerging trends are also in medical diagnostics, personality identification. The iris based recognition system rely on patterns/textures present in the iris, the color of the iris, visible features present in the iris, geometric features of the iris and the SIFT features. An overview of biometric generation is presented. Human iris can be viewed as a multilayered structure in its anterior view. The iris consists of three zones, the pupillary zone, collarette and the ciliary zone. The texture features present in the pupillary zone and collarette are used for identification. As these features are closer to the pupil they are not affected by the occlusion caused by eyelid or eyelashes. The geometric features of the iris can also be used for human identification. The structure of the iris is more related to the geometric shape and hence the extraction of these features is also possible. An overview of the performance metrics to evaluate a biometric system is also presented.

INTRODUCTION

Traditionally, identification of a genuine person was based on key, password, magnetic or chip card. However, all of these can be stolen, forgotten or forged and hence password and token-based recognition systems are nowadays replaced by biometric recognition system. Even in some systems where password and token are still used, on top of it a biometric layer is added for more secure authentication. Hence there is a tremendous growth in biometric based identification system in almost all paths round the world. Biometric includes reference to the measurement, analysis, classification, science of personal recognition and verification or identification by using distinguishable biological (physiological) or behavioural trait, features or characteristic of that person. Biometric identification is the process of associating an identity to the input biometric data by comparing it against the enrolled identities in a database (Jain et al., 2004).

DOI: 10.4018/978-1-4666-9685-3.ch010

Depending on the mode of application biometric system operate on verification or identification mode. In verification mode, the system validates a person's identity by comparing the captured biometric data with their own biometric template stored in the database; say by 1:1 matching. In identification mode, the system recognizes the person by searching the template of all the users in the database, where 1:N matching is performed. Any biometric system should possess the characteristics such as: versatility, uniqueness, permanence, measurability, performance, acceptability and circumvention. Among the various available biometric traits such as face, fingerprint, palm print, hand geometry, keystroke, signature, voice and gait, iris is proved to hold all characteristics for an identification system. Fingerprint, face and hand voice have been extensively studies for a comparatively longer period than iris, but iris is reported to be the most reliable biometric trait in identification and authentication (Bowyer & Flynn, 2008; Ross et al., 2006). It is claimed for two reasons that iris is unique and stable throughout the life time of an individual. The first is based on the biological development. The structure, appearance and colour are genetically inherited. The texture and other visible characteristics or features are epigenetic, hence the distinctive features. The second reason is based on the analysis made to the feature present in the iris. Even though there are cases like aniridia (an absences or undeveloped iris), corectopia (displacement of pupil), colobloma (missing or distortion in pupil) which are very rare and hence the uniqueness and stability of iris is taken for recognition. This chapter deals with the overview of the iris recognition system and with combination of other biometric system.

OVERVIEW OF BIOMETRICS

Biometric includes reference to the measurement, analysis, classification, science of personal recognition and verification or identification by using distinguishable biological (physiological) or behavioural trait, features or characteristic of that person.

Generation of Biometrics

The biometric system that is identifiable human dates back to the 19th century as Bertillon system. Since the evolution of the biometric system fingerprint was the only biometric traits used for identification that too only for criminal identification. The generation of biometrics (Jain & Kumar, 2010) are:

- **Zeroth Generation Biometrics System:** The biometric trait that falls in this generation is fingerprint and hand geometry. The systems were not automated and were also stand alone. The performance and usage was also very weak. These systems were only primarily used by forensic and law department.
- **First Generation Biometrics System:** In this generation the physiological and behavioral traits were encompassed. On top of forensic and law, they were used in civil aviation and commercial system. The main drawback of this generation was performance, security, privacy, poor interoperability, storage and scalability.
- **Second Generation Biometrics System:** The second generation took up all the challenging issues of the first generation. The system developed during this generation was viewed in engineering perspective and social perceptive. Apart from fingerprint, iris, face other anatomical, behavioural and physiological traits were included for identification. Some of them are ear, footprint, periocu-

lar region, finger knuckle back, keystroke dynamics, nose shape etc. The above stated biometric traits were categorized as hard biometric or simply biometric. Soft biometric were used along with hard biometric so as to improve performance or append with hard biometric such as Aadhaar number in (U. I. D. of India, 2014). The biometric system was later viewed as unimodal and multimodal. The security for biometric system and data which was a major issue was also taken care.

- **Next Generation Biometrics System:** The present biometric system addresses the major issue of security, scalability, privacy, performance and speed. Still more effort has to be taken in terms of the following:
  - **Security:** Nowadays health related data can also be computed from the biometric data and the data is available at multiple place for multiple usage.
  - Storage: A unique representation of all biometric data.
  - **Scalability:** The size of the data increases an also the applications increases.
  - **Performance:** Robust matching techniques and computational cost are to be considered.

ANATOMY OF HUMAN EYE AND IRIS

The human eye is asymmetrical globe which measures nearly an inch in diameter. The front view of the human eye (the part what we see) as shown in figure 1 includes:

- Pupil (centre of the eye),
- Iris (the pigmented darker part),
- Cornea (a dome structure over the iris),
- Sclera (white part),
- Conjunctiva (layer of tissue covering the eye).

Figure 1. Human eye

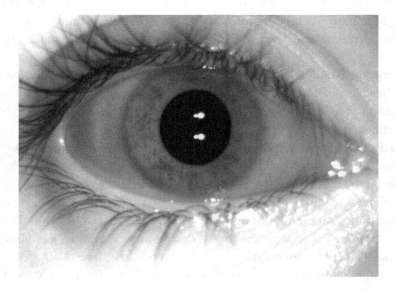

Behind the iris and pupil lies the lens, which helps to focus light on the back of the eye. Most of the eye is filled with a clear gel called the vitreous. Light projects through the pupil and the lens to the back of the eye. The inside lining of the eye is covered by special light-sensing cells that are collectively called the retina. The retina converts light into electrical impulses. Behind the eye, the optic nerve carries these impulses to the brain. The macula is a small extra-sensitive area within the retina that gives central vision. It is located in the center of the retina and contains the fovea, a small depression or pit at the center of the macula that gives the clearest vision. Iris is a Greek word means goddess of the rainbow due to many colors of the iris and hence the name. The iris is a thin circular ring region, a part of the human eye positioned between the black pupil and white sclera presenting a unique and rich texture information, such as patterns, rifts, colors, rings, spots, stripes, filaments, coronal, furrows, minutiae and recess and other detailed characteristics seen under the infrared light.

The iris is composed of loosely woven soft tissues. The iris is responsible for the amount of light reaching the retina by controlling the diameter and size of the pupil which is hole a located in the center of the iris. The Iris is the only internal organ which seen from outside. Further it is measurable internal physical feature, which is unique and cannot be easily altered due to ecological effects (Daugman, 2003). The probability of finding any two eyes identical, are approximately 1 in 10^52. It has nearly about 250 points of identification for comparison. The minute iris patterns and textures which is the phenotypic feature are determined during the foetal development and not inherited from the gene and for this reason the right and left eye of a person are not alike and same even for the identical twins. It has been proved that the color of the eye and the appearance of the eye are genetically inherited (genotype) but the texture patterns are not inherited (epigenetic).

The color of the iris can be green, blue, or brown. In some cases it can be hazel (a combination of light brown, green and gold), grey, violet, or even pink. Although there are a variety of colors in iris the dark pigment melanin is responsible for the ranges of colors in iris. The amount of melanin is the deciding factor for the iris color. The color of iris is brown or black which is due to the quantity of eumelanin when it is more. The red or yellow is because of pheomelanin caused by melanocytes which is found less in blue and green color iris. If it is moderate quantity of melanin then it is hazel. In brown color iris the surface of the iris is smooth and is heavily pigmented. With blue and hazel color iris the surface is irregular with crypts. The color of the eye may be influenced by more than 50 genes and hence the genetics of eye color are more complex than what they appear (Ivan, 2012).

Iris originates in the sixth week of gestation period (Daugman & Downing, 2001). At end of the twelfth week the rim of optic cup is formed over the lens from the pupillary membrane which later is the melanocytes, fibroblast and collagen fibers on the anterior layer. The cilliary fold are formed and by the completion of the fourth month the vascular layers of the iris is formed. During the fifth month the pupillary membrane, the iris stroma and sphincter muscle is formed. In this period the hole in the pupil is absent as the pupillary membrane covers the pupil. After seventh month the growth if epithelial layer is complete and cells in the pupillary membrane, stroma and epithelial layer become as a cell layer. At this stage the pupils formation is started. The flow of blood vessels slows down and later closes the blood supply, in this stage the pupil is free from the tissues obstructs. The development is completed by the end of eight month but the stroma layer is very thin, the cellular framework is incomplete and the collarette is very nearer to the pupil in pupillary region. During this period the patterns and structures are complete but the pigmentation process is carried out until one year after the birth. The size of the eyeball of a new born baby is about 18 mm starting from front to back. The eye grows until the age of two and increases in length to 24-25 mm for an adult approximately. The diameter of the iris is 11-12 mm, the radius is 5.5 mm approximately, circumference is about 38 mm and thickness is 0.6 mm at the pupillary margin which is collarette and at the ciliary margin the thickness is 0.5 mm. The pupil which is a hole in the center (so called) occupies one-third of the iris say about nearly 5 mm in diameter and 2.5 mm radius. The edge of the pupil is the collarette which is 1.5 mm away from the pupil.

The iris is a multilayerd structure consisting of anterior layer and posterior layer. The anterior layer is visible and the posterior layer is invisible. The anterior layer is larger and lies between the cornea and the iris. The posterior layer is smaller and lies between the iris and the lens. The anterior layer consists of the pupillary zone and the ciliary zone. The pupillary zone and the ciliary zone are separated by the collarette which is a circular ridge. The pupillary zone is relatively flat in the iris and the width varies with the degree of atrophy of the anterior border layer. The ciliary zone contains radial interlacing ridges giving an appearance of gossamer. The iris crypts are formed due to the irregular atrophy in the ciliary zone. The anterior border layer of the iris is a loose collagen tissue in which cells are densely packed. The posterior layer is a heavily pigmented epithelial cell.

The idea of using iris feature for human based recognition is over hundred years old (Bowyer & Flynn, 2008) but the automated recognition system is very young. Dr. Frank Burch an ophthalmologist in the year 1936 proposed iris for the purpose of identification of individuals. In 1985 Dr. Leonard Flom and Aran Safir found that no two irises are identical. Later in 1993 Dr. J. Daugman proceeded with the novel approach of Dr. Flom and Safir to effectively automate the iris recognition system in 1994. Then, in 1993, Dr. John Daugman proceeded using the novel approach of Flom and Safir and effectively automated an iris recognition system in 1994. The approach by (Daugman, 2002) is based on the frequency domain and he used an integro-differential operator to detect pupils and two-dimensional Gabor filter phase modulation to extract the IrisCode. The IrisCode was matched using Hamming distance. In (Wildes, 1997) approach was based on the Hough transform and the gradient edge detection method for pupil detection and a Laplacian pyramid for iris image analysis. The work in (Boles & Boashash, 1998) was based on the zero-crossing method with dissimilarity functions of matching. In (Ma et al., 2003) proposed a method to extract the pupil texture. An attempt with four types of 1-D wavelets to extract the iris features was proposed in (Kong & Zhang, 2003). In (Chin et al., 2006) proposed S-iris encoding where the iris code is generated from the inner product of the output from a 1-D Log Gabor filter. In (Schmid et al., 2006) proposed an algorithm based on the Gaussian model for a small dataset. Identification using biometric is also solved using artificial intelligence (Wang, 2008). Authentication through dynamic keystroke analysis with feed forward neural network is proposed in (Purgason & Hibler, 2012). The enhancement of biometric with artificial intelligence has a greater achievement (Saeed et al., 2007). The reader can find a thorough review of iris recognition in (Burge & Bowyer, 2013).

IRIS RECOGNITION SYSTEM

Iris recognition system is one of the emerging identification systems for the last few decades. The objective of iris recognition is to differentiate human through the feature present in the iris. The iris recognition system operated in three modes as shown in the Figure 2. The iris recognition system consist of four stages: input image acquisition, iris segmentation, iris feature extraction, and matching. The iris recognition system has been endorsed as most perfect biometric trait because of the richness in features and high degree of freedom; inner organ which is protected and accessible from outside; stable through one's life; and high accuracy rate.

Figure 2. Modes of iris recognition system

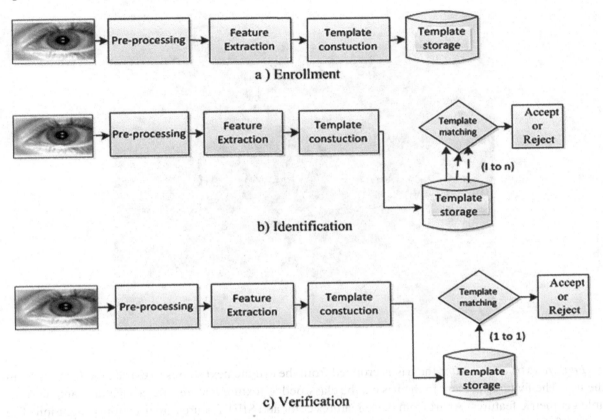

a) Enrollment

b) Identification

c) Verification

Image acquisition: Image acquisition is the first step of iris recognition system. The input image can be acquired using sensors and in some cases with high resolution cameras. The main aim of image acquisition is based on performance of the image because the better the quality of image quality, the more accurate result the system can attain. The iris acquisition devices have to accommodate a bigger size, more advance technological features and less acquisition time.

Iris segmentation: In the acquisition step the full human eye image is acquired. The iris only has to be detected from the eye and hence the iris segmentation. The iris is an annular shape i.e. there exist an inner circle and an outer circle. The inner circle is the boundary of the pupil which is inner most circle of the human eye. The outer circle lies between the boundary of the iris and sclera. So, iris is the portion between the pupil which is darker and sclera the white part of the eye as shown in Figure 3. There exist several iris segmentation techniques which are based on gradient of the image and edge detection algorithms. The iris segmentation algorithm has to satisfy the following:

- The inner and outer circle has to be correctly detected as iris is not always a circle.
- The centre of the pupil always need not be the exact center of the annular circle, as literature proves it is nasally inclined.
- Algorithms based on intensity needs to be taken care as determining the limbus boundary is difficult.

Figure 3. Segmented iris

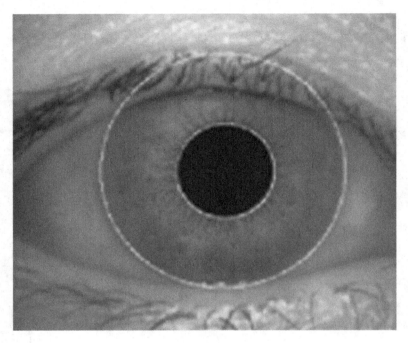

Feature extraction: After the iris is cropped from the eye the next step is to extract the features from the iris. The features present in the iris can be classified as texture features, macro features and deformable geometric features. Apart from these features color and SIFT features are used for recognition. The texture features are extracted based on statistical measures, geometrical methods, model based methods and signal processing methods. The powerful technique for feature extraction is obtained by applying filtering techniques to the image as in signal processing methods. In the literature Gabor filters, 2D-wavelet transform, circular symmetric filters, are used. The feature extraction of iris has an optional step called the normalization or unwrapping of the iris. The annular iris is transformed into a rectangular shape and Cartesian co-ordinates are linked to polar co-ordinates. This transformation is based on the Daugman rubber sheet method.

Matching: The extracted feature can be a feature vector or a binary code. The matching process can be done using distance measure or similarity score to find the genuine or imposter.

IRIS FEATURE EXTRACTION

The human iris can be distinguished based on the rich texture patterns, color of the iris, geometric features, visible features called the macro features and Scale Invariant Feature Transform (SIFT). In this section we describe these features.

Texture Features

In the proposed approach the features present in the pupillary zone are extracted. As theses feature are closer to the pupil it is not affected by the occlusion caused by eyelid or eyelashes. The patterns present in this region are denser when compared to the ciliary region. The frequency in the pupillary region is low and contains more information which can be used for recognition. In order to extract the pupillary zone the iris is first extracted. The iris is extracted based on the method proposed by Daugman. The segmentation process of detecting the inner and outer boundaries are done using active-contour model. The success of segmentation depends on the imaging quality of eye images. The pre-segmentation process involves Gaussian smoothing to remove the noise. Mathematically the Gaussian smoothing function can be used. Daugman makes use of an integro-differential operator for locating the circular iris and pupil regions, and also the arcs of the upper and lower eyelids. In the circular path the operator travels around for a maximum changes in pixel value with respect to the radius and center of x and y position in the circular contour. The operator is progressively used to smoothen in order attain precise localization. Eyelids are localized with the path of contour integration changed from circular to an arc. Once the iris is extracted from the raw image then the curvature of the pupil boundary is deducted. The center of the pupil is calculated using the boundary points on the pupil. The boundary point is fixed in all eight direction say 45°, 90°, 135°, 180°, 225°, 270°, 335°, and 360°.

The curvature is calculated for each boundary points in all eight directions. As the center of the pupil is calculated the next step is to calculate the pupillary zone. The pupillary zone is detected as the collarette is the boundary from the inner circle of the iris. The collarette located about 1.5 mm from the edge of the pupil. The next process of normalization is done based on the homogeneous rubber sheet model formulated by Daugman which remaps each point within the iris region to a pair of polar coordinates(r, θ) where r is on the interval [0, 1] and is angle [0, 2π] as shown in Figure 4. The collarette area is insensitive to pupil dilation and not affected by eyelid or eyelash. The collarette is concentric with the pupil and the radius of the area is restricted certain range. The collarette can be defined as a snaky scalloped line that splits the iris ancillary zone and cilliary zone. The collarette is restricted to the inner half of the iris and contains either radial spokes or dots as shown in Figure 5.

1. **Pupillary Zone:** In the proposed approach the features present in the pupillary zone are extracted. As theses feature are closer to the pupil it is not affected by the occlusion caused by eyelid or eyelashes. The patterns present in this region are denser when compared to the cilliary region. The frequency in the pupillary region is low and contains more information which can be used for recognition. In order to extract the pupillary zone the iris is first extracted. The iris is extracted based on the method proposed by Daugman. The segmentation process of detecting the inner and outer boundaries are done using active-contour model. The success of segmentation depends on

Figure 4. Unwrapped iris

Figure 5. Pupillary, collarette and ciliary region of iris

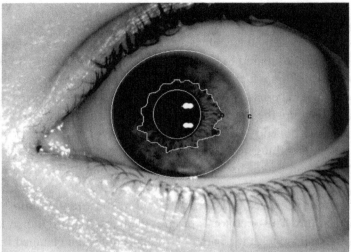

the imaging quality of eye images. The pre-segmentation process involves Gaussian smoothing to remove the noise. Mathematically the Gaussian smoothing function can be used. Daugman makes use of an integro-differential operator for locating the circular iris and pupil regions, and also the arcs of the upper and lower eyelids. In the circular path the operator travels around for a maximum changes in pixel value with respect to the radius and center of x and y position in the circular contour. The operator is progressively used to smoothen in order attain precise localization. Eyelids are localized with the path of contour integration changed from circular to an arc. Once the iris is extracted from the raw image the centre of the pupil is deducted and the curvature of the pupil boundary is deducted. The center of the pupil is calculated using the boundary points on the pupil. The boundary point is fixed in all eight direction say 45°, 90°, 135°, 180°, 225°, 270°, 335°, and 360°. The curvature is calculated for each boundary points all eight directions. As the center of the pupil is calculated the next step is to calculate the pupillary zone. The pupillary zone is detected as the collarette is the boundary from the inner circle of the iris. The collarette located about 1.5 mm from the edge of the pupil. The next process of normalization is done based on the homogeneous rubber sheet model formulated by Daugman which remaps each point within the iris region to a pair of polar coordinates (r, θ) where r is on the interval [0, 1] and θ is angle [0, 2π].

2. **Collarette:** The collarette area is insensitive to pupil dilation and not affected by eyelid or eyelash. The collarette is concentric with the pupil and the radius of the area is restricted certain range. The collarette can be defined as a snaky scalloped line that splits the iris ancillary zone and ciliary zone. The collarette is restricted to the inner half of the iris and contains either radial spokes or dots.

Geometric Features

The geometric features of the iris can also be used for human identification. The structure of the iris is more related to the geometric shape and hence the extraction of these features is also possible. The geometric features which are extracted can be used as a primary level of identification and some can be used as secondary, for example, the size of the pupil may not be unique, but when it is associated with other features say iris or collarette it becomes unique. The geometric characteristics are classified as:

1. **Pupil Based Features:** Pupil is defined to be circular or round, but they are not actually a circle. So, the geometrical properties of the circle can be used to identify the pupil and these features can be used for recognition. The following are the pupil based features:

    a. **Pupil Roundness (PR):** The roundness measurement requires tracing the iris in 360 degrees and hence the consistency of the diameter can be measured at a number of orientation points on the iris. In general roundness is defined as a measure of sharpness at the corners and edges of a circle which is related with the spherecity and compactness of the circle. In simple it is the radii around the iris at regular intervals. The roundness feature is calculated based on the diameter at various orientations, where the ratio between the maximum value and the minimum value is calculated at horizontal (h), vertical (v), left (l) and right (r) at 0°, 45°, 90° and 135° respectively. Given a circle the roundness value is 1.0 for a standard circle, for a non-circular it is less than 1.0 and greater than 1.0 for an irregular shape.

    b. **Pupil Largeness (PL):** The largeness of the pupil is described based on the radius of the pupil. As the pupil is not an actual circle the general diameter calculation of distance from the center to any point on the pupil is not sufficient. Hence, the diameter is calculated at eight direction on the pupil at 0° (horizontally), 90° (vertically), 30°, 45°, 75°, 120°, 135° and 165°.

    c. **Pupil Smoothness (PS):** Geometrically the curvature is defined as how fast the unit tangent vector to the curve rotates. If the a curve keeps close to the same direction the unit tangent vector change very little and the curvature is small whereas the curve undergoes a light turn the curvature is large.

2. **Collarette Based Feature:** The collarette area is insensitive to pupil dilation and not affected by eyelid or eyelash. The collarette is concentric with the pupil and the radius of the area is restricted certain range. The collarette can be defined as a snaky scalloped line that splits the iris ancillary zone and ciliary zone. The collarette is restricted to the inner half of the iris and contains ether radial spokes or dots. As the collarette based feature cannot be detected directly from the iris it requires some first to detect the collarette and then compute the geometric measures

    a. **Collarette Roundness (CR):** As the collarette feature is extracted from the iris, the next step is working out of geometric feature of the collarette. The roundness feature of collarette is computed as the ratio between the maximum and minimum values of the six diameter of the collarette.

    b. **Collarette Iris Ratio (CIR):** The collarette iris ratio is computed based on the diameter of the iris. The diameter of iris is nearly 10 to 11 mm. The collarette occupies one third of the iris and is located at about 1.5 mm away from the pupil. Hence the distance of the collarette and iris diameter is calculated at eight points, where the iris is divided into equal space ordinates with respect to the polar co-ordinates. For each intersection point on the edge of the iris, the distance is computed and the collarette iris ratio is computed.

Macro Features

The iris complex patterns consist of unique features such as arching ligaments, furrows, ridges, crypts, rings, corona, freckles and a zigzag collarette area. The iris macro features are marked in figure 6 as,

Figure 6. Iris features

1. Pupil
2. Sclera
3. Pupillary zone
4. Collarette
5. Ciliary zone
6. Radial furrows
7. Crypts
8. Pigment spot
9. Concentric Furrows

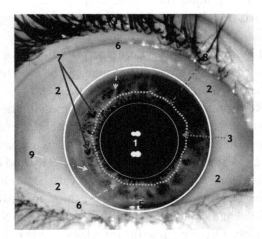

1-pupil, 2-sclera, 3-pupillary region, 4-collarette, 5-cilliary, 6-radial furrows, 7-crypts, 8-pigment spots and 9-concentric furrows. The Crypts of Fuchs is present on both the side of a collarette as a series of openings which is used to make the stroma and other in-depth iris tissues to float on aqueous humor. The pupillary ruff is found at end of the pupillary region as a series of small ridges formed by the continuation of the pigmented epithelium. The contraction furrows are the circular contraction folds are a series of circular lines or folds in the middle of the collarette and the iris. Crypts are the pit like depression or additional openings that can be observed close to the collarette and near the outermost part of the ciliary portion. The macro level features are also the visible characteristics which are the anatomical structures present in the iris and are unique to be used for identification. The macro features are usually the discontinuities that are present in the iris with respect to the size, color, texture and intensity. The macro features can be categorized based on the following characteristics:

- **Size:** The size of the features vary in size.
- **Color:** The colors of the features are not constant and they vary from feature to feature in the same iris. They can be orange, yellow, dark brown and black.
- **Texture:** The patterns present in the iris.

The features present in the anterior and posterior layer are crypts, radial furrows, pupil, pigment related feature, concentric furrows and pigmented frill. Some other features that are present in the iris are due to nevi, tumors or melanoma present in eye such as: lisch nodules, wolffin Spots, brushfield spots, yellow coloration, central heterochroma, sectrol heterochroma and bilateral heterochroma.

1. *Crypts* are chain of pit like depression or opening which appear near the collarette and the periphery of the iris. These are responsible for the flow of aqueous humor into the stroma from the anterior layer of the iris when the size of the iris alters with dilation and contraction. The crypts are identified as the regions which are invariably darker than the surrounding region. As crypts have high curvature along the contours it can be used for matching. Crypts sometime are also isolated and

they can be detected using region-growing algorithm and then obtaining center of gravity and the lower order central moments.

2. *Radial Furrows* are described as extending radially to any direction in relation to the center of pupil. They may begin near pupil and extend through collarette. Radial furrows are creases in the anterior layer of the iris form which loose tissue may protuberate outward and it is these loose tissues which permit the iris to dilate and contract. This feature is an elevation dependent feature as it bulges outward. The positions of radial furrows in relation to each other are stable. The angular position and length of the radial furrows can be used for identification.

3. *Pupil* is generally defined as a black circle but exactly not a circle which is a hole in the center of the iris of an eye. The pupil is an opening through which light is passed to the retina. The size of the pupil is equal in size but depending on lighting the size varies. In an adult it varies from 2 to 4 mm in light and 4 to 8 mm in dark. The feature that can be used for identification with respect to the pupil is the shape and the size. The size of the pupil can be measured using the peripheral points and center point of the pupil.

4. *Pigment related* features are the pigment spots, mole, freckles or nevi and crypts. The pigment spots are formed due to the random concentration of pigments on the iris surface. The color of the pigment sport is mostly black in color that is they appear to be darker than the iris brown color. The position and size of the pigment spots can be used for identification.

5. *Concentric furrows* are usually circular and these creases are concentric with the pupil. Concentric furrows are present in the ciliary zone which is near to the pupillary zone of the iris.

6. *Pigment frill* appear as dark brown color and are present at the margin of the pupil as a protruding portion of the posterior layer of the iris.

A comparative result for the above methods is given in Table 1.

RECENT RESEARCH IN IRIS

The iris recognition system is extensively used for human identification. Iris authentication is deployed in many commercial applications and government organizations, such as border crossing and social identity. The idea of systemizing iris as biometric feature is 100 years old, but automation is very young.

Table 1. Comparison of iris features

Iris Features	FRR (%)	FAR (%)	Accuracy (%)
Texture features	5.33	4.67	95.23
Pupillary features	3.45	4.35	95.81
Collarette features	2.82	3.73	96.51
Geometric features	2.75	1.23	98.32
Macro features	4.45	5.62	96.14

The earlier research works were based on stop-and-stare method, which was controlled environment. Later it was extended to on-a-move, at-a-distance and visible wavelength.

Iris for Personality Identification

Earlier research and literature survey depicts iris as an authentication feature. But personality identification based on iris is not a new idea as (Cattell, 1965), has used iris color for identifying the physiological and behavioural characteristics of persons. In (Larsson & Stattin, 2003; Larsson & Pedersen, 2004) study they have given a novel technology based on iris to identify the personality or characteristics of a person. Though iris has proved to be epigenetic but certain features are genetically inherited. The macro level features used in their research are Fuchs crypts, pigmentation dots, color of iris, the wolffin nodules and contractile furrows. The crypts were related with humanity behaviour such as the feelings, tendermindness, warmth, trust and positive emotions. The crypts frequency can be:

- Either parallel or curly fibres densely packed,
- Both parallel and curly fibres,
- Spots of wavy fibres,
- Shallow crypts.

The presences of dense crypts frequency suggest warmer, joyful and happy person when compared to open crypt structure. Contractile furrows which are more dense and thick in iris were associated with impulsiveness. Contraction furrows can emerge or appear in:

- Extension from pupil to 0.25 mm.
- Between 0.25 mm to 0.8 mm.
- Extending from 0.8 mm to border of iris, which are more distinct.

Persons with few contraction furrows are not capable of controlling their desire and urges when compared to other people with less contraction furrows.

Iris for Medical Diagnosis

The iris as medical diagnosis tool in early days was called as iridology. Iridology is defined as a study of pathological issues related to human body which enables to observe the changes in iris. The texture, color and patterns present in the iris are believed to have an impulse association with a disease sign or malfunction of a organ in the human body. Iridology enables location of toxins in the organs, inflammation in the body, weakness and strength of the organs and deficiency in human organs. The iridologist makes use of the iris chart to associate the organs in human body. The chart is divided into segments and layers where each layer and segments are correlated with the internal organs. The iridology was done manually. Recent research uses the feature extraction techniques of authentication for medical diagnosis also. In (Ma et al., 2013) proposes a semi-automated system to identify the disease in human body with deformable geometric iris features. In the experiment two diseases gastrointestinal and enteritis were diagnosed.

IRIS DATABASES

- BATH database (Dobes & Machala, 2004) is a publicly available database with a minimum of handling fees. It is maintained by university of Bath in conjunction with Smart Sensor Limited. The databases consist of 1600 eyes taken from 800 people with 20 images of each left and right eye. The iris images are with higher resolution of 1280x960 pixel stored in JPEG format.
- CASIA (Chinese Academy of Sciences, 2004) Iris Image Database for Testing Version 1.0 (or IR-TestV1) contains 10,000 iris images of 2,000 eyes from 1,000 subjects. The images are 8 bit gray-scale BMP files with a resolution of 640x480. CASIA Iris Image Database Version 1.0 (CASIA-IrisV1) includes 756 iris images from 108 eyes. For each eye, 7 images are captured in two sessions where three samples are collected in the first session and four in the second session. All images are stored as BMP format with resolution 320x280. CASIA Iris Image Database Version 2.0 (CASIA-IrisV2) includes two subsets captured with two different devices in a controlled environment. Each subset includes 1200 images from 60 classes.
- CASIA-IrisV3 includes three subsets which are labelled as CASIA-Iris-Interval, CASIA-Iris-Lamp, CASIA-Iris-Twins. CASIA-IrisV3 contains a total of 22,034 iris images from more than 700 subjects. All iris images are 8-bit gray-level JPEG files, collected under near infrared illumination. Almost all subjects are Chinese except a few in CASIA-Iris-Interval. Because the three data sets were collected in different times, only CASIA-Iris-Interval and CASIA-Iris-Lamp have a small overlap in subjects. CASIA- Iris-Twins contains iris images of 100 pairs of twins, which were collected during Annual Twins Festival in Beijing. Although iris is usually regarded as a kind of phenotypic biometric characteristics and even twins have their unique iris patterns, it is interesting to study the dissimilarity and similarity between iris images of twins.
- UBIRIS (Proenca & Alexandre, 2005), is a public and free noisy iris database managed by the Dept of CS at University of Beira Interior. The database consist of 1877 iris images collected from 372 subjects, 5 samples each in two sessions. During the first session, images are captured under a controlled environment to minimize the noise factor. In the second session images were acquired form 131 persons in a natural luminosity location. The images are stored in JPEG file format.
- ICE (Iris Challenge Evaluation, 2006) a large database used for evaluation of iris recognition system. It is conducted and managed by National Institute of Standards and Technology (NIST). The database consist of 2953 iris images form 132 subjects. The iris images are 480x640 pixel resolution. The images are acquired under near infrared (NIR) in a constrained environment. The images are stored in tiff file format. The main objective is to identify the correlation between the left and right irises for match and non-match similarity scores.
- IITK Indian Institute of Technology, Kanpur iris image database is used for the iris data. The database comprises of 1350 iris images of 150 subjects (nine images per subject) from their left eye. The images are JPEG in grey scale and are resized with 450x350 pixels resolution.

PERFORMANCE METRICS

- **Decision Error Rates:** Decision errors are due to matching errors or image acquisition errors. These fundamental errors combine to form decision errors depends on (a) whether one-to-one or one-to- many matching is required; (b) whether there is a positive or negative claim of identity.

Biometric performance has traditionally been stated in terms of the decision error rates, viz., false accept rate and false reject rate. False accept rate: The expected proportion of transactions with wrongful claims of identity or non-identity that are incorrectly confirmed. False reject rate: The expected proportion of transactions with truthful claims of identity (in a positive ID system) or non-identity (in a negative ID system) that are incorrectly denied.

- **Matching Errors:** The matching error is used to evade uncertainty with biometric systems per-mit- ting multiple attempts or taking multiple templates. Matching error is defined against a single comparison with a single enrolled template.

  - **False Match Rate (FMR):** The FMR is otherwise called the false positive. It is defined as the expected probability that a sample will be falsely declared to match a single randomly-selected template.
  - **False Non-Match Rate (FNMR):** The FNMR is also called as false negative. It is defined as the expected probability of a sample that falsely declares not to match a template of the same measure of the same user template.

In literature the decision error and matching are used interchanging. But there is a difference between decision errors and matching errors. False match/non-match rates are calculated over the number of comparisons, but false accept/reject rates are calculated over transactions and refer to the acceptance or rejection of the stated hypothesis, whether positive or negative. Further, false accept/reject rates include failure-to-acquire rates. In a positive identification system allowing a maximum of three attempts is required to be matched to an enrolled template, a false rejection will result with any combination of failures-to-acquire. For both FMR and FNMR the expectations are those for a user selected randomly from the target population. In a negative identification system, a users claim not to be enrolled in the system will be falsely rejected if an image is acquired and then falsely matched to one or more enrolled templates. Depending upon system policy, a user's claim might be falsely accepted if an image cannot be acquired or if an acquired image is falsely non-matched against the enrolled image. If each user is allowed one enrolment template and makes the same number (and pattern) of verification attempts, the observed error rates will be the best estimates of the true error rates. Note that the error rates are averaged over users as opposed to attempts. Averaging over attempts would weigh the error rates towards those of the heavy users of the system and toward those requiring multiple attempts for acceptance.

- **Image Acquisition Errors**: Irrespective of the accurateness of the matching algorithm, the con-cert of a biometric system is compromised if an individual cannot enrol or if they cannot present a satisfactory image at a later attempt. Failure to enrol rate: The failure to enrol rate is the expected proportion of the population for whom the system is unable to generate repeatable templates. This will include those unable to present the required biometric feature, those unable to produce an image of sufficient quality at enrolment, and those who cannot reliably match their template in attempts to confirm the enrolment is usable. The failure to enrol rate will depend on the enrolment policy. For example in the case of failure, enrolment might be re-attempted at a later date. The failure to acquire rate is defined as the expected proportion of transactions for which the system is unable to capture or locate an image or signal of sufficient quality. The failure to acquire rate may depend on adjustable thresholds for image or signal quality.
- **Binning Algorithm Performance:** To improve efficiency in systems requiring a one-to-many search of the enrolled database, some systems may partition template data to separate bins. An

input sample is likewise assigned to a partition and compared only to the portion of the template data contained in the same partition.

  ○ **Penetration Rate:** The penetration rate is defined as the expected proportion of the template data to be searched over all input samples under the rule that the search proceeds through the entire partition regardless of whether a match is found. Lower penetration rates indicate fewer searches and, hence, are desirable.

  ○ **Binning Error Rate:** A binning error occurs if the enrolment template and a subsequent sample from the same biometric feature on the same user are placed in different partitions. In general, the more partitioning of the database that occurs the lower the penetration rate, but the greater the probability of a binning error.

- **Receiver Operating Characteristic (ROC) Curves**: Receiver operating characteristic curves is an accepted method for summarising the performance of imperfect diagnostic, detection, and pattern matching systems. An ROC curve plots, parametrically as a function of the decision threshold, the rate of false positives (i.e. Impostor attempts accepted) on the x-axis, against the corresponding rate of true positives (i.e. genuine attempts accepted) on the y-axis. ROC curves are threshold independent, allowing performance comparison of different systems under similar conditions, or of a single system under differing conditions.

- **Detection Error Trade-Off (DET) Curves:** In the case of biometric systems, a modified ROC curve known as a detection error trade-off curve is preferred. A DET curve as shown in figure 7 plots error rates on both axes, giving uniform treatment to both types of error. The graph can then be plotted using logarithmic axes. This spreads out the plot and distinguishes different well-performing systems more clearly.

Figure 7. DET curve

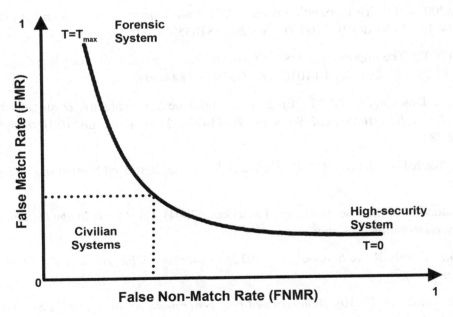

CONCLUSION

Iris biometrics is a dynamic research field in biometric based authentication system and is measured as a key biometric technology for large-scale systems. In this chapter the anatomy and formation of human iris was described. Iris recognition has been able to work well in stop-and-stare, on-a-move, at-a-distance and visible wavelength. Apart from iris used for recognition it is also viewed in other perspective as medical diagnosis and personality identification. Iris is not only used as unibiometric but also as multibiometrics i.e., with combination with other biometric traits. The iris biometric system is evaluated using FAR, FRR, FMR, FNMR and represented by ROC curve and DET curve. To evaluate the iris biometric system there exist a number of freely available databases which are presented in this chapter.

REFERENCES

Boles, W. W., & Boashash, B. (1998). A human identification technique using images of the iris & wavelet transform. *IEEE Transactions on Signal Processing, 46*(4), 1185–1188. doi:10.1109/78.668573

Bowyer, W., & Flynn, P. J. (2008). Image understanding for iris biometrics: A survey. *Computer Vision and Image Understanding, 110*(2), 281–307. doi:10.1016/j.cviu.2007.08.005

Burge, M. J., & Bowyer, K. W. (2013). *Handbook of Iris Recognition*. Springer-Verlag. doi:10.1007/978-1-4471-4402-1

Cattell, R. B. (1965). *The Scientific Analysis of Personality*. Aldine.

Chin, C., Jin, A., & Ling, D. (2006). High security iris verification system based on random secret integration. *Computer Vision and Image Understanding, 102*(2), 169–177. doi:10.1016/j.cviu.2006.01.002

Daugman, J. (2002). How iris recognition works. *IEEE Transactions on Circuits and Systems for Video Technology, 14*(1), 21–30. doi:10.1109/TCSVT.2003.818350

Daugman, J. (2003). The importance of being random: Statistical principles of iris recognition. *Pattern Recognition, 36*(2), 279–291. doi:10.1016/S0031-3203(02)00030-4

Daugman, J., & Downing, C. (2001). Epigenetic randomness, complexity, & singularity of human iris patterns. *Royal Soc. Biological Sciences, 268*(1477), 1737–1740. doi:10.1098/rspb.2001.1696 PMID:11506688

Dobes, M., & Machala, L. (2004). *UPOL Iris Image Database*. Retrieved from http:// phoenix.inf.upol.cz/iris/

Institute of Automation, Chinese Academy of Sciences. (2004). *CASIA Iris Image Database*. Retrieved from http://www.sinobiometrics.com

Ivan, R. R. D., Schwab, R., & Schobert, C. (2012). *Evolution's Witness: How Eyes Evolved*. Oxford University Press.

Jain, A. K., & Kumar, A. (2010). *Biometrics of next generation: An overview. In Second Generation Biometric*. Springer.

Jain, A. K., Ross, A., & Prabhakar, S. (2004). An introduction to biometric recognition. *IEEE Transactions on Circuits and Systems for Video Technology*, *14*(1), 4–20. doi:10.1109/TCSVT.2003.818349

Kong, W., & Zhang, D. (2003). Detecting eyelash & reflection for accurate iris Segmentation. *International Journal of Pattern Recognition and Artificial Intelligence*, *17*(6), 1025–1034. doi:10.1142/S0218001403002733

Larsson, M., & Pedersen, N. L. (2004). Genetic correlations among texture characteristics in the human iris. *Molecular Vision*, *10*, 821–831. PMID:15534585

Larsson, M., & Stattin, H. (2003). Importance of genetic effects for characteristics of the human iris. *Twin Research*, *6*(3), 192–200. doi:10.1375/136905203765693843 PMID:12855068

Ma, L., Tan, T., & Zhang, D. (2003). Personal identification based on iris texture analysis. *IEEE Transactions on Pattern Analysis and Machine Intelligence*, *25*(12), 1519–1533. doi:10.1109/TPAMI.2003.1251145

Ma, L., Zhang, D., Li, N., Cai, Y., Zuo, W., & Wang, K. (2013). Iris-based medical analysis by geometric deformation features. *IEEE Journal of Biomedical & Health Informatics*, *17*(1), 223–231. doi:10.1109/TITB.2012.2222655 PMID:23144041

National Institute of Standards and Technology, Iris Challenge Evaluation. (2006). Retrieved from http://iris.nist.gov/ICE/

Proenca, H., & Alexandre, L. A. (2005). Ubiris: A noisy iris image database. *LNCS*, *1*, 970–977.

Purgason, B., & Hibler, D. (2012). Security Through Behavioral Biometrics and Artificial Intelligence, *Procedia. Computer Science*, *12*, 398–403.

Ross, A., Nandakumar, K., & Jain, A. K. (2006). *Handbook of Multibiometrics*. New York: Springer-Verlag.

Saeed, K., Pejas, J., & Mosdorf, R. (2007). *Biometrics, Computer Security Systems and Artificial Intelligence Applications*. Springer Science & Business Media.

Schmid, N., Ketkar, M., Singh, H., & Cukic, B. (2006). Performance analysis of iris based identification system at the matching score level. *IEEE Transactions on Information Forensics & Security*, *1*(2), 154–168. doi:10.1109/TIFS.2006.873603

U. I. D. of India. (n.d.). Retrieved from www.uidai.gov.in

Wang, P. (2008). Intelligent pattern recognition and biometrics. In *Proceedings of IEEE International Conference on Intelligence and Security Informatics*, (pp. 39-40). IEEE.

Wildes, R. P. (1997). Iris recognition: An emerging biometric technology. *Proceedings of the IEEE*, *85*(9), 1348–1363. doi:10.1109/5.628669

Chapter 11
Object Classification and Tracking in Real Time:
An Overview

Amlan Jyoti Das
Gauhati University, India

Navajit Saikia
Assam Engineering College, India

Kandarpa Kumar Sarma
Gauhati University, India

ABSTRACT

Algorithms for automatic processing of visual data have been a topic of interest since the last few decades. Object tracking and classification methods are highly demanding in vehicle traffic control systems, surveillance systems for detecting unauthorized movement of vehicle and human, mobile robot applications, animal tracking, etc. There are still many challenging issues while dealing with dynamic background, occlusion, etc. in real time. This chapter presents an overview of various existing techniques for object detection, classification and tracking. As the most important requirements of tracking and classification algorithms are feature extraction and selection, different feature types are also included.

There is a growing popularity of surveillance mechanisms in public safety systems for detecting unauthorized vehicle parking, unintended luggage and unauthorized entry of persons or vehicles in a restricted area, and also in tracking of animals in forest, sport video analysis, etc. In general, the processing framework for object tracking and classification includes the four stages: detection (segmentation and modelling of the candidate object and the changing background), feature extraction (extraction of features from the object), classification (detecting the type of the object) and tracking (estimation of the possible location of the object in each frame and localization of the object in each frame).

The detection, classification and tracking of moving object are challenging tasks in the outdoor environments for various reasons like (1) incomplete details of moving object due to possible occlusions, (2)

DOI: 10.4018/978-1-4666-9685-3.ch011

Figure 1. Classification of Object detection techniques

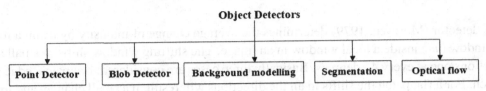

change in environment conditions like fog, rain, lighting, haze and strong shadow effects, etc. (3) very low resolution of candidate object and (4) real-time processing and high memory requirement. Further, the efficiency of classifier and tracker depend on their ability to perform under varying camera angle and to discriminate objects.

There are many techniques proposed in recent past for classifying and tracking of objects in real time. This chapter discusses about some of the popular methods available in the literature for object detection, feature extraction, classification and tracking of objects of interest from the visual data. Each section in the following considers the methods at each stage with description and discussion. A comprehensive set of references is also presented for further consultation. Section 1 discusses about object detection. Section 2 covers briefly about different aspects of feature extraction. Classification methods are included in Section 3. Tracking aspects are discussed in Section 4. The work is concluded in the last section.

1. OBJECT DETECTION

Detection of object of interest in video is the most important step in a system for tracking and classifying object. The performance of the complete system depends on the accuracy and rate of detection of the region of interest. An object can be detected either when it first appears in the video or in every frame depending on requirement. Since it is more meaningful to detect the moving objects than to detect all the static objects in a video sequence, most methods focus on detecting such objects. The common approach is to use the temporal information that highlights the difference between the consecutive frames in a video. In the following, some popular object detection techniques are discussed in the context of object classification and tracking. The different types of object detection methods commonly used may be grouped as in Figure 1.

1.1. Point Detectors

Point detectors are used to find the points of interest in video frames which have expressive photometric descriptors. These points having useful textures are important in the applications like recognition, tracking, etc. Point detectors are less sensitive to illumination changes and can perform even in occluded environment. Moreover, they do not involve segmentation while detecting objects of interest. Most commonly used point detectors include Moravec's interest operator, Harris interest point detector, KLT detector and SIFT detector and Affine invariant point detector (Mikolajczyk & Schmid, 2002).

Moravec's Detector

Moravec's detector (Moravec, 1979) determines the average change of intensity by using a rectangular shifting window (w) inside a local window in an image. The shifting window shifts in small amount in eight directions one at every 45 degrees. Basically three cases are considered: flat patch, edge patch and corner patch. For a flat patch the shifts in all the directions will result in a small change, and for a corner patch all the shifts will result in a large change. If the shift is perpendicular to the edge, an edge patch will result in a large change. Mathematically,

$$E\left(x,y\right) = \sum_{u,v} w\left(u,v\right)\left|I\left(x+u,y+v\right) - I\left(u,v\right)\right|^2, \tag{1}$$

where all elements in w are 1, and $\left(x,y\right)$ represents the shift. Since a limited set of shifts are considered, the response of Moravec's detector is anisotropic. Also, the response is highly noisy as w is rectangular and binary.

Harris Detector

In Harris detector (Harris & Stephens, 1981), all possible small shifts about the shift origin are considered for improved performance over the Moravec's detector. Here a gradient formulation is used to detect response at any shift:

$$E\left(x,y\right) = \sum_{u,v} w\left(u,v\right)\left[I\left(x+u,y+v\right) - I\left(u,v\right)\right]^2$$

$$= \sum_{u,v} w\left(u,v\right)\left[xX + yY + O\left(x^2,y^2\right)\right]^2, \tag{2}$$

where the first gradients are approximated by using the following two expressions:

X component of gradient: $X = I \otimes \left(-1,0,1\right) \approx \dfrac{\partial I}{\partial x}$ \hfill (3)

Y component of gradient: $Y = I \otimes \left(-1,0,1\right)^T \approx \dfrac{\partial I}{\partial y}$ \hfill (4)

For small shifts,

$$E\left(x,y\right) = Ax^2 + 2Cxy + By^2,$$

where $A = X^2 \otimes w, B = Y^2 \otimes w$ and $C = \left(XY\right) \otimes w$. The window used in Harris detector is Gaussian given by:

$$w\left(u,v\right) = \exp-\left(u^2 + v^2\right)/2\sigma^2,$$

here, the variation of E with the direction of shift is used in corner measures for enhanced performance. The change in E for a small shift (x, y) can be written as:

$$E(x, y) = (x, y) M (x, y)^T,$$

(5)

where $M = \begin{bmatrix} A & C \\ C & B \end{bmatrix}$.

The two eigen values of M correspond to the principal curvatures of the local autocorrelation function. The windowed image region is of approximately constant intensity when both the curvatures are small. If only one curvature is high, an edge is indicated. A corner is denoted if both the curvatures are high. The corner response is obtained by using the trace $(Tr(M))$ and determinant $(Det(M))$ of M:

$$R = Det(M) - kTr(M)^2,$$

(6)

where

$$Tr(M) = \alpha + \beta,$$

where α and β are the eigen values of M, and

$$Det(M) = \alpha\beta = AB - C^2$$

(8)

A positive R value indicates a corner and a negative indicates an edges. A small values of R indicate flat regions.

KLT Detector

As we have seen above, the Harris detector sets implicit threshold via the corner magnitude. The Kanade–Lucas–Tomasi (KLT) (Shi & Tomaski, 1994) detector sets explicit threshold on the diagonalised M. The moment matrix M in Eqn. (5) is also used here to detect the points of interest. Computing the 'interest point confidence'(R) from the minimum eigen value of M (λ_{min}), the 'interest point candidates' are selected by using a threshold λ_{thr} with the condition $\lambda_{min} > \lambda_{thr}$. From all the candidate points, the points which are appearing further in the list belonging to the neighbourhood of the detected current point are deleted. The Harris and KLT detectors are conceptually related as both are related to intensity variations. Figure2 in the following shows the results of the Harris and KLT detectors on the Cameraman image.

In Harris and KLT detectors, the locations are repeatable up to relatively small scale changes as they rely on Gaussian derivatives computed at a certain fixed base scale. If the image scale differs by a large value between the test images, then the extracted structures will be different.

SIFT Detector

Lowe (2004) has proposed SIFT (scale invariant feature transform) detector for efficient detection of points of interest which works under different scales of transformation. This detector works in four steps as under:

Figure 2. (a) Output of Harris point detector, (b) Output of KLT point detector

(a)   **(b)**

Scale-Space Extrema Detection: Here, the potential points of interest are searched over all scales and image locations. It is implemented by using a difference-of-Gaussian (DoG) function to identify the potential points of interest that are invariant to scale and orientation:

$$D\big(x,y,\sigma\big) = \Big(G\big(x,y,k\sigma\big) - G\big(x,y,\sigma\big)\Big) * I\big(x,y\big) = L\big(x,y,k\sigma\big) - L\big(x,y,\sigma\big), \tag{9}$$

where $I\big(x,y\big)$ is the input image, $L\big(x,y,\sigma\big)$ is the scale space of the image produced by convoluting variable scale Gaussian $G\big(x,y,\sigma\big) = \dfrac{1}{2\pi\sigma^2}e^{-\big(x^2+y^2\big)/2\sigma^2}$ with the input image and k is a constant. Candidate interest points are selected from the minima and maxima of the DoG images across scales.

2. **Key-Point Localization:** The location, scale and ratio of principal curvature are determined at each candidate location. Key points are selected based on their stability measures. Key points having low contrast are discarded.
3. **Orientation Assignment:** By assigning one or more orientations to each key-point location based on the local image gradient directions, the key-point descriptor can be represented relative to this orientation. The operations are then performed on the visual data that has been changed relative to the assigned orientation, scale and location for each feature for achieving invariance of these transformations.
4. **Key-Point Descriptor:** At the selected scale, the local image gradients are computed around each key-point. These are transformed into a representation that allows change in local shape distortion and change in illumination to a significant level.

1.2. Blob Detectors

The most important requirement of a scale-invariant blob detector is to efficiently detect objects under scale changes. For automatic scale selection, a scale-dependent signature function is evaluated on the key-point neighbourhood and the resulting value is plotted as a function of the scale. If two key-points correspond to the same structure, their signature functions will have similar shapes and corresponding neighbourhood sizes can be determined by searching for the scale-space extrema of the signature function.

Laplacian of Gaussian

Lindeberg (1998) has proposed a detector for blob-like features that searches for scale space extrema of a scale-normalized Laplacian-of-Gaussian (LoG) based on automatic scale selection. The 2D LoG filter mask

$$L\left(x,\sigma\right) = \sigma^2 \left(I_{ii}\left(x,\sigma\right) + I_{jj}\left(x,\sigma\right)\right), \tag{10}$$

takes the shape of a circular centre region with positive weights surrounded by another circular region with negative weights.

Difference of Gaussian

The difference of Gaussian (DoG), $D\left(x,\sigma\right)$, is used to approximate the scale-space Laplacian (Lowe, 2004) by using the difference of two adjacent scales that are separated by a factor of k:

$$D\left(x,\sigma\right) = \left(G\left(x,k\sigma\right) - G\left(x,\sigma\right)\right) * I\left(x\right), \tag{11}$$

Each scale octave is divided into an equal number (K) of intervals, such that $k = 2^{1/K}$ and $\sigma_n = k^n \sigma_0$. Finally, those regions are kept that pass a threshold and whose estimated scale falls into a certain scale range $\left[s_{min}, s_{max}\right]$. The resulting point (of interest) operator reacts to blob-like structures that have their maximal extent in a radius of approximately 1.6σ of the detected points.

SURF Detector

Bay et al. (2008) introduces the SURF (speeded up robust feature) algorithm with the scale and rotation-invariant properties for detecting points of interest and descriptors. SURF combines a Hessian-Laplace region detector with an own gradient orientation using Haar wavelet based box filters. These box filters estimates the effects of the derivative filter kernels. This algorithm is shown to be faster than SIFT.

The SURF detector basically uses integral image as defined by:

$$I_{\Sigma}\left(x\right) = \sum_{i=0}^{i \leq x} \sum_{j=0}^{j \leq y} I\left(i,j\right)$$

Points of interest are detected based on Hessian matrix defined at a point $x = \left(i, j\right)$ at scale σ by using:

$$H\left(x, \sigma\right) = \begin{bmatrix} L_{ii}\left(x, \sigma\right) & L_{ij}\left(x, \sigma\right) \\ L_{ij}\left(x, \sigma\right) & L_{jj}\left(x, \sigma\right) \end{bmatrix}, \tag{12}$$

where

$$L_{ii}\left(x, \sigma\right), L_{ij}\left(x, \sigma\right) and\, L_{jj}\left(x, \sigma\right)$$

are the convolutions of the input image in point x with the Gaussian second-order derivatives $\dfrac{\partial^2 g\left(\sigma\right)}{\partial i^2}, \dfrac{\partial^2 g\left(\sigma\right)}{\partial i \partial j}$ and $\dfrac{\partial^2 g\left(\sigma\right)}{\partial j^2}$ respectively. The box filters are approximations of a Gaussian with σ and represent the lowest scale for computing the blob response maps.

MSER Detector

Maximally stable extremal regions (MSER) (Matas, Chum, Urban, & Pajdla, 2002) is an affine covariant region detection technique which is usually used to find features in case of a large viewpoint changes which is not possible by local point detectors. Although a scale- and rotation-invariant region can be described by a circle, an affine deformation transforms this circle to an ellipse. MSER applies a watershed segmentation algorithm on image to extract homogeneous intensity regions which are stable over a large range of thresholds (maximally stable extremal regions).

BRISK Detector

Leutenegger et al. (2011) have proposed binary robust invariant scalable key-point(BRISK) detector involving the following two steps

1. **Scale-Space Key-Point Detection:** Points of interest are identified in the image and scale dimensions using a criterion. To fulfil the features from accelerated segment test (FAST) (Rosten and Drummond, 2006) criterion using 9-16 mask, which requires at least 9 consecutive pixels in the 16-pixel circle to either be sufficiently brighter or be darker than the central pixel. For efficiency boosting of computation, key-points are detected in octave layers of the image pyramid as well as in the layers in between. A quadratic function fitting is used to obtain the location and the scales of each key-point are in the continuous domain.
2. **Key-Point Description:** To retrieve gray values, a sampling pattern consisting of points lying on appropriately scaled concentric circles is applied at the neighbourhood of each key-point. Finally, pair wise brightness comparison is obtained by using the oriented BRISK sampling pattern and these comparison results are then assembled into the binary BRISK descriptor.

As shown by Leutenegger et al. (2011), the BRISK detector outperformed the SIFT and SURF detectors in some cases. However, the BRISK detectors are more sensitive to blur than other blob detectors.

1.3. Background Modelling

The background subtraction is the most popular and common approach for object motion detection in a video. The main idea is to subtract the current image from a reference background image, which is updated periodically to make the detection adaptive in changing illumination conditions. The subtraction leaves the entire silhouette region of the moving or new objects entering the scene. This approach is simple and computationally inexpensive making it suitable for real-time systems. But these algorithms are extremely sensitive to dynamic changes in the background either from lightning or extraneous event etc. Therefore it is highly dependent on a good background maintenance model. The main problem with background subtraction is that it should update the background after a particular number of frames. Moreover it should be robust enough to deal with: motion in the background, shadows, camouflages (ability to detect moving object even if the pixel characteristics are similar to that of the background).

Simple Background Subtraction

In simple background subtraction an absolute difference is taken between every current image $I_t(i,j)$ and the reference background image $R(i,j)$ to find out the motion detection mask $B(i,j)$. The reference background image is generally the first frame of a video, which should not contain any foreground object that are to be detected. Mathematically,

$$B(i,j) = \begin{cases} 1, & If\ |I_t(i,j) - R(i,j)| \geq \tau \\ 0, & otherwise \end{cases} \tag{13}$$

To make the background adaptive with the illumination changes and to prevent it from noise, running average can be used to update the background in each frame of the video sequence.

$$R_t(i,j) = (1-\alpha)R_{t-1}(i,j) + \alpha I_t(i,j), \tag{14}$$

where α is a learning rate. To minimize the computation load, the update rate can be set to less than that of the frame rate. But lower update rate will lead to a system which cannot respond to quick changing background.

Temporal/Frame Differencing

To detect moving object in the surveillance video, the frame difference is the simplest method because it has fast detection and easy implementation. In frame differencing, the pixel wise difference between two or three consecutive frames is taken to generate a difference image, where the unchanged part is removed and the changed part is kept. Mathematically it is given by:

$$|I_n(x) - I_{n-1}(x)| > T, \tag{15}$$

where $I_n(x)$ and $I_{n-1}(x)$ is the intensity of the pixel at location x and at time instant n and $n-1$ respectively and T is the threshold.

Sugandi et al. (2007) have proposed a frame differencing method where he uses three successive frames resulting in two difference images. An AND operation is performed between the difference images to create the motion mask.

It is a highly adaptive approach to dynamic scene changes however, it fails to extract all relevant pixels of a foreground object especially when the object has uniform texture or moves slowly (Sugandi, Kim, Tan, & Ishikawa, 2007). When a foreground object stops moving, temporal differencing method fails in detecting a change between consecutive frames and loses the object.

Median Filter

Median filter is also used to update the background model. Lo and Velastin (2000) have proposed a method where the median value of the last n frames is considered as the background model. Cucchiara et al. (2003) have included an adaptive factor by combining the sampled frame values and the background past values with an associated weight. These frames are then sub-sampled from the original sequence at a rate of one every 10 frames. Then, the statistical background model is computed by using the median function.

The disadvantage of median filter based approach is that the memory requirement is more as it needs to store the past frames in a buffer. Moreover median filter cannot provide a proper statistical description of the background model.

Gaussian Mixture Model

All the background update models fail to represent the background if a particular pixel in the background has not permanently changed and varying rate is faster than the background update rate, for example rain, snow, sea waves in the beach etc.

Instead of modelling the values of the pixels in the frames as one particular type of distribution, Stauffer and Grimson (2000) have modelled a particular pixel as mixture of Gaussian distribution. The Gaussians corresponding to the background colours are determined by the persistence and variance of each Gaussian distribution in the mixture. The recent history of each pixel is modelled using a mixture of K Gaussian distributions. The probability of observing the current pixel X_t at any given time t is given by:

$$P\left(X_t\right) = \sum_{i=1}^{K} \omega\left(i,t\right) * \eta\left(X_t, \mu_{i,t}, \Sigma_{i,t}\right), \tag{16}$$

where $\omega\left(i,t\right)$, is an estimate of the portion of the data accounted for by the Gaussian of the i_{th} Gaussian in the mixture at time t, $\Sigma_{i,t}$ and $\mu_{i,t}$ are the covariance matrix and mean value of the i_{th} Gaussian in the mixture at time t, and η is a Gaussian probability density function given as:

$$\eta\left(X_t, \mu, \Sigma\right) = \frac{1}{\left(2\pi\right)^{\frac{n}{2}} \left|\Sigma\right|^{\frac{1}{2}}} e^{-\frac{1}{2}\left(X_t - \mu_t\right)^T \Sigma^{-1}\left(X_t - \mu_t\right)}, \tag{17}$$

The covariance matrix is assumed to be as:

$$\sum k,t = \sigma_k^2 I \tag{18}$$

The least probable distribution is replaced with a distribution with the current value as its mean value, an initially high variance, and low prior weight, if none of the K distributions match the current pixel value. The low prior weights of the K distributions at time t are adjusted as follows:

$$\omega_{k,t} = \left(1 - \alpha\right)\omega_{k,t-1} + \alpha\left(M_{k,t}\right), \tag{19}$$

where α the learning is rate and $M_{k,t}$ is 1 for the matched model and 0 for the rest.

The μ and σ parameters for non-matching distributions remain the same, while for the matched distributions these parameters are updated by using:

$$\mu_t = \left(1 - \rho\right)\mu_{t-1} + \rho X_t, \tag{20}$$

$$\sigma_t^2 = \left(1 - \rho\right)\sigma_{t-1}^2 + \rho\left(X_t - \mu_t\right)^T\left(X_t - \mu_t\right), \tag{21}$$

where ρ is the learning factor. All the Gaussian weights are normalized after the update is performed. The K-Gaussians are then reordered based on their likelihood of existence.

The first B distributions are chosen as the background model and the remaining $\left(K - B\right)$ distributions are considered as the foreground, where,

$$B = argmin\left(\sum_{k=1}^{b}\omega_k > T\right), \tag{22}$$

where T is a threshold value which determines the proportion of the data that needs to be considered as the background and then the first B distribution are chosen as background model.

This approach is adaptive to the variation in the lighting conditions, dynamic changes in the background, tracking through cluttered regions etc. However, the major disadvantages of GMM are that it is computationally expensive and involves a tricky parameter optimization (Jalal & Singh, 2012).

Hidden Markov Model

Rittscher et al. (2000) have proposed to use the Hidden Markov Models (HMM) to classify small blocks of an image as belonging to one of the three states: background state, foreground state and shadow state. This approach has two advantages. Firstly it does not require any training data. The hidden states allow the learning of distributions for foreground and background areas and shadow regions from a mixed sequence. Here the background model is constructed on the basis of intensity values and temporal continuity. Hidden Markov Model is used to model such a temporal continuity constraint where the detected foreground object is expected to be in the foreground region in a particular number of frames. The model parameters are estimated by using a maximum likelihood approach, for a given training sequence. But, in the proposed method no criterion has been given when the parameters need to be updated in case of illumination changes.

Stenger et al. (2001) have used HMMs for the background subtraction in different lighting conditions. An online version of the HMM topology estimation algorithm has been proposed, where the HMM trained by using an online learning algorithm. The HMM was found to be useful at handling global illumination effects in case of background adaptation.

Eigen Space Representation

Oliver et al. (2000) have proposed a technique which used Eigen space decomposition, which is less sensitive to illumination changes. The eigen space model is formed by taking an N sample images and computing the mean background image and its covariance matrix. The covariance matrix is diagonalized via an eigen value decomposition as follows:

$$L_b = \Phi_b C_b \Phi_b^{\ T},$$

(23)

where, Φ_b is the eigen vector matrix of the covariance of the data and C_b is the covariance matrix. For the purpose of reducing the dimensionality of the space, only M largest eigen vectors (Φ_M) are kept by using principal component analysis (PCA). The generated principal component feature vector is given by $I_i - \Phi_{Mb}^{\ T} X_i$ where, $X_i = I_i - \mu_b$ (mean).

The background is then modelled by projecting each input images onto the space expanded by the eigen background images given by $B_i = \Phi_{Mb} X_i$. The moving objects are then computed by thresholding the Euclidian distance between the input image and the projected image. However this technique does not yield a good result when working in the dynamic background conditions.

Wallflower

Toyama et al. (1999) have proposed a three component system for background maintenance. At the pixel level component Wiener filtering is performed to make probabilistic predictions of the expected background colour. The pixel level removes some common problems like moved objects, waving of trees, camouflage, and bootstrapping. The region-level component fills in homogeneous colours of foreground objects. It removes the foreground aperture problem (when a homogeneously coloured object moves, change in the interior pixels cannot be detected. Thus, the entire object may not appear as foreground.). At the frame-level, the background is swapped to previous better approximations of the background as well as there is a sudden change in most pixels in that particular frame.

Kernel Density Estimation

Elgammal et al. (2000) have proposed to model the background distribution by a non-parametric model based on kernel density estimation (KDE) on the buffer of the last n background values. KDE offers a smoothed, continuous version of the histogram. The background probability density function is estimated using the sum of Gaussian kernels centred in the most recent n background values x_i', without any assumption about background and foreground, which is given by:

$$P(x_i) = \frac{1}{n} \sum_{i=1}^{n} \eta \left(x_i - x_i' \, \Sigma_i \right), \tag{24}$$

here, each Gaussian describes just one sample data, with n in the order of 100, and Σ_i is the same for all kernels. Classification of x_i as foreground can be given as: $P(x_i) < T$. The model is robust and has good model accuracy as compared to Gaussian mixture model in more complex scenes. However, the computation cost much high.

Recently, a method based on texture is proposed to model the background and extract moving objects (Heikkila & Pietikainen, 2006). A binary pattern calculated around the pixel in a circular region is used to model each pixel. The binary pattern indicates whether the neighbouring pixel is smaller or larger than the central pixel. A modified local binary pattern (LBP) operator is used to extract features to make the method invariance to monotonic gray-scale change. However, the method can cause poor performance on flat image areas, where the intensity values of the neighbouring pixels are similar. Though this texture based method belongs to nonparametric methods, but it is fast due to simplification of LBP computation.

1.4. Segmentation

Image segmentation is the process of partitioning an image into different regions depending on colour, intensity or texture similarity. Segmentation techniques are usually divided into five types: threshold, edge, region, watershed and energy based. This section considers the energy-based segmentation procedures (mean shift, graph cut, active contour, etc.) are discussed which are commonly used in object tracking. These procedures use an energy function which reaches a minimum value when the segmented image is close to the expected result.

Mean Shift Clustering

Mean shift clustering is first proposed by Fukunaga and Hostetler (1975), later adapted by Cheng (1995) for the purpose of image analysis and more recently extended by Comaniciu et al. (2003) to low-level vision problems including segmentation, adaptive smoothing and tracking. The mean shift algorithm is a non-parametric clustering technique without requiring prior knowledge of the number of clusters. It also does not constrain the shape of the clusters.

Given a set $x_i | i = 1, 2, \ldots . n$ in a d-dimensional space, the radially symmetric multivariate kernel density estimate with kernel $K(x)$ of radius h computed at the point x is given by:

$$\hat{f}\left(x\right) = \frac{1}{nh^d} \sum_{i=1}^{n} K\left(\frac{x - x_i}{h}\right) \qquad (25)$$

Radially symmetric kernels may be used to define the profile $k\left(x\right)$ of $K\left(x\right)$ according to:

$$K(x) = c_{k,d} k(\|x\|^2), x \geq 0. \qquad (26)$$

Here, $c_{k,d}$ represents a normalization constant (strictly positive) such that $K\left(x\right)$ integrate to 1. By taking the estimate of the density gradient as the gradient of the density estimate results:

$$\hat{\nabla} f_{h,K}\left(x\right) = \frac{2c_{k,d}}{nh^{d+2}} \sum_{i=1}^{n} \left(x_i - x\right) g\left(\left\|\frac{x - x_i}{h}\right\|^2\right)$$

$$= \frac{2c_{k,d}}{nh^{d+2}} \underbrace{\left[\sum_{i=1}^{n} g\left(\left\|\frac{x - x_i}{h}\right\|^2\right)\right]}_{1st\ term} \underbrace{\left[\frac{\sum_{i=1}^{n} x_i g\left(\left\|\frac{x - x_i}{h}\right\|^2\right)}{\sum_{i=1}^{n} g\left(\left\|\frac{x - x_i}{h}\right\|^2\right)} - x\right]}_{2nd\ term}, \qquad (27)$$

where $f_{h,K}\left(x\right)$ is the density estimator and $g\left(x\right) = -k'{}'(x)$. The first term in eqn. (27) is proportional to the density estimate at x computed with the kernel G given as $G\left(x\right) = c_{g,d} g(x^2)$. The second term is the mean shift ($m_{h,G}\left(x\right)$) that points toward the direction of maximum increase in density and is proportional to the density gradient estimate at point x obtained with kernel K. $m_{h,G}\left(x\right)$ is computed iteratively until the cluster centres do not change their positions.

Because of the unspecified bandwidth parameter (which is a major limitation of this algorithm), it requires fine tuning of colour selection, spatial kernel bandwidths and threshold for optimal performance.

Graph Cut Segmentation

The graph cut based segmentation method uses both boundary and regional information to construct the energy function. Shi and Malik (2000) have proposed a normalized cut technique which is related to graph theoretic formulation of grouping. Let a weighted undirected graph represented by $G = \left(V, E\right)$, where V is a set of vertices and E is the graph edge which is formed between every pair of neighbouring vertices. A weight $w\left(i, j\right)$ is assigned to each edge depending on the similarity between the nodes i and j. During grouping, the set of vertices is partitioned into some disjoint sets, A, B, where the similarity of the vertices in the same set is high and between the vertices of two different sets are low. The degree of dissimilarity between these two parts obtained by removing the edges between these two parts is calculated by the total weight of the edge that has been removed.

$$cut\left(A, B\right) = \sum_{u \in A, v \in B} w\left(u, v\right) \tag{28}$$

Shi and Malik (2000) have used the following steps for the grouping algorithm:

1. From an image sequence a weighted undirected graph $G = \left(V, E\right)$ and edge between two nodes is weighted according to the similarity between the two nodes.
2. Solve $\left(D - W\right)x = \lambda Dx$ for the eigen vectors with the smallest eigen values.
3. The eigenvector with the second smallest eigen value is used to bipartition the graph.
4. Repartition the segmented part of the graph if required by following the same steps.

The normalized cut requires less parameters to be selected manually, but the memory requirement is more the mean shift segmentation.

Yi and Moon (2012) have considered graph cut image segmentation as pixel labelling problems. The label of the foreground object (s-node) is set to be 1 and the background (t-node) is set to be 0. By minimizing the energy-function with the help of minimum graph cut the process of pixel labelling can be done.

Wu and Leahy (1993) have used the minimum cut criterion to obtain the partitions that minimizes a cut. In their approach, the weights are defined based on the colour similarity. One disadvantage of minimum cut is it tendency to over segment the image.

Active Contour

In an active contour framework, object segmentation is achieved by generating a closed contour governed by an energy function on the object's boundary. Let $v\left(s\right) = \left(x\left(s\right), y\left(s\right)\right)$ represent the position of the contour where s is the arc length. The energy function for contour evolution can be written as:

$$E\left("\right) = \int_0^1 E_{int}\left(v\right) + E_{image}\left(v\right) + E_{ext}\left(v\right) ds \tag{29}$$

where E_{int} is internal energy involving the regularisation constraints, E_{image} is image or appearance-based energy and E_{ext} is energy due to the additional external constraints. The internal energy is given by,

$$E_int = (\alpha(s) \mid v_s(s) \mid^2 + \beta(s) \mid v_s(s) \mid^2) / 2, \tag{30}$$

which comprises of one first-order and one second-order terms weighted by $\alpha\left(s\right)$ and $\beta\left(s\right)$ respectively so that the shortest contour can be found.

The image energy E_{image} is locally or globally computable. Local computation involves computation of an image gradient around the contour. The colour and/or texture features computed from both inside and outside of the contour are used to calculate E_{image} globally. While computing locally, the image energy can be expressed as a weighted combination of the three components:

$$E_{image} = w_{line}E_{line} + w_{edge}E_{edge} + w_{term}E_{term},$$

where E_{line} is computed from by the image intensity, $E_{edge} = -\left|\nabla I\left(x, y\right)\right|^2$ is computed from the image gradient and E_{term} is the termination function. Kass et al. (1988) have modified the E_{edge} component to $E_{edge} = -\left(G_\sigma \nabla^2 I\right)^2$, where G_σ is the Gaussian of the standard deviation σ. Minima of this function on the zero crossing of $G_\sigma \nabla^2 I$ represents the edge. Caselles et al. (1995) have used only the image gradient as the image energy. Here, the object contour is represented as a geodesic curve in the Riemannian space with a function of the gradient. Sensitivity of the image gradients to the local minima is a drawback of this method. To overcome this problem of sensitivity, Zhu and Yuille (1996) have used region information (colour) instead of the image gradient. Paragios and Deriche (2002) have derived the image energy as a convex combination of the gradient and region-based energies according to:

$$E_{image} = \lambda E_{boundary} + \left(1 - \lambda\right) E_{region}, \tag{31}$$

where E_{region} is modelled by a mixture of Gaussians. In gradient-based approaches, the contour initialization is placed outside the object region while in region-based methods, the contour can be initialized either inside or outside the object with prior knowledge of contour initialisation.

1.5. Optical Flow

Optical flow is a commonly used technique for object motion segmentation. Evaluation of optical flow of 2D image motion, makes the following approximation:

$$I\left(x, t\right) \approx I\left(x + dx, t + dt\right), \tag{32}$$

where $I\left(x, t\right)$ is the spatio-temporal function of image intensity i.e. illumination changes are not supported. By expanding the above equation by using Taylor's theorem and neglecting the higher order terms we get:

$$\nabla^T I.V + I_t = 0, \tag{33}$$

where $\nabla I = \left(I_x, I_y\right)^T$ is the gradient, I_t, is the temporal derivative of the $I\left(x, t\right)$ and $V = \left(u, v\right)^T$ is the image velocity. But to determine the two dimensional velocity, one dimensional constraint equation is insufficient.

Barron et al. (1994) have given argumentation on several proposed works and the quantitative analysis showed that the method proposed by Lucas and Kanade (1981) gives the most accurate results.

This method is based on minimizing a weighted sum-of-squares error function in a spatial local region. All pixels in this region are supposed to have the same velocity, and the error equation is given by:

$$E = \sum_{i \in R} |w_i| \left[\nabla^T I(x_i, t).V + I_t(x_i, t) \right]^2, \tag{34}$$

where R is a spatial local region and $|w_i|$ is a positive weight of each pixel of the region R. Then the velocity is estimated as:

$$\hat{v} = -M^{(-1)}b, \tag{35}$$

where

$$M = \begin{bmatrix} \sum |w_i| I_x^2 & \sum |w_i| I_x I_y \\ \sum |w_i| I_x I_y & \sum |w_i| I_y^2 \end{bmatrix} \text{ and } b = \begin{bmatrix} \sum |w_i| I_x I_t \\ \sum |w_i| I_y I_t \end{bmatrix}.$$

But, the method proposed in [37] does not work well in changing illumination conditions.

2. FEATURE EXTRACTION AND REPRESENTATION

Selection of efficient and effective features plays a crucial role in object classification and tracking. The most desirable property of a visual feature is its uniqueness so that the objects can be easily distinguished in the feature space. The most commonly used features are colour, shape, texture, edges, etc. Usually classification and tracking algorithms considers a combination of these features. In the following, some of the popular visual features are considered. Different types features are classified as shown in Figure 3.

Figure 3. Classification of features

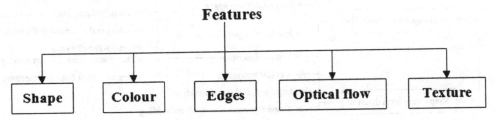

2.1. Shape

Content description of detected moving regions can be provided by the shape-based features having the desirable properties such as identifiability, geometric invariance (translation, rotation and scale), affine invariance, noise resistance, occultation invariance, statistical independence, reliability, etc. Shape feature extraction are classified into two categories, contour based and region based. The contour-based approach calculates shape features only from the boundary of the shape and the region-based methods extract features from the entire region of interest. Yang et al. (2008) have presented a survey on various available shape-feature extraction procedures. These techniques are classified by Yang et al. (2008) as under in Figure 4.

Figure 4. Classification of different shape-based features

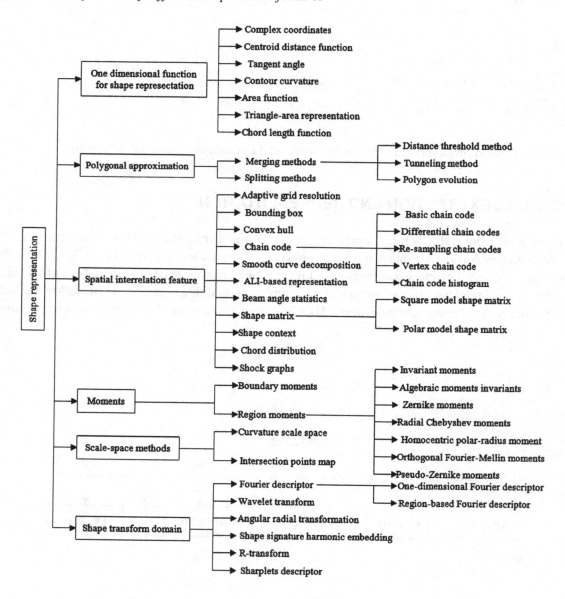

2.2. Colour

Primarily, the colour of an object depends two physical factors: i) the spectral power distribution of the illuminant and ii) the surface reflectance properties of the object. Various colour spaces RGB, HSV, LUV, HMMD, etc. have been used in the literature. The RGB space is not a perceptually uniform colour space, that is, the differences between the colours in the RGB space do not correspond to the colour differences perceived by human (Paschos, 2001). Additionally, the RGB dimensions are highly correlated. In contrast, LUV and HSV are perceptually uniform colour spaces. However, these colour spaces are sensitive to noise and illumination changes (Song, Kittler, & Petrou, 1996). The colour features that are popularly used in the literature includes colour histogram (Jain & Vailaya, 1996) (Swain & Ballard, 1991), colour moments (CM) (Flickner, Sawhney, Niblack, Ashley, Huang, Dom, Gorkani, Hafner, Lee, Petkovic, Steele, & Yanker, 1995), colour coherence vector (CCV) (Pass & Zabith, 1996), colour correlogram (Huang, Kumar, Mitra, Zhu, & Zabith, 1997), etc. MPEG-7 (Manjunath, Salembier, & Sikora, 2002) also standardizes a number of colour features including dominant colour descriptor (DCD), colour layout descriptor (CLD), colour structure descriptor (CSD), and scalable colour descriptor (SCD). Zhang et al. (2012) have described a comparative study of the colour features, where it is concluded that DCD is sufficient to represent the colour information of the region. Moreover feature dimension of DCD is low and the computational complexity is also relatively low.

2.3. Edges

Edge detection is used to identify the intensity changes along the object boundaries. The main advantage of edge based features is that they are less sensitive to illumination changes compared to colour features. Methods that track the boundary of the objects usually use edges as the feature. Popular edge detectors include Sobel, Canny (1986), Bergholm (1987), Sarkar and Boyer (1991), Heitger (1995), Rothwell et al. (1995), Black et al. (1998), Smith and Brady (1997), Iverson and Zucker (1995), Bezdek et al. (1998), and Tabb and Ahuja (1997). Because of the simplicity and accuracy, Canny Edge detector is the most commonly used edge detection approach. An evaluation of the edge detection algorithms is provided by Bowyer et al. (1999).

2.4. Optical Flow

Translation of each pixel in a region can be found by using a field of displacement vectors defined by optical flow. It is computed by considering the brightness constraint (brightness constancy of corresponding pixels in consecutive frames) (Horn & Schunck, 1981). Optical flow is commonly used as a feature in motion-based object detection and tracking applications. Some of the popular techniques for computing dense optical flow are presented by Horn and Schunck (1981), Lucas and Kanade (1981), Black and Anandan (1996), and Szeliski and Couglan (1997). Barron et al. (1994) have presented a survey on the performance evaluation of the optical flow methods.

2.5. Texture

Texture is a measure of the intensity variation of a surface which is used to compute properties such as smoothness and regularity. Compared to colour, texture requires a processing step to generate the texture descriptors such as: Gray-Level Co-occurrence Matrices (GLCM's) (Haralick, Shanmugam, & Dinstein, 1973) (a 2D histogram which shows the co-occurrences of intensities in a specified direction and distance), Laws' texture measures (Laws, 1980) (twenty-five 2D filters generated from five 1D filters corresponding to level, edge, spot, wave, and ripple), wavelets (Mallat, 1989) (orthogonal bank of filters), and steerable pyramids (Greenspan, Belongie, Goodman, Perona, Rakshit, & Anderson, 1994). The texture features are also less sensitive to illumination changes compared to colour. Local binary patterns (LBP) texture feature are known as one of the efficient features.

Feature selection is one of the most important step in determining the performance of a classification and tracking algorithm. Usually features are selected manually by the user based on the application requirement. The features can also be selected automatically. Automatic feature selection can be done in two ways: filter methods and wrapper methods (Blum & Langley, 1997). The filter methods try to select the uncorrelated features. Principal component analysis (PCA) is an example of the filter methods for the feature selection. The wrapper methods select the features based on the importance of the features in a specific problem domain, for example, the classification performance using a subset of features. Adaboost (Tieu & Viola, 2004) algorithm is a wrapper method of selecting the discriminatory features for tracking a particular class of objects.

3. SUPERVISED LEARNING BASED DETECTION/ SEGMENTATION (CLASSIFICATION)

Object detection can be performed by learning different object views automatically from a set of template images by means of supervised learning. Using a set of learning samples, the supervised learning methods generate a function that maps inputs to desired outputs (classification). Selection of features plays an important role in the performance of the classifier. The learning samples are composed of pairs of object features and an associated object class which are manually defined. Once the features are selected, different appearances of an object can be learned by choosing an efficient classifier. Some of the popular learning approaches include neural networks (Rowley, Baluja, & Kanade, 1998), adaptive boosting (Viola, Jones, & Snow, 2003), decision trees (Pal & Mather, 2001), support vector machines (Papageorgiou, Oren, & Poggio, 1998), fuzzy logic, etc. These methods compute a hypersurface that separates one object class from the other in a high-dimensional space. The different types of commonly used supervised classification techniques are shown in Figure 5.

Figure 5. Classification of supervised classification techniques

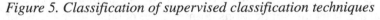

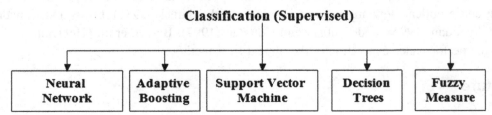

3.1. Neural Network

Neural network is a data driven self-adaptive technique which efficiently handles noisy input. Neural network consists of a sequence of layers, each of which consist of a set of neurones. All the neurones of every layer are linked by weighted connections to all neurons on the preceding and succeeding layers. Rowley et al. (1998) have proposed a neural network based algorithm for face detection. The neural network is trained with both "images containing faces" and "images without faces" so as to output both the presence and absence of a face. A neural network based filtering window is applied at each pixel location with varying scales. To detect faces larger than the window size, the input image is sub-sampled and then filter is applied to it. The eyes, tip of the nose, centre of the mouth are labelled manually on each face which in turn are used to normalize each face to the same scale, orientation and position. In the initial iteration, network's weights are selected randomly. Then the weights are computed by training in the previous iteration as the starting point. False detections are eliminated by ANDing the outputs of different networks over different positions and scales. Voting, AND and OR distance is used to indicate a close detection. Voting requires two out of three networks to detect a face, AND requires two out of two and OR requires one out of two to detect a face. But, the training of neural network is time consuming and prone to over-fitting.

3.2. Adaptive Boosting

Boosting is an iterative method for generating an accurate classifier by combining many weak classifiers, each of which may only be moderately accurate (Freund, & Schapire, 1995).

$$f(x) = \sum_{t=1}^{T} \alpha_t h_t(x),$$

(36)

where $h(t)$ are weak classifier and α_t is the weight associated with the weak classifier. AdaBoost performs even in the case of variety of efficient classifiers (such as neural networks, linear discriminants, etc.). In the training phase of the Adaboost algorithm, the first step is to form an initial distribution of weights over the training set. A base classifier is then selected by the boosting algorithm which gives the least error (error is proportional to the weights of the misclassified data). Next, the weights associated with the misclassified data are increased. Thus, in the next iteration, the algorithm boosts the selection of another classifier that performs better on the misclassified data.

In the perspective of object detection, weak classifiers can be simple operators such as a set of thresholds, applied to the object features extracted from the image. Viola et al. (2003) have used the Adaboost framework to detect pedestrians. The training phase uses AdaBoost to select a subset of features and construct the classifier. In their approach, perceptrons are selected as the weak classifiers which are trained on image features extracted by a combination of spatial and temporal operators. The operators in the temporal domain are in the form of frame differencing which encode some form of motion information. Frame differencing, when used as an operator in the temporal domain, reduces the number of false detections by enforcing object detection in the regions where the motion occurs.

Adaboost algorithm has been widely used in object classification and tracking algorithms in the literature. Elhoseiny et al. (2013) have used Adaboost classifier for object recognition by using geometric and HOG (histogram of oriented gradients) features. Li et al. (2008) have proposed a multiple overlapping camera-based approach which uses Adaboost algorithm for evaluating the relative importance of the shape and motion features.

3.3. Support Vector Machines

Support vector machine (SVM) computes the maximum marginal hyperplane to group data into two classes (Boser, Guyon, & Vapnik, 1992). The margin of the maximum marginal hyperplane is calculated by the distance between the hyperplane and the closest data points. The data points on the boundary of the margin of the hyperplane are called the support vectors. In the object detection framework, these classes correspond to the object class and the non-object class. Quadratic programming is used for deriving the hyperplane from among an infinite number of possible hyperplanes, from manually generated training examples labelled as object and non-object.

By applying the kernel trick to the input feature vector, SVM can also be used as a nonlinear classifier. Application of the kernel trick to a set of linearly non-separable data, transforms the data to a higher dimensional space which is expected to be separable. Polynomial kernels or radial basis functions are generally used for kernel trick. Once a kernel is chosen, its classification performance is tested for a set of parameters and by introducing new observation to the sample set.

Papageorgiou et al. (1998) have used SVM for pedestrian and face detection in images. For feature extraction, Haar wavelets is applied to the sets of positive and negative training examples. The search space reduction is done by using the discontinuities in the optical flow to initiate the search for possible objects resulting in a reduced number of false positives.

3.4. Decision Trees

A decision tree classifier (Pal & Mather, 2001) uses a multistage or sequential hierarchical decision approach instead of using the usual approach of using a common set of features jointly in a single decision step. Hierarchical classifier is a special type of multistage classifier that allows rejection of class labels at intermediate stages. These hierarchical classifiers can be implemented using classification trees. It is assumed that a data set consisting of feature vectors and their corresponding class labels are available. The features are then identified based on problem-specific knowledge. The decision tree is defined by recursively partitioning a dataset into homogeneous subset based on the tests applied to one or more attribute values at each branch or node of the tree. This procedure basically involves three steps: splitting nodes, determining which node is a terminal node, and assignment of class label to the terminal node. The labels are assigned based on a weighted vote. Because of the simplicity, automatic feature selection and efficiency to classify new data, decision tree classifier has been increasingly used in the literature.

3.5. Fuzzy Measure

In fuzzy classification, various stochastic associations are determined to describe characteristics of an image. The various types of stochastic are combined (set of properties) in which the members of this set of properties are fuzzy in nature. It provides the opportunity to describe different categories of stochastic characteristics in the similar form. Performance and accuracy of fuzzy classifier depends upon the threshold selection and fuzzy integral.

4. OBJECT TRACKING

The primary objective of object tracking is to find the motion trajectory of the detected object by locating its position with respect to time along the successive frames in video. A tracking algorithm should detect all the objects that enter or change location in a video scene irrespective of their velocities. Yilmaz et al. (2006) has classified the object tracking algorithms as follows:

4.1. Point Tracking

In point tracking, detected objects are represented by points and the association of the points in the present frame is dependent on the point or object's position and its motion in the previous frame. The correspondence of the detected objects is not accurate (Correspondence problem (Sethi & Jain, 1987)) in the case of occlusion, misdetection, entries and exits of the detected objects. Yilmaz et al. (2006) have subdivided the point tracking into two categories: Deterministic method and Statistical method.

4.1.1. Deterministic Approach for Point Correspondence

In deterministic method, qualitative motion heuristics are used to constrain possible tracks and to identify the optimal track set, instead of using probability density functions. Deterministic methods for point correspondence use a set of motion constraints to compute the cost of associating each object in frame $t - 1$ to a single object in frame t. The most common methods for minimization of the correspondence cost are Hungarian algorithm (Kuhn, 1955) or greedy exchange algorithm (Sethi & Jain, 1987).The constraints that are used to define the correspondence cost are: proximity, maximum velocity, small velocity, common motion, rigidity, proximal uniformity (combination of proximity and small velocity constraint).

Figure 6. Classification of object tracking algorithms

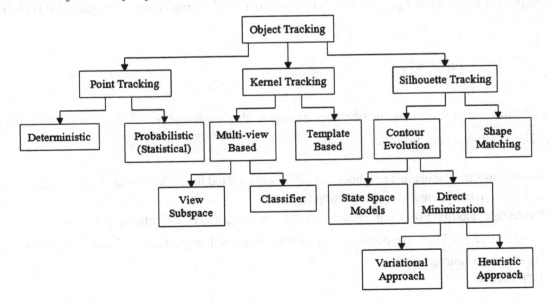

Figure 7. Different motion constraints (a) proximity, (b) maximum velocity (r denotes radius), (c) small velocity change, (d) common motion, (e) rigidity constraints. Δ *denotes object position at frame* $t-2$, $^{\circ}$ *denotes object position at frame* $t-1$, $\times$ *denotes object position at frame* t.

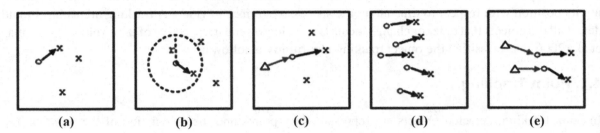

(a)	(b)	(c)	(d)	(e)

Greedy Exchange Algorithm

Sethi and Jain (1987) has made use of a greedy approach based on the proximity and rigidity constraints to solve the correspondence problem. The algorithm extends the trajectories up to $(k+1)^{th}$ frame, considering that the trajectories up to k^{th} frame have been acquired. The criterion for the expected trajectories for the $(k+1)^{th}$ frame is given by:

$$D = \sum_{p=1}^{m} D_p = \sum_{p=1}^{m}\sum_{q=2}^{k} d_p^{\ q} \ . \tag{37}$$

For i^{th} and j^{th} trajectories, the equation can be written as:

$$D = \sum_{p=1;p\neq i,j}^{m} D_p + \sum_{q=2}^{k-1} d_i^{\ q} + \sum_{q=2}^{k-1} d_j^{\ q} + d_i^{\ k} + d_j^{\ k} \ , \tag{38}$$

Now the points are exchanged from $(k+1)^{th}$ frame to i^{th} and j^{th} trajectories. The gain of this exchange is given by:

$$g_{i,j}^{\ k} = d_i^{\ k} + d_j^{\ k} - \left(\underline{d_i^{\ k}} + \underline{d_j^{\ k}} \right), \tag{39}$$

where $\underline{d_i^{\ k}}$ and $\underline{d_j^{\ k}}$ are the new patch coherence measures after exchange for i^{th} and j^{th} trajectories respectively. The algorithm is as follows:

1. **Initialization:** The nearest neighbour in X^{k+1} is calculated for each point in $X^k, k = 1,2,....,n-1$ and m trajectories are initialized using them.
2. **Exchange Loop:** For each frame $k = 2....n-1$, $g_{i,j}^{\ k}$ is calculated for $i = 1,..,m-1$ and $j = i+1,...,m$. Then, the points in $(k+1)^{th}$ frame are exchanged on the T_i and T_j trajectories having the maximum gain.
3. Termination.

The major disadvantage of this method is its inefficiency in handling occlusions, object entries, or exits. This problem is compensated by a method proposed by Salari and Sethi (1990) where, the correspondence for the detected points are first established and then extend the tracking of the missing objects by adding a number of hypothetical points. Rangarajan and Shah (1991) have proposed a non-iterative greedy approach, which is constrained by proximal uniformity to solve the correspondence problem. The authors have used gradient-based optical flow in the first two frames for establishing the initial correspondence. If this algorithm detects occlusion then it covers the missing point in frame k + 1 using the correspondence in the frames k - 1 and k. But this approach does not address the entry and exit of objects. Intille et al. (1997) have proposed a modified approach by using informations like size, colour, velocity, current and past position etc. of the object for matching each object in the last frame to a blob in the new frame. Image blobs are computed in each frame using background differencing. The system uses knowledge about the global closed world, which stores information about the objects in the entire scene. But in this approach, the change in the number of objects is explicitly handled in specific regions of the image.

Greedy Optimal Assignment Tracker

Veenman et al. (2001) have proposed to use the greedy optimal assignment (GOA) tracker which uses the common motion constraint for solving the correspondence problem. Common motion constraint assumes the velocity of the objects to be similar in a small neighbourhood region. As this constraint is suitable for representing objects by multiple points, it is helpful for coherent tracking of points lying on the same object. Occlusion and misdetection can be handled using this approach. But the disadvantage of this approach is its assumption of no entry and exit of objects.

First, the cost matrix D_λ^k is achieved by computing all costs c_{ij}^k (individual motion criteria). True tracks are assigned to true measurements. If the maximum speed (d_{max}) constraint is not maintained then, $c_{ij}^k = \phi_{max} + \epsilon$, else c_{ij}^k will follow individual motion model. Secondly, a bipartite graph is constructed based on the cost matrix and all edges are pruned which have weights above ϕ_{max}. Then, the edge weights w_{ij} are adjusted to satisfy the combined motion model (average deviation model (Veenman et al. 2001) and average deviation conditioned by competition and alternatives model). The cost function minimization is done by applying Hungarian algorithm (Kuhn, 1955) to this graph. The resulting edges correspond to an output square matrix A_λ^k.

Non-Iterative Greedy Algorithm

Shafique and Shah (2003) have introduced an algorithm which is very similar to the GOA tracker proposed by Veenman et al. (2001), for detecting point correspondences in multiple frames. Correspondence problem is solved by finding a set of vertex disjoint directed paths of length 0 or more, so as to maximise the total gain among all the paths. The generated directed graph is transformed to a bipartite graph by splitting each node into two nodes and the directed edges are represented as undirected edges. The problem of finding maximum path cover is solved using the theorem: *The edges of maximum matching of the split graph G of an acyclic edge-weighted digraph D correspond to the edges of a maximum path cover of D.* Greedy algorithm is then used to establish the correspondence. This method solves the problem of occlusion by using window of frames during point correspondence whose durations are shorter than the temporal window used to perform matching. The result of this algorithm is shown in Figure 8:

Figure 8. Result of tracking algorithm proposed by Shafique and Shah (2003) (a) Paths generated for rotating dish sequence. (b) Paths generated for flock of fish.

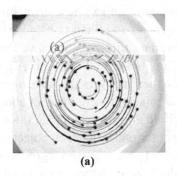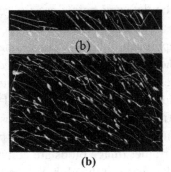

(a)   **(b)**

4.1.2. Statistical Approach for Point Correspondence

Statistical correspondence methods solves the problem of random movement of the detected objects by taking the state space approach to model object properties like position, velocity, acceleration etc. In this section, the state estimation techniques for the tracking of the detected points are discussed. These techniques are widely used in various object tracking and surveillance applications. Some of the popular statistical approaches are Kalman filter, Extended Kalman filter, particle Filter, multiple hypothesis tracking (MHT), joint probability data association filter (JPDAF), probabilistic MHT (PMHT). Out of these, the first three techniques are for single object tracking and rest are for multiple object tracking in the scene.

The main objective of statistical approach is to estimate the state of the object at any specific time t, X^t and all the measurements up to that particular time should be available. It is also equivalent to calculate the probability density function $p\left(X^t|Z^{1,2,...t-1}\right)$, where, the change in state over time is given by: $X^t = f^t\left(X^{t-1}\right)+W^t$. W^t is the process noise and the measurement equation $Z^t = h^t\left(X^t,\ N^t\right)$, where N^t is the associated white noise. This probability density function is calculated using two steps: prediction step and correction step. In prediction step, a dynamic equation and the computed pdf of the state at time $t-1$ is used to derive the prior pdf of the state at time t, that is, $p\left(X^t|Z^{1,2,...t-1}\right)$. In correction step, the likelihood function $p\left(Z^t|X^t\right)$ of the current measurement is used to compute the posterior pdf $p\left(X^t|Z^{1,2,...t-1}\right)$.

Kalman Filtering

Kalman filter was first introduced in 1960s and it is considered as a powerful state estimation method. Kalman filter is an optimal filter for non-smooth signal, dynamic time varying systems. It is basically used to estimate the state of a linear system which is assumed to be Gaussian. However, Kalman filter does not work with non-linear, non-Gaussian distributed models. In prediction step a state model is used to estimate the new state:

$$\overline{X}^t = DX^{t-1}+W, \tag{40}$$

$$\overline{\pounds}^t = D\pounds^{t-1}D^T + Q^T, \tag{41}$$

where D is the state transition matrix defining the relationship between states at time $t-1$ and t, $\overline{X}^t$ is the state prediction and $\overline{\Sigma}^t$ is the covariance prediction at time t. In the correction step, Riccati equation is used as Kalman gain K given by:

$$K^t = \overline{\Sigma}^t M^T \left[M\overline{\Sigma}^t M^T + R^t \right]^{-1}, \tag{42}$$

where M is the measurement matrix. The updated state after the correction step is given by:

$$X^t = \overline{X}^t + K^t \underbrace{\left[Z^t - M\overline{X}^t \right]}_{v}, \tag{43}$$

$$\Sigma^t = \overline{\Sigma}^t - K^t M\overline{\Sigma}^t \tag{44}$$

where, v is the associated innovation. Kalman filter has been widely used in various tracking applications. Li et al. (2013) have used Kalman filter for the tracking of vehicles, Lu et al. (2009) have used 4 states Kalman filter based tracking algorithm by introducing FSM for tracking of vehicles in a crowded environment, Johnson et al. (2009) have used Kalman filter for the tracking of both human and vehicles, Beymer and Konolige (1999) have used the Kalman filter for predicting object's position and speed. Li et al (2008) have used Adaptive Kalman filter for tracking which used number of corner point variations in consecutive frames to automatically adjust the estimate parameters of Kalman filter.

Extended Kalman Filtering

Kalman filter may not give an optimum result if the system is highly non-linear. In order to deal with the non-linear functions, it is linearized around the predicted values by first order approximation of Taylor series expansion, which is known as extended Kalman filter (EKF) proposed by Bar-Shalom and Foreman (1988). But, because of its first-order approximation of Taylor series expansion, the success rate in tracking visual objects is less. Julier and Uhlmann (1997) have introduced an unscented Kalman filter (UKF) that can accurately compute the mean and covariance of a function, up to the second order of the Taylor series expansion which performs much better than EKF. Rosales and Sclaroff (1999) have used the extended Kalman filter to estimate 3D trajectory of an object from 2D motion.

Particle Filtering

Particle filter proposed by Tanizaki (1987), overcomes the major limitation of Kalman filter in case of non-Gaussian state variable estimation. In particle filtering, a set of samples $s_t^{(n)} : n = 1, \dots, N$ (particles) represents the conditional state density, $p\left(X_t|Z_t\right)$ at time t with a weight $\pi_t^{(n)}$ (sampling probability) which defines the importance of a sample (Isard & Blake, 1998). Based on different sampling schemes (MacKay, 1998), the new samples a time t are drawn from the set of samples, weights and cumulative weight ($c^{(n)}$), at the previous time $(t-1)$ step. The most commonly used sampling scheme is the importance sampling which is a generalization of the uniform sampling method. The algorithm for importance sampling is as follows:

1. **Selection:** N random samples $\widehat{S}_t^{(n)}$ are selected from S_{t-1} by generating a random number $r \in [0,1]$, and finding the smallest j such that $c_{t-1}^{(j)} > r$ and setting $\widehat{S}_t^{(n)} = s_{t-1}^{(j)}$.

2. **Prediction:** A new sample is generated for the selected samples $\widehat{S}_t^{(n)}$ by using $s_t^{(n)} = f\left(\widehat{S}_t^{(n)}, W_t^{(n)}\right)$, where, f is a non-negative function and $W_t^{(n)}$ is the zero mean Gaussian error.

3. **Correction:** The weights of the new samples are computed using:

$$\pi_t^{(n)} = p\left(z_t | x_t = s_t^{(n)}\right)$$

These new samples can be used to estimate the new object position by using:

$$\varepsilon_t = \sum_{n=1}^{N} \pi_t^{(n)} f\left(s_t^{(n)}, W\right), \tag{45}$$

The particle filters can be initialized by either using first parameters, $s_0^{(n)} \sim X_0$ and $\pi_0^{(n)} = \frac{1}{N}$ or by training the system using sample dataset.

Zhang et al. (2014) have used a modified particle filter for object tracking in low frame rate video sequence. The authors have used the object detection and extraction to locate tracked object, instead of using motion transitions to model the movement of the target as done in traditional particle filtering. Then, the sample set is propagated around the detected regions where, the samples are assumed to be uniformly distributed in the neighbourhoods of the detected region. The likelihood between the target model and the candidate regions are based on colour histogram distances. Lu et al. (2012) have modelled the object's rough location by colour histogram and Harris corner features fusion method in particle filter framework. Region based object contour extraction is done to extract the contours. Zhang and Fei (2011) have tracked a target with a particle filter by comparing its histogram with the histograms of the sample positions using the Bhattacharyya distance. Chen et al. (2008) have used the Markov chain Monte Carlo (MCMC) particle filter and object colour distribution for object tracking. This scheme is robust to clutter, rotation invariant and can handle partial occlusion.

The disadvantage of particle filter is that the computational complexity is more. For tracking multiple objects, a joint solution of data association and state estimation is required which can be done by using tracking algorithms like JPDAF, MHT etc.

The easiest approach to solve the correspondence problem is to use the nearest neighbour. But, if the objects lie very close to each other the correspondence may be incorrect. The above mentioned data association techniques like JPDAF, MHT etc. solve this problem.

Joint Probability Data Association Filter

The Joint probability data association filter (JPDAF) algorithm extends the original probabilistic data association algorithm by using a fixed known number of target objects, which is described below:

Suppose we have cluster of N tracks and m measurements are detected in the combined validation region of these tracks at time t,

$$Z(t) = \{z_1(t), \ldots, z_{m_t}(t)\}.$$

Let $\hat{z}^l$ be the predicted measurement calculated from track l and $v_{i,l}$ be the innovation associated with track l for the measurement z_i. The JPDAF associates all measurements with all tracks to generate a combined weighted innovation given by:

$$v^l = \sum_{i=1}^{m_k} \beta_i^l v_{i,l}, \qquad (46)$$

where β_i^l denotes the posterior probability that the measurement i originated from geometric feature l and is given by:

$$\beta_i^l = \sum_{\theta} P\left(\theta_l(k)|Z^k\right)\tau_{i,l}(\theta) \begin{cases} i = 1, \ldots, m_k \\ l = 0, 1, \ldots, T \end{cases}, \qquad (47)$$

where θ is the set of assignment and $\tau_{i,l}(\theta)$ is the indicator variable and is unity if the measurement $z_i(k)$ is associated with track l in the assignment $\theta_l(k)$ otherwise the value is zero. The weighted innovation v^l is then applied into the standard Kalman filter update equations given in eqn. (43) for each track l.

Chang and Aggarwal (1991) have used JPDA filter to maintain tracking in subsequent images to perform 3D structure reconstruction from ego motion sequence. Rasmussen and Hager (2001) have used a constrained JPDAF to track multiple and compound objects. Gorji and Menhaj (2007) have used JPDAF for tracking the position of multiple robots, which used two models to characterize the motion: constant velocity and variable velocity model. JPDAF based tracking is prone to estimation coalescence when close neighbouring objects share measurements. To overcome this limitation, Kaufman et al. (2014) have proposed Coalescence Avoiding JPDAF (C-JPDAF) that minimizes the weighted sum of the posterior uncertainty and a measure of similarity between estimated probability densities. Since JPDAF performs data association of a fixed number of objects in the field of view, any change in the number of objects due to new entry may cause errors. To overcome this limitation, Multiple Hypothesis Tracking (MHT) can be used.

Multiple Hypothesis Tracking

The Multiple Hypothesis Tracking (MHT) algorithm proposed by Reid (1979) provides the capability to initialize tracks when a new object enters the field of vision and terminate tracks when the objects exits the field of vision. MHT maintains several correspondence hypotheses for each object at each time frame since correspondence established by using first two frames may lead to incorrect correspondence result. The final track of the object is a set of correspondences over the time period. Moreover, the occlusion related problems can also be handled using MHT. The flowchart of the MHT algorithm is shown in the Figure 9.

An iteration begins with a set of current track hypotheses from iteration $(k-1)$. Each hypotheses contains a collection of disjoint active tracks. A prediction is made for each hypotheses to estimate each

Figure 9. MHT algorithm

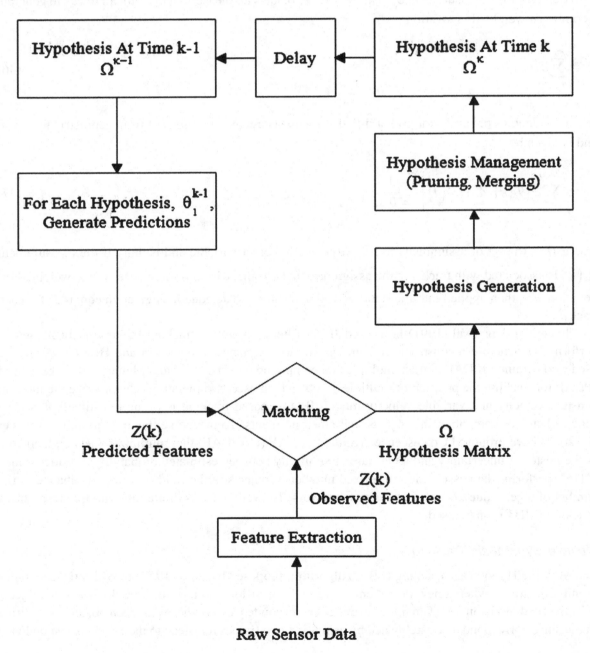

object's position in the next frame. Mahalanobis distance measure is used to compare the predictions with the actual measurements. New hypotheses for the next iteration are then introduced by forming a set of correspondences for each hypotheses based depending on the distance measure. Each measurement may belong to either a previously tracked object or a new object entering the field of vision or a false alarm when the object have exited or if a measurement corresponding to an object is not obtained due to occlusion or noise in the scene.

The main disadvantage of MHT is its computational load as it is exponential both in memory and time. To overcome this limitation, Streit and Luginbuhl (1994) have introduced probabilistic MHT (PMHT), Hue et al. (2002) have proposed to use particle filter that handles multiple measurements to track multiple objects. Cham and Rehg (1999) have used the MHT framework for the purpose of tracking complete human body. Pu et al. (2011) have used a combination of colour feature and contour information in the particle filter based probabilistic multi-hypothesis tracking algorithm. Zulkifley et al. (2012) have enhanced the performance of multiple hypothesis tracker by successfully resolving the limitations of split and merge, occlusion by using hierarchical approach. Foreground segmentation and clustered optical flow are used as the first-level tracker input. Only track associated with the first level is fed to the second level. Occlusion predictor obtained from the predicted data of each track is used to distinguish between merge and occlusion. Kalman filter is used to predict the state of the track. Gaussian modelling is used to compute the quality of the hypotheses.

4.2. Kernel Tracking

Kernel tracking is basically dependent on the motion of the object and the object is usually represented by primitive object region (rectangular or elliptical). The kernel-based tracking algorithms differ in terms of the techniques used to estimate the object motion, appearance representation used, and number of object to be tracked. The most common kernel based tracking algorithms are template matching, mean shift or CAMshift, Appearance tracking, KLT, Layering, Bramble, Eigen tracker and SVM etc.

Template Matching

Template matching is a most commonly used kernel tracking algorithm. But due to brute force searching of a matched region in each frame of the video sequence, it is computationally expensive. Let O_t denotes the object template defined in the previous frame. Then, the position of the template object in the current image I_w is given by a similarity measure like cross correlation given by:

$$argmax_{dx,dy} \frac{\sum_x \sum_y \left(O_t\left(x,y\right) \times I_w\left(x+dx, y+dy\right)\right)}{\sqrt{\sum_x \sum_y \left(O_t^2\left(x,y\right)\right)}}, \tag{48}$$

where $\left(dx, dy\right)$ denotes the position of the candidate template. Birchfield (1998) has used gradient images as templates since intensity and colour images are highly sensitive to the illumination changes. Schweitzer et al. (2002) have proposed an efficient template matching algorithm to overcome the limitation of computation complexity of the template matching algorithms. The authors have developed a match measure that uses the local algebraic moments. Fieguth and Terzopoulos (1997) have used colour histogram or mixture models for object representation instead of templates. The authors generated object models by taking the mean value of the pixels inside the rectangular region. Then, the similarity of the object model M and each of the eight neighbouring positions H is calculated by taking the ratio between M and H. The position with the highest ratio is selected as the position of the object in the current frame.

Mean-Shift

Mean shift is one of the most popularly used object tracking algorithm. Comaniciu and Meer (2003) have introduced mean-shift based tracking. The authors have used weighted histogram computed from a circular region to represent the object. For detecting the location of the object mean shift procedure (described in the previous section 1.4) has been used. Appearance similarity is maximized by iteratively comparing the histograms of the object Q, and the window around the hypothesized object location, P. The histogram similarity is achieved by defining a distance in terms of Bhattacharya coefficient among target model and candidates. The iteration process is repeated until it achieves convergence.

The main advantage of mean-shift tracking is that brute force search is not required as in the case of template matching and computation involved in translation of the object. But, the mean shift tracking requires a portion of the object to be inside the elliptical region during at initialization. Moreover, it is designed to find local maxima for tracking objects. So, if the target object moves a large distance between two consecutive frames, it may fail. In [69], the author has proposed to use a multiband with process to help simple mean shift tracker to reach the global mode of the density function using any starting points. Dargazany et al. (2010) a fusion scheme has been proposed to fuse multiple spatially distributed fragments. Under the fusion scheme, a mean shift type algorithm is used for efficient target tracking with very low computational load. Lucena et al. (2010) have proposed a mean shift based multiple model tracking algorithm. Fang et al. (2011) have proposed an efficient and robust fragment based multiple kernels tracking algorithm. Ning et al. (2009) have extended the mean-shift tracking algorithm by combing a LBP (Local Binary Pattern) texture feature with colour histogram features. Shen et al. (2010) have extended the use of support vector machines for object localization and tracking. A probabilistic kernel based SVM is used to represent the template model for mean shift algorithm. Zhang et al. (2013) have combined canny edge detector and mean shift algorithm for object tracking. Firstly, the change tendency of the object is determined using canny edge detection. Then, Kernel-bandwidth of the Mean Shift is adjusted using the proper ratio increment. Finally, the object can be located accurately with proper kernel-bandwidth. Tang and Zhang (2011) have proposed a novel object tracking method by combining both mean-shift and particle filter.

Bradski (1998) has proposed an adaptive version of mean-shift algorithm called CAMShift (Continuously Adaptive Mean-shift). A known hue value in colour image sequences is used to track the head and face movement. Mean shift algorithm is used with adaptive region sizing step. The kernel having simple step function is applied to a skin probability map. At each iteration, centroid with the search window is computed as zero and first order moment. The algorithm consumes less time due to the consideration of a single channel (hue). However, the algorithm may fail to track objects where hue value is not sufficient to discriminate the object from background.

KLT Transform Based Tracking

Optical flow based methods are also used to track regions defined by a primitive shape (rectangular or elliptical). Horn and Schunk (1981) have introduced a method for computing optical flow from a sequence of images. The flow velocity has two components and that the basic equation for the rate of change of image brightness provides one constraint. The flow vector is computed in the neighbourhood of the pixel either algebraically (Lucas & Kanade, 1981) or geometrically (Schunk, 1986). Shi and Tomaski (1994) have proposed the iterative KLT tracker which iteratively calculates the translation (du, dv) of the region centred at the interest point detected by the point detector. The quality of the tracked patch is obtained by calculating an affine transform when a new location of the interest point is detected. The tracking of the feature is done if the sum of squared distance between the current and projected patch is small, otherwise the feature is eliminated.

Appearance Tracking

Jepsonet al. (2003) have proposed an object tracker which used a robust, adaptive appearance model for kernel based tracking of complex natural objects. It maintains a natural measure of the stability of the observed object structure during tracking. By identifying stable properties of appearance, weight is assigned to them more heavily. The model for appearance is formulated as a mixture of three components, namely, a stable component that is learned with a relatively long time-course which identifies the most reliable structure for motion estimation, a 2-frame transient component to provide additional information during appearance model initialization, and an outlier process which handles the outliers in the object appearance caused due to noise. The parameters of this three component mixture are learned efficiently with an on-line version of the EM algorithm. The authors have used steerable pyramidal response as features for appearance representation. Primitive elliptical representation is used to denote the object shape. Frame-to-frame parameterized image warps are used to represent motion. The warping transformation consists of translation, rotation and scale.

Using this technique, more weights can be assigned to the more stable features for tracking. It can also handle partial occlusion very efficiently. Wang and Ji (2007) have presented a new appearance model for object tracking. The object is modelled using the colour features and the distribution of object sub-regions partitioned using k-means clustering.

In the techniques discussed so far, objects are modelled individually which does not take into account the interaction between different objects in the scene and between objects and background during tracking. The techniques given in the following, explicitly track the background and the moving objects.

Layering

Tao et al. (2002) have proposed a multi-object tracking algorithm based on modelling the whole image I^t as a set of 2D motion layers. Regions of homogeneous motion in an image sequence represented by motion layers. Each of the layers have features like shape of the layer, Φ_t, motion of the layer, Θ_t, and appearance of the layer A_t. The main objective is to maintain coherency between motion, appearance, and shape of each layer over time. 2D rigid motion (Translation + Rotation) is used for motion model.

A Gaussian prior function (elliptical) is used to handle objects with compact shapes and layer appearance is the intensity value of a pixel in the layer modelled using Gaussian distribution. Layering is done by compensating the background motion modelled by using projective motion which is then employed for estimating the object's motion by using 2D- parametric motion model. Each pixel's probability of belonging to the object layer is determined based on the object's previous shape and motion characteristics. This probability is mixed with the object's appearance probability to estimate the final layer. The problem of data association that establishes the correspondences between pixels and layers and the computation of the optimal layer parameters at a specific time is solved by the EM (expectation maximization) algorithm. Since it is difficult to optimize Φ_t, Θ_t and A_t simultaneously, the authors have individually improved one set and kept the other two fixed and finally the layer ownership is updated.

Bramble

Bramble is a Bayesian multiple-blob tracker. Isard and MacCormick (2001) have proposed a multi-blob likelihood function that assigns directly comparable likelihoods to hypotheses containing different numbers of objects which is computed using a variation on the Bayesian correlation scheme presented by Sullivan et al. (1999).It uses a unified approach to background and foreground modelling. Both background and foreground appearance were modelled using 4 component mixture of Gaussians. A generalised-cylinder model is used for modelling the shape of the objects. A particle filtering of a Bayesian multiple-object tracker is implemented where the state vector includes 3D position, shape, and velocity of all the objects. But the maximum number of objects in the scene is predefined. A modified prediction and correction algorithm for particle filter is also introduced that can increase or decrease the size of the state vector to handle the entry and exit of the objects. This method can efficiently handle full occlusion between objects. Moreover, it requires training for modelling the foreground objects since same appearance model is used for all the foreground objects.

Eigen Tracker

The method proposed by Black and Jepson (1998) is a multiview appearance model in which views of the object from different directions can be learnt. It overcomes the limitation of the previous approaches in which the appearance model of the object may not be valid if the view of the object changes during tracking.

Black and Jepson (1998) have computed the affine transform of the current scene of the object to the reconstructed image using a subspace based approach using eigenvectors. Eigen spaces are considered as one promising candidate for an appearance-based object representation which is based on principal component analysis (PCA). First the position, orientation, and scale of the object must be estimated. Then, the object must be segmented from the background using robust formulation of the eigen space matching. Sub-space constancy assumption is then formulated and minimized to transform the image to the eigen space. Minimization is done in two steps: subspace coefficients are calculated and affine parameters are computed. For tracking, the affine parameters are estimated iteratively until the difference between the input image and the projected image is minimized.

Support Vector Tracking

Avidan (2001) has integrated an optic-flow-based tracker and an SVM classifier for tracking objects. Optic flow based tracker (Anandan, Bergen, Hanna, & Hingorani, 1993) minimizes the intensity difference between a pair of successive frames by using a gradient descent method to search for transformation parameters. SVM (Vapnik, 1995) is a general classification scheme that generates the separating hyperplane between the object and the background, when the object of interest (positive) and background (negative) training samples are provided. A Gaussian pyramid termed as 'Support vector pyramid' allows support vector tracking (SVT) to handle large motions in the image plane. SVT fuses the computational efficiency of optic-flow based tracking with the efficiency of a general SVM classifier, to enhance the power of both the tracker and the classifier.

However, SVT suffers from several drawbacks like: the method cannot handle partial occlusions and SVT may switch from one vehicle to another in case of two close vehicles.

4.3. Silhouette Tracking

Silhouette Tracking was introduced to efficiently describe the complex shapes like hands, head, shoulders etc. which is not well described by the geometric shapes. These object models are represented using colour histogram, edges or contours. It is classified into two types: Shape matching and Contour tracking.

4.3.1 Shape Matching

Shape matching is performed by searching for a matched silhouette of the associated object model based on the previous frame, in the current frame. To avoid problems related to illumination and viewpoint changes, the object model is reinitialized in every frame after the detection.

Huttenlocher et al. (1993) have performed intensity edge-based representation for shape matching. The authors have used the minimum Hausdorff distance (Hausdorff) for the object matching. Li et al. (2001) have proposed to use Hausdorff metric for the matching procedure used for pose estimation as well as the identification and verification problem. Image sequence stabilization is based on the optical flow-based approach, where the optical flow is modelled using a weighted sum of basis functions, and is found to achieve an accurate and fast motion computation. The computed flow field is then used to estimate the motion parameters. Kang et al. (2004) have proposed a technique where the moving objects colour and shape are represented by a multi polar representation. A reference circle is set defined by the smallest circle containing the object silhouette. The defined model is rotation, translation, and scale invariant. The scale invariance is achieved by taking a larger number of control points along the reference circle and normalizing the reference circle to unit circle. The authors have used three types of similarity functions: cross-correlation, Bhattacharyya distance, and Kullback-Leibler distance, for computing the similarity of the computed appearance models. Sato and Aggarwal (2004) have proposed temporal spatio-velocity (TSV) transform for tracking where, the object tracks are generated by applying Hough transform in the velocity space to the object silhouette in the consecutive frames. The voting matrices obtained by applying Hough transform provide the TSV image. The TSV image encodes the dominant motion of a moving region and represents a measure of the likelihood of occurrence of a pixel with instantaneous velocity in the current position in terms of votes. It provides the regions with similar motion patterns.

4.3.2 Contour Tracking

Tracking of the complete object can be achieved by employing the active contours. In contour tracking, an initial contour from the previous frame is evolved to its new position in the current frame. But, it requires a portion of the object in the current frame to be inside the object region in the previous frame. Contour tracking can either be done by using state space models or by the minimization of the contour energy functional.

By Using State Space Models

In state space models, the state of an object is represented in terms of the shape and motion parameters of the contour which is updated at each frame to maximize the contour's posteriori probability. This posterior probability in turn is dependent on the prior state and the likelihood function defined in terms of the distance of the contour from the edges.

Terzopoulos and Szeliski (1992) have fused the snakes (active contour models) and Kalman filter for the purpose of tracking objects. The Kalman snake uses snake dynamics as a system model to constrain and possible motion predicted. Image gradients are used for the correction step. Isard and Blake (1998) have used spline shape parameters and affine motion parameters to define the object state and particle filter is used for state update. The initial samples for the particle filter are obtained by computing the state variables from the extracted contours in the training step. MacCormick and Blake (2000) have used exclusion principle for handling occlusion. Chen et al. (2001) have proposed a new HMM framework for contour-based object tracking. A joint probability data association filter (JPDAF) is used for the computation of HMM's state transition probabilities, taking into account the inter relationship between neighbouring measurements. Next, the contour tracking using minimization of energy functional will be discussed.

By Direct Minimization of Contour Energy Functional

The contour energy is defined in terms of temporal information in the form of either the temporal image gradient (optical flow), or appearance statistics generated by the object and the background regions. Both the contour based segmentation and tracking methods minimize the energy functional either by greedy methods or by gradient descent.

Bertalmio et al. (2000) have used the optical flow constraint to evolve the contour in consecutive frames. With an objective to compute the flow vector iteratively for each contour position using the level set representation. At each iteration, contour speed in the normal direction is computed by projecting the gradient magnitude in normal direction. Two energy functionals are basically used: contour tracking and intensity morphing. Mansouri (2002) has applied the optical flow constraint to compute the flow vector for each pixel inside the complete object region. The contour energy is then evaluated based on brightness constancy constraint. The energy is minimized by iteratively performing this process. Cremers and Schnorr (2003) have also used the optical flow for contour evolution, and homogeneous flow vectors constraint inside the object region. The shape priors are generated from a set of object contours such that each control point on the contour has an associated Gaussian with a mean and standard deviation of the spatial positions of the corresponding control points on all the object contours. This approach can handle partial occlusion efficiently.

The techniques discussed so far have used the temporal gradient to define the contour energy. Instead of this appearance statistics of the regions inside and outside the object can be computed to define the contour energy, from one frame to the next. But, this approach requires initialization of the contour using its previous location. Yilmaz and Shah (2004) have evolved the object contour from frame to frame by minimizing some energy functional evaluated in the contour vicinity defined by a band. Semi-parametric models are used to define visual features (colour, texture) and are fused using independent opinion polling. Shape priors consist of shape level sets so as to recover the missing object regions during occlusion.

Recently, contour tracking has been widely used in the literature for the purpose of object tracking. Chen (2009) has employed the active contour models and neural fuzzy network method to track moving objects of the same kind. To extract object feature vector, it has used contour-based model. Chen et al. (2010) have proposed an object tracking method consisting of two-stages. Firstly, the kernel-based method is used to locate the object in complex environment like partial occlusions, clutter etc. To improve the tracking result they have again used contour based method and have tracked the object contour precisely after the target localization. In the target localization step, the authors have used Kalman filter and the Bhattacharyya coefficient for the prediction of initial target position. Hu et al. (2013) have presented a framework for active contour-based visual tracking using level sets. Initialization of contour-based tracking is done using an optical flow-based algorithm for automatically initializing contours at the first frame. Colour based contour evolution is done using Markov Random Field (MRF) theory. Global shape information and the local color information is used for adaptive shape-based contour evolution.

CONCLUSION

In this chapter, we have discussed some of the existing popularly used techniques for object detection, feature extraction, classification, and tracking. We have also discussed the advantages, disadvantages and context of use of these techniques.

In the Section 1 we have discussed the various object detectors such as: point detector, blob detector, background modelling based detector, segmentation, and optical flow based detector. These detectors are used depending on their accuracy, computational complexity and application requirement. Among all these detectors, the most popularly used technique is background modelling, since, it is suitable for real time applications because of its less computation time. But, it requires an efficient background maintenance model to deal with the changing background conditions. Moreover, mean shift detector, active contour based detectors are also efficient enough for real time operations. The point detectors have the ability to deal with the changing illumination conditions, but the whole object region cannot be detected. The optical flow detectors provide moderate accuracy, but require more computation time.

In the Section 2, we have given a brief description of the feature types. Shape features are used to provide the content description of the detected region. Different colour spaces are used to provide colour features. But, the colour features are prone to illumination changes. Object boundaries are also used as edge feature as edges are less sensitive to illumination changes. Similar to the edge features, texture feature are also less sensitive to the illumination conditions as it is used to quantify properties like smoothness and regularity.

In the Section 3, we have presented some of the popular classification techniques. The neural network based classifier high computation rate and efficient for handling noisy input. AdaBoost classifier is one of the popular classifier in real time applications because of its simplicity and robustness. The over fitting problem in case of neural network is eliminated in SVM classifier. Moreover, reduction in computational complexity makes it efficient for real time applications. However, the training in SVM classifier is time consuming. The decision tree classifier provides hierarchical associations between input variables to forecast class labels. This classifier is computationally efficient and requires less training time. But the computation becomes complex when various outcomes are correlated. Fuzzy based classifier efficiently handles uncertainty, but the output is not good in the absence of prior knowledge.

In the Section 4, we have classified the tracking algorithms into three types: Point tracking, Kernel tracking and Silhouette tracking. The point trackers are useful in tracking of small objects that can be represented using a single point. For handling occlusion or missing observation, the deterministic point trackers normally use a combination of the motion constraints, while the statistical methods used model uncertainties to handle the noise. Kalman filtering, multiple hypothesis tracking and particle filtering are some the widely used tracking methods. The main objective of kernel based tracker is the object motion estimation. The motion may be either translational or affine or projective. In some algorithms, the estimation process is defined by brute force search or gradient descent based minimization. Region based representation and primitive shape based representation is usually used to represent the object. One of the drawbacks of primitive geometric shape for object representation is that parts of the objects may be outside the defined shape while parts of the background may reside inside the shape. Object appearance is also modelled by using probability density functions of colour or texture and assigns weights to pixels residing inside the shape based on conditional probability of the observed colour or texture. Template matching, mean shift, Appearance tracking, and SVM tracker are some of the popularly used kernel based tracker. Silhouette tracking is used to track objects having complex shapes or when tracking of the complete region of the object is required. The silhouette trackers use various features like edge template, colour histogram, silhouette, gradient magnitude, temporal gradient, region statistics etc. Some silhouette trackers use object boundary while some others use complete region inside the boundary for the purpose of tracking. The silhouette based trackers either use motion model representation or appearance model representation, shape model representation or combination of these. Some of the silhouette trackers can also handle occlusion efficiently. Another important aspect related to silhouette tracker is its ability to handle object split and merge. Contour based silhouette tracking proposed by Yilmaz et al. (2004) can split and merge the objects efficiently.

REFERENCES

Anandan, P., Bergen, J., Hanna, K., & Hingorani, R. (1993). Hierarchical Model-Based Motion Estimation. In Motion Analysis and Image Sequence Processing. Kluwer Academic. doi:10.1007/978-1-4615-3236-1_1

Avidan, S. (2001). Support vector tracking. In *IEEE Conference on Computer Vision and Pattern Recognition (CVPR)*, (pp. 184–191). IEEE.

Bar-Shalom, Y., & Foreman, T. (1988). *Tracking and Data Association*. Academic Press Incorporation.

Barron, J., Fleet, D., & Beauchemin, S. (1994). Performance of optical flow techniques. *International Journal of Computer Vision*, *12*(1), 43–77. doi:10.1007/BF01420984

Bay, H., Ess, A., Tuytelaars, T., & Van Gool, L. (2008). *SURF*: Speeded Up Robust Features. *Computer Vision and Image Understanding, 110*(3), 346–359. doi:10.1016/j.cviu.2007.09.014

Bergholm, F. (1987). Edge Focussing. *IEEE Transactions on Pattern Analysis and Machine Intelligence, 9*(6), 726–741. doi:10.1109/TPAMI.1987.4767980 PMID:21869435

Bertalmio, M., Sapiro, G., & Randall, G. (2000). Morphing active contours. *IEEE Transactions on Pattern Analysis and Machine Intelligence, 22*(7), 733–737. doi:10.1109/34.865191

Beymar, D., & Konolige, K. (1999). Real-time tracking of multiple people using continuous detection. In *IEEE International Conference on Computer Vision (ICCV) Frame-Rate Workshop*. IEEE.

Bezdek, J. C., Chandrasekhar, R., & Attikiouzel, Y. (1998). A geometric approach to edge detection. *IEEE Transactions on Fuzzy Systems, 6*(1), 52–75. doi:10.1109/91.660808

Birchfield, S. (1998). Elliptical head tracking using intensity gradients and color histograms. In *IEEE Conference on Computer Vision and Pattern Recognition (CVPR)*. doi:10.1109/CVPR.1998.698614

Black, M., & Anandan, P. (1996). The robust estimation of multiple motions: Parametric and piece-wise smooth flow fields. *Computer Vision and Image Understanding, 63*(1), 75–104. doi:10.1006/cviu.1996.0006

Black, M., & Jepson, A. (1998). Eigentracking: Robust matching and tracking of articulated objects using a view-based representation. *International Journal of Computer Vision, 26*(1), 63–84. doi:10.1023/A:1007939232436

Black, M. J., Sapiro, G., Marimont, D. H., & Heeger, D. (1998). Robust anisotropic diffusion. *IEEE Transactions on Image Processing, 7*(3), 421–432. doi:10.1109/83.661192 PMID:18276262

Blum, A. L., & Langley, P. (1997). Selection of relevant features and examples in machine learning. *Artificial Intelligence, 97*(1-2), 245–271. doi:10.1016/S0004-3702(97)00063-5

Boser, B., Guyon, I. M., & Vapnik, V. (1992). A training algorithm for optimal margin classifiers. In *ACM Workshop on Conference on Computational Learning Theory (COLT)*, (pp. 142–152). doi:10.1145/130385.130401

Bowyer, K., Kranenburg, C., & Dougherty, S. (1999). Edge Detector Evaluation using Empirical ROC Curves. In *IEEE Computer Society Conference on Computer Vision and Pattern Recognition*. doi:10.1109/CVPR.1999.786963

Bradski, G. (1998). Computer vision face tracking for use in a perceptual user interface. *Intel Technology Journal, 2*(2), 1–15.

Canny, J. (1986). A computational approach to edge detection. *IEEE Transactions on Pattern Analysis and Machine Intelligence, 8*(6), 679–698. doi:10.1109/TPAMI.1986.4767851 PMID:21869365

Caselles, V., Kimmel, R., & Sapiro, G. (1995). Geodesic active contours. In *IEEE International Conference on Computer Vision (ICCV)*, (pp. 694–699). doi:10.1109/ICCV.1995.466871

Cham, T., & Rehg, J. M. (1999). A multiple hypothesis approach to figure tracking. In *IEEE International Conference on Computer Vision and Pattern Recognition*, (pp. 239–245).

Chang, Y. L., & Aggarwal, J. K. (1991). 3D Structure Reconstruction from an Ego Motion Sequence using Statistical Estimation and Detection Theory. In *Workshop on Visual Motion*, (pp. 268–273). doi:10.1109/WVM.1991.212797

Chen, Q., Sun, Q. S., Heng, P. A., & Xia, D.-S. (2010). Two-Stage Object Tracking Method Based on Kernel and Active Contour. *IEEE Transactions on Circuits and Systems for Video Technology, 20*(4), 605–609. doi:10.1109/TCSVT.2010.2041819

Chen, T. (2009). Object Tracking Based on Active Contour Model by Neural Fuzzy Network. *IITA International Conference on Control Automation and Systems Engineering*, (pp. 570-574). doi:10.1109/CASE.2009.165

Chen, Y., Rui, Y., & Huang, T. (2001) Jpdaf based hmm for real-time contour tracking. In *IEEE Conference on Computer Vision and Pattern Recognition (CVPR)*, (pp. 543–550).

Chen, Y., Yu, S., Fan, J., Chen, W., & Li, H. (2008). An Improved Color-Based Particle Filter for Object Tracking. *International Conference on Genetic and Evolutionary Computing*, (pp. 360-363). doi:10.1109/WGEC.2008.110

Cheng, Y. (1995, August). Mean shift, mode seeking, and clustering. *IEEE Transactions on Pattern Analysis and Machine Intelligence, 17*(8), 790–799. doi:10.1109/34.400568

Comaniciu, D., Ramesh, V., & Meer, P. (2003). Kernel-based object tracking. *IEEE Transactions on Pattern Analysis and Machine Intelligence, 25*(5), 564–575. doi:10.1109/TPAMI.2003.1195991

Cremers, D., & Schnorr, C. (2003). Statistical shape knowledge in variational motion segmentation. *Israel Nent. Cap. J, 21*, 77–86.

Cuccharina, R., Grana, C., Piccardi, M., & Prati, A. (2003). Detecting Moving Objects, Ghosts, and Shadows in Video Streams. Transactions on Pattern Analysis and Machine Intelligence.

Dargazany, A., Soleimani, A., & Ahmadyfard, A. (2010). Multi-bandwidth kernel-based object tracking. *Journal of Advances in Artificial Intelligence*, Article ID.175603.

Elgammal, A., Harwood, D., & Davis, L. (2000). Non-parametric model for background subtraction. In *European Conference on Computer Vision (ECCV)*, (pp. 751–767).

Elhoseiny, M., Bakry, A., & Elgammal, A. (2013, June). Multi-Class Object Classication in Video Surveillance Systems Experimental Study. *IEEE Conference on Computer Vision and Pattern Recognition Workshops*, (pp. 788-793).

Fang, J., Yang, J., & Liu, H. (2011). Efficient and robust fragments-based multiple kernels track. *International Journal of Electronics and Communications, Elsevier, 65*(11), 915–923. doi:10.1016/j.aeue.2011.02.013

Fieguth, P., & Terzopoulos, D. (1997). Color-based tracking of heads and other mobile objects at videoframe rates. In *IEEE Conference on Computer Vision and Pattern Recognition (CVPR)* (pp. 21–27). doi:10.1109/CVPR.1997.609292

Flickner, M., Sawhney, H., Niblack, W., Ashley, J., Huang, Q., Dom, B., & Yanker, P. et al. (1995, September). Query byimage and video content: The QBIC system. *IEEE Computer*, *28*(9), 23–32. doi:10.1109/2.410146

Freund, Y., & Schapire, R. (1995). *A decision-theoretic generalization of on-line learning and an application to boosting*. Computatational Learning Theory.

Fukunaga, K., & Hostetler, L. D. (1975). The Estimation of the Gradient of a Density Functions, with Applications in Pattern Recognition. *IEEE Transactions on Information Theory*, *21*(1), 32–40. doi:10.1109/TIT.1975.1055330

Gorji, A., & Menhaj, M. B. (2007). Multiple Target Tracking for Mobile Robots Using the JPDAF Algorithm. *19th IEEE International Conference on Tools with Artificial Intelligence*, (vol. 1, pp. 137-145). IEEE.

Greenspan, H., Belongie, S., Goodman, R., Perona, P., Rakshit, S., & Anderson, C. (1994). Over complete steerable pyramid filters and rotation invariance. In *IEEE Conference on Computer Vision and Pattern Recognition (CVPR)*, (pp. 222–228). doi:10.1109/CVPR.1994.323833

Haralick, R., Shanmugam, B., & Dinstein, I. (1973). Textural features for image classification. *IEEE Transactions on Systems, Man, and Cybernetics*, *33*(3), 610–622. doi:10.1109/TSMC.1973.4309314

Harris, C., & Stephens, M. (1981). A combined corner and edge detector. In *4th Alvey Vision Conference*, (pp. 147-151).

Hausdorff, F. (n.d.). *Set Theory*. Chelsea.

Heikkila, M., & Pietikainen, M. (2006). A texture-based method for modeling the background and detecting moving objects. *IEEE Transactions on Pattern Analysis and Machine Intelligence*, *28*(4), 657–662. doi:10.1109/TPAMI.2006.68 PMID:16566514

Heitger, F. (1995). *Feature Detection using Suppression and Enhancement: TR 163*. ETH-Zurich.

Horn, B., & Schunk, B. (1981). Determining optical flow. *Artificial Intelligence*, *17*(1-3), 185–203. doi:10.1016/0004-3702(81)90024-2

Hu, W., Zhou, X., Li, W., Luo, W., Zhang, X., & Maybank, S. (2013). Active Contour -Based Visual Tracking by Integrating Colors, Shapes, and Motions. *IEEE Transactions on Image Processing*, *22*(5), 1778–1792. doi:10.1109/TIP.2012.2236340 PMID:23288333

Huang, J., Kumar, S., Mitra, M., Zhu, W. J., & Zabith, R. (1997). Image indexing usingcolour correlogram. *Proceedings of the*, *CVPR97*, 762–765.

Hue, C., Cadre, J. L., & Prez, P. (2002). Sequential monte carlo methods for multiple target tracking and data fusion. *IEEE Transactions on Signal Processing*, *50*(2), 309–325. doi:10.1109/78.978386

Huttenlocher, D., Noh, J., & Rucklidge, W. (1993). Tracking non rigid objects in complex scenes. In *IEEE International Conference on Computer Vision (ICCV)*, (pp. 93–101). doi:10.1109/ICCV.1993.378231

Intille, S., Davis, J., & Bobick, A. (1997). Real-time closed-world tracking. In *IEEE Conference on ComputerVision and Pattern Recognition (CVPR)*, (pp. 697–703). doi:10.1109/CVPR.1997.609402

Isard, M., & Blake, A. (1998). Condensation - conditional density propagation for visual tracking. *International Journal of Computer Vision, 29*(1), 5–28. doi:10.1023/A:1008078328650

Isard, M., & Maccormick, J. (2001). Bramble: A bayesian multiple-blob tracker. In *IEEE International Conference on Computer Vision (ICCV)*, (pp. 34–41).

Iverson, L. A., & Zucker, S. W. (1995). Logical/linear operations for image curves. *IEEE Transactions on Pattern Analysis and Machine Intelligence, 17*(10), 982–996. doi:10.1109/34.464562

Jain, A. K., & Vailaya, A. (1996). Image retrieval using colour and shape. *Pattern Recognition, 29*(8), 1233–1244. doi:10.1016/0031-3203(95)00160-3

Jalal, A. S., & Singh, V. (2012). The State-of-the-Art in Visual Object Tracking. *Informatica, 36*, 227–248.

Jepson, A., Fleet, D., & Elmaraghi, T. (2003). Robust online appearance models for visual tracking. *IEEE Transactions on Pattern Analysis and Machine Intelligence, 25*(10), 1296–1311. doi:10.1109/TPAMI.2003.1233903

Johnsen, S., & Tews, A. (2009, May). *Real-Time Object Tracking and Classification Using a Static Camera*. IEEE ICRA 2009 Workshop on People Detection and Tracking.

Julier, S. J., & Uhlmann, J. K. (1997, July). A New Extension of the Kalman Filter to Nonlinear Systems. *Proceedings of the Society for Photo-Instrumentation Engineers, 3068*.

Kang, J., Cohen, I., & Medioni, G. (2004). Object reacquisition using geometric invariant appearance model. In *International Conference on Pattern Recongnition (ICPR)*, (pp. 759–762).

Kass, M., Witkin, A., & Terzopoulos, D. (1988). Snakes: Active contour models. *International Journal of Computer Vision, 1*(4), 321–332. doi:10.1007/BF00133570

Kaufman, E., Lovell, T. A., & Lee, T. (2014). Optimal joint probabilistic data association filter avoiding coalescence in close proximity. *European Control Conference (ECC)*, (pp. 2709-2714). doi:10.1109/ECC.2014.6862602

Kuhn, H. (1955). The hungarian method for solving the assignment problem. *Naval Research Logistics Quart., 2*(1-2), 83–97. doi:10.1002/nav.3800020109

Laws, K. (1980). *Textured image segmentation*. (PhD thesis). Electrical Engineering, University of Southern California.

Leutenegger, S., Chli, M., & Siegwart, R. Y. (2011). BRISK: Binary Robust Invariant Scalable Keypoints. In *International Conference on Computer Vision*, (pp. 2548-2555). doi:10.1109/ICCV.2011.6126542

Li, B., Chellappa, R., Zheng, Q., & Der, S. (2001). Model-based temporal object verification using video. *IEEE Transactions on Image Processing, 10*(6), 897–908. doi:10.1109/83.923286

Li, N., Liu, L., & Xu, D. (2008). Corner feature based object tracking using Adaptive Kalman Filter. In *9th International Conference on Signal Processing*, (pp. 1432 – 1435).

Li, X., & Guo, X. (2013, July). Vision-Based Method for Forward Vehicle Detection and Tracking. *IEEE International Conference on Mechanical and Automation Engineering*, (pp. 128-131). doi:10.1109/MAEE.2013.41

Li, Z., Tian, X., Xie, L., & Chen, Y. (2008, August). Improved Object Classification and Tracking Based on Overlapping Cameras in Video Surveillance. *ISECS International Colloquium on Computing, Communication, Control, and Management*. IEEE. doi:10.1109/CCCM.2008.125

Lindeberg, T. (1998). Feature Detection with Automatic Scale Selection. *International Journal of Computer Vision*, *30*(2), 77–116.

Lo, B. P. L., & Velastin, S. A. (2000). Automatic Congestion Detection System for Underground Platforms. In *Proceeding of International Symposium on Intelligent Multimedia, Video, and Speech Processing*, (pp. 158-161).

Lowe, D. (2004, November). Distinctive image features from scale-invariant keypoints. *International Journal of Computer Vision*, *60*(2), 91–110. doi:10.1023/B:VISI.0000029664.99615.94

Lu, W., Wang, S., & Ding, X. (2009, October). Vehicle Detection and Tracking in Relatively Crowded Conditions. *IEEE International Conference on Systems, Man, and Cybernetics*, (pp. 4136-4141). doi:10.1109/ICSMC.2009.5346721

Lu, X., Song, L., Yu, S., & Ling, N. (2012). Object Contour Tracking Using Multi-feature Fusion based Particle Filter. *IEEE Conference on Industrial Electronics and Applications (ICIEA)*, (pp. 237 –242). doi:10.1109/ICIEA.2012.6360729

Lucas, B. D., & Kanade, T. (1981). An iterative image registration technique with an application to stereo vision. In *International Joint Conference on Artificial Intelligence*.

Lucena, M., Fuertes, J. M., Blanca, N., Manuel, J. & Jimenez, M. (2010). Tracking people in video sequences using multiple model. *Multimedia Tools and Applications*, *49*(2), 371-403.

Maccormick, J., & Blake, A. (2000). Probabilistic exclusion and partitioned sampling for multiple object tracking. *International Journal of Computer Vision*, *39*(1), 57–71. doi:10.1023/A:1008122218374

MacKay, D. J. C. (1998). Introduction to Monte Carlo methods. In N. A. T. O. Science Series (Ed.), *Learning in Graphical Models, M. I. Jordan* (pp. 175–204). Kluwer Academic Press. doi:10.1007/978-94-011-5014-9_7

Mallat, S. (1989). A theory for multiresolution signal decomposition: The wavelet representation. *IEEE Transactions on Pattern Analysis and Machine Intelligence*, *11*(7), 674–693. doi:10.1109/34.192463

Manjunath, B. S., Salembier, P., & Sikora, T. (2002). *Introduction to MPEG-7: Multimedia Content Description Language*. John Wiley & Sons Ltd.

Mansouri, A. (2002). Region tracking via level set pdes without motion computation. *IEEE Transactions on Pattern Analysis and Machine Intelligence*, *24*(7), 947–961. doi:10.1109/TPAMI.2002.1017621

Matas, J., Chum, O., Urban, M., & Pajdla, T. (2002). Robust wide baseline stereo from maximally stable extremal regions. In *Proceeding of British Machine Vision Conference*, (pp. 384-396). doi:10.5244/C.16.36

Mikolajczyk, K., & Schmid, C. (2002). An affine invariant interest point detector. In *European Conference on Comuter Vision (ECCV)*, (vol. 1, pp. 128-142).

Moravec, H. (1979). Visual mapping by a robot rover. In *Proceedings of the International Joint Conference on Artificial Intelligence (IJCAI)*, (pp. 598-600).

Ning, J., Zhang, L., Zhang, D., & Wu, C. (2009). Robust object tracking using joint color-texture histogram. *International Journal of Pattern Recognition and Artificial Intelligence, 23*(7), 1245–1263. doi:10.1142/S0218001409007624

Oliver, N., Rosario, B., & Pentland, A. (2000). A bayesian computer vision system for modeling human interactions. *IEEE Transactions on Pattern Analysis and Machine Intelligence, 22*(8), 831–843. doi:10.1109/34.868684

Pal, M., & Mather, P. M. (2001, November). Decision Treebased Classification on Remotely sensed Data. *22nd Asian Conference on Remote Sensing*.

Papageorgiou, C., Oren, M., & Poggio, T. (1998). A general framework for object detection. In *IEEE International Conference on Computer Vision (ICCV)*, (pp. 555–562). doi:10.1109/ICCV.1998.710772

Paragios, N., & Deriche, R. (2002). Geodesic active regions and level set methods for supervised texture Segmentation. *International Journal of Computer Vision, 46*(3), 223–247. doi:10.1023/A:1014080923068

Paschos, G. (2001). Perceptually uniform color spaces for color texture analysis: An empirical evaluation. *IEEE Transactions on Image Processing, 10*(6), 932–937. doi:10.1109/83.923289

Pass, G., & Zabith, R. (1996). Histogram refinement for content-based image retrieval. In *Proceedings of the IEEE Workshop on Applications of Computer Vision*, (pp. 96–102). doi:10.1109/ACV.1996.572008

Pu, B., Zhou, F., & Bai, X. (2011). Particle Filter Based on Color Feature with Contour Information Adaptively Integrated for Object Tracking. *Fourth International Symposium on Computational Intelligence and Design*, (pp. 359-362). doi:10.1109/ISCID.2011.192

Rangarajan, K., & Shah, M. (1991, June). Establishing motion correspondence. *IEEE Computer Society Conference on Computer Vision and Pattern Recognition*, (pp. 103-108).

Rasmussen, C., & Hager, G. (2001). Probabilistic data association methods for tracking complex visual Objects. *IEEE Transactions on Pattern Analysis and Machine Intelligence, 23*(6), 560–576. doi:10.1109/34.927458

Reid, D. B. (1979). An algorithm for tracking multiple targets. *IEEE Transactions on Automatic Control, 24*(6), 843–854. doi:10.1109/TAC.1979.1102177

Rittscher, J., Kato, J., Joga, S., & Blake, A. (2000). A probabilistic background model for tracking. In *European Conference on Computer Vision (ECCV)*, (vol. 2, pp. 336–350).

Rosales, R., & Sclaroff, S. (1999). 3D trajectory recovery for tracking multiple objects and trajectory guided recognition of actions. *IEEE Computer Society Conference on Computer Vision and Pattern Recognition*, (vol. 2). doi:10.1109/CVPR.1999.784618

Rosten, E., & Drummond, T. (2006, May). Machine learning for highspeed corner detection. In *Proceedings of the European Conference on Computer Vision (ECCV)*, (vol. 3951, pp. 430-443).

Rothwell, C., Mundy, J. L., Hoffman, W., & Nguyen, V. D. (1995). Driving Vision by Topology. *IEEE International Symposium on Computer Vision*, (pp. 395-400). doi:10.1109/ISCV.1995.477034

Rowley, H., Baluja, S., & Kanade, T. (1998). Neural network-based face detection. *IEEE Transactions on Pattern Analysis and Machine Intelligence, 20*(1), 23–38. doi:10.1109/34.655647

Salari, V., & Sethi, I. K. (1990). Feature point correspondence in the presence of occlusion. *IEEE Transactions on Pattern Analysis and Machine Intelligence, 12*(1), 87–91. doi:10.1109/34.41387

Sarkar, S., & Boyer, K. (1991). Optimal Infinite Impulse Response Zero-Crossing Based Edge Detection. *Computer Vision Graphics and Image Processing, 54*(2), 224–243.

Sato, K., & Aggarwal, J. (2004). Temporal spatio-velocity transform and its application to tracking and Interaction. *Computer Vision and Image Understanding, 96*(2), 100–128. doi:10.1016/j.cviu.2004.02.003

Schunk, B. (1986). The image flow constraint equation. *Computer Vision Graphics and Image Processing, 35*(1), 20–46. doi:10.1016/0734-189X(86)90124-6

Schweitzer, H., Bell, J. W., & Wu, F. (2002). Very fast template matching. In *European Conference on Computer Vision (ECCV)*, (pp. 358–372).

Sethi, I., & Jain, R. (1987). Finding trajectories of feature points in a monocular image sequence. *IEEE Transactions on Pattern Analysis and Machine Intelligence, 9*(1), 56–73. doi:10.1109/TPAMI.1987.4767872 PMID:21869377

Shafique, K., & Shah, M. (2003). A non-iterative greedy algorithm for multi-frame point correspondence. In *IEEE International Conference on Computer Vision (ICCV)*, (pp. 110–115). doi:10.1109/ICCV.2003.1238321

Shen, C., Kim, J., & Wang, H. (2010). Generalized kernel-based visual tracking. *IEEE Transactions on Circuits and Systems for Video Technology, 20*(1), 119–130. doi:10.1109/TCSVT.2009.2031393

Shi, J., & Malik, J. (2000). Normalized cuts and image segmentation. *IEEE Transactions on Pattern Analysis and Machine Intelligence, 22*(8), 888–905. doi:10.1109/34.868688

Shi, J., & Tomaski, C. (1994). Good features to track. In *IEEE Conference on Computer Vision and PatternRecognition (CVPR)*, (pp. 593–600).

Smith, S., & Brady, M. (1997). SUSAN- A new approach to low level image processing. *International Journal of Computer Vision, 23*(1), 45–78. doi:10.1023/A:1007963824710

Song, K. Y., Kittler, J., & Petrou, M. (1996). Defect detection in random color textures. *Israel Verj. Cap. J, 14*(9), 667–683.

Stauffer, C., & Grimson, W. E. L. (2000). Learning Patterns of Activity Using Real-Time Tracking. IEEE Transactions on Pattern Analysis and Machine Intelligence, 747–757. doi:10.1109/34.868677

Stenger, B., Ramesh, V., Paragios, N., Coetzee, F., & Buhmann, J. (2001). Topology free hidden markovmodels: Application to background modeling. In *IEEE International Conference on Computer Vision (ICCV)*, (pp. 294–301).

Streit, R. L., & Luginbuhl, T. E. (1994). Maximum likelihood method for probabilistic multi-hypothesis tracking. In *Proceedings of the International Society for Optical Engineering (SPIE)*, (vol. 2235, pp. 394–405).

Sugandi, B., Kim, H., Tan, J. K., & Ishikawa, S. (2007, September). Tracking of moving objects by using a low resolution image. *Second International Conference on Innovative Computing, Information and Control (ICICIC)*. IEEE. doi:10.1109/ICICIC.2007.600

Sullivan, J., Blake, A., Isard, M., & MacCormick, J. (1999). Object localization by bayesian correlation. In *Proceeding of 7th International Conference on Computer Vision*, (vol. 2, pp. 1068-1075). doi:10.1109/ICCV.1999.790391

Swain, M. J., & Ballard, D. H. (1991). Colour indexing. *International Journal of Computer Vision, 7*(1), 11–32. doi:10.1007/BF00130487

Szeliski, R., & Coughlan, J. (1997). Spline-based image registration. *International Journal of Computer Vision, 16*(1-3), 185–203.

Tabb, M., & Ahuja, N. (1997). Multiscale Image segmentation by integrated edge and region detection. *IEEE Transactions on Image Processing, 6*(5), 642–655. doi:10.1109/83.568922 PMID:18282958

Tang, D., & Zhang, Y. J. (2011). Combining Mean-Shift and Particle Filter for Object Tracking. *Sixth International Conference on Image and Graphics (ICIG)*, (pp. 771-776). doi:10.1109/ICIG.2011.118

Tanizaki, H. (1987). Non-gaussian state-space modeling of nonstationary time series. *Journal of the American Statistical Association, 82*, 1032–1063.

Tao, H., Sawhney, H., & Kumar, R. (2002). Object tracking with bayesian estimation of dynamic layer representations. *IEEE Transactions on Pattern Analysis and Machine Intelligence, 24*(1), 75–89. doi:10.1109/34.982885

Terzopoulos, D., & Szeliski, R. (1992). Tracking with kalman snakes. In Active Vision. MIT Press.

Tieu, K., & Viola, P. (2004). Boosting image retrieval. *International Journal of Computer Vision, 56*(1), 17–36. doi:10.1023/B:VISI.0000004830.93820.78

Toyama, K., Krumm, J., Brumitt, B., & Meyers, B. (1999). Wallflower: Principles and practices of background maintenance. In *IEEE International Conference on Computer Vision (ICCV)*, (pp. 255–261). doi:10.1109/ICCV.1999.791228

Vapnik, V. (1995). *The Nature of Statistical Learning Theory*. New York: Springer. doi:10.1007/978-1-4757-2440-0

Veenman, C., Reinders, M., & Backer, E. (2001). Resolving motion correspondence for densely moving points. *IEEE Transactions on Pattern Analysis and Machine Intelligence, 23*(1), 54–72. doi:10.1109/34.899946

Viola, P., Jones, M., & Snow, D. (2003). Detecting pedestrians using patterns of motion and appearance. In *IEEE International Conference on Computer Vision (ICCV)*, (pp. 734–741). doi:10.1109/ICCV.2003.1238422

Wang, F. L., Yu, S. Y. & Yang, J. (2009). Robust and efficient fragments-based tracking using mean shift. *International Journal of Electronics and Communications*, 1-10.

Wang, S. P., & Ji, H. B. (2007). A new appearance model based on object sub-region for tracking. *International Conference on Wavelet Analysis and Pattern Recognition*, (pp. 929-932). doi:10.1109/ICWAPR.2007.4420802

Wu, Z., & Leahy, R. (1993, November). An Optimal Graph Theoretic Approach to Data Clustering: Theory and Its Application to Image Segmentation. *IEEE Transactions on Pattern Analysis and Machine Intelligence, 15*(11), 1,101-1,113.

Yang, M., Kpalma, K., & Ronsin, J. (2008). A survey of shape feature extraction techniques. Pattern Recognition, 43-90.

Yi, F., & Moon, I. (2012). Image Segmentation: A Survey of Graph-cut Methods. *International Conference on Systems and Informatics (ICSAI 2012)*. doi:10.1109/ICSAI.2012.6223428

Yilmaz, A., Javed, O., & Shah, M. (2006, December). Object tracking: A survey. *ACM Computing Surveys, 38*(4).

Yilmaz, A., Li, X., & Shah, M. (2004). Contour based object tracking with occlusion handling in video acquired using mobile cameras. *IEEE Transactions on Pattern Analysis and Machine Intelligence, 26*(11), 1531–1536. doi:10.1109/TPAMI.2004.96 PMID:15521500

Zhang, D., Islam, M. M., & Lu, G. (2012). A review on automatic image annotation techniques. *Pattern Recognition, 45*(1), 346–362. doi:10.1016/j.patcog.2011.05.013

Zhang, L., Zhang, D., Su, Y., & Long, F. (2013). Adaptive kernel-bandwidth object tracking based on Mean-shift algorithm. *Fourth International Conference on Intelligent Control and Information Processing (ICICIP)*, (pp. 413-416). doi:10.1109/ICICIP.2013.6568108

Zhang, T., & Fei, S. (2011). Improved particle filter for object tracking. *Chinese Control and Decision Conference (CCDC)*, (pp. 3586-3590).

Zhang, T., Fei, S., & Wang, L. (2014). Modified Particle filter for object tracking in low frame rate video. *33rd Chinese Control Conference (CCC)*, (pp. 4936-4941). doi:10.1109/ChiCC.2014.6895777

Zhu, S., & Yuille, A. (1996). Region competition: Unifying snakes, region growing, and bayes/mdl for multiband image segmentation. *IEEE Transactions on Pattern Analysis and Machine Intelligence, 18*(9), 884–900. doi:10.1109/34.537343

Zulkifley, M. A., Moran, B., & Rawlinson, D. (2012, October). Robust hierarchical multiple hypothesis tracker for multiple object tracking. *19th IEEE International Conference on Image Processing (ICIP)*, (pp. 405-408). doi:10.1109/ICIP.2012.6466881

Chapter 12
Gait Based Biometric Authentication System with Reduced Search Space

L. R. Sudha
Annamalai University, India

R. Bhavani
Annamalai University, India

ABSTRACT

Deployment of human gait in developing new tools for security enhancement has received growing attention in modern era. Since the efficiency of any algorithm depends on the size of search space, the aim is to propose a novel approach to reduce the search space. In order to achieve this, the database is split into two based on gender and the search is restricted in the identified gender database. Then highly discriminant gait features are selected by forward sequential feature selection algorithm in the confined space. Experimental results evaluated on the benchmark CASIA B gait dataset with the newly proposed combined classifier kNN-SVM, shows less False Acceptance Rate (FAR) and less False Rejection Rate (FRR).

INTRODUCTION

From the early days of mankind, humans have struggled with the problem of protecting their assets. So there is an ever-growing need to authenticate and identify legitimate users in many important areas such as military, airport, hospital, digital right management systems, commercial applications etc. Due to the increasing number of crimes from robbery to terrorist attacks, surveillance cameras are deployed in these security sensitive areas which may help to identify the individuals suspected of committing crimes. But since the level of security breaches increases, definitely these systems are vulnerable to the wiles of an impostor, in the absence of robust personal recognition schemes. So in order to reduce future crimes, efficient authentication systems should be developed for early recognition of suspicious individuals who may pose security threats, before the crime is about to happen.

DOI: 10.4018/978-1-4666-9685-3.ch012

The goal of this chapter is to investigate the information contained in the video sequences of human gait and to extract and represent the information in ways that helps to authenticate human, when they enter into a surveillance area. Human gait which is nothing but walking style is a complex set of coordinated activities involving both voluntary and involuntary body systems. The brain, nerves, muscles and bones all work together so that body balance and stability are maintained while the weight of the body is continually shifted between the left and right foot. The muscles must contract and lengthen in a precise sequence to maintain a smooth and steady forward motion. During walking, more than 1000 muscles are synchronized to move over 200 bones around 100 moveable joints. Early medical studies says that there are 24 different components of human gait and if all movements are considered, gait is unique (Kale et al. 2002).

There are three challenging tasks in this work: First, generating a common representation insensitive to lighting, clothing and carrying condition; second, generating a compact motion representation; third, the algorithm has to be reasonably fast, to have the potential to be used in real-time without excessive computational power.

The rest of this chapter is organized as follows. Background provides the different types of authentication techniques, motivation of using gait in the proposed authentication system, challenges of using gait and the literatures available in gait based recognition system. Then the issues identified in the literature are discussed along with the proposed approach to address the issues and analyzed the experimental results. Following this, future scope of this proposed system is discussed and then the chapter is concluded and the references are listed.

BACKGROUND

Authentication is a process of verifying the identity of the user in order to determine whether to allow an individual to access the system. This is the first line of defense for protecting any resource. It is an area which has grown before last two decades and become most widely used today, by finding applications in many places. The three factors in which authentication methods based on are what you know (Knowledge based), what you have (Object based) and what you are (Biometric based).

Knowledge Based Authentication

Password or secret phrase or PIN-based authentication schemes are examples of knowledge based type (Conklin et al. 2004). People can prove their identity by providing passwords or PINs. User name and password is the most common form for authenticating users to control access to personal computers, networks and internet. PIN codes are another example of authentication used to get access bank account and withdraw money from an ATM machine. For a long time it was the only one type of authentication used, because it is cheap, easy to implement and also very fast. Due to this, it is used in many different applications.

So an average person has many password protected accounts today. Because of the difficulty in remembering all passwords, people either use the same password for multiple accounts, or choose passwords that are easy to remember. Unfortunately, easy to remember usually means easy to guess. Some users select difficult passwords but then write them down where unauthorized eyes can find them. Thus, attempting to achieve greater security can actually result in worse security. Passwords can also be stolen by one system masquerading as another and by key loggers (whether hardware or software), or malware. So weakness in this type of authentication system is, passwords can often be forgotten, stolen, accidentally revealed or can be guessed.

Object Based Authentication

In object based authentication, the user possesses a unique piece of hardware that can be matched to his identity (O'Gorman et al. 2003). Examples of such hardware are keys, tokens, SIM cards, smart cards, bank cards, etc. Instead of knowing or remembering long and difficult passwords which can be forgotten, in this case the user does no longer need to remember any password, which is an advantage. The only thing the user needs for authentication is this unique piece of hardware. For an attacker to gain access he must copy or steal the hardware item, which is in most cases very hard to copy and in case of stealing, it cannot go unnoticed.

The disadvantage of this authentication factor is that not only the hardware items are expensive, but also the equipment used to verify these items in the verification side. In case of loss or theft of items, it is very important to take required action to not be used any longer. The lost key must be blocked from the list of accepted key identifiers. This type of authentication is not capable of verifying whether the person is the authorized user or not. According to it, only the person carrying the token and knows the PIN is the authorized user.

Biometric Based Authentication

Since people forget things and lose things, there is growing interest in the last few decades in using the factor "something you are" which is known as biometric, for authentication. Most of biometric characteristics are unique to each individual and they are found in almost all people. The chances that two different persons possess same biometric characteristic are very small, even among identical twins. It is a secure and a convenient authentication tool. It can't be borrowed, stolen and forgotten. Also forging is not so easy.

Biometric technologies are automated methods of verifying or identifying the identity of a living person based on physiological or behavioral characteristics (Jain et al., 2005). Many biometric technologies have emerged for identifying and verifying individuals by analyzing face, fingerprint, palmprint, iris, gait or a combination of these traits. At its simplest, biometric authentication works by comparing two sets of human features to figure out if they come from the same person. The use of biometric technologies for authentication has been an ongoing topic of research, mainly due to the increasing number of real-world applications requiring reliable authentication of humans.

Because biometrics can't be guessed, lost or shared, it is the only way for reliable verification. Also, biometric characteristics are permanent and not changeable. It is also not easy to change one's fingerprint, iris or other biometric characteristics. Users cannot pass their biometric characteristics to other users as easily as they do with their cards or passwords. Biometric objects cannot be stolen as tokens, keys, cards or other objects used for the traditional user authentication. Biometric characteristics are not secret and therefore the availability of a user's fingerprint or iris pattern does not break security the same way as availability of the user's password.

Although biometric authentication has been extensively used in high-security systems, its use in everyday applications, such as access control in buildings, tracking attendance or user personalization, was until recently rather limited. This can be mainly attributed to the fact that high performance biometrics such as the iris or fingerprint do not enjoy user acceptance, since they are highly obtrusive. The targeted subjects are required to closely cooperate with the measurement scheme, which can easily lead to human rights disputes. Also Face, fingerprints and iris can be obscured in most situations where serious crimes are involved.

Motivation of Using Gait

Although gait recognition is still a new biometric and is not sufficiently mature to be deployed in real world applications such as visual surveillance, it has the potential to overcome most of the limitations that other biometrics suffer from. Also it provides salient information about people, including features of individuality, gender, age and pathologies. Human gait has the following advantages.

- **Non-Obtrusive:** The main characteristic of gait features comparing with other biometric features is that they can be used unobtrusively without direct contacting with the sensing devices in capturing the features. Other commercially available biometrics such as face, fingerprint and iris compel the person to touch or to be at a very close distance from the acquisition sensor.
- **Difficult to Conceal and Replicate:** As the purpose of any reliable biometric system is to be robust enough to reduce the possibility of signature forgery, a gait signature which is based on human motion is hard to conceal and forge. Many established biometrics are obscured in various person identification applications. The face may be at low resolution or hidden with makeup or glasses, the palm could be obscured or hands may be cut off and the ears might be covered by hair. But people need to walk; and the manner of walking is usually observable and more difficult to obscure or disguise.
- **Non-Intrusive:** Some biometric modalities, like fingerprint and iris recognition, have already been commercially deployed in large-scale applications (access control in airports and other public access areas and the issuance of passports and ID cards). However, these modalities, in their current state, are not sufficient for all society needs and concerns as they are highly intrusive, i.e., they require the cooperation of the individuals to be identified or controlled. Although fingerprint and iris recognition have proved to be robust for applications where authentication or verification is required, such biometrics are inapplicable to situations where the subject's consent and cooperation are impossible to obtain.
- **Distant Capture:** Unlike other biometrics, gait can be captured from a distant camera. Although face identification is a sort of unobtrusive biometric identification, face images have to be captured at short distances with high enough image resolution. Furthermore, another major drawback of face identification in security applications is, its low recognition rates in poor illumination. This is because most of the facial features cannot be recovered at large distances even using night vision capability. Fortunately, gait features can still be acquired at certain far enough distance with only low resolution to successfully accomplish the identification task.

Challenges of Using Gait

Gait possesses some apparent constraints because of large intrapersonal variations. Human gait is a complex biological process that involves nervous and musculo-skeletal systems. So gait patterns and dynamics can be affected and the discriminating power is reduced by many variability factors both internal and external (Jeffrey et al. 2005).

- **External Factors:** These factors mostly impose challenges on the recognition approach. For example, viewing angles (e.g. frontal view, lateral view, oblique view), lighting conditions (e.g. day, night), outdoor/indoor environments (e.g. sunny, rainy days), clothes, walking surface conditions (e.g. hard/soft, dry/wet, grass/concrete, level/stairs, etc.), shoe types (e.g. mountain boots, sandals), object carrying (e.g. backpack, briefcase) and so on.
- **Internal Factors:** These factors cause changes of the natural gait due to sickness (e.g. foot injury, lower limb disorder, Parkinson disease etc.) or other physiological changes in body due to aging, drunkenness, pregnancy, gaining or losing weight and so on.

From computational perspective, it is quite difficult to accurately extract some of the components such as angular displacements of thigh, leg and foot using current computer vision system, and some others are not consistent over time for the same person. Furthermore segmentation errors and different viewpoints post a substantial challenge for accurate joint localization. Hence, the problem of representing and recognizing gait turns out to be a challenging one. Methods that attain good performance for normal walk suffers with viewpoint constraints, clothing variety, carrying object, different walking speed, low quality silhouettes and insufficient dynamic characteristics.

Literature Survey

Current gait recognition methods are mainly classified into two major categories, namely model-based approaches and model-free approaches. In model-based methods, human body structure or motion is modeled first, and then the image features are extracted by the measure of structural components of models or by the motion trajectories of body parts. A structural model is a model that basically relies on the topology or the shape of human body parts such as head, torso, hip, thigh, knee and ankle. This model is made up of sticks or shapes such as cylinders, cones, truncated cone and quadrangles or arbitrary shapes describing the edge of the body parts (Boulgouris et al., 2005; Goffredo et al., 2010; Jane & De Paor, 2010; Lu et al., 2008). These methods are view invariant and scale independent. But they are sensitive to quality of gait sequences and it needs large computations for parameter calculations. Also due to the highly flexible structure of non-rigid human body and self-occlusion, the performance of these methods is usually limited.

Majority of current approaches are model free. Model-free approaches do not assume an explicit model of the human body, but focus on binary silhouettes and analyze the spatio-temporal shape and motion characteristics of silhouettes (Sarkar et al., 2006; Barnich & Droogenbroeck, 2009; Zheng et al., 2010). These approaches are insensitive to the quality of silhouettes, easy to implement with low computational complexity and have simplified feature space when comparing to model-based approaches. However, they are usually not robust to viewpoints and scaling. This spatiotemporal method characterizes both spatial and temporal characteristics of gait by collapsing the entire 3D spatiotemporal (XYT) data over an entire sequence into 1D or 2D signals.

Initially, in model free approaches raw silhouette was used for human identification as in baseline algorithm (Phillips et al., 2002). Then, authors represent gait using methods such as Radon transform

(Boulgouris & Chi, 2007), Wavelet Transform (Zhang & Jing, 2006), Zernike velocity moments (Shutter & Nixon, 2006) and vector data scanned in horizontal, vertical and diagonal direction (Bo Ye & Yu-mei wen, 2007). Zhang and Liu presented a new gait identification and authentication method based on Haar wavelet and Radon transform. Horizontal and vertical features were acquired by Haar wavelet, and then feature vectors were obtained by Radon transform. Amin & Hatzinakos (2009), extracted area of the lower half of the silhouettes as gait signature. Then they applied I-D Discrete Wavelet Transform (DWT) to extract statistical features from low frequency and high frequency subbands to form the gait signature. In this approach, feature set was low dimensional and hence the recognition stage was computationally very efficient. Eigenspace transformation and canonical space analysis are widely used in these methods to reduce the dimensionality of input feature space and optimize class discrimination.

To address the problem of low quality silhouettes and to reduce computational cost and storage space, there are methods which compress a gait cycle into one static image before feature extraction. Bobick & Davis (2001) first proposed Motion Energy Image(MEI) and Motion History Image(MHI) for robust static representation of human motion. Han & Bhanu (2006) later extended this idea to gait representation and developed a new feature named as Gait Energy Image (GEI). GEI reflects major shapes of silhouettes and their changes over a gaitcycle. It keeps both the static information and motion information but loses intrinsic dynamic characteristics and detailed information of the gait pattern. Yang et al. (2008), proposed dynamic region in gait energy image which reflects the walking manner of an individual, called enhanced GEI .

To preserve the temporal information besides the spatial information, Gait History Image(GHI) was proposed in (Liu & Zheng, 2007). Later, Gait Moment Image(GMI) (Ma et al., 2007) was developed, which is the gait probability image at each key moment of all gait cycles. The gait images over all possible gait cycles corresponding to a key moment are averaged as the GEI of this key moment. In order to improve the performance further, some other methods were proposed by directly modifying the basic GEI, namely Enhanced GEI(EGEI) (Yang et al., 2008), Frame Difference Energy Image(FDEI) (Chen et al. 2009) and Mean Gait Energy Image (MGEI) (Sruti Das & Tardi, 2012) . The method in (Wang et al., 2010) captures temporal information of the gait sequence into a single color image called Chrono Gait Image (CGI).

Zhang et al. (2010) proposed Active Energy Image (AEI) for gait representation to include more dynamic information for recognition. To further enhance the discriminative power of AEI, they applied a newly proposed two-Dimensional Locality Preserving Projections (2DLPP) method. This is to reduce feature dimension and improve the separable capability of features. Euclidean distance between gallery and probe dataset was calculated to perform recognition by using the Nearest Neighbor rule.

Lam et al. (2011) proposed a representation called as Gait Flow Image (GFI), which contains motion information for gait recognition without constructing any model and performing any transformation. They first determined optical flow field from two consecutive silhouette images. In a gait cycle, if there are N silhouette images, there will be N-1 binary flow images. Then they created GFI by averaging the binary flow images. For classification they adopted the Nearest Neighbor technique.

Aditi Roy et al. (2012) proposed a novel feature called Pose Energy Image (PEI) from the chain of key poses of a gait cycle. Processing speed and space requirement are higher for PEI than the conventional GEI methods. To overcome this shortcoming, another novel feature named as Pose Kinematics was introduced. This represents the percentage of time spent in each key pose state over a gait cycle. At first, they have applied Pose Kinematics to select a set of most probable classes and then, PEI was used on those selected classes to get the final classification using Nearest Neighbor criteria.

All the above methods can attain good performance under controlled conditions but not under factors, such as viewpoint constraint, clothing variety, carrying object, different walking speed, low quality silhouettes and insufficient dynamic characteristics. Chen et al. (2010) applies a part-based feature extraction strategy to achieve substantial clothing invariance and uses an adaptive weight control mechanism to identify the subject. Active Energy Image (AEI) is used to alleviate the effect caused by low quality silhouettes, carrying object and clothing variety in (Zhang et al., 2010).

The gait recognition method in (Bashir et al., 2010) computes Gait Entropy Image (GEnI) from a sequence of images of a subject's gait period to identify non cooperating individuals in unconstrained environment with varying covariate conditions for gallery and probe sequences. Hu et al. (2013) proposed a novel approach based on optical flow. Local Binary Pattern (LBP) was employed to describe the texture information of optical flow and flow pyramid was designed to reduce the computational time during the processes of recognition. In order to accelerate flow computation, uninteresting region in the coarsest layer of the image pyramid was eliminated by the authors. However, these improvements are still affected by the covariates and there is some room to obtain further improvement.

Issues in the Existing Literature

While analyzing the literature, we found that most of the approaches are affected by variability factors such as wearing coats and carrying bags. The techniques which give very good performance for normal video sequences perform poorly under these covariates. So to improve the performance of gait recognition system under such covariates; highly discriminative spatio-temporal, anatomical and binary moment features are selected based on their contribution in identification and employed a combined classifier for identification.

PROPOSED APPROACH

A machine vision based, model free biometric system using gait is proposed for authentication. A critical task in this system is feature extraction. A careful analysis of gait reveals that it has two important components, a structural component which captures the physical build of a person and a dynamic component which captures the transitions that the body undergoes, during walking. In the proposed approach, these static and dynamic components are extracted from the silhouette parts which are not affected by covariate factors and then recognized by pattern classifiers for authentication.

Different from traditional authentication approaches, identification mode of authentication is followed in the proposed system. In this mode, when a person enters into the surveillance area, his identity will be established based on his/her gait by one-to-many comparisons. This identity will be matched with the identity claimed by the person requesting authentication. This makes the system more robust against attacks of imposters who know the closest person in the database in terms of gait similarity. The reason is in the case of identification, template with maximum similarity score will be selected as the class of test data. In verification mode, a threshold must be determined accurately to prevent the attack of imposters getting authorized, by mimicking the gait of genuine user. Accurately determining threshold is a challenging task in the case of gait biometric because of intrapersonal variations of gait.

In any classification problem increase in search space will degrade the performance of the classification system (Mhatre et al. 2005). It has been shown that the number of false positives in a biometric identification system grows geometrically with the size of the database. Also by restricting the final identification with only a fraction of the entire database, the system will ensure not only good response time, but also improved accuracy. Based on this analysis, the search space is reduced in the proposed approach by splitting the database into two based on gender.

The input to the system is gait video sequences captured by a static camera. These sequences are then processed to extract the binary silhouettes of the walker by using a background subtraction process which includes two important steps, background modeling and foreground extraction.

In the training phase, features for gender classification are extracted and a gender classifier is created first. Then gender of the training gait sequences is determined by this classifier and based on the gender, gait representing features are extracted and stored in two different databases, one for male and the other for female along with the identity of the walker. During the testing phase, two different classifiers are employed. First one is to determine the gender of the test video and the other one is to verify the individual by comparing the obtained features with the ones previously stored in the corresponding gender database.

Background Modeling

Extracting moving objects from a video sequence captured using a static camera is a critical task in visual surveillance. Unfortunately extracting moving objects quickly and exactly from a real time monitoring video is quite difficult, because of the complexity of the objects, environment and device. To detect moving objects, each incoming frame must be compared with the background model to classify the scene into foreground and background. So a common approach to detect moving object is to first perform background modeling to yield a reference model. The simplest way to model the background is to acquire a background image which doesn't include any moving object. Much research has been devoted to develop a background model that is robust and sensitive enough to identify moving object of interest. Among the various methods introduced in the literature, based on their representation models, these methods can be divided into three categories, namely Median-based (Cheng et al. 2008), Gaussian-based (Tang et al. 2007)and KDE (Kernel Density Estimation) based approaches (Zhang et al. 2009).

Foreground Segmentation

After background modeling, moving objects from the video sequence must be segmented out for further processing. The most common approach for this segmentation is frame differencing which uses the video frame at time t-1 as the background model for the frame at time t (Tang et al. 2007). In this method a pixel is marked as foreground if the difference between background and the current frame is greater than the threshold. A major flaw of this method is that for objects with uniformly distributed intensity values, the pixels are interpreted as part of the background. Another problem is that objects must be continuously moving. If an object stays still for more than a frame period (1/fps), it becomes part of the background. But this is highly adaptive since the background is based on previous frame and computationally efficient. In order to reduce the problem created by this approach, background model generated by background modeling technique is used for finding frame difference.

The algorithm is:

Step 1: Find the difference between current frame and background image.

fr_diff(x,y) = |I(x,y)-B(x,y)|

Step 2: Check the value of frame difference image (fr_diff (x,y)) with threshold Th, and set foreground pixel as below.

If (fr_diff(x,y) > Th)

Fg(x,y) = I(x,y)

Else

Fg(x,y) = 0

where B(x,y) is Background image, I(x,y) is Current frame and Fg(x,y) is Foreground image. The determined threshold value is 40 for the test video and it varies from 1 video to other.

Sillhouette Generation

A silhouette is the image of a person, an object or scene represented as a solid shape using a single color, usually white with its edges matching the outline of the subject. The interior of a silhouette is featureless, and the whole is typically presented on a dark background, usually black. The silhouette differs from an outline which depicts the edge of an object in a linear form, while a silhouette appears as a solid shape. This is obtained by thresholding the foreground image with a suitable threshold value T as in Equation 1. In order to be robust to changes in color and texture of clothing and illumination, it is reasonable to consider the binarized silhouette of the object.

$$Sil(x, y) = \begin{cases} 0 \ Background \ \ if \ Fg(x, y) > T \\ 1 \ Foreground \ else \end{cases}. \tag{1}$$

where Sil(x,y) is silhouette image and Fg(x,y) is the foreground image. The estimated threshold value is 35.

Gaitcycle Estimation

A single gait cycle can be regarded as the time between two identical events during the human walking and usually measured from heel strike to heel strike of one leg. Human gait is treated as a periodic activity within each gait cycle. Estimating gait cycle is an important step before feature extraction. This is to divide the video sequence which contains around 75 frames into subsequences of gait cycle length. Aspect ratio of the silhouettes bounding box is used to estimate the gait cycle in (Wang et al., 2003). In this proposed method, width of the bounding box of the moving object (Sharmila et al., 2010) is used for gait cycle estimation. During walking the width of the bounding box will be larger when the legs are farthest apart and thinner when the legs are together. Using this periodic nature, the gait cycle is estimated by using the following algorithm.

Step 1: Find width of the bounding box of each frame.
Step 2: Create an array 'a' using the following logic.

If bounding box width of frame n <= bounding box width of frame n+1

a = 0, else a = 1.

Step 3: There will be sequence of 0's and 1's in the array as below.

a = 0 0 0 0 0 0 0 1 1 1 1 1 0 0 0 0 0 0 0 1 1 1 1 1 0 0 0 0 0....

Step 4: Count the number of 0's and 1's for first 2 alternate 0's and 1's sequence.

Eg. count = 23

Step 5: Number of frames in a gait cycle is 23.

Feature Extraction

Knowing the number of frames in a gait cycle, the sequence of binary silhouettes is divided into subsequences of gait cycle length. Frames in one gait cycle are then considered for feature extraction. Three different types of features namely binary moment features, anatomical features and spatiotemporal features are extracted from a single gait cycle. Moments are features of the object, which do not have a direct understandable geometrical meaning (Rocha et al. 2004). So it is used to extract features from gait silhouette which does not have a definite geometry. As human anatomy is very much related with gender discrimination, anatomical features are used. To include time dependant gait features, spatiotemporal features are used in our approach. The process of extracting these features is discussed below.

Binary Moment Feature Computation

Moment functions have a broad spectrum of applications in image analysis. For a 2D continuous function f(x,y) the moment (sometimes called "raw moment") of order (p + q) is defined as in Equation 2.

$$M_{pq} = \int\limits_{-\infty}^{\infty}\int x^p y^q f(x, y) dx dy \tag{2}$$

Adapting this to grayscale image with pixel intensities f(x,y), raw image moments M_{pq} are calculated by Equation 3.

$$M_{pq} = \sum_x \sum_y x^p y^q f(x, y) \tag{3}$$

For binary image since f(x,y) = 1, the raw image moments are calculated by Equation 4.

$$M_{pq} = \sum_x \sum_y x^p y^p \tag{4}$$

The moments computed with respect to the object centroid are called central moments and are defined as Equation 5.

$$\mu_{pq} = \int\limits_{-\infty}^{\infty} \int (x - \overline{x})^p (y - \overline{y})^q f(x, y) dx dy \tag{5}$$

where $\overline{x}$ and $\overline{y}$ is defined as Equations 6 and 7.

$$\overline{x} = \frac{M_{10}}{M_{00}} \tag{6}$$

$$\overline{y} = \frac{M_{01}}{M_{00}} \tag{7}$$

If $f(x, y)$ is a digital image, then Equation 5 becomes Equation 8.

$$M_{pq} = \sum_x \sum_y (x - \overline{x})^p (y - \overline{y})^q f(x, y) \tag{8}$$

The central moments of order up to 2 expressed in terms of raw moments are given by Equations 9, 10, 11, 12, 13 and 14.

$$\mu_{00} = M_{00} \tag{9}$$

$$\mu_{01} = 0 \tag{10}$$

$$\mu_{10} = 0 \tag{11}$$

$$\mu_{01} = M_{11} - \overline{x} M_{01} = M_{11} - \overline{y} M_{10} \tag{12}$$

$$\mu_{20} = M_{20} - \overline{x} M_{10} \tag{13}$$

$$\mu_{02} = M_{02} - \overline{y} M_{01} \tag{14}$$

Above moments computed from a digital image generally represent global characteristics of the image shape and provide a lot of information about different types of geometrical features of the image such as area, centroid (xmean and ymean), length of major and minor axis, aspect ratio, eccentricity and orientation angle. These geometrical features can be calculated using 0th, 1st and 2nd order moments as given from Equations 15, 16, 17, 18, 19 and 20.

$$Area = \mu_{00} \tag{15}$$

$$xmean = \frac{M_{10}}{M_{00}} \tag{16}$$

$$ymean = \frac{M_{01}}{M_{00}} \tag{17}$$

$$Aspect\ ratio = \frac{major\ axis\ length}{min\ or\ axis\ length} \tag{18}$$

$$Eccentriciy = \frac{(\mu_{01} - \mu_{02})^2 - 4\mu_{11}{}^2}{(\mu_{20} + \mu_{02})^2} \tag{19}$$

$$Angle = 0.5\ atan\left(\frac{2\mu_{11}}{\mu_{20} - \mu_{02}}\right) \tag{20}$$

Anatomical Feature Computation

To estimate physical parameters, different positions of the human body are obtained as a fraction of height (H) by measuring the height of the bounding rectangle which encloses the silhouette contour. The vertical positions of ankle, knee, hip, waist, chest, shoulder and head are then estimated as a fraction of the body height following anatomical studies as in (winter, 2004) as 0.039H, 0.285H, 0.530H, 0.535H, 0.720H, 0.818H and 0.870H measured from the bottom of the bounding rectangle, respectively. Bounding rectangle's mean height 'H' is obtained by averaging the difference between upper and bottom points on y axis at each time instant t as given by Equation 21.

$$H = \frac{\sum_{i=1}^{N} [Y_{up}(t) - Y_{bp}(t)]_i}{N} \tag{21}$$

where Yup is the upper point on y axis, Ybp is the bottom point on y axis and N is the number of frames in the gait cycle.

Spatio-Temporal Feature Computation

Bounding rectangle's height and width over a gait cycle is used for obtaining spatial features. Height 'H' is obtained by Equation 21. Width 'W' is obtained by averaging the difference between left and right points on x axis and is given by Equation 22.

$$W = \frac{\sum\limits_{i=1}^{N} [X_{rp}(t) - X_{lp}(t)]_i}{N} \tag{22}$$

where Xrp is the right point on x axis, Xlp is the left point on x axis and N is the number of frames in the gait cycle. These features are then used for obtaining Aspect ratio and Diagonal angle as in Equations 23 and 24.

$$A = \frac{\sum\limits_{i=1}^{N} \left[tan^{-1} \left(\frac{H(t)}{W(t)} \right) \right]_i}{N} \tag{23}$$

$$A = \frac{\sum\limits_{i=1}^{N} \left[\left(\frac{H(t)}{W(t)} \right) \right]_i}{N} \tag{24}$$

Stride length, Step length, Cadence and Velocity are considered as temporal components. Stride length is the distance travelled by a person during one stride (or cycle) and can be measured as the length between the heels from one heel strike to the next heel strike on the same side. Two step lengths (left plus right) make one stride length. Step length and stride lengths are computed by finding the number of frames in a step and stride. Cadence is number of steps per minute and velocity is calculated by the Equation 25.

$$Velocity = stridelength \times 0.5 cadence \tag{25}$$

Feature Selection

In majority of real-world classification problems, many candidate features are introduced to better represent the domain. Unfortunately many of these are either partially or completely irrelevant / redundant to the target concept. Selecting appropriate features is one of the most important factors to achieve high classification performance in classification systems. Reducing the number of irrelevant/redundant features drastically reduces the running time of a learning algorithm and yields a more general concept. In the proposed system sequential forward selection (Dash et al. 1997) is used to select features for gender discrimination and authentication. This method has two components.

Components of sequential feature selection are

1. An objective function, called the criterion, which the method seeks to minimize over all feasible feature subsets. Common criteria are mean squared error and misclassification rate.
2. A sequential search algorithm, which adds or removes features from a candidate subset while evaluating the criterion.

Starting from an empty feature set, this approach creates candidate feature subsets by sequentially adding each of the features not yet selected. Each candidate feature subset is evaluated with an objective function to minimize misclassification rate. 10-fold cross-validation is performed with different training subsets of training database and test subsets of testing database to test the validity of the selected subset.

Algorithm of sequential feature selection:

```
Step 1: Start from empty feature subset SS = 0
Step 2: For each feature F in Feature Set FS
        a)  SS' = {SS} U {F}
        b)  eval(SS')
        c)  if minimum classification error
        d)  SS = SS'
Step 3: Selected feature set is SS
```

The selected features are then normalized using Equation 26.

$$y = x - xmean\left(\frac{ystd}{xstd}\right) + ymean \tag{26}$$

Gender Classification

Gait based gender classification has received great attention from researchers in the biometric society in the vision field due to its potential in different applications. This will help a human authentication system to focus only on the identified gender related features, which can improve search speed and efficiency of the retrieval system by limiting the subsequent searching space into either a male database or female database.

In this method, features are extracted based on binary moments and anatomical division. A total of 26 parameters are considered as gait features initially and removed irrelevant and redundant features. As a result, 9 important features are selected from all the frames in one gait cycle and then calculated the average of each feature for gender discrimination.

Extracted 26 features are

- 6 binary Moment features area, xmean, ymean, aspectratio, orientation, eccentricity from 3 different regions upper, lower and whole body.
- 8 anatomical features Shoulder width, head width, chest width, hip width, hip chest ratio, hip height ratio, chest height ratio and shoulder height ratio.

Selected features are

- 5 binary moment features area, meanx, meany, aspect ratio and angle of inclination.
- 4 anatomical features are shoulder width, head width, chest width and hip_chest ratio.

Human Authentication

Enrollment phase and authentication phase are the two phases of authentication process. Biometric templates of all users must be captured and stored in a reference database during enrollment phase and the test template must be matched against the database information during authentication phase. A biometric system for user authentication operates in two modes: (i) Identification Mode: The biometrics captured of an unknown individual goes through a "one-to-many comparison" with those enrolled in the database and the identity is established if there is a match. (ii) Verification Mode: The biometrics captured of an individual, who is already identified through another means of authentication, goes through a "one-to-one comparison" with a stored template in the database to verify whether the individual is the person who claims to be. In the proposed approach, identification mode of authentication is followed.

Feature extraction is a critical process in authentication. Since gait of a person varies with covariates, it is important to extract features which are invariant to the covariate factors. Keeping this in mind a total of 76 parameters are extracted from three different types of features (binary moment, anatomical, spatio-temporal) initially and removed irrelevant and indiscriminant features by applying sequential feature selection technique. As a result, 19 important features for male and 12 features for female are selected from all the frames in one gait cycle and then calculated the average of each feature for gait representation of a video. The male feature set contains 11 binary moment features, 3 anatomical features and 5 spatiotemporal features. The female feature set contains 10 binary moment features and 2 spatiotemporal features.

Extracted 76 features are:

- 9 binary moment features (area, xmean, ymean, aspectratio, orientation, eccentricity, length of major axis, length of minor axis, stdofymean from Head, Shoulder, Chest, Ankle, Whole body.
- 6 binary moment features (ymean, orientation, eccentricity, length of major axis, length of minor axis, stdofymean) from Hip and Knee.
- 9 Anatomical features (Shoulder width, head width, chest width, hip width, hip chest ratio, hip height ratio, chest height ratio, shoulder height ratio, hip waist ratio).
- 10 Spatiotemporal features (Height, width, stdofwidth, aspectratio, diagonal angle, stridelength, steplength, cadence, velocity, stdheight).

Selected features for male are:

- Binary moment features(11): 5 features from head, (xmean, angle, minor axis length, eccentricity, standard deviation of ymean), 3 features from shoulder (angle, area, major axis length) and 3 from the whole body silhouette (xmean, standard deviation of ymean and angle).
- Anatomical features(3): chest height ratio, hip height ratio, hip waist ratio.
- Spatio-temporal features(5): Standard deviation of height and width, Height, Step length, Stride length.

Selected features for female are:

- Binary moment features(10): All features of male except standard deviation of ymean from whole body.
- Spatio-temporal features(2): Height and Step length.

In the proposed authentication system, Probabilistic Neural Network (PNN) is used for gender determination and kNN-SVM for authentication. PNN is a Bayesian statistical classifier that uses Parzen estimator to approximate class dependent probability density function (pdf). It is a multilayer feed forward neural network with four layers, input layer, pattern layer, summation layer and decision layer. kNN-SVM is a new model as shown in Figure 1 formed by combining the predictions of two different classifiers; first one is the Cityblock distance based k Nearest Neighbor (kNN) classifier and the other one is Radial Basis Function based Support Vector Machine (SVM) classifier by mean vote method. Mean vote method combines the binary output labels of classifiers.

kNN is a method for classifying objects based on closest training examples in the feature space. It is the simplest of all algorithms for predicting the class of a test example. The algorithm contains three steps to classify objects:

Step 1: Calculate distances of all training vectors to test vector.

Step 2: Pick k closest vectors.

Step 3: Calculate average/majority.

In SVM the original input space is mapped into a high dimensional dot product space called feature space, and in the feature space the optimal hyper plane is determined to maximize the generalization ability of the classifier. The primary advantage of SVM is its ability to minimize both structural and empirical risks leading to better generalization for new data classification even when the dimension of input data is high with limited training dataset.

To authenticate a person, from the corresponding test gait video, gender related features are extracted after preprocessing and the gender is determined first. Then features for authentication are extracted and the identity is established by kNN and SVM independently. Then the established identity is verified with

Figure 1. Block diagram of kNN-SVM

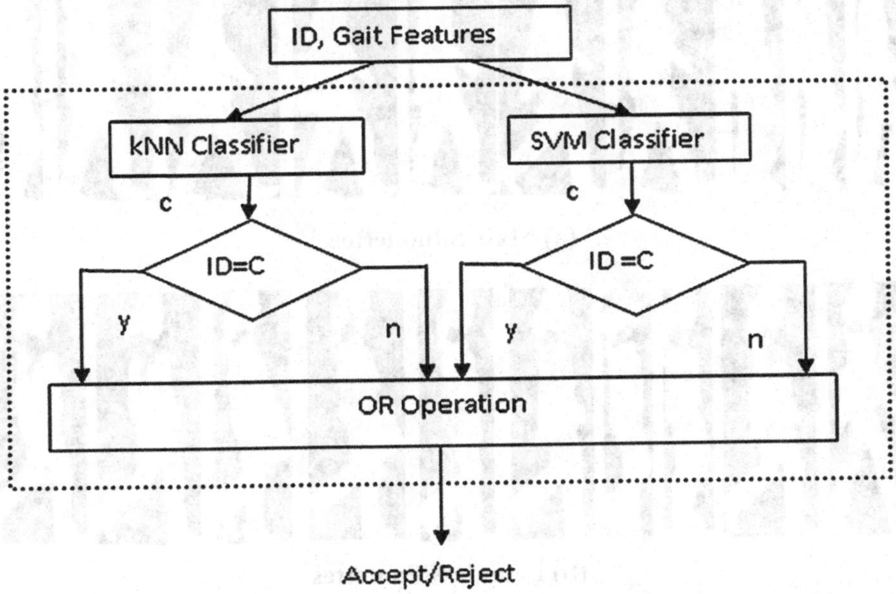

the claimed identity by the proposed system. It was found that the decision of kNN and SVM differs for some probe data. The accepted person by one classifier is rejected by the other classifier. In order to improve accuracy of the system, the decisions of both classifiers are utilized by the kNN-SVM Classifier. So a person is treated as an authenticated user if he/she is accepted by any one classifier.

SOLUTIONS AND RECOMMENDATIONS

To justify the discriminating capability of our proposed approach, a series of experiments were conducted based on CASIA B gait dataset. In this database there are 124 subjects (93 males and 31 females) from 11 views. Every subject walked 10 times in the scene including 6 normal walking sequences, 2 clothes-varying sequences and 2 bag-carrying sequences, CASIA gait datasets also provide the preliminary segmented foreground sequences. Data of all the 31 females and 31 randomly selected males, from lateral view are covered in this experiment. Sample cropped silhouettes from 10 different video sequences of a male and female are shown in Figure 2.

For training, only normal walking scenario are used, while the normal walking scenario and the other two scenarios (carrying bags, wearing coats) were used for testing. This test protocol allows us to assess the ability of the classifiers to unseen data both under the same training scenario and under other scenarios. For training 4 normal walking sequences are used. Hence we have 4 x 62 = 248 video sequences for training. For testing there are 124 sequences from all the three test cases. Only few results are reported on the same dataset and with the same test protocol as this. Three fold cross validation is used to evaluate the performance of the proposed system.

Figure 2. Sample lateral view male and female silhouettes from CASIA-B database

(a) Male Silhouettes

(b) Female Silhouettes

Gender Classification Results

Table 1 summarizes the classification rates for gender classification obtained by PNN classifier under three test cases by using Equation 27 and it can be noted that the CCR of our method for normal/normal and normal/bag test case is 100%, which confirms that the proposed approach is effective for gender classification.

$$CCR = \left(\frac{No\ of\ correctly\ classified\ test\ data}{Total\ number\ of\ test\ data} \right) \times 100 \tag{27}$$

Figure 3 shows the representing capability and robustness of the proposed approach in cloth varying and carrying conditions. Results are compared with the results in (Hu et al., 2010).

Table 1. Correct classification rate for gender classification by PNN classifier

Test Case Train/Test	No. of Sequences Train/Test	CCR (%)
Normal	248/124	100
Carrying Bag	248/124	100
Wearing Coat	248/124	82.5

Figure 3. Comparison chart of proposed gender classification algorithm with the results reported by Hu et al. (2010)

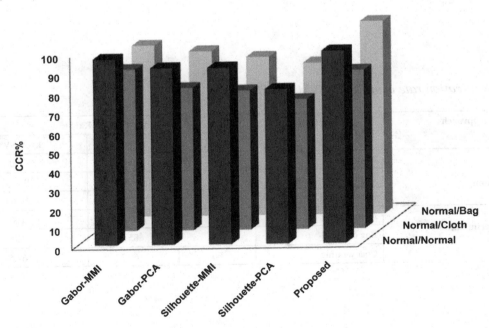

Human Authentication Results

Two types of experiments (with gender discrimination and without gender discrimination) are conducted to evaluate the performance of proposed authentication approach. Table 2 summarizes the verification rates obtained by the above said two experiments under the three test cases for kNN, SVM and kNN-SVM classifiers.

Experimental results obtained using the proposed approach is compared with Bashir et al. (2010), Zhang et al. (2010) & Hu et al. (2013) in terms of identification rates and reported in Table 3 for all the three test cases.

It can be noted that CCR of our method for normal/normal test case is 100% and there are 2 more approaches with 100%. But when compared the results of other test cases of those approaches, ours is superior for both the test cases. This shows the representing capability and robustness of the proposed approach in cloth varying and bag carrying conditions. Achievement of improved performance with less processing time is due to the splitting of database based on gender and less dimension feature set by the selection of significant gait characteristics.

Other performance measures such as Precision, Recall, and F-measure are also calculated using Equations 28, 29 and 30. The results are reported in Table 4.

$$\Pr ecision = \frac{TP}{TP + FP} \times 100 \tag{28}$$

$$\mathrm{Re}\, call = \frac{TP}{TP + FN} \times 100 \tag{29}$$

$$F\, measure = 2 \times \frac{\Pr ecision \times \mathrm{Re}\, call}{\Pr ecision + \mathrm{Re}\, call} \times 100 \tag{30}$$

Table 2. Verification rate using kNN, SVM and kNN-SVM

Approach	Test Case	Verification Rate (%)		
		kNN	SVM	kNN-SVM
With Gender Discrimination	Normal	100	100	100
	Bag carrying	87.5	92.5	92.74
	Coat wearing	72.5	67.5	80.64
Without Gender Discrimination	Normal	100	97.5	100
	Bag carrying	87	85	92.5
	Coat wearing	60	60	67.5

Table 3. Comparison of verification rate of the proposed approach with other reported approaches using CASIA B database

Authors	Methods	Verification Rate (%)		
		Normal	Bag Carrying	Coat Wearing
Bashir et al. (2010)	M_G^{ji} +CDA	100	78.3	44
	M_G^{ji} +ACDA	100	77.8	43.1
Zhang et al. (2010)	AEI + 2DLPP	98.39	91.94	72.18
	AEI + 2DLDA	94.35	81.85	68.95
Hu et al. (2013)	LBP Flow	94	45.2	42.9
Proposed		100	92.74	80.64

Table 4. Comparison of different performance measures

Classifiers	Test Cases (Train/Test)	Performance Measures (%)		
		Precision	Recall	F-Measure
kNN	Normal	100	100	100
	Bag Carrying	82.5	87.5	84.77
	Coat Wearing	69.17	72.5	70.8
SVM	Normal	100	100	100
	Bag Carrying	73.34	92.5	91.63
	Coat Wearing	57.92	65	61.25
kNN-SVM	Normal	100	100	100
	Bag Carrying	90.12	92.74	91.41
	Coat Wearing	72.34	80.64	76.26

Performance Metrics: FAR and FRR

Performance of the system is evaluated by FAR and FRR. FAR is the probability of wrongly accepting an impostor, while FRR represents the probability of wrongly rejecting a genuine user. FAR and FRR are estimated by using Equations 31 and 32.

$$FAR = \frac{Number\ of\ accepted\ impostor\ attempts}{Total\ Number\ of\ impostor\ attempts} \qquad (31)$$

$$FRR = \frac{Number\ of\ rejected\ genuine\ attempts}{Total\ Number\ of\ genuine\ attempts} \qquad (32)$$

In the proposed system, for a single impostor, maximum possible number of attempts is 62 and possible number of accepted attempts is 2. The probability of accepting an impostor is 2/62. Therefore FAR

= .032. Varying from other authentication systems, the probability of accepting an imposter decreases with the increase of enrolled users as shown in Figure 4. Also increase in number of impostors will not increase FAR of the system as shown in Table 5.

False Rejection Rate for different test cases of the system is tabulated in Table 6.

Overall FRR of the proposed authentication system (considering all the test cases) is calculated as below.

Total Sample = 372
Rejected = 33
FRR = 8.87%

Figure 4. FAR curve for various number of enrolled users

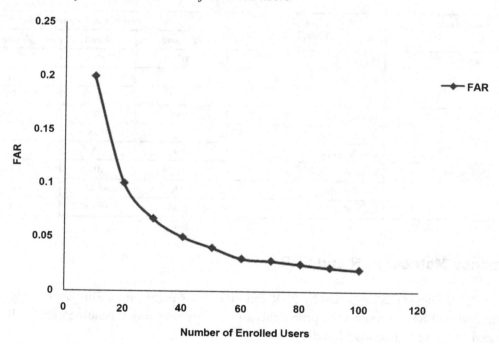

Table 5. FAR for various number of impostors

Number of Impostor Users	Possible Attempts	Accepted Attempts	FAR
1	62	2	2/62 = 0.032
2	124	4	4/124 = 0.032
3	186	6	6/186 = 0.032

Table 6. FRR of the proposed system

Test Case	Total Sample	Rejected	FRR (%)
Normal	124	0	0
Bag carrying	124	9	7.26
Coat wearing	124	24	19.35

Experimental results evaluated on the benchmark CASIA-B dataset show that this proposed method can effectively capture gait characteristics. Though, the performance of the system degrades when the training and testing data differ in clothing it is least affected by variation in carrying condition. False Acceptance Rate of the proposed system is only 0.032. Varying from other authentication systems, the probability of accepting an imposter decreases with the increase of enrolled users in the proposed system. False Rejection Rate of the system is 0%, 7.26%, 19.35% for Normal, Bag carrying and Coat wearing test cases respectively. Performance of the combined classifier outperforms many gait classification approaches. Achievement of improved performance with less processing time is due to the splitting of database based on gender, stable and discriminant gait representing features, less dimension feature set by employing feature selection algorithm and combined classifier approach for utilizing decisions of both kNN and SVM classifier.

FUTURE RESEARCH DIRECTIONS

- Develop view transformation algorithms to make the system view invariant because in realistic surveillance scenarios, it is unreasonable to assume that a person could always present a lateral view to the camera. Therefore, further work is required to address the different viewpoint angles for gait recognition.
- Although the method brings closer to goal, we are still at a far distance because the real world data are very complex.
- Fusion of model free and model based approaches to yield better results.
- Consider other external factors varying gait.

CONCLUSION

A machine vision based, model free approach is proposed for authentication in reduced search space by splitting the database into two based on gender. Given the video of an individual, the moving object is segmented out by a background subtraction technique first. Then gait representing spatiotemporal, anatomical and part based binary moment features are extracted from human silhouette. As the gait characteristics vary significantly by intrapersonal variations due to covariates such as carrying bag and wearing coat, a representation which is stable and discriminant is used. Also, a combined classifier approach was applied for utilizing the decisions of more than one classifier. Experimental results evaluated on CASIA B gait dataset showed that this proposed method can effectively capture gait characteristics.

REFERENCES

Amin, T., & Hatzinakos, D. (2009). Wavelet Analysis of Cyclic Human Gait for Recognition. *16th IEEE International Conference on Digital Signal Processing*. doi:10.1109/ICDSP.2009.5201167

Barnich, O., & Droogenbroeck, M. V. (2009). Frontal-view gait recognition by intra- and inter-frame rectangle size distribution. *Pattern Recognition Letters*, *30*(9), 893–901. doi:10.1016/j.patrec.2009.03.014

Bashir, K., Xiang, T., & Gong, S. (2010). Gait recognition without subject cooperation. *Pattern Recognition Letters*, *31*(13), 2052–2060. doi:10.1016/j.patrec.2010.05.027

Bo, Y., & Wen. (2007). Gait Recognition based on DWT and SVM. *Proc. Int'l Conf. on Wavelet Analysis and Pattern Recognition 3*, (pp. 1382-1387). IEEE. doi:10.1109/ICWAPR.2007.4421650

Bobick, A. F., & Davis, J. W. (2001). The recognition of human movement using temporal templates. *IEEE Transactions on Pattern Analysis and Machine Intelligence*, *23*(3), 257–267. doi:10.1109/34.910878

Boulgouris, N. V., & Chi, Z. X. (2007). 'Gait Recognition Using Radon Transform and Linear Discriminant Analysis. *IEEE Transactions on Image Processing*, *16*(3), 731–740. doi:10.1109/TIP.2007.891157 PMID:17357733

Boulgouris, N. V., Hatzinakos, D., & Plataniotis, K. N. (2005). Gait recognition: A Challenging signal processing technology for Biometric identification. *IEEE Signal Processing Magazine*, *22*(6), 78–90. doi:10.1109/MSP.2005.1550191

Boyd, J. E., & Little, J. J. (2005). *Biometric Gait Recognition. LNCS 3161* (pp. 19–42). Berlin: Springer-Verlag.

Chen, C., Liang, J., Zhao, H., Hu, H., & Tian, J. (2009). Frame difference energy image for gait recognition with incomplete silhouettes. *Pattern Recognition Letters*, *30*(11), 977–984. doi:10.1016/j.patrec.2009.04.012

Chen, X., Fan, Wang, & Li. (2010). Automatic Gait Recognition using Kernel Principal Component Analysis. *International Conference on Biomedical Engineering and Computer Science* (pp.1 – 4). IEEE. doi:10.1109/ICBECS.2010.5462298

Cheng, Q., & Fu, B. (2008), Gait Recognition Based on Hilbert-Huang Descriptors. *Proceedings of the 7th World Congress on Intelligent Control and Automation*, (pp. 7640-7643).

Conklin, A., Dietrich, G., & Walz, D. (2004). Password-based authentication: A system perspective. *Int. Conference on System Sciences* (HICSS- 37 2004).

Courtney, J., & de Paor, A. M. (2010). Monocular Marker- Free Gait Measurement System. *IEEE Transactions on Neural Systems and Rehabilitation Engineering*, *18*(4), 453–460. doi:10.1109/TNSRE.2010.2041792 PMID:20144920

Das Choudhury, S., & Tjahjadi, T. (2012). Silhouette-based gait recognition using Procrustes shape analysis and elliptic Fourier descriptors. *Pattern Recognition*, *45*(9), 3414–3426. doi:10.1016/j.patcog.2012.02.032

Dash, M., & Liu, H. (1997). Feature Selection for Classification. *Intelligent Data Analysis*, *1*(1-4), 1–4, 131–156. doi:10.1016/S1088-467X(97)00008-5

Goffredo, M., Bouchrika, I., Carter, J. N., & Nixon, M. S. (2010). Self-calibrating view- invariant gait biometrics. *IEEE Transactions on Systems, Man, and Cybernetics*, *40*(4), 997–1008. doi:10.1109/TSMCB.2009.2031091 PMID:19884085

Han, J., & Bhanu, B. (2006). Individual recognition using gait energy image. *IEEE Transactions on Pattern Analysis and Machine Intelligence*, *28*(2), 316–322. doi:10.1109/TPAMI.2006.38 PMID:16468626

Hu, M., Wang, Y., Zhang, Z., De, D., & Little, J. J. (2013). Incremental Learning for Video-Based Gait Recognition With LBP Flow. *IEEE Transactions on Systems, Man, and Cybernetics. Part B, Cybernetics, 43*, 77–89. PMID:22692925

Hu, M., Wang, Y., Zhang, Z., & Wang, Y. (2010). Combining spatial and temporal information for gait based gender classification. *Proc. IEEE/IAPR Int. Conf. Pattern Recognition* (pp. 3679–3682). IEEE. doi:10.1109/ICPR.2010.897

Jain, A. K., Bolle, R., & Pankanti, S. (1999). *Biometrics: Personal Identication in Networked Society.* Springer. doi:10.1007/b117227

Kale, A., RajaGopalan, A.N., Cuntoor, N., & Kruger, V. (2002). Gait Based Recognition of Humans using continuous HMMs. *Proc. Int'l Conf. on Automatic Face and Gesture Recognition.* doi:10.1109/AFGR.2002.1004176

Lam, T. H. W., Cheung, K. H., & Liu, J. N. K. (2011). Gait flow image: A silhouette-based gait representation for human identification. *Pattern Recognition, 44*(4), 973–987. doi:10.1016/j.patcog.2010.10.011

Lu, H., Plataniotis, K. N., & Venetsanopoulos, A. N. (2008). A full-body layered deformable model for automatic model-based gait recognition. *EURASIP Journal on Advances in Signal Processing*, 1–13.

Lu, J., Zhang, E., & Jing, C. (2006). Gait Recognition using wavelet descriptors and independent component analysis. *Proc.of 3rd International Symposium on Neural Network* (pp. 232-237). Springer Berlin Heidelberg. doi:10.1007/11760023_34

Ma, Q., Wang, S., Nie, D., & Qiu, J. (2007). Recognizing humans based on gait moment image. *ACIS International Conference on SNPD 2*, (pp.606–610). IEEE. doi:10.1109/SNPD.2007.307

Mhatre, A., Palla, S., Chikkerur, S., & Govindaraju, V. (2005). Efficient Search and Retrieval in Biometric Databases. *SPIE Defense and Security Symposium, 5779*, 265-273.

O'Gorman, L. (2003). Comparing passwords, tokens, and biometrics for user authentication. *Proceedings of the IEEE, 91*(12), 2019–2020. doi:10.1109/JPROC.2003.819605

Phillips, P., Sarkar, S., Robledo, I., Grother, P., & Bowyer, K. (2002). Baseline Results for Challenge Problem of Human ID Using Gait Analysis. *Proc. Int'l Conf. Automatic Face and Gesture Recognition* (pp. 130-135). IEEE.

Ran, Y., Zheng, Q., Chellappa, R., & Stat, T. M. (2010). Applications of a simple characterization of human gait in surveillance. *IEEE Transactions on Systems, Man, and Cybernetics*, 1009–1019. PMID:20363680

Rocha, L., Velho, L., Cezar, P., & Carvalho, P. (2004). Motion Eecognition using Moments Analysis. *Proceedings of 17th Brazilian Symposium on Computer Graphics and Image Processing*, (354-361). doi:10.1109/SIBGRA.2004.1352981

Roy, A., Sural, S., & Mukherjee, J. (2012). Gait recognition using Pose Kinematics and Pose Energy Image. *Signal Processing, 92*(3), 780–792. doi:10.1016/j.sigpro.2011.09.022

Sarkar, S., Philips, P. J., Liu, Z., Vega, I., Grother, P., & Bowyer, K. (2006). The HumanID gait challenge problem: Data sets, performance, and analysis. *IEEE Transactions on Pattern Analysis and Machine Intelligence, 27*(2), 162–177. doi:10.1109/TPAMI.2005.39 PMID:15688555

Sharmila, D., & Kirubakaran, V. (2010). Image and Formula Based Gait Recognition Methods. *International Journal of Computer and Electrical Engineering, 2*(2), 1793–8163.

Shutter, J. D., & Nixon, M. S. (2006). Zernike velocity moments for sequence-based description of moving features. *Image and Vision Computing, 24*(4), 343–356. doi:10.1016/j.imavis.2005.12.001

Tang, Z., & Miao, Z., & Wan. (2007). *Background Subtraction Using Running Gaussian Average and Frame Difference, Entertainment Computing*. ICEC 2007, *6th International Conference*, Shanghai, China.

Wang, C., Zhang, J., Pu, J., Yuan, X., & Wang, L. (2010). Chrono Gait Image: a novel temporal template for gait recognition. *European Conference on Computer Vision, 6311*, 257–270. doi:10.1007/978-3-642-15549-9_19

Wang, L., Tan, T., Ning, H., & Hu, W. (2003). Silhouette analysis-based gait recognition for human identification. *IEEE Transactions on Pattern Analysis and Machine Intelligence, 25*(12), 1505–1518. doi:10.1109/TPAMI.2003.1251144

Winter, D. A. (2004). *Biomechanics a nd Motor Control of Human Movement* (3rd ed.). John Wiley & Sons.

Yang, X. C., Zhou, Y., Zhang, T. H., Shu, G., & Yang, J. (2008). Gait recognition based on dynamic region analysis. *Signal Processing, 88*(9), 2350–2356. doi:10.1016/j.sigpro.2008.03.006

Zhang, E., Zhao, Y., & Xiong, W. (2010). Active energy image plus 2DLPP for gait recognition. *Signal Processing, 90*(7), 2295–2302. doi:10.1016/j.sigpro.2010.01.024

Zhang, S., Yao, H., & Liu, V. (2009), *Spatial-Temporal Nonparametric Background Subtraction in Dynamic Scenes*. Multimedia and Expo ICME 2009, *IEEE International Conference*, New York, NY.

Chapter 13

Lung Disease Classification by Novel Shape–Based Feature Extraction and New Hybrid Genetic Approach:
Lung Disease Classification by Shape–Based Method

Bhuvaneswari Chandran
Annamalai University, India

P. Aruna
Annamalai University, India

D. Loganathan
Pondicherry Engineering College, India

ABSTRACT

The purpose of the chapter is to present a novel method to classify lung diseases from the computed tomography images which assist physicians in the diagnosis of lung diseases. The method is based on a new approach which combines a proposed M2 feature extraction method and a novel hybrid genetic approach with different types of classifiers. The feature extraction methods performed in this work are moment invariants, proposed multiscale filter method and proposed M2 feature extraction method. The essential features which are the results of the feature extraction technique are selected by the novel hybrid genetic algorithm feature selection algorithms. Classification is performed by the support vector machine, multilayer perceptron neural network and Bayes Net classifiers. The result obtained proves that the proposed technique is an efficient and robust method. The performance of the proposed M2 feature extraction with proposed hybrid GA and SVM classifier combination achieves maximum classification accuracy.

DOI: 10.4018/978-1-4666-9685-3.ch013

INTRODUCTION

The lung diseases are one of the major health challenges faced in the world. The lung diseases are diagnosed and treated by the physician with the use of imaging modalities like chest X-Ray, CT scans and the required medications. According to Susanstandring (2005) majority of the lung diseases fall into three major categories

1. Obstructive lung diseases such as asthma, bronchiectasis, chronic bronchitis, etc.
2. Restrictive lung diseases include sarcoidosis, amyotrophic lateral sclerosis, chronic pleural effusion, kyphoscoliosis, etc.
3. Pulmonary vascular diseases or pulmonary embolism, pulmonary artery hypertension, etc.

Mehta, P.J. (2001) discussed smoking, infections, inhaling polluted air and genetics are responsible for most lung diseases that affect any age group of people. The continued ill health in lung problem, if left untreated for a long time will lead to major problems. Computer programs are supporting doctors in diagnosing the diseases. The medical diagnostic software serves as a consultant to the physician. Computer technology can be used to detect the complexity of the disease, thus reducing the number of transience. The software system deals with medical data and knowledge domain in detecting the diseases. With regard to a limited medical staff, an automated system can significantly decrease the manual labor involved in diagnosing the lung diseases with additional care. For assisting the doctors in rapid finding of the diseases, the proposed work has been carried out in an appropriate manner

This chapter focuses on assisting the doctors to diagnose the lung diseases, by a computed approach in a more precise manner. The normal lung and diseases such as pleural effusion, emphysema, bronchitis and pneumonia are suggested in this work as these diseases require CT imaging for diagnosing and these diseases are some of the most common lung diseases which affect the human community widely. Data collection is done. Preprocessing of the images is performed by median filter and morphological smoothening. Feature extraction is done by the proposed shape based filter method, feature selection is performed by a novel hybrid feature selection method and the classification is performed by SVM, MLP and Bayes Net classifiers. The proposed feature extraction method deals with the shape based methods. The moment invariants method, proposed multiscale filter method and the combination of the both methods M^2 feature extraction are used for feature extraction. The genetic algorithm promises convergence but not optimality. The choice of stopping the genetic algorithm is not well-defined and there is no guarantee of optimality of successive runs of the GA. The proposed hybrid GA outstands well than the genetic algorithm as the search space is limited to a small area for best search and thereby top ranked features are selected. The classification accuracy, sensitivity, specificity and F-measure values are calculated for each classifier.

OBJECTIVE OF THE CHAPTER

The objective of the work is as follows

- To apply the proposed shape based feature extraction technique for extracting the features of normal lung CT images and lung diseases, namely bronchitis, emphysema, pleural effusion and pneumonia.

- To implement proposed hybrid genetic algorithm method for selecting the top ranked features for lung diseases.
- To evaluate the various classifiers for the proposed methods and to estimate the performance measures, including classification accuracy, sensitivity, specificity, etc.
- By using the proposed feature extraction and proposed feature selection methods, different classifiers are used to diagnose the lung diseases using computed tomography images.

BACKGROUND

Swarnalatha and Tripathy (2013) study presents a vital role in the significance of the analysis of an image in medical image processing field. Chowdhury et al.(2012) proposed method was put forward for classification based on Bayesian rules which makes use of image features in order to classify medical X-ray images. Shape features such as Fourier descriptor, invariant moments and Zernike moments were extracted from the image. Chowdhury et al. proposed classification algorithm obtained the accuracy rate of 82.87% for a 28-class classification problem. Lung image patch classification with automatic feature learning was dealt in Song et al.(2013) to create multi-scale feature extractors based on unsupervised learning algorithm obtaining image feature vectors by convolving feature extractors with image patches.

Zhu et al.(2011) proposed, a new image based system for classification of lung tissue patterns was. In the first stage lung images is separated using a set of thresholding, filtering and morphological operators. In the second stage, two sets of over complete wavelet filters and in the third stage the fuzzy k-Nearest Neighbor algorithm is employed to perform the pattern classification.A method was proposed in Korfiatis et al. (2009) that focused on the shape and distribution of the area of lesions in the lung CT images for the classification of three kinds of pulmonary emphysema. It calculated five features to classify the emphysema types by neural network classifier.

An algorithm was proposed by Nandakumar L (2013) that incorporated scale-space features based on Gaussian derivative filters and multi-dimensional, multi-scale features based on wavelet and contourlet transforms of the original images. The average sensitivity and specificity achieved were 94.16% and 98.68% respectively. The effectiveness and efficiency of hybridizing genetic algorithms with various techniques are available in a wide variety of hybrid genetic approaches. Chen et al. (2005) shows that hybridizing is one possible way to build a competent genetic algorithm that solves hard problems quickly, reliably and accurately without the need for any form of human intervention. Tarek et al. (2006) stated hybridization has been utilized to construct competent genetic algorithms that belong to two of the three main approaches for building competent genetic algorithms, i.e., perturbation, linkage adaptation, and probabilistic model-building. Calle et al. (2013) states hybridization is also one of the four main techniques for efficiency enhancement of genetic algorithms. Hybridization can also be used as a tool to achieve evaluation relaxation, which in turn is another main technique for efficiency enhancement.

An image classification system that is able to discriminate between normal and pathological images was presented in Markus et al.(2012). Different feature spaces for discrimination are investigated and evaluated using a support vector machine.A fast indexing method proposed by Ruizhe et al.(2010) was stated using anatomical feature classification. In our method, the brain CT scan is divided into 6 height levels along the axial direction so that slices in each level share similar anatomical structure. In this way, the indexing problem becomes a classification problem that one series of scan slices are to be classified into 6 classes. Experimental results showed this method was effective and efficient.Three soft computing techniques were used viz., fuzzy logic, neural network and genetic algorithm to design alternative control schemes for switching the advance policy firewall. The models for these control schemes were designed and simulated in MATLAB. A comparative study of the results obtained using these artificial-intelligence-based schemes was presented Kumar et al. (2009).

In this section, literature pertaining to different methods for diagnosing various lung diseases is discussed. The literature gathered so far has focused mainly on the specific methods and the results are discussed. The methodology adopted in this work is a combination of the methods that yields best results than the other methods. This study will definitely help the doctors in easy and earlier diagnosis.

METHODOLOGY

Thoracic computed tomography is an imaging method that uses X-rays to create cross-sectional pictures of the chest and upper abdomen. The lung CT images are obtained using 16 slice MX16 ^{EVO} Philips CT scanner at the radiology department of Sri Manakula Vinayagar Medical College and Hospital, Madagadipet, Puducherry. The dataset comprises normal, bronchitis, emphysema, pleural effusion and pneumonia CT lung images. These images are used as input, preprocessing is performed to obtain the enhanced image, median filter and morphological smoothening are applied in the image. The output of the preprocessed image is given as input to the feature extraction technique. The selection of the relevant features is done by the proposed hybrid feature selection method and the classifiers are used to classify the images into respective diseases. The block diagram of the proposed work is presented as follows (see Figure 1).

DATA COLLECTION

Valid information can be obtained by structured and systematic process of data collection. Once the data are collected, decisions based on that information are to be obtained. The lung CT images are obtained using 16 slice MX16 ^{EVO} Philips CT scanner at the radiology department of Sri Manakula Vinayagar Medical College and Hospital, Madagadipet, Puducherry. The dataset comprises normal, bronchitis, emphysema, pleural effusion and pneumonia CT lung images. For each dataset 200 images are taken and hence totaling about 1000 images are used as the image dataset for this research work.

The sample input CT images are represented in Figure 2: Normal lung (a_1), bronchitis (b_1), emphysema (c_1), pleural effusion (d_1) and pneumonia (e_1).

PREPROCESSING TECHNIQUES

Noise reduction is a process to remove the noise from a corrupted image and preferably keep the structures of the original image simultaneously. Preprocessing methods use a small neighborhood of a pixel in an input image to get a new brightness value in the output image. Smoothening is one of the preprocessing operations that suppress noise or other small fluctuations in the image, equivalent to the suppression of high frequencies in the frequency domain. The detection of lung diseases using CT images is to be preprocessed in order to remove noise, enhance the contrast and to correct the uneven illumination. Pre-

Figure 1. Block diagram of the proposed work

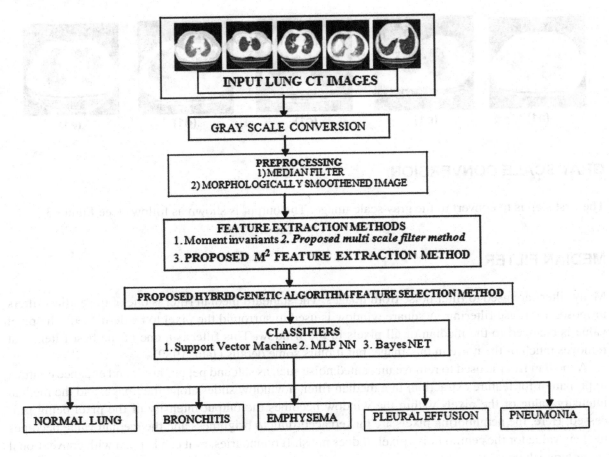

processing phase of the images is necessary to improve the quality of the images and make the feature extraction phase more reliable. The methods involved in the preprocessing are

1. Gray scale conversion
2. Median filter
3. Morphological smoothening

Figure 2. (a_1) – (e_1) Sample input images of lung CT

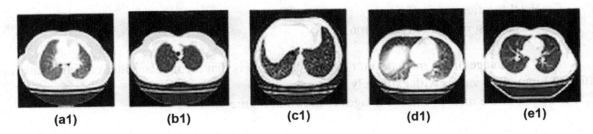

(a1)   (b1)   (c1)   (d1)   (e1)

Figure 3. (a₁) – (e₁) Gray scale images of lung CT

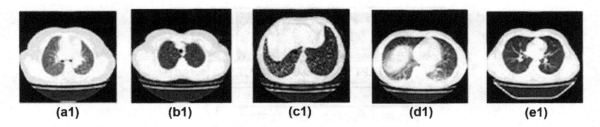

(a1)　　　(b1)　　　(c1)　　　(d1)　　　(e1)

GRAY SCALE CONVERSION

The first step is to convert to the gray scale image. The output is shown as follows (see Figure 3).

MEDIAN FILTER

Many filters are used to filter noise from images. The standard median filter is one of the earliest filters proposed for noise filtering. A square window is used to surround the pixel to be de-noised. The pixel value is changed to the median of all pixels in the window. This filter is a one of the best filters that removes much of the noise in the image, but it blurs some details (Jain, 1989) .

A median filter is used to remove unwanted noise such as salt and pepper noise and enhance contrast to prepare it for feature extraction. In a median filter, a window slides along the image, and the median intensity value of the pixels within the window becomes the output intensity of the pixel being processed. Here, the neighboring pixels are ranked according to brightness and the median value becomes the new value for the central noisy pixel. It does not shift boundaries, as it can happen with conventional smoothing filters.

The formula for the median filter is given as

$$Y\left(t\right) = median\left(\left(x(t - T\,/\,2\right), x\left(t - T_1 + 1\right), ..., x\left(t\right), ..., x\left(t + T\!\big/\!2\right)\right)\right) \tag{1}$$

where

- Y - Median filter at the moment t
- t - Size of the window of the median filter
- x - Represents the Image
- T - Pixel location
- T_1 - Pixel at first row and first column (r_1, c_1).

A major advantage of the median filter over linear filters is that the median filter can eliminate the effect of input noise values with extremely large magnitudes.

The output of the median filtered images is shown in Figure 4.

Figure 4. $(a_1) - (e_1)$ Median filtered image of lung CT

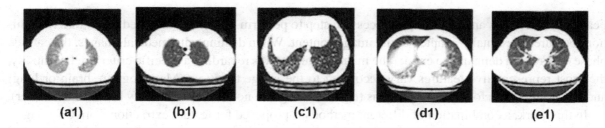

| (a1) | (b1) | (c1) | (d1) | (e1) |

MORPHOLOGICAL SMOOTHENING

Image enhancement is one of the main areas in digital image processing. The main purpose of image enhancement is to bring out details which are hidden in an image or to increase the contrast in a low contrast image.

The most general translation-invariant morphological dilation and erosion of a gray level image $f(x)$ by another image g are:

$$(f \oplus g)(x) \equiv \bigvee_{y \in \mathbb{D}} f(x - y) + g(y) \tag{2}$$

$$(f ? g)(x) \equiv \bigwedge_{y \in \mathbb{D}} f(x + y) - g(y) \tag{3}$$

If the erosion is followed by dilation is known as opening operation which suppresses the bright details smaller and eliminates small features resulting in smoother edges. Where dilation followed by erosion is closing operation that suppresses the dark details to remove the narrow gaps. By performing these operations, the images are smoothened to improve the edges. In this work, the darker details are suppressed where the dilation is performed followed by erosion. The preprocessed image is obtained by applying the median filter and morphological smoothening (see Figure 5).

Figure 5. $(a_1) - (e_1)$ Morphologically smoothened images of lung CT

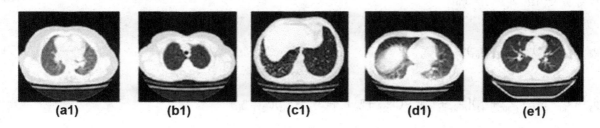

| (a1) | (b1) | (c1) | (d1) | (e1) |

FEATURE EXTRACTION METHODS

Feature extraction is an essential preprocessing step to perform classification based on pattern recognition. Features are usually adapted to the image content. When dealing with medical images, the earliest phase of a system demands to extract the main image features regarding a specific criterion. Essentially, the most representative features vary according to the image type (e.g. Mammogram, brain or lung) and according to the focus of the analysis (e.g. to distinguish nodules or to identify brain white matter).

In this work, a combination of different methods is proposed for feature extraction from CT images. The shape features are extracted by moment invariants to extract seven shape features. The proposed multiscale filter is used to extract filtered coefficient values of an image. The proposed M^2 (combination of **M**oment invariants, proposed **M**ultiscale filter method) feature extraction method results in producing the proposed feature extraction method.

MOMENT INVARIANTS

An effective shape descriptor is a key component of an image, since the shape is a fundamental property of an object. Some simple geometric features can be used to describe shapes. Usually, the simple geometric features can only discriminate shapes with large differences. Therefore, they are usually used as filters to eliminate false hits or combined with other shape descriptors to discriminate shapes. The moment invariants are one of the best methods for finding the shape features in the medical images. Moment invariants have been frequently used as features for image processing, remote sensing, shape recognition and classification. Moments can provide characteristics of an object that uniquely represent its shape. Invariant shape recognition is performed by classification in the multidimensional moment invariant feature space.

Hu derived six absolute orthogonal invariants and one skew orthogonal invariant based upon algebraic invariants, which are not only independent of position, size and orientation, but also independent of parallel projection.

$$\varphi_1 = \eta_{20} + \eta_{02} \tag{4}$$

$$\varphi_2 = (\eta_{20} - \eta_{02})^2 + 4\eta_{11}^2 \tag{5}$$

$$\varphi_3 = (\eta_{30} - 3\eta_{12})^2 + (3\eta_{21} - \mu_{03})^2 \tag{6}$$

$$\varphi_4 = (\eta_{30} + \eta_{12})^2 + (\eta_{21} + \mu_{03})^2 \tag{7}$$

$$\varphi_5 = (\eta_{30} - 3\eta_{12})^2 (\eta_{30} + \eta_{12})[(\eta_{30} + \eta_{12})^2 - (3\eta_{21} + \eta_{03})^2 + (3\eta_{21} - \eta_{03})(\eta_{21} + \eta_{03})$$

$$[3(\eta_{30} + \eta_{12})^2 - (\eta_{21} + \eta_{03})^2] \tag{8}$$

$$\varphi_6 = (\eta_{20} - \eta_{02}) [(\eta_{30} + \eta_{12})^2 - (\eta_{21} + \eta_{03})^2] + 4\eta_{11}(\eta_{30} + \eta_{12}) (\eta_{21} + \eta_{03}) \qquad (9)$$

$$\varphi_7 = (3\eta_{21} - \eta_{03})(\eta_{30} + \eta_{12}) [(\eta_{30} + \eta_{12})^2 - 3(\eta_{21} + \eta_{03})^2] - (\eta_{30} - 3\eta_{12}) (\eta_{21} + \eta_{03})$$

$$[3(\eta_{30} + \eta_{12})^2 - (\eta_{21} + \mu_{03})^2] \qquad (10)$$

The φ_1, is analogous to the moment of inertia around the image's centroid, where the pixel intensities are analogous to physical density. In this research work centroid values of the images are found. The last one, φ_7, is skew invariant, which enables it to distinguish mirror images of identical images. Image geometric transformation is a popular technique in image processing, which usually involves image translation, scaling and rotation to obtain all the possible values from the image in various orientations. The translation operator maps the position of each pixel in an input image into a new position in an output image. The scale operator is used to shrink or zoom the size of an image, that is achieved by subsampling or interpolating to the input image. The rotation operator maps the position of each pixel onto a new position by rotating it through a specified angle, which may produce non-integer coordinates.

Region moment representations interpret a normalized gray level image function as a probability density of a 2D random variable. Properties of this random variable can be described using statistical characteristics - moments. A moment of order (p + q) is dependent on scaling, translation, rotation and even on gray level transformations and is given by Amr et.al. (2010).

Moment invariants are features of the image which are calculated in terms of ordinary moments and have the property that they retain their exact values (i.e., they are invariant) when the image is shifted, scaled or rotated. Moment invariants were originally established from the relation between moments and the mathematically developed algebraic invariants (see Figure 6).

PROPOSED MULTISCALE FILTER BASED METHOD

Image filtering refers to modifying the pixels in an image based on some function of a local neighborhood of the pixels for obtaining the best features. Gaussian filter removes high frequency components from the image to low frequency components. Larger σ (standard deviation) representing the width of the Gaussian distribution removes more irrelevant details. It involves various properties such as commutative, associative, linear, shift variance and differentiation. It is also possible to use second order derivatives to extract the features. A very popular second order operator is the Laplacian operator. Laplacian does

Figure 6. (a_1) – (e_1) Output of the moment invariants

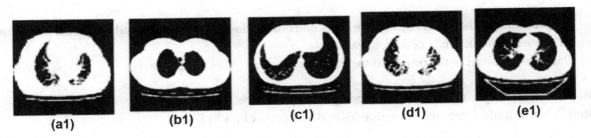

| (a1) | (b1) | (c1) | (d1) | (e1) |

Figure 7. Convolution mask of Laplacian

0	1	0
1	-4	1
0	1	0

not take out edges in any particular direction, but it takes out edges in following classification as inward mask or outward mask. The positive Laplacian operator is used to take out outward edges in an image. The discrete difference approximations are used to estimate the derivatives and represent the Laplacian operator with the convolution mask (see Figure 7).

Multiscale filters are filter banks created using Gaussian functions, where the goal is to evaluate the capability of different filter banks, based on Gaussian functions. They help to represent image features by giving the response of the image to a particular filter bank. In the proposed work, the second order Gaussian derivatives and Laplacian transform are averaged to produce the proposed multiscale filter.

The formula for the second order Gaussian derivatives is given by

$$G^2(x,y) = \frac{y^2 - \sigma_y^2}{2\pi\sigma_x\sigma_y^5} \exp\left(-\frac{x^2}{2\sigma_x^2} - \frac{y^2}{2\sigma_y^2}\right) \tag{11}$$

Laplacian transform is given by

$$LG(x,y) = \frac{(x^2 + y^2 - 2\sigma^2)}{2\pi\sigma^6} \exp\left(-\frac{x^2 + y^2}{2\sigma^2}\right) \tag{12}$$

The proposed multiscale filter can be obtained by averaging the equations, second order Gaussian derivatives (11) and Laplacian transform (12).

$$\text{Proposed Multiscale filter} = \frac{G^2(x,y) + LG(x,y)}{2} \tag{13}$$

The proposed method is a combination of second order Gaussian derivatives and Laplacian transform which results in the filtered coefficient values.

The steps involved in the proposed method are:

Step 1: Create u by v multi filters each being a m by n matrix.
Step 2: Show multi filters with magnitudes and real parts of multi filters.

Step 3: Create multiscale filter of filter size 0.25 to extract feature vector from the input image.

Step 4: Normalize to zero mean, unit variance and arrange the values.

Step 5: Calculate the median, average, standard deviation and compute the Laplacian transform of the pixels.

The second order Gaussian derivatives (with aspect-ratio equals 0.25) oriented at 0°, 45°, 90° and 135° are implemented. All the filter bank contains 16 scales. The standard deviation used for the Gaussian filter banks is equal to a quarter of the filter mask size. Each image generates minimum, maximum and average features with 39 different values of filter coefficients. Two banks are used and hence the output is 3 features x 39 filter coefficients x 2 parts of multi filter (magnitude and real) which results in 234 best filtered co-efficient values for lung CT images (see Figure 8).

PROPOSED M² FEATURE EXTRACTION METHOD

In this research work, combinations of two methods are combined to form proposed M² feature extraction method. The shape features are extracted by moment invariants. The proposed multiscale filter is used to extract filtered co-efficient values. All the features of the above methods are combined to give a novel M² (combination **M**oment invariants and **M**ultiscale filter methods) feature extraction method. The shape features are extracted by the proposed M² feature extraction method that results in best extracted features. To perform a rigorous validation with the proposed system, training and testing of the datasets are done after the feature selection process.

FEATURE SELECTION

Feature selection is a dimensionality reduction technique widely used for data mining and knowledge discovery. It also allows eliminating irrelevant features, while retaining the underlying discriminatory information. Feature selection implies less data transmission and efficient data mining. It is one of the key topics in machine learning and other related fields.

The wrapper methods utilize the classifier as a black box to score the subsets of features based on their predictive power. It uses a backward feature elimination scheme to remove insignificant features

Figure 8. Sample output screen of the proposed multiscale filter

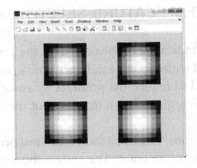
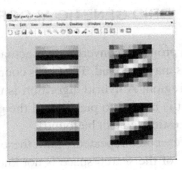

from subsets of features. In each recursive step, it ranks the features based on the amount of reduction in the objective function. It eliminates the bottom ranked feature from the results.

WRAPPER METHODS

Though many feature selection techniques are available, choice of this work depends on various filter methods, dimensionality reduction and evolutionary approaches. Univariate filter based model is performed by information gain, dimensionality reduction is done by principal component analysis, multivariate filter based model is chosen for correlation based feature selection, wrapper randomized evolutionary model is evaluated by genetic algorithm and a proposed hybrid genetic algorithm feature selection method is developed in this work.

HYBRID GENETIC ALGORITHM

Hybrid Genetic Algorithm (HGA) has received significant interest in recent years and is being increasingly used to solve real-world problems. Hybrid genetic algorithms are based on the complementary view of search methods. The authors of Mathew et al. (1996), Sastry et al. (2005), Carvalho et al. (2014), Kumar et al. (2014) discuss in their research about Genetic and other search methods can be seen as complementary tools that can be brought together to achieve an optimal goal. In these hybrids, a genetic algorithm incorporates one or more methods to improve the performance of the genetic search.

There are several ways in which a search or optimization technique can complement the genetic search. Population size is crucial in a genetic algorithm. It determines the memory size and the convergence speed in serial genetic algorithms and affects the speed of search in the case of parallel genetic algorithms. Efficient population sizing is critical for getting the most out of a fixed budget of function evaluations.

If the fitness function is excessively slow or complex to evaluate, approximation function evaluation techniques can be utilized to accelerate the search without disrupting search effectiveness. This is because genetic algorithms are robust enough to achieve convergence in the face of noise produced by the approximation process. Fitness approximation schemes replace high cost, accurate fitness evaluation with a low cost approximate fitness assignment procedure. This can be achieved either by evolutionary approximation, where the fitness of a chromosome is estimated from its parent's fitness or function approximation, where the fitness function is replaced by an alternate simpler model.

PROPOSED HYBRID GENETIC ALGORITHM FEATURE SELECTION

The schema which promises convergence is actually indicative of the regions in the search space where good chromosomes may be found. The GA is coupled with a local search mechanism to find the optimal chromosome in a region. A hybrid algorithm is used to reduce the problem by ensuring the GA runs as many times as it is needed to pick out all the good regions. With the shape of the search space, the number of regions estimated can be found.

The GA can be executed repeatedly until these regions have been found. In most practical problems, however, the shape of the search space is not known before hand. The systematic approach is then to repeat GA runs until the best chromosomes are found and starts to repeat with some regularity. GA's are not good at identifying the optimal value of a chromosome for a problem, but do very well in identifying the regions where those optima lie. Therefore, the usage of proposed hybrid GA for every ten generations, anneals the best 10% of the population.

This has the effect of moving the top chromosomes in that generation (which are the result of exponential convergence towards the best regions) to the local maximum in their region. The exploring ability of the genetic algorithm can be improved by utilizing local search to ensure fair representation of different regions of a search. The goal of the hybridization, which is the effectiveness of search, can be satisfied if a genetic algorithm and a local search method cooperates in the manner. Researchers have proposed different techniques to enable the hybrid to mix both methods wisely or at least to reduce the consequences of the improper use of the expensive local search. Modifying the parameters of the local search, such as the frequency of local search, the duration of local search, and the probability of local search can help the hybrid to strike the balance between the two search methods.

WORKING OF THE PROPOSED HYBRID GENETIC ALGORITHM

The proposed model is done to select the optimal features of the images. The working principle of the genetic algorithm is as follows:

1. **Solution Encoding:** In the feature subset selection problem, a solution is specific feature subset that can be encoded as a string of n binary digits (bits). Each feature is represented by binary digits of 1 or 0. If a bit is equal to 1, the feature is selected. Consequently, if a bit is equal to 0, the feature is not selected. For example, in the lung disease dataset if the solution is 0110010000100000 strings of 16 binary digits, it indicates that features 2, 3, 6, and 11 are selected as the feature subset.

2. **Initial Population:** The initial population is generated randomly to select a subset of variables (solutions). If the variables are all different, the subset is included in the initial population. If not, it generates again until an initial population with desired size has been created.

3. **Fitness Function:** The function is used to classify between five groups of the dataset. The error rate of the classification will be calculated using a 10 fold cross-validation. The fitness function is the final error rate obtained. The subset of variables with the lowest error rate will be selected.

4. **Selection:** Selection is a process to select the parent chromosome from the population to reproduce the next generation. In this work, the roulette wheel selection is chosen where the fittest individuals have a higher chance of being selected than weaker ones.

5. **Crossover:** The crossover function used in this work is crossover scattered. It creates a random binary vector and selects the genes where the vector is a 1 from the first parent, and the genes where the vector is a 0 from the second parent and combines the genes to form the child. Two point crossover with crossover rate of 0.7 is used. In addition, the crossover function is set to ensure that it does not return the repeated variables.

6. **Mutation:** Same as crossover, the mutation is set to ensure that it does not return the repeated variables. Mutation uniform is used, where the algorithm selects a fraction of an individual for mutation, where each entry has a probability rate of being mutated. Next, the algorithm replaces each selected entry by a random number selected uniformly from the range for that entry. The mutation rate is set at 0.01.

7. **Stopping Criteria:** The stopping criteria used in this study are the number of generations and RMSE. The number of generation is set at 500 and the RMSE is 0.001, whichever occur first for the GA to stop.

The steps for creating new generation are

- Initialize mut_prob, cross_prob, pop_size, elitism, delta, epsilon, max_generation.
- For the populations find fitness, sum_fitness, ave_fitness.
- Sort the fitness and rearrange the population according to their fitness.
- Return the values best_fitness, best_features and search_fitness from the equally spaced pointers find the crossover and mutation and create the next generation.

The top ranked features are selected by the proposed hybrid genetic algorithm and fed into classifiers for classifying in to respective dataset.

ADVANTAGES OF THE PROPOSED WORK

- A local 3D greedy search is initiated for finding optimal solutions after the first iteration by using the random parameter.
- The usage of proposed hybrid GA for every ten generations, anneals the best 10% of the population for finding the top ranked features.

CLASSIFIERS

The top ranked features are classified using the SVM, MLP and Bayes Net classifiers. The classification accuracy, sensitivity, specificity and F-measure values are calculated for each classifier.

SVM CLASSIFIER

Support Vector Machine (SVM) is a classification and regression prediction tool, that uses machine learning theory to maximize predictive accuracy while automatically avoiding over-fit to the data. Support Vector machine uses the hypothesis space of a linear function in a high dimensional feature space, trained with a learning algorithm from optimization theory that implements a learning bias derived from statistical learning theory was proposed by Jakkula.V (2012). SVM uses pixel maps as input. It gives an accuracy comparable to sophisticated neural networks with elaborate features in a handwriting recognition task. It is also being used for many applications such as handwriting analysis, phase analysis and so forth, especially for pattern classification and regression based applications (see Figure 9).

The SVM is developed by Vapnik and colleagues at Bell laboratories with further algorithm improvements by others. For a binary problem the training data points are $\{x_i, y_i\}$, $i=1,...,l$, $y_i \in \{-1, 1\}$, $x_i \in R^d$.

Figure 9. Representation of SVM

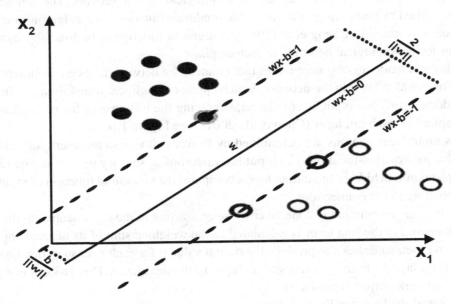

For the linearly separable case, the support vector algorithm simply looks for the separating hyperplane with the largest margin. This can be formulated as follows

$$X_i \cdot w + b \geq +1 \ for \ y_i = +1$$
$$X_i \cdot w + b \leq -1 \ for \ y_i = -1$$

(14)

These can be combined into one set of inequalities:

$$y_i(X_i \cdot w + b) - 1 \geq 0 \ \forall i$$

(15)

An important property of the SVM classifier, called sparseness, is a number of the resulting Lagrange multipliers, α_i, equal to zero. As such, the sum in the resulting classifier which should only be taken over all nonzero α_i values, i.e. support values, instead of all data points Luts et al(2010). The corresponding vectors x_i are referred to as the support vectors. These data points are located close to the decision boundary and contribute to the construction of the separating hyperplane (Priya,2014).

MULTILAYER PERCEPTRON NEURAL NETWORK CLASSIFIER

The MLP is a layered feed-forward network with a direct acyclic graph as shown in Figure.11. Each node represents MLP artificial neuron, and every directed arc represents a connection between two neurons and MLP signal flow direction. Labels used with arcs in graph denote the MLP's synaptic connections strengths, also called weights. Each MLP layer consists of specific neurons, each connected with neurons of following layer to replicate synaptic connections of biological Neural Network. The biological neuron's functions are modified by computing a differentiable nonlinear function (like a sigmoid) for MLP's each artificial neuron was stated in Cheng et al.(1999). A sigmoid function is biologically motivated, as it tries to account for the biological neurons' refractory phase.

The input layer is made up of source nodes that connect the network to its environment. The second layer has only one hidden layer in the network, which applies a nonlinear transformation from the input layer to the hidden layer. The output layer is linear, supplying the response of the network to the activation pattern applied to the input layer (Chen et al., 2001) (see Figure 10).

The MLP's input layer neurons are determined by features chosen to represent relevant patterns in feature space for pattern classification. The input layer neurons as sensory units compute identity function, $y = x$. Each neuron in hidden and output layers computes the sigmoidal function of input and weight values corresponding to the connections.

In this network, the calculation is done layer by layer, starting at the layer nearest to the inputs. The s value of each neuron in the first layer is calculated as the weighted sum of its neurons inputs. The activation function f then squashes s to produce the output value o for each neuron in that layer. Once the set of outputs for a layer is found, it serves as an input to the next layer. This process is repeated until the final set of network output is produced.

This is expressed mathematically as follows:

$$s_j = \sum_{i=1}^{n} x_i V_{ij} \tag{16}$$

Figure 10. Representation of a 2-layer MLP

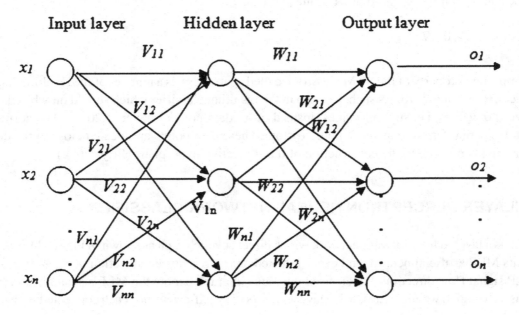

$$o_n = f(s_j) = \frac{1}{(1 + \exp(-s_j))} \tag{17}$$

where

- x_i : i^{th} element of the input pattern
- V_{ij}: weight from i^{th} input to j^{th} neuron in the hidden layer
- s_j : activation value of the jth hidden neuron

The MLP output layer neurons are determined by possible pattern classes to be dealt with, for problems of interest. The class label of output neuron producing highest output value determines the input pattern class supplied to MLP. The output of the hidden layer is given as an input to the output layer.

In this work, the number of features is equal to the number of input neurons. For example, in the proposed hybrid genetic algorithm method the number of input neuron is 27. The number of neurons in the hidden layer is two third of the number of neurons in the input layer. The Sigmoidal activation function with the initial random weights between 0 and 1 are used and the bias value is set to zero. The number of classes constituted the number of neurons in the output layer. The output will result in five classes of labels namely normal lung, bronchitis, emphysema, pleural effusion and pneumonia.

In MLP algorithm, different structures are considered for example, in the proposed M^3 feature extraction with proposed hybrid genetic algorithm the number of inputs is 27, so the number of neurons in the input layer is 27. After considering different number of neurons in the hidden layers like 14, 18 and 20 the optimal structure is found in the 18 number of neurons in the hidden layer (i.e.,) two third of the number of input. The number of output is the five classes namely normal lung, bronchitis, emphysema, pleural effusion and pneumonia.

BAYES NET CLASSIFIER

A Bayesian Network (BN) can be used to compute the conditional probability of one node, given values assigned to the other nodes hence, a BN can be used as a classifier that gives the posterior probability distribution of the classification node given the values of other attributes. When learning Bayesian networks from dataset, nodes are used to represent dataset attributes (Beniwal et.al., 2001).

There are two ways to view a BN each suggesting a particular approach to learning. First a BN is a structure that encodes the joint distribution of the attributes. Second, the BN structure encodes a group of conditional independence relationships among the nodes, according to the concept of d-separation . This suggests learning the BN structure by identifying the conditional independence relationships among the nodes. These algorithms are referred as computational intelligence based algorithms or constraint-based algorithms.

A Bayesian network defines a unique joint probability distribution over X given by

$$P_B(X_1, ..., X_n) = \prod_{i=1}^{n} \theta_{X_i | \pi_{X_i}} \tag{18}$$

The set of all Bayesian networks with n variables is given by B_n. Informally, a Bayesian network encodes the independence assumptions over the component random variables of X. An edge (i, j) in E represents a direct dependency of Xj to Xi. Moreover Xi is independent of its non-descendants given its parents $\prod_{Xi}$ in G.

A *Bayesian network classifier* is a Bayesian network where $X = (X_1,..., X_n:C)$ where

- Variables $X_1.....Xn$ are called *attributes*
- C is called the *class variable*.
- Moreover, the graph structure G is such that the class variable has no parents, that is, $\prod_C = \varnothing$ and all attributes have at least the class variable as parent, that is, $C \in \prod_{Xi}$.

The corresponding classifier is defined as $\arg\max_C P_B(C \mid X_1,..., X_n)$.

Bayes Nets or Bayesian networks are graphical representation of probabilistic relationships among a set of random variables. A Bayesian network is an annotated directed acyclic graph (DAG) G that encodes a joint probability distribution over X. The nodes of the graph correspond to the random variables. The links of the graph correspond to the direct influence from one variable to the other. If there is a directed link from variable A to variable B, variable A will be a parent of variable B. Each node is annotated with a conditional probability distribution (CPD) that represents a link, where A denotes the parents. The pair (G, CPD) encodes the joint distribution. Recursive function to determine the number of possible DAGs that contain n nodes is given by

$$f(n) = \sum_{i=1}^{n} (-1)^{i+1} c_i^n 2^{i(n-i)} f(n-i) \tag{19}$$

One way to construct Bayesian networks is from domain knowledge. There are three main steps to construct a Bayesian network by domain knowledge

1. Determine the number of the variables in the interested domain.
2. Determine the direct influence relationships among variables in the domain.
3. Determine the conditional probabilities given the structure of the Bayesian networks from step 2.

It is a combination of the Bayes network and decision tree based method.

RESULTS AND DISCUSSIONS

This section presents the details of the results obtained from the proposed feature extraction and selection method with classifiers. The result reveals that the promising output is obtained by the proposed method with SVM classifier.

The research work is performed in the Intel (R) core (TM) i5 processor - 2410M CPU @ 2.30 GHz speed with memory 4.00 GB. The MATLAB version R2010a is used to develop the proposed work.

PERFORMANCE MEASURES

The following terminologies are used as performance indicators:

Classification Accuracy: The number of cases correctly classified

$$Classification\ Accuracy = \frac{TP + TN}{TP + FP + TN + FN} \qquad (20)$$

where

- **True Positive (TP):** Positive cases that are correctly identified in a dataset.
- **False Positive (FP):** Negative cases that are incorrectly classified as positive in a dataset.
- **True Negative (TN):** Negative cases that are correctly identified in a dataset.
- **False Negative (FN):** Negatives cases that are incorrectly classified as negative in a dataset.
  Sensitivity: Measures the proportion of actual positives which are correctly identified as such.

$$Sensitivity = \frac{TP}{(FP + TN)} \qquad (21)$$

Specificity: Measures the proportion of negatives which are correctly identified as such.

$$Specificity = \frac{TN}{(FP + TN)} \qquad (22)$$

F-Measure: Defined as a harmonic mean of Precision (P) and Recall (R).

$$F - measure = 2 * \frac{precision * recall}{precision + recall} \qquad (23)$$

where

- Precision (P) is the proportion of the predicted positive cases that are correct.
- Recall (R) is the proportion of positive cases that are correctly identified.

F-measures are commonly used in tasks where it is important to retrieve elements belonging to a particular class correctly without including too many elements of other classes.

Performance Measures of Moment Invariants

The results of the performance measures of moment invariants are presented as follows (see Table 1).

The classification accuracy of moment invariants are presented in Table 1. The SVM classifier gives classification accuracy of 88.9%, 84.4% for MLP and 72.6% for Bayes Net classifier. The sensitivity of moment invariants using various classifiers is observed. For SVM classifier, the sensitivity is 88.56%, MLP gives 85.31%, Bayes Net gives 73.11%. It is observed that the maximum sensitivity for moment invariants is obtained by SVM classifier. The specificity of moment invariants using various classifiers is observed.For SVM classifier, the specificity is 89.17%, MLP gives 86.44% and Bayes Net gives 78.51% (see Figure 11).

The classification accuracy, sensitivity and specificity of moment invariants. The results of the SVM classifier are 88.9%, 88.56%, 89.17% and 88.16% respectively.

It is observed that the precision value of moment invariants using SVM classifier is 89.22%, MLP classifier is 85.16% and Bayes Net is 73.12%. The recall value of moment invariants using SVM clas-

Table 1. Performance measures of moment invariants

Classifiers	Classification Accuracy (%)	Sensitivity (%)	Specificity (%)
MLP	84.4	85.31	86.44
Bayes Net	72.6	73.11	78.51
SVM	**88.9**	**88.56**	**89.17**

Figure 11. Performance measures of moment invariants

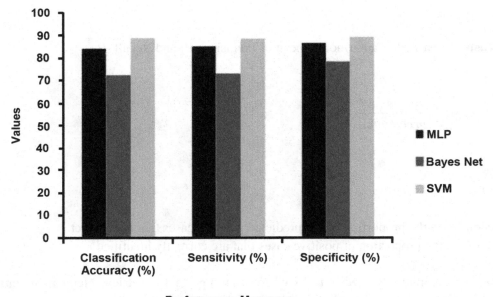

sifier is 87.14%, MLP classifier is 84.11% and Bayes Net classifier is 73.34%. The F-measure obtained by SVM classifier is 88.56%, MLP classifier is 84.34% and Bayes Net is 72.43%.

It is observed from the results of classification accuracy, sensitivity, specificity, precision, recall and F-measure values that the moment invariants with SVM classifier is performing better than the other classifiers.

Performance Measures of the Proposed Multiscale Filter Method

The classification accuracy of the proposed multiscale filter is presented. The sample true positive, true negative, false positive, false negative values for the proposed multiscale filter for the emphysema disease are presented in Table 2.

Table 2 infers true positive, true negative, false positive and false negative values for the emphysema disease calculated for hybrid genetic algorithm method.

From the true positive, true negative, false positive, false negative values, the classification accuracy for the proposed multiscale filter method is calculated. The SVM classifier achieves satisfactory results when compared with other classifiers such as MLP and Bayes Net.

Table 3 shows the classification accuracy of the proposed multiscale filter method. The features are reduced using proposed HGA feature selection method. Different classifiers like MLP, Bayes Net and SVM classifier are used to classify the lung diseases. The proposed HGA feature selection is 91.67% for MLP classifier and 87.43% for Bayes Net classifier. The classification accuracy of SVM classifier is 92.75%. The sensitivity of the multiscale filter with proposed hybrid feature selection using various classifiers is observed. The SVM classifier gives the sensitivity of 93.12%, MLP classifier gives the sensitivity of 92.12% and Bayes Net classifier gives the sensitivity of 88.14%. The maximum sensitivity value is obtained by SVM classifier (see Figure 12).

From Table 3, the specificity of SVM with the proposed HGA feature selection is observed. The maximum specificity value of 92.11% is obtained by SVM classifier. The maximum precision, recall value of proposed multiscale filter feature extraction technique with the proposed hybrid genetic algorithm using SVM is 94.01%, 93.00% respectively. The F-measure of multiscale filter with HGA feature selection is 93.21% for SVM classifier, 92.36% for MLP classifier and 87.43% for Bayes Net classifier.

Table 2. Proposed multiscale filter method with hybrid genetic algorithm for emphysema disease

Classifiers	True Positive	True Negative	False Positive	False Negative
MLP	186	730	14	70
Bayes Net	178	696	22	104
SVM	**192**	**742**	**8**	**58**

Table 3. Performance measures of the proposed multiscale filter

HGA Feature Selection Method	MLP (%)	Bayes Net (%)	SVM (%)
Classification Accuracy	91.67	87.43	**92.75**
Sensitivity	92.12	88.14	**93.12**
Specificity	92.14	88.14	**92.11**
F-measure	92.36	87.43	**93.21**

Figure 12. Performance measures of proposed multiscale filter

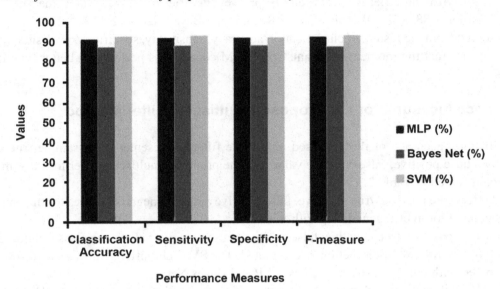

Performance Measures of the Proposed M² Feature Extraction Method

The performance of the various methods has been discussed so far. The classification accuracy of the proposed M² feature extraction method is presented as follows (see Table 4).

The results ensure that the proposed M² feature extraction method with proposed hybrid genetic algorithm feature selection and SVM classifier results in *94.21%* of classification accuracy. The true positive, true negative, false positive, false negative values for all methods are found. The sensitivity, specificity, F-measure of the proposed method is 93.55%, 93.16%, 94.21% respectively. The proposed method performs better than the other methods (see Figure 13).

In this work, different types of classifiers are used. Multilayer perceptron neural networks use the soft computing technique. Bayes Net classifier deals with probability and distance based techniques.

Support vector machine classifier uses classification and regression methodology. SVM outperforms better than the other available classifiers in terms of true positive, true negative, false positive, false negative, classification accuracy, sensitivity, specificity, precision, recall and F-measure values.

This study classifies the five datasets, four different lung diseases and normal lung images by the proposed M² feature extraction, proposed hybrid genetic algorithm feature selection method by using various classifiers. This combination of work is not available in the literature Thus, the proposed method

Table 4. Performance measures of the proposed M² feature extraction method

HGA Feature Selection Method	MLP (%)	Bayes Net (%)	SVM (%)
Classification Accuracy	92.11	88.53	**94.82**
Sensitivity	92.14	89.14	**93.55**
Specificity	92.05	88.34	**93.16**
F-measure	92.45	86.23	**94.21**

Figure 13. Performance measures of proposed M^2 feature extraction method

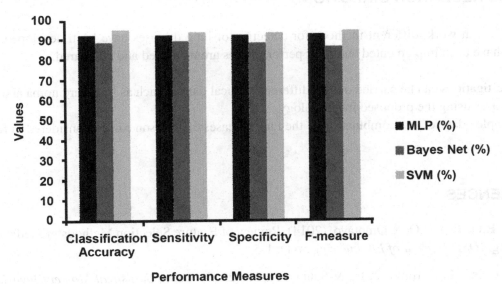

is performing better than the other available literatures. These types of lung diseases are common among human beings, and this automated system will be useful for the medical community to assist the physicians in diagnosing the lung diseases in an effective manner.

CONCLUSION

Computer aided diagnosis methods are developed at the present time to diagnose the disease well in advance and quicker manner. multiscale filter method and M^3 feature extraction method are developed for the feature extraction methods. A novel hybrid genetic algorithm feature selection method is proposed to select the top ranked features. Performance analysis of various classifiers is done in terms of true positive, true negative, false positive, false negative, sensitivity, specificity, precision, recall and F-measure. The moment invariant method is used to extract the shape features that returns moments value and the proposed multiscale filter is used to extract filtered co-efficient values using second order Gaussian derivatives and Laplacian transform. The proposed M^2 feature extraction method is proposed to combine the shape features of moments and proposed multiscale filter so as to extort all the essential features of a lung CT image. In this work, feature selection model using a hybrid genetic algorithm is proposed. Classification is undertaken through support vector machine, MLP and Bayes Net. The testing and training of the dataset are done using the 10 fold cross validation method where all the dataset is trained and tested. The performance of various methods is calculated and the results show that the proposed M^3 feature extraction method with proposed hybrid genetic algorithm feature selection and classification by the support vector machine gives **94.82%** of classification accuracy. The sensitivity, specificity, F-measure of the proposed method are 93.55%, 93.16%, 94.21% respectively.

FUTURE RESEARCH DIRECTIONS

In this research work, different methods for detection of lung diseases have been developed. All the methods have been implemented and their performances are measured and compared.

- Investigations can be carried out for different medical dataset such as lung carcinoma and chronic diseases using the proposed methodology.
- Complex dataset i.e., combination of the lung diseases of a person can be considered in future.

REFERENCES

Adegoke, B.O., Ola, B.O, & Omotayo. (2014). Review of Feature Selection Methods in Medical Image Processing. *IOSR Journal of Engineering, 4*(1), 1-5.

Amr, I., Amin, M., Kafrawy, P. E., & Sauber, A. M. (2010). *Using Statistical Moment Invariantsand Entropy in Image Retrieval*. arXiv preprint arXiv: 1002.2193

Beniwal, S., & Arora, J. (2012). Classification and feature selection techniques in data mining. *International Journal of Engineering Research and Technology., 1*(6), 1–6.

Calle-Alonso, F., Perez, C.J., Arias-Nicolás, J.P., & Martín, J. (2013). Computer-aided diagnosis system: A Bayesian hybrid classification method. *Computer Methods and Programs in Biomedicine, 112*(1), 104-113.

Chen, J., & Greiner, R. (2001). Learning bayesian belief network classifiers. In Proceedings of Advances in Artificial Intelligence Algorithms and System (pp. 141-151). Springer Berlin Heidelberg.

Chen, Y., & Goldberg, D. (2005). Convergence time for the linkage learning genetic algorithms. *Journal of Evolutionary Computation, 13*(3), 279-302.

Cheng, J., & Greiner, R. (1999). Comparing Bayesian network classifiers. In *Proceedings of Fifteenth Conference on Uncertainty in Artificial Intelligence.* (pp. 101-108). Morgan Kaufmann Publishers.

Chowdhury, M. S., Das, & Kundu, M.K. (2012). Effective Classification of Radiographic Medical Images Using LS-SVM and NSCT based Retrieval System Constraints. In *Proceedings of 5th International Conference on Computers and Devices for Communication* (pp. 1-4).

De Carvalho Filho, A. O., De Sampaio, W. B., Silva, A. C., de Paiva, A. C., Nunes, R. A., & Gattass, M. (2014). Automatic detection of solitary lung nodules using quality threshold clustering, genetic algorithm and diversity index. *Artificial Intelligence in Medicine, 60*(3), 165–177. doi:10.1016/j.artmed.2013.11.002 PMID:24332156

Gonzalez & Woods. (2008). Digital Image Processing. Pearson Prentice Hall.

Jain, A. K. (1989). *Fundamentals of Digital Image Processing* (1st ed.). Prentice Hall of India.

Jakkula, V. (2012). *Tutorial on support vector machine (SVM)*. School of EECS. Washington State University.

Korfiatis, P., Karahaliou, A., & Costaridou, L. (2009). Automated vessel tree segmentation: challenges in computer aided quantification of diffuse parenchyma lung diseases In *Proceeding of 9th IEEE International Conference on Information Technology and Applications in Biomedicine*, (pp. 1-4). IEEE. doi:10.1109/ITAB.2009.5394323

Kumar, P., & Mahajan, A. (2009). Soft computing techniques for the control of an active power filter. *IEEE Transactions on Power Delivery*, 2(1), 452–461. doi:10.1109/TPWRD.2008.2005881

Kumar, & Kumar. (2014). A Detailed Review of Feature Extraction in Image Processing Systems. In *Proceeding of Fourth International Conference on Advanced Computing and Communication Technologies* (pp.5-12). Academic Press.

Kuruvilla, & Gunavathi. (2014). Lung cancer classification using neural networks for CT images. *Computer Methods and Programs in Biomedicine, 113*(1), 202–209.

Li-dong, F., & Yi-fei, Z. (2010). Medical Image Retrieval and Classification Based on Morphological Shape Feature. In *Proceedings of IEEE 3rd International Conference on Intelligent Networks and Intelligent Systems*. (pp. 116-119). IEEE.

Liu, Li., Tan, Pang, Lim, Lee, … Zhang. (2010). Fast traumatic brain injury CT slice indexing via anatomical feature classification. In *Proceeding of 17th IEEE International Conference on Image Processing*, (pp.4377-4380).

Luts, J., Ojeda, F., Van de Plas, R., De Moor, B., Van Huffel, S., & Suykens, J. A. (2010). A tutorial on support vector machine-based methods for classification problems in chemometrics. *Analytica Chimica Acta, 665*(2), 129–145. doi:10.1016/j.aca.2010.03.030 PMID:20417323

Markus, B. (2012). Texture feature ranking with relevance learning to classify interstitial lung disease patterns. *Artificial Intelligence in Medicine, 56*(2), 91–97. doi:10.1016/j.artmed.2012.07.001 PMID:23010586

Mathew, T. V. (1996). *Genetic Algorithm. In Lecture notes* (pp. 1–15). Mumbai: Indian Institute of Technology.

Mehta, P. J. (2001). *Practiced medicine* (19th ed.). The National Book Depot.

Melanie, M. (1999). An introduction to genetic algorithms. MIT Press.

Nandakumar, L. (2013) A novel algorithm for spirometric signal processing and classification by evolutionary approach and its implementation on an ARM embedded platform In *Proceedings of IEEE International Conference on Control Communication and Computing*, (pp. 384-387). doi:10.1109/ICCC.2013.6731684

Priya, R., & Aruna, P. (2014). Automated Diagnosis Of Age-Related Macular Degeneration Using Machine Learning Techniques. *International Journal of Computer Applications in Technology, 49*(2), 157–165. doi:10.1504/IJCAT.2014.060527

Sastry, K., Goldberg, D., & Kendall, G. (2005). Genetic algorithms- In Search Methodologies. Springer US.

Song, Y., Ca, W., Zhou, Y., & Feng, D. (2013). Feature-based Image Patch Approximation for Lung Tissue Classification. *IEEE Transactions on Medical Imaging, 32*(4), 814–818. PMID:23340591

SusanStandring. (2005). *Gray's Anatomy The Anatomical Basis of Clinical Practice* (39th ed.). Elsevier.

Swarnalatha, P., & Tripathy, B. K. (2013). A novel fuzzy, c-means approach with a bit plane algorithm for classification of medical images. In *Proceedings of IEEE International Conference on Emerging Trends in Computing, Communication and Nanotechnology* (pp. 360-365). doi:10.1109/ICE-CCN.2013.6528524

Tarek, A., El-Mihoub, A. A. Hopgood, L. N., & Batters, A. (2006). Hybrid Genetic Algorithms: A Review. *Engineering Letters, 13*(2), 1–12.

Vo, K. T., & Sowmya, A. (2011). Multiscale sparse representation of high-resolution computed tomography (HRCT) lung images for diffuse lung disease classification. In *Proceedings of 18th IEEE International Conference on Image Processing (ICIP)* (pp. 441-444). IEEE. doi:10.1109/ICIP.2011.6116545

Zhu, X., Yang, X., Zhou, Q., Wang, L., Yuan, F., & Bian, Z. (2011). A Wavelet Multiscale De-Noising Algorithm Based on Radon Transform. *Measurement Science & Technology, 22*(2), 1–26.

Chapter 14
Fingerprint Iris Palmprint Multimodal Biometric Watermarking System Using Genetic Algorithm-Based Bacterial Foraging Optimization Algorithm

S. Anu H. Nair
Annamalai University, India

P. Aruna
Annamalai University, India

ABSTRACT

With the wide spread utilization of Biometric identification systems, establishing the authenticity of biometric data itself has emerged as an important issue. In this chapter, a novel approach for creating a multimodal biometric system has been suggested. The multimodal biometric system is implemented using the different fusion schemes such as Average Fusion, Minimum Fusion, Maximum Fusion, Principal Component Analysis Fusion, Discrete Wavelet Transform Fusion, Stationary Wavelet Transform Fusion, Intensity Hue Saturation Fusion, Laplacian Gradient Fusion, Pyramid Gradient Fusion and Sparse Representation Fusion. In modality extraction level, the information extracted from different modalities is stored in vectors on the basis of their modality. These are then blended to produce a joint template which is the basis for the watermarking system. The fused image is applied as input along with the cover image to the Genetic Algorithm based Bacterial Foraging Optimization Algorithm watermarking system. The standard images are used as cover images and performance was compared.

DOI: 10.4018/978-1-4666-9685-3.ch014

INTRODUCTION

Digital watermarking is the technology of embedding information (i.e., watermark or host image) into the multimedia data (such as image, audio, video, and text), called cover image. It is realized by embedding data that is invisible to the human visual system into a host image. Hence, the term digital image watermarking is a procedure by which watermark data is covered inside a host image which imposes imperceptible changes to the picture. Watermarking techniques have been used in multimodal biometric systems for the purpose of protecting and authenticating biometric data and enhancing accuracy of identification. A multimodal biometric system combines two or more biometric data recognition results such as a combination of a subject's fingerprint, face, iris and voice. This increases the reliability of personal identification system that discriminates between an authorized person and a fraudulent person.

Multimodal biometric system has addressed some issues related to unimodal such as, (a) Non-universality or insufficient population coverage (reduce failure to enroll rate which increases population coverage). (b) It becomes more and more unmanageable for an impostor to imitate multiple biometric traits of a legitimately enrolled individual. (c) Multimodal-biometric systems effectively address the problem of noisy data (illness affecting voice, scar affecting fingerprint).

In this chapter, a novel approach for creating a multimodal biometric system has been proposed. The multimodal biometric system is implemented using the different fusion schemes such as Average Fusion, Minimum Fusion, Maximum Fusion, PCA Fusion, DWT Fusion, SWT Fusion, IHS Fusion, Laplacian Gradient Fusion, Pyramid Gradient Fusion and Sparse Representation Fusion to improve the performance of the system. In feature extraction level, the information extracted from different modalities is stored in vectors on the basis of their modality. These modalities are then blended to produce a joint template which is the basis for the watermarking system. Fusion at feature extraction level generates a homogeneous template for fingerprint, iris and palmprint features. The fused image is applied as input along with the cover image to the GA based BFOA watermarking system.

RELATED WORK

Jing-Ming Guo et.al(2014) proposed a fingerprint classification method where types of singular points and the number of each type of point are chosen as features. Kai Caoet.al (2013) designed an orientation diffusion model for fingerprint extraction where corepoints and ridgeline flow are used. Ayman Mohammad Bahaa-Eldin (2013) created a novel minutiae based fingerprint matching system which creates a feature vector template from the extracted core points and ridges. Kamlesh Tiwariet.al (2013) modeled a palmprint based recognition system which uses texture and dominant orientation pixels as features. XiumeiGuo(2014) identified a palmprint recognition method which uses blanket dimension for extracting image texture information. Feng Yueet.al (2014) presented a typical palmprint identification system which constructed a pattern from the orientation and response features. O. Niboucheet.al (2013) designed a new palmprint matching system based on the extraction of feature points identified by the intersection of creases and lines. Jing Liet.al (2013) proposed a competent representation method which can be used for classification. Anne M.P et.al(2013) created a model that fused voice and iris biometric features. This model acted as a new representation of existing biometric data. Norman Pohet.al (2013) proposed user specific and selective fusion strategy for an enrolled user. Mohd Shahrimie et.al(2014) identified a new geometrical feature width centroid contour distance for finger geometry biometric. Zengxi Huanget.al

(2013) developed a face and ear biometric system which uses a feature weighing scheme called Sparse Coding error ratio.Meng Ding et.al (2013)proposed the fusion method based on a compressive sensing theory which contains over complete dictionary, an algorithm for sparse vector approximation and fusion rule. J.Aravinth et.al(2012) identified the feature extraction techniques for three modalities viz. fingerprint, iris and face. The extracted data is stored as a template which can be fused using density based score level fusion. SumitShekharet.al (2013) proposed a multimodal sparse representation method, which understands the test data by a sparse linear combination of training data, while restricting the observations from different modalities of the test subject to share their sparse representations. Vidhi Khanduja et.al (2013) demonstrated a novel method for watermarking relational databases for recognition and validation of ownership based on the secure embedding of blind and multi-bit watermarks using Bacterial Foraging Optimization Algorithm (BFOA). Riya Mary Thomas(2013) provided an outline of bacterial Foraging optimization Algorithm (BFOA) and its intermediated operations in grid scheduling. Vipul Sharma et.al (2012)presented an application based review of variants of BFOA that have come up with faster convergence with higher accuracy and will be useful for new researchers exploring its use in their research problems.

PROPOSED WORK

The proposed work describes the feature extraction of multimodal biometric images such as, fingerprint, palmprint, and iris. The extracted information is fused together using Average Fusion, Minimum Fusion, Maximum Fusion, PCA Fusion, DWT Fusion, SWT Fusion, IHS Fusion, Laplacian Gradient Fusion, Pyramid Gradient Fusion and Sparse Representation Fusion. The best fused template is then watermarked into a host image using GA based BFOA algorithm and extracted further.

Figure 1. Proposed model

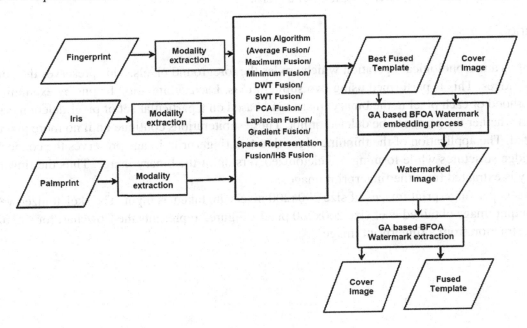

BIOMETRIC MODALITY EXTRACTION

In this chapter fingerprint, iris and palmprint modalities are extracted individually. The processes are explained below.

Fingerprint Modality Extraction

Fingerprint identification is also known as dactyloskopy or also hand identification is the process of comparing the two examples of friction ridge skin impression from human fingers.

Pre-Processing

Image enhancement techniques are used to refine a given image so that the desired features become easier to perceive for the human visual system or more likely to be detected by automated image analysis system. Enhancement algorithms are used to reduce image noise and increase the contrast of the region of interest. The histogram - equalization method usually enhances the global contrast of the image, especially when the usable data of the image are represented by close contrast values. Through this adjustment, the intensities can be better distributed on the histogram. This allows areas of lower local contrast to obtain a greater contrast. Histogram equalization achieves this by effectively spreading out the most frequent intensity values.

Binarisation

This is a process of converting gray level image into a binary image. This improves the contrast between ridges in a fingerprint image. The binarisation process involves examining the gray-level value of each pixel in the enhanced image, and, if the value is greater than the global threshold, then the pixel value is set to a binary value one; otherwise, it is set to zero.

Thinning

Thinning is a morphological operation which erodes the foreground pixels. This preserves the connectivity of ridges. This is performed using two subiterations. Each subiteration begins by examining the neighborhood of each pixel in the binary image, and based on a particular set of pixel-deletion criteria, it checks whether the pixel can be deleted or not. These subiterations continue until no more pixels can be deleted. The application of the thinning algorithm to a fingerprint image preserves the connectivity of the ridge structures while forming a skeletonized version of the binary image. Thus the fingerprint modality is extracted from the fingerprint image.

In this paper fingerprint images of size 200x200 pixels are taken as input. The skeletonized version of the output image obtained is of size 200x200 pixels. Figure2 represents the flowchart for singularity region extraction from a fingerprint image

Figure 2. Flow diagram of fingerprint modality extraction

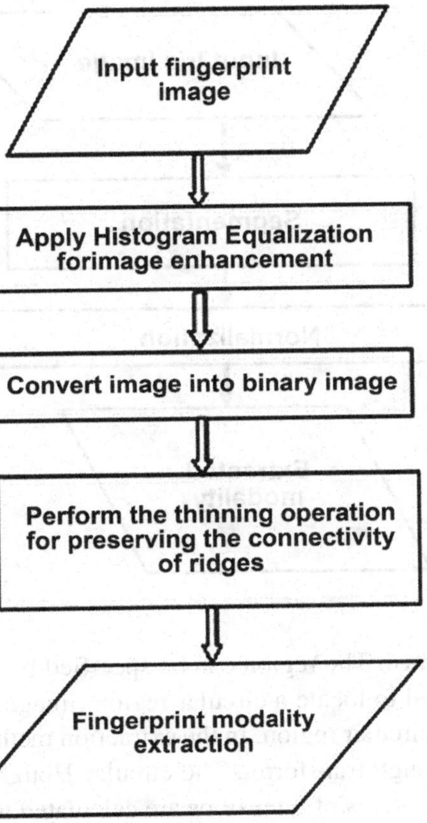

Iris Modality Extraction

Iris recognition is an automated method of biometric identification that uses mathematical pattern-recognition techniques on video images of the irises of an individual's eyes, whose complex random patterns are unique and can be seen from some distance.

Many millions of individuals in several nations about the globe have been enrolled in iris recognition systems, for convenience purposes such as passport-free automated border-crossings, and some national ID systems based on this technology are being deployed. A central advantage of iris recognition, besides its speed of matching and its extreme opposition to false matches, is the stableness of the iris as an inner, protected, yet externally visible organ of the optic.

Segmentation

The iris segmentation is the initial stage of iris extraction. This stage isolates the actual iris region from an image. In this research work, segmentation of iris is the first phase of iris extraction. Here, the actual

Figure 3. Flow diagram of iris modality extraction

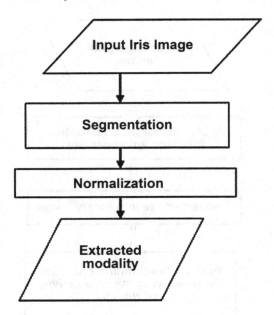

region is separated from the image. The region can be specified by 2 circles. The occlusion by eyelids and eyelashes is to be eliminated to locate a circular region. Imaging quality plays a major role in the success of the extraction of the circular region. In the extraction method, biometric shapes like lines and circles, are identified by the Hough transform.. The circular Hough transform extracts the centre and radius iris region. The first derivatives of intensities are calculated to produce an edge map.

The definition of a circle is

$$x^2 + y^2 = r^2 \tag{1}$$

where, x and y are the coordinates of centre and r is the radius.

The definition of Hough Transform is

$$H\left(x_c, y_c, r\right) = \sum_{j=1}^{n} h(x_j, y_j, x_c, y_c, r) \tag{2}$$

where

$$h(x_j, y_j, x_c, y_c, r) = \begin{cases} 1, if \ g\left(xj, yj, xc, yc, r\right) \\ 0, Otherwise \end{cases}$$

$$y_i = \ centre\left(y\right) + \left[innerradius * sin\left(\theta\right)\right]$$

with

$$g\left(x_j, y_j, x_c, y_c, r\right) = \left(x_j - x_c\right)^2 + \left(y_j - y_c\right)^2 - r^2$$

The linear Hough transform fits a line to the upper and lower eyelid. The second line which is horizontal is drawn. The first line intersects with the second at the edge of the iris. This allows maximum isolation of regions of eyelids. Canny edge detection is utilized to produce an edge map.

Normalization

Generally, normalization is a linear procedure and it is implemented to negate the variable's impact on the information. Here, the output of the segmentation process provides a polar form of the iris modality. The iris modality is preferred to be a rectangular form for the fusion of images. Therefore, normalization appears to be a conversion process for this research work.

The rectangular coordinates are obtained using equations (3) to (8).

$$x_i = centre(x) + \left[innerradius * cos(\theta)\right] \tag{3}$$

$$y_i = centre(y) + \left[innerradius * sin(\theta)\right] \tag{4}$$

$$x_o = centre(x + \left[outerradius * cos(\theta)\right] \tag{5}$$

$$y_o = centre(y) + \left[outerradius * sin(\theta)\right] \tag{6}$$

$$x = x_i + \left[(x_o - x_i) * Y\right] / m \tag{7}$$

$$y = x_i + \left[(x_o - x_i) * Y\right] / m \tag{8}$$

where

- $\theta = (2 * \pi * X)/n$
- x_i, y_i - Midpoint of the inner circle,
- x_o, y_o - Midpoint of outer circle,
- (x, y) - Midpoint of iris image,

Equations (3) and (4) denote the calculation of the inner circle and equations (5) and .6) depict calculation of the outer circle.

In this chapter iris images of size 150x200 are taken as input. The rectangular iris image obtained is of size 64x512.

Palmprint Modality Extraction

Palmprint has its own advantages comparing with other methods of biometrics. Palmprint is hardly affected by age (the problem of age is the main problem for face recognition). Palmprint contains more information and can use low resolution devices (in comparison with fingerprinting). Palmprint cannot make harm to the health of people, and many people prefer palmprinting to iris recognition based on this very reason. Palmprinting is a rapidly developed method of biometrics. Palmprints contain more information than fingerprint, so they are more distinctive; palmprint capture devices are much cheaper than iris devices. Palmprints also contain additional distinctive features, such as principal lines and wrinkles, which can be extracted from low-resolution images; a highly accurate biometrics system can be built by combining all features of palms, such as palm geometry, ridge and valley features, and principal lines and wrinkles, etc. It is for these reasons that palmprint recognition has recently attracted an increasing amount of attention from researchers.

Pre-Processing

Histogram-equalization method usually increases the global contrast of the image, especially, when the usable data of the image is represented by close contrast values. Through this adjustment, the intensities can be better distributed on the histogram. This allows for areas of lower local contrast to gain a higher contrast. Histogram equalization accomplishes this by effectively spreading out the most frequent intensity values.

Binarisation

This is a process of converting gray level image into a binary image. This improves the contrast between ridges in an image. The binarisation process involves examining the gray-level value of each pixel in the enhanced images and converting them to either 0 or 1.

Cropping and Convolving

The image is subjected to cropping process for the selection of the region of interest. The obtained image is convolved with the Sobel operator.

The Sobel Operator is [12 1 0 0 0 -1 -2 -1].

The resultant would be the extracted modality of palmprint. In this paper palmprint images of size 640 x 480 pixels are taken as input. The skeletonized version of the output image obtained is of size 233 x 287 pixels.

MULTIMODAL BIOMETRIC SYSTEMS

A multimodalbiometric system is one in which multiple categories of data are collected and used for various purposes, including but not limited to fusion:

- Selection, in which the best or most useful data is retained for use, while the other data is ignored or discarded. Selection is frequently based on quality metrics.
- Validation, in which some of the data is used to check the integrity of the other data.
- Fusion, which is based on combining data at various levels.

Biometric fusion is generally classified in terms of both categories and levels.

The categories define what inputs or processes are being used for fusion; the levels define how the fusion performed.

Categories of Fusion

The types of data or methods of processing used constitute the categories of fusion:

- **Multi-sample:** Fusion of multiple samples (images) acquired from the same source, such as multiple images of a single fingerprint, images of the same face, or recordings of a speaker.
- **Multi- instance:** Fusion of multiple instances of the same type of biometric, such as fingerprints from multiple fingers, or images of both irises.
- **Multimodal:** Fusion of multiple types (or modalities) of biometrics, such as a combination of a subject's fingerprints, face, irises, and voice.
- **Metadata:** Fusion of biometric inputs with other information, such as measures of sample quality, or demographic information such as gender, height, or age. Demographic information is sometimes described as soft biometrics.
- **Multialgorithm:** Fusion of multiple methods of processing for each individual sample. In practice, this usually means the use of multiple matchers, but can also apply to multiple methods of feature extraction.

Image Fusion Techniques

Image fusion is collecting image data from a variety of image information on the same target after the image processing and computing technology, to maximize the extraction of useful information from each channel, and finally integrated into high-quality images to improve image information utilization and the computer interpretation accuracy and reliability. Algorithm will often combine with some evaluation information values such as image fusion, average entropy value, standard deviation, and average gradient, which reflect the tiny details in the image contrast and texture variation, and also reflect the sharpness of the image.

Image Fusion (also called synthesis) is the process of combining two or more distinct entities into a new whole entity. Image fusion is the process of merging relevant information from two or more images into a single image. The resulting image will be more informative than any of the input images. Data fusion is a formal framework in which are expressed means and tools for the alliance of data originating from different sources. It aims at obtaining information of greater quality; the exact definition of greater quality will depend upon the application.

Figure 5. Fusion of fingerprint, iris and palmprint modalities

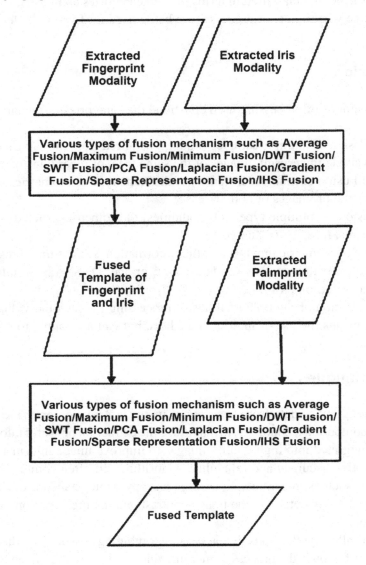

Various Image Fusion Methods

There are various methods that have been developed to perform image fusion. Some well-known image fusion methods are listed below:

1. Simple Image Fusion
    a. Simple Average
    b. Simple Maximum/minimum
    c. Intensity-hue-saturation (IHS) transform based fusion
    d. Principal component analysis (PCA) based fusion

2. Multi scale transform based fusion
   a. Pyramid method
      i. Laplacian Pyramid
      ii. Gradient pyramid
   b. Wavelet transforms
      i. Discrete wavelet transforms (DWT)
      ii. Stationary wavelet transforms
3. Sparse Representation Fusion

Implementation of Image Fusion Algorithms

To obtain a homogenous template, fusion process is used. The modalities are extracted individually and combined together using fusion methods explained below.

Simple Average

Generally, areas in focus have greater intensity. This procedure acquires infocus areas. In this research work, the pixel value P (i, j) in each modality is chosen and summed. This total is then halved to get the average (Deepak Kumar Sahu et al 2012). The pixels of the output image are assigned the average values. Equation (9) gives the same. This is iterated for all pixel values.

$$K\left(i, j\right) = \left\{ X\left(i, j\right) + Y\left(i, j\right) \right\} / 2 \tag{9}$$

where X (i, j) and Y (i, j) are two input images.

Select Maximum

An infocus image has greater pixel values. Therefore, this procedure chooses the greatest value to obtain infocus areas. The pixel values of input images are compared and the greatest value is assigned to the output image (Deepak Kumar Sahu et al 2012). In this research work, the input images are extracted biometric modalities.

$$F(i, j) = \sum_{i=1}^{m} \sum_{j=1}^{n} \max(A(i, j), B(i, j)) \tag{10}$$

where A (i, j) and B (i, j) are different biometric modalities and F (i, j) is the fused image

Select Minimum

This algorithm chooses the lowest pixel values among the two input images. The output image is assigned the lower values. (Deepak Kumar Sahu et al 2012). In this research work, the input images are extracted biometric modalities.

$$F(i, j) = \sum_{i=1}^{m} \sum_{j=1}^{n} \min(A(i, j), B(i, j)) \tag{11}$$

where $A(i, j)$ and $B(i, j)$ are different biometric modalities and $F(i, j)$ is the fused image

Intensity Hue Saturation Fusion (IHS Fusion)

The IHS fusion technique is utilized in image fusion to endeavor the complementary nature of MS images. First red, green and blue space is changed into IHS space using IHS fusion strategy and then the intensity band is replaced by the image. This is converted into RGB space. Similarly the above process is applied for the other input image which are added together resulting in the fused image.

In this research work, the IHS fusion for every pixel can be modeled by the following process. The steps are as follows:

$$\begin{bmatrix} I \\ v_1 \\ v_2 \end{bmatrix} = \begin{bmatrix} \dfrac{1}{3} & \dfrac{1}{3} & \dfrac{1}{3} \\ \dfrac{-\sqrt{2}}{6} & \dfrac{-\sqrt{2}}{6} & \dfrac{2\sqrt{2}}{6} \\ \dfrac{1}{\sqrt{2}} & \dfrac{-1}{\sqrt{2}} & 0 \end{bmatrix} \begin{bmatrix} R \\ G \\ B \end{bmatrix} \tag{12}$$

$$H = \tan^{-1}\left(\frac{v_2}{v_1}\right) \tag{13}$$

$$S = \sqrt{v_1^2 + v_2^2} \tag{14}$$

The corresponding inverse transform is defined as

$$v_1 = S \cos\left(H\right) \tag{15}$$

$$v_2 = S \sin(H) \tag{16}$$

$$\begin{bmatrix} R' \\ G' \\ B' \end{bmatrix} = \begin{bmatrix} \dfrac{1}{\sqrt{3}} & \dfrac{-1}{\sqrt{6}} & \dfrac{-1}{\sqrt{2}} \\ \dfrac{1}{\sqrt{3}} & \dfrac{-1}{\sqrt{6}} & \dfrac{1}{\sqrt{2}} \\ \dfrac{1}{\sqrt{3}} & \dfrac{-1}{\sqrt{6}} & 0 \end{bmatrix} \begin{bmatrix} I \\ v_1 \\ v_2 \end{bmatrix} \tag{17}$$

Equations (12) to (17) state that the fused image can be obtained from the original image by adding the values of the IHS images. That is, the IHS method is efficiently implemented by this process. This algorithm is called the fast IHS fusion algorithm.

Principal Component Analysis (PCA)

PCA is a mathematical tool which changes various correlated variables into a number of uncorrelated variables. The applications of PCA are in areas like image compression and image classification. It calculates a compact and optimal description of the data set. The first principal component represents for as much of the variance in the data as possible and each succeeding component represents for as much of the remaining variance as possible. (Deepak Kumar Sahu, 2012).

First principal component is taken to be along the direction with the maximum variance. The second principal component is constrained to lie in the subspace perpendicular of the first. Within this subspace, this component points the direction of maximum variance. The third principal component is taken in the maximum variance direction in the subspace perpendicular to the first two and so on. Its basis vectors rely on the data set. In this research work, the biometric modalities are given as input images. The stepwise description of the PCA algorithm for fusion is explained below.

Step 1: The column vectors are generated from the input image matrices.

Step 2: The mean along each column is calculated which is subtracted from each column. The column vectors form a matrix X.

Step 3: The covariance matrix of the column vectors found in step 1 is calculated.

$$C = XX^T \tag{18}$$

Step 4: The diagonal elements of the 2x2 covariance vector contain the variance of each column vector with itself, respectively.

Step 5: The Eigen values and the Eigen vectors of the covariance matrix are computed.

Step 6: Normalization of the column vector with the larger Eigen value is implemented by dividing each element with the mean of the Eigen vector.

Suppose $(x,y)^T$ is a vector of the eigenvectors of the image A and B, the weight value of image A and image B are

$$\omega_A = \frac{x}{x+y} \tag{19}$$

$$\omega_B = \frac{y}{x+y} \tag{20}$$

Step 7: The normalized Eigen vectors act as the weights that are multiplied with every pixel values of the input images respectively.

Step 8: The total value of the two matrices calculated in step 7 is the fused image. Then, the fusion is accomplished using a weighted average as

$$I_F = \omega_A I_A + \omega_B I_B \tag{21}$$

where I_F is the fused image and I_A and I_B represent images A and B respectively.

Pyramid Fusion Algorithm

An image pyramid comprises of a set of low pass or band pass copies of an image, each copy depicting pattern information on a different scale. The size of the pyramid is halved in the preceding level and the higher levels will focus on the lower spatial frequencies. The basic idea is to create the pyramid transform of the fused image from the pyramid transforms of the source images and then the fused image is retrieved by applying inverse pyramid transform (Sukhpreet Singh, 2014).

Every pyramid transform comprises of three major stages:

1. **Decomposition:** Implement decomposition where a pyramid is produced subsequently at every level of the fusion. The 3 steps are
    a. The biometric modality images are subjected to Low pass filtering using W = [1/16, 4/16, 6/16, 4/16, 1/16].
    b. The low pass filtered images obtained are subtracted and the pyramid is created.
    c. The input images are decimated by dividing the number of rows and columns by 2.
2. Formation of the initial image for recomposition.
    a. The input images are merged after the process of decomposition.
    b. The output of this process is the input for the process of recomposition.
    Step 3.   Recomposition
    a. I/P image is undecimated.
    b. The image is undecimated by copying every row and column and convolves the undecimated image with the filter vector's transpose.
    c. The output of the step (ii) is merged with the pyramid formed at the level of decomposition.
    d. The output is the fused image.

Laplacian Pyramids Image Fusion

Laplacian pyramid is a set of band pass images, in which each is a band pass filtered copy of its antecedent. The difference between low pass images at subsequent levels of a guassian pyramid is calculated. In Laplacian fusion approach the Laplacian pyramids for input images are utilized. In this research work, the input images are extracted biometric modalities (N. Indhumadhi, 2011).

Gradient Pyramid Image Fusion

A gradient pyramid is acquired by implementing a set of 4 directional gradient filters (horizontal, vertical and 2 diagonal) to the Gaussian pyramid at every level. Merging of 4 directional gradient pyramids results in a combined pyramid in each level. The combined gradient is used instead of Laplacian pyramid. In this research work, the inputs are extracted biometric modalities. (N. Indhumadhi, 2011).

Discrete Wavelet Transform (DWT)

The wavelets-based methodology is suitable for performing fusion tasks for the following reasons: - (1) Appropriate for different image resolutions. (2) Preserves image formation even during image decomposition. (3) Data is preserved even though IDWT is applied (Meng Ding et al 2013).

$$y[n] = (x * g)[n] = \sum_{k=-\infty}^{\infty} x[k] g[n-k] \tag{22}$$

$$y_{low}[n] = \sum_{k=-\infty}^{\infty} x[k] g[2n-k] \tag{23}$$

$$y_{high}[n] = \sum_{k=-\infty}^{\infty} x[k] h[2n-k] \tag{24}$$

where x is the DWT signal, g is the low pass filter, h is the high pass filter.

The 2×2 Haar matrix associated with the Haar wavelet is $\begin{bmatrix} 1 & 1 \\ 1 & -1 \end{bmatrix}$.

The wavelet transform transforms the image into low-high, high-low, high-high spatial frequency bands at different scales and the low-low band at the coarsest scale which is demonstrated in Figure 4.11. The average image data is present in LL band. Directional data is available in other bands because spatial orientation causes directional data. Edges or lines are depicted in higher bands of the image. In this research work, the basic steps performed in image fusion given are as follows:

- Perform independent wavelet decomposition of the two images until level 2.
- Fusion of two input image's DWT coefficients take place by calculating appropriate coefficient's average.
- The fused image is procured by applying inverse DWT.

Stationary Wavelet Transform

This method fuses two biometric modality images by the means of Stationary Wavelet Transform (DSWT or SWT). The Stationary Wavelet Transform is a wavelet transform procedure which is modeled to overcome the absence of translation invariance of the Discrete Wavelet Transform. Translation Invariance is accomplished by eliminating the down samplers and the up samplers in the DWT and up-sampling

Figure 4. Flow diagram for Palmprint extraction modality

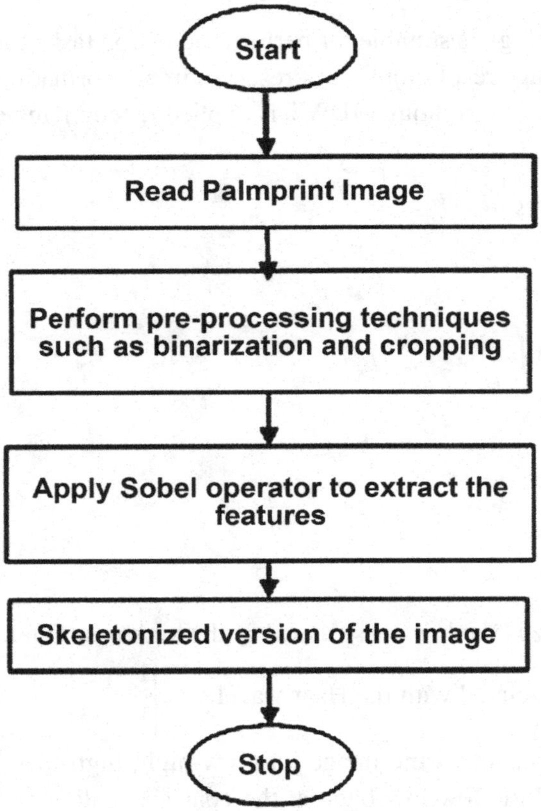

the filter coefficients by a component of *2(j-1)* in the *j*th level of the procedure. In summary, the SWT method can be described as follows

- Decompose the two source images utilizing SWT at one level resulting in three details subbands and one approximation subband (HL, LH, HH and LL bands).
- Then the approximate parts are averaged.
- Choose the absolute values of horizontal details of the image and subtract the second part of image from first.

$$D = (abs (H1L2)-abs (H2L2))>=0 \qquad (25)$$

For fused horizontal part perform element wise multiplication of D and horizontal detail of first image and then subtract another horizontal detail of second image multiplied by logical not of D from first.

- Find D for vertical and diagonal parts and acquire the fused vertical and details of the image.
- Fused image is retrieved by applying ISWT.

Figure 6. Sparse representation method

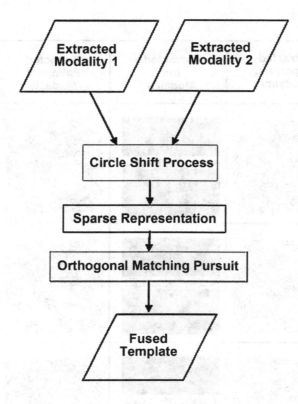

Sparse Representation Fusion

The extracted features are fed as the input of the sparse fusion methodology. The input features were converted into matrix format to perform sparse representation (S.Anu H Nair, 2013).

The algorithm is as follows:

Step 1: The images are fed as input.
Step 2: The values of input image 1 and input image 2 are convolved.
Step 3: The resultant matrix is converted into sparse representation by squeezing out the zero elements.
Step 4: The sparse representation is further transformed into an image using orthogonal matching pursuit.

The fused template is obtained.

Figure 7. Output of different Fusion Methods like Average, Maximum, Minimum, Intensity Hue Saturation Fusion and PCA Fusion

Fusion Method	Extracted Fingerprint Modality	Extracted Iris Modality	Extracted Palmprint Modality	Fused Image
Average Fusion			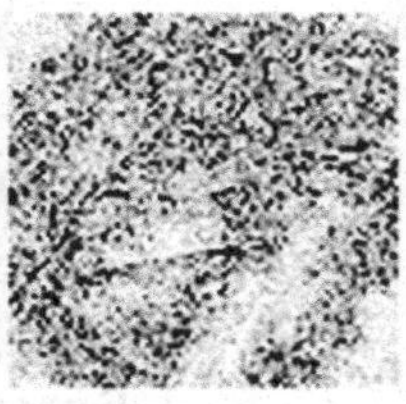	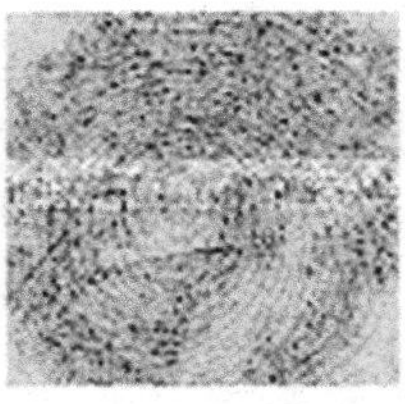
Maximum Fusion		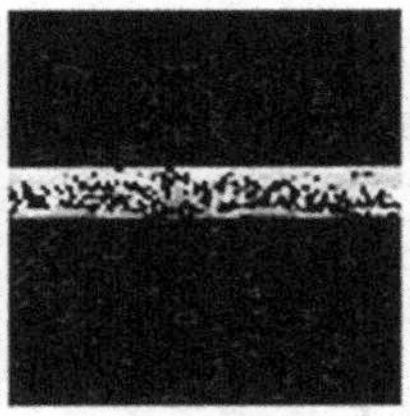	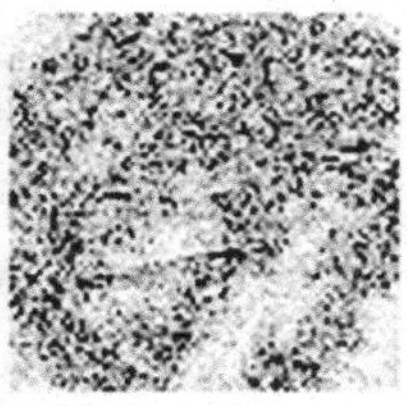	
Minimum Fusion			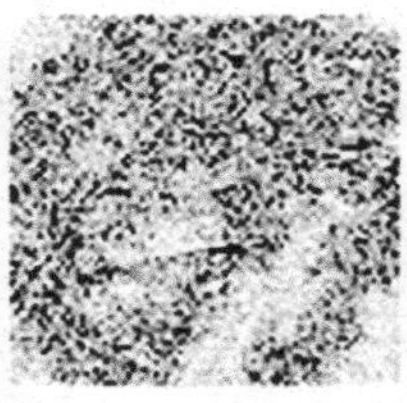	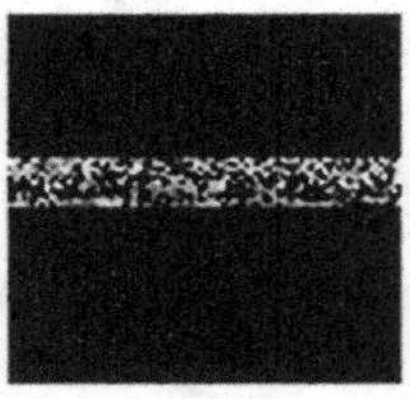
Intensity Gue Saturation Fusion			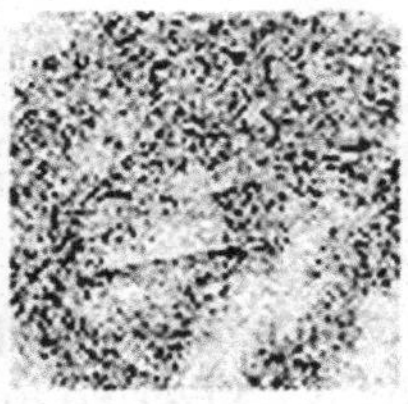	
PCA Fusion			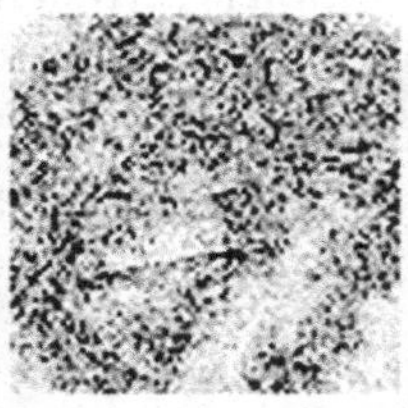	

Figure 8. Output of different Fusion Methods like Laplacian Pyramid, Gradient Pyramid, DWT, SWT and Sparse Representation Fusion

Fusion Method	Extracted Fingerprint Modality	Extracted Iris modality	Extracted Palmprint Modality	Fused Image
Laplacian Pyramid fusion			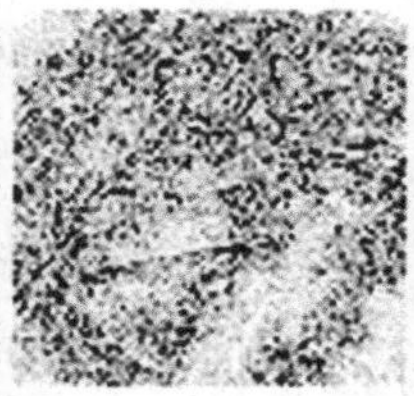	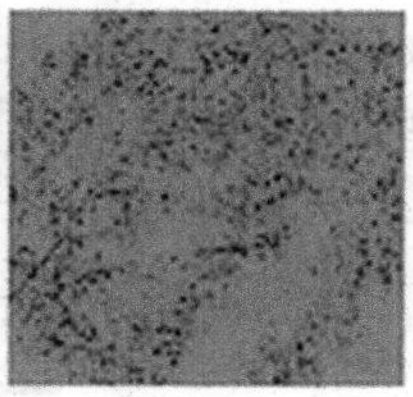
Gradient Pyramid fusion			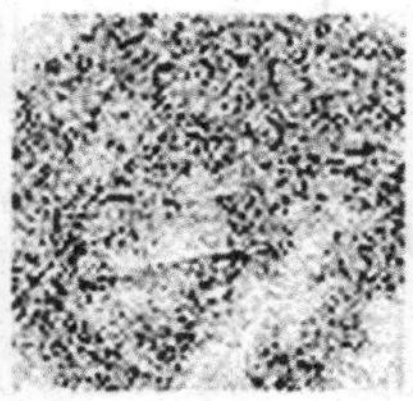	
Discrete Wavelet Transform (DWT)			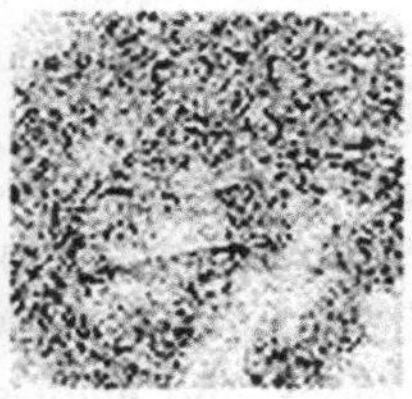	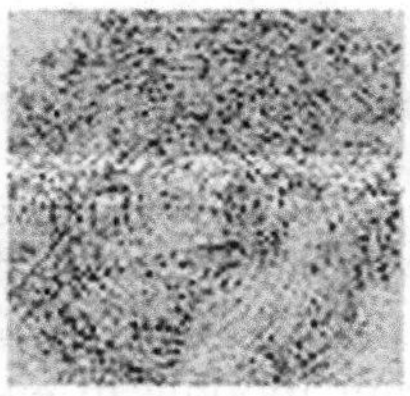
Stationary Wavelet Transform			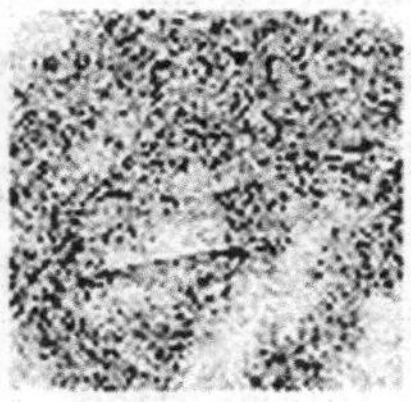	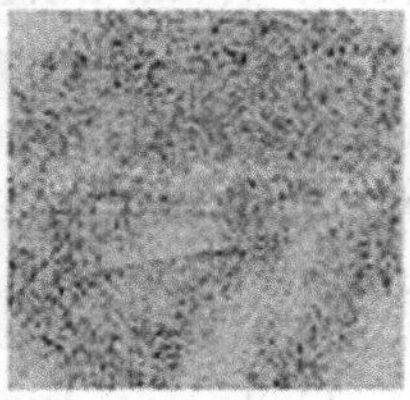
Sparse representation Fusion			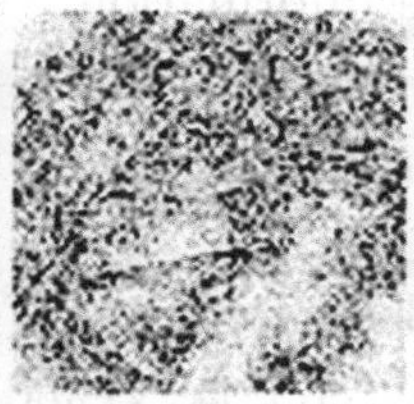	

PERFORMANCE METRICS USED

To analyze and find the best fused image some performance metrics are used. This identifies the best fused template which is fed as input to the watermarking model.

Xydeas and Petrovic Metric - Q$_{abf}$

A normalized weighted performance metric of a given process p that fuses A and B into F, is given as (Nedeljko Cvejic, 2006)

$$Q^{AB/F} = \frac{\sum_{m=1}^{M} \sum_{n=1}^{N} \left[Q^{AF}(m,n) w^{A}(m,n) + Q^{BF}(m,n) w^{B}(m,n) \right]}{\sum_{m=1}^{M} \sum_{n=1}^{N} \left[w^{A}(m,n) + w^{B}(m,n) \right]} \tag{26}$$

where *A, B* and *F* represent the input and fused images respectively. The definition of Q^{AF} and Q^{BF} are same and given as

$$Q^{AF}(m,n) = Q_g^{AF}(m,n) Q_\alpha^{AF}(m,n) \tag{27}$$

where Q^{*F}_g, Q^{*F}_α are the edge strength and orientation values at location *(m, n)* for images A and B. The dynamic range for $Q^{AB/F}$ is [0, 1] and it should be close to one for better fusion.

Visual Information Fidelity (VIF)

VIF first decomposes the natural image into several sub-bands and parses each sub-band into blocks (Yu Han, 2013). Then, VIF measures the visual information by computing mutual information in the different models in each block and each sub-band. Finally, the image quality value is measured by integrating visual information for all the blocks and all the sub-bands. This relies on modeling of the statistical image source, the image distortion channel and the human visual distortion channel. Image quality assessment is done based on information fidelity where the channel imposes fundamental limits on how much information could flow from the source (the reference image), through the channel (the image distortion process) to the receiver (the human observer).

$$VIF = \frac{\text{Distorted Image Information}}{\text{Reference Image Information}} \tag{28}$$

Fusion Mutual Information

Mutual Information calculates the degree of dependence of two images (Manjusha Deshmukh et al 2011). If the joint histogram between I$_1$ (x, y) and I$_f$ (x, y) is defined as $h_{I_1 I_f}(i, j)$ and I$_2$(x, y) and I$_f$ (x, y) is defined as $h_{I_2 I_f}(i, j)$ then Fusion Mutual Information (FMI) is given as

$$FMI = MI_{I_1 I_f} + MI_{I_2 I_f} \tag{29}$$

where

$$MI_{I_{1}I_{f}} = \sum_{i=1}^{M}\sum_{j=1}^{N} h_{I_{1}I_{f}}(i,j) \log_2 \log_2 \left(\frac{h_{I_{1}I_{f}}(i,j)}{h_{I_{1}}(i,j) h_{I_{f}}(i,j)} \right) \tag{30}$$

$$MI_{I_{2}I_{f}} = \sum_{i=1}^{M}\sum_{j=1}^{N} h_{I_{2}I_{f}}(i,j) \log_2 \log_2 \left(\frac{h_{I_{2}I_{f}}(i,j)}{h_{I_{2}}(i,j) h_{I_{f}}(i,j)} \right) \tag{31}$$

Average Gradient

The Average Gradient is applied to measure the detailed information in the images.

$$g = \frac{1}{(M-1)(N-1)} \sum_{x=1}^{M-1}\sum_{y=1}^{N-1} \sqrt{\left(\frac{\partial f(x,y)}{\partial x}\right)^2 + \left(\frac{\partial f(x,y)}{\partial y}\right)^2} \tag{32}$$

where M and N are the rows and colums of images.

Higher the average gradient describes better the fused template.

Entropy

Entropy is defined as amount of information contained in a signal. The entropy of the image can be evaluated as

$$H = - \sum P(i) * log_2 \left(P(d_i) \right) \tag{33}$$

where G is the number of possible gray levels, $P(d_i)$ is probability of occurrence of a particular gray level d_i. If entropy of fused image is higher than parent image then it indicates that the fused image contains more information

The results shown in Table 1 indicate that the DWT fusion method gave better results than other fusion algorithms. This fused template is fed into the watermarking model along with the cover image.

INTRODUCTION TO WATERMARKING

Digital watermarking is the technology of embedding information (watermark or host signal) into the multimedia data (such as image, audio, video, and text), called cover signal, in order to produce watermarked signal for use in certain applications such as copyright protection, content authentication,

Table 1. Quality of fingerprint, iris and palmprint fused template

Metrics Fusion Methods	Qabf	VIF	MI	Average Gradient	Entropy
DWT Fusion	**0.44**	**0.32**	**4.01**	**30.10**	**7.66**
IHS Fusion	0.42	0.31	3.91	28.06	7.15
PCA Fusion	0.35	0.23	3.84	15.16	7.14
Average Fusion	0.35	0.22	3.08	15.15	6.76
SWT Fusion	0.27	0.10	2.74	13.01	5.70
Minimum Fusion	0.22	0.10	1.88	9.61	4.02
Maximum Fusion	0.21	0.09	1.82	8.89	3.97
Sparse representation Fusion	0.12	0.07	1.32	5.60	2.80
Laplacian Pyramid Fusion	0.09	0.04	0.54	4.94	2.49
Gradient Pyramid Fusion	0.03	0.00	0.49	24.94	0.57

copy protection, broadcast monitoring, and so on. It is realized by embedding data that is invisible to the human visual system into a host image. Thus digital image watermarking is the process by which watermark data is hidden within a host image imposing imperceptible changes to the image. The root of watermarking as an information hiding technique can be traced from ancient Greece as steganography .The application of watermarking ranges from copyright protection, file tracking and monitoring. Watermarking techniques have been used in multimodal biometric systems for the purpose of protecting and authenticating biometric data and enhancing accuracy of recognition. A multimodal biometric system combines two or more biometric data which increases the reliability of personal recognition systems that discriminate between an authorized person and a fraudulent person. The applications of Multimodal biometric systems are law enforcement, e-commerce, smart cards, passports and visa etc.

In optimization of a design, the design objective could be simple to minimize the cost of production or to maximize the efficiency of production. An optimization algorithm is a procedure which is executed iteratively by comparing various solutions till an optimum or a satisfactory solution is found. With the advent of computers, optimization has become a part of computer-aided design activities.

Genetic Algorithm Based Bacterial Foraging Algorithm

The novel approach of combining GA with the Bacterial foraging algorithm is proposed. Here the crossover and mutation operations are involved to perform reproduction operation in bacterial foraging. The other operations are similar to bacterial foraging operation.

The procedure utilized in this work is as follows (Algorithm 1).

Algorithm 1 identifies the best block and the watermark is embedded in it. The extraction is the reverse process of the above process.

Figure 9. Optimized watermarking method

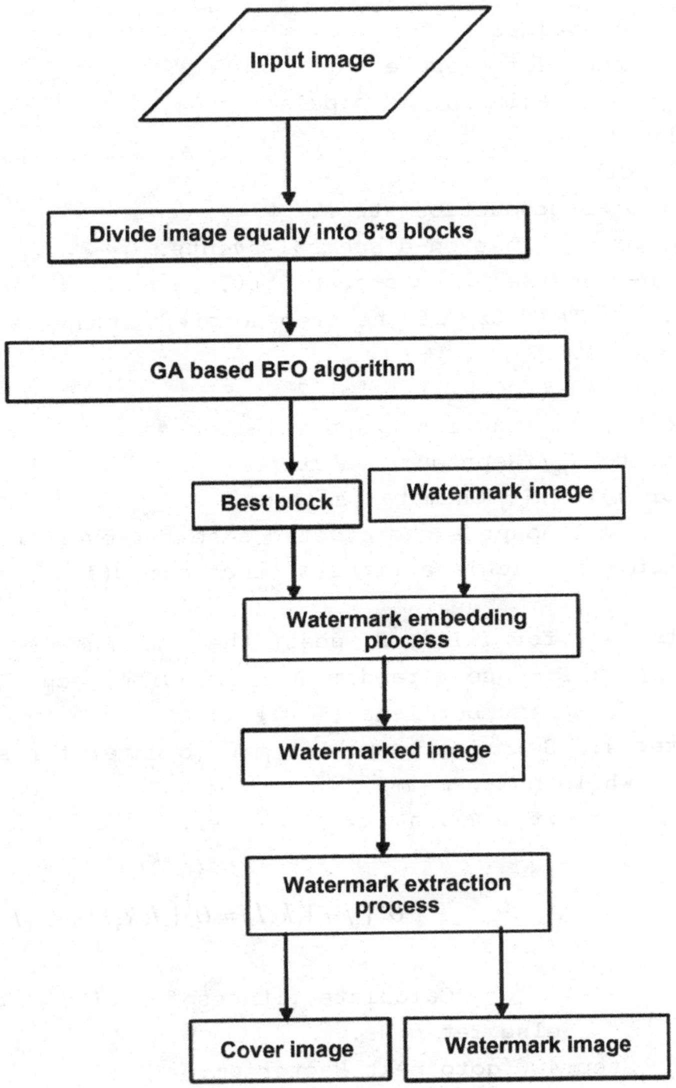

PERFORMANCE METRICS

Peak Signal-to-Noise Ratio (PSNR)

Peak Signal Noise Ratio represents the measure of peak error. Inorder to compute PSNR the mean squared error (MSE) is first calculated.

$$MSE = \frac{1}{MN} \sum_{i=0}^{M-1} \sum_{j=0}^{N-1} \left[A(i,j) - B(i,j) \right]^2 \tag{34}$$

Algorithm 1. Genetic algorithm based bacterial foraging optimization algorithm

Step 1. Initialize the values

    p: Dimension of the search space.

    S: The number of bacteria in the population.

    N_c: Chemotactic steps.

    N_s: Swimming length.

    N_{re}: The number of reproduction steps.

    N_{ed}: The number of elimination-dispersal events.

    P_{ed}: Elimination-dispersal with probability.

    C(i) (i=1,2,…..S): The size of the step adopted in the random direction specified by the tumble.

    P(j,k,l):P(j,k,l)={θ (i,j,k,l) | i=1,2,…..S}.

Step 2. **for** *l*=1 to N_{ed}//Elimination Dispersal loop

    Step 3. **for** *k*=1 to N_{re}//Reproduction loop

        Step 4. **for** *j*=1to N_c//Chemotaxis loop

            Step 4.1 Adapt a chemotactic step for every bacterium (*i*).

            Step 4.2 Calculate fitness function: *J(i, j, k, l)* and assign *Jlast=J(i,j,k,l)*.

            Step 4.3 **for** *i*=1 to S, adapt the tumbling/ swimming decision

            Tumble: Produce a random number Δ with each element Δ*m (i)* where *m*=1, 2….p the random number lies [0, 1].

            Step 4.4 Swimming loop: Let m=0 (counter for swim length).

                while *m<Ns, m=m+1*.

                    if *J (i, j, k, l) <Jlast*.

                        Let *Jlast=J (i, j, k, l)*,

$$\theta^i \left(j+1,k,l \right) = \theta^i \left(j,k,l \right) + C\left(i\right) \frac{\Delta\left(i\right)}{\sqrt{\Delta\left(i\right)\Delta\left(i\right)^T}}$$

                    Calculate fitness function *J (i, j, k, l)*,

                else let *m*=Ns.

            Step 4.6 **goto** next Bacterium.

    Step 5. **end for** (Chemotaxis loop)

    Step 6. Reproduction: Compute the health of the bacterium *i*. Arrange bacteria and chemotactic parameters *C (i)* in the order of ascending cost *Jhealth*. Apply crossover and mutation to the highest values of *Jhealth* for creating the child of the bacteria.

    Step 7. **end for** (Reproduction loop)

    Step 8. Elimination-dispersal: Eliminate and disperse bacteria with probability P_{ed}.

Step 9. **end for** (Elimination Dispersal loop).

Figure 10. The structure of bacterial foraging-genetic algorithm

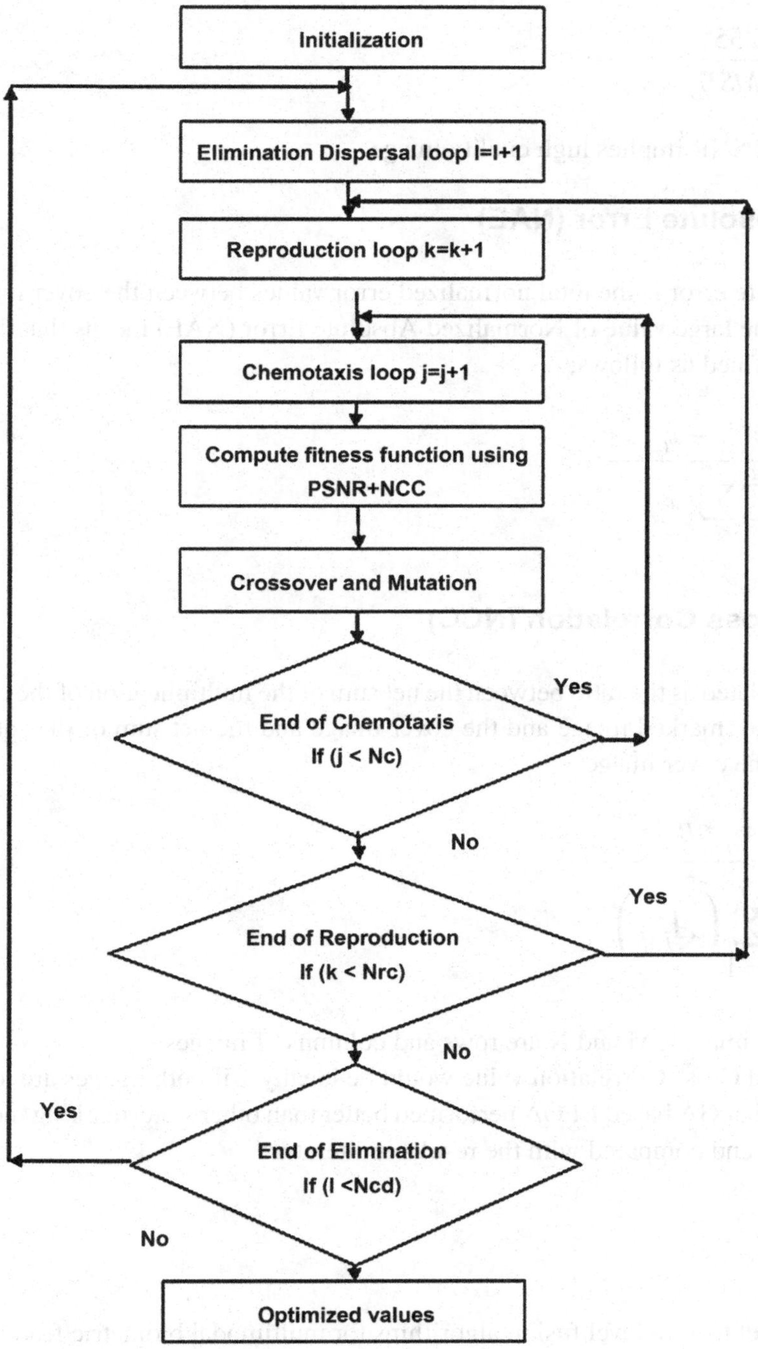

where A, B are watermarked and cover images respectively, M, N are rows and columns of images.

$$PSNR = 10\log_{10}\frac{255^2}{MSE}$$ (35)

An increase in PSNR implies high quality image.

Normalized Absolute Error (NAE)

Normalized absolute error is the total normalized error values between the cover image and the watermarked images. The large value of Normalized Absolute Error (NAE) means that the image is of poor quality. NAE is defined as follows:

$$NAE = \sum_{j=1}^{M}\sum_{k=1}^{N}\frac{|x_{(j,k)} - x_{(j,k)}'|}{\sum_{j=1}^{M}\sum_{k=1}^{N}|x_{(j,k)}|}$$ (36)

Normalized Cross Correlation (NCC)

The metric is calculated as the ratio between the net sum of the multiplication of the corresponding pixel densities of the watermarked image and the cover image and the net sum of the squared values of the pixel densities of the cover image.

$$NCC = \sum_{i=1}^{M}\sum_{j=1}^{N}\frac{\left(A_{i,j}*B_{i,j}\right)}{\sum_{i=1}^{M}\sum_{j=1}^{N}\left(A_{i,j}\right)^2}$$ (37)

where A and B are images, M and N are rows and columns of images

The Normalized Cross Correlation value would be ideally 1 if both images are identical.

Table 3 shows that GA based BFOA performed better than other watermarking models. The standard images were taken and compared with the results in literature.

CONCLUSION

In this chapter novel feature level fusion algorithms for multimodal biometric features and Genetic Algorithm based Bacterial Foraging Optimization Algorithm for watermarking of images were proposed. Each biometric modality was individually extracted and the obtained modalities were fused together. As a result the fusion methods produced successfully the fused templates and the best fused template has been identified. The best fused template had been watermarked in different cover images using Genetic Algorithm based BFOA watermarking system. Various metrics such as PSNR, NAE, and NCC are used

Figure 11. Sample output obtained by applying GA based BFOA watermarking system on different cover Images

Table 2. Performance Analysis for different watermarked images using GA based BFOA watermarking system

Standard Images	PSNR(dB)	NCC	NAE
BOAT	59.72	0.974	0.0015
BABOON	60.35	0.987	0.0013
LENA	62.92	0.978	0.0016
COUPLE	68.13	0.983	0.0011

Table 3. Comparison of PSNR (dB) of GA based BFOA method with other methods

Standard Images	PSNR (dB)	(Sikander. B, 2010)	(A. Khan, 2004)	(A. Khan, 2005)
BOAT	59.72	43.9381	40.94	39.16
LENA	60.35	45.292	44.45	41.5125
COUPLE	62.92	45.637	39.59	37.881
BABOON	68.13	39.635	36.28	36.06

to measure the image quality. CASIA database is chosen for the biometric images. All the images are 8 bit gray-level JPEG image with the resolution of 320*280.The experimental results show that the Genetic Algorithm based Bacterial Foraging Optimization Algorithm for watermarking provided better results than other watermarking methods.

FUTURE RESEARCH DIRECTIONS

In this chapter the biometric features like fingerprint, iris and palmprint are taken. There are several other biometric features like voice, ear, genes etc. These can be combined to create the multimodal biometric system. The watermarking models can be implemented and outputs can be compared.

REFERENCES

Anne, M. P. (2013). Investigating fusion approaches in multi-biometric cancellable recognition. *Expert Systems with Applications, Elsevier, 40*(6), 1971–1980. doi:10.1016/j.eswa.2012.10.002

Anu, S., Nair, H., Aruna, P., & Sakthivel, K. (2013). Sparse Representation Fusion of Fingerprint, Iris and Palmprint Biometric Features. *International Journal of Advanced ComputerResearch, 4*(1), 46–53.

Aravinth, J. &Dr.S.Valarmathy. (2012). A Novel Feature Extraction Techniques for Multimodal Score Fusion Using Density Based Gaussian Mixture Model Approach. *International Journal of Emerging Technology and Advanced Engineering, 2*(1), 189–197.

Bahaa-Eldin, A. M. (2013). A medium resolution fingerprint matching system. *Ain Shams Engineering Journal,Elsevier, 4*(3), 393–408. doi:10.1016/j.asej.2012.10.001

Cao, K., Pang, L., Liang, J., & Tia, J. (2013). Fingerprint classification by a hierarchical classifier. *Pattern Recognition,Elsevier, 46*(12), 3186–3197. doi:10.1016/j.patcog.2013.05.008

Cvejic, Łoza, Bull, & Canagarajah. (2006). A Similarity Metric for Assessment of Image Fusion Algorithms. *International Journal of Information and Communication Engineering, 2*(3).

Ding, M., Wei, L., & Wang, B. (2013). Research on fusion method for infrared and visible images via compressive sensing. *Infrared Physics & Technology, Elsevier, 57,* 56–67. doi:10.1016/j.infrared.2012.12.014

Guo, J.-M., Liu, Y.-F., Chang, J.-Y., & Lee, J.-D. (2014). Fingerprint classification based ondecision tree from singular points and orientation field. *Expert Systems with Applications,Elsevier, 41*(2), 752–764. doi:10.1016/j.eswa.2013.07.099

Guo, Zhou & Wang. (2014). Palmprint recognition algorithm with horizontally expanded blanket dimension. *Neurocomputing, 127,* 152–160.

Han, Cai, Cao, & Xu. (2013). A new image fusion performance metric based on visual information fidelity. Information Fusion, 14, 127–135.

Huang, Z., Liu, Y., Li, C., Yang, M., & Chen, L. (2013). A robust face and ear based multimodal biometric system using sparse representation. *Pattern Recognition, Elsevier, 46*(8), 2156–2168. doi:10.1016/j.patcog.2013.01.022

Indhumadhi, N., & Padmavathi, G. (2011). Enhanced Image fusion algorithm Using Laplacian Pyramid and Spatial Frequency Based Wavelet algorithm. *International Journal of Soft Computing And Engineering, 1*(5).

Khan, Mirza, & Majid. (2006). Intelligent perceptual shaping of a digital watermark: exploiting characteristics of human visual system. *International Journal of Knowledge-Based Intelligent Engineering Systems, 9,* 1-11.

Khan, A., Mirza, A. M., & Majid, A. (2004). Optimizing Perceptual shaping of a digital watermark using Genetic Programming. *Iranian Journal of Electrical and Computer Engineering, 3*(2), 1251–1260.

Khanduja, Verma, & Chakraverty. (2013). Watermarking relational databases using bacterial foraging algorithm. *Multimedia Tools and Applications, 73*(2).

Li, Cao, & Lu. (2013). Improve the two-phase test samples representation method for palmprint recognition. *Optik - International Journal for Light and Electron Optics, 124*(24), 6651–6656.

Mohd Asaari, M. S., Suandi, S. A., & Rosdi, B. A. (2014). Fusion of Band Limited Phase Only Correlation and Width Centroid Contour Distance for finger based biometrics. *Expert Systems with Applications, Elsevier, 41*(7), 3367–3382. doi:10.1016/j.eswa.2013.11.033

Nibouche, O., & Jiang, J. (2013). Palmprint matching using feature points and SVD factorization. *Digital Signal Processing Elsevier, 23*(4), 1154–1162. doi:10.1016/j.dsp.2013.02.011

Poh, N., Ross, A., Lee, W., & Kittle, J. (2013). A user-specific and selective multimodal biometric fusion strategy by ranking subjects. *Pattern Recognition, Elsevier, 46*(12), 3341–3357. doi:10.1016/j.patcog.2013.03.018

Sahu, D. K., & Parsai, M. P. (2012). Different Image Fusion Techniques –A Critical Review. *International Journal of Modern Engineering Research*, *2*(5), 4298–4301.

Sharma, Pattnaik, & Garg. (2012). A Review of Bacterial Foraging Optimization and Its Applications. In *Proceedings on Future Aspects of Artificial intelligence in Industrial Automation (NCFAAIIA 2012)* (pp. 9-12). International Journal of Computer Applications (IJCA).

Shekhar, Patel, & Nasrabadi. (2013). Joint Sparse Representation for Robust Multimodal Biometrics Recognition. *IEEE Transactions on Pattern Analysis and Machine Intelligence, 36*(1), 113-126.

Sikander, B., Ishtiaq, M., Jaffar, M.A., Tariq, M., & Mirza, A.M. (2010). Adaptive Digital Watermarking of Images Using Genetic Algorithm. In *Proceedings on Information Science and Applications* (pp. 1-8). IEEE.

Singh, S., & Rajput, R. (2014). A Comparative Study of Classification of Image Fusion Techniques. *International Journal Of Engineering And Computer Science*, *3*(7), 7350–7353.

Thomas, R. M. (2013). Survey of Bacterial Foraging Optimization Algorithm. *International Journal of Science and Modern Engineering*, *1*(4), 11–12.

Tiwari, K., Arya, D. K., Badrinath, & Gupta. (2013). Designing palmprint based recognition system using local structure tensor and force field transformation for human identification. Neurocomputing, 116, 222–230.

Yue, F., & Zuo, W. (2013). Consistency analysis on orientation features for fast and accurate palmprint identification. *Information Sciences, Elsevier, 268*, 78–90. doi:10.1016/j.ins.2013.08.021

Section 4
Image and Video Classification, Clustering, and Applications

Chapter 15
Color Features and Color Spaces Applications to the Automatic Image Annotation

Vafa Maihami
Semnan University, Iran

Farzin Yaghmaee
Semnan University, Iran

ABSTRACT

Nowadays images play a crucial role in different fields such as medicine, advertisement, education and entertainment. Describing images content and retrieving them are important fields in image processing. Automatic image annotation is a process which produces words from a digital image based on the content of this the image by using a computer. In this chapter, after an introduction to neighbor voting algorithm for image annotation, we discuss the applicability of color features and color spaces in automatic image annotation. We discuss the applicability of three color features (color histogram, color moment and color Autocorrelogram) and three color spaces (RGB, HSI and YCbCr) in image annotation. Experimental results, using Corel5k benchmark annotated images dataset, demonstrate that using different color spaces and color features helps to select the best color features and spaces in image annotation area.

INTRODUCTION

Technology, in the form of inventions such as photography and television, has played a major role in facilitating the capture and communication of image data. Nowadays images play a crucial role in fields as diverse as medicine, journalism, advertisement, design, education and entertainment. The application of images in human communications is hard and the process of digitization does not in itself make image collections easier to manage. Images have low level features (color, texture, shape, etc.), while high level features are understood words from image. The gap between low level and high level features can be removed by image annotation (Dengsheng Zhang, 2012) (R. Datta, 2008) (Y. Liu, 2007). Image annotation is a process which produces metadata (text or keywords) from a digital image based on visual

DOI: 10.4018/978-1-4666-9685-3.ch015

Figure 1. Image annotation process

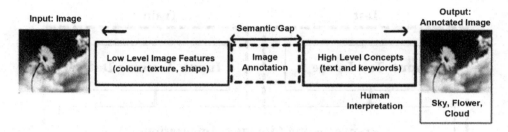

content of an image (Dengsheng Zhang, 2012); (Wang, 2011). The aim of image annotation is to assign the appropriate words to describe the images, see Figure 1. Image annotation can be done by both machines or by humans, but performing this action by humans is boring, costly and it is usually erroneous or ambiguous. In fact image annotation refers to an action which is automatic and performed by machines.

Most of existing methods of automatic image annotation make use of the visual content and they often rely heavily on supervised machine learning methods (J. Liu, 2009) (Su, 2011) (Y. Han, 2012) (Yang, 2012) (Zenghai Chen, 2013). The block diagram of an image annotation system is shown in Figure 2. To get the annotation model training phase is performed. An image dataset is used in this phase. Images are segmented and important feature are extracted to the learning model based on global feature-based or regional feature-based methods. Learning models are usually derived by machine learning algorithms such as neural networks, support vector machines and decision tree. An image annotation model is obtained from the dataset in the final step of the training phase. The second phase in image annotation is testing. The images that we want annotated can be used as input. The next stage is to perform pre-processing and feature extraction on the images. The existing features of the model are given and based on the model learned in the previous phase; finally image annotation is displayed in the output.

But in modern applications, especially real-time applications with a large and diverse visual content, a weak supervision which effectively and efficiently estimates tag/keywords relevance is needed. This paradigm is recently developed (X. Li, 2009) (Ro, 2013) (Lei Wu, 2013).

Generally, the same tags/keywords are used to describe similar images. From this fact, a method called neighbor voting is proposed to annotate images (X. Li, 2009) . Neighbor voting is a popular technique to estimates the relevance of image keywords/tags. Neighbor voting comes with a simple effective mathematical model and with a low computational complexity. Also this method has no limit on the number of images and tags (X. Li, 2009) (Ro, 2013). These advantages have recently attracted substantial research attention.

Color is one of important features in image annotation system. Number of color features are color histogram, color moment and color correlogram. The choice of the color space can be also a very important decision which can dramatically influence the results of the processing. Several popular color spaces are used for image and video processing that the most important of them is RGB color space, HSV color space and YCbCr color space. The right choice of these two parameters has an important impact on improving the results of the image annotation algorithms. Accordingly, the objective of this chapter is to present an algorithm for image annotation using similarity distance and by the help of different color features and spaces. In addition, comparisons have done between state of the art researches to motivate research in new trend-setting directions to select the best color features and spaces.

Figure 2. The block diagram of an image annotation system

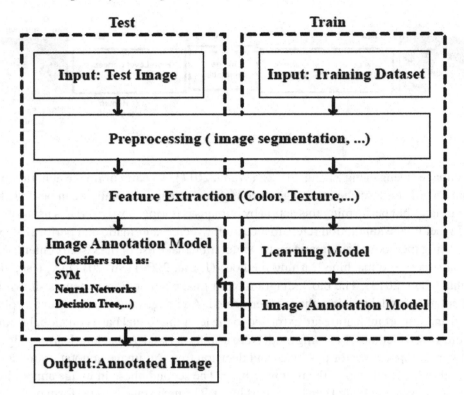

In this chapter, after an introduction on neighbor voting algorithm for image annotation, different color features, and color spaces, simulation studies are performed to illustrate the capability of proposed intelligent approach in real-time image annotation applications. We have done various tests on these features in equal conditions to obtain the best feature based experimental results. A comparison between image annotation based on different color spaces and color histograms is also presented. This mechanism shows an appropriate color space in image annotation.

The contributions of this chapter are summarized as follows:

- We propose approache for automatic image annotation by color similarity distance similar to the algorithm proposed by (X. Li, 2009). In order to do, we use Euclidean distance to obtain the similarity.
- Introducing three widely used color features included: color histogram, color moment and color correlogram. Doing various tests on these features in equal conditions to obtain the best feature based experimental results.
- Introducing three popular color spaces included: RGB, HSV and YCbCr. Comparisons between image annotation based on different color spaces and color histogram are also presented. It shows the appropriate color space to image annotation.
- We have done sensitivity analysis on the main parameters of the annotation algorithm presented.

The rest of this chapter is organized as follows: background of image annotation approaches, color features, and color spaces are described in Section II. Image annotation using color similarity measure is explained in section III. The experimental results of proposed method based on different color features and color spaces are in Section IV and conclusion of paper is presented in Section V.

BACKGROUND

This section, describes the backgrounds of image annotation, color features and color spaces. First, related works of image annotation are presented and the classification of the automatic image annotation is discussed. In continue section two, three famous color features are introduced. In section three, three popular color spaces are introduced.

Related Works

The overall image annotation approaches can be usually done either manually or automatically. The manually approach has high accuracy. Occasionally manual annotation process of images by human is expensive, time- consuming and fully dependent on personality, knowledge and personal view against the subject. In automatic image annotation (AIA) the attempt is to use the machines instead of humans. The accuracy in this approach is lower than image annotation by human but it is much faster and the cost is low. Image annotation in automatic/semi-automatic is divided into text-based methods and image-based methods. In Text-based methods image annotation is based on some texts which are near the image (like an image in a web page.) This approach cannot make use of image contents and it is usually divided in two categories: based on ontology (S. Dasiopoulou, 2007) and based on field (Zh. Hua, November 06-11, 2005).

Furthermore, image-based methods use low level features such as color, texture, shape and ... to obtain annotation. Image-based methods are usually classified into two approaches: Global feature-based methods (features extraction, annotation using single feature vector per image), Regional feature-based methods (segmentation process, features extraction applied for every segment, annotation using a set of feature vectors per image - single feature vector per each segment). The approaches of AIA can be classified into three models (Wang, 2011) (M. Han, 2012) (Zhang, 2012):

- **Generative Models:** The generative model learns a joint distribution over image features and concepts (or annotation keywords). To annotate a new image, the learned generative model computes the conditional probability over keywords given the visual features (K. Barnard, 2003).
- **Discriminative Models:** The discriminative model trains a separate classifier from visual features for each keyword. These classifiers are used to predict whether the test image belongs to the class of images that is annotated with each particular keyword.
- **Nearest-Neighbor-Based Models:** In this method, image annotation is solved as a retrieval problem. Nearest neighbors are determined by the average of several distances such as fuzzy measures (T. Chaira, 2005), histogram intersection (F. Long, 2003) and Euclidean distance (S. Jeong, 2004). Keywords are then transferred from neighbors to the given image.

A comparative study of the aforementioned schemes has been done recently in (Dengsheng Zhang, 2012). In paper (Dengsheng Zhang, 2012) the most focus on the two major aspects of automatic image annotation, feature extraction and semantic learning/annotation.

COLOR FEATURES

Color Histogram

Color histogram describes the distribution of colors within a whole or within an interest region of image. Color histograms are flexible constructs that can be built from images in various color spaces. The main drawback of histograms for classification is that the representation is dependent of the color of the object being studied, ignoring its shape and texture. On the other hand, histogram based descriptors are either too high dimensional or too expensive to compute and are sensitive to noise. The histogram method is widely used for visual feature representation due to many advantages in image retrieval and image annotation such as its robustness, effectiveness, implementation and computational simplicity (Dengsheng Zhang, 2012) (A.K. Jain, 1996).

A digital image is commonly seen as a 2D mapping $I : X \rightarrow V$ from $M \times N$ pixel X [i, j] to value V. (where $i = 1, \ldots, M$ and $j = 1, \ldots, N$ correspond to y-axis and x-axis respectively). Often the values V are discrete intensity values in the range [0-255]. In order to design a descriptor of an image its histogram is calculated. An image histogram can be generated as follows:

$$His_t = \sum_{i=1}^{M} \sum_{j=1}^{N} p_{(i,j)}, \forall t \in V \tag{1}$$

where $p_{(i,j)} = 1$ if the V at pixel location [i,j] falls in t, and $p_{(i,j)} = 0$ otherwise.

Color Moment

Color moments are very effective for color-based image analysis. They are especially important for classification of images based on color, image retrieval, and identification of Image angle (0, 90, 180, or 270 degrees). Color moments to be calculated are in fact, statistical moments. The mean, variance and standard deviation of an image are known as color moments. (Dengsheng Zhang, 2012) (M. Flickner, 1995).

Following equations define the mean, variance and standard deviation of an image of size $M \times N$:

$$\text{Mean} = \sum_{i=1}^{M} \sum_{j=1}^{N} \frac{P_{(i,j)}}{M \times N} \tag{2}$$

$$Variance = 1 / (M \times N) \sum\nolimits_{(i=1)}^{M} \sum\nolimits_{(j=1)}^{N} (p_{(i,j)}) - Mean)^2 \tag{3}$$

$$\text{stddev} = \sqrt{\text{Variance}} \tag{4}$$

where $p_{(i,j)}$ is the Pixel value of the ith row and j^{th} column.

Among the various color features, color moments are not sufficient to represent the regions.

Color Correlogram

In the analysis of data, a correlogram is an image of correlation statistics (Dengsheng Zhang, 2012). Color correlogram is useful for whole image representation. A color correlogram can be treated as a 3D histogram where the first two dimensions represent the colors of any pixel pair and the third dimension is their spatial distance. A color correlogram of an image is a table indexed by color pairs, where the k-th entry for (i,j) specifies the probability of finding a pixel of color j at a distance k from a pixel of color i in the image. Color correlogram is a variant of histogram that accounts for local spatial correlation of colors Based on estimation of the probability of finding a pixel of color j at a distance k from a pixel of color i in an image.

$$\text{Image} : I \tag{5}$$

$$\text{Quantized colors} : c_1, c_2, ..., c_m \tag{6}$$

$$\text{Distance between two pixels} : |p_1 - p_2| = \max \left| x_1 - x_2 \right|, \left| y_1 - y_2 \right| \tag{7}$$

$$\text{Pixel set with color } c : I_c = p \mid I_{(p)} = c \tag{8}$$

$$\text{Given distance} : k \tag{9}$$

The color correlogram is defined as

$$3_{c_i,c_j}^{(k)}(I) = \Pr_{p_1 \mu I_{c_i}, p_2 \mu I_{c_j}} [p_2 \mu I_{c_j} \parallel p_1 - p_2 \mid = k] \tag{10}$$

The auto-correlogram is

$$\pm_c^{(k)}(I) = 3_{c,c}^{(k)}(I) \tag{11}$$

The drawbacks of Autocorrelogram are Very high computation cost, sensitive to noise, rotation and scale (Dengsheng Zhang, 2012) (J. Huang, 1997).

COLOR SPACES

The color of an image is represented through some color space (model). There exist various color spaces to describe color information. The more commonly used color models are RGB (red, green, blue), HSI (hue, saturation, value) and YCbCr (luminance and chrominance). In continue briefly described any one.

RGB (Red Green Blue)

The RGB color format is based on the three color components red (R), green (G) and blue (B). The RGB color model describes a color space with additive color composition as it is used in CRT or LCD monitors. Thus, the RGB color format is very popular in computer graphics and image processing.

HSV

The HSV color model describes a color by using the three color components hue (H), saturation (S) and Value (V). This color format is very popular for designing and editing (e.g. within graphics design tools) because it gives the user a good impression about the resulting color for a certain color value: Hue defines the pure color tone out of the color spectrum, saturation defines the mixture of the color tone with gray and finally value defines the lightness of the resulting color. In HSV color space, colors are mapped onto cylindrical coordinates: Hue [0..360] – angle on cylinder, Saturation [0..100] – radius of cylinder and Intensity [0..255] – height of cylinder. Conversion is done by rotating RGB space so white is at top and black at bottom and then stretching space into a double cone or cylinder. Calculating color differences in HSV space is much harder than most other color spaces. Hue, saturation, and intensity all have different value ranges [0..360], [0..100], [0..255] so we need to introduce three scale factors. Change in hue must take into account angle wrap around from 0 to 360 degrees (the angle difference between (5 and 355 is 10 degrees, not 350). The given values in RGB color space R, G, B are in [0, 255] can be then converted into values H, S and I in HSV color space.

YCbCr

The YCbCr color format is consists of a luminance component (Y) and two chrominance components (Cb and Cr). The term YCbCr is often used in the context of digital image and video processing, especially, for JPEG images and MPEG video encoding.

YCbCr, describe a color by using luminance and chrominance. The given values in RGB color space R, G, B are in [0, 255] can be then converted into values Y, Cb and Cr in YCbCr color space.

SOLUTIONS AND RECOMMENDATIONS

In this design an image annotation scheme like the algorithm proposed by (X. Li, 2009), to find best keywords to query image has been described. In Figure 3 the model of this approach is presented. Like any other automatic image annotation system, the algorithm in this chapter is composed of two steps training and testing. In accordance with the iterative solution, as shown in this algorithm, training step is initialized with a set of inputs. In continue training step, each of the images in the training dataset is read and the work below being done on it:

1. First, read the keywords for each image dataset and associate them with of related images.
2. Next, read the images which are transferred to the desired color space. In the previous section, three popular color spaces including: RGB, HSV and YCbCr were introduced. In this part, the images are transferred to one of three color space.
3. And finally, obtain color features from read images. In the previous section, three color features including: color histogram, color moment and color correlogram were introduced. In this part, one of this color features is obtained from the images.

But in phase testing in addition to the above, additional work needs to be done that is explained in the following. First, calculate similarity any test image with training images using

$$\mathrm{ED}\left(\mathrm{M}^k, \mathrm{M}^t\right) = \sqrt{\sum_{n=1}^{N}(\mathrm{M}_i^k, \mathrm{M}_i^t)^2} \tag{12}$$

where M^k and M^t are image query and image database respectively, i is a feature range. Closer distance represents the higher similarity between images. Next, Find N image with max similarity. Calculate repeat keywords from N image with max similarity and write N keywords with max repeat (Image annotation results).

The main advantage of this model is a simple effective mathematical model with a low computational complexity. This advantage causes that it can be used in real-time applications such as smart phones, search engines and etc.

Experimental Results

Dataset

One of the benchmark for evolutionary image annotation is Corel5k image dataset. This set contains 5000 images in 50 categories. In each category, there are 100 almost similar images, such as cars, sunset, animals, flowers and so on. The images are stored in JPEG format with size 192x128. The set split into 4500 training and 500 test examples. From each image category exist in test images. All images are also annotated from a dictionary of 374 keywords, with each image having been annotated between 1 to 5 keywords. Distribution number of images for keywords between 1 to 5 are 25, 341, 1416, 2708 and 18, respectively (P. Duygulu, 2002).

To evaluated the performance annotation results we used three measures: average Precision (P), average Recall (R) and F-score (F+). The annotation precision for a test image is defined as the number of keywords that assigned correctly, divided by the total number of keywords predicted to have the image. The annotation recall is defined as the number of keywords that assigned correctly, divided by the

Figure 3. The model of proposed method

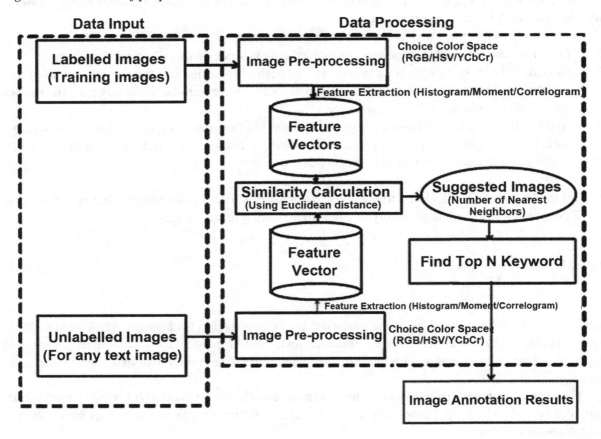

number of manual keywords image. The averaged precision and recall over all test images as well as the number of individual images with positive recall are used for evaluation.

$$Precision = \frac{\# \, of \, keywords \, that \, assigned \, correctly}{Total \; \# \, of \, keywords \, predicted} \qquad (13)$$

$$Recall = \frac{\# \, of \, keywords \, that \, assigned \, correctly}{\# \, of \, manual \, keywords \, image} \qquad (14)$$

Another measure is F-score, which is obtained from a relation between precision and recall. F-score is defined as:

$$F - score = \frac{2 \times Precision \times Recall}{Precision + Recall} \qquad (15)$$

Results

Numerical results of proposed algorithm are provided in this section. We consider presented algorithm on Corel5k dataset. Number of images nearest neighbor similarity and number of words to any test image are assumed to be 50 and 4, respectively. In Table 1, we compare the annotation performances of different color features. The Comparison showed that color moment has the better performance than other color features. Combined features together and using each of three features in feature vector also showed the best performance.

In Table 2, we compare the annotation performances of different color spaces. The color histogram feature is used in all three space because of being simple to compute. Results show that YCbCr color space has a better performance than other color spaces. And that it has the highest accuracy, recall and F-score among other color spaces in image annotation.

Table 3 compares the best proposed models in this article with those in previous traditional annotation models such as CMRM (Jeon J, 2003), CRM (Lavrenko V, 2003), NPDE (A. Yavlinsky, 2005), MIL (Zhu S, 2011), and RFC-PSO (Nashwa El-Bendary, 2013). Table 3 shows that the proposed method is one of the most accurate methods and F-score AIA models, however is not the best one on Corel5k. It is also the best model in recall measures. In Figure 4, we compared the performance of various annotation models on Corel5k vs. the best proposed method.

Table 1. Comparison of different color spaces in proposed image annotation

Color Spaces	Recall	Precision	F-Score
Histogram	0.2188	0.1884	0.2024
Moment	0.2239	0.1939	0.2078
Correlogram	0.2233	0.1934	0.2072
Any three features	0.2333	0.2014	0.2161

Table 2. Comparison of different color spaces in proposed image annotation

Color Spaces	Recall	Precision	F-Score
RGB	0.2188	0.1884	0.2024
HSV	0.2194	0.1894	0.2032
YCbCr	0.2249	0.1949	0.2088

Table 3. Performance of various annotation models on Corel5k vs. The best proposed method

Models	Recall	Precision	F-score
CMRM	0.09	0.10	0.094
CRM	0.19	0.16	0.173
NPDE	0.21	0.18	0.193
MIL	0.22	0.20	0.209
RFC-PSO	0.22	0.26	0.238
The best Proposed method	0.24	0.21	0.224

Figure 4. Compare performance of various annotation models on Corel5k vs. the best proposed method

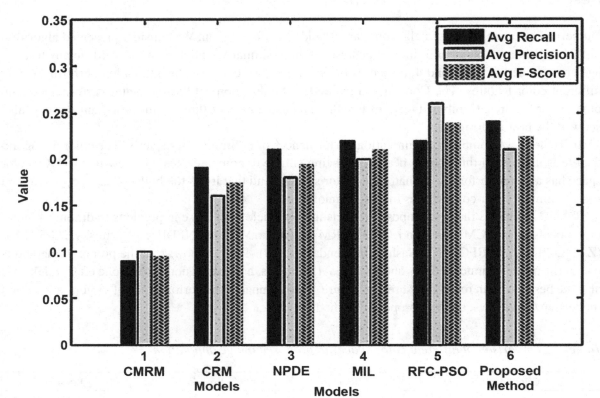

Sensitivity Analysis

Number of Neighbor Analysis

The evaluation of the different number of nearest neighbor performance is available in Table 4 and Figure 5 for any test, when the number of nearest neighbors varies between 5 and 200. Number of keywords equals 4 in different color features. Recall and Precision increases as the number of nearest neighbor's increases, but in number of nearest neighbor's 200, Recall and Precision decreases. In the other words, the system performance increases when the number of nearest neighbors increases. Among different color features, color Moment has better performances than other features and its change range is less than that of other features too. Approximate the number of nearest neighbors 50 is the best choice in all features. Figure 6 shows the performance f-score different color features.

Evaluation of the performance of different Number of nearest neighbor for any test is available in Table 5 and Figure 7, when the number of nearest neighbors varies between 5 and 200. Number of keywords equals 4 in different color spaces. Recall and Precision increases as the number of nearest neighbor's increases, but in number of nearest neighbors 200 Recall and Precision decreases. In the other words, the system performance increases when the number of nearest neighbors increases. Among different color spaces, YCbCr has a better performances than other spaces and its change range is less than that of other spaces. Approximate the number of nearest neighbors 50 is the best choice in all spaces. Figure.8

Table 4. Comparison of different number of nearest neighbor in different color spaces image annotation

Color Space # of Nearest Neighbor	RGB			HSV			YCbCr		
	Recall	Precision	F-score	Recall	Precision	F-score	Recall	Precision	F-score
5	0.2138	0.1839	0.1977	0.2154	0.1859	0.1995	0.2007	0.1728	0.1857
10	0.2164	0.1864	0.2003	0.2194	0.1894	0.2032	0.2181	0.1879	0.2018
20	0.2181	0.1879	0.2019	0.2223	0.1919	0.2059	0.2191	0.1899	0.2034
50	0.2188	0.1884	0.2024	0.2239	0.1939	0.2078	0.2233	0.1934	0.2072
100	0.2209	0.1904	0.2045	0.2229	0.1929	0.2068	0.2248	0.1944	0.2084
200	0.2216	0.1899	0.2045	0.2233	0.1929	0.2069	0.2224	0.1924	0.2063

Figure 5. Comparison of different number of nearest neighbor in different color features image annotation. a. Recall, b. Precision.

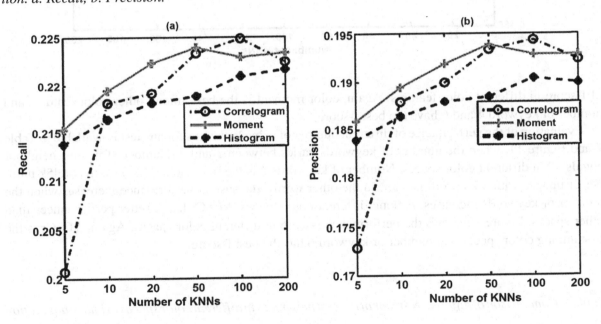

shows the performance f-score different color spaces. The figure shows all three color spaces. Being similar to other results of color spaces, YCbCr has the best result.

Number of Keywords Analysis

The evaluation of the performance of different Number of using keywords for any test is available in Table 6 and Figure 9, when the number of keywords varies between 3 and 7. Number of nearest neighbor equals 50 in different color features. Number of keywords 4 is the best choice; because of in corel5k number of images with 4 keyword is a lot. In the other words, the system performance increases when the Number of Keywords increases. Among different color features Color Moment has a better performances than other features. Its change range is less than that of other features. Figure 10 shows the performance

Figure 6. Compare f-score different color features on Corel5k

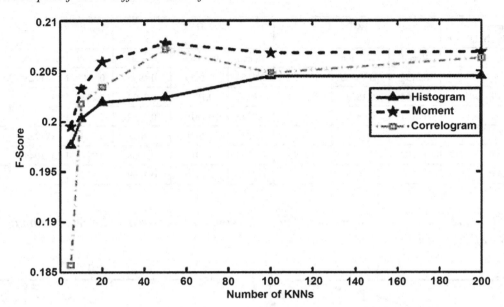

of f-score in different color features. Again, color moment is the best among other color features and number of keyword 4 and 6 have the best f-score.

Evaluation of the performance of different number of using keywords for any test is available in Table 7 and Figure 11, when the number of keywords varies between 3 and 7. Number of nearest neighbor equals 50 in different color spaces. Number of keywords 4 is the best choice; because in corel5k number of images with 4 keyword is a lot. In the other words, the system performance increases when the number of keywords increases. Among different color spaces, YCbCr has a better performances than other spaces. Figure 12 shows the performance f-score in different color spaces. Again, YCbCr is the best among color spaces and number of keyword 6 has the best f-score.

Table 5. Comparison of different Number of nearest neighbors in different color spaces in image annotation

Color Space # of Nearest Neighbor	RGB			HSV			YCbCr		
	Recall	Precision	F-score	Recall	Precision	F-score	Recall	Precision	F-score
5	0.2138	0.1839	0.1977	0.2126	0.1824	0.1963	0.2159	0.1864	0.2001
10	0.2164	0.1864	0.2003	0.2143	0.1839	0.1979	0.2221	0.1919	0.2059
20	0.2181	0.1879	0.2019	0.2166	0.1859	0.2001	0.2196	0.1909	0.2042
50	0.2188	0.1884	0.2024	0.2194	0.1894	0.2033	0.2249	0.1949	0.2088
100	0.2209	0.1904	0.2045	0.2209	0.1904	0.2045	0.2253	0.1949	0.2090
200	0.2216	0.1899	0.2045	0.2213	0.1894	0.2041	0.2243	0.1939	0.2080

Figure 7. Comparison of different Number of nearest neighbor in different color spaces image annotation. a. Recall, b. Precision.

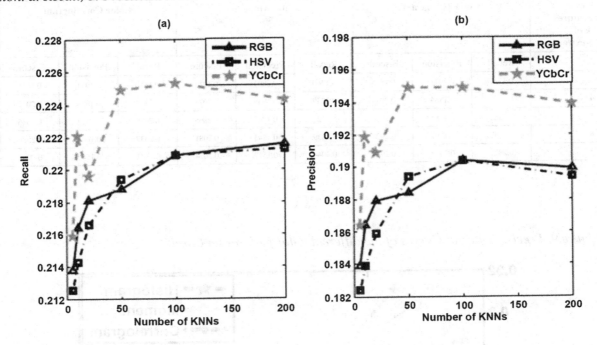

Figure 8. Compare f-score different color spaces on Corel5k

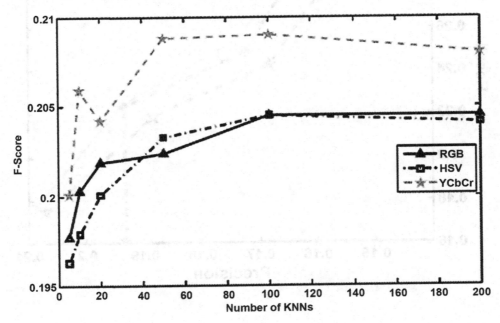

Table 6. Comparison of different keyword Number in different color featuress in image annotation

Color Features # of Keywords	Color Histogram			Color Moment			Color Correlogram		
	Recall	Precision	F-score	Recall	Precision	F-score	Recall	Precision	F-score
3	0.1747	0.2071	0.1895	0.1760	0.2091	0.1911	0.1610	0.1931	0.1755
4	0.2188	0.1884	0.2024	0.2239	0.1939	0.2078	0.2233	0.1934	0.2072
5	0.2425	0.1683	0.1987	0.2527	0.1747	0.2065	0.2488	0.1723	0.2036
6	0.2752	0.1597	0.2021	0.2839	0.1643	0.2081	0.2837	0.1643	0.2080
7	0.2877	0.1434	0.1914	0.3044	0.1517	0.2024	0.3121	0.1555	0.2075

Figure 9. Precision-Recall Curves of the different color features on Corel5k

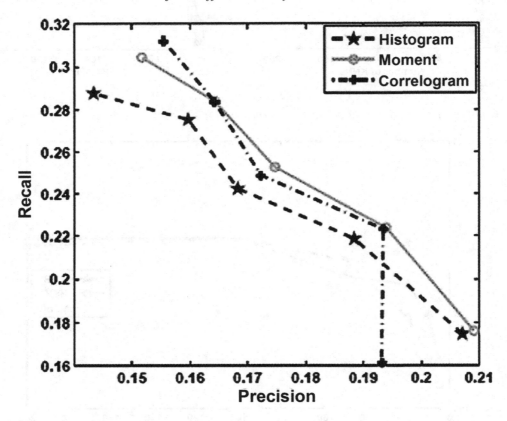

Figure 10. Compare f-score measure in different color features

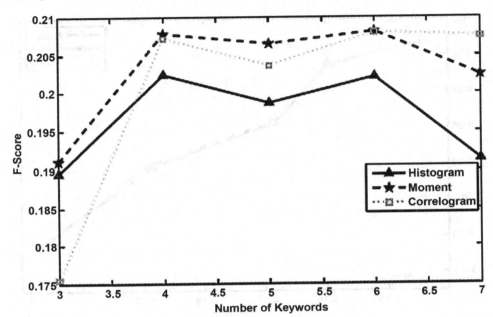

Table 7. Comparison of different keyword Number in different color spaces in image annotation

Color Spaces # of Keywords	RGB			HSV			YCbCr		
	Recall	Precision	F-score	Recall	Precision	F-score	Recall	Precision	F-score
3	0.1747	0.2071	0.1895	0.1743	0.2071	0.1893	0.1754	0.2084	0.1905
4	0.2188	0.1884	0.2024	0.2194	0.1894	0.2033	0.2249	0.1949	0.2088
5	0.2425	0.1683	0.1987	0.2432	0.1687	0.1992	0.2537	0.1760	0.2078
6	0.2752	0.1597	0.2021	0.2740	0.1593	0.2015	0.2861	0.1660	0.2101
7	0.2877	0.1434	0.1914	0.2884	0.1440	0.1921	0.2993	0.1492	0.1991

FUTURE RESEARCH DIRECTIONS

As a future work there are many new applications of image annotation and intelligent schemes in industry, medicine, arts, etc which researchers have not focused on them yet. Some of these areas are as follows:

1. *Analysis other image features.* In this chapter, we discuss applicable different color features and color spaces on automatic image annotation. Future works can be researches into different texture, shape, edge as well as algorithm on image annotation.
2. *Other application color features and spaces.* Here, we analyzed the effect of the application of different color features and color spaces on image annotation. One important open issue in this area is the analysis of color features and spaces vs. other applications from image processing and computer vision.

Figure 11. Precision-Recall Curves of the different color spaces on Corel5k

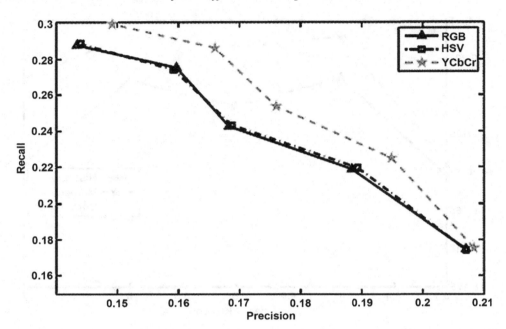

3. *New datasets in image annotation.* One of main challenges in automatic image annotation is a general shortage of standard image datasets and benchmarks in all applications. Unfortunately, a standard database that covers all applicable image categories is not accessible. Create new datasets in special application are open.

4. *Image annotation real-time application.* Nowadays, the popularity of massive visual data in many computer vision and multimedia based applications is clear. In order to effectively and automatically annotate the images in large-scale computer vision applications, a new algorithm with low complexity is required. Researches in this area have been developed recently (Ro, 2013) (X. Li, 2009) (Lei Wu, 2013).

CONCLUSION AND DISCUSSION

Automatic image annotation is a process of producing metadata (text or keywords) for a digital image based on its visual content. Image annotation can fill the gap between low level features (color, texture, shape, etc.) extraction and high level semantically features (text and keywords about image).

Indeed, finding an optimal solution to achieve a high accurate annotator is very difficult. This chapter presented an algorithm for automatic image annotation using similarity distance and by the help of different color features and color spaces. The experimental results show that proposed annotation approach is effective and efficient in facing data consisting the color features and color spaces.

On one hand, we reflected how to choice the best color features in image annotation, and on the other hand, how to choice the best color spaces presented. Results show YCbCr is the best color space and color moment is the best color feature for automatic image annotation. We also had done sensitivity

Figure 12. Compare f-score measure in different color spaces

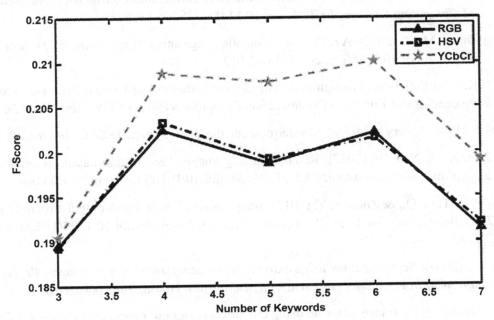

analysis on a number of nearest neighbor images and keywords in each image test. It shows that the best number of the nearest neighbor image is 50 and the best number of keywords to each image test is 4, because of having a balance for precision and recall.

NOMENCLATURE

AIA: Automatic Image Annotation.
RGB : Red Green Blue.
HSV: Hue Saturation Value.
stddev : Standard Deviation.

REFERENCES

Barnard, , P. D. (2003). Matching words and pictures. *Journal of Machine Learning Research*, *3*, 1107–1135.

Chaira, T., & Ray, A. K. (2005). Fuzzy measures for colour image retrieval. *Fuzzy Sets and Systems*, *150*(3), 545–560. doi:10.1016/j.fss.2004.09.003

Dasiopoulou, S. C. D. (2007). Semantic- Based Visual Information Retrieval, An Ontology-Based Framework for Semantic Image Analysis and Retrieval. Idea Group Inc.

Datta, R., Joshi, D., Li, J., & Wang, J. Z. (2008). Image retrieval: Ideas, influences, and trends of the new age. *ACM Computing Surveys*, *40*(2), 5. doi:10.1145/1348246.1348248

Dengsheng Zhang, M. M. (2012). A review on automatic image annotation techniques. *Pattern Recognition*, *45*(1), 346–362. doi:10.1016/j.patcog.2011.05.013

Duygulu, P. K. B. (2002). Object recognition as machine translation:learning a lexicon for a fixed image vocabulary. Proceedings of European Conferenceon Computer Vision (ECCV), (pp. 97-112).

Flickner, H. S. (1995). Query by image and video content: the QBIC system. *IEEE Computer*, *28*(9), 23-32.

Han, M., Zhu, X., & Yao, W. (2012). Remote sensing image classification based on neural network ensemble algorithm. *Neurocomputing*, *78*(1), 133–138. doi:10.1016/j.neucom.2011.04.044

Han, Y., Wu, F., Tian, Q., & Zhuang, Y. (2012). Image annotation by input-output structural grouping sparsity. *IEEE Transactions on Image Processing*, *21*(6), 3066–3079. doi:10.1109/TIP.2012.2183880 PMID:22262682

Hua, Z. X. W. (2005). Semantic knowledge extraction and annotation for web images. *Proceedings of the 13th annual ACM international conference on Multimedia*. Hilton, Singapore: ACM.

Huang, J. S. K.-J. (1997). Image indexing using colour correlogram. *Proceedings of the CVPR97*, (pp. 762-765).

Jain, A. K., & Vailaya, A. (1996). Image retrieval using colour and shape. *Pattern Recognition*, *29*(8), 1233–1244. doi:10.1016/0031-3203(95)00160-3

Jeon, J. L. V. (2003). Automatic image annotation and retrieval using cross-media relevance models. *26th Annual International ACM SIGIR Conference on Research and Development in Information Retrieval* (pp. 119-126). Toronto: ACM.

Jeong, S., Won, C. S., & Gray, R. M. (2004). Image retrieval using colour histograms generated by Gauss mixture vector quantization. *Computer Vision and Image Understanding*, *94*(13), 44–66. doi:10.1016/j.cviu.2003.10.015

Lavrenko, V. M. R. (2003). model for learning the semantics of pictures. *16th conference on advances in neural information processing systems (NIPS 16)*. Vancouver, Canada: MIT Press.

Lei Wu, R. J., Rong Jin, , & Jain, A. K. (2013). Tag Completion for Image Retrieval. *IEEE Transactions on Pattern Analysis and Machine Intelligence*, *35*(3), 716–727. doi:10.1109/TPAMI.2012.124 PMID:22641703

Li, C. S. (2009). Learning Social Tag Relevance by Neighbor Voting. *IEEE Trans. Multimedia*, *11*(7), 1310-1322.

Liu, D. Z. (2007). Survey of content-based image retrieval with high-level semantics. *Pattern Recognition*, *40*(1), 262–282.

Liu, J., Li, M., Liu, Q., Lu, H., & Ma, S. (2009). Image annotation via graph learning. *Pattern Recognition*, *42*(2), 218–228. doi:10.1016/j.patcog.2008.04.012

Long, F. H. Z. (2003). Fundamentals of content-based image retrieval. In Multimedia Information Retrieval and Management: Technological Fundamentals and Applications. Springer.

Nashwa El-Bendary, T.-K. (2013). Automatic image annotation approach based on optimization of classes scores. *Computing*.

Ro, S. L. (2013). *Visually weighted neighbor voting for image tag relevance learning*. Multimed Tools App.

Su, J.-H. e. (2011). Effective semantic annotation by image-to-concept distribution model. *IEEE Transactions on Multimedia, 13*(3), 530–538. doi:10.1109/TMM.2011.2129502

Wang, F. (2011). A survey on automatic image annotation and trends of the new age. *Procedia Engineering, 23*, 434–438. doi:10.1016/j.proeng.2011.11.2526

Yang, Y. Z., Huang, Z., Yang, Y., Liu, J., Shen, H. T., & Luo, J. (2012). Local image tagging via graph regularized joint group sparsity. *Pattern Recognition, 46*(5), 1358–1368. doi:10.1016/j.patcog.2012.10.026

Yavlinsky, A. E. S. (2005). Automated image annotation using global features and robust nonparametric density estimation. *Proc. ACM Int. Conf. Image Video Retrieva*, (pp. 507-517). doi:10.1007/11526346_54

Zenghai Chen, Z. C. (2013). Multi-instance multi-label image classification: A neural approach. *Neurocomputing, 99*, 298–306. doi:10.1016/j.neucom.2012.08.001

Zhang, S. J. (2012). Automatic image annotation and retrieval using group sparsity. *IEEE Transactions on Systems, Man, and Cybernetics. Part B, Cybernetics, 42*(3), 838–849. doi:10.1109/TSMCB.2011.2179533 PMID:22249744

Zhu, S. T. X., & Tan, X. (2011). A novel automatic image annotation method based on multi-instance learning. *Procedia Eng, 15*, 3439–3444. doi:10.1016/j.proeng.2011.08.644

ADDITIONAL READING

Barata, C., Figueiredo, M. A., Celebi, M. E., & Marques, J. S. (2014, May). Color identification in dermoscopy images using gaussian mixture models. InAcoustics, Speech and Signal Processing (ICASSP), 2014 IEEE International Conference on (pp. 3611-3615). IEEE. doi:10.1109/ICASSP.2014.6854274

Bovik, A. C. (2010). *Handbook of image and video processing*. Academic Press.

Bratasanu, D., Nedelcu, I., & Datcu, M. (2011). Bridging the semantic gap for satellite image annotation and automatic mapping applications. Selected Topics in Applied Earth Observations and Remote Sensing. *IEEE Journal of, 4*(1), 193–204.

Daneshfar, F., & Maihami, V. (2014). *Distributed Learning Algorithm Applications to the Scheduling of Wireless Sensor Networks. A book chapter in: Handbook of Research on Novel Soft Computing Intelligent Algorithms: Theory and Practical Applications* (P. Vasant, Ed.). IGI Global Publisher.

Fathi, M., & Maihami, V. (in press). Operational State Scheduling of Relay Nodes in Two-Tiered Wireless Sensor Networks. *IEEE System Journal*.

Fathi, M., Maihami, V., & Moradi, P. (2013). Reinforcement Learning for Multiple Access Control in Wireless Sensor Networks: Review, Model, and Open Issues. *Wireless Personal Communications*, *72*(1), 535–547. doi:10.1007/s11277-013-1028-9

Feng, Y., Xiao, J., Zha, Z., Zhang, H., & Yang, Y. (2012). Active learning for social image retrieval using Locally Regressive Optimal Design. *Neurocomputing*, *95*, 54–59. doi:10.1016/j.neucom.2011.06.037

Fu, Z., Lu, G., Ting, K. M., & Zhang, D. (2011). A survey of audio-based music classification and annotation. Multimedia. *IEEE Transactions on*, *13*(2), 303–319.

Gao, Y., Wang, M., Zha, Z. J., Shen, J., Li, X., & Wu, X. (2013). Visual-textual joint relevance learning for tag-based social image search. Image Processing. *IEEE Transactions on*, *22*(1), 363–376.

Gonzalez, R. C., & Woods, R. E. (2002). Digital image processing.

Gonzalez, R. C., Woods, R. E., & Eddins, S. L. (2004). Digital image processing using MATLAB. Upper Saddle River, NJ Jensen: Prentice Hall

Gupta, M., Li, R., Yin, Z., & Han, J. (2010). Survey on social tagging techniques. *ACM SIGKDD Explorations Newsletter*, *12*(1), 58–72. doi:10.1145/1882471.1882480

Gupta, M., Li, R., Yin, Z., & Han, J. (2011). An overview of social tagging and applications. In Social network data analytics (pp. 447-497). Springer US. doi:10.1007/978-1-4419-8462-3_16

Hou, J., Zhang, D., Chen, Z., Jiang, L., Zhang, H., & Qin, X. (2010). Web Image Search by Automatic Image Annotation and Translation. In *Proceedings of the 17th International Conference on Systems, Signals and Image Processing (IWSSIP'10)* (pp. 105-108).

Im, D. H., & Park, G. D. (2014). Linked tag: Image annotation using semantic relationships between image tags. *Multimedia Tools and Applications*, 1–15.

Kekre, H. B., Sarode, T., & Natu, P. J. (2014). Color Image Compression using hybrid Haar-DCT wavelet in Different color spaces. *Advances in Image and Video Processing*, *2*(4), 1–11. doi:10.14738/aivp.24.371

Li, X., Snoek, C. G., & Worring, M. (2010, July). Unsupervised multi-feature tag relevance learning for social image retrieval. In *Proceedings of the ACM International Conference on Image and Video Retrieval* (pp. 10-17). ACM. doi:10.1145/1816041.1816044

Liu, D., Hua, X. S., & Zhang, H. J. (2011). Content-based tag processing for internet social images. *Multimedia Tools and Applications*, *51*(2), 723–738. doi:10.1007/s11042-010-0647-3

Liu, Z. (2011). A Survey on Social Image Mining. In Intelligent Computing and Information Science (pp. 662-667). Springer Berlin Heidelberg. doi:10.1007/978-3-642-18129-0_100

Ma, Z., Nie, F., Yang, Y., Uijlings, J. R., & Sebe, N. (2012). Web image annotation via subspace-sparsity collaborated feature selection. *Multimedia. IEEE Transactions on*, *14*(4), 1021–1030.

Moran, S., & Lavrenko, V. (2014). A sparse kernel relevance model for automatic image annotation. International Journal of Multimedia Information Retrieval, 1-21.

Qian, X., Liu, X., Zheng, C., Du, Y., & Hou, X. (2013). Tagging photos using users' vocabularies. *Neurocomputing, 111*, 144–153. doi:10.1016/j.neucom.2012.12.021

Qin, C., Bao, X., Choudhury, R. R., & Nelakuditi, S. (2014). TagSense: Leveraging Smartphones for Automatic Image Tagging. Mobile Computing. *IEEE Transactions on, 13*(1), 61–74.

Sonka, M., Hlavac, V., & Boyle, R. (2014). *Image processing, analysis, and machine vision*. Cengage Learning.

Sumana, I. J., Lu, G., & Zhang, D. (2012, July). Comparison of curvelet and wavelet texture features for content based image retrieval. In Multimedia and Expo (ICME), 2012 IEEE International Conference on (pp. 290-295). IEEE. doi:10.1109/ICME.2012.90

Sun, A., Bhowmick, S. S., Nguyen, N., Tran, K., & Bai, G. (2011). Tag-based social image retrieval: An empirical evaluation. *Journal of the American Society for Information Science and Technology, 62*(12), 2364–2381. doi:10.1002/asi.21659

Tang, J., Chen, Q., Wang, M., Yan, S., Chua, T. S., & Jain, R. (2013). Towards optimizing human labeling for interactive image tagging. [TOMCCAP]. *ACM Transactions on Multimedia Computing, Communications, and Applications, 9*(4), 29. doi:10.1145/2501643.2501651

Truong, B. Q., Sun, A., & Bhowmick, S. S. (2012, June). Content is still king: the effect of neighbor voting schemes on tag relevance for social image retrieval. In *Proceedings of the 2nd ACM International Conference on Multimedia Retrieval*(p. 9). ACM. doi:10.1145/2324796.2324808

Ulges, A., Worring, M., & Breuel, T. (2011). Learning visual contexts for image annotation from flickr groups. Multimedia. *IEEE Transactions on, 13*(2), 330–341.

Wang, M., Ni, B., Hua, X. S., & Chua, T. S. (2012). Assistive tagging: A survey of multimedia tagging with human-computer joint exploration. *ACM Computing Surveys, 44*(4), 25. doi:10.1145/2333112.2333120

Wang, Y., Ostermann, J., & Zhang, Y. Q. (2002). *Video processing and communications* (Vol. 5). Upper Saddle River: Prentice Hall.

Weston, J., Bengio, S., & Usunier, N. (2010). Large scale image annotation: Learning to rank with joint word-image embeddings. *Machine Learning, 81*(1), 21–35. doi:10.1007/s10994-010-5198-3

Wu, P., Hoi, S. C. H., Zhao, P., & He, Y. (2011, February). Mining social images with distance metric learning for automated image tagging. InProceedings of the fourth ACM international conference on Web search and data mining (pp. 197-206). ACM. doi:10.1145/1935826.1935865

Yaghmaee, F., & Jamzad, M. (2008, August). Introducing a new method for estimation image complexity according to calculate watermark capacity. InIntelligent Information Hiding and Multimedia Signal Processing, 2008. IIHMSP'08 International Conference on (pp. 981-984). IEEE. doi:10.1109/IIH-MSP.2008.185

Yaghmaee, F., & Jamzad, M. (2010). Estimating watermarking capacity in gray scale images based on image complexity. *EURASIP Journal on Advances in Signal Processing, 2010*, 8. doi:10.1155/2010/851920

Yang, Y., Huang, Z., Shen, H. T., & Zhou, X. (2011). Mining multi-tag association for image tagging. *World Wide Web (Bussum)*, *14*(2), 133–156. doi:10.1007/s11280-010-0099-8

Yao, B., Bradski, G., & Fei-Fei, L. (2012, June). A codebook-free and annotation-free approach for fine-grained image categorization. In Computer Vision and Pattern Recognition (CVPR), 2012 IEEE Conference on (pp. 3466-3473). IEEE.

Zhang, D., Islam, M., & Lu, G. (2013). Structural image retrieval using automatic image annotation and region based inverted file. *Journal of Visual Communication and Image Representation*, *24*(7), 1087–1098. doi:10.1016/j.jvcir.2013.07.004

Zhang, X., Zhao, X., Li, Z., Xia, J., Jain, R., & Chao, W. (2013). Social image tagging using graph-based reinforcement on multi-type interrelated objects. *Signal Processing*, *93*(8), 2178–2189. doi:10.1016/j.sigpro.2012.05.021

Zhou, N., Cheung, W. K., Qiu, G., & Xue, X. (2011). A hybrid probabilistic model for unified collaborative and content-based image tagging. Pattern Analysis and Machine Intelligence. *IEEE Transactions on*, *33*(7), 1281–1294.

KEY TERMS AND DEFINITIONS

Automatic Image Annotation: Perform image annotation action automatically and by machine (computer).

Color Feature: An important feature of the image which has many applications in image processing and computer vision. Number of color features are color histogram, color moment and color correlogram.

Color Space: The color of an image is represented through some color space (model). There exist various color spaces to describe color information. The more commonly used color models are RGB (red, green, blue), HSI (hue, saturation, value) and YCbCr (luminance and chrominance).

Corel5k Dataset: One of the benchmark for evolutionary image annotation.

Image Annotation: Image annotation is a process produces metadata (text or keywords) to a digital image based on visual content of this image.

Machine Learning Methods: Machine learning is programming computers to optimize a performance criterion using example data or past experience. Three approaches of this learning are as follows. 1) *Supervised learning.* In this approach, the agent utilizes a stream of educational data from a supervisor to learn a specific behavior using artificial neural networks, fuzzy logic or genetic algorithm. 2) *Unsupervised learning.* In contrast to the first approach, the agent learns without any human intervention or feedback from the environment. For example clustering. 3) *Reinforcement Learning.* The agent interacting with an environment attempts to increase its knowledge and to improve its actions incrementally.

Neighbor Voting: A real-time algorithm to automatic image annotation with weakly supervision and low complexity.

Semantic Gap: Distance between the human visual perception and the low-level visual features.

Chapter 16
Biomedical Imaging Techniques

Shanmuga Sundari Ilangovan
VIT University, India

Biswanath Mahanty
INHA University, Republic of Korea

Shampa Sen
VIT University, India

ABSTRACT

Biomedical imaging techniques had significantly improved the health care of patients. Image guided therapy has reduced the high risk of human errors with improved accuracy in disease detection and surgical procedures. The chapter provides an overview of existing imaging methods and current imaging approaches and their potential to unravel the challenges in medical field. First part of the chapter picture outs the basic concepts and mechanism of various imaging techniques that are currently in use. The second part explains about the features of image processing system and future trends in image guided therapy extended with a short discussion on radiation exposure in medical imaging. The authors trust the chapter to be beneficial to the beginners in the area of medical science and to the clinicians.

INTRODUCTION

Image and video processing finds its broad application in medical science. Biomedical imaging techniques have their prominent role both in diagnostic and therapeutic arenas. These techniques had significantly helped to improve the health care of patients. Image guided therapy has drastically reduced the high risk of human errors with improved accuracy in disease detection and surgical procedures. The history of medical imaging started since 1890's, gradually raised in 1980's and considerably explored in recent years with technological advancements. The main objective of this chapter is to provide a basic knowledge to the novices of various biomedical imaging on techniques and their advancements in today's world.

DOI: 10.4018/978-1-4666-9685-3.ch016

BACKGROUND

Discovery of X-rays by Wilhelm Conrad Rontgen was the beginning era for medical imaging. In 1895, Wilhelm Conrad Rontgen discovered the occurrence of electromagnetic radiation in the wavelength range while undertaking an experiment with Hittorf – Crookes tube. He named the new ray as X-rays, with which he took the first picture of his wife Anna Bertha's hand. The X-rays were later developed by William Coolidge with the invention of Coolidge tube which gave more powerful visualization of deep-rooted anatomy and tumours. Use of Coolidge tube with tungsten filament by Coolidge was one of the biggest exploitation of X-rays in the field of radiology. In 1946, Nuclear magnetic Resonance (NMR) in a condensed matter was discovered by Felix Bloch and Edward Purcell. This was the initial footstep towards the discovery of Magnetic Resonance Imaging (MRI).

With the advent of NMR, Raymond Vahan Damadian proposed the first MR body scanner in 1969. He discovered that tumour can be distinguished from normal cells using NMR. Godfrey Hounsfield came up with the idea to create an object in slices using X- rays at various angles around the object. He built the first prototype Computed Tomographic (CT) scanner and obtained first CT image of a preserved human brain. The first MRI body scanner on humans came into picture in 1977. With the assist of mathematics, and computer algorithms and with technological expansion in digital and communications system, new imaging techniques were developed. This moulded biomedical imaging to be an interdisciplinary field which collaborate physicist, biologist, mathematician, pharmacologist and computational biologist.

IMAGING TECHNIQUES

The basic principles of all imaging techniques are same. A beam of wave passes through the body/area under diagnosis, transmits or reflects back the radiation which will be captured by a detector and processed to get an image pattern. The type of wave differs for different modalities. CT involves the use of X-rays, whereas radio frequency waves and gamma rays are used for MRI and SPECT (Single-Photon Emission Computed Tomography) respectively.

Conventional Film Radiography

With the development of X-rays, the first radiographic image was obtained through conventional film radiography. Conventional radiography contains X-ray film placed in between two screen supports and fluorescent screens. The setup is placed in between a couple of cassettes as shown in Figure 1. A beam of X-ray passes though the human body, hits the fluorescent screen and produces a photographic image pattern. The film is later removed, processed and developed with automated chemical film processor (Brant & Helms, 2012) in a dark room and a visible image pattern is obtained.

Computed Radiography

Conventional film radiography was modified with the use of a reusable phosphor imaging plate and was named as Computed Radiography (CR). Instead of film cassette, a photostimulable phosphor imaging plate was placed in the cassette. The radiographic shadow falls, gets projected on the imaging plate and the plate is placed on a reading device or a CR reader. The reading device consists of a helium neon laser

Figure 1. X-ray film cassette of conventional radiography

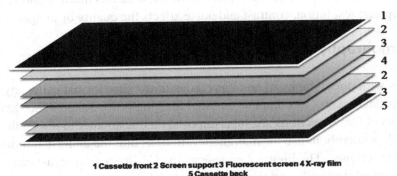

**1 Cassette front 2 Screen support 3 Fluorescent screen 4 X-ray film
5 Cassette back**

and a photomultiplier tube. The laser reads the imaging plate and emits the light which is passed to the photomultiplier tube and processed with the help of system software to get a digital image. An example could be the image of a male chest taken by CR shown in Figure 2.

With the advent of CR, Direct or Digital Radiography (DR) was developed. DR is also known as direct imaging and CR is known as indirect imaging. The major difference between CR and DR would be; CR a cassette system within which the imaging plate is hosted to capture the image, whereas DR directly captures the image. DR is more beneficial in eliminating the cost with reliable storage and easy film processing. But both CR and DR have advantages of specific representation of anatomy and

Figure 2. X ray image of chest by Computed Radiography
Source: Image was obtained directly from the patient with patient's authorization

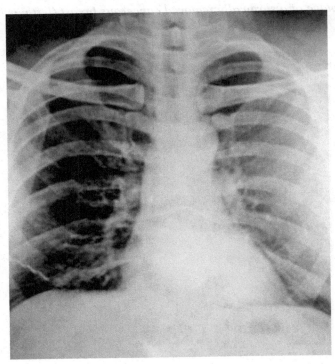

specific algorithms to envisage various diseases. However, few factors like detection efficiency, dynamic range, spatial sampling, resolution, contrast and noise affects the quality of images in both CR and DR.

Computed Tomography (CT)

Tomography deals with photography of an object in sections/ slice format using any type of wave. CT provides cross sectional images by computer assisted imaging process, and hence known as Computed Tomography. Slices of image sections are superimposed on one another to obtain the 3D digital image using software. CT is notably in use for malignancy, in detecting the abnormal tumour growth, stages in tumour or their recurrence. The Figure 3 represents the CT image of a breast cancer patient. The left side breast was removed surgically and the scan was taken for any recurrence of tumour after a month. CT is also widely employed in coronary artery disease (atherosclerosis), blood vessel aneurysms, blood clots, inflammations and enlargement, injuries in parts of head, skeletal system and internal organs. An example could be the CT scan of liver enlargement, hepatomegaly, depicted in Figure 4. For abdomen and pelvis scan CT is of best choice as compared to MRI.

Advancements with CT as spiral or multi – slice imaging achieved the resolution of 1 mm and scans the whole body in 10 sec (Sakas, 2002). Bone or surface images are more clearly visualized in CT. Recently, Electron Beam CT (EBCT) is used, where distinct images/snapshots can be produced without any moving object. EBCT has more benefits compared to normal CT including quicker image acquisition.

To get clear visualization for some parts/moving objects like brain, blood vessels etc contrast medium are employed. Iodinated contrast medium is commonly employed for CT. Contrast agent can be given intravenously or orally depending on the part of the body. In case of poor kidney functioning, intravenous

Figure 3. Represents image of a surgically removed cancerous breast (left portion) and normal breast (right portion) of CT

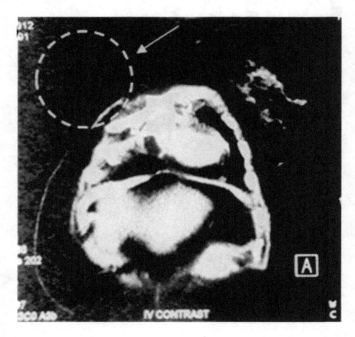

Figure 4. Shows enlarged liver (Hepatomegaly). Both the images are taken from 256 slice whole body CT scan. Source: Images were obtained directly from the patient with patient's authorization

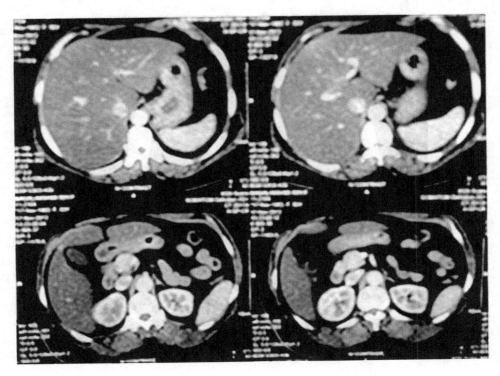

injection of contrast medium is avoided as it could further depress the kidney function. In few cases, it will cause mild allergic reactions. Persons allergic to iodine will be requested to inform the radiologist as an early precaution. Contrast agents will pass through the urine and are mostly harmless to the patients. However, mild to adverse reactions are reported less frequently (Jingu et al., 2014).

Magnetic Resonance Imaging (MRI)

MRI is a powerful diagnostic technique for soft tissues. MRI system implies strong and uniform magnetic field together with radiofrequency waves. Suitable resonant radiofrequency is applied to the patient from the scanner. The waves pass through the tissues or any region that hold hydrogen atoms in the body, *viz.,* water molecules. The atom gets excited and return back to the equilibrium state using the energy from oscillating magnetic field which will be captured by the scanner and digitally processed. Hence MRI is best suited for visualization of soft tissues, tendons and ligaments. MRI is also applicable in detection of some lesions in brain as shown in Figure 5. Contrast agents like gadolinium are used to distinguish minute differences/changes in structures of the body. The major advantage of using MRI is to vary the contrast of the image. Minute alteration in the radiowave frequency and the magnetic field can alter the contrast of the image which highlights different types of tissues. Another advantage of MRI is that it can construct images in any plane (axial/horizontal) which is unfeasible in CT.

There are diverse types of MRI. MRI exploited in the measurement of diffusion of water molecules inside the body is known as Diffusion MRI. This MRI is valuable in diagnosis of neurological disorders

Figure 5. MRI Image of a brain showing lesions (indicated by arrow). Source: Image was obtained directly from the patient with patient's authorization

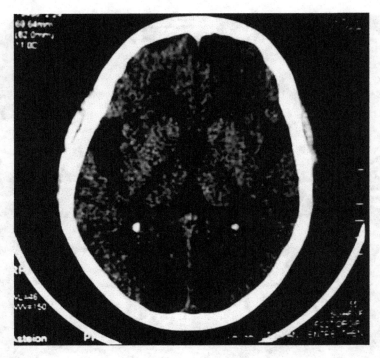

like multiple sclerosis and in stroke (Bihan et al., 1986). The change in neural activity can be diagnosed using functional MRI (fMRI), hence widely applied is neurological disorders. Other application would be the real time MRI, as the name indicates; it monitors the moving objects in real time.

Ultrasonography

Ultrasonography is a real time imaging technique which uses ultrasound frequency for visualizing internal body structures. Ultrasound gel is placed on the transducer, a device that converts energy into ultrasound and is directly kept on the place of visualization (on the skin). The gel avoids air bubble formation and transmits the sound waves. High frequency sound waves are transmitted into the body. The sound that bounces back (echoes) from the tissues or organs are collected by an ultrasound transducer and with the assistance of computer, images are obtained with good axial and lateral resolutions. The images obtained are known technically as sonogram.

Ultrasound with low frequencies (1- 6 MHz) have long wavelength with less resolution and has higher penetration profundity in tissues. Organs such as liver, kidney are visualized with low frequencies. High frequencies (7-18 MHz) have short wavelength and can scatter or reflect small structures and are capable of imaging superficial structures like tendons and neonatal brain. The only constraint with this imaging technique is that organs blocked with bowel or air filled bowel are impossible to diagnose, as the ultrasound waves are disturbed. In addition, ultrasound waves cannot penetrate bones.

New techniques with the existing Ultrasonography were developed which are far more advanced than the conventional method. Ultrasonography has different names based on the place they are imaged/visualized. In visualization of the developing foetus, as illustrated in Figure 6 and 7 it is known as obstetrical sonography while, imaging of the eyes are known as Ocular Ultrasonography. Arterial sonography, diagnosis arteries, and venosonography image the venous, its severity and deficiency. Thromosonography plays role in visualization of deep vein thrombosis. Carotid Ultrasonography diagnoses the blood flow and stenoses in the arteries of carotid.

Figure 6. Shows image of a foetus taken at 7 weeks of gestational stage by transvaginal ultrasonography

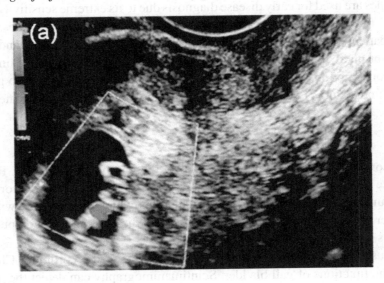

Figure 7. Shows the image of foetus developed corresponding to a gestational stage of 12 weeks obtained from transabdominal ultrasonography. Source: Images were obtained directly from the patient with patient's authorization

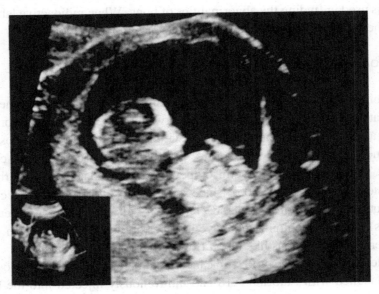

Nuclear Medicine

All the other imaging modalities discussed earlier helps to visualize or image the anatomy of the body structures. Nuclear medicine or nuclear imaging is the visualization of functions of the organs. Labelling of radionuclides (radioactive substances/ radioisotopes) together with pharmaceutical compounds in analyzing functions of specific organs and detecting the minute changes at molecular and cellular level is known as nuclear medicine. Scintigraphy, Positron emission tomography (PET) / Single-photon emission computed tomography (SCECT) are the standard nuclear imaging modalities currently in use.

Nuclear medicines are used for early disease diagnosis due to its extreme sensitivity; in early detection of different stages of cancer or the exact location of cancer and other abnormalities. With the assist of nuclear medicine, patient's response to administered drugs or recurrence of disease and their management with quick treatment plans for advanced diseases are easily possible. The major limitation of nuclear medicine is time consumption. It takes several hours to days for the radiotracer to get accumulated in the specific region under study. Further the resolutions of the images are not as greater as in MRI or CT.

Scintigraphy

Scintigraphy is a conventional method used to visualize the internal body tissues. Radiopharmaceuticals/radiotracers are given internally to the patients either as injection, swallowed or inhaled subjected to specific region under study. Radiotracers emit radiations which are captured with gamma camera also known as anger camera. The images are processed with the assistance of computer to produce two dimensional images.

Scintigraphy is used in diagnosis of most of the organs and named accordingly. Cholescintigraphy is done to diagnose the functions of gall bladder. Scintimammography can detect the presence of cancer in the breast, also known as nuclear medicine breast imaging or molecular breast imaging. Radionuclide angiography or radionuclide ventriculography plays role in detection of heart failure as it detects the function of right and left ventricles of heart. Radioisotope renography is used to evaluate the function of kidney. Sestamibi parathyroid scintigraphy is used in localization of parathyroid adenoma while bone scintigraphy is used in finding the abnormalities of bone. When radioactive labeled antibodies are injected to detect the presence of cancer cells, it is known as Immunoscintigraphy.

Positron Emission Tomography (PET)

PET is similar to scintigraphy except that positron emitting radiotracer is used. The radiotracer differs based on the application, oncology or neuro or cardiology. Once injected, the positron radiotracer travels through the tissue, a few millimetres and combines with free electrons to form positronium which on decay results in generation of pair of gamma rays, detected, reconstructed by the computer system to produce the images. The commonly used radioisotopes are short lived isotopes of carbon-11, oxygen-15, nitrogen-13, and fluorine-18 (Ziegler, 2005). Since short lived isotopes are used, a cyclotron is mandatory for PET. Cyclotron is a type of particle accelerator. It will produce positron emitters (short lived radioactive isotopes) when stable non-radioactive isotopes are fed into a cyclotron. PET is commonly used in the measurement of functions like blood flow and glucose metabolism.

The best example could be the use of PET in cancer treatment. Fluorodeoxyglucose (FDG) is a sugar analogue. FDG is labelled with Fluorine – 18 and intravenously injected into the body. Cancer cells

Table 1. An overview of imaging techniques

	CT	MRI	Ultrasound	Nuclear Medicine
Source	X-rays	Radiofrequency waves	Ultrasound frequency	Radiotracers
Time taken for scanning	> 30 sec. Depends on the part under investigation. Completed in 10 minutes	10 min to 1hr depending on the part of the body	depends on the part of the body abdominal – 20 min pelvic – 30 min	depends on the type of scan two to several hours after injection
Radiation dose	2 to 10 mSv	1-100 MHz	1 -18 MHz	Differs based on the isotope ex: Tc 99 m
Advantages	distinguish tissues differing in physical density cost effective	high sensitivity accuracy	non – exposure to radiations	high sensitivity accuracy
Applications	neurology cardiology gastroenterology measures bone strength	all parts of the body	neonatal brain, thyroid, muscle joints, tendons heart, liver, kidney, spleen, urinary bladder, pancreas, blood vessels	bladder, bowel, spleen, adrenal medulla, colon, thyroid tumour detection
Risk/ Precautions	health conditions pregnancy claustrophobia	pregnancy claustrophobia unsuitable for patients with metal chips/ devices pacemakers)	Nil	children < 14 yrs. are not allowed pregnant women should stop breast feeding on the day of scan should not do within 24rhs of gadolinium MRI scan

will have higher uptake of glucose compared to normal cells. Hence, the injected radiotracer will enter cancer cells; gets accumulated which will take approximately 40 mins. SPECT has the same principles of PET except that lower energy emitting isotopes Technetium-99m and Iodine – 123 are used. SPECT is cheaper and widely used, as it does not employ cyclotron.

The most commonly used imaging techniques are given in a precise format with their advantages and disadvantages in Table 1.

OTHER IMAGING TECHNIQUES

A number of new imaging techniques are currently available and are still getting developed. Few of the techniques are listed below. These techniques are often less common in the field of medical imaging due to lack of some important factors needed for efficient imaging or they are in the developing process. However, because of their unique properties each of these imaging techniques are gaining significant importance day by day.

- Electrical Impedance Tomography
- Optical Coherence Tomography
- Photoacoustic/ Thermoacoustic Imaging
- Microwave Imaging

- Elastography
- Magnetic Resonance Elastography

Electrical Impedance Tomography (EIT)

EIT is a technique which uses surface electrodes with low frequency electric current that observes the changes in biological tissues during the occurrence of electrical conductivity. The amount of free ion content in the body tissues are the basis for EIT. Usually, muscle tissues and body fluids such as blood are monitored here. EIT results in two dimensional images which are obtained from the conductivity of small altering current passed/diffused through the biological samples. At higher frequencies, due to changes in dielectric constant the images results are obtained as slices of two dimensional images. Hence, this method is in general known as Impedance tomography.

The imaging technique is safe and cost effective when compared to MRI. As EIT is based on applying small current without use of radiations, this technique is considered to be the safest with no side effects. EIT is currently employed in screening of breast cancer, real time usage in lung ventilation inside Intensive Care Unit (ICU), functioning of cardiac, brain, cervix etc.

EIT measures the electrical conductivity; however, it cannot measure interior conductivity inside the biological tissues. Hence, to overcome these hurdles, MRI is united together with EIT. The ensuing imaging modality is Magnetic Resonance Electrical Impedance Tomography (MREIT). This involves the application of both electrical field and magnetic field which results in high resolution images. The resulting two dimensional images can be reconstructed to three dimensional images by reconstruction of algorithms. MREIT is more advantageous and have wider applications, when compared to EIT.

Optical Coherence Tomography (OCT)

OCT is an imaging technique that employs back reflecting and scattering light waves of long wavelength which can enter deeper the diagnosing area, scatters the light rays and produces a typical tomogram of higher resolution. The images are obtained in micrometer resolution with the assistance of low coherence interferometry. It is commonly used in diagnosing early detection of the retina in ophthalmology. OCT is also used to diagnose plaques in coronary arteries, in dermatology and in dentaology for root canal treatment. The main advantages of OCT include direct imaging with no radiation exposure, ease of use and are cost effective. The imaging depth in OCT is less than imaging of Ultrasound; however, OCT has much higher resolution. As OCT has no radiation effects and are economically feasible, they can be integrated with other diagnostic imaging techniques. One such example is the integration of OCT with endoscopic and catheter units. The main use of OCT in these techniques is the ability of OCT to enter inside the body, as OCT is of fiber optic based technology. Due to the immense applications of this technique, its integration with other diagnostic techniques for earlier detection and prevention of diseases are being studied.

Photoacoustic/Thermoacoustic Imaging

Photoacoustic Imaging is based on the principle of photoacoustic effect. Photoacoustic imaging employs laser pulse that passes through the biological sample, absorbs the energy and converts to heat, resulting in generation of ultrasound waves. These waves are captured by transducers and are converted to images.

Thermoacoustic imaging has the same principle of Photoacoustic imaging, but uses radio frequency waves. Photoacoustic imaging is widely applied in detection of brain lesions, measurement of concentration of hemoglobin, screening of breast cancer etc. Combination of thermo and photo acoustic imaging are widely used in diagnosis of breast cancer. Since, it does not use radiation, will not affect normal cells. There is an increasing preference to use this technique in detection of cancers.

Microwave Imaging

Microwave imaging is an emerging imaging modality especially in diagnosis of breast cancer. Compared to photoacoustic imaging and ultrasound imaging, microwave imaging has promising future for breast cancer diagnosis. Microwave imaging depends on the water content in tissue samples. Due to angiogenesis, cancer cells usually have high water content compared to normal cells and better diagnosed in microwave imaging. A high electrical contrast is obtained between the cancerous cells and normal cells in microwave imaging, making this more appropriate for cancer detection. Microwave imaging is also applied in osteoporosis, where it detects the variation in mineral density of bone. As the imaging method is cost effective, user friendly and safe, considerable interest is shown by the researchers to develop this technique for other cancer detection and in diagnosis of other diseases.

Elastography

Elastography or elastic imaging is an imaging modality that involves the use of mechanical properties of soft tissues. In general, imaging techniques such as CT, MRI fails to diagnose breast cancer in early stages, mainly due to the firm lesions which are often undetectable in these techniques. Cancer tissues possess more stiffness compared to normal tissues. Elastic stiffness is the main factor which is analyzed using elastic imaging, as breast cancer tissues often undergo palpitation in early breast cancer detection. Apart from cancer, the main organ diagnosed is liver. Damaged liver will have more stiffness compared to normal liver. Hence, elastography is the common imaging technique used for detecting liver damages. Other organs like muscles, tendons are also diagnosed using this technique based on the elastic properties.

Magnetic Resonance Elastography (MRE)

MRE is an emerging technique that employs magnetic resonance principle together with elastography. MRE uses elastic waves of 10–1000 Hz together with phase contrast MRI. The changes in the wave patterns and the values of shear modulus are calculated from elastic stiffness, and from these values the results are obtained as images. MRE is commonly used for hepatic fibrosis. However, use of MRE as a standard imaging modality is still at its infancy.

NEED FOR SEVERAL IMAGING MODALITIES

A single imaging technique can give the view of a particular tissue or an organ. For example, a CT scan can show the presence of stone or an abnormality of urinary tract, but techniques like MRI, PET and Ultrasound are used for the same purpose. Further, to visualize kidney arteries (in case of artery stenosis) Magnetic resonance angiogram is used, whereas to find a cyst, tumour or an infection CT is used. A voiding cystourethrogram is used to find the abnormal flow of urine in children and abnormal bladder position in women. All these techniques are used to image regions within the urinary tract. Even though several imaging modalities exists, based on the patient's history, symptoms, requirements, quality and resolution of the photograph, a particular imaging mode is preferred. Other examples could be the use of Sonography, which gives report on 53 – 77% lesions whereas, MRI could better discriminate 91% of malignant tumour and PET could be used for its high sensitivity in tumour detection.

Each technique has its unique characteristics in diagnosis of a particular disease. But they have their own disadvantage too; MRI could give the blood flow and activity of brain cells, whereas CT cannot. Hence, hybrid techniques emerged to integrate the advantages of each imaging modality and to confer the exact interpretation of the diagnosed disease. For example, CT coupled MRI gives useful information both on the bone and soft tissues nearby/around the bone. This helps the doctors in interpretation of the disease in that particular locality. Multimodality imaging currently in use are PET-MRI/ CT-PET coupled MRI/CT scan gives the functional characteristics of the organs/tissues together with detailed anatomical structures like tissue density, organ size etc. Hence dual and multimodality imaging gives better diagnosis.

IMAGE QUALITY, IMAGE PROCESSING, AND VISUALIZATION OF IMAGES

The images obtained from various imaging modalities makes way for doctors to plan a surgery, radiotherapy or to identify any malignancy or other dysfunctions. Image quality, resolution and interpretation of the results from an image are more important as, minute variation in diagnosis could change the treatment to be done for the patient. Exact diagnosis and treatment relies to a great extent on the quality of the image as it plays a major role in biomedical image interpretation. Hence, considering the importance of the image, the entire process of receiving data/signal from the object to acquiring final images from the imaging modality are discussed here.

Components of Image Processing System

The signal received from the patient's body to finally processed image as displayed in the monitor all together constitutes the main components of the image processing system. Figure 8 represents the block diagram of image processing system.

- **Image Sensors:** Images are captured by a sensor such as videos, camera or scanner. The captured image is converted to digital form by digitizer (analogue-to-digital converter).
- **Image Processing Hardware:** Specialized image processing hardware consists of digitizer and hardware. The main purpose of the hardware is to speed up the process.
- **Computer:** Based on the need, a simple PC to super computer can be used as an image processing system.
- **Mass Storage:** Images acquired from each patient has to be stored in a storage system. Though most of the images are compressed before storing, enough space is required to store thousands/ millions of images. Hence adequate storage is required.
- **Hardcopy Devices:** Mainly used for recording the images.

Figure 8. Components of image processing system

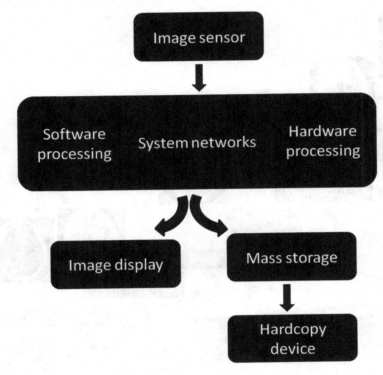

- **Image Processing Software:** Software specific to image processing are commercially available which performs required tasks in the processing system.
- **Image Display:** The device to project the output of the image and its information, such as monitor or television.

Image Processing

The image obtained from the scanning devices may usually have some geometric deformation, blur, noise etc. due the sensitivity of the equipments. Hence once the images are retrieved from the sensor, they are fed into the computer. The image processing software converts the original scan into an improved image for better visualization. The flow chart of the image processing steps are portrayed in Figure 9. performed using system networks

1. **Image Acquisition:** Images are acquired from videos of camera or from the scanner of the imaging modality.
2. **Image Restoration:** Restoration is primarily considered to get back the quality of digital image that has been degraded during the digital image formation that usually comes from motion blur or due to instrumental noise or some misfocus of the sensor. Various methods such as inverse filtering, wiener filtering are used to restore the original images.
3. **Image Enhancement:** Enhancement is done to give better appearance to the image. Enhancement techniques include image sharpening, noise reduction, manipulating the greyscale levels, improv-

Figure 9. Steps in image processing

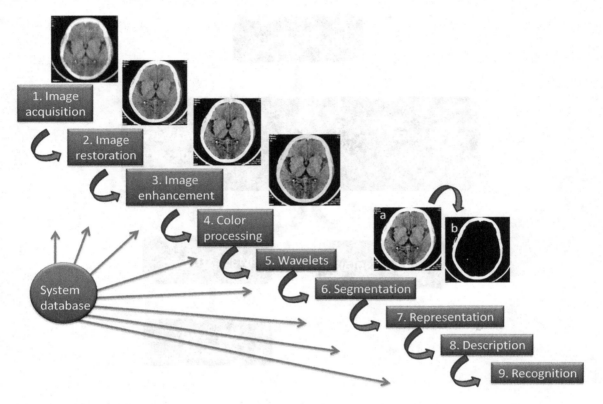

ing image brightness and contrast to increase the quality of the image. Mathematical concepts like Fourier transforms and algorithms for halftoning, zooming are applied to enhance the appearance of the image.

4. **Colour Processing:** To simplify the image analysis, such as, extraction of an image based on colour, colour processing is done. The common model implemented is RGB (red, green, blue) model which transforms each RGB colour plane in the image to give a coloured image.

5. **Wavelets:** Images obtained are usually of greater size and requires large storage space. Hence, the images are compressed by minimizing their size (bytes) without degrading the quality of the image. Wavelet transform is an important technique used to compress images and to recover weak signals from noises.

6. **Segmentation:** Partitioning of images into multiple segments or regions to represent the meaningful areas from the whole image is known as segmentation. Segmentation algorithms such as clustering algorithms, line and arc detectors, and region growing are used for this purpose. Figure 9, step 6a represents the original image and 6b represent the segmented region showing clear visualization of lesion.

7. **Representation:** After segmentation, the multiple segments of pixels are represented for further processing. It may be boundary representation which focus on the external areas (corners) or regional representation which focus on internal properties (pixels containing region)

8. **Description**: Describing the region based on the representation suitable for further processing. This highlights the quantitative information and the features of interest.
9. **Recognition:** Recognizing individual characters or labelling using algorithms.

All the steps are guided by system database which plays role in processing and interaction of each module. To perform the entire operation, specialized software are available for image processing (Gonzalez & Woods, 2001). These software perform the tasks ranging from few seconds to minutes to give the best quality images.

RADIATION EXPOSURE AND RADIATION PROTECTION IN MEDICAL IMAGING

Development of CT, MRI and other diagnostic techniques has drastically increased the use of radiation in the medical field. About 62 million CT scans were taken in 2006 which were less than 20 million in 1995 (Brenner & Hall, 2007) and has increased two fold at current scenario. These radiation exposures could significantly affect the human population. In 2007, guidelines were framed by the United States government as, International Commission for Radiological Protection, 2007 and National Council on Radiation Protection and Measurements to understand the possible risks of exposure to radiations and to follow measures for the protection of human welfare (Kase, 2004). Hence radiation protection can be achieved by utilizing minimum amount of radiation to get maximum relevant information on the particular diagnosis. Few measures that can be considered are proper shielding of examination room and patient's anatomical area. This avoids the exposure of radiation in other parts of the room and patients body respectively. Radiation dose monitors are used by the clinicians/ radiologist and in the room to examine the radiation levels. Enhanced reconstruction algorithms and image processing are widely under research to minimize the direct exposure of radiation from the instruments.

GENERAL APPLICATIONS OF MEDICAL IMAGING

Application of Imaging towards Diseases

Alzheimer's Disease (AD)

Quantitative MRI is the diagnosis of AD, which facilitates both the doctors and patients in treatment and prevention. Doctors, on using MRI as potential biomarker could diagnose the stages of disease and its progression. This helps the doctor to increase or decrease the drug dosages and to change the combination of drugs to be given for each stages of AD. Patients on the other hand, could directly see the images of their own body, say lesions or strokes from the MRI images. This creates awareness towards the changes in life style of AD patients such as smoking, stress or depression in anticipation of AD. About 10% reduction changes in life style of AD patients could prevent the disease progression to minimum. Hence, application of MRI in diagnosis of AD could significantly benefit the patients.

Cancer

Cancer is the foremost emerging disease involving millions of death per year. Cancer is the abnormal growth of normal cells leading to formation of malignant tumour. These cancer cells can raid over the other parts of the body creating it to be a life threatening disease. Liver cancer is one of the leading cancers causing more than six lakhs death all over the world. In general tumor/cancer cells possess a pressurized environment which potentially eliminates the foreign materials that may be the drugs or contrast agents. As the contrast agents are rapidly eliminated, cancer imaging becomes tricky. Further, liver cancer cells undergo rapid metabolism and makes early detection of liver cancer to be a complicated process.

Scientists have developed new bioimaging markers to rectify these problems. Protein based contrast agent viz. ProCA32 was developed by the researchers of Georgia State University for detection of early stage liver cancer and metastases. ProCA32 measures tumor of smaller size, less than 0.24 nm using T_1- and T_2-weighted or T_2/T_1 ratio MRI (Shenghui et al., 2015). The authors believe that ProCA32 are capable of providing both positive and negative images with higher accuracy and resolutions. Since these agents are proven to afford high resolution MRI images, ProCA32 can also be applied to other liver diseases and to other diseases such as brain tumors and Alzheimer's disease.

Another problem in early detection of cancer is the use of contrast MRI. This MRI cannot detect the structure of tumors, as the contrast agent flowing through the blood gets repelled from tumor tissues. Though, diffusion MRI is used to solve this problem, as it measures the diffusion of water in cancer cells, they suffer from magnetic deviations resulting in wrong prediction of exact tumor location. A new MRI technique, Restriction Spectrum Imaging-MRI (RSI-MRI) was developed by the researchers from University of California to detect early stages of prostate cancer (Rakow-Penner et al., 2015). RSI- MRI predicts the exact location of tumor solving the problem of magnetic field distortions occurring in diffusion MRI scans. RSI – MRI can be applied to other cancers for earlier detection of aggressive cancers.

Cardiovascular Diseases

SPECT imaging is the most common technique used in diagnosis of heart related problems. SPECT imaging utilizes higher amount of radiotracer to take images. The major drawback of this technique is the low quality images and more exposure to radiation. Further, the radioactive tracer has long half life and gets eliminated in 2 days. Further patients having high levels of liver and gastrointestinal activity and obese patients are not diagnosed through SPECT for cardiovascular diseases. Hence, additional imaging techniques are required for such patients. To overcome the drawbacks of SPECT imaging, Intermountain Medical Centre Heart Institute, Salt Lake City signifies the use PET/CT for cardio related diseases (Intermountain Medical Centre, 2015). PET/CT can solve all the drawbacks of SPECT, providing to be more accurate and cost effective method. PECT/CT has short half life of two minutes and the radiotracers are eliminated in 20 minutes from the body. In addition, it can diagnose all kinds of patients with high quality images. Hence, projecting these variations to clinicians and using PE/CT for cardiovascular disease provides safe imaging with reliable results.

Till date it is impossible to exactly analyze the three dimensional structure of artery plaques, because the current imaging techniques are not able to penetrate deeper the tissues to provide three dimensional structure of plaques. Wang and his co-workers developed new imaging technology to view the 3D structure of plaques. The main concept of their work is to predict the specific chemical bonds in the diagnosis area. Finding out the carbon-hydrogen bonds which forms lipids in the plaque arteries, can lead to the diagnosis of plaque by this technique (Wang et al., 2015).

Fetal Alcohol Syndrome (FAS)

FAS is the symptom arises due to drinking of alcohol by pregnant women. The syndrome is characterized by heart problems, growth retardation and other abnormalities in developing stages of the foetus. Women drinking at pregnancy can leads to several child birth defects. These symptoms which are due to the consumption of alcohol were proved in model organism Quail. Injecting known quantity of alcohol in quail embryos resulted in adverse effects. Imaging through optical coherence tomography (OCT) to observe the structural anatomy and blood flow of heart showed remarkable effects in hatching and blood flow. Hence, diagnosing the functional changes in pregnant women in early developing foetus through OCT helps in preventing heart and other child birth defects.

Another study using MRI to predict the effects of alcohol on FAS disclosed the consequence of alcohol consumption by pregnant women in group study of children with their mother consumed alcohol during their fetal development. From the MRI imaging, it was observed that a considerably thinning occurred compared to control group in the corpus callosum of brain, which are directly related to child psychological problems (Radiological Society of North America, 2012). Other problems in FAS studied by other researchers of same Radiological society, explained the effects in neurological disorders. Diffusion weighted imaging (DWI) which observes the diffusion of water can perceive tissue deformities. Further, proton (hydrogen) magnetic resonance spectroscopy (HMRS) can give details of metabolic changes specifically to the brain. These techniques can be used in early diagnosis of FAS to avoid child birth defects.

Imaging in Drug Development

Drug discovery and drug development is a long term process where the world invests billions of dollars every year. It takes 15 to 20 years to get one FDA approved drug from thousands of drugs screened in clinical trials. The need for safety and efficacy increases the time duration of preclinical and clinical trials thereby delaying the progress in drug development. Medical imaging can play vital role in preclinical trials where, imaging techniques are used to develop new imaging biomarkers, responders to the therapy. Imaging biomarkers which are highly responding to the therapeutic drug can reveal either the success or the failure of drug at some points in Phase I/II or Phase III clinical trials; supporting the clinical outcomes (Wang and Deng, 2010). Improving a single step in clinical trial would increase the early drug outcome to the market. For example, in phase I clinical trials, imaging agents helps in obtaining pharmacokinetic data of a single dose. In phase II clinical trials imaging agents are used to predict the dose regimen, standardizing the image acquisition data progression, deeper evaluation of medical imaging agents etc. These studies help in a smooth progress of phase III clinical trials. Phase III studies further confirm the efficacy and safety of imaging agents and authorize the formulation proposed for marketing purposes (FDA, Guidance for industry Part III, 2004).

Patients with kidney damage, specifically renal papillary necrosis (RPN) are diagnosed usually at advanced stages, where the damage cannot be reversible with current therapies. Medical imaging such as contrast-enhanced multi-phasic CT scan can be used for early identification of RPN and can be further used in post treatment to monitor disease progression (Lang et al., 2004)

Superparamagnetic iron oxide nanoparticles (SPION) are magnetic nanoparticles that exhibit super-paramagnetism when they act as a single domain magnetic material. SPION can image cells in MRI by acting as contrast agents. SPION exhibit large magnetic moment under external magnetic field and no magnetic moment in its absence. This basic principle of SPION is used in MRI; predominantly for cancer diagnosis. Ferumoxide/AMI-25 is a contrast agent used for MRI imaging to differentiate cancerous and normal liver tissues. Cancerous cells do not phagocytize SPION, whereas healthy liver cells phagocytize SPIONs leading to darkening of liver parenchyma cells (Joshua et al., 2012). Hence, SPIONs act as imaging marker in cancer detection.

Imaging in Medical Device Manufacturing

Industries manufacturing medical devices strictly follow the regulations of FDA, where cost effective and high quality products are desirable. In general, errors occur during the development of medical devices, such as in cardiac stent (Kulbago, 2013). Those errors require manual inspections which are far more inaccurate in detection. Instead, imaging techniques such as high resolution CT scan can aid in visualizing the three dimensional structure of each fine sections of the medical device. Further, image analysis software when integrated into these manufacturing processes could render in observation of breaks in structures of the material. High end image analysis software facilitates the earlier detection of errors in manufacturing process prior to manual inspection thus saving the time and cost of the manufacturing process.

Imaging techniques plays role not only in inspecting the manufacturing devices, also in designing the entire medical devices for patients. SEIMENS company introduces "image to implant integrated technology" where medical devices are to be designed in automated fashion according to the patients anatomy using product lifecycle management softwares (SEIMENS, 2015). Introduction of such personalized medical devices will aid in more effective treatment and therapies.

Further, enhancing the personalized operation of medical imaging for individual patients helps faster diagnosis and further medication procedures. Medical imaging devices can be fitted in bathrooms, so that change in colour and composition of urine content can give an alarm to the patients, such as frequent pink or red coloured urine indicating the haemolysis of blood, indirectly relating to the formation of stone in kidney or urinary tract. Instead of approaching a doctor to perform different scans such as ultrasound, such kind of medical devices integrated within the home can indicate the severeness of the disease to the patients, leading to earlier treatment. Recently, FDA approved the usage of mobile application, "Visage Ease Pro ™" app developed by Visage Imaging (Richmond, VIC, Australia). Visage Ease Pro is a free app and can be downloaded from Apple App. Store. This mobile diagnostic app can interpret all imaging modalities except mammography. When a full diagnostic setup is unavailable, this mobile application can be used for diagnosis. However, following the regulations of FDA, this app should be performed only on iPads (Visage imaging, 2015).

FUTURE ASPECTS OF MEDICAL IMAGING

Though multimodality imaging resulted in better diagnosis, new challenges have been arisen. There are ongoing researches to overcome the arising challenges by (1) integrating diagnostic imaging with molecular techniques (2) developing new methods far more advanced than the existing ones. Examples of such research could be the use of Radiogenomic imaging. Radiogenomic imaging involves the molecular profiling of biological tissues together with molecular techniques. Radiogenomic imaging is currently in use for tumour detection and associated studies. The expression of genes, projects as biomarkers that can be determined using radiation oncology. A study was done for 353 breast cancer patients for their gene expression studies together with MRI to analyse the correlation between gene expression and the imaging data. The results correlated 12 imaging traits with breast cancer genes and 11 traits with prostate cancer genes (Yamamoto et al., 2012). Such investigation facilitates to understand the underlying roots of molecular biology in cancer.

Techniques were developed to enhance the contrast agents which will rapidly increase the efficiency of imaging techniques. A new tracer, F-18 Florbetapir (Amyvid™) was approved by Food and Drug Administration (FDA) to detect beta amyloid plaque in the brain of patients with Alzheimer's disease (AD). This tracer functions with PET to detect AD at earlier stages which is critical normally (Abraham, 2013).

New explorations such as digital photon counting developed by the company, Philips overcome the biomedical instrumental limitations. In 2013, Philips introduced an advanced fully digital PET instrument known as Vereos PET/CT. They used digital photon counting enabled by all-digital silicon photomultiplier detectors. This photon counting could twice increase the sensitivity gain, volumetric resolution, and quantitative accuracy compared to analog systems (Nabeel, 2013). Likewise, to improve the image resolution, signal to noise ratio and the acquisition time, several approaches and algorithms are being developed. Super – resolution (SR) techniques are the one developed using interpolation, frequency domain, regularization, and learning-based approaches (Thapa et al., 2014).

CONCLUSION

Early detection of vital diseases like cancer could save the life of millions of people and happiness of their family. This needs advancements and new findings not only in imaging techniques, but in all other medical fields. The major challenge that should be addressed is the economical use of all imaging techniques considerable for the human society.

REFERENCES

Abraham, B. (2013). Imaging's Role in the Future of Alzheimer's Disease. *Electroindustrty, 18*(3), 11.

Bihan, D. L., Breton, E., Lallemand, D., Grenier, P., & Cabanis, E. (1986). MR imaging of intravoxel incoherent motions: Application to diffusion and perfusion in neurologic disorders. *Radiology, 161*(2), 401–407. doi:10.1148/radiology.161.2.3763909 PMID:3763909

Brant, W. E., & Helms, C. A. (2012). *Fundamentals of Diagnostic Radiology* (4th ed.). Lippincott Williams & Wilkins.

Brenner, D. J., & Hall, E. J. (2007). Computed Tomography — An Increasing Source of Radiation Exposure. *The New England Journal of Medicine, 357*(22), 2277–2284. doi:10.1056/NEJMra072149 PMID:18046031

FDA. (2004). *Guidance for industry, Part III*. Retrieved June 10, 2015, from http://www.fda.gov/Drugs/DevelopmentApprovalProcess/DevelopmentResources/ucm092895.htm

Gonzalez, R. C., & Woods, R. E. (2001). *Digital Image Processing*. Upper Saddle River, NJ: Prentice Hall Inc.

Intermountain Medical Centre. (n.d.). New imaging tool to diagnose heart conditions is dramatically more accurate, less expensive and safer. *ScienceDaily*. Retrieved March 16, 2015, from www.sciencedaily.com/releases/2015/03/150316113323. htm

Jingu, A., Fukuda, J., Takahashi, A. T., & Tsushima, Y. (2014). Breakthrough reactions of iodinated and gadolinium contrast media after oral steroid premedication protocol. *BMC Medical Imaging*, *14*(1), 34. doi:10.1186/1471-2342-14-34 PMID:25287952

Joshua, E. (2012). Iron oxide nanoparticles for targeted cancer imaging and diagnostics. *Nanomedicine; Nanotechnology, Biology, and Medicine*, *8*(3), 275–290. doi:10.1016/j.nano.2011.08.017 PMID:21930108

Kase, K. R. (2004). Radiation protection principles of NCRP. *Health Physics*, *87*(3), 251–257. doi:10.1097/00004032-200409000-00005 PMID:15303061

Kulbago, T. (2013). *Imaging in Medical Device Manufacturing*. Retrieved June 15, 2015, from http://www.bonezonepub.com/component/content/article/742-the-use-of-imaging-analytics-in-medical-device-manufacturing

Lang, E. K., Thomas, R., Davis, R., Shore, B., Ruiz-Deya, G., & Macchia, R. J. (2004). Multiphasic helical CT diagnosis of early medullary and papillary necrosis. *Journal of Endourology*, *18*, 167–171. doi:10.1089/089277904322959815 PMID:15006054

Nabeel, U. A. (2013). *New Innovations in Medical Imaging Technology: Live from RSNA*. Retrieved December 18, 2013, from http://in-training.org/new-innovations-in-medical-imaging-technology-live-from-rsna-3961

Radiological Society of North America. (2012). Fetal alcohol exposure affects brain structure in children. *ScienceDaily*. Retrieved November 25, 2012, from www.sciencedaily.com/releases/2012/11/121125103949. htm

Radiological Society of North America. (2015). Retrieved June 12, 2015, from http://www.sciencedaily.com/releases/2015/05/150527095440.htm

Rakow-Penner, R. A., White, N. S., Parsons, J. K., Choi, H. W., Liss, M. A., Kuperman, J. M., & Dale, A. M. et al. (2015). Novel technique for characterizing prostate cancer utilizing MRI restriction spectrum imaging: Proof of principle and initial clinical experience with extraprostatic extension. *Prostate Cancer and Prostatic Diseases*, *18*(1), 81–85. doi:10.1038/pcan.2014.50 PMID:25559097

Sakas, G. (2002). Trends in medical imaging: from 2D to 3D. *Computers & Graphics*, *26*(4), 577–587. doi:10.1016/S0097-8493(02)00103-6

SEIMENS. (2015). Retrieved June 12, 2015, from http://www.bonezonepub.com/component/content/article/1193

Shenghui, X., Hua, Y., Jingjuan, Q., Fan, P., Jie, J., & Kendra, H. (2015). Protein MRI contrast agent with unprecedented metal selectivity and sensitivity for liver cancer imaging. *Proceedings of the National Academy of Sciences of the United States of America*, *112*(21), 6607–6612. doi:10.1073/pnas.1423021112 PMID:25971726

Thapa, D., Raahemifar, K., Bobier, W. R., & Lakshminarayanan, V. (2014). Comparison of super-resolution algorithms applied to retinal images. *Journal of Biomedical Optics*, *19*(5), 056002. doi:10.1117/1.JBO.19.5.056002 PMID:24788371

Visage Imaging. (2015). Retrieved June 12, 2015, from www.visageimaging.com/visage-imaging-receives-fda-clearance-visage-ease-pro/

Wang, T., McElroy, A., Halaney, D., Vela, D., Fung, E., & Hossain, S. et al.. (2015). Detection of Plaque Structure and Composition Using OCT Combined With Two-photon Luminescence (TPL) Imaging. *Lasers in Surgery and Medicine*, 1–10. doi:10.1002/lsm.22366

Wang, Y. X., & Deng, M. (2010). Medical imaging in new drug clinical development. *Journal of Thoracic Disease*, *2*(4), 245–252. PMID:22263053

Yamamoto, S., Maki, D., Korn, R. L., & Kuo, M. D. (2012). Radiogenomic analysis of breast cancer using MRI: A preliminary study to define the landscape. *AJR. American Journal of Roentgenology*, *199*(3), 654–663. doi:10.2214/AJR.11.7824 PMID:22915408

Ziegler, S. I. (2005). Positron Emission Tomography: Principles, Technology, and Recent Developments. *Nuclear Physics. A.*, *752*, 679c–687c. doi:10.1016/j.nuclphysa.2005.02.067

KEY TERMS AND DEFINITIONS

Anger Camera: A device specifically used for imaging gamma radiation emitting isotopes.
Artery Plaque: Mass of substance occurs in arteries usually lumped together with fat and cholesterol.
Claustrophobia: Unusual dread occurs when subjected in closed space or room.
Haemolysis: Demolition of red blood cells.
Imaging Biomarker: An indicator used to quantify the abnormality or diseased conditions in biomedical imaging process.
Modality: A diagnostic method commonly used in treatment of diseases.
Palpitation: Irregular heart beat; a sensation occurs when the heart omits or add up a heart beat.
Radiation Dose: The measurable degree of ionizing radiations absorbed by the tissues.

Chapter 17

A New EYENET Model for Diagnosis of Age–Related Macular Degeneration:
Diagnosis of Age–Related Macular Degeneration

Priya Kandan
Annamalai University, India

P. Aruna
Annamalai University, India

ABSTRACT

Age-related macular degeneration is an eye disease, that gradually degrades the macula, a part of the retina, which is responsible for central vision. It occurs in one of the two types, DRY and WET age-related macular degeneration. In this chapter, to diagnose Age-related macular degeneration, the authors have proposed a new EYENET model which was obtained by combining the modified PNN and modified RBFNN and hence it poses the advantages of both the models. The amount of the disease spread in the retina can be identified by extracting the features of the retina. A total of 250 fundus images were used, out of which 150 were used for training and 100 images were used for testing. Experimental results show that PNN has an accuracy of 87%, modified PNN has an accuracy of 90% RBFNN has an accuracy of 80%, modified RBFNN has an accuracy of 85% and the proposed EYENET Model has an accuracy of 94%. This infers that the proposed EYENET model outperforms all other models.

INTRODUCTION

Age-related macular degeneration [ARMD] is defined as an ocular disease leading to loss of central vision in the elderly stage. Therefore, regular Screening of ARMD affected patients retina is very important. With the advent of computing techniques, the automated segmentation and analysis is expected to support

DOI: 10.4018/978-1-4666-9685-3.ch017

the ophthalmologist in the clinical decision making process. Automated or computer-assisted analysis of ARMD affected patients retina can help eye care specialist to screen larger populations of patients. Dry ARMD is characterized by thinning of the retina and drusen, small yellowish-white deposits that form with-in the retina. It results in slow, gradual progressive "dimming" of the central vision. Wet ARMD is characterized by abnormal growth of new blood vessel under the retina called "Neovascularization". Blood vessels are unusually weak in their structure and prone to leaky and be easily break and bleed. During the recent years, there have been many studies on automatic diagnosis of ARMD using several features and techniques.

Hoover, A.,et al. (2000) described an automated method to locate the optic nerve in images of the ocular fundus. Zakaria Ben Sbeh et al. (2001) proposed a new segmentation method based on new transformations, they introduced in mathematical morphology. It is based on the search for a new class of regional maxima components of the image. These maxima correspond to the regions inside the drusen. Rapantzikos.K et al. 2003 developed a novel segmentation technique for the detection of drusen in retina images. They introduced and tested a histogram-based enhancement technique, which uses histogram equalization as its core operator and a histogram-based segmentation technique (HALT) to segment areas that differ slightly from their background regions. Zhu Hong Qing, (2004) presented a novel automated method for the segmentation of blood vessels in retinal images based upon the enhancement and maximum entropy thresholding. Ingrid E. Zimmer-Galler and Ran Zeimer, (2005) detected the presence of age-related macular degeneration(AMD) at a level requiring referral to an ophthalmologist for further evaluation and possible treatment. Nageswara Rao Pv et al. (2005-2009), proposed a new approach for protein classification based on a PNN and feature selection. Ana Maria Mendonca and Aurelio Campilho, (2006) presented an automated method for the segmentation of the vascular network in retinal images. The outputs of four directional differential operators are processed in order to select connected sets of candidate points to be further classified as centerline pixels using vessel derived features. Niall Patton et al. 2006 described current techniques used to automatically detect landmark features of the fundus, such as the optic disc, fovea and blood vessels.

W.Kenneth et al. 2007 proposed optic nerve and localization of the macula using digital red-free fundus photography. Maria Garcia et al, 2007 extracted a set of features from image regions and selected the subset which best discriminates between Hard Exudates and the retinal background. The selected features were then used as inputs to a multilayer perceptron classifier to obtain a final segmentation of Hard Exudates in the image. Saurabh Garg et al. 2008 explained two methods namely texture- based detection and model based approach that they have developed to reliably detect and count drusens. O Sheba et al. 2008 developed an automated method using the principle of mathematical morphology for finding the drusen exudates using retinal image analysis. JieTian et al. 2009 used PNN as a classifier for the automated classification of underwater objects. LiliXu and Shuqian Luo, 2009 presented a novel method to identify hard exudates from digital retinal images. A feature combination based on stationary wavelet transform and gray level co-occurrence matrix was used to characterize hard exudates candidates. Maria Garcia et al. 2009 automatically detected one of these lesions, hard exudates, in order to help ophthalmologists in the diagnosis and follow-up of the disease. Three NN classifiers were investigated: multilayer perceptron, RBFNN and support vector machine (SVM). Alireza Osareh & BitaShadgar, 2010 proposed an automated method for identification of blood vessels in color images of the retina. For every image pixel, a feature vector is computed that utilizes properties of scale and orientation selective Gabor filters. The extracted features are then classified using generative Gaussian mixture model and discriminative support vector machine classifiers. D. Jayanthi et al. 2010 gave only the frame work for diagnosing human retinal diseases. UsmanAkram M and Aasia Khanum, 2010 proposed a wavelet based method for vessel enhancement, piecewise threshold probing and adaptive thresholding for vessel localization and segmentation respectively.

Retinal imaging has rapidly grown within ophthalmology in the past twenty years. The availability of cameras to take direct images of the retina, fundus photography, makes it possible to examine the eye for the presence of many different eye diseases with a simple, non-invasive method. Research has focused on automatic early detection of ARMD from fundus photographs. We are currently also applying the computer-aided detection and quantification techniques, we have developed to diagnosis and quantification of ARMD. A mass screening facility with teleophthalmology or telemedicine in combination with computer-aided analysis for large rural-based communities may identify more individuals suitable for early stage ARMD prevention. Digital imaging of the retina is useful for detection and classification of ARMD. Also, so far in the literature only drusen detection has been done, but ARMD classification of Dry and Wet images using pattern classification models have not been proposed. So this work differs from previous methods in that we have used five classifiers and found a more suitable classifier for classification of ARMD.

MAIN FOCUS OF THE CHAPTER

In this chapter, an automated approach for classification of the disease ARMD using fundus images is presented. In order to diagnose the disease ARMD, number of features such as area, mean, standard deviation etc of the pre-processed images are extracted to study the image content. Then Modeling Techniques like Probabilistic Neural Network [PNN] which is a probabilistic model, Radial Basis Function Neural Network [RBFNN] which is a neural network model and our proposed EYENET models are used and their performances are compared. The classifiers are applied to analyze the training data to find an optimal way to classify images into their respective classes namely Dry ARMD, Wet ARMD or Normal. The main goal is to detect automatically and segment the disease ARMD in retina without any human supervision and interaction. *Figure 1*. illustrates the block diagram for comparison between five classifiers for diagnosis of ARMD.

Blood Vessel Detection

A combination of normal and ARMD affected images are taken for processing. The size of the input retinal images is 1280×1024 pixels.

1. Green Component

First, the green component is extracted from the color retinal image. The green channel is considered in several works as the basis for vessel segmentation because it normally presents a higher contrast between vessels and retinal background.

Figure 1.

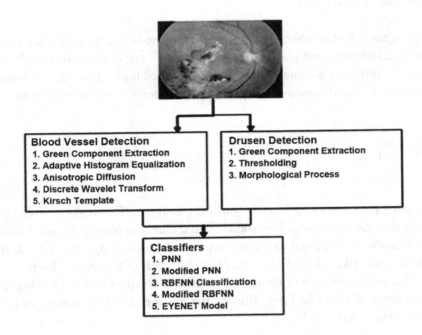

2. Histogram Equalization

After green component extraction, histogram equalization is used to enhance the contrast and improve the quality of the retinal image. It enhances the contrast of images by transforming the values in the intensity image. It operates on small data regions (tiles), rather than the entire image. Each tile's contrast is enhanced, so that the histogram of the output region approximately matches the specified histogram.

3. Anisotropic Diffusion

Anisotropic diffusion is a non-linear and space-variant transformation of the original image. The filter iteratively uses diffusion equation in combination with information about the edges. As a consequence, the homogenic (but noisy) areas are blurred and the edges are preserved. The anisotropic diffusion equation is defined as,

$$I\ div(c\left(x,\ y,\ t\right)\nabla I)\ =\ c\left(x,\ y,\ t\right)\ \Delta I\ +\nabla c\nabla I \tag{1}$$

where div is the divergence operator, ∇ is a gradient and Δ is a Laplacian operator, c represented the conduction coefficient function. Index 't' denotes the time (iterations). The filtering or non-linear smoothing approach using anisotropic diffusion is applied on green band of fundus image after histogram equalization to smooth unwanted data, such as small and tiny capillaries. Finally an-isotropic diffusion is applied to enhance the blood vessel structure.

4. Discrete Wavelet Transform

The transform of a signal is just another form of representing the signal. The Discrete Wavelet Transform (DWT), which is based on sub-band coding, is found to yield a fast computation of Wavelet Transform. Wavelet transform decomposes a signal into a set of basis functions. These basis functions are called wavelets. Wavelets are obtained from a single prototype wavelet ψ(t) called mother wavelet by dilations and shifting:

$$\psi_{a,b}(t) = \frac{1}{\sqrt{a}}\psi(\frac{t-b}{a})$$ (2)

where 'a' is the scaling parameter and 'b' is the shifting parameter. The mother wavelet used to generate all the basis functions is designed based on some desired characteristics associated with that function. Discrete wavelet Transform is applied to the an-isotropic diffused image. As a result of applying this DWT, four types of filters like 2-D lowpass filter to the top left of the image, horizontal highpass and vertical lowpass filter to the top right of the image, horizontal lowpass and vertical highpass filter to the lower left of the image and a 2-D highpass filter to the lower right of the image are applied. Also the size of the images are reduced to half.

5. The Kirsch Operator

The Kirsch operator is made up of a number of templates. Each template focuses on the edge strength in one direction. This edge detector performs convolution with 8 masks calculating gradients. The Kirsch edge detection algorithm uses a 3×3 table of pixels to store a pixel and its neighbors while calculating the derivatives. The 3×3 table of pixels is called a convolution table, because it moves across the image in a convolution-style algorithm . The Kirsch edge detection algorithm identifies both the presence of an edge and the direction of the edge and finally detects the blood vessels. For a convolution table, calculating the presence and direction of an edge is done in three major steps:

1. Calculate the derivative for each of the eight directions.
2. Find the value and direction of the maximum derivative.

$$EdgeMax = Maximum of eight derivatives$$ (3)

$$DirMax = Direction of EdgeMax$$ (4)

3. Check if the maximum derivative is above the threshold.

The templates of the Kirsch operator are shown in *Figure 2*. The threshold value used here is 30 which is obtained by trial and error method. The kirsch operator is applied to the discrete wavelet transformed image to segment the blood vessels. *Figure 3*. (a),(b) and (c) shows the original eye images which is a

Figure 2.

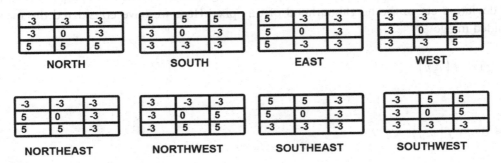

Kirsch Operator

combination of Normal, Dry ARMD and Wet ARMD. (d),(e) and (f) shows their corresponding blood vessel detected images.

Drusen Detection

Drusens are accumulation of lipid and other waste material from different layers of the retina. These are markers of ARMD as their increasing number generally indicates risk for ARMD. So the criterion for finding the abnormal images are drusen present in the Dry and Wet images.

1. Green Component

The retinal image is taken in the RGB form by fundus camera. The green channel of the RGB space is extracted and chosen for detection of exudates because exudates appear most contrasted in this channel.

2. Thresholding

Thresholding is a simple shape extraction technique, where the images could be viewed as the result of trying to separate the eye from the background. Thresholding is a method of producing regions of uniformity within an image based on some threshold criterion, T. T can be defined as

$$T = T\{x, y, A(x, y), f(x, y)\} \tag{5}$$

Figure 3.

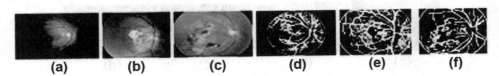

(a)   (b)   (c)   (d)   (e)   (f)

where f(x,y) is the gray level of the pixel at (x,y) and A(x,y) denotes some local property such as mean, standard deviation etc in the neighbourhood of this pixel.Here we have considered the mean value. Athresholded image

$$g(x,y) = 1 if \ f(x,y) \geq T \tag{6}$$

$$g(x,y) = 0 \ if \ f(x,y) \ < \ T \tag{7}$$

A Local thersholding technique is one that partitions the given image into sub-images and determines the threshold for each of this sub-images.

$$T = T\left\{A(x,y), f(x,y)\right\} \tag{8}$$

where T is dependent upon a neighbourhood property of the pixel as well as its grey-level value. The main task of thresholding is to highlight high values of wavelet coefficients which almost correspond to the drusen areas and suppress small values which correspond to noise or unimportant structures in the image. To the green component extracted image, local thresholding is applied. Here the threshold value is chosen to be in the range 50-60 by trial and error method.

3. Morphological Processing

Erosion involves the removal (alteration) of pixels at the edges of regions, for example changing binary 1 values to 0, while dilation is the reverse process with regions growing out from their boundaries. These two processes are often carried out using a form of kernel known as a structural element. A structural element is an NxN kernel with entries classified according to a binary scheme, typically as 0 or 1. If all entries are coded 1 then the structural element is a solid square block, the center of which is laid over each pixel in the source image in turn The shape of the structural element may vary, for example as a vertical bar, horizontal bar, cross shape or a user-defined pattern. If dilation is followed by erosion the process is described as a closing operation, while erosion followed by dilation is known as opening. Here dilation is used after thresholding and the Drusen is detected. Disk shaped structuring element is used here. *Figure 4.* (a) and (b) gives the Dry and Wet ARMD affected images and (c),(d) their corresponding Drusen detected images.

Figure 4.

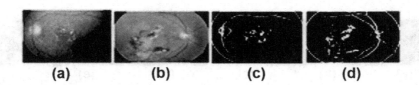

(a)   (b)   (c)   (d)

Feature Extraction

1. Features Detecting the Optic Nerve

After applying the pre-processing techniques, we obtain a better contrast image.

Vessel Density, A(x,y)

Vessel density is defined as the number of vessels existing in a unit area of the retina. Since the vasculature that feeds the retina enters the eye, the vessels tend to be most dense in this region.

$$\rho(x,y) = b_t(x,y) \bullet w_v(x,y) \tag{9}$$

where, $b_t(x,y)$ is the skeletonized image. we have used the morphological method to get the skeletonized image. $w_v(x,y)$ is the convolution window also known as morphologically skeletonized window. This window can be considered as a structuring element that searches for long, narrow, and vertical vessels entering the optic nerve. The value of $w_v(x,y)$ is 0.6×3.0.

Average Vessel Thickness, t(x,y)

Vessels are also observed to be thickest near the optic nerve since most branching of both the arterial and venous structure does not take place until the tree is more distal from the optic nerve

$$t(x,y) = \frac{b(x,y) \bullet w_v(x,y)}{b_t(x,y) \bullet w_v(x,y)} \tag{10}$$

where $b(x,y)$ is the binary representation of the vascular tree image.

2. Features Detecting Diseases

Some of the features that are extracted for detecting diseases are Area, Radius, Diameter, Perimeter, Centre angle, Arc length, Radian, Chord length, Half range area. Binary radian, Navigation, Hour angle and Minutes of arc.

Area

Area is determined by the formula.

$$Area = \pi r^2 \tag{11}$$

Radius

The radius of the circle is determined by the formula

$$Radius, r = \frac{\sqrt{Area}}{\pi} \tag{12}$$

Diameter

The diameter of the circle is determined by the formula

$$Diameter, d = 2r \tag{13}$$

Perimeter

The formula to find the perimeter is given by

$$perimeter, p = 2\pi r (or) p = \pi d \text{ Perimeter, } p = 2Àr \left(or \right) p = Àd \tag{14}$$

Centre Angle

The formula to find the center angle is given by

$$CA = \left(perimeter / 360 \right) * \left(2 * \pi * radius \right) \tag{15}$$

Arc Length

The formula to find the arc length is given by

$$AL = \left(radius \right) * \left(\left(2 * \pi * center\ angle \right) / 360 \right) \tag{16}$$

Radian

The formula to find the radian is given by

$$Rad = radius * center\ angle \tag{17}$$

Chord Length

The formula to find the chord length is given by

$$CL = \left(area * 360 \right) / \left(center\ angle * \pi * radius \right) \tag{18}$$

Half Range Area

The formula to find the half range area is given by

$$HA = 1 / 2 * Area \tag{19}$$

Binary Radian

$$BR = Area \,/\, 256 \tag{20}$$

Navigation

$$N = Area \,/\, 32 \tag{21}$$

Hour Angle

$$HR = Area \,/\, 24 \tag{22}$$

Minutes of Arc

$$MA = hour\ angle * 15 \tag{23}$$

Classifiers

In our experiments we apply five different classifiers namely PNN, RBFNN, modified PNN, modified RBFNN and our proposed EYENET model.

1. PNN

There were thirteen input features, which created a thirteen dimensional input vector $(x_1, x_2, x_3, \ldots x_{13},)$. Each image had a combination of specific values of the input vector—called an input pattern—that described the operating features of the image. The PNN model classifies that image from its input pattern into one of three categories (Normal, Dry ARMD, Wet ARMD) as follows: In the input layer, the number of neurons is equal to the number of input features. In the pattern layer, the total number of neurons is the sum of the numbers of neurons used to represent the patterns for each category. Each category may contain many training patterns (training vectors) whose dimension is equal to the number of input factors, and taking a set of specific values of input factors. The training vectors are imported from sample data and hence they are not always necessarily representative of all existing patterns for that class. The activation function used in the pattern layer, is the Gaussian kernel. In the summation layer, the number of neurons is equal to the number of categories. The activation is simply a weighted sum function. In the output layer, there is one neuron to represent the classification result. The activation function is an arg max function, which outputs the category associated with the largest value between incoming signals. Suppose, h_{dn} is the input to the pattern layer for 'd' varies from 1, 2, ... 100, corresponding to 100 tested images and 'n' varies from 1, 2, ...,13 corresponding to the feature vector. The pattern layer can be processed and the output layer has a node for each pattern classification. The sum for each hidden node is sent to the output layer and the highest values wins. This method has been done for three classes namely normal, Dry ARMD and Wet ARMD.

2. Modified PNN

PNN are slower than multilayer perceptron networks at classifying new cases. PNN requires more memory space to store the model. In modified PNN the manhattan distance is used instead of Euclidean distance and netinverse transfer function is used instead of radial basis transfer function. Since the manhattan distance follows a grid like path, the accuracy obtained is more. Transfer functions calculate a layer's output from its net input. Inverse function handles both continuous and discrete data. So the netinverse transfer function gives better results than Radial basis Functions.

We have applied the preprocessing techniques to all the 200 images and obtained the feature values. These feature values are used as input to the classifiers. we have used the 400 images data set values and trained the classifier. For PNN, we obtain a set of results after training and testing. The values obtained are given as inputs for training. Then we fed the testing values and evaluated the classifier performance from the results obtained during testing. In Cartesian coordinates, if p = $(p_1, p_2,..., p_n)$ and q = $(q_1, q_2,..., q_n)$ are two points in Euclidean n-space, then the distance from p to q, or from q to p is given by:

$$d(p,q) = d(q,p) = \overline{)q_1 - p_1)^2 + (q_2 - p_2)^2 + ... + (q_n - p_n)^2} = \sqrt{\sum_{i=1}^{n}(q_i - p_i)^2} \tag{24}$$

The formula for manhattan distance between a point $X=(X1, X2,$ etc.) and a point $Y=(Y1, Y2,$ etc.) is:

$$d = \sum_{i=1}^{n}\left|X_i - Y_i\right| \tag{25}$$

The results of the PNN and modified PNN classification Procedures are shown in *Table 1. Table 2* shows the result of Sensitivity, Specificity and Percentage of accuracy for the three classes of eye images. Sensitivity and specificity are statistical measures of the performance of a binary classification test, also known in statistics as classification function. Sensitivity measures the proportion of actual positives which are correctly identified. Specificity measures the proportion of negatives which are correctly identified.

Table 1. Results of PNN and modified PNN classification

Models	Methods Used	True Positive	True Negative	False Positive	False Negative
PNN	Euclidean distance radial basis transfer function	62	25	8	5
Modified PNN	Manhattan distance Radial basis for PNN	67	23	6	4

Table 2. Results of sensitivity, specificity, % of accuracy

Models	Sensitivity	Specificity	Accuracy
PNN	92.54	75.76	87
Modified PNN	94.37	79.31	90

1. **True Positive:** ARMD affected images are correctly identified as ARMD.
2. **False Positive:** Normal image incorrectly identified as ARMD.
3. **True Negative:** Normal image correctly identified as normal.
4. **False Negative:** ARMD image incorrectly identified as normal.

Sensitivity: Sensitivity of the test is the proportion of the images that have the disease test positive for it.

$$sensitivity = \frac{NumberofTruePositive}{NumberofTruePositive + NumberofFalseNegative} \tag{26}$$

Specificity: Specificity of the test is the proportion of the images that do not have the disease test negative for it.

$$specificity = \frac{NumberofTrueNegative}{NumberofTrueNegative + NumberofFalsePositive} \tag{27}$$

Accuracy: Accuracy of the measurement system is the degree of closeness of measurements of the quantity to the quantity's actual (true) value. Accuracy is also used as a statistical measure of how well a binary classification test correctly identifies or excludes a condition. Accuracy is the proportion of true results in the population.

$$Accuracy = \frac{NumberofTP + NumberofTN}{NumberofTP + NumberofFP + NumberofFN + NumberofTN} \tag{28}$$

3. RBFNN

The RBFNN consists of three layers with extremely different roles. The input to an RBFNN is non-linear while the output of the network is linear combination of outputs from the radial basis functions. The input layer is made up of source nodes that connect the network to its environment. The second layer has only one hidden layer h_{rl} in the network, which applies a nonlinear transformation from the input layer to hidden layer. The output layer is linear, supplying the response of the network to the activation pattern applied to the input layer. RBFNN is an artificial neural network that uses radial basis function as an activation function. It is a linear combination of radial basis functions. The most common one is the Gaussian function defined by,

$$g_i\left(x_j\right) = \exp\left(\frac{-\left\|x_j - \mu_i\right\|^2}{2\sigma_i^2}\right) \tag{29}$$

where σ is the width parameter, μ is the vector determining the center of basis function f and x is the d–dimensional input vector. The input layer of this network has x_i units which is a x_{13} dimensional input vector corresponding to thirteen features. The input units are fully connected to the h_n hidden layer units, which are in turn fully connected to the y_c output layer units, where y_c is the number of output classes for three classes namely normal, Dry ARMD and Wet ARMD.

4. Modified RBFNN

RBFNN, possess slower execution of the network and requires a representative training set. In the case of modified RBFNN, Manhattan distance is used instead of Euclidean distance and triangular basis transfer function is used instead of linear transfer function. The triangular function can be seen as the convolution of two half-size rectangular windows giving it twice the width of the rectangular windows. Since the convolution operator is used in triangular basis function, the system gives the better results than the linear model.

The results of the RBFNN and modified RBFNN classification Procedures are shown in *Table 3*. *Table 4* shows the result of Sensitivity, Specificity and Percentage of accuracy for the three classes of eye images.

5. EYENET Model

EYENET model was obtained by combining modified PNN and modified RBFNN and hence it posses the advantages of both the methods. The EYENET model took both modified PNN and modified RBFNN models as inputs and the perceptron training algorithm was used for combining both the models. The main reasons for combining the models are to increase the efficiency and accuracy for which

Table 3. Results of RBFNN and modified RBFNN classification

Models	Methods Used	True Positive	True Negative	False Positive	False Negative
RBFNN	Linear transfer for RBFNN	60	20	12	8
Modified RBFNN	Triangular basis for RBFNN	68	17	11	6

Table 4. Results of sensitivity, specificity, % of accuracy

Models	Sensitivity	Specificity	Accuracy
RBFNN	88.24	62.5	80
Modified RBFNN	93.15	62.96	85

multistage combination rules can be adopted. Figure 5 gives the Architecture of EYENET Model. The perceptron is the simplest form of a neural network. Basically it consists of a single neuron with a number of adjustable weights. The neuron is the fundamental processor of a neural network. It has three basic elements: A set of connecting links, each link carries a weight w_0 to w_n. A summation unit that sums the input signals after they are multiplied by their respective weights. An activation function f(x), limits the output of the neuron. Typically the output is limited to the interval 0 to 1 or alternatively -1 to 1. The basic building block of a perceptron is an element that accepts a number of inputs x_i, i=1 to n and computes a weighted sum of these inputs where, for each input, its fixed weight β can be only 1 or +1. Here the input to the perceptron is the output of radial basis function neural network and probabilistic neural network. The output layer corresponds to one of three classes namely normal, DRY ARMD and WET ARMD. Moreover the inputs and outputs to the perceptron classifier correspond to the binary inputs and outputs respectively. Mathematically the input to the neuron is represented by a vector $x=x_1$ to x_n, and the output is a scalar y=f(x). The weights of the connections are represented by the vector $w= w_0$ to w_n, where w_0 is the offset. The output is calculated as,

$$y = \begin{cases} 1 & if [\sum_{i=1}^{n} \beta_i x_n] \geq 0 \\ 0 & if [\sum_{i=1}^{n} \beta_i x_n] < 0 \end{cases} \tag{30}$$

To test the model, the test data were applied to modified PNN and modified RBFNN. The tested outputs of both the models were applied to the perceptron network of the EYENET model. Then the classifier performance was evaluated from the results obtained during testing. The results of the EYENET

Figure 5.

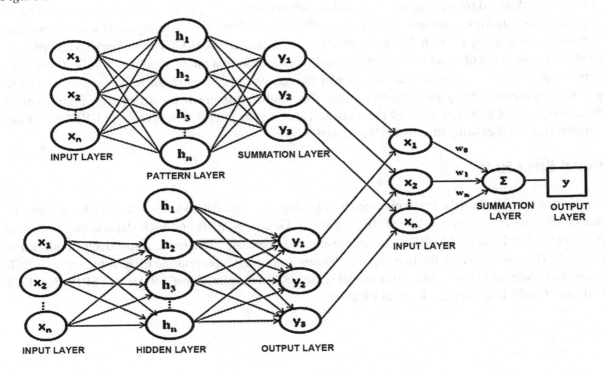

Table 5. Results of EYENET classification

Model	True Positive	True Negative	False Positive	False Negative
EYENET Model	76	18	4	2

Table 6. Results of sensitivity, specificity, % of accuracy

Model	Sensitivity	Specificity	Accuracy
EYENET Model	97.44	81.82	94

classification Procedure are shown in Table 5. Table 6 shows the result of Sensitivity, Specificity and Percentage of accuracy for the three classes of eye images using the EYENET classifier. Clearly, the proposed EYENET model produces encouraging results. Our system is far better as compared to the other works discussed so far.

SOLUTIONS AND RECOMMENDATIONS

The Proposed method was implemented in Matlab and Microsoft visual basic 6.0. We have used a set of 250 images for processing out of which 150 images were used for training and 100 images were used for testing. Experimental results show that PNN has an accuracy of 87%, modified PNN has an accuracy of 90%, RBFNN Classifier has an accuracy of 80%, modified RBFNN has an accuracy of 85% and the proposed EYENET model has an accuracy of 94%.

ROC Curve

The ROC curve is a graphical representation of the sensitivity and specificity for a model with continuous predictions, obtained by plotting the observed sensitivity versus 1- specificity. Each point on the curve represents the sensitivity and specificity for a prediction based on classifying a patient with disease and without diseases using a threshold. Receiver operating characteristic (ROC) curve analysis can provide an objective measure of a model's sensitivity and specificity over a range of output cutoffs. The overall performance can be expressed as the area under the receiver operating characteristic curve. The ROC graphs are a useful technique for organizing classifiers and visualizing their performance. Figure.6 gives the comparison of ROC curve for all the models. These results infer that the proposed EYENET model outperforms other existing models PNN and RBFNN.

Equal Error Rate

Equal error rate (EER) is the result obtained by adjusting the system threshold such that false acceptance rate (FAR) and false rejection rate (FRR) are equal. Generally, FAR and FRR depend on the system threshold t. The FAR(t) and FRR(t) are increasing and decreasing functions, respectively, as shown in Figure 7. The error at which the two curves in Figure 7 intersect represent the EER. If the value of EER is the least, then the performance of the model is the best. In the plot, ZeroFAR denotes FRR when FAR = 0, and ZeroFRR denotes FAR when FRR = 0.

Figure 6.

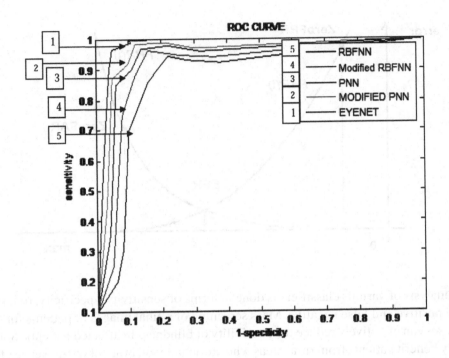

The EER value of the EYENET model for diagnosing ARMD is 0.06 as shown in Figure 8. In this work, normal, Dry ARMD and Wet ARMD cases of the ARMD are correctly identified with an accuracy of more than 79% and a sensitivity of more than 88% in all the five models.

FUTURE RESEARCH DIRECTIONS

The system can be further used for diagnosis of other retinal diseases such as eye cancer, cataract diseases, etc. The database and our system can be hosted in the medical websites for online diagnosis of the diseases. Due to the limitation of medical facilities and the number of ophthalmologists, the data regarding the screening can be transmitted via satellite links to the ophthalmologists at the hospitals and the result can be communicated via these links. This can be further enhanced by the use of wifi long distance networks which provide video conferencing facility between the patients at the rural camp and the doctors at the hospital. These systems can be interfaced with an ophthalmoscope from which the retinal image is given as input and a separate display device can be used to display the result regarding the presence or absence of the disease. Further the algorithms can be enhanced to produce results regarding the grade and the severity of the disease.

CONCLUSION

Advanced techniques in image processing and analysis are being extensively used to assist clinical diagnosis. Digital color retinal fundus images are widely utilized to investigate various eye diseases.

Figure 7.

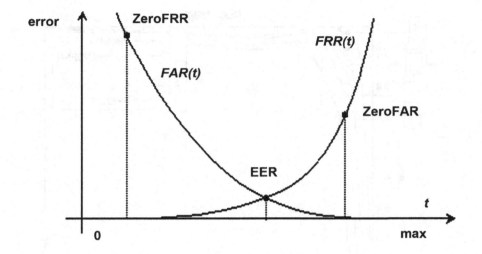

Performance analysis of various classifiers is done in terms of sensitivity, specificity, true positive, true negative, false positive and false negative. Mass screening of retinal images of patients for the presence of retinal diseases can effectively reduce the possibility of blindness in affected patients. Such screening systems mainly benefit patients from rural areas who are actually unaware of the presence of the disease. The performance of the models are evaluated using area under curve of roc which is one of the best performance measuring techniques. The five classifiers are developed for diagnosis of ARMD. A user

Figure 8.

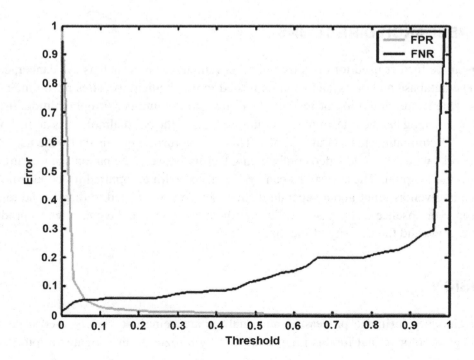

friendly model was developed for diagnosing ARMD and its performance is analyzed. Thus this work has given a successful age-related macular degeneration diagnosing method which helps to diagnose the disease in early stage which mutually reduces the manual work.

REFERENCES

Akram, & Khanum. (2010). Retinal Images: Blood Vessel Segmentation by Threshold Probing. *IEEE Symposium On Industrial Electronics And Applications(ISIEA)*.

Ben Sbeh, Z., Cohen, L. D., Mimoun, G., & Coscas, G. (2001). A New Approach of Geodesic Reconstruction for Drusen Segmentation in Eye Fundus Images. *IEEE Transactions on Medical Imaging*, *20*(12), 1321–1333. doi:10.1109/42.974927 PMID:11811832

Zimmer-Galler, & Zeimer. (2005). Feasibility of Screening for High-Risk Age- Related Macular Degeneration With an Internet-Based Automated Fundus Camera. *Ophthalmic Surgery, Lasers & Imaging*, *36*(3), 228–236. PMID:15957480

García, Hornero, Sanchez, Lopez, & Díez. (2007). Feature Extraction and Selection for the Automatic Detection of Hard Exudates in Retinal Images. *Proceedings of the 29th Annual International Conference of the IEEE EMBS*.

Garcia, Sanchez, Lopez, Abasolo, & Hornero. (2009). Neural network based detection of hard exudates in retinal images. *Computer Methods and Programs in Biomedicine*, *93*, 9-19.

Garg, Sivaswamy, & Joshi. (2008). Automatic Drusen Detection from Color Retinal Images. Center for Visual Information Technology, IIT Hyderabad.

Hoover, A., Kouznetsova, V., & Goldbaum, M. (2000). Locating blood vessels in retinal images by piecewise threshold probing of matched filter response. *IEEE Transactions on Medical Imaging*, *19*(3), 203–209. doi:10.1109/42.845178 PMID:10875704

Jayanthi, Devi, & Parvathi. (2010). Automatic Diagnosis of Retinal Diseases from Color Retinal Images. *International Journal of Computer Science and Information Security*, *7*(1), 234-238.

Mendonca, A. M., & Campilho, A. (2006). Segmentation of Retinal Blood Vessels By Combining the Detection of Centerlines and Morphological Reconstruction. *IEEE Transactions on Medical Imaging*, *25*(9), 1200–1213. doi:10.1109/TMI.2006.879955 PMID:16967805

Nageswara, Uma, Dsvgk, Sridhar, & Rao. (n.d.). A Probabilistic Neural Network Approach For protein Super family Classification. *Journal of Theoretical and Applied Information Technology*, *6*(1), 101–105.

Osareh & Shadgar. (2010). An Automated tracking approach for extraction of retinal vasculature in fndus images. *Journal of Ophthalmic And Vision Research*, *5*(1), 20–26. PMID:22737322

Patton, N., Aslam, T. M., MacGillivray, T., Deary, I. J., Dhillon, B., Eikelboom, R. H., & Constable, I. J. et al. (2006). Retinal image analysis: Concepts, applications and potential. *Progress in Retinal and Eye Research*, *25*(1), 99–127. doi:10.1016/j.preteyeres.2005.07.001 PMID:16154379

Qing. (2004). Segmentation Of Blood Vessels In Retinal Images Using 2-D Entropies Of Gray Level-Gradient Co-Occurrence Matrix. *ICASSP*, III-509 – III-512.

Rapantzikos, K., Zervakis, M., & Balas, K. (2003). Detection and Segmentation of Drusen Deposits on Human Retina: Potential in the diagnosis of age-related macular degeneration. *Medical Image Analysis*, *7*(1), 95–108. doi:10.1016/S1361-8415(02)00093-2 PMID:12467724

Sheba, O., & Sukesh Kumar, A. (2008). Automated Diagnosis of Macular Degeneration through Image Processing. *IE(I) Journal-CP*, *3-6*, 89.

Tian, Xue, & Huang. (2009). Classification of Underwater Objects Based on Probabilistic Neural Network. *Fifth International Conference on Natural Computation*, (pp. 38-42).

Xu & Luo. (2009). Support Vector Machine Based Method For Identifying Hard Exudates In Retinal Images. Academic Press.

Chapter 18
Automatic Detection and Classification of Ischemic Stroke Using K–Means Clustering and Texture Features

N. Hema Rajini
Annamalai University, India

R. Bhavani
Annamalai University, India

ABSTRACT

Computed tomography images are widely used in the diagnosis of ischemic stroke because of its faster acquisition and compatibility with most life support devices. This chapter presents a new approach to automated detection of ischemic stroke using k-means clustering technique which separates the lesion region from healthy tissues and classification of ischemic stroke using texture features. The proposed method has five stages, pre-processing, tracing midline of the brain, extraction of texture features and feature selection, classification and segmentation. In the first stage noise is suppressed using a median filtering and skull bone components of the images are removed. In the second stage, midline shift of the brain is calculated. In the third stage, fourteen texture features are extracted and optimal features are selected using genetic algorithm. In the fourth stage, support vector machine, artificial neural network and decision tree classifiers have been used. Finally, the ischemic stroke region is extracted by using k-means clustering technique.

INTRODUCTION

Clinical diagnosis of ischemic stroke is still challenging and its accuracy has been an issue of concern especially with lesions. Medical imaging plays an important role in the early detection and treatment of medical diagnosis. It provides physicians with information essential for efficient and effective diagnosis of various diseases. Less attention is paid towards detection of ischemic stroke with small lesions (la-

DOI: 10.4018/978-1-4666-9685-3.ch018

cunar stroke) due to its challenging nature. It is relatively difficult to identify, as it manifests as a small hypodense area of less than 15mm in diameter on Computed Tomography (CT). Therefore, early detection of ischemic stroke with small lesions is important and this necessitates a more efficient method to improve the detection rate.

The objective of this work is to provide a robust technique for automatic segmentation of ischemic stroke lesions from brain CT images. It also focuses on using textural analysis in the classification process. In the present chapter the purpose is to improve the level of accuracy of the diagnostic detection and classification of ischemic stroke. In this chapter, different techniques used for ischemic stroke detection and classification are discussed and the quantitative analysis is described along with the results of segmentation for diagnosing ischemic stroke.

BACKGROUND

Stroke or cerebrovascular accident is a disease, which affects the vessels that supply blood to the brain. The stroke occurs when a blood vessel either bursts or there is a blockage of the blood vessel. Due to loss of oxygen, nerve cells in the affected brain area are not able to perform basic functions which lead to death of the brain tissue. Stroke leads to serious long term disability or death. This can be due to ischemia (lack of blood flow) caused by blockage (thrombosis, arterial embolism), or a hemorrhage (leakage of blood). In an ischemic stroke, blood supply to part of the brain is decreased leading to death of the brain tissue in that region (Adam et al., 2005).

According to the World Health Organization (WHO), 15 million people are affected by stroke; of these 5 million die and another 5 million (2002 estimates) are permanently disabled. As the average human life span has increased, stroke has become the third leading cause of death worldwide after heart disease and cancer. Between these, ischemic stroke accounts for about 80 percent of all strokes (Thom et al., 2006). A lacunar stroke, a subtype of ischemic stroke, is relatively difficult to identify, as it manifests as a small hypodense area of less than 15 mm in diameter on CT (Toni et al., 2000). There are various classification systems for acute ischemic stroke. The Oxford Community Stroke Project (OCSP) classification relies primarily on the initial symptoms; the stroke episode is classified as Total Anterior Circulation Infarct (TACI), Partial Anterior Circulation Infarct (PACI), Lacunar Infarct (LACI) or Posterior Circulation Infarct (POCI).

Clinical diagnosis of ischemic stroke is difficult within the first few hours after the onset of stroke. Therefore, early detection of ischemic stroke is crucial. Early detection solely relies on some important early abnormal signs, including Loss of Insular Ribbon (LIR), loss of gray-white matter Attenuation of the Lentiform Nucleus (ALN), Hemispherical Sulcus Effacement (HSE) and the Hyperdense Middle Cerebral Artery Sign (HMCAS) (Tomura et al., 1988). Hypo dense changes are found to be the most frequent sign of early ischemia. However, its detection is difficult, since the early infarct sign is subtle hypo attenuation. An early and rapid diagnosis of stroke is critical for proper treatment of the patients. Definitive therapy is aimed to remove the blockage by breaking the clot (thrombolysis) or by removing it mechanically (thrombectomy), where immediately the blood flow is restored to the affected tissue.

MRI is the most sensitive diagnostic method in detecting ischemic stroke, especially in very early stages and to determine whether thrombolysis is needed or not. In most instances, CT provides information required to make decisions during emergency. Compared to MRI, brain imaging with CT is more accessible, less expensive and quicker especially in severely ill patients. Non-enhanced CT is often the first radiologic examination performed in case of suspicion of stroke (Von Kumar, 2005).

In CT images, an ischemic stroke appears as a dark region (hypo dense) well contrasted against its surrounds. Accordingly, stroke is characterized as a distortion between the two halves of the brain in terms of tissue density and texture distribution. The human head is roughly bilaterally symmetric. For many focal brain diseases manifested as intracranial mass (e.g. Hematoma, tumor, abscess, etc.) clinicians rely on a Midline Shift (MLS) to quantify the change of symmetry for diagnosis and outcome prediction. The amount of midline shift can be used to measure the "mass effect" of the brain lesion and has been shown to correlate well with the outcome of the patients. Therefore, MLS is considered as the 'gold standard' by neurologists, neurosurgeons and neuro radiologists.

In the last decade, a number of algorithms have been proposed to segment and classify the brain in MR and CT images. This chapter reviews the various methods available in the literature for medical diagnosis. It presents a survey that covers a computer-aided detection system for ischemic stroke. Both the advantages and disadvantages of these methods are pointed out, from which it was found that most of them have problem to serve as full automatic segmentation of the brain in MRI and CT. Therefore, to extract the abnormality accurately and classify the type of the medical images, segmentation and classification are very important for clinical research, diagnosis and applications, leading to requirement of robust, reliable and adaptive techniques.

There are many computer-aided detection systems for brain images in the literature, most of them are used to detect stroke in CT images. Lee et al. (2006) proposed a method to detect early sign of acute stroke on brain CT images using an adaptive partial smoothing filter. To improve the detectability of the early infarct sign, an image processing was used to reduce local noise with edges preserved. The results showed that the detectability of early infarct signs was much improved. Przelaskowski et al. (2007) introduced a method to detect acute ischemic stroke using wavelet based image processing. It enhanced the contrast and denoises the subtlest signs of hypodensity of the image locally.

Chawla et al. (2009) proposed a method to detect and classify all types of stroke in brain CT images. It was a two-level classification scheme used to detect abnormalities using features derived in the intensity and the wavelet domain. Usinskas et al. (2004) proposed a method to segment the ischemic stroke region on CT images by utilizing joint features from mean, standard deviation, histogram and gray level co-occurrence matrix methods. Maldjian and Chalela (2001) analyzed the stroke using segmentation approach. This approach successfully identified hypodensity within the lentiform nucleus and insula in patients with acute middle cerebral artery stroke. Fauzi et al. (2008) introduced a method to extract abnormality using two phase segmentation. In the first phase segmentation, the combination of k-means and Fuzzy C-Means (FCM) methods were implemented to partition the images into the binary images. From the binary images, a decision tree was then utilized to annotate the connected component into normal and abnormal regions. For the second phase segmentation, the obtained experimental results had shown that modified FCM with population-diameter independent segmentation was more feasible and yield satisfactory results. Fuk Hay et al. (2011) proposed a method for early detection of ischemic stroke with small lesions using image feature characteristics. A circular adaptive region of interest method was proposed to analyze CT images of the brain. The accuracy of ANN classifier was 86.96%.

We propose a method for stroke detection to locate the small region of ischemia for a definite diagnosis and to classify whether the image is having stroke or not. In our method an efficient MLS method is used to measure the degree of symmetry of the brain. The application of the proposed method for early detection of ischemic stroke is demonstrated to improve efficiency and accuracy of clinical practice. A quantitative analysis is not performed in the existing method and different classifiers are used to train and test the dataset. The classifier which gives the best result is identified for our dataset.

PROPOSED APPROACH FOR ISCHEMIC STROKE

Developing an efficient method may help physicians to diagnose ischemic stroke at an appropriate time. The proposed system has been developed using Matlab (The MathWorks, Inc., Natick, MA, USA). Considering CT images as input data, the proposed method has five stages, pre-processing, tracing midline of the brain, extraction of texture features using Gray Level Co-Occurrence Matrix (GLCM) and feature selection, classification and segmentation.

In the first stage noise is suppressed using a median filtering and skull bone components of the images are removed by a global thresholding method. In the second stage, midline shift of the brain is calculated. In the third stage, fourteen texture features are extracted using GLCM. The optimal features are extracted from the left and right side of the brain using Genetic Algorithm (GA). The optimal features are used to train the binary classifier, which can automatically infer whether the image is that of a normal brain or an ischemic brain. The methodology of the proposed technique for ischemic stroke detection and classification is illustrated in Figure 1.

Figure 1. Methodology of the proposed technique

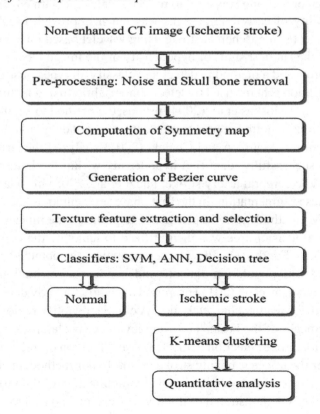

In the fourth stage, Support Vector Machine (SVM), Artificial Neural Network (ANN) and decision tree classifiers have been used to classify normal brain and ischemic brain. Finally, the ischemic stroke region is extracted by using k-means clustering technique.

The research protocol is approved by the Human Ethics Committee of the Rajah Muthiah Medical College, Annamalai University and informed consent is signed by all participants. The dataset of brain CT images is collected from Rajah Muthaiah Medical College Hospital (RMMCH) in Chidambaram to develop the algorithm. All brain CT scans are performed using a standard protocol according to the guideline, with some variations in slice spacing (Bullock et al., 2006). The Field of View (FOV) is 25x25 cm. Each image is 512x512 pixels in size, resulting in an in-plane resolution of 0.488mm per pixel. The original CT number (Hounsfield Unit, HU) is transformed with brain window (center 40HU, width 150HU) into 256 gray levels.

Consecutive Digital Imaging and Communications in Medicine (DICOM) CT slices are imported into the Matlab workspace automatically. The proposed system is experimented and tested using 21 cases. The thickness of brain CT images is 5 mm. All are emergency brain CT scans performed on a single detector CT scanner (Mx 8000 Dual, Philips). All images are axial images obtained parallel to the orbitomeatal line, at 120kV and 80–200mA. A region of ischemic stroke identified by an experienced radiologist is used as gold standard.

Pre-Processing for Ischemic Stroke

To detect the abnormality in the brain, the unwanted background information has to be removed. To enhance the accuracy of segmentation and to save computational time, it is useful to eliminate the artifacts that might be present in the image. The following are the examples of the artifacts commonly seen in CT images.

1. Streek artifacts are usually produced by metal and patient motion.
2. A partial volume artifact occurs when a volumetric pixel contains two very different materials like bone and soft tissue.

Noise Removal

To reduce noise, median filtering using a 3-by-3 square kernel is applied. Median filter is chosen because it is less sensitive to extreme values and able to remove outliers without reducing sharpness of the image. This produces a more homogeneous background in which abnormalities become more conspicuous. Median filters are quite popular because they provide excellent noise-reduction capabilities, with considerably less blurring than linear smoothing filters of similar size. The median filter considers each pixel and its neighbors in the image to decide whether or not it is a representation of the surroundings. It replaces the pixel value with the median of the neighboring pixel values. Calculate the median by first sorting all the pixel values from the neighborhood in numerical order and then replace the pixel being considered with the middle pixel value. (If the neighborhood under consideration contains an even number of pixels, the average of the two middle pixel values is the median.) It preserves sharp edges of the image. The three different input images are shown in Figure 2(a-c) and the noise removed images are presented in Figure 3(a-c) after applying the median filter for the input images.

Figure 2. Input CT brain images (a-c)

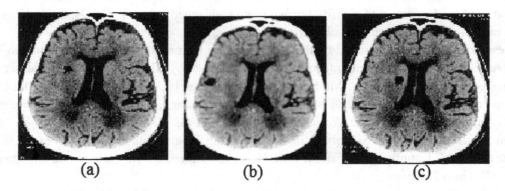

Figure 3. Images after median filtering (a-c)

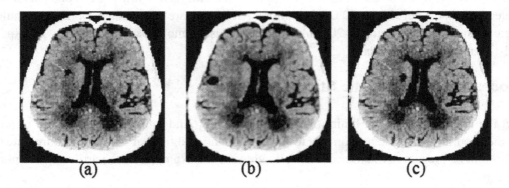

Skull Bone Removal Using Global Thresholding

The bony skull has to be removed with preservation of cranial content of the brain. Skull, by virtue of its exceptionally high attenuation values, is first removed using global thresholding with a threshold value of 110. Intracranial contents, including both the brain and CSF containing spaces, are first segmented. There are two simple anatomical facts to pick out the brain and the skull in the given CT study: (a) the skull is the largest connected region with bone density in the whole imaging volume; (b) the brain is the largest connected region with brain density within the skull. The CT image is converted to binary image with pixel value (0, 1) using a global threshold. The bony skull of the image is removed with reference to the binary image. Thus in order to detect the abnormality in the brain, the bony skull has to be removed as shown in Figure 4(a-c).

$$level = \; graythresh\left(I\right) \tag{1}$$

Eq. 1 computes a global threshold (level) that can be used to convert an intensity image to a binary image. Level is a normalized intensity value that lies in the range [0, 1]. The graythresh function uses

Figure 4. Images after skull bone removal (a-c)

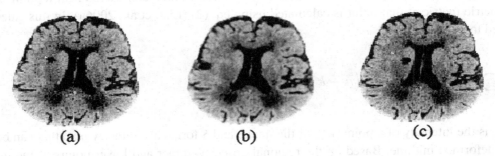

(a)   (b)   (c)

the Otsu's method, which chooses the threshold to minimize the intraclass variance of the black and white pixels (Nobuyuki Otsu, 1979).

Midline of the Brain

The tracing midline of the brain is a good indicator for measuring the symmetry of the brain. The classification of the images into normal and abnormal depends on the features of left and right side of the image. So in the case of asymmetric brain the left and right features should be extracted accurately to classify it correctly. For automatic detection, the following method is applied for tracing the midline of the brain. The human head is roughly bilaterally symmetric. For many focal brain diseases manifested as intracranial mass clinicians rely on a midline shift to quantify the change of symmetry for diagnosis and outcome prediction. The remarkable feature of a normal human brain is the symmetry. Asymmetry in an axial CT brain image strongly indicates abnormality. Hence the symmetry in non-enhanced CT images are an important feature that needs to be considered in deciding whether the CT image at hand is of a normal or an abnormal brain.

Midline shift is the most important quantitative measure clinicians use to evaluate the severity of brain compression by various pathologies. The deformed midline model used is according to the biomechanical properties of different types of intracranial tissues (Liao et al., 2006a, 2006b). There is functional difference between the hemispheres of the brain. Both cerebrum and cerebellum are symmetric with lobes, ventricles and deep nuclei of similar size and shape in both hemispheres. Therefore, they rely on MLS to quantify the change of symmetry for diagnosis and outcome prediction. The most commonly used landmarks for MLS measurement is septum pellucidum, the structure between both frontal horns of the lateral ventricles. In general, the anatomical midline could only be judged by human eyes. For automatic detection, the following method is used for tracing the midline of the brain.

Symmetry Map

The abnormality mostly occurs only on one side of the brain. The difference along the horizontal direction is considered because of bilateral symmetry of the brain and the head. The symmetry metric in an image of a point is quantized by measuring the intensities of points on both sides of it. Typically, the diameter of the brain is about 300 pixels. Weighted sum of squared difference of the 48 pixels on each side is calculated for each brain pixel value. This corresponds to about 2.4 cm laterally and usually covers anatomical structures around the midline, such as frontal horns of the lateral ventricles and the basal ganglia. Let n denote the number of pixels on each side to be considered near a point *(i, j)*, then the symmetric metric at that point is calculated using eq. (2) (Liao et al., 2006a). In this calculation n is assigned to be 48.

$$S_{i,j} = \sum_{k=1}^{n-1}((P_{i+k,j} - P_{i-k,j})^2 * (n-k)/n); k = 1\,to\,47 \tag{2}$$

where $P_{i,j}$ is the intensity of a point *(i, j)* of the image and S forms a symmetry map that can be used to trace the deformed midline. Based on the regional property, upper and lower points of the midline of the brain image are obtained. A midpoint is calculated from upper and lower points. Using these three control points (N=3) (Liao et al., 2006a) deformed midline is drawn using Bezier curves. The symmetry map of the image is shown in Figure 5(a-c).

Bezier Curve

The upper and lower control points represent the parts of tough meninges separating the two hemispheres; it can be treated as straight lines and the curved segment in between are fitted by a quadratic Bezier curve representing the intervening soft brain tissue. This quadratic Bezier curve is drawn using a De Casteljau method (Sedeberg, 2011) for N=3 using eq. (3). The label of the control point is represented by P. τ is the slope of the line. The deformed midline indicated by dashed line is shown in Figure 6(a-c).

$$P_i^j = (1-\tau)P_i^{(j-1)} + \tau P_{(i+1)}^{(j-1)}; j = 1,...,n; i = 0,...,n-1 \tag{3}$$

Texture Feature Extraction and Selection

Feature extraction is the process of extracting certain characteristic attributes and generating a set of meaningful descriptors from an image. The purpose of the feature extraction component in a computer-

Figure 5. Generation of the symmetry map (a-c)

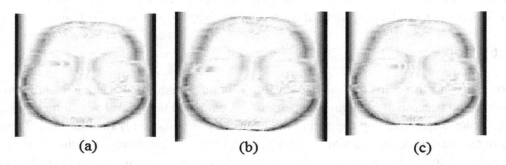

(a)   (b)   (c)

Figure 6. Generation of Bezier curve (a-c)

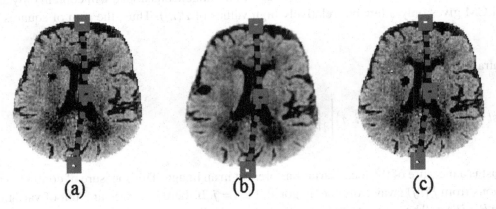

aided diagnosis system of ischemic stroke is to extract various features from a given brain image which best characterizes a given lesion as normal or abnormal. Medical images are often highly textured and texture analysis becomes crucial in medical image classification. Texture based analysis has been very successful in the diagnosis of medical images.

Texture is a repeating pattern of local variations in image intensity. The co-occurrence matrix is a statistical method used for texture analysis. As the name suggests, the co-occurrence matrix is constructed from the image by estimating the pairwise statistics of pixel intensity. The use of the co-occurrence matrix is based on the hypotheses that the same grey-level configuration is repeated in a texture. This pattern will vary more by fine textures than by coarse textures. The co-occurrence matrix $P(i, j|d,\theta)$ counts the co-occurrence of pixels with grey values i and j at a given distance d and in a given direction θ. According to the number of intensity points (pixels) in each combination, statistics are classified into first-order, second-order and higher-order statistics.

The GLCM method is a way of extracting second order statistical texture features (Haralick et al., 1973). However, the performance of a given GLCM based feature, as well as the ranking of the texture features, depends on the number of gray levels used. The following notations are used: μ is the mean value of P. μ_x, μ_y, σ_x and σ_y are the means and standard deviations of P_x and P_y. G is the size of the co-occurrence matrix. Here the number of rows and columns of the co-occurrence matrix is equal. The following GLCM features are extracted in this work: ASM, contrast, entropy, correlation, sum of squares, difference entropy, IDM, inertia, cluster prominence, cluster shade, energy, homogeneity, dissimilarity and difference in variance. They are defined in eqs. (4)-(17).

1.   Angular Second Moment

$$ASM = \sum_{i=0}^{G-1}\sum_{j=0}^{G-1}\left\{P\left(i,j\right)\right\}^2 \tag{4}$$

ASM is a measure of homogeneity of the image. A homogeneous image will contain only a few gray levels, GLCM gives only a few but relatively high values of $P(i,j)$. Thus, the sum of squares also will be high.

2. Contrast

$$Contrast = \sum_{n=0}^{G-1} n^2 \left\{ \sum_{i=1}^{G} \sum_{j=1}^{G} P(i,j) \right\}, |i-j| = n \tag{5}$$

Contrast is a measure of the local variations present in an image. This measure of contrast will favour contributions from $P(i,j)$ away from the diagonal, i.e. $i = j$. If there is a large amount of variations in an image, the $P[i,j]$'s will be concentrated away from the main diagonal and the contrast will be a high value.

3. Inverse Difference Moment

$$IDM = \sum_{i=0}^{G-1} \sum_{j=0}^{G-1} \frac{1}{1 + (i-j)^2} P(i,j) \tag{6}$$

IDM is also influenced by the homogeneity of the image. Because of the weighting factor $(1+(i-j)^2)^{-1}$ IDM will get small contributions from inhomogeneous areas $(i \; j)$. The result is a low IDM value for inhomogeneous images and higher value for homogeneous images.

4. Entropy

$$Entropy = -\sum_{i=0}^{G-1} \sum_{j=0}^{G-1} P(i,j) \times log\left(P(i,j)\right) \tag{7}$$

Entropy statistic measures the disorder or complexity of an image. Complex textures tend to have high entropy. Entropy is strong, but inversely correlated to energy.

5. Correlation

$$Correlation = \sum_{i=0}^{G-1} \sum_{j=0}^{G-1} \frac{\{i \times j\} \times P(i,j) - \{\mu_x \times \mu_y\}}{\sigma_x \times \sigma_y} \tag{8}$$

Correlation is a measure of gray level linear dependence between the pixels at the specified positions relative to each other. The correlation will be higher, if an image contains a considerable amount of linear structure.

6. Sum of Squares, Variance

$$Variance = \sum_{i=0}^{G-1}\sum_{j=0}^{G-1}(i-\mu)^2 P(i,j) \qquad (9)$$

The variance is a measure of the dispersion of the gray level differences at a certain distance, *d*. This feature puts relatively high weights on the elements that differ from the average value of *P(i,j)*.

7. Difference Entropy

$$DEnt = -\sum_{i=0}^{G-1}P_{x+y}(i)\log\left(P_{x+y}(i)\right) \qquad (10)$$

Difference entropy is a measure of histogram content and logical value between two images. If two images are identical the difference entropy will be high otherwise low. Where $P_x(i)$ is the ith entry in the marginal-probability matrix obtained by summing the rows of *P(i,j)* and $P_y(i)$ is obtained by summing the columns of *P(i,j)*.

8. Inertia

$$Inertia = \sum_{i=0}^{G-1}\sum_{j=0}^{G-1}\{i-j\}^2 \times P(i,j) \qquad (11)$$

The inertia indicates the distribution of gray scales in the image.

9. Cluster Shade

$$Shade = \sum_{i=0}^{G-1}\sum_{j=0}^{G-1}\{i+j-\mu_x-\mu_y\}^3 \times P(i,j) \qquad (12)$$

The image is not symmetric when shade is high.

10. Cluster Prominence

$$Prom = \sum_{i=0}^{G-1}\sum_{j=0}^{G-1}\{i+j-\mu_x-\mu_y\}^4 \times P(i,j) \qquad (13)$$

The image is not symmetric when prominences are high.

11. Energy

$$Energy = \sum_{i=0}^{G-1}\sum_{j=0}^{G-1} p(i,j)^2 \tag{14}$$

The energy of a texture describes the uniformity of the texture. Energy is 1 for a constant image.

12. Homogeneity

$$Homogeneity = \sum_{i=0}^{G-1}\sum_{j=0}^{G-1} \frac{P(i,j)}{1+|i-j|} \tag{15}$$

Homogeneity returns a value that measures the closeness of the distribution of elements in the GLCM to the GLCM diagonal. Homogeneity is 1 for a diagonal GLCM. A homogeneous image will result in a co-occurrence matrix with a combination of high and low $P[i,j]$'s. A heterogeneous image will result in an even spread of $P[i,j]$'s.

13. Dissimilarity

$$Dissimilarity = \sum_{i=0}^{G-1}\sum_{j=0}^{G-1} |i-j| P(i,j) \tag{16}$$

Dissimilarity is a measure of evenness between two groups.

14. Difference in variance

$$Variance = \sum_{i=0}^{G-1}\sum_{j=0}^{G-1} (i-\mu)^2 P(i,j) \tag{17}$$

Difference in variance is the sum of the difference between the intensity of the central pixel and its neighborhood.

Normalized GLCM N[i,j], is defined in eq. (18).

$$N[i,j] = \frac{P[i,j]}{\sum_i \sum_j P[i,j]} \tag{18}$$

which normalizes the co-occurrence values to lie between 0 and 1.

In a classification problem, the number of features can be quite large; many of them can be irrelevant or redundant. All the features extracted from the input images does not account for high accuracy. So the optimal solution is not occurring. To solve this problem, feature reduction is introduced to improve the classification by searching for the best feature subset, from the fixed set of the original features, according to a given processing goal and a feature evaluation criterion: classification accuracy. In this work GA is proposed to select the optimal features.

GA is an adaptive method of global-optimization searching and simulates the behaviour of the evolutionary process in nature (Siedlecki & Sklanky, 1989). The total features extracted are 14. The features selected using GA is 7. Therefore, optimized feature selection reduces data dimensionalities and computational time and increase the classification accuracy. The GA uses three basic operators to evolve the population: selection, crossover and mutation. From the experiments conducted for feature selection, it is found that the optimal feature set which gives good classification performance are ASM, contrast, entropy, correlation, IDM, variance and dissimilarity details of the image. Hence for this application domain, the above 7 features are enough for classifying images into normal and abnormal.

In the proposed method all the features of left by right ratio and right by left ratio are close to 1. Therefore in the proposed method the midline is the best indicator for measuring the degree of symmetry.

Classifiers: SVM, ANN, Decision Tree

Support Vector Machine Classifier

Support vector machine (SVM) is a powerful supervised classifier and accurate learning technique. From the statistical theory it was derived and developed by Vapnick in 1982. It yields successful classification results in various application domains, e.g. medical diagnosis. SVM is based on the structural risk minimization principle from the statistical learning theory (Cristianini and Shawe Taylor, 2000). Its kernel is to control the empirical risk and classification capacity in order to maximize the margin between the classes and minimize the true costs. A support vector machine searches an optimal separating hyper-plane between members and non-members of a given class in a higher dimension feature space. The inputs to the SVM algorithm are the features extracted and selected using the GLCM and GA. In our method, the two classes are normal and ischemic stroke image. Then classification procedure continues to divide the image into normal and abnormal; each subject is represented by a vector in all images.

Artificial Neural Network Classifier

Artificial neural network (ANN) is a mathematical model consisting of a number of highly interconnected processing elements organized into layers, geometry and functionality which have been resembled to that of the human brain. The ANN may be regarded as a massively parallel distributed processor that has a natural propensity for storing experiential knowledge and making it available for use (Baxt, 1995). The cascade-forward back propagation network which is employed as the classifier required in this work has three layers (after several trails for different hidden layers with a different number of neurons). The first layer consists of 14 input elements in accordance with the 14 feature vectors selected from left and right side of texture features. The number of hidden layers used is two. The number of neurons in the hidden layer is five. The single neuron in the output layer is used to represent normal and ischemic stroke image. The neural network has been trained to adjust the connection weights and biases in order to produce the desired mapping. In this stage, the feature vectors are applied as an input to the network and the network adjusts its variable parameters, the weights and biases, to capture the relationship between the input patterns and outputs.

Decision Tree Classifier

Decision trees are considered to be one of the most popular approaches for representing classifiers. A decision tree is a tree structured prediction model where each internal node denotes a test on an attribute; each outgoing branch represents an outcome of the test and each leaf node is labeled with a class of the image (Yun and Fu, 1983). Decision trees are often used in classification and prediction. It is simple yet a powerful way of knowledge representation. The models produced by decision trees are represented in the form of tree structure. Learning a decision tree involves deciding which split to make at each node and how deep the tree should be. A leaf node indicates the class of the image. The instances are classified by sorting them down the tree from the root node to some leaf node.

Segmentation: K-Means Clustering Technique

K-means clustering is often suitable for biomedical image segmentation. In this research work the number of clusters is 6. This method has a number of advantages, such as its ability to handle large amounts of data points and its ability to work with compact clusters. However, it has its own set of limitations as well, such as the variables must be commensurable, the number of clusters should be known beforehand and it is sensitive to outliers and noise.

In the abnormal brain imaging, the ischemic stroke region is extracted using k-means clustering technique (Hartigen et al., 1979; Hema Rajini and Bhavani, 2011).

The k-means clustering algorithm includes the following steps:

1. Select the number of clusters k with initial cluster centroid v_i, i = 1,2,..., k.
Partition the input data points into k clusters by assigning each data point x_j to the closest cluster centroid v_i using the selected distance measure, for example, Euclidean distance, defined as

$$d_{ij} = \| x_j - v_i \| \tag{19}$$

where $X = \{x_1, x_2, ...x_n\}$ is the input data set.

3. Compute a cluster assignment matrix U representing the partition of the data points with the binary membership value of the jth data point to the ith cluster such that

$$U = \lfloor u_{ij} \rfloor, \text{ where } u_{ij} \in \{0,1\} \text{ for all } i, j$$

$$\sum_{i=1}^{k} u_{ij} = 1 \text{ for all } j \text{ and } 0 < \sum_{j=1}^{n} u_{ij} < n \text{ for all } i \tag{20}$$

4.   Re-compute the centroid using the membership values by

$$v_i = \frac{\sum_{j=1}^{n} u_{ij} x_j}{\sum_{j=1}^{n} u_{ij}} \text{ for all i.} \tag{21}$$

5.   If a cluster centroid or the assignment matrix does not change from the previous iteration, stop; otherwise go to step 2.

'The k-means clustering method' optimizes the sum-of-squared-error-based objective function J_w (U, v) then

$$J_w(U,v) = \sum_{i=1}^{k}\sum_{j=1}^{n} \left\| x_j - v_i \right\|^2 \tag{22}$$

It can be spotted from the above algorithm that the k-means clustering method is quite sensitive to the initial cluster assignment and the choice of the distance measure. The additional criterion like within-cluster and between-cluster variances can be included in the objective function as constraints to force the algorithm to adapt the number of clusters k, as necessary for optimization of the objective function. The extracted stroke region using k-means clustering technique is shown in Figure 7(a-c).

Quantitative Analysis

The automatic segmentation results are compared to the manual results. The results are quantitatively evaluated by a human expert. A region of ischemic stroke identified by an experienced radiologist is the ground truth. Each pixel belongs to one of the four classes accordingly: True Positive (TP) is correctly classified as positive pixels; False Positive (FP) is incorrectly classified as negative pixels; True Negative (TN) is correctly classified as negative pixels and False Negative (FN) is incorrectly classified as positive pixels. Three quantitative measures are employed to evaluate the segmentation result: precision, recall and overlap metric. They are defined in the following eqs. (23)-(25).

$$Precision = \frac{TP}{TP + FP} \tag{23}$$

Figure 7. Ischemic stroke region using k-means clustering technique (a-c)

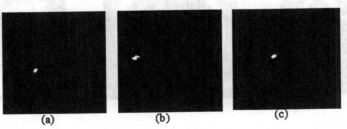

(a)   (b)   (c)

$$Recall \ or \ Sensitivity = \frac{TP}{TP + FN} \tag{24}$$

$$Overlap \ metric = \frac{2 \times TP}{2 \times TP + FP + FN} \tag{25}$$

The average overlap metric, average precision and average recall between the results obtained using the proposed approach and the ground truth are 0.98, 0.99 and 0.98.

Results and Discussion for Segmentation of Ischemic Stroke Detection

The images are collected from 15 cases of acute ischemic stroke and 6 normal cases from the Department of Radiology, RMMCH. All the input data set used for ischemic stroke detection consisted of non-enhanced 512×512 CT brain images. The CT brain images collected from the patients are acquired on Mx 8000 Dual, Philips CT scanner. The proposed method has been evaluated on a dataset of 21 patients (400 image slices). The original CT brain image without stroke is shown in Figure 8(a). CT brain image which is stained with ischemic stroke lesion is shown in Figure 8(b-f). In ischemic stroke, 50 images are considered as training set and 35 images are considered as testing set. The number of inputs to this classifier is 14 and the output is 2 as normal and abnormal (ischemic stroke). In this method, the two classes are normal image and ischemic stroke image.

Figure 8. Original CT brain images: (a) Normal brain image and (b-f) Abnormal brain images (Ischemic stroke region marked in green colour)

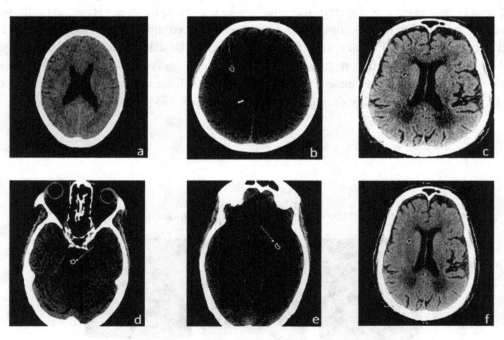

The proposed method consists of five stages. In the first stage noise is suppressed using median filtering and skull bone components of the images are removed by a global thresholding method. In the second stage, midline shift of the brain is calculated. Symmetry map is calculated at this stage and Bezier curve is drawn for the control points.

In the third stage, fourteen texture features are extracted using GLCM. The following GLCM features are extracted in this work: ASM, entropy, correlation, sum of squares, difference entropy, inertia, cluster prominence, IDM, cluster shade, energy, homogeneity, dissimilarity and difference in variance. The 7 optimal features are extracted from the left and right side of the brain using GA. The optimal features are ASM, contrast, entropy, correlation, IDM, variance and dissimilarity. The optimal features are used to train the binary classifier, which can automatically infer whether the image is that of a normal brain or an ischemic brain suffering from a brain lesion. In this method all the features values of left by right ratio and right by left ratio are close to 1. Therefore in this method the midline is the best indicator for measuring the degree of symmetry.

In the next stage, SVM, ANN and decision tree classifiers have been used to classify normal brain and ischemic brain. The cascade forward BP network which is employed as the classifier required in ischemic stroke classification has three layers (after several trails for different hidden layers with a different number of neurons). The first layer consists of 14 input elements in accordance with the 14 feature vectors selected from left and right side of texture features. The number of hidden layers used is two. The number of neurons in the hidden layers is five. The single neuron in the output layer is used to represent normal and abnormal image (ischemic stroke).

The classification performance of the proposed method tests at a slice (normal vs. abnormal case) level. The performance of the classifiers is evaluated in terms of sensitivity (also called recall in some fields), specificity and accuracy. The formulae for these are given in eqs. (24), (26-27). The three terms are defined as follows:

- *Sensitivity* (true positive fraction) is the probability that a diagnostic test is positive, given that the person has the disease.
- *Specificity* (true negative fraction) is the probability that a diagnostic test is negative, given that the person does not have the disease.

$$Specificity = \frac{TN}{TN + FP} \qquad (26)$$

- *Accuracy* is the probability that a diagnostic test is correctly performed.

$$Accuracy = \frac{TP + TN}{TP + TN + FP + FN} \qquad (27)$$

TP = An abnormal classified as abnormal. TN = A normal classified as normal. FP = A normal classified as abnormal. FN = An abnormal classified as normal. The classification performance is described using the percentages of correct or incorrect classification of normal or abnormal data.

Table 1. Classification rates of SVM classifier for ischemic stroke

Classifier	Sensitivity (%)	Specificity (%)	Accuracy (%)
SVM	96	100	97
ANN	96	90	94
Decision tree	92	90	91

The system achieves 96% of sensitivity and 100% of specificity, respectively for SVM. The system achieves 96% of sensitivity and 90% of specificity, respectively for ANN. The system achieves 92% of sensitivity and 90% of specificity, respectively for decision tree. In the proposed method the accuracy of SVM, ANN and decision tree are 97%, 94% and 91%. Thus SVM is the best classifier for this dataset. Table 1 gives the performance measures for SVM, ANN and decision tree model.

Finally, the stroke region is extracted using k-means clustering technique. The results are quantitatively evaluated by a human expert. The average overlap metric, average precision and average recall between the results obtained using the proposed approach and the ground truth are 0.98, 0.99 and 0.98. The performance of the algorithm is very good. The results of the proposed method are given in Figure 9(a-h).

The application of the proposed method for early detection of ischemic stroke is demonstrated to improve efficiency and accuracy of clinical practice. The proposed method helps to increase the accuracy in detection of ischemic stroke and hence it decreases the risk of misdiagnosis and mismanagement.

FUTURE RESEARCH DIRECTIONS

There is scope for future research work concerning to improve the performance of the CAD system.

- This method can be further extended to segment other types of images (PET, MRS and fMRI) with few modifications.
- One can incorporate the CT and MR image information together to obtain more accurate lesion segmentation.

Figure 9. An ischemic stroke detection process in brain CT image: a) Original brain CT image; b) Image after skull bone removal; c) Generation of the symmetry map; d) Generation of Bezier curve; e), f) Left and right image extraction; g) Ischemic stroke region using proposed method and h) Ischemic stroke region using manual method

Original image

Skull bone removed image

Symmetric map image

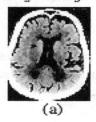

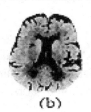

- An interesting extension of this chapter will be to investigate and quantify the patterns extracted from other modalities and fuse them with the patterns employed in the present research work.
- In this chapter, an ANN model is used to classify the types of diseases. Its network accuracy can be further improved by training it on a larger data set.

CONCLUSION

A computer aided detection system capable of identifying small ischemic stroke has been developed. We have developed an automated method for the detection of ischemic stroke in brain CT images using segmentation, texture features and tracing midline shift algorithm. This system detects ischemic stroke on routine non-enhanced brain CT images. Our system has been successfully tested on small lesion causing the ischemic stroke. This method is fully automatic as it does not require any human intervention. The proposed system can help the physicians to better diagnose human brain stroke, for further treatment. The brain region related to a lesion can be exactly separated from the brain image. This system is able to generate accurate quantitative results ready for clinical use. The average overlap metric, average precision and average recall between the results obtained using the proposed approach and the ground truth are 0.98, 0.99 and 0.98 respectively. The proposed system can help the physicians to identify the type of ischemic stroke, for further treatment. A classification with accuracy of 97%, 94% and 91% has been obtained by SVM, ANN and decision tree respectively. Among the three classifiers the SVM classifier is shown to be highly effective in the classification of brain lesions. The proposed system helps to improve the accuracy in detection of ischemic stroke and hence it decreases the risk of misdiagnosis and mismanagement.

REFERENCES

Adams, H., Adams, R., Del Zoppo, G., & Goldstein, L. B. (2005). Guidelines for the early management of patients with ischemic stroke, guidelines update. *Stroke*, *36*(4), 916–921. doi:10.1161/01. STR.0000163257.66207.2d PMID:15800252

Baxt, T. W. G. (1995). Application of Artificial Neural Networks to Clinical Medicine. *Lancet*, *346*(8983), 1135–1138. doi:10.1016/S0140-6736(95)91804-3 PMID:7475607

Bullock, M. R., Chestnut, R., Ghajar, J., Gordon, D., Hartl, R., & Newell, D. W. (2006). Post-traumatic mass volume measurement in traumatic brain injury patients. *Journal of Neurosurgery*, *58*, S2–S61.

Chawla, M., Sharma, S., Sivaswamy, J., & Kishore, L. T. (2009). A method for automatic detection and classification of stroke from brain CT images. *Annual International Conference of the IEEE Engineering in Medicine and Biology Society* (pp. 3581-3584). doi:10.1109/IEMBS.2009.5335289

Cristianini, N., & Shawe Taylor, J. (2000). *An Introduction to Support Vector Machines and Other Kernel-based Learning Methods* (1st ed.). Cambridge University Press. doi:10.1017/CBO9780511801389

Fauzi, M. F. A., Komiya, R., & Cheng Haw, S. (2008). Unsupervised abnormalities extraction and brain segmentation. In *Proceedings of the International Conference on Intel System Knowledge Engineering* (vol. 1, pp. 1185-1190).

Haralick, R. M., Shanmugam, K., & Dinstein, I. (1973). Textural features for image classification. In *Proceedings of the IEEE Transactions on Systems, Man and Cybernetics* (vol. 36, pp.610-621).

Hartigan, J. A., Wong, M. A., & Algorithm, A. S. (1979). A K-Means Clustering Algorithm. *Journal of the Royal Statistical Society. Series A (General)*, *28*(1), 100–108.

Hay, F. (2011). An image feature approach for computer-aided detection of ischemic stroke. *Computers in Biology and Medicine*, *41*(7), 529–536. doi:10.1016/j.compbiomed.2011.05.001 PMID:21605853

Hema Rajini, N., & Bhavani, R. (2011). Enhancing k-means and kernelized fuzzy c-means clustering with cluster center initialization in segmenting MRI brain images. In *Proceedings of the 3rd International Conference on Electronics Computer Technology* (pp.259-263).

Lee, Y., Takahashi, N., Tsai, D. Y., & Fujita, H. (2006). Detectability improvement of early sign of acute stroke on brain CT images using an adaptive partial smoothing filter. In *Proceedings of the Society of Photo-Optical Instrumentation Engineering and Medical Imaging* (vol. 6144, pp.2138-2145). doi:10.1117/12.654242

Liao, C. C., Chiang, I. J., Xiao, F., & Wong, J. M. (2006a). Tracing the deformed midline on brain CT. *Biomedical Engineering-Applications Basis Communications*, *18*(6), 305–311. doi:10.4015/S1016237206000452

Liao, C. C., Xiao, F., Wong, J. M., & Chiang, I. J. (2006b). A simple genetic algorithm for tracing the deformed midline on a single slice of brain CT using quadratic Bezier curves. In *Proceedings of Sixth IEEE International Conference on Data Mining Workshops*, (pp. 463-467). doi:10.1109/ICDMW.2006.22

Maldjian, J. A., & Chalela, J. (2001). Automated CT segmentation and analysis for acute middle cerebral artery stroke. *AJNR. American Journal of Neuroradiology*, *22*(6), 1050–1055. PMID:11415896

Otsu, N. (1979). A threshold selection method from gray-level histograms. *IEEE Transactions on Systems, Man, and Cybernetics*, *9*(1), 62–66. doi:10.1109/TSMC.1979.4310076

Przelaskowski, A., Sklinda, K. P., Bargie, P. J., Walecki, J., Biesiadko Matus Zewska, M., & Kazubek, M. (2007). Improved early stroke detection: Wavelet-based perception enhancement of computerized tomography exams. *Computers in Biology and Medicine*, *37*(4), 524–533. doi:10.1016/j.compbiomed.2006.08.004 PMID:16999952

Sederberg, T. W. (2011). Computer Aided Geometric Design Course Notes. Brigham Young University.

Siedlecki, W., & Sklanky, J. (1989). A note on genetic algorithms for large-scale feature selection. *Pattern Recognition Letters*, *10*(5), 335–347. doi:10.1016/0167-8655(89)90037-8

Thom, T., Haase, N., Rosamond, W., Howard, V. J., Rumsfeld, J., & Manolio, T. (2006). Heart disease and stroke statistics—2006 update: Are port from the American Heart Association Statistics Committee and Stroke Statistics Subcommittee. *Circulation*, *113*(6), e85–e151. doi:10.1161/CIRCULATIONAHA.105.171600 PMID:16407573

Tomura, N., Uemura, K., Inugami, A., Fujita, H., Higano, S., & Shishida, F. (1988). Early CT finding in cerebral infarction: Obscuration of the lentiform nucleus. *Radiology, 168*(2), 463–467. doi:10.1148/radiology.168.2.3393665 PMID:3393665

Toni, D., Iweins, F., Von Kummer, R., Busse, O., Bogousslavsky, J., Falcou, A. E., & Lenzi, G. L. et al. (2000). Identification of lacunar infarcts before thrombolysis in the ECASS 1 Study. *Neurology, 54*(3), 684–688. doi:10.1212/WNL.54.3.684 PMID:10680804

Usinskas, D. R. A., & Tomandl, B. F. (2004). Ischemic stroke segmentation on CT images using joint features. *Informatica, 15*(2), 283–290.

Von Kummer, R. (2005). The impact of CT on acute stroke treatment. In P. Lyden (Ed.), Thrombolytic Therapy for Stroke. Humana Press.

Yun, S. Q., & Fu, K. S. (1983). A method for the design of binary tree classifiers. *Pattern Recognition, 16*(6), 593–603. doi:10.1016/0031-3203(83)90076-6

Compilation of References

Procopiuc, & Agarwal, P. K. (2003). Bkd-Tree: A Dynamic Scalable kd-Tree. *LNCS, 2750*, 46–65.

1f noise, Brownian Noise. (1999). Retrieved from http://classes.yale.edu/9900/math190a/ OneOverF.html

Abbas, J., Qadri, S., Idrees, M., Awan, S., & Khan, N. A. (2010). Frame work for content based image retrieval (Textual Based) system. *Journal of American Science, 6*(9), 704–707.

Abraham, B. (2013). Imaging's Role in the Future of Alzheimer's Disease. *Electroindustrty, 18*(3), 11.

Adams, H., Adams, R., Del Zoppo, G., & Goldstein, L. B. (2005). Guidelines for the early management of patients with ischemic stroke, guidelines update. *Stroke, 36*(4), 916–921. doi:10.1161/01.STR.0000163257.66207.2d PMID:15800252

Adegoke, B.O., Ola, B.O, & Omotayo. (2014). Review of Feature Selection Methods in Medical Image Processing. *IOSR Journal of Engineering, 4*(1), 1-5.

Aggarwal, J. K., & Ryoo, M. S. (2011). Human activity analysis: A review. *ACM Computing Surveys, 43*(3), 16. doi:10.1145/1922649.1922653

Aharon, M., Elad, M., & Bruckstein, A. M. (2006). The K-SVD: An algorithm for designing of overcomplete dictionaries for sparse representation. *IEEE Transactions on Signal Processing, 54*(11), 4311–4322. doi:10.1109/TSP.2006.881199

Ah-Pine, J., Cifarelli, C., Clinchant, S., Csurka, G., & Renders, J. (2009). *XRCE's participation to ImageCLEF 2008.* Academic Press.

Akram, & Khanum. (2010). Retinal Images: Blood Vessel Segmentation by Threshold Probing. *IEEE Symposium On Industrial Electronics And Applications(ISIEA).*

Alemu, Y., Koh, J.-b., Ikram, M., & Kim, D.-K. (2009). *Image retrieval in multimedia databases: A survey.* Paper presented at the Intelligent Information Hiding and Multimedia Signal Processing, 2009. IIH-MSP'09. Fifth International Conference on. doi:10.1109/IIH-MSP.2009.159

Al-Hamami, A., & Al-Rashdan, H. (2010). Improving the Effectiveness of Color Coherehence Vector.Histogram. *The International Arab Journal of Information Technology, 7*(3), 324–332.

Ali, A., & Terada, K. (2009, September). A framework for human tracking using kalman filter and fast mean shift algorithms. In *Computer Vision Workshops (ICCV Workshops), 2009 IEEE 12th International Conference on* (pp. 1028-1033). IEEE.

Amin, T., & Hatzinakos, D. (2009). Wavelet Analysis of Cyclic Human Gait for Recognition. *16th IEEE International Conference on Digital Signal Processing.* doi:10.1109/ICDSP.2009.5201167

Amr, I., Amin, M., Kafrawy, P. E., & Sauber, A. M. (2010). *Using Statistical Moment Invariantsand Entropy in Image Retrieval.* arXiv preprint arXiv: 1002.2193

Anandan, P., Bergen, J., Hanna, K., & Hingorani, R. (1993). Hierarchical Model-Based Motion Estimation. In Motion Analysis and Image Sequence Processing. Kluwer Academic. doi:10.1007/978-1-4615-3236-1_1

Anne, M. P. (2013). Investigating fusion approaches in multi-biometric cancellable recognition. *Expert Systems with Applications, Elsevier, 40*(6), 1971–1980. doi:10.1016/j.eswa.2012.10.002

Anu, S., Nair, H., Aruna, P., & Sakthivel, K. (2013). Sparse Representation Fusion of Fingerprint, Iris and Palmprint Biometric Features. *International Journal of Advanced ComputerResearch, 4*(1), 46–53.

Aouat. (2010). Indexing binary images using quad-tree decomposition. In *Proceedings of IEEE International Conference on Systems Man & Cybernetics,* (pp. 3074-3080). IEEE.

Aravinth, J. &Dr.S.Valarmathy. (2012). A Novel Feature Extraction Techniques for Multimodal Score Fusion Using Density Based Gaussian Mixture Model Approach. *International Journal of Emerging Technology and Advanced Engineering, 2*(1), 189–197.

Arbelaez, P., Maire, M., Fowlkes, C., & Malik, J. (2011). Contour detection and hierarchical image segmentation. *Pattern Analysis and Machine Intelligence. IEEE Transactions on, 33*(5), 898–916.

Arge, L. (2002), External memory data structures. In J. Abello, P. M. Pardalos, & M. G. C. Resende (Eds.), Handbook of Massive Data Sets, (pp. 313–358). doi:10.1007/978-1-4615-0005-6_9

Arya, S., Mount, D. M., Netanyahu, N. S., Silverman, R., & Wu, A. Y. (1998). An optimal algorithm for approximate nearest neighbor searching fixed dimensions. *Journal of the ACM, 45*(6), 891–923. doi:10.1145/293347.293348

Ascenso, J., Brites, C., & Pereira, F. (2005). Improving Frame Interpolation with Spatial Motion Smoothing for Pixel Domain Distributed Video Coding.*Proc. EURASIP Conference on Speech and Image Processing, Multimedia Communications and Services.*

Atrey, P. K., Hossain, M. A., El Saddik, A., & Kankanhalli, M. S. (2010). Multimodal fusion for multimedia analysis: A survey. *Multimedia Systems, 16*(6), 345–379. doi:10.1007/s00530-010-0182-0

Avidan, S. (2001). Support vector tracking. In *IEEE Conference on Computer Vision and Pattern Recognition (CVPR),* (pp. 184–191). IEEE.

Ayatollahi, S. M., Masoud, A., Moghadam, E., & Hosseini, M. S. (2013). A taxonomy of depth map creation methods used in multiview video compression. Springer Science and Business Media.

Babenko, B., Yang, M. H., & Belongie, S. (2009, June). Visual tracking with online multiple instance learning. In *Computer Vision and Pattern Recognition, 2009. CVPR 2009. IEEE Conference on* (pp. 983-990). IEEE.

Bahaa-Eldin, A. M. (2013). A medium resolution fingerprint matching system. *Ain Shams Engineering Journal,Elsevier, 4*(3), 393–408. doi:10.1016/j.asej.2012.10.001

Baljozovic, Kovacevic, & Baljozovic. (2013). Mixed noise removal filter for multi-channel images based on halfspace deepest location. *Image Processing, 7*(4), 310-323.

Baraniuk, R. G., Candès, E. J., Elad, M., & Ma, Y. (2010). Applications of sparse representation and compressive sensing. *Proceedings of the IEEE, 98*(6), 906–909. doi:10.1109/JPROC.2010.2047424

Barnard, , P. D. (2003). Matching words and pictures. *Journal of Machine Learning Research, 3,* 1107–1135.

Barnich, O., & Droogenbroeck, M. V. (2009). Frontal-view gait recognition by intra- and inter-frame rectangle size distribution. *Pattern Recognition Letters, 30*(9), 893–901. doi:10.1016/j.patrec.2009.03.014

Barron, J., Fleet, D., & Beauchemin, S. (1994). Performance of optical flow techniques. *International Journal of Computer Vision, 12*(1), 43–77. doi:10.1007/BF01420984

Bar-Shalom, Y., & Foreman, T. (1988). *Tracking and Data Association.* Academic Press Incorporation.

Bashir, K., Xiang, T., & Gong, S. (2010). Gait recognition without subject cooperation. *Pattern Recognition Letters, 31*(13), 2052–2060. doi:10.1016/j.patrec.2010.05.027

Battiato, S., Curti, S., Cascia, M. L., Tortora, M., & Scordato, E. (2004). Depth map generation by image classification. In *Proceedings on SPIE conference on Three Dimensional Image Capture and Applications* (vol. 5302-95). SPIE. doi:10.1117/12.526634

Baxt, T. W. G. (1995). Application of Artificial Neural Networks to Clinical Medicine. *Lancet, 346*(8983), 1135–1138. doi:10.1016/S0140-6736(95)91804-3 PMID:7475607

Bay, H., Ess, A., Tuytelaars, T., & Van Gool, L. (2008). *SURF*: Speeded Up Robust Features. *Computer Vision and Image Understanding, 110*(3), 346–359. doi:10.1016/j.cviu.2007.09.014

Beckmann, N., Kriegel, H. P., Schneider, R., & Seeger, B. (1990). The R*-Tree: An efficient and robust access method for points and rectangles.*Proceedings of the ACM SIGMOD International Conference on Management of Data.* ACM. doi:10.1145/93597.98741

Ben Sbeh, Z., Cohen, L. D., Mimoun, G., & Coscas, G. (2001). A New Approach of Geodesic Reconstruction for Drusen Segmentation in Eye Fundus Images. *IEEE Transactions on Medical Imaging, 20*(12), 1321–1333. doi:10.1109/42.974927 PMID:11811832

Beniwal, S., & Arora, J. (2012). Classification and feature selection techniques in data mining. *International Journal of Engineering Research and Technology., 1*(6), 1–6.

Bentley, J. L. (1975). Multi dimensional binary search trees used for associative searching. *Communications of the ACM, 18*(9), 509–517. doi:10.1145/361002.361007

Berchtold, S., Keim, D., & Kriegel, H. P. (1996). The X-Tree: An index structure for high-dimensional data.*Proceedings of the International Conference on Very Large Databases*, (pp. 28–39).

Bergholm, F. (1987). Edge Focussing. *IEEE Transactions on Pattern Analysis and Machine Intelligence, 9*(6), 726–741. doi:10.1109/TPAMI.1987.4767980 PMID:21869435

Bertalmio, M., Sapiro, G., & Randall, G. (2000). Morphing active contours. *IEEE Transactions on Pattern Analysis and Machine Intelligence, 22*(7), 733–737. doi:10.1109/34.865191

Beymar, D., & Konolige, K. (1999). Real-time tracking of multiple people using continuous detection. In *IEEE International Conference on Computer Vision (ICCV) Frame-Rate Workshop.* IEEE.

Bezdek, J. C., Chandrasekhar, R., & Attikiouzel, Y. (1998). A geometric approach to edge detection. *IEEE Transactions on Fuzzy Systems, 6*(1), 52–75. doi:10.1109/91.660808

Bharathi, S., & Vasuki, A. (2012). 2D-To-3D Conversion of Images using Edge Information. In *Proceedings of International Conference on Recent Trends in Computational Methods, Communication and Controls.*

Bhoi, N., & Meher, D. S. (2008). Total Variation based Wavelet Domain Filter for Image Denoising.*First International Conference on Emerging Trends in Engineering and Technology.* IEEE Computer Society. doi:10.1109/ICETET.2008.6

Bihan, D. L., Breton, E., Lallemand, D., Grenier, P., & Cabanis, E. (1986). MR imaging of intravoxel incoherent motions: Application to diffusion and perfusion in neurologic disorders. *Radiology, 161*(2), 401–407. doi:10.1148/radiology.161.2.3763909 PMID:3763909

Birchfield, S. (1998). Elliptical head tracking using intensity gradients and color histograms. In *IEEE Conference on Computer Vision and Pattern Recognition (CVPR)*. doi:10.1109/CVPR.1998.698614

Black, M. J., Sapiro, G., Marimont, D. H., & Heeger, D. (1998). Robust anisotropic diffusion. *IEEE Transactions on Image Processing, 7*(3), 421–432. doi:10.1109/83.661192 PMID:18276262

Black, M., & Anandan, P. (1996). The robust estimation of multiple motions: Parametric and piecewise smooth flow fields. *Computer Vision and Image Understanding, 63*(1), 75–104. doi:10.1006/cviu.1996.0006

Black, M., & Jepson, A. (1998). Eigentracking: Robust matching and tracking of articulated objects using a view-based representation. *International Journal of Computer Vision, 26*(1), 63–84. doi:10.1023/A:1007939232436

Blum, A. L., & Langley, P. (1997). Selection of relevant features and examples in machine learning. *Artificial Intelligence, 97*(1-2), 245–271. doi:10.1016/S0004-3702(97)00063-5

Bobick, A. F., & Davis, J. W. (2001). The recognition of human movement using temporal templates. *IEEE Transactions on Pattern Analysis and Machine Intelligence, 23*(3), 257–267. doi:10.1109/34.910878

Bobin, J., Starck, J. L., Fadili, J. M., Moudden, Y., & Donoho, D. L. (2007). Morphological component analysis: An adaptive thresholding strategy. *IEEE Transactions on Image Processing, 16*(11), 2675–2681. doi:10.1109/TIP.2007.907073 PMID:17990744

Boles, W. W., & Boashash, B. (1998). A human identification technique using images of the iris & wavelet transform. *IEEE Transactions on Signal Processing, 46*(4), 1185–1188. doi:10.1109/78.668573

Boncelet, C. (2005). Image noise models. In A. C. Bovik (Ed.), *Handbook of Image and Video Processing*. Academic Press.

Borsotti, M., Campadelli, P., & Schettini, R. (1998). Quantitative evaluation of color image segmentation results. *Pattern Recognition Letters, 19*(8), 741–747. doi:10.1016/S0167-8655(98)00052-X

Boser, B., Guyon, I. M., & Vapnik, V. (1992). A training algorithm for optimal margin classifiers. In *ACM Workshop on Conference on Computational Learning Theory (COLT)*, (pp. 142–152). doi:10.1145/130385.130401

Bossu, J., Hautière, N., & Tarel, J. P. (2011). Rain or snow detection in image sequences through use of a histogram of orientation of streaks. *International Journal of Computer Vision, 93*(3), 348–367. doi:10.1007/s11263-011-0421-7

Boulgouris, N. V., & Chi, Z. X. (2007). 'Gait Recognition Using Radon Transform and Linear Discriminant Analysis. *IEEE Transactions on Image Processing, 16*(3), 731–740. doi:10.1109/TIP.2007.891157 PMID:17357733

Boulgouris, N. V., Hatzinakos, D., & Plataniotis, K. N. (2005). Gait recognition: A Challenging signal processing technology for Biometric identification. *IEEE Signal Processing Magazine, 22*(6), 78–90. doi:10.1109/MSP.2005.1550191

Bovik, A. C. (2009). *The Essential Guide to Image Processing* (2nd ed.). Academic Press.

Bowyer, K., Kranenburg, C., & Dougherty, S. (1999). Edge Detector Evaluation using Empirical ROC Curves. In *IEEE Computer Society Conference on Computer Vision and Pattern Recognition*. doi:10.1109/CVPR.1999.786963

Bowyer, W., & Flynn, P. J. (2008). Image understanding for iris biometrics: A survey. *Computer Vision and Image Understanding, 110*(2), 281–307. doi:10.1016/j.cviu.2007.08.005

Bo, Y., & Wen. (2007). Gait Recognition based on DWT and SVM. *Proc. Int'l Conf. on Wavelet Analysis and Pattern Recognition 3*, (pp. 1382-1387). IEEE. doi:10.1109/ICWAPR.2007.4421650

Boyd, J. E., & Little, J. J. (2005). *Biometric Gait Recognition. LNCS 3161* (pp. 19–42). Berlin: Springer-Verlag.

Bradski, G. (1998). Computer vision face tracking for use in a perceptual user interface. *Intel Technology Journal, 2*(2), 1–15.

Brant, W. E., & Helms, C. A. (2012). *Fundamentals of Diagnostic Radiology* (4th ed.). Lippincott Williams & Wilkins.

Breiman, L. (2001). Random forests. *Machine Learning, 45*(1), 5–32. doi:10.1023/A:1010933404324

Brenner, D. J., & Hall, E. J. (2007). Computed Tomography — An Increasing Source of Radiation Exposure. *The New England Journal of Medicine, 357*(22), 2277–2284. doi:10.1056/NEJMra072149 PMID:18046031

Bruckstein, A. M., Donoho, D. L., & Elad, M. (2009). From sparse solutions of systems of equations to sparse modeling of signals and images. *SIAM Review, 51*(1), 34–81. doi:10.1137/060657704

Buades, A., Coll, B., & Morel, J. M. (2005). A review of image denoising algorithms, with a new one. *Multiscale Modeling & Simulation, 4*(2), 490–530. doi:10.1137/040616024

Buccigrossi, R. W., & Simoncelli, E. P. (1999, December). Image compression via joint statistical characterization in the wavelet domain. *IEEE Image Process., 8*(12), 1688–1701. doi:10.1109/83.806616 PMID:18267447

Bugatti, P. H., Traina, A. J., & Traina, C., Jr. (2008). *Assessing the best integration between distance-function and image-feature to answer similarity queries.* Paper presented at the 2008 ACM Symposium on Applied Computing. doi:10.1145/1363686.1363969

Bullock, M. R., Chestnut, R., Ghajar, J., Gordon, D., Hartl, R., & Newell, D. W. (2006). Post-traumatic mass volume measurement in traumatic brain injury patients. *Journal of Neurosurgery, 58*, S2–S61.

Burge, M. J., & Bowyer, K. W. (2013). *Handbook of Iris Recognition.* Springer-Verlag. doi:10.1007/978-1-4471-4402-1

Cafforio, C., & Rocca, F. (1976). Methods for measuring small displacements of television images. *IEEE Transactions on Information Theory, 22*(5), 573–579. doi:10.1109/TIT.1976.1055602

Calle-Alonso, F., Perez, C.J., Arias-Nicolás, J.P., & Martín, J. (2013). Computer-aided diagnosis system: A Bayesian hybrid classification method. *Computer Methods and Programs in Biomedicine, 112*(1), 104-113.

Canny, J. (1986). A computational approach to edge detection. *IEEE Transactions on Pattern Analysis and Machine Intelligence, 8*(6), 679–698. doi:10.1109/TPAMI.1986.4767851 PMID:21869365

Cao, K., Pang, L., Liang, J., & Tia, J. (2013). Fingerprint classification by a hierarchical classifier. *Pattern Recognition, Elsevier, 46*(12), 3186–3197. doi:10.1016/j.patcog.2013.05.008

Cao, X., Bovik, A. C., Wang, Y., & Dai, Q. (2011). Converting 2D Video to 3D: An Efficient Path to a 3D Experience. *IEEE MultiMedia, 18*(4), 12–17. doi:10.1109/MMUL.2011.65

Caselles, V., Kimmel, R., & Sapiro, G. (1995). Geodesic active contours. In *IEEE International Conference on Computer Vision (ICCV)*, (pp. 694–699). doi:10.1109/ICCV.1995.466871

Cattell, R. B. (1965). *The Scientific Analysis of Personality.* Aldine.

Cha, G.-H., & Chung, C.-W. (2002). The GC-Tree: A High-Dimensional Index Structure for Similarity Search in Image Databases. *IEEE Transactions on Multimedia, 4*(2), 235–247. doi:10.1109/TMM.2002.1017736

Chaira, T., & Ray, A. K. (2005). Fuzzy measures for colour image retrieval. *Fuzzy Sets and Systems, 150*(3), 545–560. doi:10.1016/j.fss.2004.09.003

Chakrabarti, K., & Mehrotra, S. (1999). The hybrid Tree: An index structure for high dimensional feature spaces.*Proceedings of the International Conference on Data Engineering*, (pp. 440–447). doi:10.1109/ICDE.1999.754960

Chalmer, B. J. (1987). *Understanding statistics*. New York: Marcel Dekker, Inc.

Cham, T., & Rehg, J. M. (1999). A multiple hypothesis approach to figure tracking. In *IEEE International Conference on Computer Vision and Pattern Recognition*, (pp. 239–245).

Chanda, B., & Majumder, D. (2002). Digital Image Processing and Analysis. Prentice-Hall of India.

Chandler, D. M., & Hemami, S. S. (2007, September). VSNR: A wavelet-based visual signal-to-noise ratio for natural images. *IEEE Transactions on Image Processing, 16*(9), 2284–2298. doi:10.1109/TIP.2007.901820 PMID:17784602

Chang, N.-S., & Fu, K.-S. (1980). Query-by-pictorial-example. *Software Engineering, IEEE Transactions on*, (6), 519-524.

Chang, C. C., & Lin, C. J. (2011). LIBSVM: A library for support vector machines. *ACM Transactions on Intelligent Systems and Technology, 2*(3), 27. doi:10.1145/1961189.1961199

Chang, N.-S., & Fu, K. S. (1980). *A relational database system for images*. Springer. doi:10.1007/3-540-09757-0_11

Chang, Y. L., & Aggarwal, J. K. (1991). 3D Structure Reconstruction from an Ego Motion Sequence using Statistical Estimation and Detection Theory. In *Workshop on Visual Motion*, (pp. 268–273). doi:10.1109/WVM.1991.212797

Chang, Y. L., Fang, C. Y., Ding, L. F., & Chen, S. Y. (2007). Depth Map Generation for 2D-to-3D Conversion by Short-Term Motion Assisted Color Segmentation. In *Proceedings of IEEE International Conference on Multimedia and Expo* (pp-1958-1961). IEEE. doi:10.1109/ICME.2007.4285061

Chang, Y., Yan, L., Fang, H., & Liu, H. (2014). Simultaneous destriping and denoising for remote sensing images with unidirectional total variation and sparse representation. *IEEE Geoscience and Remote Sensing Letters, 11*(6), 1051–1055. doi:10.1109/LGRS.2013.2285124

Chavez-Roman, H., & Ponomaryov, V. I. (2014). Super resolution image generation using wavelet domain interpolation with edge extraction via a sparse representation. *IEEE Geoscience and Remote Sensing Letters, 11*(10), 1777–1781. doi:10.1109/LGRS.2014.2308905

Chawla, M., Sharma, S., Sivaswamy, J., & Kishore, L. T. (2009). A method for automatic detection and classification of stroke from brain CT images.*Annual International Conference of the IEEE Engineering in Medicine and Biology Society* (pp. 3581-3584). doi:10.1109/IEMBS.2009.5335289

Chen, H.-C., & Wang, S.-J. (2006). Visible colour difference-based quantitative evaluation of colour segmentation. *Vision, Image and Signal Processing, IEE Proceedings, 153*, 598-609.

Chen, J., & Greiner, R. (2001). Learning bayesian belief network classifiers. In Proceedings of Advances in Artificial Intelligence Algorithms and System (pp. 141-151). Springer Berlin Heidelberg.

Chen, Ma, & Chen. (1999, December). Tri-State Median Filter for Image Denoising. *IEEE Transactions On Image Processing, 8*(12), 1834-1838.

Chen, X., Fan, Wang, & Li. (2010). Automatic Gait Recognition using Kernel Principal Component Analysis. *International Conference on Biomedical Engineering and Computer Science* (pp.1 – 4). IEEE. doi:10.1109/ICBECS.2010.5462298

Chen, Y., & Goldberg, D. (2005). Convergence time for the linkage learning genetic algorithms. *Journal of Evolutionary Computation, 13*(3), 279-302.

Chen, C., Liang, J., Zhao, H., Hu, H., & Tian, J. (2009). Frame difference energy image for gait recognition with incomplete silhouettes. *Pattern Recognition Letters, 30*(11), 977–984. doi:10.1016/j.patrec.2009.04.012

Chen, D.-Y., Chen, C.-C., & Kang, L.-W. (2014). Visual depth guided color image rain streaks removal using sparse coding. *IEEE Transactions on Circuits and Systems for Video Technology, 24*(8), 1430–1455. doi:10.1109/TCSVT.2014.2308627

Cheng, P.-C., Yeh, J.-Y., Ke, H.-R., Chien, B.-C., & Yang, W.-P. (2004). *NCTU-ISU's Evaluation for the User-Centered Search Task at ImageCLEF 2004.* Paper presented at the Working notes of the 2004 CLEF workshop, Bath, UK.

Cheng, X., Sun, L., & Yang, S. (2007). Generation of Layered Depth Images from Multi-View Video. In *Proceedings of IEEE International Conference on Image Processing* (Vol. 5, pp. V‑225‑V–228). IEEE. doi:10.1109/ICIP.2007.4379806

Cheng, J., & Greiner, R. (1999). Comparing Bayesian network classifiers. In *Proceedings of Fifteenth Conference on Uncertainty in Artificial Intelligence.* (pp. 101-108). Morgan Kaufmann Publishers.

Cheng, Q., & Fu, B. (2008), Gait Recognition Based on Hilbert-Huang Descriptors. *Proceedings of the 7th World Congress on Intelligent Control and Automation*, (pp. 7640-7643).

Cheng, Y. (1995, August). Mean shift, mode seeking, and clustering. *IEEE Transactions on Pattern Analysis and Machine Intelligence, 17*(8), 790–799. doi:10.1109/34.400568

Chen, Q., Sun, Q. S., Heng, P. A., & Xia, D.-S. (2010). Two-Stage Object Tracking Method Based on Kernel and Active Contour. *IEEE Transactions on Circuits and Systems for Video Technology, 20*(4), 605–609. doi:10.1109/TCSVT.2010.2041819

Chen, T. (2009). Object Tracking Based on Active Contour Model by Neural Fuzzy Network. *IITA International Conference on Control Automation and Systems Engineering*, (pp. 570-574). doi:10.1109/CASE.2009.165

Chen, X., Udupa, J. K., Bagci, U., Zhuge, Y., & Yao, J. (2012). Medical image segmentation by combining graph cuts and oriented active appearance models. *Image Processing. IEEE Transactions on, 21*(4), 2035–2046.

Chen, Y.-L., & Hsu, C.-T. (2013). A generalized low-rank appearance model for spatio-temporally correlated rain streaks. In *Proceedings of IEEE Int. Conf. Comput. Vis.*Sydney, Australia. doi:10.1109/ICCV.2013.247

Chen, Y., Rui, Y., & Huang, T. (2001) Jpdaf based hmm for real-time contour tracking. In *IEEE Conference on Computer Vision and Pattern Recognition (CVPR)*, (pp. 543–550).

Chen, Y., Yu, S., Fan, J., Chen, W., & Li, H. (2008). An Improved Color-Based Particle Filter for Object Tracking. *International Conference on Genetic and Evolutionary Computing*, (pp. 360-363). doi:10.1109/WGEC.2008.110

Cheung, C.-H., & Po, L.-M. (2002). A novel cross-diamond search algorithm for fast block motion estimation. *IEEE Transactions on Circuits and Systems for Video Technology, 12*(12), 1168–1177. doi:10.1109/TCSVT.2002.806815

Chiang, Tsai, & Huang. (2007). An Efficient Indexing Method for Content-Based Image Retrieval. *Proceedings of IEEE International Conference on Innovative Computing, Information and Control*, (pp. 222-225). IEEE.

Chin, C., Jin, A., & Ling, D. (2006). High security iris verification system based on random secret integration. *Computer Vision and Image Understanding, 102*(2), 169–177. doi:10.1016/j.cviu.2006.01.002

Chirillo, J., & Blaul, S. (2003). *Implementing Biometric Security.* Wiley Red Books.

Choras, R. S. (2007). Image feature extraction techniques and their applications for CBIR and biometrics systems. *International Journal of Biology and Biomedical Engineering, 1*(1), 6-16.

Chowdhury, M. S., Das, & Kundu, M.K. (2012). Effective Classification of Radiographic Medical Images Using LS-SVM and NSCT based Retrieval System Constraints. In *Proceedings of 5ᵗʰ International Conference on Computers and Devices for Communication* (pp. 1-4).

Christel, M. G. (2007). *Examining user interactions with video retrieval systems.* Paper presented at the Electronic Imaging 2007.

Chui, C. K. (1992). *An Introduction to Wavelets.* London, UK: Academic Press.

Clancy, T. C., Kiyavash, N., & Lin, D. J. (2003). Secure smart cardbased fingerprint authentication. *Proceedings of the 2003 ACM SIGMM Workshop on Biometrics Methods and Application.* doi:10.1145/982507.982516

Clinchant, S., Ah-Pine, J., & Csurka, G. (2011). *Semantic combination of textual and visual information in multimedia retrieval.* Paper presented at the 1st ACM International Conference on Multimedia Retrieval. doi:10.1145/1991996.1992040

Clinchant, S., Renders, J.-M., & Csurka, G. (2007). XRCE's Participation to ImageCLEFphoto 2007. *Working Notes of the CLEFWorkshop.*

Cohen, I., Raz, S., & Malah, D. (1999). Translation invariant denoising using the minimum description length criterion. *Signal Processing, 75*(3), 201–223. doi:10.1016/S0165-1684(98)00234-5

Collins, R. T., Liu, Y., & Leordeanu, M. (2005). Online selection of discriminative tracking features. *Pattern Analysis and Machine Intelligence. IEEE Transactions on, 27*(10), 1631–1643.

Comaniciu, D., & Meer, P. (2002). Mean shift: A robust approach toward feature space analysis. *Pattern Analysis and Machine Intelligence. IEEE Transactions on, 24*(5), 603–619.

Comaniciu, D., Ramesh, V., & Meer, P. (2003). Kernel-based object tracking. *IEEE Transactions on Pattern Analysis and Machine Intelligence, 25*(5), 564–575. doi:10.1109/TPAMI.2003.1195991

Conklin, A., Dietrich, G., & Walz, D. (2004). Password-based authentication: A system perspective. *Int. Conference on System Sciences* (HICSS- 37 2004).

Costa, Humpire-Mamani, & Machado Traina. (2012). An Efficient Algorithm for Fractal Analysis of Textures. In *Proceedings of IEEE 25ᵗʰ SIBGRAPI Conference on Graphics, Patterns and Images,* (pp. 39-46). IEEE.

Courtney, J., & de Paor, A. M. (2010). Monocular Marker- Free Gait Measurement System. *IEEE Transactions on Neural Systems and Rehabilitation Engineering, 18*(4), 453–460. doi:10.1109/TNSRE.2010.2041792 PMID:20144920

Cremers, D., & Schnorr, C. (2003). Statistical shape knowledge in variational motion segmentation. *Israel Nent. Cap. J, 21,* 77–86.

Crevier, D. (2008). Image segmentation algorithm development using ground truth image data sets. *Computer Vision and Image Understanding, 112*(2), 143–159. doi:10.1016/j.cviu.2008.02.002

Cristianini, N., & Shawe-Taylor, J. (2000). *An introduction to support vector machines and other kernel-based learning methods.* Cambridge University Press. doi:10.1017/CBO9780511801389

Cuccharina, R., Grana, C., Piccardi, M., & Prati, A. (2003). Detecting Moving Objects, Ghosts, and Shadows in Video Streams. Transactions on Pattern Analysis and Machine Intelligence.

Cuevas, C., & García, N. (2013). Improved background modeling for real-time spatio-temporal non-parametric moving object detection strategies. *Image and Vision Computing*, *31*(9), 616–630. doi:10.1016/j.imavis.2013.06.003

Cvejic, Łoza, Bull, & Canagarajah. (2006). A Similarity Metric for Assessment of Image Fusion Algorithms. *International Journal of Information and Communication Engineering*, *2*(3).

Dabov, K., Foi, A., Katkovnik, V., & Egiazarian, K. (2007). Image denoising by sparse 3D transform-domain collaborative filtering. *IEEE Transactions on Image Processing*, *16*(8), 2080–2095. doi:10.1109/TIP.2007.901238 PMID:17688213

Dalal, N., & Triggs, B. (2005, June). Histograms of oriented gradients for human detection. In *Computer Vision and Pattern Recognition, 2005. CVPR 2005. IEEE Computer Society Conference on*, (pp. 886-893). IEEE.

Dalal, N., & Triggs, B. (2005). Histograms of oriented gradients for human detection. In *Proceedings of IEEE Conf. Comput. Vis. Pattern Recognit.* San Diego, CA: IEEE. doi:10.1109/CVPR.2005.177

Danafar, S., & Gheissari, N. (2007). Action recognition for surveillance applications using optic flow and SVM. In *Computer Vision–ACCV 2007* (pp. 457–466). Springer Berlin Heidelberg. doi:10.1007/978-3-540-76390-1_45

Dargazany, A., Soleimani, A., & Ahmadyfard, A. (2010). Multi-bandwidth kernel-based object tracking. *Journal of Advances in Artificial Intelligence*, Article ID.175603.

Das Choudhury, S., & Tjahjadi, T. (2012). Silhouette-based gait recognition using Procrustes shape analysis and elliptic Fourier descriptors. *Pattern Recognition*, *45*(9), 3414–3426. doi:10.1016/j.patcog.2012.02.032

Dash, M., & Liu, H. (1997). Feature Selection for Classification. *Intelligent Data Analysis*, *1*(1-4), 1–4, 131–156. doi:10.1016/S1088-467X(97)00008-5

Dasiopoulou, S. C. D. (2007). Semantic- Based Visual Information Retrieval, An Ontology-Based Framework for Semantic Image Analysis and Retrieval. Idea Group Inc.

Datta, R., Joshi, D., Li, J., & Wang, J. Z. (2008). Image retrieval: Ideas, influences, and trends of the new age. *ACM Computing Surveys*, *40*(2), 5. doi:10.1145/1348246.1348248

Daugman, J. (2002). How iris recognition works. *IEEE Transactions on Circuits and Systems for Video Technology*, *14*(1), 21–30. doi:10.1109/TCSVT.2003.818350

Daugman, J. (2003). The importance of being random: Statistical principles of iris recognition. *Pattern Recognition*, *36*(2), 279–291. doi:10.1016/S0031-3203(02)00030-4

Daugman, J., & Downing, C. (2001). Epigenetic randomness, complexity, & singularity of human iris patterns. *Royal Soc. Biological Sciences*, *268*(1477), 1737–1740. doi:10.1098/rspb.2001.1696 PMID:11506688

de Berg, M., Eindhoven, T., Cheong, O., Van Kreveld, M., & Overmars, M. (2008). Computational Geometry: Algorithms and Applications. Springer-Verlag.

De Carvalho Filho, A. O., De Sampaio, W. B., Silva, A. C., de Paiva, A. C., Nunes, R. A., & Gattass, M. (2014). Automatic detection of solitary lung nodules using quality threshold clustering, genetic algorithm and diversity index. *Artificial Intelligence in Medicine*, *60*(3), 165–177. doi:10.1016/j.artmed.2013.11.002 PMID:24332156

Debnath. (2002). *Wavelet Transforms and Their Applications. In Wavelet Transforms and Basic Properties* (pp. 382–383). Boston: Birkhauser.

Deokar, P. S., & Kaushik, A. R. (2014). Medical Image Denoising using Independent Component Analysis. *International Journal of Advanced Electronics & Communication Systems*.

Depeursinge, A., & Müller, H. (2010). *Fusion techniques for combining textual and visual information retrieval. In ImageCLEF* (pp. 95–114). Springer.

Derpanis, K. G., Sizintsev, M., Cannons, K. J., & Wildes, R. P. (2013). Action spotting and recognition based on a spatiotemporal orientation analysis. *Pattern Analysis and Machine Intelligence. IEEE Transactions on, 35*(3), 527–540.

Deselaers, T., Gass, T., Weyand, T., & Ney, H. (2007). *FIRE in ImageCLEF 2007.* Paper presented at the Working Notes for the CLEF 2007 Workshop, Budapest, Hungary.

Devernay, F., Duchene, S., & Peon, A. R. (2011). Adapting stereoscopic movies to the viewing conditions using depth-preserving and artifact-free novel view synthesis. In *Proceedings of SPIE 7863.* Stereoscopic Displays and Applications XXII. doi:10.1117/12.872883

Ding, M., Wei, L., & Wang, B. (2013). Research on fusion method for infrared and visible images via compressive sensing. *Infrared Physics & Technology, Elsevier, 57,* 56–67. doi:10.1016/j.infrared.2012.12.014

Dobes, M., & Machala, L. (2004). *UPOL Iris Image Database.* Retrieved from http:// phoenix.inf.upol.cz/iris/

Dogra, D. P., Majumdar, A. K., & Sural, S. (2012). Evaluation of segmentation techniques using region area and boundary matching information. *Journal of Visual Communication and Image Representation, 23*(1), 150–160. doi:10.1016/j.jvcir.2011.09.005

Dong, W., Shi, G., Ma, Y., & Li, X. (2015). Image restoration via simultaneous sparse coding: Where structured sparsity meets Gaussian scale mixture. *International Journal of Computer Vision, 114*(2-3), 217–232. doi:10.1007/s11263-015-0808-y

Dong, W., Zhang, L., Shi, G., & Wu, X. (2011). Image deblurring and super-resolution by adaptive sparse domain selection and adaptive regularization. *IEEE Transactions on Image Processing, 20*(7), 1838–1857. doi:10.1109/TIP.2011.2108306 PMID:21278019

Donoho, D. L. (1997). CART and best-ortho-basis: A connection. *Annals of Statistics, 25*(5), 1870–1911. doi:10.1214/aos/1069362377

Donoho, D. L., & Johnstone, I. M. (1995, December). Donoho, David L., & Johnstone, Iain M.(2001, July 27). Adapting to unknown smoothness via wavelet shrinkage. *Journal of the American Statistical Association, 90*(432), 1200–1224. doi:10.1080/01621459.1995.10476626

Dufaux, W., Gao, W., Tubaro, S., & Vetro, A. (2009). Distributed video coding: Trends and perspectives. *EURASIP Journal on Image and Video Processing, 2009,* 1–13. doi:10.1155/2009/508167

Dumais, S. T. (2004). Latent semantic analysis. *Annual Review of Information Science & Technology, 38*(1), 188–230. doi:10.1002/aris.1440380105

Duygulu, P. K. B. (2002). Object recognition as machine translation:learning a lexicon for a fixed image vocabulary. Proceedings of European Conferenceon Computer Vision (ECCV), (pp. 97-112).

Edge Detection and Image Segmentation (EDISON) System. (n.d.). Retrieved Aug 7, 2013, from https://coewww.rutgers.edu/riul/research/code/EDISON/index.html

Elad, M. (2010). *Sparse and redundant representations: from theory to applications in signal and image processing.* Springer. doi:10.1007/978-1-4419-7011-4

Elad, M. (2012). Sparse and redundant representation modeling - what next? *IEEE Signal Processing Letters, 19*(12), 922–928. doi:10.1109/LSP.2012.2224655

Elad, M., & Aharon, M. (2006). Image denoising via sparse and redundant representations over learned dictionaries. *IEEE Transactions on Image Processing*, *15*(12), 3736–3745. doi:10.1109/TIP.2006.881969 PMID:17153947

Elad, M., Figueiredo, M. A. T., & Ma, Y. (2010). On the role of sparse and redundant representations in image processing. *Proceedings of the IEEE*, *98*(6), 972–982. doi:10.1109/JPROC.2009.2037655

Elgammal, A., Harwood, D., & Davis, L. (2000). Non-parametric model for background subtraction. In *European Conference on Computer Vision (ECCV)*, (pp. 751–767).

Elhoseiny, M., Bakry, A., & Elgammal, A. (2013, June). Multi-Class Object Classication in Video Surveillance Systems Experimental Study. *IEEE Conference on Computer Vision and Pattern Recognition Workshops*, (pp. 788-793).

El-Qawasmeh, E. (2003). A quadtree-based representation technique for indexing and retrieval of image databases. *Journal of Visual Communication and Image Representation*, *14*(3), 340–357. doi:10.1016/S1047-3203(03)00034-8

Emerson, C. W., & Chinniah, S. (2006) A Region Quadtree Approach To Content Based Image Retrieval. *Proceedings of ASPRS*, (pp. 1-11).

Eng, H.-L., & Ma, K.-K. (2001). Noise adaptive soft-switching median filter. *IEEE Transactions on Image Processing*, *10*(2), 242–251. doi:10.1109/83.902289 PMID:18249615

Esakkirajanet, S. (2011, May). Removal of high density salt and pepper noise through modified decision based unsymmetric trimmed median filter. *IEEE Signal Processing Letters*, *18*(5), 287–290. doi:10.1109/LSP.2011.2122333

Everingham, M., Muller, H., & Thomas, B. (2002). Evaluating image segmentation algorithms using the pareto front. Computer Vision—ECCV 2002, (pp. 34-48).

Fadili, J. M., Starck, J. L., Bobin, J., & Moudden, Y. (2010). Image decomposition and separation using sparse representations: An overview. *Proceedings of the IEEE*, *98*(6), 983–994. doi:10.1109/JPROC.2009.2024776

Fadili, J. M., Starck, J. L., Elad, M., & Donoho, D. L. (2010). MCALab: Reproducible research in signal and image decomposition and inpainting. *IEEE Computational Science & Engineering*, *12*(1), 44–63. doi:10.1109/MCSE.2010.14

Fang, J., Yang, J., & Liu, H. (2011). Efficient and robust fragments-based multiple kernels track. *International Journal of Electronics and Communications, Elsevier*, *65*(11), 915–923. doi:10.1016/j.aeue.2011.02.013

Fan, Y. C., Chen, Y. C., & Chou, S. Y. (2014). Vivid-DIBR Based 2D–3D Image Conversion System for 3D Display. *Journal of Display Technology*, *10*(10), 887–898. doi:10.1109/JDT.2014.2331064

Farsiu, S., Robinson, M., Elad, M., & Milanfar, P. (2004). Fast and robust multiframe super resolution. *IEEE Transactions on Image Processing*, *13*(10), 1327–1344. doi:10.1109/TIP.2004.834669 PMID:15462143

Fauzi, M. F. A., Komiya, R., & Cheng Haw, S. (2008). Unsupervised abnormalities extraction and brain segmentation. In *Proceedings of the International Conference on Intel System Knowledge Engineering* (vol. 1, pp. 1185-1190).

FDA. (2004). *Guidance for industry, Part III*. Retrieved June 10, 2015, from http://www.fda.gov/Drugs/DevelopmentApprovalProcess/DevelopmentResources/ucm092895.htm

Feitosa, R., Costa, G., Cazes, T., & Feijo, B. (2006). A genetic approach for the automatic adaptation of segmentation parameters. *Proceedings of the First International Conference on Object-Based Image Analysis*, 4.

Felzenszwalb, P., & Huttenlocher, D. (n.d.). *Efficient Graph-Based Image Segmentation*. Retrieved Aug 7, 2013, from http://cs.brown.edu/~pff/segment/

Felzenszwalb, P. F., & Huttenlocher, D. P. (2004). Efficient graph-based image segmentation. *International Journal of Computer Vision, 59*(2), 167–181. doi:10.1023/B:VISI.0000022288.19776.77

Ferrara, M., Franco, A., & Maio, D. (2012). A multi-classifier approach to face image segmentation for travel documents. *Expert Systems with Applications, 39*(9), 8452–8466. doi:10.1016/j.eswa.2012.01.173

Fieguth, P., & Terzopoulos, D. (1997). Color-based tracking of heads and other mobile objects at videoframe rates. In *IEEE Conference on Computer Vision and Pattern Recognition (CVPR)* (pp. 21–27). doi:10.1109/CVPR.1997.609292

Flickner, H. S. (1995). Query by image and video content: the QBIC system. *IEEE Computer, 28*(9), 23-32.

Flickner, M., Sawhney, H., Niblack, W., Ashley, J., Huang, Q., Dom, B., & Yanker, P. et al. (1995, September). Query byimage and video content: The QBIC system. *IEEE Computer, 28*(9), 23–32. doi:10.1109/2.410146

Forouzanfar, M., Forghani, N., & Teshnehlab, M. (2010). Parameter optimization of improved fuzzy c-means clustering algorithm for brain MR image segmentation. *Engineering Applications of Artificial Intelligence, 23*(2), 160–168. doi:10.1016/j.engappai.2009.10.002

Franco, J., Bernab, G., Fernndez, J., & Acacio, M. E. (2009). A parallel implementation of the 2d wavelet transform using cuda. IEEE Computer Society.

Fredrich, C. M., & Feitosa, R. Q. (2008). Automatic adaptation of segmentation parameters applied to inhomogeneous objects detection.*Conference on geographic object-based image analysis held*, (pp. 6-7).

Freedman, G., & Fattal, R. (2011). Image and video upscaling from local self-examples. *ACM Transactions on Graphics, 30*(2), 1–11. doi:10.1145/1944846.1944852

Freeman, W. T., Jones, T. R., & Pasztor, E. C. (2002). Example-based super-resolution. *IEEE Computer Graphics and Applications, 22*(2), 56–65. doi:10.1109/38.988747

Freund, Y., & Schapire, R. (1995). *A decision-theoretic generalization of on-line learning and an application to boosting*. Computatational Learning Theory.

Fukunaga, K., & Hostetler, L. D. (1975). The Estimation of the Gradient of a Density Functions, with Applications in Pattern Recognition. *IEEE Transactions on Information Theory, 21*(1), 32–40. doi:10.1109/TIT.1975.1055330

Gaede, V., & Gunther, O. (1998). Multidimensional access methods. *ACM Computing Surveys, 30*(2), 170–231. doi:10.1145/280277.280279

Gao, Y., Wang, M., Zha, Z.-J., Shen, J., Li, X., & Wu, X. (2013). Visual-textual joint relevance learning for tag-based social image search. *Image Processing. IEEE Transactions on, 22*(1), 363–376.

García, Hornero, Sanchez, Lopez, & Díez. (2007). Feature Extraction and Selection for the Automatic Detection of Hard Exudates in Retinal Images. *Proceedings of the 29th Annual International Conference of the IEEE EMBS*.

Garcia, Sanchez, Lopez, Abasolo, & Hornero. (2009). Neural network based detection of hard exudates in retinal images. *Computer Methods and Programs in Biomedicine, 93*, 9-19.

Garg, Sivaswamy, & Joshi. (2008). Automatic Drusen Detection from Color Retinal Images. Center for Visual Information Technology, IIT Hyderabad.

Garg, K., & Nayar, S. K. (2007). Vision and rain. *International Journal of Computer Vision, 75*(1), 3–27. doi:10.1007/s11263-006-0028-6

Garnett, Huegerich, Chui, & He. (2005, November). A Universal Noise Removal Algorithm with an Impulse Detector. *IEEE Transactions on Image Processing, 14*(11), 1747-1754.

Ghabel, L., & Amindavar, H. (2002). Image Denoising Using Hidden Markov Models. *Lecture Notes in Computer Science, 2510*, 402–409. doi:10.1007/3-540-36087-5_47

Giryes, R., & Elad, M. (2014). Sparsity-based poisson denoising with dictionary learning. *IEEE Transactions on Image Processing, 23*(12), 5057–5069. doi:10.1109/TIP.2014.2362057 PMID:25312930

Glover, F., & Laguna, M. (2013). *Tabu Search*. New York: Springer.

Goel, N., & Sehgal, P. (2012). A refined hybrid image retrieval system using text and color. *Int. J. Comput. Sci*, (9), 4.

Goel, N., & Sehgal, P. (2013). *Weighted semantic fusion of text and content for image retrieval*. Paper presented at the Advances in Computing, Communications and Informatics (ICACCI), 2013 International Conference on. doi:10.1109/ICACCI.2013.6637255

Goel, N., & Sehgal, P. (2014b). Parallel Weighted Semantic Fusion for Cross-Media Retrieval. *International Journal of Computational Intelligence Studies*.

Goel, N., & Sehgal, P. (2014a). Image Retrieval Using Fuzzy Color Histogram and Fuzzy String Matching: A Correlation-Based Scheme to Reduce the Semantic Gap. In D. P. Mohapatra & S. Patnaik (Eds.), *Intelligent Computing, Networking, and Informatics* (Vol. 243, pp. 327–341). Springer India. doi:10.1007/978-81-322-1665-0_31

Goel, N., & Sehgal, P. (2015). Parallel weighted semantic fusion for cross-media retrieval. *International Journal of Computational Intelligence Studies, 4*(1), 50–71. doi:10.1504/IJCISTUDIES.2015.069832

Goffredo, M., Bouchrika, I., Carter, J. N., & Nixon, M. S. (2010). Self-calibrating view- invariant gait biometrics. *IEEE Transactions on Systems, Man, and Cybernetics, 40*(4), 997–1008. doi:10.1109/TSMCB.2009.2031091 PMID:19884085

Goh, A., & Ngo, D. C. L. (2003). Computation of cryptographic keys from face biometrics. International Federation for Information Processing. *LNCS, 2828*, 1–13.

Goldberg, D. E. (1989). *Genetic Algorithms in Search, Optimization and Machine Learning*. Boston: Addison-Wesley Longman Publishing Co., Inc.

Gonzalez & Woods. (2008). Digital Image Processing. Pearson Prentice Hall.

Gonzalez, R. C., & Woods, R. E. (2009). *Digital Image Processing* (2nd ed.). Addison Wesley.

Gonzalez, R. C., Woods, R. E., & Eddins, S. L. (2011). *Digital Image Processing Using MATLAB. In Image Compression* (2nd ed.; pp. 374–439). New Delhi: Tata McGraw Hill Education Private Limited.

Gorji, A., & Menhaj, M. B. (2007). Multiple Target Tracking for Mobile Robots Using the JPDAF Algorithm. *19th IEEE International Conference on Tools with Artificial Intelligence*, (vol. 1, pp. 137-145). IEEE.

Grabner, H., Leistner, C., & Bischof, H. (2008). Semi-supervised on-line boosting for robust tracking. In *Computer Vision–ECCV 2008* (pp. 234–247). Springer Berlin Heidelberg. doi:10.1007/978-3-540-88682-2_19

Granados, R., Benavent, X., García-Serrano, A., & Goñi, J. (2008). *MIRACLE-FI at ImageCLEFphoto 2008: Experiences in merging text-based and content-based retrievals*. Paper presented at the Working Notes of the 2008 CLEF Workshop, Aarhust, Denmark.

Greenspan, H., Belongie, S., Goodman, R., Perona, P., Rakshit, S., & Anderson, C. (1994). Over complete steerable pyramid filters and rotation invariance. In *IEEE Conference on Computer Vision and Pattern Recognition (CVPR)*, (pp. 222–228). doi:10.1109/CVPR.1994.323833

Griffiths, A., Luckhurst, H. C., & Willett, P. (1997). *Using interdocument similarity information in document retrieval systems. In Readings in Information Retrieval* (pp. 365–373). San Francisco, CA: Morgan Kaufmann Publishers.

Grosky, W. I., Agrawal, R., & Fotouchi, F. (2008). *Mind the gaps-finding the appropriate dimensional representation for semantic retrieval of multimedia assets. In Semantic Multimedia and Ontologies* (pp. 229–252). Springer.

Guan, L., Wang, Y., Zhang, R., Tie, Y., Bulzacki, A., & Ibrahim, M. (2010). Multimodal information fusion for selected multimedia applications. *International Journal of Multimedia Intelligence and Security*, *1*(1), 5–32. doi:10.1504/IJMIS.2010.035969

Gudivada, V. N., & Raghavan, V. V. (1995). Content based image retrieval systems. *Computer*, *28*(9), 18–22. doi:10.1109/2.410145

Guha, T., & Ward, R. K. (2012). Learning sparse representations for human action recognition. *IEEE Transactions on Pattern Analysis and Machine Intelligence*, *34*(8), 1576–1588. doi:10.1109/TPAMI.2011.253 PMID:22745001

Gui, C., Liu, J., Xu, C., & Lu, H. (2010). *Extended CBIR via learning semantics of query image. In Advances in Multimedia Modeling* (pp. 782–785). Springer.

Guo, D., Qu, X., Du, X., Wu, K., & Chen, X. (2014). Salt and pepper noise removal with noise detection and a patch-based sparse representation. *Advances in Multimedia*, *2014*, 682747:1–682747:14.

Guo, F., Tang, J., & Peng, H. (2014). Adaptive Estimation of Depth Map for Two-Dimensional to Three-Dimensional Stereoscopic Conversion. Journal of Optical Review, 21(1), 60–73.

Guo, J.-M., Liu, Y.-F., Chang, J.-Y., & Lee, J.-D. (2014). Fingerprint classification based ondecision tree from singular points and orientation field. *Expert Systems with Applications,Elsevier*, *41*(2), 752–764. doi:10.1016/j.eswa.2013.07.099

Guo, Y., Chai, H., & Wang, Y. (2015). A global approach for medical image denoising via sparse representation. *Int. J. of Bioscience. Biochemistry and Bioinformatics*, *5*(1), 26–35.

Guo, Zhou & Wang. (2014). Palmprint recognition algorithm with horizontally expanded blanket dimension. *Neurocomputing*, *127*, 152–160.

Guttman, A. (1984). R-Trees: a dynamic index structure for spatial searching.*Proceedings of the ACM SIGMOD International Conference on Management of Data*. Boston, MA: ACM. doi:10.1145/602259.602266

Hafiane, A., Chabrier, S., Rosenberger, C., & Laurent, H. (2007). *A new supervised evaluation criterion for region based segmentation methods. In Advanced Concepts for Intelligent Vision Systems* (pp. 439–448). Springer. doi:10.1007/978-3-540-74607-2_40

Han, & Lin. (1997). Minimum-maximum exclusive mean (MMEM) filter to remove impulse noise from highly corrupted images. *Electronics Letters*, *33*(2).

Han, C. C., & Hsiao, H. F. (2014). Depth Estimation and Video Synthesis for 2D to 3D Video Conversion. Journal of Signal Processing System, 76, 33-46.

Han, Cai, Cao, & Xu. (2013). A new image fusion performance metric based on visual information fidelity. Information Fusion, 14, 127–135.

Han, H., Lee, G., Lee, J., Kim, J., & Lee, S. (2013). A new method to create depth information based on lighting analysis for 2D/3D conversion. *Journal of Central South University*, *20*(10), 2715–2719.

Han, J., & Bhanu, B. (2006). Individual recognition using gait energy image. *IEEE Transactions on Pattern Analysis and Machine Intelligence*, *28*(2), 316–322. doi:10.1109/TPAMI.2006.38 PMID:16468626

Han, M., & Kanade, T. (2003). Multiple Motion Scene Reconstruction with Uncalibrated Cameras. *IEEE Transactions on Pattern Analysis and Machine Intelligence*, *25*(7), 884–894. doi:10.1109/TPAMI.2003.1206517

Han, M., Zhu, X., & Yao, W. (2012). Remote sensing image classification based on neural network ensemble algorithm. *Neurocomputing*, *78*(1), 133–138. doi:10.1016/j.neucom.2011.04.044

Han, Y., Wu, F., Tian, Q., & Zhuang, Y. (2012). Image annotation by input-output structural grouping sparsity. *IEEE Transactions on Image Processing*, *21*(6), 3066–3079. doi:10.1109/TIP.2012.2183880 PMID:22262682

Haralick, R. M., Shanmugam, K., & Dinstein, I. (1973). Textural features for image classification. In *Proceedings of the IEEE Transactions on Systems, Man and Cybernetics* (vol. 36, pp.610-621).

Haralick, R. M., & Shapiro, L. G. (1985). Image segmentation techniques. In *1985 Technical Symposium East* (pp. 2-9). International Society for Optics and Photonics.

Haralick, R., Shanmugam, B., & Dinstein, I. (1973). Textural features for image classification. *IEEE Transactions on Systems, Man, and Cybernetics*, *33*(3), 610–622. doi:10.1109/TSMC.1973.4309314

Harispe, S., Ranwez, S., Janaqi, S., & Montmain, J. (2013). *Semantic Measures for the Comparison of Units of Language, Concepts or Instances from Text and Knowledge Base Analysis.* arXiv preprint arXiv:1310.1285

Harris, C., & Stephens, M. (1988, August). A combined corner and edge detector. Alvey Vision Conference, 15, 50. doi:10.5244/C.2.23

Harris, C., & Stephens, M. (1981). A combined corner and edge detector. In *4th Alvey Vision Conference*, (pp. 147-151).

Hartigan, J. A., Wong, M. A., & Algorithm, A. S. (1979). A K-Means Clustering Algorithm. *Journal of the Royal Statistical Society. Series A (General)*, *28*(1), 100–108.

Hartvedt, C. (2010). *Using context to understand user intentions in Image retrieval.* Paper presented at the Advances in Multimedia (MMEDIA), 2010 Second International Conferences on. doi:10.1109/MMEDIA.2010.35

Hausdorff, F. (n.d.). *Set Theory*. Chelsea.

Hay, F. (2011). An image feature approach for computer-aided detection of ischemic stroke. *Computers in Biology and Medicine*, *41*(7), 529–536. doi:10.1016/j.compbiomed.2011.05.001 PMID:21605853

Haykin, S., & Chen, Z. (2005). The cocktail party problem. *Neural Computation*, *17*(9), 1875–1902. doi:10.1162/0899766054322964 PMID:15992485

Heber, M., Godec, M., Rüther, M., Roth, P. M., & Bischof, H. (2013). 6). Segmentation-based tracking by support fusion. *Computer Vision and Image Understanding*, *117*(6), 573–586. doi:10.1016/j.cviu.2013.02.001

Heidemann, G. (2008). Region saliency as a measure for colour segmentation stability. *Image and Vision Computing*, *26*(2), 211–227. doi:10.1016/j.imavis.2007.05.001

Heikkila, M., & Pietikainen, M. (2006). A texture-based method for modeling the background and detecting moving objects. *IEEE Transactions on Pattern Analysis and Machine Intelligence*, *28*(4), 657–662. doi:10.1109/TPAMI.2006.68 PMID:16566514

Heitger, F. (1995). *Feature Detection using Suppression and Enhancement: TR 163*. ETH-Zurich.

He, K., Sun, J., & Tang, X. (2011). Single image haze removal using dark channel Prior. *IEEE Transactions on Pattern Analysis and Machine Intelligence*, *33*(12), 2341–2353. doi:10.1109/TPAMI.2010.168 PMID:20820075

He, K., Sun, J., & Tang, X. (2013). Guided image filtering. *IEEE Transactions on Pattern Analysis and Machine Intelligence*, *35*(6), 1397–1409. doi:10.1109/TPAMI.2012.213 PMID:23599054

Hema Rajini, N., & Bhavani, R. (2011). Enhancing k-means and kernelized fuzzy c-means clustering with cluster center initialization in segmenting MRI brain images. In *Proceedings of the 3rd International Conference on Electronics Computer Technology* (pp.259-263).

He, N., Wang, J.-B., Zhang, L.-L., Xu, G.-M., & Lu, K. (2015). Non-local sparse regularization model with application to image denoising. *Multimedia Tools and Applications*. doi:10.1007/s11042-015-2471-2

Henrich, A., Six, H.-W., & Widmaye, P. (1989). The LSD tree: Spatial access to multidimensional point and non-point objects. In *Proceedings of the Fifteenth International Conference on Very Large Data Bases* (pp. 45–53).

Hong, H. (2010). Coherent Block-Based Motion Estimation for Motion-Compensated Frame Rate Up-Conversion. *International Conference on Consumer Electronics*.

Hoover, A., Kouznetsova, V., & Goldbaum, M. (2000). Locating blood vessels in retinal images by piecewise threshold probing of matched filter response. *IEEE Transactions on Medical Imaging*, *19*(3), 203–209. doi:10.1109/42.845178 PMID:10875704

Horn, B., & Schunk, B. (1981). Determining optical flow. *Artificial Intelligence*, *17*(1-3), 185–203. doi:10.1016/0004-3702(81)90024-2

Hotelling, H. (1933). Analysis of a complex of statistical variables into principal components. *Journal of Educational Psychology*, *24*(6), 417–441. doi:10.1037/h0071325

Hou, H. S., & Andrews, H. C. (1978). Cubic splines for image interpolation and digital filtering. *IEEE Transactions on Acoustics, Speech, and Signal Processing*, *26*(6), 508–517. doi:10.1109/TASSP.1978.1163154

Hsiao, J.-K., Kang, L.-W., Chang, C.-L., & Lin, C.-Y. (2015). *Learning-based leaf image recognition frameworks. In Intelligent Systems in Science and Information*. Springer International Publishing Switzerland.

Hsieh, F. Y., Han, C. C., Wu, N. S., Chuang, T. C., & Fan, K. C. (2006). A novel approach to the detection of small objects with low contrast. *Signal Processing*, *86*(1), 71–83. doi:10.1016/j.sigpro.2005.03.020

Hua, Z. X. W. (2005). Semantic knowledge extraction and annotation for web images. *Proceedings of the 13th annual ACM international conference on Multimedia*. Hilton, Singapore: ACM.

Huang, B., Li, Y., Han, X., Cui, Y., Li, W., & Li, R. (2015). Cloud removal from optical satellite imagery with SAR imagery using sparse representation. *IEEE Geoscience and Remote Sensing Letters*, *12*(5), 1046–1050. doi:10.1109/LGRS.2014.2377476

Huang, D.-A., Kang, L.-W., Wang, Y.-C. F., & Lin, C.-W. (2014). Self-learning based image decomposition with applications to single image denoising. *IEEE Transactions on Multimedia*, *16*(1), 83–93. doi:10.1109/TMM.2013.2284759

Huang, D.-A., Kang, L.-W., Yang, M.-C., Lin, C.-W., & Wang, Y.-C. F. (2012). Context-aware single image rain removal. In *Proceedings ofIEEE Int. Conf. Multimedia and Expo*. Melbourne, Australia: IEEE. doi:10.1109/ICME.2012.92

Huang, J. S. K.-J. (1997). Image indexing using colour correlogram.*Proceedings of the CVPR97*, (pp. 762-765).

Huang, J., Kumar, S., Mitra, M., Zhu, W. J., & Zabith, R. (1997). Image indexing usingcolour correlogram. *Proceedings of the, CVPR97*, 762–765.

Huang, W., Cao, X., Lu, K., & Dai, Q. (2013). Towards naturalistic depth propagation. In *Proceedings of 11th IEEE IVMSP Workshop* (pp.-1-4). IEEE.

Huang, Z., Liu, Y., Li, C., Yang, M., & Chen, L. (2013). A robust face and ear based multimodal biometric system using sparse representation. *Pattern Recognition, Elsevier, 46*(8), 2156–2168. doi:10.1016/j.patcog.2013.01.022

Hua, X.-S., Worring, M., & Chua, T.-S. (2013). *Internet Multimedia and Search Mining*. Citeseer. doi:10.2174/97816 080521581130101

Hue, C., Cadre, J. L., & Prez, P. (2002). Sequential monte carlo methods for multiple target tracking and data fusion. *IEEE Transactions on Signal Processing, 50*(2), 309–325. doi:10.1109/78.978386

Hu, M., Wang, Y., Zhang, Z., De, D., & Little, J. J. (2013). Incremental Learning for Video-Based Gait Recognition With LBP Flow. *IEEE Transactions on Systems, Man, and Cybernetics. Part B, Cybernetics, 43*, 77–89. PMID:22692925

Hu, M., Wang, Y., Zhang, Z., & Wang, Y. (2010). Combining spatial and temporal information for gait based gender classification.*Proc. IEEE/IAPR Int. Conf. Pattern Recognition* (pp. 3679–3682). IEEE. doi:10.1109/ICPR.2010.897

Hung, M. F., Miaou, S. G., & Chiang, C. Y. (2013).Dual edge-confined inpainting of 3D depth map using color image's edges and depth image's edges. In *Proceedings of IEEE International Conference on Signal and Information Processing* (pp.-1-9). doi:10.1109/APSIPA.2013.6694295

Hung, M. H., Pan, J. S., & Hsieh, C. H. (2014). A Fast Algorithm of Temporal Median Filter for Background Subtraction. *Journal of Information Hiding and Multimedia Signal Processing, 5*(1), 33–40.

Huttenlocher, D., Noh, J., & Rucklidge, W. (1993). Tracking non rigid objects in complex scenes. In *IEEE International Conference on Computer Vision (ICCV)*, (pp. 93–101). doi:10.1109/ICCV.1993.378231

Hu, W., Zhou, X., Li, W., Luo, W., Zhang, X., & Maybank, S. (2013). Active Contour -Based Visual Tracking by Integrating Colors, Shapes, and Motions. *IEEE Transactions on Image Processing, 22*(5), 1778–1792. doi:10.1109/TIP.2012.2236340 PMID:23288333

Hwang, H., & Haddad, R. A. (1995). Adaptive median filters: New algorithms and results. *IEEE Transactions on Image Processing, 4*(4), 499–502. doi:10.1109/83.370679 PMID:18289998

Hyvärinen, A., Oja, E., Hoyer, P., & Hurri, J. (1998). Image feature extraction by sparse coding and independent component analysis. In *Proc. Int. Conf. on Pattern Recognition (ICPR'98)*, (pp. 1268-1273). Brisbane, Australia. doi:10.1109/ICPR.1998.711932

Ilea, D. E., & Whelan, P. F. (2009). Colour saliency-based parameter optimisation for adaptive colour segmentation. *Image Processing (ICIP), 2009 16th IEEE International Conference on*, (pp. 973-976). IEEE.

Ince, S., & Kornad, J. (2008). Occlusion-aware view interpolation. *Journal on Image and Video Processing, 21*(1), 60–73.

Indhumadhi, N., & Padmavathi, G. (2011). Enhanced Image fusion algorithm Using Laplacian Pyramid and Spatial Frequency Based Wavelet algorithm. *International Journal of Soft Computing And Engineering, 1*(5).

Institute of Automation, Chinese Academy of Sciences. (2004). *CASIA Iris Image Database*. Retrieved from http://www.sinobiometrics.com

Intermountain Medical Centre. (n.d.). New imaging tool to diagnose heart conditions is dramatically more accurate, less expensive and safer. *ScienceDaily*. Retrieved March 16, 2015, from www.sciencedaily.com/releases/2015/03/150316113323.htm

Intille, S., Davis, J., & Bobick, A. (1997). Real-time closed-world tracking. In *IEEE Conference on ComputerVision and Pattern Recognition (CVPR)*, (pp. 697–703). doi:10.1109/CVPR.1997.609402

Isard, M., & Blake, A. (1998). Condensation - conditional density propagation for visual tracking. *International Journal of Computer Vision*, *29*(1), 5–28. doi:10.1023/A:1008078328650

Isard, M., & Maccormick, J. (2001). Bramble: A bayesian multiple-blob tracker. In *IEEE International Conference on Computer Vision (ICCV)*, (pp. 34–41).

Ivan, R. R. D., Schwab, R., & Schobert, C. (2012). *Evolution's Witness: How Eyes Evolved*. Oxford University Press.

Iverson, L. A., & Zucker, S. W. (1995). Logical/linear operations for image curves. *IEEE Transactions on Pattern Analysis and Machine Intelligence*, *17*(10), 982–996. doi:10.1109/34.464562

Jain, A. K. (2012). Fundamentals of Digital Image Processing. New Delhi: Academic Press.

Jain, R., & Sinha, P. (2010). *Content without context is meaningless*. Paper presented at the International Conference on Multimedia.

Jain, A. K. (1989). *Fundamentals of Digital Image Processing* (1st ed.). Prentice Hall of India.

Jain, A. K. (1989). *Fundamentals of digital image processing*. Prentice-Hall of India.

Jain, A. K., Bolle, R., & Pankanti, S. (1999). *Biometrics: Personal Identication in Networked Society*. Springer. doi:10.1007/b117227

Jain, A. K., & Kumar, A. (2010). *Biometrics of next generation: An overview. In Second Generation Biometric*. Springer.

Jain, A. K., Ross, A., & Prabhakar, S. (2004). An introduction to biometric recognition. *IEEE Transactions on Circuits and Systems for Video Technology*, *14*(1), 4–20. doi:10.1109/TCSVT.2003.818349

Jain, A. K., & Vailaya, A. (1996). Image retrieval using colour and shape. *Pattern Recognition*, *29*(8), 1233–1244. doi:10.1016/0031-3203(95)00160-3

Jakarta, A. (2004). *Apache Lucene-a high-performance, full-featured text search engine library*. Apache Lucene.

Jakkula, V. (2012). *Tutorial on support vector machine (SVM)*. School of EECS. Washington State University.

Jalal, A. S., & Singh, V. (2012). The State-of-the-Art in Visual Object Tracking. *Informatica*, *36*, 227–248.

Janković, M. (n.d.). *Genetic algorithm library*. Retrieved Aug 7, 2013, from http://www.codeproject.com/Articles/26203/Genetic-Algorithm-Library

Jayanthi, Devi, & Parvathi. (2010). Automatic Diagnosis of Retinal Diseases from Color Retinal Images. *International Journal of Computer Science and Information Security*, *7*(1), 234-238.

Jena, Patel, & Tripathy. (2012, October). An Efficient Adaptive Mean Filtering Technique for Removal of Salt and Pepper Noise from Images. *International Journal of Engineering Research & Technology*, *1*(8).

Jeon, J. L. V. (2003). Automatic image annotation and retrieval using cross-media relevance models. *26th Annual International ACM SIGIR Conference on Research and Development in Information Retrieval* (pp. 119-126). Toronto: ACM.

Jeong, S., Won, C. S., & Gray, R. M. (2004). Image retrieval using colour histograms generated by Gauss mixture vector quantization. *Computer Vision and Image Understanding, 94*(13), 44–66. doi:10.1016/j.cviu.2003.10.015

Jepson, A., Fleet, D., & Elmaraghi, T. (2003). Robust online appearance models for visual tracking. *IEEE Transactions on Pattern Analysis and Machine Intelligence, 25*(10), 1296–1311. doi:10.1109/TPAMI.2003.1233903

Jin, H., Sun, A., Zheng, R., He, R., Zhang, Q., Shi, Y., & Yang, W. (2007). *Content and semantic context based image retrieval for medical image grid.* Paper presented at the 8th IEEE/ACM International Conference on Grid Computing. doi:10.1109/GRID.2007.4354122

Jingu, A., Fukuda, J., Takahashi, A. T., & Tsushima, Y. (2014). Breakthrough reactions of iodinated and gadolinium contrast media after oral steroid premedication protocol. *BMC Medical Imaging, 14*(1), 34. doi:10.1186/1471-2342-14-34 PMID:25287952

Jing, X., & Chau, L.-P. (2004). An efficient three-step search algorithm for Block Motion Estimation. *IEEE Transactions on Multimedia, 6*(3), 435–438. doi:10.1109/TMM.2004.827517

Johnsen, S., & Tews, A. (2009, May). *Real-Time Object Tracking and Classification Using a Static Camera.* IEEE ICRA 2009 Workshop on People Detection and Tracking.

Joseph, T., & Cardenas, A. F. (1988). PICQUERY: A high level query language for pictorial database management. *Software Engineering. IEEE Transactions on, 14*(5), 630–638.

Joshua, E. (2012). Iron oxide nanoparticles for targeted cancer imaging and diagnostics. *Nanomedicine; Nanotechnology, Biology, and Medicine, 8*(3), 275–290. doi:10.1016/j.nano.2011.08.017 PMID:21930108

Julier, S. J., & Uhlmann, J. K. (1997, July). A New Extension of the Kalman Filter to Nonlinear Systems. *Proceedings of the Society for Photo-Instrumentation Engineers, 3068.*

Jung, A. (2001, October). An introduction to a new data analysis tool: Independent Component Analysis. *Proceedings of Workshop GK, Nonlinearity .*

Jung, C., Jiao, L., Qi, H., & Sun, T. (2012). Image deblocking via sparse representation. *Signal Processing Image Communication, 27*(6), 663–677. doi:10.1016/j.image.2012.03.002

Kaisar, Md. Sakib, Mahmud, & Rahman. (2008, June). Salt and Pepper Noise Detection and Removal by Tolerance based Selectve Arithmatic Mean Filtering Technique for Image Restoration. *International Journal of Computer Science and Network Security, 8*(6), 271-278.

Kalal, Z., Matas, J., & Mikolajczyk, K. (2010, June). Pn learning: Bootstrapping binary classifiers by structural constraints. In *Computer Vision and Pattern Recognition (CVPR), 2010 IEEE Conference on* (pp. 49-56). IEEE.

Kale, A., RajaGopalan, A.N., Cuntoor, N., & Kruger, V. (2002). Gait Based Recognition of Humans using continuous HMMs. *Proc. Int'l Conf. on Automatic Face and Gesture Recognition.* doi:10.1109/AFGR.2002.1004176

Kang, L.-W., Yeh, C.-H., Chen, D.-Y., & Lin, C.-T. (2014). Self-learning-based signal decomposition for multimedia applications: a review and comparative study. In *Proceedings of APSIPA Annual Summit and Conf.* Angkor Wat, Cambodia: APSIPA.

Kang, J., Cohen, I., & Medioni, G. (2004). Object reacquisition using geometric invariant appearance model. In *International Conference on Pattern Recongnition (ICPR),* (pp. 759–762).

Kang, L.-W., Chuang, B.-C., Hsu, C.-C., Lin, C.-W., & Yeh, C.-H. (2013). Self-learning-based single image super-resolution of a highly compressed image. In *Proceedings of IEEE Int. Workshop Multimedia Signal Process.* (pp. 224–229). Sardinia, Italy: IEEE. doi:10.1109/MMSP.2013.6659292

Kang, L.-W., Hsu, C.-C., Zhuang, B., Lin, C.-W., & Yeh, C.-H. (2015). Learning-based joint super-resolution and deblocking for a highly compressed image. *IEEE Transactions on Multimedia*, *17*(7), 921–934. doi:10.1109/TMM.2015.2434216

Kang, L.-W., Hsu, C.-Y., Chen, H.-W., Lu, C.-S., Lin, C.-Y., & Pei, S.-C. (2011). Feature-based sparse representation for image similarity assessment. *IEEE Transactions on Multimedia*, *13*(5), 1019–1030. doi:10.1109/TMM.2011.2159197

Kang, L.-W., Lin, C.-W., & Fu, Y.-H. (2012). Automatic single-image-based rain streaks removal via image decomposition. *IEEE Transactions on Image Processing*, *21*(4), 1742–1755. doi:10.1109/TIP.2011.2179057 PMID:22167628

Kang, L.-W., Lin, C.-W., Lin, C.-T., & Lin, Y.-C. (2012). Self-learning-based rain streak removal for image/video. In *Proceedings of IEEE Int. Sym. Circuits Syst.* Seoul, Korea: IEEE. doi:10.1109/ISCAS.2012.6271635

Kannan, A., Mohan, V., & Anbazhagan, N. (2010). *Image clustering and retrieval using image mining techniques.* Paper presented at the IEEE International Conference on Computational Intelligence and Computing Research.

Kappagantula, S., & Rao, K. R. (1985). Motion Compensated interframe image prediction. *IEEE Transactions on Communications*, *33*(9), 1011–1015. doi:10.1109/TCOM.1985.1096415

Karlsson, L., & Sjostrom, M. (2011). Layer assignment based on depthdata distribution for multiview-plus-depth scalable video coding. *IEEE Transaction of Circuits System and Video Technology*, *21*(6), 742–754. doi:10.1109/TCSVT.2011.2130350

Kase, K. R. (2004). Radiation protection principles of NCRP. *Health Physics*, *87*(3), 251–257. doi:10.1097/00004032-200409000-00005 PMID:15303061

Kass, M., Witkin, A., & Terzopoulos, D. (1988). Snakes: Active contour models. *International Journal of Computer Vision*, *1*(4), 321–332. doi:10.1007/BF00133570

Katayama, N., & Satoh. (1997). The SR-tree: An Index Structure for High-Dimensional Nearest Neighbor Queries. *Proceedings of ACM SIGMOD, International Conference on Data*, *26*(2), 369-380. doi:10.1145/253260.253347

Kaufman, E., Lovell, T. A., & Lee, T. (2014). Optimal joint probabilistic data association filter avoiding coalescence in close proximity. *European Control Conference (ECC)*, (pp. 2709-2714). doi:10.1109/ECC.2014.6862602

Kaur, Gupta, & Chauhan. (2002, December 22). *Image Denoising using Wavelet Thresholding*. Retrieved from https://www.ee.iitb.ac.in/~icvgip/PAPERS/202.pdf

Khan, Mirza, & Majid. (2006). Intelligent perceptual shaping of a digital watermark: exploiting characteristics of human visual system. *International Journal of Knowledge-Based Intelligent Engineering Systems, 9*, 1-11.

Khan, A., Mirza, A. M., & Majid, A. (2004). Optimizing Perceptual shaping of a digital watermark using Genetic Programming. *Iranian Journal of Electrical and Computer Engineering*, *3*(2), 1251–1260.

Khanduja, Verma, & Chakraverty. (2013). Watermarking relational databases using bacterial foraging algorithm. *Multimedia Tools and Applications, 73*(2).

Kharate, G. K. (2010, March). Colour image compression based on wavelet packet best tree. *IJCSI International Journal of Computer Science Issues, 7*, 31–35.

Khayam, S. A. (2003). *The discrete cosine transform (DCT): theory and application.* Michigan State University.

Kim, H. G., & Song, B. C. (2013). Automatic object-based 2D-to-3D conversion. In *Proceedings of 11th IEEE IVMSP Workshop* (pp.-1-4). IEEE. doi:10.1109/MEC.2011.6025855

Kim, J., & Sim, C.-B. (2011). Compression artifacts removal by signal adaptive weighted sum technique. *IEEE Transactions on Consumer Electronics, 57*(4), 1944–1952. doi:10.1109/TCE.2011.6131175

Knorr, S., Imre, E., Özkalayci, B. A., Alatan, A., & Sikora, T. (2006). A modular scheme for 2D/3D conversion of TV broadcast. *Third International Symposium on 3D Data Processing, Visualization, and Transmission* (3DPVT). doi:10.1109/3DPVT.2006.15

Knorr, S., Smolic, A., & Sikora, T. (2007). From 2D-to stereo-to multi-view video. In *Proceedings of 3DTV Conference* (pp. 1–4).

Ko, & Lee. (1991, September). Center Weighted Median Filters and Their Applications to Image Enhancement. *IEEE Transactions On Circuits And Systems, 38*(9), 984-993.

Ko, J., Kim, M., & Kim, C. (2007). Depth-map estimation in a 2D single-view image. In *Proceedings of SPIE Electronic Imaging, Applications of Digital Image Processing* (Vol. 6696, pp. 66962A-1–66962A-9). doi:10.1117/12.736131

Kodituwakku, S., & Selvarajah, S. (2004). Comparison of color features for image retrieval. *Indian Journal of Computer Science and Engineering, 1*(3), 207–211.

Ko, J., Kim, M., & Kim, C. (2007). Depth-map estimation in a 2D single-view image. In *Proceedings of SPIE Electronic Imaging—Applications of Digital Image Processing* (Vol. 6696, pp. 66962A-1–66962A-9). SPIE.

Kong, W., & Zhang, D. (2003). Detecting eyelash & reflection for accurate iris Segmentation. *International Journal of Pattern Recognition and Artificial Intelligence, 17*(6), 1025–1034. doi:10.1142/S0218001403002733

Konrad, J., Wang, M., Ishwar, P., Wu, C., & Mukherjee, D. (2013). Learning-Based, Automatic 2D-to-3D Image and Video Conversion. *IEEE Transactions on Image Processing, 22*(9), 3485–3496. doi:10.1109/TIP.2013.2270375 PMID:23799697

Konstantinidis, K., Gasteratos, A., & Andreadis, I. (2005). Image retrieval based on fuzzy color histogram processing. *Optics Communications, 248*(4), 375–386. doi:10.1016/j.optcom.2004.12.029

Korfiatis, P., Karahaliou, A., & Costaridou, L. (2009). Automated vessel tree segmentation: challenges in computer aided quantification of diffuse parenchyma lung diseases In *Proceeding of 9th IEEE International Conference on Information Technology and Applications in Biomedicine*, (pp. 1-4). IEEE. doi:10.1109/ITAB.2009.5394323

Kuhn, H. (1955). The hungarian method for solving the assignment problem. *Naval Research Logistics Quart., 2*(1-2), 83–97. doi:10.1002/nav.3800020109

Kulbago, T. (2013). *Imaging in Medical Device Manufacturing*. Retrieved June 15, 2015, from http://www.bonezonepub.com/component/content/article/742-the-use-of-imaging-analytics-in-medical-device-manufacturing

Kumar, & Kumar. (2014). A Detailed Review of Feature Extraction in Image Processing Systems. In *Proceeding of Fourth International Conference on Advanced Computing and Communication Technologies* (pp.5-12). Academic Press.

Kumar, P., & Mahajan, A. (2009). Soft computing techniques for the control of an active power filter. *IEEE Transactions on Power Delivery, 2*(1), 452–461. doi:10.1109/TPWRD.2008.2005881

Kuruvilla, & Gunavathi. (2014). Lung cancer classification using neural networks for CT images. *Computer Methods and Programs in Biomedicine, 113*(1), 202–209.

Lam, T. H. W., Cheung, K. H., & Liu, J. N. K. (2011). Gait flow image: A silhouette-based gait representation for human identification. *Pattern Recognition, 44*(4), 973–987. doi:10.1016/j.patcog.2010.10.011

Lang, E. K., Thomas, R., Davis, R., Shore, B., Ruiz-Deya, G., & Macchia, R. J. (2004). Multiphasic helical CT diagnosis of early medullary and papillary necrosis. *Journal of Endourology, 18*, 167–171. doi:10.1089/089277904322959815 PMID:15006054

Lang, M. G., Odegard, H. J. E., & Burrus, C. S. (1995, April). Nonlinear processing of a shift invariant DWT for noise reduction, in Mathematical Imaging: Wavelet Applications for Dual Use. Proc. for Image and Video Database III. *Proceedings of the Society for Photo-Instrumentation Engineers, 2420*, 165–173.

Laptev, I., Marszalek, M., Schmid, C., & Rozenfeld, B. (2008, June). Learning realistic human actions from movies. In *Computer Vision and Pattern Recognition, 2008. CVPR 2008. IEEE Conference on* (pp. 1-8). IEEE.

Laptev, I. (2005). On space-time interest points. *International Journal of Computer Vision, 64*(2-3), 107–123. doi:10.1007/s11263-005-1838-7

Larsson, M., & Pedersen, N. L. (2004). Genetic correlations among texture characteristics in the human iris. *Molecular Vision, 10*, 821–831. PMID:15534585

Larsson, M., & Stattin, H. (2003). Importance of genetic effects for characteristics of the human iris. *Twin Research, 6*(3), 192–200. doi:10.1375/136905203765693843 PMID:12855068

Lavrenko, V. M. R. (2003). model for learning the semantics of pictures. *16th conference on advances in neural information processing systems (NIPS 16).* Vancouver, Canada: MIT Press.

Laws, K. (1980). *Textured image segmentation.* (PhD thesis). Electrical Engineering, University of Southern California.

Lee, J.-S. (2014). On designing paired comparison experiments for subjective multimedia quality assessment. *IEEE Transactions on Multimedia, 16*(2), 564–571. doi:10.1109/TMM.2013.2292590

Lee, Y., Takahashi, N., Tsai, D. Y., & Fujita, H. (2006). Detectability improvement of early sign of acute stroke on brain CT images using an adaptive partial smoothing filter. In *Proceedings of the Society of Photo-Optical Instrumentation Engineering and Medical Imaging* (vol. 6144, pp.2138-2145). doi:10.1117/12.654242

Lei Wu, R. J., Rong Jin, , & Jain, A. K. (2013). Tag Completion for Image Retrieval. *IEEE Transactions on Pattern Analysis and Machine Intelligence, 35*(3), 716–727. doi:10.1109/TPAMI.2012.124 PMID:22641703

Lepetit, V., & Fua, P. (2006). Keypoint recognition using randomized trees. *Pattern Analysis and Machine Intelligence. IEEE Transactions on, 28*(9), 1465–1479.

Leutenegger, S., Chli, M., & Siegwart, R. Y. (2011). BRISK: Binary Robust In variant Scalable Keypoints. In *International Conference on Computer Vision,* (pp. 2548-2555). doi:10.1109/ICCV.2011.6126542

Levenshtein, V. I. (1966). *Binary codes capable of correcting deletions, insertions, and reversals.* Paper presented at the Soviet Physics Doklady.

Levine, M. D., & Nazif, A. M. (1985). Dynamic measurement of computer generated image segmentations. *Pattern Analysis and Machine Intelligence, IEEE Transactions on,* (2), 155-164.

Li, C. S. (2009). Learning Social Tag Relevance by Neighbor Voting. *IEEE Trans. Multimedia, 11*(7), 1310-1322.

Li, Cao, & Lu. (2013). Improve the two-phase test samples representation method for palmprint recognition. *Optik - International Journal for Light and Electron Optics, 124*(24), 6651–6656.

Li, D., Dimitrova, N., Li, M., & Sethi, I. K. (2003). *Multimedia content processing through cross-modal association.* Paper presented at the Eleventh ACM International Conference on Multimedia. doi:10.1145/957013.957143

Li, Z., Tian, X., Xie, L., & Chen, Y. (2008, August). Improved Object Classification and Tracking Based on Overlapping Cameras in Video Surveillance. *ISECS International Colloquium on Computing, Communication, Control, and Management*. IEEE. doi:10.1109/CCCM.2008.125

Li, Z., Xie, X., & Liu, X. (2009). An efficient 2D to 3D video conversion method based on skeleton line tracking. In Proceedings of IEEE 3DTVCON (pp. 1–4). IEEE.

Liao, C. C., Chiang, I. J., Xiao, F., & Wong, J. M. (2006a). Tracing the deformed midline on brain CT. *Biomedical Engineering-Applications Basis Communications*, *18*(6), 305–311. doi:10.4015/S1016237206000452

Liao, C. C., Xiao, F., Wong, J. M., & Chiang, I. J. (2006b). A simple genetic algorithm for tracing the deformed midline on a single slice of brain CT using quadratic Bezier curves. In *Proceedings of Sixth IEEE International Conference on Data Mining Workshops*, (pp. 463-467). doi:10.1109/ICDMW.2006.22

Liao, M., Gao, J., Yang, R., & Gong, M. (2012). Video stereolization: Combining motion analysis with user interaction. *IEEE Transactions on Visualization and Computer Graphics*, *18*(7), 1079–1088. doi:10.1109/TVCG.2011.114 PMID:21690648

Li, B., Chellappa, R., Zheng, Q., & Der, S. (2001). Model-based temporal object verification using video. *IEEE Transactions on Image Processing*, *10*(6), 897–908. doi:10.1109/83.923286

Li-dong, F., & Yi-fei, Z. (2010). Medical Image Retrieval and Classification Based on Morphological Shape Feature. In *Proceedings of IEEE 3rd International Conference on Intelligent Networks and Intelligent Systems*. (pp. 116-119). IEEE.

Lin, D. (1998). *An information-theoretic definition of similarity*. Paper presented at the ICML.

Li, N., Liu, L., & Xu, D. (2008). Corner feature based object tracking using Adaptive Kalman Filter. In *9th International Conference on Signal Processing*, (pp. 1432 – 1435).

Lindeberg, T. (1998). Feature Detection with Automatic Scale Selection. *International Journal of Computer Vision*, *30*(2), 77–116.

Linden, G., Smith, B., & York, J. (2003). Amazon. com recommendations: Item-to-item collaborative filtering. *IEEE Internet Computing*, *7*(1), 76–80. doi:10.1109/MIC.2003.1167344

Lin, G. S., Huang, H. Y., Chen, W. C., Yeh, C. Y., Liu, K. C., & Lie, W. N. (2012). *A stereoscopic video conversion scheme based on spatio-temporal analysis of MPEG videos. EURASIP Journal on Advances in Signal Processing*.

Lin, K., Jagadish, H. V., & Faloutsos, C. (1994). The TV-Tree: An index for high dimensional data. *The VLDB Journal*, *3*(4), 517–543. doi:10.1007/BF01231606

Lin, X., Suo, J., & Dai, Q. (2014). Extracting Depth and Radiance from a Defocused Video Pair. *IEEE Transactions on Circuits and Systems for Video Technology*.

List, P., Joch, A., Lainema, J., Bjontegaard, G., & Karczewicz, M. (2003). Adaptive deblocking filter. *IEEE Transactions on Circuits and Systems for Video Technology*, *13*(7), 614–619. doi:10.1109/TCSVT.2003.815175

Liu, D. Z. (2007). Survey of content-based image retrieval with high-level semantics. *Pattern Recognition*, *40*(1), 262–282.

Liu, Li., Tan, Pang, Lim, Lee, … Zhang. (2010). Fast traumatic brain injury CT slice indexing via anatomical feature classification. In *Proceeding of 17ᵗʰ IEEE International Conference on Image Processing*, (pp.4377-4380).

Liu, W., Wu, Y., Guo, F. & Hu, Z. (2013). An efficient approach for 2D to 3D video conversion based on structure from motion. *Journal of the Visual Computer*.

Liu, B., Gould, S., & Koller, D. (2010). Single image depth estimation from predicted semantic labels. In *Proceedings of IEEE International Conference on Computer Vision and Pattern Recognition (CVPR)* (pp. 1253 – 1260). IEEE. doi:10.1109/CVPR.2010.5539823

Liu, J., Li, M., Liu, Q., Lu, H., & Ma, S. (2009). Image annotation via graph learning. *Pattern Recognition, 42*(2), 218–228. doi:10.1016/j.patcog.2008.04.012

Liu, J., Xu, C., & Lu, H. (2010). Cross-media retrieval: State-of-the-art and open issues. *International Journal of Multimedia Intelligence and Security, 1*(1), 33–52. doi:10.1504/IJMIS.2010.035970

Liu, J., & Yang, Y.-H. (1994). Multiresolution color image segmentation. *Pattern Analysis and Machine Intelligence. IEEE Transactions on, 16*(7), 689–700.

Liu, M., Chen, X., & Wang, X. (2015). Latent fingerprint enhancement via multi-scale patch based sparse representation. *IEEE Trans. Information Forensics and Security, 10*(1), 6–15. doi:10.1109/TIFS.2014.2360582

Liu, Q., & Zhang, C., Guo, Xu, H., & Zhou, Y. (2015). Adaptive sparse coding on PCA dictionary for image denoising. *The Visual Computer.*

Liu, Y., Zhang, D., Lu, G., & Ma, W.-Y. (2007). A survey of content-based image retrieval with high-level semantics. *Pattern Recognition, 40*(1), 262–282. doi:10.1016/j.patcog.2006.04.045

Li, X., & Guo, X. (2013, July). Vision-Based Method for Forward Vehicle Detection and Tracking. *IEEE International Conference on Mechanical and Automation Engineering*, (pp. 128-131). doi:10.1109/MAEE.2013.41

Lizuka, S., Endo, Y., Kanamori, Y., Mitani, J., & Fukui, Y. (2014). Efficient Depth Propagation for Constructing a Layered Depth Image from a Single Image. In *Proceedings of Computer Graphics Forum* (Vol.33, No.7, pp. 279-288). doi:10.1111/cgf.12496

Lo, B. P. L., & Velastin, S. A. (2000). Automatic Congestion Detection System for Underground Platforms. In *Proceeding of International Symposium on Intelligent Multimedia, Video, and Speech Processing*, (pp. 158-161).

Long, F. H. Z. (2003). Fundamentals of content-based image retrieval. In Multimedia Information Retrieval and Management: Technological Fundamentals and Applications. Springer.

Long, F., Zhang, H., & Feng, D. D. (2003). *Fundamentals of content-based image retrieval. In Multimedia Information Retrieval and Management* (pp. 1–26). Springer. doi:10.1007/978-3-662-05300-3_1

Lord, P. W., Stevens, R. D., Brass, A., & Goble, C. A. (2003). Investigating semantic similarity measures across the Gene Ontology: The relationship between sequence and annotation. *Bioinformatics (Oxford, England), 19*(10), 1275–1283. doi:10.1093/bioinformatics/btg153 PMID:12835272

Lowe, D. G. (2004). Distinctive image features from scale-invariant key points. *International Journal of Computer Vision, 60*(2), 91–110. doi:10.1023/B:VISI.0000029664.99615.94

Lu, J., Zhang, E., & Jing, C. (2006). Gait Recognition using wavelet descriptors and independent component analysis. *Proc. of 3rd International Symposium on Neural Network* (pp. 232-237). Springer Berlin Heidelberg. doi:10.1007/11760023_34

Lu, C., Adluru, N., Ling, H., Zhu, G., & Latecki, L. J. (2010). Contour based object detection using part bundles. *Computer Vision and Image Understanding, 114*(7), 827–834. doi:10.1016/j.cviu.2010.03.009

Lucas, B. D., & Kanade, T. (1981). An iterative image registration technique with an application to stereo vision. In *International Joint Conference on Artificial Intelligence.*

Lucena, M., Fuertes, J. M., Blanca, N., Manuel, J. & Jimenez, M. (2010). Tracking people in video sequences using multiple model. *Multimedia Tools and Applications, 49*(2), 371-403.

Lu, G., & Kudo, M. (2014). Learning action patterns in difference images for efficient action recognition. *Neurocomputing, 123*, 328–336. doi:10.1016/j.neucom.2013.06.042

Lu, H., Plataniotis, K. N., & Venetsanopoulos, A. N. (2008). A full-body layered deformable model for automatic model-based gait recognition. *EURASIP Journal on Advances in Signal Processing*, 1–13.

Luo, B., Wang, X., & Tang, X. (2003). *World Wide Web Based Image Search Engine Using Text and Image Content Features*. Academic Press.

Luts, J., Ojeda, F., Van de Plas, R., De Moor, B., Van Huffel, S., & Suykens, J. A. (2010). A tutorial on support vector machine-based methods for classification problems in chemometrics. *Analytica Chimica Acta, 665*(2), 129–145. doi:10.1016/j.aca.2010.03.030 PMID:20417323

Lu, W., Wang, S., & Ding, X. (2009, October). Vehicle Detection and Tracking in Relatively Crowded Conditions. *IEEE International Conference on Systems, Man, and Cybernetics*, (pp. 4136-4141). doi:10.1109/ICSMC.2009.5346721

Lu, X., Song, L., Yu, S., & Ling, N. (2012). Object Contour Tracking Using Multi-feature Fusion based Particle Filter. *IEEE Conference on Industrial Electronics and Applications (ICIEA)*, (pp. 237–242). doi:10.1109/ICIEA.2012.6360729

Maccormick, J., & Blake, A. (2000). Probabilistic exclusion and partitioned sampling for multiple object tracking. *International Journal of Computer Vision, 39*(1), 57–71. doi:10.1023/A:1008122218374

Machin, D. (2004). Building the world's visual language: The increasing global importance of image banks in corporate media. *Visual Communication, 3*(3), 316-336.

MacKay, D. J. C. (1998). Introduction to Monte Carlo methods. In N. A. T. O. Science Series (Ed.), *Learning in Graphical Models, M. I. Jordan* (pp. 175–204). Kluwer Academic Press. doi:10.1007/978-94-011-5014-9_7

Madhu, N. S., Revathy, K., & Tatavarti, R. (2008). An Improved Decision Based Algorithm for Impulse Noise Removal. In *Proceedings of International Congress on Image and Signal Processing* (CISP 2008), (pp. 426–431). IEEE Computer Society Press.

Mairal, J., Bach, F., & Ponce, J. (2012). Task-driven dictionary learning. *IEEE Transactions on Pattern Analysis and Machine Intelligence, 34*(4), 791–804. doi:10.1109/TPAMI.2011.156 PMID:21808090

Mairal, J., Bach, F., Ponce, J., & Sapiro, G. (2010). Online learning for matrix factorization and sparse coding. *Journal of Machine Learning Research, 11*, 19–60.

Mairal, J., Elad, M., & Sapiro, G. (2008). Sparse representation for color image restoration. *IEEE Transactions on Image Processing, 17*(1), 53–69. doi:10.1109/TIP.2007.911828 PMID:18229804

Mairal, J., Sapiro, G., & Elad, M. (2008). Learning multiscale sparse representation for image and video restoration. *SIAM Multiscale Modeling and Simulation, 7*(1), 214–241. doi:10.1137/070697653

Ma, L., Tan, T., & Zhang, D. (2003). Personal identification based on iris texture analysis. *IEEE Transactions on Pattern Analysis and Machine Intelligence, 25*(12), 1519–1533. doi:10.1109/TPAMI.2003.1251145

Ma, L., Zhang, D., Li, N., Cai, Y., Zuo, W., & Wang, K. (2013). Iris-based medical analysis by geometric deformation features. *IEEE Journal of Biomedical & Health Informatics, 17*(1), 223–231. doi:10.1109/TITB.2012.2222655 PMID:23144041

Maldjian, J. A., & Chalela, J. (2001). Automated CT segmentation and analysis for acute middle cerebral artery stroke. *AJNR. American Journal of Neuroradiology*, 22(6), 1050–1055. PMID:11415896

Malfait, M., & Roose, D. (1997, April). Wavelet-based image denoising using a Markov random field a priori model. *Image Processing, IEEE Transactions on*, 6(4), 549 – 565.

Mallat, S. (1989). A theory for multiresolution signal decomposition: The wavelet representation. *IEEE Transactions on Pattern Analysis and Machine Intelligence*, 11(7), 674–693. doi:10.1109/34.192463

Mallat, S., & Zhang, Z. (1993). Matching pursuits with time-frequency dictionaries. *IEEE Transactions on Signal Processing*, 41(12), 3397–3415. doi:10.1109/78.258082

Manjunath, B. S. (1998). Image Browsing in the Alexandria Digital Library (ADL) Project. *Proceedings of IEEE International Forum on Research and Technology Advances in Digital Libraries*, (pp. 180-187). IEEE. doi:10.1109/ADL.1998.670393

Manjunath, B. S., & Ma, W. Y. (1996). Texture features for browsing and retrieval of image data. *Pattern Analysis and Machine Intelligence. IEEE Transactions on*, 18(8), 837–842.

Manjunath, B. S., Salembier, P., & Sikora, T. (2002). *Introduction to MPEG-7: Multimedia Content Description Language*. John Wiley & Sons Ltd.

Manning, C. D., Raghavan, P., & Schütze, H. (2008). *Introduction to information retrieval* (Vol. 1). Cambridge University Press.

Mansouri, A. (2002). Region tracking via level set pdes without motion computation. *IEEE Transactions on Pattern Analysis and Machine Intelligence*, 24(7), 947–961. doi:10.1109/TPAMI.2002.1017621

Ma, Q., Wang, S., Nie, D., & Qiu, J. (2007). Recognizing humans based on gait moment image. *ACIS International Conference on SNPD 2*, (pp.606–610). IEEE. doi:10.1109/SNPD.2007.307

Markus, B. (2012). Texture feature ranking with relevance learning to classify interstitial lung disease patterns. *Artificial Intelligence in Medicine*, 56(2), 91–97. doi:10.1016/j.artmed.2012.07.001 PMID:23010586

Marteen, J. (2000, April). *Wavelet thresholding and noise reduction*. (Ph. D. Thesis). Katholieke Universiteit Leuven.

Martin, M. B., & Bell, A. E. (2001, April). New image compression techniques using multiwavelets and multiwavelet packets. *IEEE Transactions on Image Processing*, 10(4), 500–510. doi:10.1109/83.913585 PMID:18249640

Matas, J., Chum, O., Urban, M., & Pajdla, T. (2002). Robust wide baseline stereo from maximally stable extremal regions. In *Proceeding of British Machine Vision Conference*, (pp. 384-396). doi:10.5244/C.16.36

Mathew, T. V. (1996). *Genetic Algorithm. In Lecture notes* (pp. 1–15). Mumbai: Indian Institute of Technology.

Matsuyama, T. (2004), Exploitation of 3D video technologies. In *International Conference on Informatics Research for Development of Knowledge Society Infrastructure*, (pp. 7-14). doi:10.1109/ICKS.2004.1313403

Matusik, W., & Pfister, H. (2004). 3D TV: A scalable system for real-time acquisition, transmission, and autostereoscopic display of dynamic scenes. *ACM Transactions on Graphics*, 24(3), 811–821.

Mehta, P. J. (2001). *Practiced medicine* (19th ed.). The National Book Depot.

Meil, M. (2005). Comparing clusterings: an axiomatic view. *Proceedings of the 22nd international conference on Machine learning* (pp. 577-584). ACM.

Melanie, M. (1999). An introduction to genetic algorithms. MIT Press.

Mendonca, A. M., & Campilho, A. (2006). Segmentation of Retinal Blood Vessels By Combining the Detection of Centerlines and Morphological Reconstruction. *IEEE Transactions on Medical Imaging, 25*(9), 1200–1213. doi:10.1109/TMI.2006.879955 PMID:16967805

Meur, O. L., Baccino, T., & Roumy, A. (2011). Prediction of the inter-observer visual congruency (IOVC) and application to image ranking. In *Proceedings of ACM Conf. Multimedia*. ACM.

Mhatre, A., Palla, S., Chikkerur, S., & Govindaraju, V. (2005). Efficient Search and Retrieval in Biometric Databases. *SPIE Defense and Security Symposium, 5779*, 265-273.

Mihcak, M. K. I., & Kozintsev, K. R., & Moulin. (1999, December). Low-Complexity Image Denoising Based On Statistical Modeling of Wavelet Coefficients. *IEEE Signal Processing Letters, 6*(12).

Mikolajczyk, K., & Schmid, C. (2002). An affine invariant interest point detector. In *European Conference on Comuter Vision (ECCV)*, (vol. 1, pp. 128-142).

Miller, G. A., & Charles, W. G. (1991). Contextual correlates of semantic similarity. *Language and Cognitive Processes, 6*(1), 1–28. doi:10.1080/01690969108406936

Min, J., Powell, M., & Bowyer, K. W. (2004). Automated performance evaluation of range image segmentation algorithms. *Systems, Man, and Cybernetics, Part B: Cybernetics. IEEE Transactions on, 34*(1), 263–271.

Mitchell, T. M. (1997). *Machine learning*. WCB.

Mohd Asaari, M. S., Suandi, S. A., & Rosdi, B. A. (2014). Fusion of Band Limited Phase Only Correlation and Width Centroid Contour Distance for finger based biometrics. *Expert Systems with Applications, Elsevier, 41*(7), 3367–3382. doi:10.1016/j.eswa.2013.11.033

Monrose, F., Reiter, M. K., Li, Q., & Wetzel, S. (2001, May).Cryptographic key generation from voice.*Proceedings of the IEEE Symposium on Security and Privacy 2001*. IEEE.

Monteiro, F. C., & Campilho, A. C. (2006). *Performance evaluation of image segmentation. In Image Analysis and Recognition* (pp. 248–259). Springer.

Moravec, H. (1979). Visual mapping by a robot rover. In *Proceedings of the International Joint Conference on Artificial Intelligence (IJCAI)*, (pp. 598-600).

Motiian, S., Feng, K., Bharthavarapu, H., Sharlemin, S., & Doretto, G. (2013). Pairwise kernels for human interaction recognition. In *Advances in Visual Computing* (pp. 210–221). Springer Berlin Heidelberg. doi:10.1007/978-3-642-41939-3_21

Motwani, Gadiya, Motwani, & Harris. (2004). Survey of Image. Denoising Techniques. *Proc. of GSPx*.

Moulin, P., & Liu, J. (1999, April). Analysis of multiresolution image denoising schemes using generalized Gaussian and complexity priors. *IEEE Infor. Theory, 45*(3), 909–919. doi:10.1109/18.761332

Mourato, A. S., & Jesus, R. (2014). Clip Art Retrieval Using a Sketch Tablet Application. *Procedia Technology, 17*, 368–375. doi:10.1016/j.protcy.2014.10.246

Mulhem, P., Chevallet, J.-P., Quenon, G., & Al Batal, R. (2009). MRIM-LIG at ImageCLEF 2009: Photo Retrieval and Photo Annotation tasks. *CLEF Working Notes*.

Müller, H., Michoux, N., Bandon, D., & Geissbuhler, A. (2004). A review of content-based image retrieval systems in medical applications—clinical benefits and future directions. *International Journal of Medical Informatics, 73*(1), 1–23. doi:10.1016/j.ijmedinf.2003.11.024 PMID:15036075

Müller, H., Ruch, P., & Geissbühler, A. (2004). Enriching content-based image retrieval with multilingual search terms. *Swiss Medical Informatics, 21*(54), 6–11.

Musmann, H. G., Pirsch, P., & Grallert, H.-J. (1985). Advances in picture coding. *Proceedings of the IEEE, 73*(4), 523–548. doi:10.1109/PROC.1985.13183

Nabeel, U. A. (2013). *New Innovations in Medical Imaging Technology: Live from RSNA*. Retrieved December 18, 2013, from http://in-training.org/new-innovations-in-medical-imaging-technology-live-from-rsna-3961

Nageswara, Uma, Dsvgk, Sridhar, & Rao. (n.d.). A Probabilistic Neural Network Approach For protein Super family Classification. *Journal of Theoretical and Applied Information Technology, 6*(1), 101 – 105.

Nair, M. S., & Raju, G. (2010). *A new fuzzy-based decision algorithm for high-density impulse noise removal. Journal of Signal*. Image and Video Processing; doi:10.1007/s11760-010-0186-4

Nakamura, J. (2005). *Image Sensors and Signal Processing for Digital Still Cameras*. CRC Press. doi:10.1201/9781420026856

Nandakumar, L. (2013) A novel algorithm for spirometric signal processing and classification by evolutionary approach and its implementation on an ARM embedded platform In *Proceedings of IEEE International Conference on Control Communication and Computing*, (pp. 384-387). doi:10.1109/ICCC.2013.6731684

Napster. (2001). *Napster*. Retrieved from http://www. napster. com

Nashwa El-Bendary, T.-K. (2013). Automatic image annotation approach based on optimization of classes scores. *Computing*.

Nason, G. P. (2002). Choice of wavelet smoothness, primary resolution and threshold in wavelet shrinkage. *Journal: Statistics and Computing, 12*, 219–227.

National Institute of Standards and Technology, Iris Challenge Evaluation. (2006). Retrieved from http://iris.nist.gov/ICE/

Navarro, G. (2001). A guided tour to approximate string matching. *ACM Computing Surveys, 33*(1), 31–88. doi:10.1145/375360.375365

Netravali, A. N., & Limb, J. O. (1980). Picture Coding: A review. *Proceedings of the IEEE, 68*(3), 366–406. doi:10.1109/PROC.1980.11647

Netravali, A. N., & Robbins, J. D. (2004). Motion Compensated television coding: Part I. *The Bell System Technical Journal*, 631–670.

Ng, & Ma. (2006, June). A Switching Median Filter With Boundary Discriminative Noise Detection for Extremely Corrupted Images. *IEEE Transactions on Image Processing, 15*(6), 1506-1516.

Niblack, W., Barber, R., Equitz, W., Flickner, M., Glasman, E. H., Petkovic, D., & Taubin, G. et al. (1993). The QBIC project: Querying images by content using color, texture, and shape. *Proceedings of the SPIE: Storage and Retrieval for Image and Video Databases, 1908*, 173–187. doi:10.1117/12.143648

Nibouche, O., & Jiang, J. (2013). Palmprint matching using feature points and SVD factorization. *Digital Signal Processing Elsevier, 23*(4), 1154–1162. doi:10.1016/j.dsp.2013.02.011

Niebner, M., Henry, S., & Marc, S. (2010). Fast indirect illumination using Layered Depth Images. *Journal of The Visual Computer, 26*, 679–686.

Ning, J., Zhang, L., Zhang, D., & Wu, C. (2009). Robust object tracking using joint color-texture histogram. *International Journal of Pattern Recognition and Artificial Intelligence, 23*(7), 1245–1263. doi:10.1142/S0218001409007624

Nuruzzaman, M. (2005). *Digital Image Fundamentals in MATLAB*. Author House.

O'Gorman, L. (2003). Comparing passwords, tokens, and biometrics for user authentication. *Proceedings of the IEEE, 91*(12), 2019–2020. doi:10.1109/JPROC.2003.819605

Ogle, V. E., Stonebraker, M., & Chabot. (1995). Retrieval from a relational database of images. *IEEE Computer, 28*(9), 40–48.

Ohm, J. R., Sullivan, G. J., Schwarz, H., Tan, T. K., & Wiegand, T. (2012). Comparison of the coding efficiency of video coding standards – Including High Efficiency Video Coding (HEVC). *IEEE Transactions on Circuits and Systems for Video Technology, 22*(12), 1668–1683. doi:10.1109/TCSVT.2012.2221192

Ohta, J. (2007). *Smart CMOS Image Sensors and Applications*. CRC Press. doi:10.1201/9781420019155

Oliver, N., Rosario, B., & Pentland, A. (2000). A bayesian computer vision system for modeling human interactions. *IEEE Transactions on Pattern Analysis and Machine Intelligence, 22*(8), 831–843. doi:10.1109/34.868684

Olshausen, B. A., & Field, D. J. (1996). Emergence of simple-cell receptive field properties by learning a sparse code for natural images. *Nature, 381*(13), 607–609. doi:10.1038/381607a0 PMID:8637596

Osareh & Shadgar. (2010). An Automated tracking approach for extraction of retinal vasculature in fndus images. *Journal of Ophthalmic And Vision Research, 5*(1), 20–26. PMID:22737322

Otsu, N. (1979). A threshold selection method from gray-level histograms. *IEEE Transactions on Systems, Man, and Cybernetics, 9*(1), 62–66. doi:10.1109/TSMC.1979.4310076

Ozuysal, M., Fua, P., & Lepetit, V. (2007, June). Fast keypoint recognition in ten lines of code. In *Computer Vision and Pattern Recognition, 2007. CVPR'07. IEEE Conference on* (pp. 1-8). IEEE.

Pal, M., & Mather, P. M. (2001, November). Decision Treebased Classification on Remotely sensed Data. *22nd Asian Conference on Remote Sensing*.

Pandey. (2008, April). An Improved Switching Median filter for Uniformly Distributed Impulse Noise Removal. *Proceedings of World Academy of Science, Engineering and Technology, 28*.

Papageorgiou, C., Oren, M., & Poggio, T. (1998). A general framework for object detection. In *IEEE International Conference on Computer Vision (ICCV)*, (pp. 555–562). doi:10.1109/ICCV.1998.710772

Paragios, N., & Deriche, R. (2002). Geodesic active regions and level set methods for supervised texture Segmentation. *International Journal of Computer Vision, 46*(3), 223–247. doi:10.1023/A:1014080923068

Park, S. C., Park, M. K., & Kang, M. G. (2003). Super-resolution image reconstruction: A technical overview. *IEEE Signal Processing Magazine, 20*(3), 21–36. doi:10.1109/MSP.2003.1203207

Parra, L., & Sajda, P. (2003). Blind source separation via generalized eigenvalue decomposition. *Journal of Machine Learning Research, 4*, 1261–1269.

Paschos, G. (2001). Perceptually uniform color spaces for color texture analysis: An empirical evaluation. *IEEE Transactions on Image Processing, 10*(6), 932–937. doi:10.1109/83.923289

Pass, G., & Zabith, R. (1996). Histogram refinement for content-based image retrieval. In *Proceedings of the IEEE Workshop on Applications of Computer Vision*, (pp. 96–102). doi:10.1109/ACV.1996.572008

Patel, P., Tripathi, A., Majhi, B., & Tripathy, C.R. (2011, February). *A New Adaptive Median Filtering Technique for Removal of Impulse Noise from Images.* International Conference on Communication, Computing & Security (ICCCS-2011), Department of Computer Science & Engineering, National Institute of Technology, Rourkela, India.

Patil, C., & Dalal, V. (2011). *Content based image retrieval using combined features.* Paper presented at the International Conference & Workshop on Emerging Trends in Technology. doi:10.1145/1980022.1980043

Patton, N., Aslam, T. M., MacGillivray, T., Deary, I. J., Dhillon, B., Eikelboom, R. H., & Constable, I. J. et al. (2006). Retinal image analysis: Concepts, applications and potential. *Progress in Retinal and Eye Research, 25*(1), 99–127. doi:10.1016/j.preteyeres.2005.07.001 PMID:16154379

Patwardhan, S., & Pedersen, T. (2006). *Using WordNet-based context vectors to estimate the semantic relatedness of concepts.* Paper presented at the EACL 2006 Workshop Making Sense of Sense-Bringing Computational Linguistics and Psycholinguistics Together.

Pavlidis, T. (2008). *Limitations of content-based image retrieval.* Paper presented at the Invited Plenary Talk at the 19th Internat. Conf. on Pattern Recognition, Tampa, FL.

Peleg, T., & Elad, M. (2014). A statistical prediction model based on sparse representations for single image super-resolution. *IEEE Transactions on Image Processing, 23*(6), 2569–2582. doi:10.1109/TIP.2014.2305844 PMID:24815620

Peng, B., & Zhang, L. (2012). Evaluation of image segmentation quality by adaptive ground truth composition. *Computer Vision–ECCV, 2012,* 287–300.

Peng, B., Zhang, L., & Zhang, D. (2011). Automatic image segmentation by dynamic region merging. *Image Processing. IEEE Transactions on, 20*(12), 3592–3605.

Pengcheng, W., Hoi, Nguyen, & He. (2011). Randomly Projected KD-Trees with Distance Metric Learning for Image Retrieval. *The 17th International Conference on Multi Media Modeling,* 1-11.

Peng, X., Wu, X., Peng, Q., Qi, X., Qiao, Y., & Liu, Y. (2013, August). Exploring dense trajectory feature and encoding methods for human interaction recognition. In *Proceedings of the Fifth International Conference on Internet Multimedia Computing and Service* (pp. 23-27). ACM. doi:10.1145/2499788.2499795

Pentland, A. P., Picard, R., & Sclaroff, S. (1994). Photobook: Tools for Content-Based Manipulation of Image databases. In *Proceedings of the SPIE: Storage and Retrieval for Image and Video Databases II.* doi:10.1117/12.171786

Person, K. (1901). On lines and planes of closest fit to systems of points in space. *Philosophical Magazine, 2*(6), 559–572. doi:10.1080/14786440109462720

Petrou, M., & Bosdogianni, P. (2003). *Image Processing the Fundamentals* (1st ed.). John Wiley and Sons.

Peyré, G., Fadili, J., & Starck, J. L. (2007). Learning adapted dictionaries for geometry and texture separation. In *Proceedings of SPIE.* SPIE.

Philipp-Foliguet, S., & Guigues, L. (2008). Multi-scale criteria for the evaluation of image segmentation algorithms. *Journal of Multimedia, 3*(5), 42–56. doi:10.4304/jmm.3.5.42-56

Phillips, P., Sarkar, S., Robledo, I., Grother, P., & Bowyer, K. (2002). Baseline Results for Challenge Problem of Human ID Using Gait Analysis.*Proc. Int'l Conf. Automatic Face and Gesture Recognition* (pp. 130-135). IEEE.

Poh, N., & Bengio, S. (2005). How do correlation and variance of base-experts affect fusion in biometric authentication tasks? *Signal Processing. IEEE Transactions on, 53*(11), 4384–4396. doi:10.1109/TSP.2005.857006

Poh, N., Ross, A., Lee, W., & Kittle, J. (2013). A user-specific and selective multimodal biometric fusion strategy by ranking subjects. *Pattern Recognition, Elsevier, 46*(12), 3341–3357. doi:10.1016/j.patcog.2013.03.018

Pok, G., & Liu, J.-C. (1999). Decision based median filter improved by predictions. *Proc. ICIP, 2*, 410–413. doi:10.1109/ICIP.1999.822928

Polat, Ö., & Yýldýrým, T. (2008). Hand geometry identification without feature extraction by general regression neural network. *Expert Systems with Applications, 34*(2), 845–849. doi:10.1016/j.eswa.2006.10.032

Poppe, R. (2010). A survey on vision-based human action recognition. *Image and Vision Computing, 28*(6), 976–990. doi:10.1016/j.imavis.2009.11.014

Prajapati, H. B., & Vij, S. K. (2011). Analytical study of parallel and distributed image processing. In *Proceedings of the 2011 International conference on Image Information Processing*. doi:10.1109/ICIIP.2011.6108870

Priya, R., & Aruna, P. (2014). Automated Diagnosis Of Age-Related Macular Degeneration Using Machine Learning Techniques. *International Journal of Computer Applications in Technology, 49*(2), 157–165. doi:10.1504/IJCAT.2014.060527

Proenca, H., & Alexandre, L. A. (2005). Ubiris: A noisy iris image database. *LNCS, 1*, 970–977.

Przelaskowski, A., Sklinda, K. P., Bargie, P. J., Walecki, J., Biesiadko Matus Zewska, M., & Kazubek, M. (2007). Improved early stroke detection: Wavelet-based perception enhancement of computerized tomography exams. *Computers in Biology and Medicine, 37*(4), 524–533. doi:10.1016/j.compbiomed.2006.08.004 PMID:16999952

Pu, B., Zhou, F., & Bai, X. (2011). Particle Filter Based on Color Feature with Contour Information Adaptively Integrated for Object Tracking. *Fourth International Symposium on Computational Intelligence and Design*, (pp. 359-362). doi:10.1109/ISCID.2011.192

Purgason, B., & Hibler, D. (2012). Security Through Behavioral Biometrics and Artificial Intelligence, *Procedia. Computer Science, 12*, 398–403.

Purnachand, N., Alves, & Navarro. (2012). Fast Motion Estimation Algorithm for HEVC. *Proc. IEEE Second International Conference on Consumer Electronics (ICCE)*.

Qing. (2004). Segmentation Of Blood Vessels In Retinal Images Using 2-D Entropies Of Gray Level-Gradient Co-Occurrence Matrix. *ICASSP*, III-509 – III-512.

Radiological Society of North America. (2012). Fetal alcohol exposure affects brain structure in children. *ScienceDaily*. Retrieved November 25, 2012, from www.sciencedaily.com/releases/2012/11/121125103949.htm

Radiological Society of North America. (2015). Retrieved June 12, 2015, from http://www.sciencedaily.com/releases/2015/05/150527095440.htm

Rahman, M., Desai, B. C., & Bhattacharya, P. (2007). Multi-modal interactive approach to imageCLEF 2007 photographic and medical retrieval tasks by CINDI. *Working Notes of CLEF, 7*.

Rajan, J., & Kaimal, M.R (1996). Image Denoising Using Wavelet Embedded Anisotropic Diffusion (Wead). In *Proceedings of IEE International Conference on Visual Information Engineering* (VIE), (pp. 589 – 593). IEE.

Rakow-Penner, R. A., White, N. S., Parsons, J. K., Choi, H. W., Liss, M. A., Kuperman, J. M., & Dale, A. M. et al. (2015). Novel technique for characterizing prostate cancer utilizing MRI restriction spectrum imaging: Proof of principle and initial clinical experience with extraprostatic extension. *Prostate Cancer and Prostatic Diseases, 18*(1), 81–85. doi:10.1038/pcan.2014.50 PMID:25559097

Rangarajan, K., & Shah, M. (1991, June). Establishing motion correspondence. *IEEE Computer Society Conference on Computer Vision and Pattern Recognition*, (pp. 103-108).

Ran, Y., Zheng, Q., Chellappa, R., & Stat, T. M. (2010). Applications of a simple characterization of human gait in surveillance. *IEEE Transactions on Systems, Man, and Cybernetics*, 1009–1019. PMID:20363680

Rapantzikos, K., Zervakis, M., & Balas, K. (2003). Detection and Segmentation of Drusen Deposits on Human Retina: Potential in the diagnosis of age-related macular degeneration. *Medical Image Analysis*, 7(1), 95–108. doi:10.1016/S1361-8415(02)00093-2 PMID:12467724

Rasmussen, C., & Hager, G. (2001). Probabilistic data association methods for tracking complex visual Objects. *IEEE Transactions on Pattern Analysis and Machine Intelligence*, 23(6), 560–576. doi:10.1109/34.927458

Rehna, V. J., & Jaya Kumar, M. K. (2012, August). Wavelet Based Image Coding Schemes: A Recent Survey. *International Journal on Soft Computing*, 3(3), 101–118. doi:10.5121/ijsc.2012.3308

Reid, D. B. (1979). An algorithm for tracking multiple targets. *IEEE Transactions on Automatic Control*, 24(6), 843–854. doi:10.1109/TAC.1979.1102177

Ren, J., & Hao, J. (2012, October). Mean shift tracking algorithm combined with Kalman Filter. In *Image and Signal Processing (CISP), 2012 5th International Congress on* (pp. 727-730). IEEE.

Ren, J., Liu, J., & Guo, Z. (2013). Context-aware sparse decomposition for image denoising and super-resolution. *IEEE Transactions on Image Processing*, 22(4), 1456–1469. doi:10.1109/TIP.2012.2231690 PMID:23221827

Resnik, P. (2011). *Semantic similarity in a taxonomy: An information-based measure and its application to problems of ambiguity in natural language*. arXiv preprint arXiv:1105.5444

Resnik, P. (1999). Semantic Similarity in a Taxonomy: An Information-Based Measure and its Application to Problems of Ambiguity in Natural Language. *Journal of Artificial Intelligence Research*, 11, 95–130.

Richardson, I. E. G. (2003). *H.264 and MPEG-4 Video Compression. In The MPEG-4 and H.264 Standards* (pp. 85–98). Jhon Wiley and Sons, Ltd. doi:10.1002/0470869615.ch4

Rittscher, J., Kato, J., Joga, S., & Blake, A. (2000). A probabilistic background model for tracking. In *European Conference on Computer Vision (ECCV)*, (vol. 2, pp. 336–350).

Robinson, J. T. (1981) The k-D-B-Tree: A Search Structure for Large Multidimensional Dynamic Indexes.*Proc. ACM SIGMOD*, 10-18. doi:10.1145/582318.582321

Rocha, L., Velho, L., Cezar, P., & Carvalho, P. (2004). Motion Eecognition using Moments Analysis. *Proceedings of 17th Brazilian Symposium on Computer Graphics and Image Processing*, (354-361). doi:10.1109/SIBGRA.2004.1352981

Romano, Y., Protter, M., & Elad, M. (2014). Single image interpolation via adaptive nonlocal sparsity-based modeling. *IEEE Transactions on Image Processing*, 23(7), 3085–3098. doi:10.1109/TIP.2014.2325774 PMID:24860029

Romberg, J. K., Choi, H., & Baraniuk, R. G. (2001). Bayesian tree-structured image modeling using wavelet-domain hidden Markov models. *IEEE Image Process.*, 10(7), 1056–1068. doi:10.1109/83.931100 PMID:18249679

Ro, S. L. (2013). *Visually weighted neighbor voting for image tag relevance learning*. Multimed Tools App.

Rosales, R., & Sclaroff, S. (1999). 3D trajectory recovery for tracking multiple objects and trajectory guided recognition of actions. *IEEE Computer Society Conference on Computer Vision and Pattern Recognition*, (vol. 2). doi:10.1109/CVPR.1999.784618

Ross, A., Nandakumar, K., & Jain, A. K. (2006). *Handbook of Multibiometrics*. New York: Springer-Verlag.

Rosten, E., & Drummond, T. (2006, May). Machine learning for highspeed corner detection. In *Proceedings of the European Conference on Computer Vision (ECCV)*, (vol. 3951, pp. 430-443).

Rotem, E., Wolowelsky, K., & Pelz, D. (2005). Automatic video to stereoscopic video conversion. In *Proceedings of SPIE Electronic Imaging—Stereoscopic Displays and Virtual Reality Systems XII* (Vol. 5664, pp. 198– 206). doi:10.1117/12.586599

Rothwell, C., Mundy, J. L., Hoffman, W., & Nguyen, V. D. (1995). Driving Vision by Topology. *IEEE International Symposium on Computer Vision*, (pp. 395-400). doi:10.1109/ISCV.1995.477034

Rowley, H., Baluja, S., & Kanade, T. (1998). Neural network-based face detection. *IEEE Transactions on Pattern Analysis and Machine Intelligence*, *20*(1), 23–38. doi:10.1109/34.655647

Roy, A., Sural, S., & Mukherjee, J. (2012). Gait recognition using Pose Kinematics and Pose Energy Image. *Signal Processing*, *92*(3), 780–792. doi:10.1016/j.sigpro.2011.09.022

Roy, V., & Shukla, S. (2012). Image Denoising by Data Adaptive and Non-Data Adaptive Transform Domain Denoising Method Using EEG Signal.*Proceedings of All India Seminar on Biomedical Engineering*. Springer.

Rubinstein, R., Bruckstein, A. M., & Elad, M. (2010). Dictionaries for sparse representation modeling. *Proceedings of the IEEE*, *98*(6), 1045–1057. doi:10.1109/JPROC.2010.2040551

Rubinstein, R., Peleg, T., & Elad, M. (2013). Analysis K-SVD: A dictionary-learning algorithm for the Analysis sparse model. *IEEE Transactions on Signal Processing*, *61*(3), 661–677. doi:10.1109/TSP.2012.2226445

Russ, J. C. (2002). *The Image Processing Hand Book* (4th ed.). CRC Press.

Ryoo, M. S. (2011, November). Human activity prediction: Early recognition of ongoing activities from streaming videos. In *Computer Vision (ICCV), 2011 IEEE International Conference on* (pp. 1036-1043). IEEE.

Ryoo, M. S., Chen, C. C., Aggarwal, J. K., & Roy-Chowdhury, A. (2010). An overview of contest on semantic description of human activities (SDHA) 2010. In *Recognizing Patterns in Signals, Speech, Images and Videos* (pp. 270–285). Springer Berlin Heidelberg. doi:10.1007/978-3-642-17711-8_28

Saeed, K., Pejas, J., & Mosdorf, R. (2007). *Biometrics, Computer Security Systems and Artificial Intelligence Applications*. Springer Science & Business Media.

Sahu, D. K., & Parsai, M. P. (2012). Different Image Fusion Techniques –A Critical Review. *International Journal of Modern Engineering Research*, *2*(5), 4298–4301.

Sakas, G. (2002). Trends in medical imaging: from 2D to 3D. *Computers & Graphics*, *26*(4), 577–587. doi:10.1016/S0097-8493(02)00103-6

Sakurai, Y., Yoshikawa, M., Uemura, S., & Kojima, H. (2000). The A-tree: An index Structure for High-Dimensional Spaces Using Relative Approximation.*Proceedings of the 26th VLDB Conference*.

Salari, V., & Sethi, I. K. (1990). Feature point correspondence in the presence of occlusion. *IEEE Transactions on Pattern Analysis and Machine Intelligence*, *12*(1), 87–91. doi:10.1109/34.41387

Salton, G., Wong, A., & Yang, C.-S. (1975). A vector space model for automatic indexing. *Communications of the ACM*, *18*(11), 613–620. doi:10.1145/361219.361220

Samet, H. (1984). The quadtree and related hierarchical data structure. *ACM Computing Surveys, 16*(2), 187–260. doi:10.1145/356924.356930

Saranya, G., Porkumaran, K., & Prabakar, S. (2014, March). Mixed noise removal of a color image using simple fuzzy filter. In *Proceedings of International Conference on Green Computing Communication and Electrical Engineering* (ICGCCEE), (pp. 1-6).

Sarkar, S., & Boyer, K. (1991). Optimal Infinite Impulse Response Zero-Crossing Based Edge Detection. *Computer Vision Graphics and Image Processing, 54*(2), 224–243.

Sarkar, S., Philips, P. J., Liu, Z., Vega, I., Grother, P., & Bowyer, K. (2006). The HumanID gait challenge problem: Data sets, performance, and analysis. *IEEE Transactions on Pattern Analysis and Machine Intelligence, 27*(2), 162–177. doi:10.1109/TPAMI.2005.39 PMID:15688555

Sastry, K., Goldberg, D., & Kendall, G. (2005). Genetic algorithms- In Search Methodologies. Springer US.

Sato, K., & Aggarwal, J. (2004). Temporal spatio-velocity transform and its application to tracking and Interaction. *Computer Vision and Image Understanding, 96*(2), 100–128. doi:10.1016/j.cviu.2004.02.003

Schmid, N., Ketkar, M., Singh, H., & Cukic, B. (2006). Performance analysis of iris based identification system at the matching score level. *IEEE Transactions on Information Forensics & Security, 1*(2), 154–168. doi:10.1109/TIFS.2006.873603

Schunk, B. (1986). The image flow constraint equation. *Computer Vision Graphics and Image Processing, 35*(1), 20–46. doi:10.1016/0734-189X(86)90124-6

Schweitzer, H., Bell, J. W., & Wu, F. (2002). Very fast template matching. In *European Conference on Computer Vision (ECCV)*, (pp. 358–372).

Sederberg, T. W. (2011). Computer Aided Geometric Design Course Notes. Brigham Young University.

Seetharaman, K., & Sathiamoorthy, S. (2014). Color image retrieval using statistical model and radial basis function neural network. *Egyptian Informatics Journal, 15*(1), 59–68. doi:10.1016/j.eij.2014.02.001

SEIMENS. (2015). Retrieved June 12, 2015, from http://www.bonezonepub.com/component/content/ article/1193

Sellis, T. K., Roussopoulos, N., & Faloutsos, C. (1987). The Rb-Tree: A dynamic index for multi-dimensional objects. *Proceedings of the 13th International Conference on Very Large Data Bases*, (pp. 507–518).

Sethi, I., & Jain, R. (1987). Finding trajectories of feature points in a monocular image sequence. *IEEE Transactions on Pattern Analysis and Machine Intelligence, 9*(1), 56–73. doi:10.1109/TPAMI.1987.4767872 PMID:21869377

Sethi, J., Mishra, S., Dash, P. P., Mishra, S. K., & Meher, S. (2011, January). Image compression using wavelet packet tree. *ACEEE Int. J. on Signal and Image Processing, 2*(1), 41–43.

Shafique, K., & Shah, M. (2003). A non-iterative greedy algorithm for multi-frame point correspondence. In *IEEE International Conference on Computer Vision (ICCV)*, (pp. 110–115). doi:10.1109/ICCV.2003.1238321

Shakhnarovich, G., Darrell, T., & Indyk, P. (2006). *Nearest-Neighbor Methods in Learning and Vision: Theory and Practice.* The MIT Press.

Shao, L., Gao, R., Liu, Y., & Zhang, H. (2011). Transform based spatio-temporal descriptors for human action recognition. *Neurocomputing, 74*(6), 962–973. doi:10.1016/j.neucom.2010.11.013

Shao, L., Yan, R., Li, X., & Liu, Y. (2014). From heuristic optimization to dictionary learning: A review and comprehensive comparison of image denoising algorithms. *IEEE Trans. Cybernetics*, *44*(7), 1001–1013. doi:10.1109/TCYB.2013.2278548 PMID:24002014

Sharma, Pattnaik, & Garg. (2012). A Review of Bacterial Foraging Optimization and Its Applications. In *Proceedings on Future Aspects of Artificial intelligence in Industrial Automation (NCFAAIIA 2012)* (pp. 9-12). International Journal of Computer Applications (IJCA).

Sharmila, D., & Kirubakaran, V. (2010). Image and Formula Based Gait Recognition Methods. *International Journal of Computer and Electrical Engineering*, *2*(2), 1793–8163.

Sheba, O., & Sukesh Kumar, A. (2008). Automated Diagnosis of Macular Degeneration through Image Processing. *IE(I) Journal-CP*, *3-6*, 89.

Shehata, M. S., Cai, J., Badawy, W. M., Burr, T. W., Pervez, M. S., Johannesson, R. J., & Radmanesh, A. (2008). Video-based automatic incident detection for smart roads: The outdoor environmental challenges regarding false alarms. *IEEE Transactions on Intelligent Transportation Systems*, *9*(2), 349–360. doi:10.1109/TITS.2008.915644

Sheikh, H. R., & Bovik, A. C. (2006). Image information and visual quality. *IEEE Transactions on Image Processing*, *15*(2), 430–444. doi:10.1109/TIP.2005.859378 PMID:16479813

Shekhar, Patel, & Nasrabadi. (2013). Joint Sparse Representation for Robust Multimodal Biometrics Recognition. *IEEE Transactions on Pattern Analysis and Machine Intelligence, 36*(1), 113-126.

Shen, C., Kim, J., & Wang, H. (2010). Generalized kernel-based visual tracking. *IEEE Transactions on Circuits and Systems for Video Technology*, *20*(1), 119–130. doi:10.1109/TCSVT.2009.2031393

Shenghui, X., Hua, Y., Jingjuan, Q., Fan, P., Jie, J., & Kendra, H. (2015). Protein MRI contrast agent with unprecedented metal selectivity and sensitivity for liver cancer imaging. *Proceedings of the National Academy of Sciences of the United States of America*, *112*(21), 6607–6612. doi:10.1073/pnas.1423021112 PMID:25971726

Shen, M.-Y., & Kuo, C.-C. J. (1998). Review of postprocessing techniques for compression artifacts removal. *Journal of Visual Communication and Image Representation*, *9*(1), 2–14. doi:10.1006/jvci.1997.0378

Shen, S., Sandham, W., Granat, M., & Sterr, A. (2005). MRI fuzzy segmentation of brain tissue using neighborhood attraction with neural-network optimization. *Information Technology in Biomedicine. IEEE Transactions on, 9*(3), 459–467.

Shi, Y. Q., & Sun, H. (2008). Image and Video Compression for Mutimedia Engineering Fundamental Algorithm and Standards. CRC Press Taylor & Francis Group. doi:10.1201/9781420007268

Shi, J., & Malik, J. (2000). Normalized cuts and image segmentation. *IEEE Transactions on Pattern Analysis and Machine Intelligence*, *22*(8), 888–905. doi:10.1109/34.868688

Shi, J., & Tomaski, C. (1994). Good features to track. In *IEEE Conference on Computer Vision and PatternRecognition (CVPR)*, (pp. 593–600).

Shutter, J. D., & Nixon, M. S. (2006). Zernike velocity moments for sequence-based description of moving features. *Image and Vision Computing*, *24*(4), 343–356. doi:10.1016/j.imavis.2005.12.001

Siedlecki, W., & Sklanky, J. (1989). A note on genetic algorithms for large-scale feature selection. *Pattern Recognition Letters*, *10*(5), 335–347. doi:10.1016/0167-8655(89)90037-8

Sikander, B., Ishtiaq, M., Jaffar, M.A., Tariq, M., & Mirza, A.M. (2010). Adaptive Digital Watermarking of Images Using Genetic Algorithm. In *Proceedings on Information Science and Applications* (pp. 1-8). IEEE.

Simpson, M., Rahman, M. M., Demner-Fushman, D., Antani, S., & Thoma, G. R. (2009). *Text-and content-based approaches to image retrieval for the ImageCLEF 2009 medical retrieval track.* Paper presented at the CLEF2009 Working Notes. CLEF 2009 Workshop.

Singh, P. K., Singh, R. S., Rai, K. N., & Jaiswal, S. (February, 2014). *Comparative study of Image Compression Technique based on Wavelet Transform and Wavelet Packet Transfor.* Paper Presented at International Conference on Recent Trends in Computer Science and Engineering, Bihar, India.

Singhai, N., & Shandilya, S. K. (2010). A Survey On: Content Based Image Retrieval Systems. *International Journal of Computers and Applications, 4*(2), 22–26. doi:10.5120/802-1139

Singh, , & Prakash, . (2014). Modified Adaptive Median Filter for Salt & Pepper Noise. *International Journal of Advanced Research in Computer and Communication Engineerin, 3*(1), 5067–5071.

Singh, S., & Rajput, R. (2014). A Comparative Study of Classification of Image Fusion Techniques. *International Journal Of Engineering And Computer Science, 3*(7), 7350–7353.

Smeulders, A. W., Worring, M., Santini, S., Gupta, A., & Jain, R. (2000). Content-based image retrieval at the end of the early years. *Pattern Analysis and Machine Intelligence. IEEE Transactions on, 22*(12), 1349–1380.

Smith, J. R., & Chung, S.-F. (1994). Quad-tree segmentation for texture-based image query.*Proceedings of ACM second International Conference on Multimedia*, (pp. 1-9). ACM.

Smith, S. W. (1999). *The Scientist and Engineer's Guide to Digital Signal Processing.* San Diego, CA: California Technical Publishing.

Smith, S., & Brady, M. (1997). SUSAN- A new approach to low level image processing. *International Journal of Computer Vision, 23*(1), 45–78. doi:10.1023/A:1007963824710

Soman, K. P., Ramachandran, K. I., & Resmi, N. G. (2011). *Insight into Wavelets – From Theory to Practice.* PHI Learning Private Limited.

Song, K. Y., Kittler, J., & Petrou, M. (1996). Defect detection in random color textures. *Israel Verj. Cap. J, 14*(9), 667–683.

Song, Y., Ca, W., Zhou, Y., & Feng, D. (2013). Feature-based Image Patch Approximation for Lung Tissue Classification. *IEEE Transactions on Medical Imaging, 32*(4), 814–818. PMID:23340591

Song, Y., Goncalves, L., & Perona, P. (2003). Unsupervised learning of human motion. *Pattern Analysis and Machine Intelligence. IEEE Transactions on, 25*(7), 814–827.

Squire, D. M., Müller, W., Müller, H., & Raki, J. (1998). *Content-based query of image databases, inspirations from text retrieval: inverted files, frequency-based weights and relevance feedback.* Academic Press.

Srinivasan, K. S., & Ebenezer, D. (2007). A new fast and efficient decision-based algorithm for removal of high-density impulse noises. *Signal Processing Letters, IEEE, 14*(3), 189-192.

Starck, J. L., Elad, M., & Donoho, D. L. (2005). Image decomposition via the combination of sparse representations and a variational approach. *IEEE Transactions on Image Processing, 14*(10), 1570–1582. doi:10.1109/TIP.2005.852206 PMID:16238062

Starck, J. L., Fadili, J., Elad, M., Nowak, R. D., & Tsakalides, P. (2011). Introduction to the issue on adaptive sparse representation of data and applications in signal and image processing. *J. Sel. Topics Signal Process., 5*(5), 893–895. doi:10.1109/JSTSP.2011.2162154

Stata, R., Bharat, K., & Maghoul, F. (2000). The term vector database: Fast access to indexing terms for web pages. *Computer Networks, 33*(1), 247–255. doi:10.1016/S1389-1286(00)00046-3

Stauffer, C., & Grimson, W. E. L. (2000). Learning Patterns of Activity Using Real-Time Tracking. IEEE Transactions on Pattern Analysis and Machine Intelligence, 747–757. doi:10.1109/34.868677

Stenger, B., Ramesh, V., Paragios, N., Coetzee, F., & Buhmann, J. (2001). Topology free hidden markovmodels: Application to background modeling. In *IEEE International Conference on Computer Vision (ICCV)*, (pp. 294–301).

Streit, R. L., & Luginbuhl, T. E. (1994). Maximum likelihood method for probabilistic multi-hypothesis tracking. In *Proceedings of the International Society for Optical Engineering (SPIE)*, (vol. 2235, pp. 394–405).

Stricker, M. A., & Orengo, M. (1995). *Similarity of color images.* Paper presented at the IS&T/SPIE's Symposium on Electronic Imaging: Science & Technology.

Struyf, & Rousseeuw. (2000). High-dimensional computation of the deepest location. *Computational Statistics & Data Analysis, 34*, 415-426.

Strzalkowski, T. (1995). Natural language information retrieval. *Information Processing & Management, 31*(3), 397–417. doi:10.1016/0306-4573(94)00055-8

Sugandi, B., Kim, H., Tan, J. K., & Ishikawa, S. (2007, September). Tracking of moving objects by using a low resolution image. *Second International Conference on Innovative Computing, Information and Control (ICICIC)*. IEEE. doi:10.1109/ICICIC.2007.600

Suhasini, P., & Krishna, K., & Krishna, M. (2009). CBIR using color histogram processing. *Journal of Theoretical & Applied Information Technology, 6*(1).

Su, J.-H. e. (2011). Effective semantic annotation by image-to-concept distribution model. *IEEE Transactions on Multimedia, 13*(3), 530–538. doi:10.1109/TMM.2011.2129502

Sullivan, G. J., Ohm, J. R., Han, W. J., & Wiegand, T. (2012). Overview of high efficiency video coding (HEVC) standard. *IEEE Transactions on Circuits and Systems for Video Technology, 12*(12), 1649–1668. doi:10.1109/TCSVT.2012.2221191

Sullivan, J., Blake, A., Isard, M., & MacCormick, J. (1999). Object localization by bayesian correlation. In *Proceeding of 7th International Conference on Computer Vision*, (vol. 2, pp. 1068-1075). doi:10.1109/ICCV.1999.790391

Sun, D., Gao, Q., Lu, Y., Huang, Z., & Li, T. (2014). A novel image denoising algorithm using linear Bayesian MAP estimation based on sparse representation. *Signal Processing, 100*, 132–145. doi:10.1016/j.sigpro.2014.01.022

SusanStandring. (2005). *Gray's Anatomy The Anatomical Basis of Clinical Practice* (39th ed.). Elsevier.

Swain, M. J., & Ballard, D. H. (1991). Colour indexing. *International Journal of Computer Vision, 7*(1), 11–32. doi:10.1007/BF00130487

Swarnalatha, P., & Tripathy, B. K. (2013). A novel fuzzy, c-means approach with a bit plane algorithm for classification of medical images. In *Proceedings of IEEE International Conference on Emerging Trends in Computing, Communication and Nanotechnology* (pp. 360-365). doi:10.1109/ICE-CCN.2013.6528524

Szántó, B., Pozsegovics, P., Vámossy, Z., & Sergyán, S. (2011). *Sketch4match—Content-based image retrieval system using sketches.* Paper presented at the Applied Machine Intelligence and Informatics (SAMI), 2011 IEEE 9th International Symposium on.

Szeliski, R., & Coughlan, J. (1997). Spline-based image registration. *International Journal of Computer Vision, 16*(1-3), 185–203.

Tabb, M., & Ahuja, N. (1997). Multiscale Image segmentation by integrated edge and region detection. *IEEE Transactions on Image Processing*, 6(5), 642–655. doi:10.1109/83.568922 PMID:18282958

Tam, W. J., & Zhang, L. (2006). 3D-TV Content Generation: 2D-to-3D Conversion. In *Proceedings of IEEE International Conference on Multimedia and Expo* (pp. 1869 – 1872). IEEE.

Tam, W. J., Vazquez, C., & Speranza, F. (2009). Three-dimensional TV: A novel method for generating surrogate depth maps using colour information. In *Proceedings of SPIE Electronic Imaging—Stereoscopic Displays and Applications XX* (Vol. 7237, pp. 72371A-1–72371A-9). SPIE. doi:10.1117/12.807147

Tang, D., & Zhang, Y. J. (2011). Combining Mean-Shift and Particle Filter for Object Tracking. *Sixth International Conference on Image and Graphics (ICIG)*, (pp. 771-776). doi:10.1109/ICIG.2011.118

Tang, Z., & Miao, Z., & Wan. (2007). *Background Subtraction Using Running Gaussian Average and Frame Difference, Entertainment Computing*. ICEC 2007, *6th International Conference*, Shanghai, China.

Tanizaki, H. (1987). Non-gaussian state-space modeling of nonstationary time series. *Journal of the American Statistical Association*, 82, 1032–1063.

Tao, H., Sawhney, H., & Kumar, R. (2002). Object tracking with bayesian estimation of dynamic layer representations. *IEEE Transactions on Pattern Analysis and Machine Intelligence*, 24(1), 75–89. doi:10.1109/34.982885

Tarek, A., El-Mihoub, A. A. Hopgood, L. N., & Batters, A. (2006). Hybrid Genetic Algorithms: A Review. *Engineering Letters*, 13(2), 1–12.

Terzopoulos, D., & Szeliski, R. (1992). Tracking with kalman snakes. In Active Vision. MIT Press.

Thapa, D., Raahemifar, K., Bobier, W. R., & Lakshminarayanan, V. (2014). Comparison of super-resolution algorithms applied to retinal images. *Journal of Biomedical Optics*, 19(5), 056002. doi:10.1117/1.JBO.19.5.056002 PMID:24788371

Thomas, R. M. (2013). Survey of Bacterial Foraging Optimization Algorithm. *International Journal of Science and Modern Engineering*, 1(4), 11–12.

Thom, T., Haase, N., Rosamond, W., Howard, V. J., Rumsfeld, J., & Manolio, T. (2006). Heart disease and stroke statistics—2006 update: Are port from the American Heart Association Statistics Committee and Stroke Statistics Subcommittee. *Circulation*, 113(6), e85–e151. doi:10.1161/CIRCULATIONAHA.105.171600 PMID:16407573

Thyagarajan, K. S. (2011). *Still Image and Video Compression with MATLAB*. Wiley. doi:10.1002/9780470886922.ch4

Tian, Xue, & Huang. (2009). Classification of Underwater Objects Based on Probabilistic Neural Network. *Fifth International Conference on Natural Computation*, (pp. 38-42).

Tieu, K., & Viola, P. (2004). Boosting image retrival. *International Journal of Computer Vision*, 56(1), 17–36. doi:10.1023/B:VISI.0000004830.93820.78

Tiwari, K., Arya, D. K., Badrinath, & Gupta. (2013). Designing palmprint based recognition system using local structure tensor and force field transformation for human identification. Neurocomputing, 116, 222–230.

Toh, K. K. V., & Nor, A. M. I. (2010). Cluster-based adaptive fuzzy switching median filter for universal impulse noise reduction. *IEEE Transactions on Consumer Electronics*, 56(4), 2560–2568. doi:10.1109/TCE.2010.5681141

Tomasi, C., & Manduchi, R. (1998). Bilateral filtering for gray and color images. In *Proceedings of the IEEE Int. Conf. Comput. Vis*. Bombay, India: IEEE. doi:10.1109/ICCV.1998.710815

Tomura, N., Uemura, K., Inugami, A., Fujita, H., Higano, S., & Shishida, F. (1988). Early CT finding in cerebral infarction: Obscuration of the lentiform nucleus. *Radiology, 168*(2), 463–467. doi:10.1148/radiology.168.2.3393665 PMID:3393665

Tong, X., Liu, Y., Shi, Z., Zeng, B., & Yu, H. B. (2013). SR-Tree: An index structure of sensor management system for spatial approximate query. *Advanced Materials Research, 756*, 885–889. doi:10.4028/www.scientific.net/AMR.756-759.885

Toni, D., Iweins, F., Von Kummer, R., Busse, O., Bogousslavsky, J., Falcou, A. E., & Lenzi, G. L. et al. (2000). Identification of lacunar infarcts before thrombolysis in the ECASS 1 Study. *Neurology, 54*(3), 684–688. doi:10.1212/WNL.54.3.684 PMID:10680804

Toufik, B., & Mokhtar, N. (2012). Advances in Wavelet Theory and Their Applications in Engineering, Physics and Technology. In The Wavelet Transform for Image Processing Applications, (pp 395-422). In Tech.

Toyama, K., Krumm, J., Brumitt, B., & Meyers, B. (1999). Wallflower: Principles and practices of background maintenance. In *IEEE International Conference on Computer Vision (ICCV)*, (pp. 255–261). doi:10.1109/ICCV.1999.791228

Trucco, E., & Verri, A. (1998). Stereopsis. In Introductory Techniques for 3-D Computer Vision (1st ed.). Prentice Hall.

Tsai, Y. M., Chang, Y. L., & Chen, L. G. (2009), Block-based Vanishing Line and Vanishing Point Detection for 3D Scene Reconstruction. In Proceedings of IEEE 3DTVCON (pp. 1–4). IEEE.

Tsai, C.-Y., Huang, D.-A., Yang, M.-C., Kang, L.-W., & Wang, Y.-C. F. (2012). Context-aware single image super-resolution using locality-constrained group sparse representation. In *Proceedings of IEEE Visual Commun. Image Process.* San Diego, CA: IEEE. doi:10.1109/VCIP.2012.6410851

Tsai, L.-W., Hsieh, J.-W., Chuang, C.-H., Tseng, Y.-J., Fan, K.-C., & Lee, C.-C. (2008). Road sign detection using eigen colour. *IET Comput. Vis., 2*(3), 164–177. doi:10.1049/iet-cvi:20070058

Tzoumas, S., Rosenthal, A., Lutzweiler, C., Razansky, D., & Ntziachristos, V. (2014). Spatio-spectral denoising framework for multispectral optoacoustic imaging based on sparse signal representation. *Medical Physics, 41*(113301). PMID:25370669

U. I. D. of India. (n.d.). Retrieved from www.uidai.gov.in

Umamaheswari, J., & Radhamani. (2012). Hybrid Denoising Method for Removal of Mixed Noise in Medical Images. *International Journal of Advanced Computer Science and Applications, 3*(5), 44-47.

Unnikrishnan, R., Pantofaru, C., & Hebert, M. (2007). Toward objective evaluation of image segmentation algorithms. *Pattern Analysis and Machine Intelligence. IEEE Transactions on, 29*(6), 929–944.

Usinskas, D. R. A., & Tomandl, B. F. (2004). Ischemic stroke segmentation on CT images using joint features. *Informatica, 15*(2), 283–290.

Vahdat, A., Gao, B., Ranjbar, M., & Mori, G. (2011, November). A discriminative key pose sequence model for recognizing human interactions. In *Computer Vision Workshops (ICCV Workshops), 2011 IEEE International Conference on* (pp. 1729-1736). IEEE.

Van Rijsbergen, C. J., Robertson, S. E., & Porter, M. F. (1980). *New models in probabilistic information retrieval.* Computer Laboratory, University of Cambridge.

Vapnik, V. (1995). *The Nature of Statistical Learning Theory.* New York: Springer. doi:10.1007/978-1-4757-2440-0

Vázquez, C., & Tam, W. J. (2010). 2D to 3D conversion using colour-based surrogate depth maps. In *Proceedings of International Conference on 3D System and. Application (3DSA).*

Veenman, C., Reinders, M., & Backer, E. (2001). Resolving motion correspondence for densely moving points. *IEEE Transactions on Pattern Analysis and Machine Intelligence, 23*(1), 54–72. doi:10.1109/34.899946

Véhel. (2000, May). *Website*. Retrieved from Fraclabwww-rocq.inria.fr/fractales/

Vijaykumar, V.R., Vanathi, P.T., Kanagasabapathy, P., & Ebenezer, D. (2008). High Density Impulse Noise Removal Using Robust Estimation Based Filter. *International Journal of Computer Science, 35*(3).

Viola, P., Jones, M., & Snow, D. (2003). Detecting pedestrians using patterns of motion and appearance. In *IEEE International Conference on Computer Vision (ICCV)*, (pp. 734–741). doi:10.1109/ICCV.2003.1238422

Visage Imaging. (2015). Retrieved June 12, 2015, from www.visageimaging.com/visage-imaging-receives-fda-clearance-visage-ease-pro/

Vo, K. T., & Sowmya, A. (2011). Multiscale sparse representation of high-resolution computed tomography (HRCT) lung images for diffuse lung disease classification. In *Proceedings of 18th IEEE International Conference on Image Processing (ICIP)* (pp. 441-444). IEEE. doi:10.1109/ICIP.2011.6116545

Von Kummer, R. (2005). The impact of CT on acute stroke treatment. In P. Lyden (Ed.), Thrombolytic Therapy for Stroke. Humana Press.

Walha, R., Drira, F., Lebourgeois, F., Garcia, C., & Alimi, A. M. (2015). Resolution enhancement of textual images via multiple coupled dictionaries and adaptive sparse representation selection. *Int. J. Document Analysis and Recognition, 18*(1), 87–107. doi:10.1007/s10032-014-0235-6

Waltisberg, D., Yao, A., Gall, J., & Van Gool, L. (2010). Variations of a hough-voting action recognition system. In *Recognizing Patterns in Signals, Speech, Images and Videos* (pp. 306–312). Springer Berlin Heidelberg. doi:10.1007/978-3-642-17711-8_31

Wang, & Qu. (2010, June). A Novel Improved Median Filter for Salt-and-Pepper Noise from Highly Corrupted Images. In *Proceedings of 3rd International Symposium on Systems and Control in Aeronautics and Astronautics* (ISSCAA 2010), (pp. 718-722). IEEE.

Wang, F. L., Yu, S. Y. & Yang, J. (2009). Robust and efficient fragments-based tracking using mean shift. *International Journal of Electronics and Communications*, 1-10.

Wang, H., & Perng. (2001). The S2-Tree: An index structure for subsequence matching of spatial objects. *Fifth Pacific-Asic Conference on Knowledge Discovery and Data Mining(PAKDD)*, (LNAI), (vol. 2035, pp. 312-323). Springer.

Wang, H., Yang, Y., Zhang, L., & Yang, Y. (2011). 2D-to-3D conversion based on depth from motion. In Proceedings of International Conference on Mechatronic Science, Electric Engineering and Computer (MEC) (pp.-1892-1895).

Wang, P. (2008). Intelligent pattern recognition and biometrics. In *Proceedings of IEEE International Conference on Intelligence and Security Informatics*, (pp. 39-40). IEEE.

Wang, C., Chen, T., & Qu, Z. (2010). A Novel Improved Median Filter for Salt-and-Pepper Noise from Highly Corrupted Images.*3rd International Symposium on Systems and Control in Aeronautics and Astronautics (ISSCAA 2010)*. Harbin, China: IEEE.

Wang, C., Zhang, J., Pu, J., Yuan, X., & Wang, L. (2010). Chrono Gait Image: a novel temporal template for gait recognition.*European Conference on Computer Vision, 6311*, 257–270. doi:10.1007/978-3-642-15549-9_19

Wang, F. (2011). A survey on automatic image annotation and trends of the new age. *Procedia Engineering, 23*, 434–438. doi:10.1016/j.proeng.2011.11.2526

Wang, L., Tan, T., Ning, H., & Hu, W. (2003). Silhouette analysis-based gait recognition for human identification. *IEEE Transactions on Pattern Analysis and Machine Intelligence*, 25(12), 1505–1518. doi:10.1109/TPAMI.2003.1251144

Wang, L., Wang, Y., Jiang, T., Zhao, D., & Gao, W. (2013). Learning discriminative features for fast frame-based action recognition. *Pattern Recognition*, 46(7), 1832–1840. doi:10.1016/j.patcog.2012.08.016

Wang, M. J., Chen, C. F., & Lee, G. G. (2013). Motion-based depth estimation for 2D-to-3D video conversion. In *Proceedings of IEEE Conference on Visual Communications and Image Processing (VCIP)* (pp.1-6). doi:10.1109/VCIP.2013.6706329

Wang, O., Lang, M., Frei, M., Hornung, A., Smolic, A., & Gross, M. (2011). StereoBrush: Interactive 2D to 3D Conversion Using Discontinuous Warps.*EUROGRAPHICS Symposium on Sketch-Based Interfaces and Modeling*. doi:10.1145/2021164.2021173

Wang, S. (2001). *A robust CBIR approach using local color histograms*. University of Alberta.

Wang, S. P., & Ji, H. B. (2007). A new appearance model based on object sub-region for tracking. *International Conference on Wavelet Analysis and Pattern Recognition*, (pp. 929-932). doi:10.1109/ICWAPR.2007.4420802

Wang, T., McElroy, A., Halaney, D., Vela, D., Fung, E., & Hossain, S. et al.. (2015). Detection of Plaque Structure and Composition Using OCT Combined With Two-photon Luminescence (TPL) Imaging. *Lasers in Surgery and Medicine*, 1–10. doi:10.1002/lsm.22366

Wang, Y. X., & Deng, M. (2010). Medical imaging in new drug clinical development. *Journal of Thoracic Disease*, 2(4), 245–252. PMID:22263053

Wang, Z., & Bovik, A. C. (2002, March). A Universal Image Quality Index. *IEEE Signal Processing Letters*, 20.

Wang, Z., Bovik, A. C., Sheikh, H. R., & Simoncelli, E. P. (2004, April). Image quality assessment: From error visibility to structural similarity. *IEEE Transactions on Image Processing*, 13(4), 600–612. doi:10.1109/TIP.2003.819861 PMID:15376593

Wang, Z., Simoncelli, E. P., & Bovik, A. C. (2003, November). Multi-scale structural similarity for image quality assessment. In *37th Proc. IEEE Asilomar Conf. on Signals, Systems and Computers*. Pacific Grove, CA: IEEE. doi:10.1109/ACSSC.2003.1292216

Wang, Z., & Zhang, D. (1999). Progressive switching median filter for the removal of impulse noise from highly corrupted images. Circuits and Systems II: Analog and Digital Signal Processing. *IEEE Transactions on*, 46(1), 78–80.

Wang, Z., & Zhang, D. (1999, January). Progressive Switching Median Filter for the Removal of Impulse Noise from Highly Corrupted Images. *IEEE Transactions On Circuits And Systems—II:Analog And Digital Signal Processing*, 46(1), 78–80.

Watanabe, T., Kitahara, I., Kameda, Y., & Ohta, Y. (2003). 3D Free-Viewpoint Video Capturing Interface by using Bimanual Operation. *ACM Transactions on Graphics*, 22(3), 569–577.

Wei, Q. (2005). *Converting 2D to 3D: A survey. In Project Report* (pp. 1–34). Delft University of Technology.

Westman, S., Lustila, A., & Oittinen, P. (2008). *Search strategies in multimodal image retrieval*. Paper presented at the Second International Symposium on Information Interaction in Context. doi:10.1145/1414694.1414700

White, D. A., & Jain, R. (1997). *Similarity Indexing: Algorithms and Performance. In Visual Computing Laboratory* (pp. 1–7). San Diego, CA: University of California.

Wildes, R. P. (1997, September). Iris recognition: An emerging biometric technology. *Proceedings of the IEEE, 85*(9), 1348–1363. doi:10.1109/5.628669

Winter, D. A. (2004). *Biomechanics a nd Motor Control of Human Movement* (3rd ed.). John Wiley & Sons.

Witten, I. H., & Frank, E. (2005). *Data Mining: Practical machine learning tools and techniques*. Morgan Kaufmann.

Wright, J., Yang, A., Ganesh, A., Sastry, S., & Ma, Y. (2009). Robust face recognition via sparse representation. *IEEE Transactions on Pattern Analysis and Machine Intelligence, 31*(2), 210–227. doi:10.1109/TPAMI.2008.79 PMID:19110489

Wu, C., Er, G., Xie, X., Li, T., Cao, X., & Dai, Q. (2008). A novel method for semi-automatic 2D to 3D video Conversion. In Proceedings of IEEE 3DTVCON (pp. 65–68). IEEE.

Wu, J., & Ruan, Q. (2006). Combining Adaptive PDE and Wavelet Shrinkage in Image Denoising with Edge Enhancing Property. In *Proceedings of 18th International Conference on Pattern Recognition* (ICPR'06), (Vol. 3).

Wu, Z., & Leahy, R. (1993, November). An Optimal Graph Theoretic Approach to Data Clustering: Theory and Its Application to Image Segmentation. *IEEE Transactions on Pattern Analysis and Machine Intelligence, 15*(11), 1,101-1,113.

Wu, D., & Shao, L. (2013). Silhouette analysis-based action recognition via exploiting human poses. *Circuits and Systems for Video Technology. IEEE Transactions on, 23*(2), 236–243.

Wu, J., & Tang, C. (2014, February). Random-valued impulse noise removal using fuzzy weighted non-local means. *Signal, Image and Video Processing, 8*(2), 349–355. doi:10.1007/s11760-012-0297-1

Xu & Luo. (2009). Support Vector Machine Based Method For Identifying Hard Exudates In Retinal Images. Academic Press.

Xu, J., Xu, B., & Men, S. (2010). *Feature-based Similarity Retrieval in Content-based Image Retrieval*. Paper presented at the Web Information Systems and Applications Conference (WISA), 2010 7th. doi:10.1109/WISA.2010.46

Yamada, K., Suehiro, K., & Nakamura, H. (2005). Pseudo 3D image generation with simple depth models. In *Proceedings of International Conference on Consumer Electronics, Digest of Technical Papers* (pp. 277–278). doi:10.1109/ICCE.2005.1429825

Yamamoto, S., Maki, D., Korn, R. L., & Kuo, M. D. (2012). Radiogenomic analysis of breast cancer using MRI: A preliminary study to define the landscape. *AJR. American Journal of Roentgenology, 199*(3), 654–663. doi:10.2214/AJR.11.7824 PMID:22915408

Yan, X., Yang, Y., Guihua, E., & Dai, Q. (2011). Depth map generation for 2D-to-3D conversion by limited user inputs and depth propagation. In *Proceedings of 3DTV Conference: The True Vision - Capture, Transmission and Display of 3D Video (3DTV-CON)* (pp. 1-4).

Yanagawa, A., Hsu, W., & Chang, S. F. (2006). Brief descriptions of visual features for baseline trecvid concept detectors. *Columbia University ADVENT Technical Report*, 219-2006.

Yang, M., Kpalma, K., & Ronsin, J. (2008). A survey of shape feature extraction techniques. Pattern Recognition, 43-90.

Yang, C.-Y., Huang, J.-B., & Yang, M.-H. (2010). Exploiting self-similarities for single frame super-resolution. In *Proceedings of Asian Conf. Comput. Vis.* (pp. 497–510). Queenstown, New Zealand.

Yang, J., Wang, Z., Lin, Z., Cohen, S., & Huang, T. S. (2012). Coupled dictionary training for image super-resolution. *IEEE Transactions on Image Processing, 21*(8), 3467–3478. doi:10.1109/TIP.2012.2192127 PMID:22481818

Yang, J., Wright, J., Huang, T. S., & Ma, Y. (2010). Image super-resolution via sparse representation. *IEEE Transactions on Image Processing*, *19*(11), 2861–2873. doi:10.1109/TIP.2010.2050625 PMID:20483687

Yang, M.-C., & Wang, Y.-C. F. (2013). A self-learning approach to single image super-resolution. *IEEE Transactions on Multimedia*, *15*(3), 498–508. doi:10.1109/TMM.2012.2232646

Yang, X. C., Zhou, Y., Zhang, T. H., Shu, G., & Yang, J. (2008). Gait recognition based on dynamic region analysis. *Signal Processing*, *88*(9), 2350–2356. doi:10.1016/j.sigpro.2008.03.006

Yang, Y. Z., Huang, Z., Yang, Y., Liu, J., Shen, H. T., & Luo, J. (2012). Local image tagging via graph regularized joint group sparsity. *Pattern Recognition*, *46*(5), 1358–1368. doi:10.1016/j.patcog.2012.10.026

Yavlinsky, A. E. S. (2005). Automated image annotation using global features and robust nonparametric density estimation.*Proc. ACM Int. Conf. Image Video Retrieva*, (pp. 507-517). doi:10.1007/11526346_54

Yeh, C.-H., Kang, L.-W., Chiou, Y.-W., Lin, C.-W., & Fan Jiang, S.-J. (2014). Self-learning-based post-processing for image/video deblocking via sparse representation. *Journal of Visual Communication and Image Representation*, *25*(5), 891–903. doi:10.1016/j.jvcir.2014.02.012

Yeh, C.-H., Kang, L.-W., Lee, M.-S., & Lin, C.-Y. (2013). Haze effect removal from image via haze density estimation in optical model. *Optics Express*, *21*(22), 27127–27141. doi:10.1364/OE.21.027127 PMID:24216937

Yeh, C.-H., Ku, T.-F., Fan Jiang, S.-J., Chen, M.-J., & Jhu, J.-A. (2012). Post-processing deblocking filter algorithm for various video decoders. *IET Image Process.*, *6*(5), 534–547. doi:10.1049/iet-ipr.2010.0545

Yi, F., & Moon, I. (2012). Image Segmentation: A Survey of Graph-cut Methods. *International Conference on Systems and Informatics (ICSAI 2012)*. doi:10.1109/ICSAI.2012.6223428

Yilma, A., & Shah, M. (2005, October). Recognizing human actions in videos acquired by uncalibrated moving cameras. In *Computer Vision, 2005. ICCV 2005. Tenth IEEE International Conference on*, (pp. 150-157). IEEE. doi:10.1109/ICCV.2005.201

Yilmaz, A., Javed, O., & Shah, M. (2006, December). Object tracking: A survey. *ACM Computing Surveys*, *38*(4).

Yilmaz, A., Li, X., & Shah, M. (2004). Contour based object tracking with occlusion handling in video acquired using mobile cameras. *IEEE Transactions on Pattern Analysis and Machine Intelligence*, *26*(11), 1531–1536. doi:10.1109/TPAMI.2004.96 PMID:15521500

Yuan, X.-T., Liu, X., & Yan, S. (2012). Visual classification with multitask joint sparse representation. *IEEE Transactions on Image Processing*, *21*(10), 4349–4360. doi:10.1109/TIP.2012.2205006 PMID:22736645

Yue, F., & Zuo, W. (2013). Consistency analysis on orientation features for fast and accurate palmprint identification. *Information Sciences, Elsevier*, *268*, 78–90. doi:10.1016/j.ins.2013.08.021

Yue, J., Li, Z., Liu, L., & Fu, Z. (2011). Content-based image retrieval using color and texture fused features. *Mathematical and Computer Modelling*, *54*(3), 1121–1127. doi:10.1016/j.mcm.2010.11.044

Yun, S. Q., & Fu, K. S. (1983). A method for the design of binary tree classifiers. *Pattern Recognition*, *16*(6), 593–603. doi:10.1016/0031-3203(83)90076-6

Zenghai Chen, Z. C. (2013). Multi-instance multi-label image classification: A neural approach. *Neurocomputing*, *99*, 298–306. doi:10.1016/j.neucom.2012.08.001

Zhang, D., Islam, M. M., Lu, G., & Hou, J. (2009). *Semantic image retrieval using region based inverted file*. Paper presented at the Digital Image Computing: Techniques and Applications, 2009. DICTA'09. doi:10.1109/DICTA.2009.48

Zhang, H., Fritts, J. E., & Goldman, S. A. (2008). Image segmentation evaluation: A survey of unsupervised methods. *Computer Vision and Image Understanding, 110*(2), 260-280.

Zhang, H., Jiang, M., & Zhang, X. (2009). *Exploring image context for semantic understanding and retrieval.* Paper presented at the Computational Intelligence and Software Engineering, 2009. CiSE 2009. International Conference on. doi:10.1109/CISE.2009.5364019

Zhang, Y. J. (2001). A review of recent evaluation methods for image segmentation. *Signal Processing and its Applications, Sixth International, Symposium on* (pp. pp. 148-151). IEEE.

Zhang, Y.-J. (2006). A summary of recent progresses for segmentation evaluation. *Advances in Image and Video Segmentation, 423.*

Zhang, D., He, J., Zhao, Y., & Du, M. (2015). MR image super-resolution reconstruction using sparse representation, nonlocal similarity and sparse derivative prior. *Computers in Biology and Medicine, 58*, 130–145. doi:10.1016/j.compbiomed.2014.12.023 PMID:25638262

Zhang, D., Islam, M. M., & Lu, G. (2012). A review on automatic image annotation techniques. *Pattern Recognition, 45*(1), 346–362. doi:10.1016/j.patcog.2011.05.013

Zhang, D., & Lu, G. (2001). Content-Based Shape Retrieval Using Different Shape Descriptors: A Comparative Study. *Proceedings of IEEE Conference on Multimedia and Expo*, (pp. 1139-1142).

Zhang, E., Zhao, Y., & Xiong, W. (2010). Active energy image plus 2DLPP for gait recognition. *Signal Processing, 90*(7), 2295–2302. doi:10.1016/j.sigpro.2010.01.024

Zhang, H., Fritts, J. E., & Goldman, S. A. (2003). An entropy-based objective evaluation method for image segmentationc. *Electronic Imaging, 2004*, 38–49.

Zhang, J., Zhao, D., & Gao, W. (2014). Group-based sparse representation for image restoration. *IEEE Transactions on Image Processing, 23*(8), 3336–3351. doi:10.1109/TIP.2014.2323127 PMID:24835225

Zhang, L., Vázquez, C., & Knorr, S. (2011). *3D-TV Content Creation: Automatic 2D-to-3D Video Conversion. IEEE Transactions on Broadcasting, 57*(2).

Zhang, L., Zhang, D., Su, Y., & Long, F. (2013). Adaptive kernel-bandwidth object tracking based on Mean-shift algorithm. *Fourth International Conference on Intelligent Control and Information Processing (ICICIP)*, (pp. 413-416). doi:10.1109/ICICIP.2013.6568108

Zhang, N., & Song, Y. (2008). *An image indexing and searching system based both on keyword and content. In Advanced Intelligent Computing Theories and Applications. With Aspects of Theoretical and Methodological Issues* (pp. 1032–1039). Springer.

Zhang, Q., Li, S., Guo, W., Wang, P., & Huang, J. (2015). Refinement of Kinect Sensor's Depth Maps Based on GMM and CS Theory. *International Journal of Signal Processing, Image Processing and Pattern Recognition, 8*(5), 87–92.

Zhang, R., Ouyang, W., & Cham, W.-K. (2011). Image postprocessing by non-local Kuan's filter. *J. Vis. Commun. Image R., 22*(3), 251–262. doi:10.1016/j.jvcir.2010.12.007

Zhang, S. J. (2012). Automatic image annotation and retrieval using group sparsity. *IEEE Transactions on Systems, Man, and Cybernetics. Part B, Cybernetics, 42*(3), 838–849. doi:10.1109/TSMCB.2011.2179533 PMID:22249744

Zhang, S., Yao, H., & Liu, V. (2009), *Spatial-Temporal Nonparametric Background Subtraction in Dynamic Scenes.* Multimedia and Expo ICME 2009, *IEEE International Conference*, New York, NY.

Zhang, T., & Fei, S. (2011). Improved particle filter for object tracking. *Chinese Control and Decision Conference (CCDC)*, (pp. 3586-3590).

Zhang, T., Fei, S., & Wang, L. (2014). Modified Particle filter for object tracking in low frame rate video. *33rd Chinese Control Conference (CCC)*, (pp. 4936-4941). doi:10.1109/ChiCC.2014.6895777

Zhang, Y., Liu, J., Yang, W., & Guo, Z. (2015). Image super-resolution based on structure-modulated sparse representation. *IEEE Transactions on Image Processing*, *24*(9), 2797–2810. doi:10.1109/TIP.2015.2431435 PMID:25966473

Zhang, Y., Liu, X., Chang, M. C., Ge, W., & Chen, T. (2012). Spatio-temporal phrases for activity recognition. In *Computer Vision–ECCV 2012* (pp. 707–721). Springer Berlin Heidelberg. doi:10.1007/978-3-642-33712-3_51

Zhao, Y., & Yang, J. (2015). Hyperspectral image denoising via sparse representation and low-rank constraint. *IEEE Transactions on Geoscience and Remote Sensing*, *53*(1), 296–308. doi:10.1109/TGRS.2014.2321557

Zhou, X., Eggel, I., & Müller, H. (2010). *The MedGIFT group at ImageCLEF 2009. In Multilingual Information Access Evaluation II. Multimedia Experiments* (pp. 211–218). Springer.

Zhu, C., Lin, X., Chau, L., & Po, L.-M. (2004). Enhanced Hexagonal search for fast block motion estimation. *IEEE Transactions on Circuits and Systems for Video Technology*, *14*(10), 1210–1214. doi:10.1109/TCSVT.2004.833166

Zhu, S. T. X., & Tan, X. (2011). A novel automatic image annotation method based on multi-instance learning. *Procedia Eng*, *15*, 3439–3444. doi:10.1016/j.proeng.2011.08.644

Zhu, S., & Ma, K.-K. (2000). A new diamond search algorithm for fast block-matching motion estimation. *IEEE Transactions on Image Processing*, *9*(3), 287–290. doi:10.1109/TIP.2000.826791 PMID:18255398

Zhu, S., & Yuille, A. (1996). Region competition: Unifying snakes, region growing, and bayes/mdl for multiband image segmentation. *IEEE Transactions on Pattern Analysis and Machine Intelligence*, *18*(9), 884–900. doi:10.1109/34.537343

Zhu, X., Yang, X., Zhou, Q., Wang, L., Yuan, F., & Bian, Z. (2011). A Wavelet Multiscale De-Noising Algorithm Based on Radon Transform. *Measurement Science & Technology*, *22*(2), 1–26.

Ziegler, S. I. (2005). Positron Emission Tomography: Principles, Technology, and Recent Developments. *Nuclear Physics. A.*, *752*, 679c–687c. doi:10.1016/j.nuclphysa.2005.02.067

Zimmer-Galler, & Zeimer. (2005). Feasibility of Screening for High-Risk Age- Related Macular Degeneration With an Internet-Based Automated Fundus Camera. *Ophthalmic Surgery, Lasers & Imaging*, *36*(3), 228–236. PMID:15957480

Zulkifley, M. A., Moran, B., & Rawlinson, D. (2012, October). Robust hierarchical multiple hypothesis tracker for multiple object tracking. *19th IEEE International Conference on Image Processing (ICIP)*, (pp. 405-408). doi:10.1109/ICIP.2012.6466881

About the Contributors

V. Santhi has received her Ph.D. in Computer Science and Engineering from VIT University, Vellore, India. She has pursued her M.Tech. in Computer Science and Engineering from Pondicherry University, Puducherry. She has received her B.E. in Computer Science and Engineering from Bharathidasan University, Trichy, India. Currently she is working as Associate Professor in the School of Computing Science and Engineering, VIT University, Vellore, India. She has authored many national and international journal papers. She is currently in the process of editing two books. Also, she has published many chapters in different books published by International publishers. She is senior member of IEEE and she is holding membership in many professional bodies like CSI, ISTE, IACSIT, IEEE and IAENG. Her areas of research include Image Processing, Digital Signal Processing, Digital Watermarking, Data Compression and Computational Intelligence.

D. P. Acharjya received his PhD in computer science from Berhampur University, India. He has been awarded with Gold Medal in M. Sc. from NIT, Rourkela. Currently he is working as a Professor in the School of Computing Science and Engineering, VIT University, Vellore, India. He has authored many national and international journal papers, book chapters, and five books to his credit. Additionally he has edited four books to his credit. He is reviewer of many international journals such as Fuzzy Sets and Systems, Knowledge Based Systems, and Applied Soft Computing. He has been awarded with Gold Medal from NIT, Rourkela; Eminent Academician Award from Khallikote Sanskrutika Parisad, Berhampur, Odisha; and Outstanding Educator and Scholar Award from National Foundation for Entrepreneurship Development, Coimbatore. Dr. Acharjya is actively associated with many professional bodies like CSI, ISTE, IMS, AMTI, ISIAM, OITS, IACSIT, CSTA, IEEE and IAENG. He was founder secretary of OITS Rourkela chapter. His current research interests include rough sets, formal concept analysis, knowledge representation, data mining, granular computing, bio-inspired computing, and business intelligence.

M. Ezhilarasan was born on May 30, 1968. He has obtained Bachelor of Technology in Computer Science and Engineering, Master of Technology in Computer Science and Engineering and Ph. D. in Computer Science and Engineering from Pondicherry University in 1990, 1996 and 2007 respectively. He is a Professor of the Department of Information Technology, Pondicherry Engineering College, Puducherry, India. He is a life member of Indian Society for Technical Education (ISTE). He has published 60 papers in National and International Conference Proceedings and Journals. His research interests include Multimedia Data Compression and Multi-Biometrics.

* * *

Mongi A. Abidi directs activities in the Imaging, Robotics, and Intelligent Systems (IRIS) Laboratory. Dr. Abidi has been conducting research in the field of three-dimensional imaging, specifically in the areas of scene building, scene description, and data visualization. Dr. Abidi is also involved in the areas of robotic multi-sensing, landmark tracking and sensor calibration, data fusion and probabilistic reasoning, and enhancement of medical images. Since joining UTK as a faculty member in 1986, Dr. Abidi has acted as either principal investigator or co-principal investigator for research contracts totaling more $30 million. He published more than 320 papers. He co-authored or co-edited a total of 4 books. Dr. Abidi has been active with many multi-institution programs. The first program is the 3D Imaging and Data Fusion for Robotic Manipulation and Inspection, part of the DOE's multi-university Research Program in Robotics. The second program is the 3D Imaging and Data Fusion for Automotive Simulation and Design, part of a multi-university program with the U.S. Army TACOM. The third program involves two projects, Gate-to-Gate Automated Video Tracking and Location and Operator Assisted Threat Assessment for Carry-on Luggage Inspection, both with National Safe Skies. He also performed work or US Air Force, Office of Naval Research, NASA, and NSF. In addition to his research duties, Dr. Abidi teaches senior and graduate courses at UTK in the fields of pattern recognition, image processing, computer vision, and robotics. He has developed three courses in image processing and robotics. He has also taught industrial courses in the areas of mathematical transforms for engineers, data fusion, fuzzy logic, and neural networks. Dr. Abidi is a member of Tau Beta Pi, Phi Kappa Phi, Eta Kappa Nu, and the Order of the Engineer. He received the First State Award in primary graduation, the First State Award in secondary graduation, and the First Presidential Principal Engineer Award. He holds memberships in the IEEE Computer Society, IEEE Institute of Electrical and Electronic Engineering, IEEE Robotics and Automation Society, Pattern Recognition Society, Association of Computing Machinery, and the International Society of Optical Engineering. Dr. Abidi is the recipient of the following awards: 2002-2003 Dun & Bradstreet Who's Who in Executives and Business, 2002 United Who's Who in Empowering Executives and Professionals, 2002 Marquis Who's Who in America, Strathmore's Lifetime Who's Who Award, 2001-2003 Philips Professorship Award, 2001 Science Alliance Faculty Award, 2001 Brooks Distinguished Professor Award, 1999-2001 Weston Fulton Professorship, 1997-2000 Magnavox Professorship, and 1995 and 2010. He has received "Most Cited Paper Award for Computer Vision and Image Understanding" for 2006 and 2007. He has received Engineering Research Fellow Award for 2003 and 2011.

P. Aruna received her B.E. from Madras University, M.Tech from IIT Delhi and the Ph.D degree from Annamalai University. Presently she is working as a Professor in the Department of Computer Science and Engineering of Annamalai University. She has published thirty five research papers in International journals and seven research papers in national journals. She has published twenty four research papers in International conferences and seventeen research papers in national conferences. She has twenty two years of teaching experience and thirteen years of research experience. Her area of specialization includes Neural networks & Fuzzy systems, Data Mining and Image processing.

J. Arunnehru is a senior research scholar at the Speech and Vision Lab in Department of Computer Science and Engineering, Annamalai University. He received his M.E and B.E in Computer Science and Engineering from Annamalai University, India. Currently, he is working on UGC sanctioned Major Research Project on video surveillance. He has published more than 20 papers in international conferences and journals. He is a life time member of ISTE. His current research interests include image and video processing, pattern recognition, data mining and machine intelligence and learning.

Manami Barthakur is PhD Scholar in the the department of electronics and communication engineering. She received her M.Sc. degree in Electronics and Communication Technology from Gauhati University in 2009. She had completed M.Tech. in Bio-electronics from Tezpur University in 2011. Her area of interests are computer vision and Image processing.

R. Bhavani received her B.E degree in Computer Science and Engineering in the year 1989 and the M.E Degree in Computer Science and Engineering in the year 1992 from Regional Engineering College, Trichy. She received her Ph.D degree in Computer Science and Engineering from Annamalai University, Chidambaram, in the year 2007. She worked in Mookambigai College of Engineering, Keeranur from 1990 to 1994, and she is now working as Professor in Annamalai University. She has published more than 75 papers in international conferences and journals. Her research interest includes image processing, image segmentation, image compression, image classification, steganography, pattern classification, medical imaging, content-based image retrieval and software metrics.

C. Bhuvaneswari received her Bachelor degree from Madras University, Post graduate from Bharathidasan University and Masters of Philosophy from Madurai Kamaraj University, Madurai. At present she is pursuing Ph.D at Annamalai University,Chidambaram. She has nine years of teaching experience and 6 years of research experience. Her main research areas include image processing and data mining. She has published ten research papers in international journals and six papers in international conferences and ten papers in national conferences.

Chung-Hao Chen received his Ph.D. in Electrical Engineering at the University of Tennessee, Knoxville in August 2009, and his B.S. and M.S. in Computer Science and Information Engineering from Fu-Jen Catholic University, Taiwan in 1997 and 1999, respectively. After receiving his M.S. degree, he was enlisted in National Military Academy from 1999 to 2001 to fulfill his civil duty/military service. In April 2001, he joined the Panasonic Taiwan Laboratory Company, Ltd. as a research and development engineer where he remained until August 2003. In August 2009, he joined in the department of Math and Computer Science at North Carolina Central University as an assistant professor. Since August 2011, he is an assistant professor in the department of Electrical and Computer Engineering at Old Dominion University. His research interests include robotics, automated surveillance systems, pattern recognition, image processing, artificial intelligent systems, and data analysis and mining.

Jacob D'Avy is an Image Processing Engineer at SolVIS, Inc. His work involves applying multispectral imaging, laser technology, and photogrammetry to solve industrial automation problems.

Amlan Jyoti Das received B.Tech. degree in Electronics and Telecommunication Engineering from Girijananda Chowdhury Institute of Management and Technology, Guwahati in 2011 and M.Tech degree in Electronics and Communication Technology from Gauhati University, Guwahati in 2013. Currently, he is pursuing Ph. D. in the Dept. of Electronics and Communication Engineering, Gauhati University. His areas of interest are Image Processing, computer vision and human computer interaction.

A. Geetha obtained her under graduate degree in computer science and engineering from the Periyar Maniammai University, Thanjavur in 1994 and her post graduate degree in computer science from National Institute of Technology, Trichy in 1997. She completed her Ph.D in computer science and engineering from Annamalai University in 2014. She started her services at Annamalai University in the year 1991 as a faculty member and is presently serving as associate professor in the Department of computer science and engineering. She has published 18 papers in national and international conferences and journals. She is a member of ISTE, CSI and IE technical bodies. Her areas of interest are image processing and parallel processing.

M. Kalaiselvi Geetha received her Ph. D in computer science and engineering from Annamalai University, India; M. Tech degree in computer technology from Indian Institute of Technology (IIT), Delhi; and B.E in computer science and engineering from Bharathiar University, India. Currently she is working as Associate Professor in department of computer science and engineering, Annamalai University, Chidambaram, India. She has authored more than 40 research papers in national and international journals and conferences. Currently, she is working on UGC sanctioned research project on video surveillance. She is acting as editorial board member of International Journal of Rough Computing and Intelligent Systems and International Journal of Modern Education and Information Technology and reviewer of Machine Vision and Applications (Springer) and International Journal of Computer Applications Technology and Research. She is associated with the professional bodies CSI and ISTE. She has organized national/state level seminars, workshops and SDPs. Recently she has organized an international conference as organising secretary. Her current research interests include video processing, pattern recognition, data mining and machine intelligence.

Nidhi Goel graduated in Physics from University of Delhi in 2006, received MCA degree from GGS Indraprastha University, Delhi in 2009 and is currently pursuing Ph.D. in Computer Science from the Department of Computer Science, University of Delhi. She was lecturer in Delhi Institute of Advanced studies, GGS Indraprastha University.

Wei-Wen Hsu received his master degree from National Taiwan University, and now he engages a Ph.D. program in Old Dominion University.

Shanmuga Sundari Ilangovan completed Bachelor of Technology, Biotechnology from PSR Engineering College, affiliated to Anna University in 2010 and Master of Technology, Biotechnology from Udaya School of Engineering, affiliated to Anna University in 2012. At present Ms. Sundari is doing Ph.D in VIT University under the guidance of Dr. Shampa Sen on Synthesis and Application of Magnetic nanoparticles.

Bibekananda Jena is a Senior Lecturer in the department of Electronics and Telecommunication Engineering, Purushottam Institute of Engineering and Technology, Rourkela, India. His research interests are image processing, signal processing, wireless and sensor network, mobile communication. He has published many research papers in national and international conferences and journals.

Priya Kandan received her B.E. from Madurai Kamaraj University, M.E from Annamalai University and the Ph.D degree from Annamalai University. Presently she is working as an Associate Professor in the Department of Computer Science and Engineering of Annamalai University. She has published nine research papers in International journals and one research paper in national journal. She has published seven research papers in International conferences and four research papers in national conferences. She has fifteen years of teaching experience and seven years of research experience. Her area of specialization includes Image processing and Pattern classification Techniques.

Li-Wei Kang received his B.S., M.S., and Ph.D. degrees in Computer Science from National Chung Cheng University, Chiayi, Taiwan, in 1997, 1999, and 2005, respectively. Since February 2013, he has been with the Graduate School of Engineering Science and Technology-Doctoral Program, and the Department of Computer Science and Information Engineering, National Yunlin University of Science and Technology, Yunlin, Taiwan, as an Assistant Professor. Before that, he worked for the Institute of Information Science, Academia Sinica (IIS/AS), Taipei, Taiwan, as an Assistant Research Scholar during 2010–2013, and as a postdoctoral research fellow during 2005–2010. His research interests include multimedia content analysis and multimedia communications. Dr. Kang has served as the Editor-in-Chief of the Gate to Multimedia Processing (Science Gate Publishing) and a Guest Editor of the International Journal of Distributed Sensor Networks. He served as an Editorial Board Member of the International Journal of Distributed Sensor Networks, an Editorial Advisory Board Member of a book entitled Visual Information Processing in Wireless Sensor Networks: Technology, Trends and Applications (IGI Global), a Guest Editor of the International Journal of Electrical Engineering (Taiwan), the Special Session Co-Chair of APSIPA ASC 2012, and the Registration Co-Chair of APSIPA ASC 2013. He serves as the Demo/Exhibition Co-Chair of the IEEE ICCE-TW 2015. He received a top 10% Paper Award from the IEEE MMSP 2013.

Andreas Koschan received his M.Sc. (Diplom) in Computer Science in 1985 and a Ph.D. (Dr.-Ing.) in Computer Engineering in 1991, both from the Technical University Berlin, Germany. In 2000, he joined the Department of Electrical and Computer Engineering at The University of Tennessee, Knoxville, where he is a Professor of Practice. His interests include computer vision, three-dimensional imaging, color image processing, and robotics. He has published over 50 papers in these areas. He co-authored two textbooks on Three-dimensional Computer Vision, one textbook on Color Image Processing, and one text book on safety and security applications of computer vision. Dr. Koschan is or has been a member in professional societies including IEEE, Computer Society, ASEE, IS&T, and SPIE.

Chih-Yang Lin received the B.S. degree in computer science and information engineering from Tung-Hai University, Taichung, in 1998, the master degree in information management from National Chi-Nan University, Nantou, in 2000. In 2006, he received a Ph.D. degree from Dept. Computer Science and Information Engineering at National Chung-Cheng University, Chiayi. After graduated, he servered in Advanced Technology Center of Industrial Technology Research Institute of Taiwan (ITRI) from 2007 to 2009. Then, he joined the Institute of Information Science (IIS), Academia Sinica, as a postdoctoral fellow. Currently, he is an Associate Professor in the Department of Computer Science and Information Engineering, Asia University. His research interests include computer vision, digital rights management, image processing, and data mining.

D. Loganathan received the Post-Graduate Degree from Birla Institute of Technology and Science, and obtained Doctorate from Anna University, Chennai. Currently, he is a professor and Head in the

Department of Computer Science and Engineering at Pondicherry Engineering College, Puducherry, INDIA. His research interests are information security, image processing. Earlier deputed for TEN week training at CICC Tokyo, Japan. He has been associated with a number of National, International Conferences and workshops and acted as Panel Member for AICTE and NBA. He is also associated with many Professional bodies.

Biswanath Mahanty completed Bachelor of Pharmacy, Pharmaceutical Technology from Jadavpur University, Kolkata, India in 2001, Master of Technology, Biotechnology from Jadavpur University, Kolkata, India in 2003 and Doctor of Philosophy, Biotechnology from Indian Institute of Technology (IIT) Guwahati, India in 2009. Dr. Mahanty is working as Assistant Professor in Department of Environmental Engineering, INHA University, Incheon, Republic of Korea. Dr. Mahanty has 21 International publications and 1 national publication.

Vafa Maihami received the M.S. degree in computer engineering from the University of Kurdistan, Sanandaj, Iran, in 2012. He is currently working toward the Ph.D. degree in computer engineering at Semnan University, Semnan, Iran, working on Artificial Intelligence algorithms. His research interests include image Processing, machine learning, machine vision, and wireless sensor networks.

Banshidhar Majhi is presently working as a Professor in the Department of Computer Science & Engineering, NIT Rourkela, India. He has produced eight PhD students and published sixty papers in referred journals. His research interests include soft computing, image processing, biometrics, network security, wireless sensor networks. He has executed five different research projects sponsored by DeitY, ISRO, India. He is a member of FIE, FIETE, IEEE, ACM, and LMCSI. He has been received many awards/medals for research paper presentation.

S. Anu H. Nair is an Assistant Professor in the Department of Computer Science and Engineering of Annamalai University. She received her Bachelor degree in 2002 and Master Degree at Manonmaniam Sundaranar University,Tirunelveli in 2005. Her main research areas include image processing, pattern classification techniques and neural networks. She has published papers on these topics.

Pritam Patel is pursuing his M.Tech in the department of Electrical Engineering, National Institute of Technology, Agartala, India. His research interest are Power Electronics and Image Processing.

Punyaban Patel, male, completed his Bachelor degree in Electrical Engineering (1996), M.E. (Computer Sc., 1999), and PhD (Computer Sc & Engineering, 2014) with more than 15 years of teaching and research experience in Under graduate and Post graduate level of Computer Science & Engineering. He has published many research papers in national and international conferences and journals. He has been associated and working with many journals and conferences in editorial and reviewer board and organizes many international conferences and workshop. His research interests are Image Processing, Software Engineering, Data Mining, Cloud Computing, Wireless and Sensor Network.

N. Poonguzhali is currently a Research Scholar at Pondicherry Engineering College, Pondicherry University. She received her M.C.A and M.Tech degree from Pondicherry University during the year 1999 and 2009 respectively. She has a teaching experience of 8 years. She is a life member of CSI, ISTE and student member of IEEE. She has published more than 10 papers in national, international journals and conferences. Her area of interest include multi- biometric and data mining.

N. Puviarasan is working as Associate Professor, Dept.of Computer Science and Engineering, Annamalai University. He has 26 years of teaching experience and 9 years research experience. He has published 10 papers in international journals, 3 papers in national journal and 7 papers in international conferences and 8 papers in national conferences.

K. N. Rai was Professor in Department of Mathematical Sciences, IIT- BHU, Varanasi, India. He had completed his M.Sc. in Mathematics and Ph.D. in mathematics both from Banaras Hindu University. He had more than 39 years of teaching and research experience and published more than 70 research papers in reputed national and international. Twelve students awarded Ph.D. under his supervision and eight are working for Ph.D. degree. His area of interest is heat mass transfer, Biotransport process, moving boundry problems and application of wavelets and numerical techniques.

N. Hema Rajini received her B.E., and M.E., degrees in Computer Science and Engineering from Annamalai University, Tamil Nadu in the year 2000 and 2005, respectively. Currently she is an Assistant Professor of the Department of Computer Science and Engineering at the Annamalai University, Tamil Nadu, India. Her current research interests include image processing, segmentation, pattern recognition and medical imaging.

Bibhudatta Sahoo is Assistant Professor in the Department of Computer Science & Engineering, NIT Rourkela, India. His technical interests include performance evaluation methods and modeling techniques distributed computing system, networking algorithms, scheduling theory, cluster computing and web engineering. He has been awarded two government of India research grants and associated with several R & D projects sponsored from government of India. He has been received many awards/medals for research paper presentation. He is a member of IEEE, ACM and CSI.

Navajit Saikia is presently an assistant professor in the Department of Electronics and telecommunication Engineering, Assam Engineering College, India. His research interests include image processing, speech processing, computer vision, application of signal processing techniques, reversible logic circuit, etc. He has co-authored several research papers in journals and conference proceedings.

Kandarpa Kumar Sarma, currently Associate Professor in Department of Electronics and Communication Technology, Gauhati University, Guwahati, Assam, India, has over seventeen years of professional experience. He has covered all areas of UG/PG level electronics courses including soft computing, mobile communication, digital signal and image processing. He obtained M.Tech degree in Signal Processing from Indian Institute of Technology Guwahati in 2005 and subsequently completed PhD programme in the area of Soft-Computational Application in Mobile Communication. He has authored six books, several book chapters, around three hundred peer reviewed research papers in international conference proceedings and journals. His areas of interest are Soft-Computation and its Applications, Mobile Communication, Antenna Design, Speech Processing, Document Image Analysis and Signal Processing Applications in High Energy Physics, Neuro-computing and Computational Models for Social-Science Applications. He has been conferred upon the IETE N. V. Gadadhar Memorial Award

2014 for contribution towards wireless communication. He is a senior member of IEEE (USA), Fellow IETE (India), Member International Neural Network Society (INNS, USA), Life Member ISTE (India) and Life Member CSI (India). He serves as an Editor-in-Chief of International Journal of Intelligent System Design and Computing (IJISDC, UK), guest editor of several international journals, reviewer of over thirty international journals and over hundred international conferences.

Priti Sehgal received her Ph.D. in Computer Science from the Department of Computer Science, University of Delhi, India in 2006 and her M. Sc. in Computer Science from DAVV, Indore, India in 1994. She is an Associate Professor in the Department of Computer Science, Keshav Mahavidyalaya, University of Delhi. She has about 19 years of teaching and 9 years of research experience and has published about 25 papers in National/International Journals/Conferences. Dr. Sehgal has been a member of the program committee of the CGIV International Conference and is a life member of Computer Society of India. Her research interests include Computer Graphics, Image Processing, Biometrics, Computer Vision and Image Retrieval.

Shampa Sen had completed Bachelor of Engineering in Chemical Engineering from Utkal University, Bhubaneswar, India in 1998, Master of Technology in Biotechnology from Jadavpur University, Kolkata, India in 2003 and Doctor of Philosophy in Environment from Indian Institute of Technology, Guwahati, India in 2010. Dr. Sen has teaching cum research experience since 1998 and presently working as Associate Professor in the School of Bio Sciences and Technology, VIT University, Vellore, India. She has 14 publications cited 151 times totally to her credit. At present, PI research works are focused on metallic nanoparticles synthesis, with specific reference to silver and magnetic nanoparticles, their environmental and medical applications.

Piyush Kumar Singh has completed his master degree in computer applications from RSMT, varanasi affiliated with GBTU, Lucknow, India. He is currently doing Ph.D. at DST-Centre for Interdisciplinary Mathematical Sciences, Banaras Hindu University, Varanasi, India. His area of interest is wavelet transform and its application in image processing algorithms, wavelet packets and its application in image processing and parallel algorithms.

R. S. Singh has academic qualification M.Tech. and Ph.D. He is Assistant Professor in Department of Computer Science and Engineering, IIT-BHU, Varanasi, India. His area of interest is Data Structures, Algorithms and High Performance Computing, Parallel Algorithms, Image Processing and cloud computing. Currently four Ph.D. research scholars are under his guidance. He has also played major role in his institution's academic and administrative works.

L. R. Sudha received her B.E degree in Computer Science and Engineering from Madras University, Chennai, India in 1991, and M.E & Ph.D degrees in Computer Science and Engineering from Annamalai University, Chidambaram, India in 2007 and 2014 respectively. She is currently working as Assistant Professor in Annamalai University. Her research work is focused on video and image processing, pattern classification, computer vision, human gait analysis and their applications in biometrics. She has more than 25 technical publications to her credit.

Farzin Yaghmaee received his PhD in 2010 and MSc in 2002 both in Artificial Intelligence from Sharif University of Technology, Iran and received BSc from AmirKabir University of Technology. He is now a faculty member of Electrical and Computer Engineering Department of Semnan University. His research interests are: image and video processing, text mining and Persian language processing tools.

Chia-Hung Yeh (M'03-SM'12) received his B.S. and Ph.D. degrees from National Chung Cheng University, Taiwan, in 1997 and 2002, respectively, both from the Department of Electrical Engineering. Dr. Yeh joined the Department of Electrical Engineering, National Sun Yat-sen University (NSYSU) as an assistant professor in 2007 and became an associate professor in 2010. In Feb. 2013, Dr. Yeh is promoted to a full professor. Dr. Yeh's research interests include multimedia communication, multimedia database management, and image/audio/video signal processing. He served on the Editorial Board of the Journal of Visual Communication and Image Representation, and the EURASIP Journal on Advances in Signal Processing. In addition, he has rich experience in organizing various conferences serving as keynote speaker, session chair, and technical program committee and program committee member for international/domestic conferences. Dr. Yeh has co-authored more than 150 technical international conferences and journal papers and holds 42 patents in the U.S., Taiwan, and China. He received the 2007 Young Researcher Award of NSYSU, the 2011 Distinguished Young Engineer Award from the Chinese Institute of Electrical Engineering, the 2013 Distinguished Young Researcher Award of NSYSU, the 2013 IEEE MMSP Top 10% Paper Award, and the 2014 IEEE GCCE Outstanding Poster Award.

Chia-Mu Yu received his Ph.D. degree from the Computer Science Group, Department of Electrical Engineering, National Taiwan University, in 2012. He was a research assistant at the Institute of Information Science, Academia Sinica, from 2005 to 2010, a visiting scholar at Harvard University from September 2010 to September 2011, a visiting scholar at Imperial College London from January 2012 to September 2012, and a postdoc researcher at IBM Thomas J. Watson Research Center from October 2012 to July 2013. He is currently an assistant professor in Department of Computer Science and Engineering, Yuan Ze University. Since 2014 he has served as an associate editor for IEEE Access, Security and Communication Networks, and Gate to Multimedia Processing. His research interests include cloud storage security, sensor network security, and smart grid security.

Index

Information Resources Management Association

Become an IRMA Member

Members of the **Information Resources Management Association (IRMA)** understand the importance of community within their field of study. The Information Resources Management Association is an ideal venue through which professionals, students, and academicians can convene and share the latest industry innovations and scholarly research that is changing the field of information science and technology. Become a member today and enjoy the benefits of membership as well as the opportunity to collaborate and network with fellow experts in the field.

IRMA Membership Benefits:

- **One FREE Journal Subscription**

- **30% Off Additional Journal Subscriptions**

- **20% Off Book Purchases**

- Updates on the latest events and research on Information Resources Management through the IRMA-L listserv.

- Updates on new open access and downloadable content added to Research IRM.

- A copy of the Information Technology Management Newsletter twice a year.

- A certificate of membership.

IRMA Membership $195

Scan code to visit irma-international.org and begin by selecting your free journal subscription.

Membership is good for one full year.

Printed in the United States
By Bookmasters